A SOURCE BOOK
FOR ANCIENT CHURCH HISTORY

A SOURCE BOOK

FOR

ANCIENT CHURCH HISTORY

FROM THE APOSTOLIC AGE
TO THE
CLOSE OF THE CONCILIAR PERIOD

BY

JOSEPH CULLEN AYER, Jr., Ph.D.

AMS PRESS
NEW YORK

BR
160
A2
A9
1970

Reprinted from the edition of 1913, New York
First AMS EDITION published 1970
Manufactured in the United States of America

International Standard Book Number: 0-404-00436-9

Library of Congress Catalog Card Number: 70-113546

AMS PRESS, INC.
NEW YORK, N.Y. 10003

PREFACE

THE value of the source-book has long been recognized in the teaching of general history. In ecclesiastical history quite as much use can be made of the same aid in instruction. It is hoped that the present book may supply a want increasingly felt by teachers employing modern methods in teaching ecclesiastical history. It has grown out of classroom work, and is addressed primarily to those who are teaching and studying the history of the Christian Church in universities and seminaries. But it is hoped that it may serve the constantly increasing number interested in the early history of Christianity.

In the arrangement of the selected illustrative material, a chronological analysis and grouping of topics has been followed, according to the lines of treatment employed by K. Müller, F. Loofs, Von Schubert in his edition of Moeller's text-book, and by Hergenröther to some extent. The whole history of ancient Christianity has accordingly been divided into comparatively brief periods and subdivided into chapters and sections. These divisions are connected and introduced by brief analyses and characterizations, with some indications of additional source material available in English.

A bibliography originally prepared for each chapter and section has been omitted. When the practical question arose of either reducing the amount of source material to admit a bibliography, or of making the book too expensive for general use by students, the main purpose of the book determined the only way of avoiding two unsatisfactory solutions of the problem, and the bibliography has been omitted. In this there may be less loss than at first appears. The student of ecclesiastical history is fortunately provided with ample bibliographical material for the ancient Church in the universally available theological and other encyclopædias which have very recently appeared or are in course of publication, and in the recent works on patristics. Possibly the time has come when, in place of duplicating bibliographies, reliance in such matters upon the work of others may not be regarded as mortal sin against the ethics of scholarship. A list of works has been given in the General Bibliographical Note, which the student is expected to consult and to which the instructor should encourage him to go for further information and bibliographical material.

The book presupposes the use of a text-book of Church history, such as those by Cheetham, Kurtz, Moeller, Funk, or Duchesne, and a history of doctrine, such as those of Seeberg, Bethune-Baker, Fisher, or Tixeront. Readings in more elaborate treatises, special monographs, and secular history may well be left to the direction of the instructor.

The translations, with a few exceptions which are noted, are referred for the sake of convenience to the *Patrology* of Migne or Mansi's *Concilia*. Although use has been freely made of the aid offered by existing translations, especially those of the *Ante-Nicene* and *Post-Nicene Fathers*, yet all translations have been revised in accordance with the best critical texts available. The aim in the revision has been accuracy and closeness to the original without too gross violation of the English idiom, and with exactness in the rendering of ecclesiastical and theological technical terms. Originality is hardly to be expected in such a work as this.

An author may not be conscious of any attempt to make his selection of texts illustrate or support any particular phase of Christian belief or ecclesiastical polity, and his one aim may be to treat the matter objectively and to render his book useful to all, yet he ought not to flatter himself that in either respect he has been entirely successful. In ecclesiastical history, no more than in any other branch of history, is it possible for an author who is really absorbed in his work to eliminate completely the personal equation. He should be glad to be informed of any instance in which he may have unwittingly failed in impartiality, that when occasion presented he might correct it. The day has gone by in which ecclesiastical history can not be treated save as a branch of polemical theology or as an apologetic for any particular phase of Christian belief or practice. It has at last become possible to teach the history of the Christian Church, for many centuries the greatest institution of Western Europe, in colleges and universities in conjunction with other historical courses.

This volume has been prepared at the suggestion of the American Society of Church History, and valuable suggestions have been gained from the discussions of that society. To Professor W. W. Rockwell, of Union Theological Seminary, New York, Professor F. A. Christie, of Meadville Theological School, the late Professor Samuel Macauley Jackson, of New York, and Professor Ephraim Emerton, of Harvard University, I have also been indebted for advice. The first two named were members with me of a committee on a *Source-Book for Church History* appointed several years ago by the American Society of Church History.

That the book now presented to the public may be of service to the teacher and student of ecclesiastical history is my sincere wish. It may easily happen that no one else would make just the same selection of sources here made. But it is probable that the principal documents, those on which the majority would agree and which are most needed by the teacher in his work, are included among those presented. There are, no doubt, slips and defects in a book written at intervals in a teacher's work. With the kind co-operation of those who detect them, they may be corrected when an opportunity occurs.

JOSEPH CULLEN AYER, JR.

CONTENTS

	PAGE
PREFACE	vii
GENERAL BIBLIOGRAPHICAL NOTE	xix

ANCIENT CHRISTIANITY

DIVISION ONE.—THE CHURCH UNDER THE HEATHEN EMPIRE:
TO A. D. 324. 3

PERIOD I.—THE APOSTOLIC AGE: TO CIRCA A. D. 100 . . . 5

§ 1. The Neronian Persecution 6
§ 2. The Death of Peter and Paul 8
§ 3. The Death of the Apostle John. 9
§ 4. The Persecution under Domitian 11

PERIOD II.—THE POST-APOSTOLIC AGE: A. D. 100–A. D. 140   13

§ 5. Christianity and Judaism 14
§ 6. The Extension of Christianity 18
§ 7. Relation of the Roman State to Christianity 19
§ 8. Martyrdom and the Desire for Martyrdom 22
§ 9. The Position of the Roman Community of Christians
      in the Church 23
§ 10. Chiliastic Expectations 25
§ 11. The Church and the World 27
§ 12. Theological Ideas 30
§ 13. Worship in the Post-Apostolic Period 32
§ 14. Church Organization 36
§ 15. Church Discipline 42
§ 16. Moral Ideas in the Post-Apostolic Period 45

xi

PAGE

PERIOD III.—THE CRITICAL PERIOD: A. D. 140 TO A. D. 200   50

*Chapter I.   The Church in Relation to the Empire and Heathen
Culture*   51

§ 17. The Extension of Christianity   52
§ 18. Heathen Religious Feeling and Culture in Relation to
        Christianity   55
§ 19. The Attitude of the Roman Government toward
        Christians, A. D. 138 to A. D. 192   64
§ 20. The Literary Defence of Christianity   69

*Chapter II.   The Internal Crisis: The Gnostic and Other Heret-
ical Sects*   75

§ 21. The Earlier Gnostics: Gnosticism in General   76
§ 22. The Greater Gnostic Systems: Basilides and Valen-
        tinus   82
§ 23. Marcion 102
§ 24. Encratites 105
§ 25. Montanism 106

Chapter III.   The Defence against Heresy 109

§ 26. Councils as a Defence against Heresy 110
§ 27. The Apostolic Tradition and the Episcopate 111
§ 28. The Canon or the Authoritative New Testament
        Writings 117
§ 29. The Apostles' Creed 123
§ 30. Later Gnosticism 126
§ 31. The Results of the Crisis 128

Chapter IV.   The Beginnings of Catholic Theology 129

§ 32. The Apologetic Conception of Christianity 130
§ 33. The Asia Minor Conception of Christianity 135

PERIOD IV.—THE AGE OF THE CONSOLIDATION OF THE CHURCH:
200 TO 324 A. D. 140

*Chapter I.   The Political and Religious Conditions of the Em-
pire* 141

§ 34. State and Church under Septimius Severus and Cara-
        calla 142
§ 35. Religious Syncretism in the Third Century 150

PAGE

§ 36. The Religious Policy of the Emperors from Heliogabalus to Philip the Arabian, 217–249   151

§ 37. The Extension of the Church at the Middle of the
Third Century   156

Chapter II. The Internal Development of the Church in Doctrine, Custom, and Constitution   159

§ 38. The Easter Controversy and the Separation of the
Churches of Asia Minor from the Western Churches   161

§ 39. The Religion of the West: Its Moral and Juristic
Character   165

§ 40. The Monarchian Controversies   171

(A) Dynamistic Monarchianism   172

(B) Modalistic Monarchianism   175

§ 41. Later Montanism and the Consequences of Its Exclusion from the Church   181

§ 42. The Penitential Discipline   183

§ 43. The Catechetical School of Alexandria: Clement and
Origen   189

§ 44. Neo-Platonism   202

Chapter III. The First General Persecution and Its Consequences   205

§ 45. The Decian-Valerian Persecution   206

§ 46. Effects of the Persecution upon the Inner Life of
the Church   212

Chapter IV. The Period of Peace for the Church: A. D. 260
to A. D. 303   218

§ 47. The Chiliastic Controversy   219

§ 48. Theology of the Second Half of the Third Century
under the Influence of Origen   221

§ 49. The Development of the Cultus   231

§ 50. The Episcopate in the Church   237

§ 51. The Unity of the Church and the See of Rome . . .   240

§ 52. Controversy over Baptism by Heretics   245

§ 53. The Beginnings of Monasticism   248

§ 54. Manichæanism   252

Chapter V. The Last Great Persecution   256

§ 55. The Reorganization of the Empire by Diocletian . .   257

§ 56. The Diocletian Persecution   258

§ 57. Rise of Schisms in Consequence of the Diocletian Persecution   265

CONTENTS

PAGE

DIVISION TWO.—THE CHURCH UNDER THE CHRISTIAN EMPIRE:
FROM 312 TO CIRCA 750 272

PERIOD I.—THE IMPERIAL STATE CHURCH OF THE UNDIVIDED
EMPIRE, OR UNTIL THE DEATH OF THEODOSIUS THE
GREAT, 395 276

Chapter I. The Church and Empire under Constantine 276

§ 58. The Empire under Constantine and His Sons . . . 277
§ 59. The Favor Shown the Church by Constantine . . . 281
§ 60. The Repression of Heathenism under Constantine . 285
§ 61. The Donatist Schism under Constantine 287
§ 62. Constantine's Endeavors to Bring about the Unity of
the Church by Means of General Synods: the Councils of Arles and Nicæa 289

*Chapter II. The Arian Controversy until the Extinction of the
Dynasty of Constantine* 297

§ 63. The Outbreak of the Arian Controversy and the Council of Nicæa A. D. 325 299
§ 64. The Beginnings of the Eusebian Reaction under Constantine 306
§ 65. The Victory of the Anti-Nicene Party in the East . . 310
§ 66. Collapse of the Anti-Nicene Middle Party; the Renewal of Arianism; the Rise of the Homoousian
Party 315
§ 67. The Policy of the Sons of Constantine toward Heathenism and Donatism 320
§ 68. Julian the Apostate 325

*Chapter III. The Triumph of the New-Nicene Orthodoxy over
Heterodoxy and Heathenism* 336

§ 69. The Emperors from Jovian to Theodosius and Their
Policy toward Heathenism and Arianism 337
§ 70. The Dogmatic Parties and Their Mutual Relations . 348
§ 71. The Emperor Theodosius and the Triumph of the
New Nicene Orthodoxy at the Council of Constantinople A. D. 381 352

Chapter IV. The Empire and the Imperial State Church . . . 356

§ 72. The Constitution of the State Church 358
(A) The Ecumenical Council 358
(B) The Hierarchical Organization 360
§ 73. Sole Authority of the State Church 370

§ 74. The Position of the State Church in the Social Order
     of the Empire 380
§ 75. Social Significance of the State Church 384
§ 76. Popular Piety and the Reception of Heathenism in
     the Church 396
§ 77. The Extension of Monasticism throughout the Empire 401
§ 78. Celibacy of the Clergy and the Regulation of Clerical
     Marriage 411
     (A) Clerical Marriage in the East 412
     (B) Clerical Celibacy in the West 415

PERIOD II.—THE CHURCH FROM THE PERMANENT DIVISION OF
   THE EMPIRE UNTIL THE COLLAPSE OF THE WESTERN EM-
   PIRE AND THE FIRST SCHISM BETWEEN THE EAST AND THE
   WEST, OR UNTIL ABOUT A. D. 500 419

Chapter I. The Church at the Beginning of the Permanent
Separation of the Two Parts of the Roman Empire. 420

   § 79. The Empire of the Dynasty of Theodosius 421
   § 80. The Extension of the Church about the Beginning of
     the Fifth Century 425

Chapter II. The Church of the Western Empire in the Fifth
Century 429

   § 81. The Western Church toward the End of the Fourth
     Century 430
   § 82. Augustine's Life and Place in the Western Church . 433
   § 83. Augustine and the Donatist Schism 445
   § 84. The Pelagian Controversy 455
   § 85. The Semi-Pelagian Controversy 466
   § 86. The Roman Church as the Centre of the Catholic
     Roman Element of the West 476

Chapter III. The Church in the Eastern Empire 481

   § 87. The First Origenistic Controversy and the Triumph
     of Traditionalism. 483
   § 88. The Christological Problem and the Theological
     Tendencies 493
   § 89. The Nestorian Controversy; the Council of Eph-
     esus, A. D. 431. 504
   § 90. The Eutychian Controversy and the Council of Chal-
     cedon A. D. 451 511

PAGE

§ 91. Results of the Decision of Chalcedon: the Rise of
Schisms from the Monophysite Controversy . . . 522

§ 92. The Church of Italy under the Ostrogoths and during
the First Schism between Rome and the Eastern
Church 529

PERIOD III.—THE DISSOLUTION OF THE IMPERIAL STATE
CHURCH AND THE TRANSITION TO THE MIDDLE AGES: FROM
THE BEGINNING OF THE SIXTH CENTURY TO THE LATTER
PART OF THE EIGHTH 538

Chapter I. The Church in the Eastern Empire 540

§ 93. The Age of Justinian 541
§ 94. The Byzantine State Church under Justinian . . . 553
§ 95. The Definitive Type of Religion in the East: Dionysius the Areopagite 560

Chapter II. The Transition to the Middle Ages. The Foundation of the Germanic National Churches 564

§ 96. The Celtic Church in the British Isles 566
§ 97. The Conversion of the Franks. The Establishment of
Catholicism in the Germanic Kingdoms 570
§ 98. The State Church in the Germanic Kingdoms . . . 579
§ 99. Gregory the Great and the Roman Church in the
Second Half of the Sixth Century 590
§ 100. The Foundation of the Anglo-Saxon Church . . . 602

Chapter III. The Foundation of the Ecclesiastical Institutions
of the Middle Ages 615

§ 101. Foundation of the Mediæval Diocesan and Parochial Constitution 616
§ 102. Western Piety and Thought in the Period of the Conversion of the Barbarians 620
§ 103. The Foundation of the Mediæval Penitential System 624
§ 104. The New Monasticism and the Rule of Benedict of
Nursia 630
(A) Benedict of Nursia, Regula 631
(B) Formulæ 641
§ 105. Foundation of Mediæval Culture and Schools . . . 644

CONTENTS

PAGE

Chapter IV. The Revolution in the Ecclesiastical and Political Situation Due to the Rise of Islam and the Doctrinal Disputes in the Eastern Church 652

§ 106. The Rise and Extension of Islam 653

§ 107. The Monothelete Controversy and the Sixth General Council, Constantinople, A. D. 681 660

§ 108. Rome, Constantinople, and the Lombard State Church in the Seventh Century 672

§ 109. Rome, Constantinople, and the Lombards in the Period of the First Iconoclastic Controversy; the Seventh General Council, Nicæa, A. D. 787 . . . 684

INDEX 699

GENERAL BIBLIOGRAPHICAL NOTE

UNDER each period special collections of available sources are to be found. The student is not given any bibliography of works bearing on the topics, but is referred to the following accessible works of reference of recent date for additional information and bibliographies:

The New Schaff-Herzog Encyclopædia of Religious Knowledge, edited by S. M. Jackson, New York, 1908–12.

The Catholic Encyclopædia, New York, 1907–12.

The Encyclopædia Britannica, eleventh edition, Cambridge, 1910.

The Encyclopædia of Religion and Ethics, edited by J. Hastings, Edinburgh and New York, 1908 ff. (In course of publication.)

For the patristic writers, their lives, works, editions, and other bibliographical matter, see:

G. Krüger, *History of Early Christian Literature in the First Three Centuries,* English translation by C. R. Gillett, New York, 1897. Cited as Krüger.

B. Bardenhewer, *Patrologie,* Freiburg-i.-B., 1911, English translation of second edition (1901) by T. J. Shahan, St. Louis, 1908. Cited as Bardenhewer.

In addition to the encyclopædias the following are indispensable, and should be consulted:

Smith and Wace, *Dictionary of Christian Biography, Literature, Sects, and Doctrines,* London, 1877–87. (The Condensed Edition of 1911 by no means takes the place of this standard work.) Cited DCB.

Smith and Cheetham, *Dictionary of Christian Antiquities,* London, 1875–80. Cited DCA.

Advanced students and those capable of using French and German are referred to the following, which have admirable and authoritative articles and ample bibliographies:

Realencyclopædie für protestantische Theologie, edited by A. Hauck, Leipsic, 1896 *ff.* Two supplementary volumes appeared in 1913. Cited PRE.

Kirchenlexicon oder Encyclopædie der katholischen Theologie und ihrer Hilfswissenschaften, second edition, by J. Hergenröther und F. Kaulen, Freiburg-i.-B., 1882–1901. Cited KL.

Dictionnaire de Théologie Catholique, edited by A. Vacant and E. Mangenot, Paris, 1903 *ff.*

Dictionnaire d'Archéologie Chrétienne et de Liturgie, edited by F. Cabrol, 1903 *ff.*

Dictionnaire d'Histoire et de Géographie Ecclesiastiques, edited by A. Baudrillart, A. Vogt, and U. Roziès, Paris, 1909 *ff.*

Collections of sources in the original languages, easily procured and to be consulted for texts and to some extent for bibliographies:

C. Mirbt, *Quellen zur Geschichte des Papsttums und des römischen Katholizismus*, third edition, Tübingen, 1911. Cited as Mirbt.

C. Kirch, S. J., *Enchiridion fontium historiæ ecclesiasticæ antiquæ*, Freiburg-i.-B., 1910. Cited as Kirch.

H. Denziger, *Enchiridion symbolorum, definitionum et declarationum de rebus fidei et morum*, eleventh edition, edited by Clemens Bannwart, S. J., Freiburg-i.-B., 1911. Cited as Denziger.

A. Hahn, *Bibliothek der Symbole und Glaubensregeln der alten Kirche*, third edition, Breslau, 1897. Cited as Hahn.

G. Krüger, *Sammlung ausgewählter kirchen und dogmengeschichtlicher Quellenschriften*, Freiburg-i.-B.

    Of this useful collection especially important are the following of more general application:

E. Preuschen, *Analecta: Kürzere Texte zur Geschichte der alten Kirche und des Kanons*, second edition, 1909–10.

F. Lauchert, *Die Kanones der wichtigsten altkirchlichen Concilien nebst den apostolischen Kanones.*

R. Knopf, *Ausgewählte Märtyreracten.*   Cited as Knopf.

Other volumes are cited in connection with topics.

H. T. Bruns, *Canones apostolorum et conciliorum sæculorum IV, V, VI, VII*, Berlin, 1839. Cited as Bruns.

Although not source-books, yet of very great value for the sources they contain should be mentioned:

J. C. L. Gieseler, *A Text-Book of Church History*, English translation, New York, 1857.

K. R. Hageñbach, *A History of Christian Doctrines*, English translation, Edinburgh, 1883–85.

C. J. Hefele, *Conciliengeschichte*, Freiburg-i.-B., 1855–70. Second edition, 1873 *et seq.* A new French translation with admirable supplementary notes has just appeared. The English translation (*History of the Councils*), Edinburgh, 1876–95, extends only through the eighth century. Cited as Hefele.

A SOURCE BOOK
FOR ANCIENT CHURCH HISTORY

THE FIRST DIVISION OF ANCIENT CHRISTIANITY

THE CHURCH UNDER THE HEATHEN EMPIRE: TO A. D. 324

By the accession of Constantine to the sole sovereignty of the Roman Empire, A. D. 324, ancient Christianity may be conveniently divided into two great periods. In the first, it was a religion liable to persecution, suffering severely at times and always struggling to maintain itself; in the second, it became the religion of the State, and in its turn set about to repress and persecute the heathen religions. It was no longer without legal rights; it had the support of the secular rulers and was lavishly endowed with wealth. The conditions of the Church in these two periods are so markedly different, and the conditions had such a distinct effect upon the life and growth of the Christian religion, that the reign of Constantine is universally recognized as marking a transition from one historical period to another, although no date which shall mark that transition is universally accepted. The year 311, the year in which the Diocletian persecution ceased, has been accepted by many as the dividing point. The exact date adopted is immaterial.

The principal sources in English for the history of the Christian Church before A. D. 324 are:

The Ante-Nicene Fathers. Translations of the Writings of the Fathers down to A. D. 325. American edition, Buffalo and New York, 1885–1896; new edition, New York, 1896 (a reprint). The collection, cited as ANF, contains the bulk of

the Christian literature of the period, with the exception of
the less important commentaries of Origen.
Eusebius, *Church History*. Translated with Prolegomena
and Notes by Arthur Cushman McGiffert. In *A Select Library
of the Nicene and Post-Nicene Fathers of the Christian Church.*
Second series, New York, 1890. The *Church History* of
Eusebius is the foundation of the study of the history of the
Church before A. D. 324, as it contains a vast number of cita-
tions from works now lost. The edition by Professor Mc-
Giffert is the best in English, and is provided with scholarly
notes, which serve as an elaborate commentary on the text.
It should be in every library. This work is cited as Eusebius,
Hist. Ec. The text used in the extracts given in this source
book is that of Ed. Schwartz, in *Die Griechischen Christlichen
Schriftsteller der ersten drei Jahrhunderte.* Kleine Ausgabe,
Leipsic, 1908. This text is identical with the larger and less
convenient edition by the same editor.

PERIOD I

THE APOSTOLIC AGE: TO CIRCA A. D. 100

The period in the Church before the clash with Gnosticism and the rise of an apologetic literature comprises the apostolic and the post-apostolic ages. These names have become traditional. The so-called apostolic age, or to circa 100, is that in which the Apostles lived, though the best tradition makes John the only surviving Apostle for the last quarter of a century.

The principal sources for the history of the Church in this period are the books of the New Testament, and only to a slight degree the works of contemporaneous Jewish and heathen writers. It is hardly necessary to reproduce New Testament passages here. The Jewish references of importance will be found in the works on the life of Christ and of St. Paul. As the treatment of this period commonly falls under a different branch of study, New Testament exegesis, it is not necessary in Church history to enter into any detail. There are, however, a few references to events in this period which are to be found only outside the New Testament, and are of importance to the student of Church history. These are the Neronian persecution (§ 1), the death of the Apostles (§§ 2, 3), and the persecution under Domitian (§ 4). The paucity of references to Christianity in the first century is due chiefly to the fact that Christianity appeared to the men of the times as merely a very small Oriental religion, struggling for recognition, and contending with many others coming from the same region. It had not yet made any great advance either in numbers or social importance.

§ 1. The Neronian Persecution.
§ 2. The Death of Peter and Paul.
§ 3. The Death of John.
§ 4. The Persecution of Domitian.

§ 1. The Neronian Persecution

The Neronian persecution took place A. D. 64. The occasion was the great fire which destroyed a large part of the city of Rome. To turn public suspicion from himself as responsible for the fire, Nero attempted to make the Christians appear as the incendiaries. Many were put to death in horrible and fantastic ways. It was not, however, a persecution directed against Christianity as an unlawful religion. It was probably confined to Rome and at most the immediate vicinity, and there is no evidence that it was a general persecution.

Additional source material: Lactantius, *De Mortibus Persecutorum*, ch. 2 (ANF, VII); Sulpicius Severus, *Chronicon*, II, 28 (PNF, ser. II, vol. XI).

(a) Tacitus, *Annales*, XV, 44. Preuschen, *Analecta*, I, § 3 : 1. Mirbt, n. 3.

Tacitus (c. 52–c. 117), although not an eye-witness of the persecution, had exceptionally good opportunities for obtaining accurate information, and his account is entirely trustworthy. He is the principal source for the persecution.

Neither by works of benevolence nor the gifts of the prince nor means of appeasing the gods did the shameful suspicion cease, so that it was not believed that the fire had been caused by his command. Therefore, to overcome this rumor, Nero put in his own place as culprits, and punished with most ingenious cruelty, men whom the common people hated for their shameful crimes and called Christians. Christ, from whom the name was derived, had been put to death in the reign of Tiberius by the procurator Pontius Pilate. The deadly superstition, having been checked for a while, began to break out again, not only throughout Judea, where this mischief first arose, but also at Rome, where from all sides all things scandalous and shameful meet and become fashionable. Therefore, at the beginning, some were seized who made confessions; then, on their information, a vast multitude was convicted, not so much of arson as of hatred of the human race. And they were not only put to death, but subjected to insults, in that they were either dressed up in the skins of wild beasts and perished by the cruel mangling of dogs, or else put on crosses to be set on fire, and, as day declined, to be burned, being used as lights by night. Nero had thrown open his gardens for that spectacle, and gave a circus play, mingling with the people dressed in a charioteer's costume or driving in a chariot. From this arose, however, toward men who were, indeed, criminals and deserving extreme penalties, sympathy, on the ground that they were destroyed not for the public good, but to satisfy the cruelty of an individual.

(b) Clement of Rome, *Ep. ad Corinthios*, I, 5, 6. Funk, *Patres Apostolici*, 1901. (MSG, 1 : 218.) Preuschen, *Analecta*, I, § 3 : 5.

The work known as the First Epistle of Clement to the Corinthians was written in the name of the Roman Church about 100. The occasion was the rise of contentions in the Corinthian Church. The name of Clement does not appear in the body of the epistle, but there is no good ground for questioning the traditional ascription to Clement, since before the end of the second century it was quoted under his name by several writers. This Clement was probably the third or fourth bishop of Rome. The epistle was written soon after the Domitian persecution (A. D. 95), and refers not only to that but also to an earlier persecution, which was very probably that under Nero. As the reference is only by way of illustration, the author gives little detail. The passage translated is of interest as containing the earliest reference to the death of the Apostles Peter and Paul, and the language used regarding Paul has been thought to imply that he labored in parts beyond Rome.

Ch. 5. But to leave the ancient examples, let us come to the champions who lived nearest our times; let us take the noble examples of our generation. On account of jealousy and envy the greatest and most righteous pillars of the Church were persecuted, and contended even unto death. Let us set before our eyes the good Apostles: Peter, who on account of unrighteous jealousy endured not one nor two, but many sufferings, and so, having borne his testimony, went to his deserved place of glory. On account of jealousy and strife Paul pointed out the prize of endurance. After he had been seven times in bonds, had been driven into exile, had been stoned, had been a preacher in the East and in the West, he received the noble reward of his faith; having taught righteousness unto the whole world, and having come to the farthest bounds of the West, and having borne witness before rulers, he thus departed from the world and went unto the holy place, having become a notable pattern of patient endurance.

Ch. 6. Unto these men who lived lives of holiness was gathered a vast multitude of the elect, who by many indignities and tortures, being the victims of jealousy, set the finest examples among us. On account of jealousy women, when they had been persecuted as Danaïds and Dircæ, and had suffered cruel and unholy insults, safely reached the goal in the race of faith and received a noble reward, feeble though they were in body.

§ 2. THE DEATH OF PETER AND PAUL

Eusebius, *Hist. Ec.*, II, 25. (MSG, 20 : 207.) *Cf.* Mirbt, n. 33.

For an examination of the merits of Eusebius as a historian, see McGiffert's edition, PNF, ser. II, vol. I, pp. 45–52; also J. B. Lightfoot, art. "Eusebius (23) of Cæsarea," in DCB.

The works of Caius have been preserved only in fragments; see Krüger, § 90. If he was a contemporary of Zephyrinus, he probably lived during the pontificate of that bishop of Rome, 199–217 A. D. The Phrygian heresy which Caius combated was Montanism; see below, § 25.

Dionysius, Bishop of Corinth, was a contemporary of Soter, Bishop of Rome, 166–174 A. D., whom he mentions in an epistle to the Roman Church. Of his epistles only fragments have been preserved; see Krüger, § 55. The following extract from his epistle to the Roman Church is the earliest explicit statement that Peter and Paul suffered martyrdom at the same time or that Peter was ever in Italy. In connection with this extract, that from Clement of Rome (see § 1, a) should be consulted; also Lactantius, *De Mortibus Persecutorum*, ch. 2 (ANF).

It is therefore recorded that Paul was beheaded at Rome itself, and that Peter was crucified likewise at the same time. This account of Peter and Paul is confirmed by the fact that their names are preserved in the cemeteries of that place even to the present time. It is confirmed no less by a member of the Church, Caius by name, a contemporary of Zephyrinus, Bishop of Rome. In carrying on a discussion in writing with Proclus, the leader of the Phrygian heresy, he says as follows concerning the places where the sacred corpses of the aforesaid Apostles are laid: "But I am able to show the trophies of the Apostles. For if you will go to the Vatican or to the Ostian Way, you will find the trophies of those who laid the foundations of this church." And that they two suffered martyrdom at the same time is stated by Dionysius, Bishop of Corinth, corresponding with the Romans in writing, in the following words: "You have thus by such admonition bound together the planting of Peter and Paul at Rome and at Corinth. For both planted in our Corinth and likewise taught us, and in like manner in Italy they both taught and suffered martyrdom at the same time."

§ 3. THE DEATH OF THE APOSTLE JOHN

(a) Irenæus, *Adversus Hæreses*, II, 22, 5; III, 3, 4. (MSG, 7 : 785, 854.)

Irenæus was bishop of Lyons soon after 177. He was born in Asia Minor about 120, and was a disciple of Polycarp (ob. circa 155) and of other elders who had seen John, the disciple of the Lord.

II, 22, 5. Those in Asia associated with John, the disciple of the Lord, testify that John delivered it [a tradition regarding the length of Christ's ministry] to them. For he remained among them until the time of Trajan [98–117 A. D.].

III, 3, 4. But the church in Ephesus also, which was

founded by Paul, and where John remained until the time of
Trajan, is a faithful witness of the apostolic tradition.

(b) Jerome, *Comm. ad Galat.* (MSL, 26 : 462.)

The following extract from Jerome's commentary on Galatians is
of such late date as to be of doubtful value as an authority. There is,
however, nothing improbable in it, and it is in harmony with other
traditions. It is to be taken as a tradition which at any rate represents the opinion of the fourth century regarding the Apostle John.
Cf. Jerome, *De Viris Inlustribus*, ch. 9 (PNF, ser. II, vol. III, 364).

When the holy Evangelist John had lived to extreme old
age in Ephesus, he could be carried only with difficulty by the
hands of the disciples, and as he was not able to pronounce
more words, he was accustomed to say at every assembly,
"Little children, love one another." At length the disciples
and brethren who were present became tired of hearing always
the same thing and said: "Master, why do you always say
this?" Thereupon John gave an answer worthy of himself:
"Because this is the commandment of the Lord, and if it is
observed then is it enough."

(c) Eusebius, *Hist. Ec.*, III, 31. (MSG, 20 : 279.)

Polycrates was bishop of Ephesus and a contemporary of Victor of
Rome (189-199 A. D.). His date cannot be fixed more precisely.
The reference to the "high priest's mitre" is obscure; see J. B. Light-
foot, *Commentary on the Epistle to the Galatians*, p. 345. A longer ex-
tract from this epistle of Polycrates will be found under the Easter
Controversy (§ 38).

The time of John's death has been given in a general way,[1]
but his burial-place is indicated by an epistle of Polycrates
(who was bishop of the parish of Ephesus) addressed to Victor
of Rome, mentioning him, together with the Apostle Philip
and his daughters, in the following words: "For in Asia also
great lights have fallen asleep, which shall rise again at the
last day, at the coming of the Lord, when he shall come with

---

[1] See Eusebius, *Hist. Ec.*, III, 23, who gives quotations from Irenæus. This
passage also gives a lengthy extract from the work of Clement of Alexandria,
Quis dives salvetur, bearing on St. John's life at Ephesus (ANF, II, 591-604).

glory from heaven and seek out all the saints. Among these are Philip, one of the twelve Apostles, who sleeps at Hierapolis, and his two aged virgin daughters, and another daughter who lived in the Holy Spirit and now rests at Ephesus; and moreover John, who was both a witness and a teacher, who reclined upon the bosom of the Lord, and being a priest wore the high priest's mitre, also sleeps at Ephesus."

§ 4. THE PERSECUTION UNDER DOMITIAN

What is commonly called the persecution under Domitian (81–96) does not seem to have been a persecution of Christianity as such. The charges of atheism and superstition may have been due to heathen misunderstanding of the Christian faith and worship. There is no sufficient ground for identifying Flavius Clemens with the Clemens who was bishop of Rome. For bibliography of the persecution under Domitian, see Preuschen, *Analecta*, second ed., I, 11.

(*a*) Cassius Dio (excerpt. per Xiphilinum), *Hist. Rom.*, LXVII, 14 *f.* Preuschen, *Analecta*, I, § 4 : 11.

For Cassius Dio, see *Encyc. Brit.*, art. "Dio Cassius."

At that time (95) the road which leads from Sinuessa to Puteoli was paved. And in the same year Domitian caused Flavius Clemens along with many others to be put to death, although he was his cousin and had for his wife Flavia Domitilla, who was also related to him. The charge of atheism was made against both of them, in consequence of which many others also who had adopted the customs of the Jews were condemned. Some were put to death, others lost their property. Domitilla, however, was only banished to Pandataria.

(*b*) Eusebius, *Hist. Ec.*, III, 18. (MSG, 20 : 252.)

To such a degree did the teaching of our faith flourish at that time[1] that even those writers who were far from our

---
[1] Reign of Domitian, 81–96.

religion did not hesitate to mention in their histories the persecutions and martyrdoms which took place during that time. And they, indeed, accurately indicate the time. For they record that, in the fifteenth year of Domitian, Flavia Domitilla, daughter of a sister of Flavius Clemens, who was at that time one of the consuls of Rome, was exiled with many others to the island of Pontia[1] in consequence of testimony borne to Christ.

[1] Pontia was an island near Pandataria. The group is known as Pontiæ Insulæ. See DCB, art. "Domitilla, Flavia"; Eusebius, *Hist. Ec.*, ed. McGiffert (PNF, ser. II, vol. I), III, 18, notes 4–6; also Lightfoot, *Commentary on the Epistle to the Philippians*, p. 22, n. 1.

PERIOD II

THE POST–APOSTOLIC AGE: A. D. 100–A. D. 140

The post-apostolic age, extending from circa 100 to circa
140, is the age of the beginnings of Gentile Christianity on an
extended scale. It is marked by the rapid spread of Christianity, so that immediately after its close the Church is found
throughout the Roman world, and the Roman Government is
forced to take notice of it and deal with it as a religion (§§ 6,
7); the decline of the Jewish element in the Church and extreme
hostility of Judaism to the Church (§ 5); the continuance of
chiliastic expectations (§ 10); the beginnings of the passion
for martyrdom (§ 8); as well as the appearance of the forms
of organization and worship which subsequently became
greatly elaborated and remained permanently in the Church
(§§ 12–15); as also the appearance of religious and moral
ideas which became dominant in the ancient Church (§§ 11,
12, 16). The literature of the period upon which the study
of the conditions and thought of the Church of this age must
be based is represented principally by the so-called Apostolic
Fathers, a name which is convenient, but misleading and to
be regretted. These are Clement of Rome, Barnabas, Ignatius,
Polycarp, Papias, Hermas; with the writings of these are commonly included two anonymous books known as the *Didache*,
or *Teaching of the Twelve Apostles*, and the *Epistle to Diognetus*.
From all of these selections are given.[1]

[1] There are three leading critical editions of the Apostolic Fathers:
Patrum Apostolicorum Opera, edited by A. von Gebhardt, A. Harnack, and
Th. Zahn, Leipsic, 1876, 1877, reprinted 1894 and since.
Opera Patrum Apostolicorum, edited by F. X. Funk, Tübingen, 1881.
There is a very inexpensive reprint of the text in Krüger's *Sammlung ausge-
wählter kirchen- und dogmengeschichtlicher Quellenschriften*, 2te Reihe, 1 Heft.

§ 5. Christianity and Judaism.
§ 6. The Extension of Christianity.
§ 7. Relation of the Roman State to Christianity.
§ 8. Martyrdom and the Desire for Martyrdom.
§ 9. Position of the Roman Church.
§ 10. Chiliastic Expectations.
§ 11. The Church and the World.
§ 12. Theological Ideas.
§ 13. Worship in the Post-Apostolic Age.
§ 14. Church Organization.
§ 15. Church Discipline.
§ 16. Moral Ideas.

§ 5. CHRISTIANITY AND JUDAISM

The Christian Church grew up not on Jewish but on Gentile soil. In a very short time the Gentiles formed the overwhelming majority within the Church. As they did not become Jews and did not observe the Jewish ceremonial law, a problem arose as to the place of the Jewish law, which was accepted without question as of divine authority. One solution is given by the author of the so-called Epistle of Barnabas, which should be compared with the solution given by St. Paul in his epistles to the Galatians and to the Romans. The number of conversions from Judaism rapidly declined, and very early an extreme hostility toward Christianity became common among the Jews.

(a) Barnabas, *Epistula*, 4, 9.

The epistle attributed to Barnabas is certainly not by the Apostle of that name. Its date is much disputed, but may be safely placed within the first century. The author attempts to show the contrast

Funk's text is used in the following sections, but as the Apostolic Fathers are everywhere accessible no references are given to Migne.

The Apostolic Fathers, edited by J. B. Lightfoot, second ed., part I, 2 vols. (Clement of Rome), London, 1890; part II, 3 vols. (Ignatius and Polycarp), London, 1889; smaller ed. (containing all the Apostolic Fathers), London, 1890.

The most recent edition of the Apostolic Fathers is that of Kirsopp Lake, in the *Loeb Classical Library*, 1912 (text and translation on opposite pages).

between Judaism and Christianity by proving that the Jews wholly misunderstood the Mosaic law and had long since lost any claims supposed to be derived from the Mosaic covenant. The epistle is everywhere marked by hostility to Judaism, of which the writer has but imperfect knowledge. The book was regarded as Holy Scripture by Clement of Alexandria and by Origen, though with some hesitation. The position taken by the author was undoubtedly extreme, and not followed generally by the Church. It was, however, merely pushing to excess a conviction already prevalent in the Church, that Christianity and Judaism were distinct religions. For a saner and more commonly accepted position, see Justin Martyr, *Apol.*, I, 47–53 (ANF, I, 178 *ff.*). A translation of the entire epistle may be found in ANF, I, 137–149.

Ch. 4. It is necessary, therefore, for us who inquire much concerning present events to seek out those things which are able to save us. Let us wholly flee, then, from all the works of iniquity, lest the works of iniquity take hold of us; and let us hate the error of the present times, that we may set our love on the future. Let us not give indulgence to our soul, that it should have power to run with sinners and the wicked, that we become not like them. The final occasion of stumbling approaches, concerning which it is written as Enoch speaks: For this end the Lord has cut short the times and the days, that His beloved may hasten and will come to his inheritance.[1] . . . Ye ought therefore to understand. And this also I beg of you, as being one of you and with special love loving you all more than my own soul, to take heed to yourselves, and not be like some, adding largely to your sins, and saying: "The covenant is both theirs and ours." For it is ours; but they thus finally lost it, after Moses had already received it.[2]

Ch. 9. . . . But also circumcision, in which they trusted, has been abrogated. He declared that circumcision was not of the flesh; but they transgressed because an evil angel deluded them.[3] . . . Learn, then, my beloved children, concerning all

[1] *Cf.* Matt. 24 : 6, 22; Mark 13 : 7, 20. These words do not occur in the book of Enoch.
[2] The writer quotes Ex. 31 : 18; 34 : 28; 32 : 7; Deut. 9 : 12.
[3] *I. e.*, so that they believed that circumcision should be made in the flesh and not taken spiritually.

things richly, that Abraham, the first who enjoined circumcision, looking forward in spirit to Jesus, circumcised, the teaching of the three letters having been received. For the Scripture saith: "Abraham circumcised eighteen and three hundred men of his household." What, then, was the knowledge [*gnosis*] given to him in this? Learn that he says the eighteen first and then, making a space, the three hundred. The eighteen are the Iota, ten, and the Eta, eight; and you have here the name of Jesus. And because the cross was to express the grace in the letter Tau, he says also, three hundred. He discloses therefore Jesus in the two letters, and the cross in one. He knows this who has put within us the engrafted gift of his teaching. No one has learned from me a more excellent piece of knowledge, but I know that ye are worthy.[1]

(*b*) Justin Martyr, *Dialogus cum Tryphone*, 17. J. C. T. Otto, *Corpus Apologetarum Christianorum Sæculi Secundi*, third ed., 1876–81. (MSG, 6 : 511.)

Justin Martyr was born about 100 in Samaria. He was one of the first of the Gentiles who had been trained in philosophy to become a Christian. His influence upon the doctrinal development of the Church was profound. He died as a martyr between 163 and 168. His principal works are the two Apologies written in close connection under Antoninus Pius (138–161), probably about 150, and his dialogue with Trypho the Jew, which was written after the first Apology. All translations of Justin Martyr are based upon Otto's text, *v. supra*.

For the other nations have not been so guilty of wrong inflicted on us and on Christ as you have been, who are in fact the authors of the wicked prejudices against the Just One and against us who hold by Him.[2] For after you

---

[1] IH or Iη = 'Ιησοῦς. T was taken as a picture of a cross. For the Tau or Egyptian cross, see DCA, art. "Cross." The method of allegorical interpretation here used is that species known as gematria, in which the numerical equivalence of letters composing a word is employed as a key to mystic meaning. This differs somewhat from the ordinary gematria, for which see Farrar, *History of Interpretation*, 1886, pp. 98 *ff.*, 445 *f.* Barnabas is by no means singular among early Christians in resorting to Jewish allegorical interpretation.

[2] For the same charge brought against the Jews of stirring up hostility against the Christians, see Tertullian, *Ad Nationes*, I, 14; *Adv. Marcionem*, III, 23; *Adv. Judæos*, 13; Origen, *Contra Celsum*, VI, 27.

had crucified Him, the only blameless and righteous Man, through whose stripes there is healing to those who through Him approach the Father, when you knew that He had risen from the dead and ascended into heaven, as the prophecies foretold would take place, not only did you not repent of those things wherein you had done wickedly, but you then selected and sent out from Jerusalem chosen men through all the world to say that the atheistical heresy of the Christians had appeared and to spread abroad those things which all they who know us not speak against us; so that you are the cause of unrighteousness not only in your own case, but, in fact, in the case of all other men generally. . . . Accordingly, you show great zeal in publishing throughout all the world bitter, dark, and unjust slanders against the only blameless and righteous Light sent from God to men.

(c) *Martyrdom of Polycarp*, 12, 13.

Polycarp, Bishop of Smyrna, died at Smyrna February 2, 155, at the age of at least eighty-six, but he was probably nearer one hundred years old. He was the disciple of John, probably same as the Apostle John. His epistle was written circa 115, soon after the death of Ignatius of Antioch. At present it is generally regarded as genuine, though grave doubts have been entertained in the past. The martyrdom was written by some member of the church at Smyrna for that body to send to the church at Philomelium in Phrygia, and must have been composed soon after the death of the aged bishop. It is probably the finest of all the ancient martyrdoms and should be read in its entirety. Translation in the ANF, I, 37-45.

Ch. 12. The whole multitude both of the heathen and the Jews who dwelt at Smyrna cried out with uncontrollable fury and in loud voice: "This is the teacher of Asia, the father of the Christians and the overthrower of our gods, who teaches many neither to sacrifice nor to worship." Saying these things, they cried out and demanded of Philip, the Asiarch, to let a lion loose upon Polycarp. But he said he could not do this, since the sports with beasts had ended. Then it pleased them to cry out with one consent that he should burn Polycarp alive. . . .

Ch. 13. These things were carried into effect more rapidly than they were spoken, and the multitude immediately gathered together wood and fagots out of the shops and baths, and the Jews especially, as was their custom, assisted them eagerly in it.

§ 6. THE EXTENSION OF CHRISTIANITY

It is impossible to determine with accuracy even the principal places to which Christianity had spread in the first half of the second century. Ancient writers were not infrequently led astray by their own rhetoric in dealing with this topic.

Justin Martyr, *Dialogus cum Tryphone,* 117. (MSG, 6 : 676.)

The following passage is of significance as bearing not only upon the extent to which Christianity had spread, after making due allowance for rhetoric, but also upon the conception of the eucharist and its relation to the ancient sacrifices held, by some Christians at least, in the first half of the second century. *Cf.* ch. 41 of the same work, *v. infra*, §§ 12 *f.*

Therefore, as to all sacrifices offered in His name, which Jesus Christ commanded to be offered, *i. e.,* in the eucharist of the bread and cup, and which are offered by Christians in all places throughout the world, God, anticipating them, testified that they are well-pleasing to Him; but He rejects those presented by you and by those priests of yours, saying: And your sacrifices I will not accept at your hands; for from the rising of the sun unto the going down of the same my name is great among the Gentiles (He says), but ye have profaned it.[1] But since you deceive yourselves, both you and your teachers, when you interpret what was said as if the Word spoke of those of your nation who were in the dispersion, and that it said that their prayers and sacrifices offered in every place are pure and well-pleasing, you should know that you are speaking falsely and are trying to cheat

[1] *Cf.* Mal. 1 : 10–12.

yourselves in every way; for, in the first place, not even yet does your nation extend from the rising to the setting sun, for there are nations among which none of your race ever dwelt. For there is not a single race of men, whether among barbarians or Greeks, or by whatever name they may be called, of those who live in wagons or are called nomads or of herdsmen living in tents, among whom prayers and thanksgivings are not offered through the name of the crucified Jesus to the Father and Maker of all things. For, furthermore, at that time, when the prophet Malachi said this, your dispersion over the whole earth, as you are now, had not taken place, as is evident from the Scriptures.

§ 7. RELATION OF THE ROMAN STATE TO CHRISTIANITY

The procedure of the Roman Government against the Christians first took a definite form with the rescript of Trajan addressed to Pliny circa A. D. 111–113, but there is no formal imperial edict extant before Decius on the question of the Christian religion. In an addition to the rescript of Trajan addressed to Pliny there is a letter of Hadrian on the Christians (*Ep. ad Servianum*) which is of interest as giving the opinion of that Emperor, but the rescript addressed to Minucius Fundanus is probably spurious, as is also the Epistle of Antoninus Pius to the Common Assembly of Asia.

Additional source material: The text of the rescripts may be found in Preuschen, *Analecta*, I, §§ 6, 7; translations, ANF, I, 186 *f*., and Eusebius, *Hist. Ec.* (ed. McGiffert), IV, 9, and IV, 13.

(*a*) Plinius Junior, *Epistulæ*, X, 96, 97. Preuschen, *Analecta*, I, 12 *ff*. *Cf*. Mirbt, nn. 14, 15.

Caius Cæcilius Secundus is commonly known as Pliny the Younger, to distinguish him from his uncle, Pliny the Naturalist, whose wealth he inherited and whose name he seems to have borne. He was propraetor of Bithynia under Trajan (98–117), with whom he stood on terms of friendship and even intimacy. His letter to the Emperor requesting advice as to the right mode of dealing with Christians was written between 111 and 113.

This correspondence is of the first importance, as it is unimpeachable evidence as to the spread of Christianity in the province in which Pliny was placed, to the customs of the Christians in their worship, and to the method of dealing with the new religion, which was followed for a long time with little change. It established the policy that Christianity, as such, was not to be punished as a crime, that the State did not feel called upon to seek out Christians, that it would not act upon anonymous accusations, but that when proper accusations were brought, the general laws, which Christians had violated on account of their faith, should be executed. Christianity was not to be treated as a crime. The mere renunciation of Christianity, coupled with the proof of renunciation involved in offering sacrifice, enabled the accused to escape punishment.

Ep. 96. It is my custom, my lord, to refer to you all questions about which I have doubts. Who, indeed, can better direct me in hesitation, or enlighten me in ignorance? In the examination of Christians I have never taken part; therefore I do not know what crime is usually punished or investigated or to what extent. So I have no little uncertainty whether there is any distinction of age, or whether the weaker offenders fare in no respect otherwise than the stronger; whether pardon is granted on repentance, or whether when one has been a Christian there is no gain to him in that he has ceased to be such; whether the mere name, if it is without crimes, or crimes connected with the name are punished. Meanwhile I have taken this course with those who were accused before me as Christians: I have asked them whether they were Christians. Those who confessed I asked a second and a third time, threatening punishment. Those who persisted I ordered led away to execution. For I did not doubt that, whatever it was they admitted, obstinacy and unbending perversity certainly deserve to be punished. There were others of the like insanity, but because they were Roman citizens I noted them down to be sent to Rome. Soon after this, as it often happens, because the matter was taken notice of, the crime became wide-spread and many cases arose. An unsigned paper was presented containing the names of many. But these denied that they were or had been Christians, and I thought it right to let them go, since at my dictation they prayed to the gods and made supplication with incense and wine to your statue, which I had ordered to be brought into the court for the purpose, together with the images of the gods, and in addition to this they cursed Christ, none of which things, it is said, those who are really Christians can be made to do. Others who were named by an informer said that they were Christians, and soon afterward denied it, saying, indeed, that they had been, but had ceased to be Christians, some three years ago, some many years, and one even twenty years ago. All these also not only worshipped your statue and the images of the gods, but also cursed Christ. They asserted, however, that the amount of their fault or error was this: that they had been accustomed to assemble on a fixed day before daylight and sing by turns [*i. e.*, antiphonally] a hymn to Christ as a god; and that they bound themselves with an oath, not for any crime, but to commit neither theft, nor robbery, nor adultery, not to break their word and not to deny a deposit when demanded; after these things were done, it was their custom to depart and meet together again to take food, but ordinary and harmless food; and they said that even this had ceased after my edict was issued, by which, according to your commands, I had forbidden the existence of clubs. On this account I believed it the more necessary to find out from two maid-servants, who were called deaconesses [*ministræ*], and that by torture, what was the truth. I found nothing else than a perverse and excessive superstition. I therefore adjourned the examination and hastened to consult you. The matter seemed to me to be worth deliberation, especially on account of the number of those in danger. For many of every age, every rank, and even of both sexes, are brought into danger; and will be in the future. The contagion of that superstition has penetrated not only the cities but also the villages and country places; and yet it seems possible to stop it and set it right. At any rate, it is certain enough that the temples, deserted until quite recently, begin to be frequented, that the ceremonies of religion, long disused, are restored, and that fodder for the victims comes to market, whereas buyers of it were until now very few. From this it may easily be supposed what a multitude of men can be reclaimed if there be a place of repentance.

(b) Ep. 97 (*Trajan to Pliny*). You have followed, my dear Secundus, the proper course of procedure in examining the cases of those who were accused to you as Christians. For, indeed, nothing can be laid down as a general law which contains anything like a definite rule of action. They are not to be sought out. If they are accused and convicted, they are to be punished, yet on this condition, that he who denies that he is a Christian and makes the fact evident by an act, that is, by worshipping our gods, shall obtain pardon on his repentance, however much suspected as to the past. Papers, however, which are presented anonymously ought not to be admitted in any accusation. For they are a very bad example and unworthy of our times.

§ 8.   MARTYRDOM AND THE DESIRE FOR MARTYRDOM

Ignatius of Antioch, *Ep. ad Romanos*, 4.

Ignatius was bishop of Antioch in the opening years of the second century. According to tradition, he suffered martyrdom in Rome under Trajan, circa 117. Having been sent from Antioch to Rome by command of the Emperor, on his way he addressed letters to various churches in Asia, exhorting them to seek unity and avoid heresy by close union with the local bishop. His aim seems to have been practical, to promote the welfare of the Christian communities rather than the exaltation of the episcopal office itself. Doubts have arisen as to the authenticity of these epistles on account of the frequent references to the episcopate and to heresy. Further difficulty has been caused by the fact that the epistles of Ignatius appear in three forms or recensions, a longer Greek recension forming a group of thirteen epistles, a short Greek of seven epistles, and a still shorter Syriac version of only three. After much fluctuation of opinion, due to the general reconstruction of the history of the whole period, which has gone through various marked changes, the opinion of scholars has been steadily settling upon the short Greek recension of seven epistles as authentic, especially since the critical re-examination of the whole question by Zahn and Lightfoot.

I write to all the churches and impress on all, that I shall willingly die for God unless ye hinder me. I beseech you not to show unseasonable good-will toward me.[1] Permit me to be the food of wild beasts, through whom it will be granted me to attain unto God. I am the wheat of God and I am ground by the teeth of wild beasts, that I may be found the pure bread of Christ. Rather entice the wild beasts, that they may become my tomb and leave nothing of my body, so that when I have fallen asleep I may be burdensome to no one. Then I shall be truly a disciple of Jesus Christ, when the world sees not my body. Entreat Christ for me, that by these instruments I may be found a sacrifice to God. Not as Peter and Paul[2] do I issue commandments unto you. They were Apostles, I a condemned man; they were free, I even until now a slave.[3] But if I suffer, I shall be the freedman of Jesus Christ, and shall rise again free in Him. And now, being in bonds, I learn not to desire anything.

§ 9. THE POSITION OF THE ROMAN COMMUNITY OF CHRISTIANS IN THE CHURCH

The Roman Church took very early a leading place in the Christian Church, even before the rise of the Petrine tradition, and its importance was generally recognized. Its charity was very widely known and extolled. It was a part of its care for Christians everywhere, a care which found expression later in the obligation of maintaining the faith in the great theological controversies. On the position of the Roman Church in this period, see the address of the Epistle of Ignatius to the Romans (ANF, I, 73), as also the relation of Polycarp

---

[1] The Christians at Rome seem, according to this statement, to have been in such a position that they might be able to interfere in the case of prisoners.

[2] A possible reference to the presence of Peter and Paul at Rome, but by no means certain, as epistolatory commands would fulfil the conditions better. The connection of Peter with Rome, however, is very significant.

[3] It can not be concluded from this that Ignatius was of servile condition. His journey to Rome in chains might be enough here to explain the language, especially when the style of Ignatius is considered.

to the Roman Church in connection with the question of the date of Easter (see § 38, below).

Dionysius of Corinth, "Epistle to the Roman Church," in Eusebius, *Hist. Ec.*, IV, 23. (MSG, 20 : 388.)   For text, see Kirch, n. 49 *f*.

Moreover, there is still current an Epistle of Dionysius to the Romans, addressed to Soter, bishop at that time. But there is nothing like quoting its words in which, in approval of the custom of the Romans maintained until the persecution in our own time, he writes as follows: "For you have from the beginning this custom of doing good in different ways to all the brethren, and of sending supplies to many churches in all the cities, in this way refreshing the poverty of those in need, and helping brethren in the mines with the supplies which you have sent from the beginning, maintaining as Romans the customs of the Romans handed down from the fathers, which your blessed bishop Soter has not only kept up, but also increased, helping the saints with the abundant supply he sends from time to time, and with blessed words exhorting, as a loving father his children, the brethren who come up to the city." In this same epistle he also mentions the Epistle of Clement to the Corinthians, showing that from the first it was read by ancient custom before the Church. He says, therefore: "To-day, then, being the Lord's day we kept holy; in which we read your letter; for reading it we shall always have admonition, as also from the former one written to us through Clement." Moreover, the same writer speaks of his own epistles as having been falsified, as follows: "For when the brethren asked me to write letters, I wrote them. And these the apostles of the devil have filled with tares, taking away some things and adding others. For them there is woe in store. So it is not marvellous that some have tried to falsify even the dominical scriptures [*i. e.*, the Holy Scriptures], when they have conspired against writings of another sort."

§ 10. CHILIASTIC EXPECTATIONS

Primitive Christianity was marked by great chiliastic enthusiasm, traces of which may be found in the New Testament. By chiliasm, strictly speaking, is meant the belief
that Christ was to return to earth and reign visibly for one
thousand years. That return was commonly placed in the
immediate future. With that reign was connected the bodily
resurrection of the saints. This belief, in somewhat varying
form, was one of the great ethical motives in apostolic and
post-apostolic times. It was a part of the fundamental
principles of Montanism. It disappeared with the rise of a
"scientific theology" such as that of Alexandria, the exclusion of Montanism, and the changed conception of the
relation of the Church and the world, due to the lapse of
time and the establishment of Christianity as the religion
of the State. From the fourth century it ceased to be a
living doctrine.

(a) Papias, in Eusebius, *Hist. Ec.*, III, 39. (MSG, 20 : 300.)

Papias, from whom two selections have been taken, was bishop of
Hierapolis in Phrygia during the first part of the second century. He
was, therefore, an elder contemporary of Justin Martyr. His work,
The Exposition of the Oracles of the Lord, has perished, with the exception of a few fragments. The comments of Eusebius in introducing
the quotations of Papias are characteristic of the change that had come
over the Church since the post-apostolic period. That Papias was not
to be regarded as a man of small power simply because he held chiliastic
ideas is sufficiently refuted by the fact that Justin Martyr falls but
little behind Papias in extravagance of expression.

"I shall not hesitate, also, to set in order for you with my
interpretations whatsoe-er things I have ever learned carefully from the elders and carefully remembered, guaranteeing
the truth of them. . . . For I did not think that what was to
be gotten from the books would profit me as much as what
came from the living and abiding voice. . . ." The same
writer gives also other accounts which he says came to him

through unwritten traditions, certain strange parables and teachings of the Saviour and some other more mythical things. Among these he says that there will be a period of some thousand years after the resurrection of the dead, when the kingdom of Christ will be set up in a material form on this very earth. I suppose he got these ideas through a misunderstanding of the apostolic accounts, not perceiving that the things said by them were spoken mystically in figures. For he appears to have been of very limited understanding, as one can see from his discourses, though so many of the Church Fathers after him adopted a like opinion, urging in their support the antiquity of the man; as, for instance, Irenæus and any one else that may have proclaimed similar views.

(b) Irenæus, *Adv. Hæreses*, V, 33. (MSG, 7 : 1213.)

The elders who saw John, the disciple of the Lord, relate that they heard from him how the Lord used to teach in regard to those times, and say: "The days will come in which vines shall grow, each having ten thousand branches, and in each branch ten thousand twigs, and in each twig ten thousand shoots, and in each one of the shoots ten thousand clusters, and on every cluster ten thousand grapes, and every grape when pressed will yield five-and-twenty metretes of wine. And when any one of the saints shall lay hold of a cluster, another shall cry out, 'I am better cluster, take me; bless the Lord through me.' In like manner [the Lord declared] that a grain of wheat would produce ten thousand ears, and that every ear would produce ten thousand grains, and every grain would yield ten pounds of clear, pure, fine flour; and that all other fruit-bearing trees, and seeds and grass would produce similar proportions, and that all animals feeding [only] on the productions of the earth would [in those days] become peaceful and harmonious with each other and be in perfect subjection to men." And these things are borne witness to in writing by Papias, the hearer of John, and a companion of Polycarp, in his fourth book; for there were five books compiled by him. And he says in addition: "Now these things are credible to believers."

(c) Justin Martyr, *Dialogus cum Tryphone*, 80 f. (MSG, 6 : 665.)

Ch. 80. Although you have fallen in with some who are called Christians, but who do not admit this truth [the resurrection] and venture to blaspheme the God of Abraham and the God of Isaac and the God of Jacob,[1] and who say that there is no resurrection of the dead and that their souls, when they die, are taken to heaven, be careful not to regard them as Christians. . . . But I and whoever are on all points right-minded Christians know that there will be a resurrection of the dead and a thousand years in Jerusalem, which will then be built, adorned, and enlarged as the prophets Ezekiel and Isaiah and the others declare.

Ch. 81. And, further, a certain man with us, named John, one of the Apostles of Christ, predicted by a revelation that was made to him that those who believed in our Christ would spend a thousand years in Jerusalem, and thereafter the general, or to speak briefly, the eternal resurrection and judgment of all men would likewise take place.

§ 11. THE CHURCH AND THE WORLD

So long as chiliastic expectations were the basis of the Christian's hope and his judgment of the order of this present world, the Christian felt that he was but a stranger and sojourner in the world, and that his real home was the kingdom of Christ, soon to be established here on earth. With such a view the Christian would naturally define his relation to the world as being in it, yet not of it. As time passed, the opinion became more common that the kingdom of Christ was not a future world-order to be set up on His return, but the Church here on earth. This thought, which is the key to

---

[1] Such were evidently Gnostics, as shown by their rejection of the God of the Jews.

the *City of God* by St. Augustine, was not to be found in the first century and a half of the Church.

Ep. ad Diognetum, 5, 6.

The Epistle to Diognetus is one of the choicest pieces of ante-Nicene literature. Although it is commonly included among the Apostolic Fathers, the date is uncertain, it is anonymous, and the reason for its inclusion is not clear. The weight of opinion is in favor of an early date. It was preserved in but one manuscript, which was unfortunately destroyed in 1870. The main themes of the epistle are the faith and manners of the Christians, and an attempt to explain the late appearance of Christianity in the world. The work, therefore, is of the nature of an apology, and should be compared with *The Apology of Aristides*. A translation of the epistle may be found in ANF, I, 23.

Ch. 5. The Christians are distinguished from other men neither by country, nor language, nor the customs which they observe. For they neither inhabit cities of their own, nor employ a peculiar form of' speech, nor lead a life which is marked out by any singularity. The course of conduct which they follow has not been devised by any speculation or deliberation of inquisitive men; nor do they, like some, proclaim themselves the advocates of any merely human doctrines. But, inhabiting Greek as well as barbarian cities, according as the lot of each of them has been determined, and following the customs of the natives in respect to clothing, food, and the rest of their ordinary conduct, they display to us their wonderful and confessedly striking method of life. They dwell in their own countries, but simply as sojourners. As citizens, they share in all things with others, and yet endure all things as if foreigners. Every foreign country is to them as their native land, and every land of their birth as a land of strangers. They marry as do all; they beget children; but they do not commit abortion. They have a common table, but not a common bed. They are in the flesh, but they do not live after the flesh. They pass their days on earth, but they are the citizens of heaven. They obey the prescribed laws, and at the same time surpass the laws by their lives. They love all men, and are persecuted by all. They are unknown and condemned; they are put to death and restored to life. They are poor, yet they make many rich; they are in lack of all things, and yet abound in all. They are dishonored, and yet in their very dishonor are glorified. They are evil-spoken of, and yet are justified. They are reviled and bless; they are insulted and repay insult with honor; they do good, yet are punished as evil-doers. When punished they rejoice as if quickened into life; they are assailed by the Jews as foreigners and are persecuted by the Greeks; yet those who hate them are unable to assign a reason for their hatred.

Ch. 6. What the soul is in the body, that the Christians are in the world. The soul is spread through all the members of the body, and Christians through the cities of the world. The soul dwells in the body, but is not of the body; so Christians dwell in the world, but they are not of the world. The invisible soul is guarded in the visible body; so Christians are known as existing in the world, but their religion remains invisible. The flesh hates the soul and wages war on it, though it has received no wrong, because it is forbidden to indulge in pleasures; so the world hates Christians, though it receives no wrong from them, because they are opposed to its pleasures. The soul loves the flesh which hates it, and it loves the members; so Christians love those who hate them. The soul is enclosed in the body, yet itself holds the body together; so the Christians are kept in the world as in a prison-house, yet they themselves hold the world together. The immortal soul dwells in a mortal tabernacle; so Christians sojourn amid corruptible things, looking for the incorruptibility in the heavens. The soul when hardly treated in the matter of meats and drinks is improved; so Christians when punished increase more and more daily. In so great an office has God appointed them, which it is not lawful for them to decline.

§ 12. Theological Ideas

In the post-apostolic period are to be traced the begin·
nings of distinctive forms of religious and ethical ideas as distinguished from mere repetition of New Testament phrases.
The most influential writer was Ignatius of Antioch, the
founder, or earliest representative, of what may be called the
Asia Minor theology, which is to be traced through Irenæus,
Methodius, and Athanasius to the other great theologians
of the Nicene period, becoming the distinctive Eastern type
of piety.   It probably persisted in Asia Minor after Ignatius.
Among its characteristic features was the thought of redemption as the imparting to man of incorruptibility through the
incarnation and the sacraments.

(a) Ignatius, *Ep. ad Ephesios*, 18 *ff.*

The Epistle to the Ephesians is doctrinally the most important of
the writings of Ignatius.   In the passage that follows there is a remarkable anticipation of a part of the Apostles' Creed (*cf.* Hahn, § 1).
The whole passage contains in brief the fundamental point of the
writer's teachings.

Ch. 18.   My spirit is an offering[1] of the cross, which is
a stumbling-block to unbelievers, but to us salvation and
life eternal.   "Where is the wise man? where the disputer?"
[I Cor. 1 : 20.]   Where is the boasting of those called prudent?
For our God, Jesus Christ, was, according to the dispensation
of God, conceived in the womb of Mary of the seed of David,
but of the Holy Ghost.   He was born and baptized, that by
His passion He might purify the water.
Ch. 19.   And the virginity of Mary was hidden from the
Prince of this World, and her bringing forth, and likewise the
death of the Lord; three mysteries of shouting, which were
wrought in silence of God.   How, then, was He manifested to
the world?   A star shone forth from heaven above all other
stars, and its light was inexpressible, while its novelty struck

[1] Piaculum.

men with astonishment, but all the rest of the stars, with the sun and moon, formed a chorus to this star, and its light was exceedingly great above them all. And there was agitation whence this novelty, so unlike to everything else. Hence every kind of magic was destroyed and every bond of wickedness disappeared; ignorance was removed and the old kingdom abolished, for God had been manifested in human form for the renewal of eternal life. And now that took a beginning which had been prepared by God. Henceforth all things were in a state of tumult because He meditated the abolition of death.

Ch. 20. . . . Especially [will I write again] if the Lord make known to me that ye all, man by man, through grace given to each, agree in one faith and in Jesus Christ, who was of the family of David according to the flesh, the Son of Man and the Son of God, so that ye obey the bishop and the presbytery with an undivided mind, breaking one bread, which is the medicine of immortality, and the antidote to prevent dying, but which is life forever in Jesus Christ.

(b) Ignatius, *Ep. ad Smyrnæos*, 7.

The following passage may be regarded as a parallel to part of the preceding extract from the same writer's Epistle to the Ephesians.

They abstain from the eucharist and from prayer, because they confess not that the eucharist is the flesh of our Saviour Jesus Christ, which suffered for our sins, and which the Father, of His goodness, raised up again. Those, therefore, who speak against this gift of God, die while disputing. But it were better for them to love it, that they also may rise again. It is fitting, therefore, that ye should keep aloof from such persons, and not speak of them either in private or public, but to give heed to the prophets and, above all, to the Gospel, in which the passion has been revealed to us and the resurrection fully proved. But avoid all divisions as the beginning of evils.

(c) Ignatius, *Ep. ad Trallianos*, 9, 10.

The heresy which the writer fears is that known as Docetism, which denied the reality of the body of Jesus. Reference is made to it in the New Testament, I John 4 : 2. It was based upon the same philosophical idea as much of the later Gnostic speculation, that matter is essentially evil, and therefore a pure spirit could not be united to a real body composed of matter. See J. B. Lightfoot, *Apostolic Fathers*, pt. II, vol. II, p. 173 *ff.*

Ch. 9. Be ye therefore deaf when any one speaks to you apart from Jesus Christ, who was of the race of David, who was born of Mary, who was truly born and ate and drank, who was truly persecuted under Pontius Pilate, who was truly crucified and died while those in heaven and those on earth and those under the earth looked on; who, also, was truly raised from the dead, His Father having raised Him, who in like fashion will raise us who believe in Him; His Father, I say, will raise us in Christ Jesus, apart from whom we have not true life.

Ch. 10. But if it were as certain persons who are godless, that is, unbelievers, say, that He only appeared to suffer, they themselves being only in appearance, why am I bound? And why, also, do I desire to fight with wild beasts? I therefore die in vain. Truly, then, I lie against the Lord.

§ 13. WORSHIP IN THE POST-APOSTOLIC PERIOD

The worship of the Christian Church in the earliest period centred in the eucharist. There are references to this in the New Testament (*cf.* Acts 2 : 42; 20 : 7; I Cor. 10 : 16). How far the agape was connected with the eucharist is uncertain.

Additional source material: See Pliny's letter to Trajan (*v. supra*, § 7); the selections from Ignatius already given (*v. supra*, § 12) and the *Didache* (*v. infra*, § 14, *a*).

Justin Martyr, *Apologia*, I, 61 : 65-67. (MSG, 6 : 428 *ff.*)
Cf. Mirbt, n. 18.

The *First Apology* of Justin Martyr was written probably about 150. As Justin's work is dated, and is of indisputable authenticity, his account of the early worship of the Christians is of the very first importance. It should be noted, however, that, inasmuch as he is writing for non-Christians, he uses no technical terms in his description, and therefore nothing can be determined as to the exact significance of the titles he applies to the presiding officer at the eucharist. The following passage is of importance, also, as a witness to the custom of reading, in the course of Christian public worship, books that appear to be the Gospels. Irenæus, thirty years later, limits the number of the Gospels to four, *v. infra*, § 28. On the eucharist, *v. infra*, § 33.

Ch. 61. But I will explain the manner in which we who have been made new through Christ have also dedicated ourselves to God, lest by passing it over I should seem in any way to be unfair in my explanation. As many as are persuaded and believe that the things are true which are taught and said by us, and promise that they are able to live accordingly, they are taught to pray and with fasting to ask God forgiveness of their former sins, while we pray and fast with them. Thereupon they are brought by us to where there is water, and are born again in the same manner of a new birth as we, also, ourselves were born again. For in the name of God the Father and Lord of all, and of our Saviour Jesus Christ, and of the Holy Spirit, they then receive the washing in the watèr. For Christ said: "Except ye be born again, ye shall not enter into the kingdom of heaven." But that it is impossible for those once born to enter into the wombs of their mothers is manifest to all. . . . And this washing is called enlightenment, because those who learn these things have their understandings enlightened. But, also, in the name of Jesus Christ who was crucified under Pontius Pilate, and in the name of the Holy Spirit who by the prophets foretold all things pertaining to Jesus, he who is illuminated is washed.

Ch. 65. But after we have thus washed him who is persuaded and has assented, we bring him to those who are called the brethren, to where they are gathered together, making earnest prayer in common for ourselves and for him who is enlightened, and for all others everywhere, that we may be accounted worthy, after we have learned the truth, by our works also to be found right livers and keepers of the

commandments, that we may be saved with the eternal salvation. We salute each other with a kiss when we conclude
our prayers. Thereupon to the president of the brethren
bread and a cup of water and wine are brought, and he takes
it and offers up praise and glory to the Father of the universe through the name of the Son and the Holy Spirit, and
gives thanks at length that we have been accounted worthy
of these things from Him; and when he has ended the prayers
and thanksgiving the whole people present assent, saying
"Amen." Now the word Amen in the Hebrew language
signifies, So be it. Then after the president has given thanks
and all the people have assented, those who are called by
us deacons give to each one of those present to partake of
the bread and of the wine and water for which thanks have
been given, and for those not present they take away a
portion.

Ch. 66. And this food is called by us eucharist, and it is
not lawful for any man to partake of it but him who believes
the things taught by us to be true, and has been washed with
the washing which is for the remission of sins and unto a new
birth, and is so living as Christ commanded. For not as
common bread and common drink do we receive these; but
just as Jesus Christ our Saviour, being made flesh through
the word of God, had for our salvation both flesh and blood,
so, also, we are taught that the food for which thanks are given
by the word of prayer which is from Him, and from which by
conversion our flesh and blood are nourished, is the flesh and
blood of that Jesus who was made flesh. For the Apostles
in the memoirs composed by them, which are called Gospels,
thus delivered what was commanded them: that Jesus took
bread and gave thanks and said, This do in remembrance of
Me, this is My body; and that He likewise took the cup,
and when He had given thanks, said, This is My blood, and
gave only to them. And this the evil demons imitating, commanded it to be done also in the mysteries of Mithras; for
that bread and a cup of water are set forth with certain ex-

planations in the ceremonial of initiation, you either know or can learn.

Ch. 67. But we afterward always remind one another of these things, and those among us who are wealthy help all who are in want, and we always remain together. And for all things we eat we bless the Maker of all things through His Son Jesus Christ and through the Holy Spirit. And on the day called the Day of the Sun there is a gathering in one place of us all who live in cities or in the country, and the memoirs of the Apostles or the writings of the prophets are read as long as time allows. Then, when the reader has ceased, the president gives by word of mouth his admonition and exhortation to imitate these excellent things. Afterward we all rise at once and offer prayers; and as I said, when we have ceased to pray, bread is brought and wine and water, and the president likewise offers up prayers and thanksgivings as he has the ability, and the people assent, saying "Amen." The distribution to each and the partaking of that for which thanks were given then take place; and to those not present a portion is sent by the hands of the deacons. Those who are well-to-do and willing give, every one giving what he will, according to his own judgment, and the collection is deposited with the president, and he assists orphans and widows, and those who through sickness or any other cause are in want, and those who are in bonds, and the strangers that are sojourning, and, in short, he has the care of all that are in need. Now we all hold our common meeting on the Day of the Sun, because it is the first day on which God, having changed the darkness and matter, created the world; and Jesus Christ our Saviour on the same day rose from the dead. For on the day before Saturn's they crucified Him; and on the day after Saturn's, which is the Day of the Sun, having appeared to his Apostles and disciples, He taught them these things which we have offered you for consideration.

§ 14. Church Organization

No subject in Church history has been more hotly discussed than the organization of the primitive Christian Church. Each of several Christian confessions have attempted to justify a polity which it regarded as *de fide* by appeal to the organization of the Church of the primitive ages. Since it has been seen that the admission of the principle of development does not invalidate claims for divine warrant for a polity, the acrimonious debate has been somewhat stilled. There seems to have been in the Church several forms of organization, and to some extent the various contentions of conflicting creeds and polities have been therein justified. The ultimately universal form, episcopacy, may in some parts of the Church be traced to the end of the apostolic age, but it seems not to have been universally diffused at that time. Since Christian communities sprang up without official propaganda, at least in many instances, and were due to the work of independent Christian believers moving about in the Empire, this variety of organization was what might have been expected, especially as the significance of the organization was first felt chiefly in connection with the danger from heresy. That various external influences affected the development is also highly probable.

(a) Clement of Rome, *Ep. ad Corinthios*, I, 42, 44.

Ch. 42. The Apostles have preached the Gospel to us from the Lord Jesus Christ; Jesus Christ was sent forth from God. Christ, therefore, was from God, and the Apostles from Christ. Both these appointments, then, came about in an orderly way, by the will of God. Having, therefore, received their orders, and being fully assured by the resurrection of our Lord Jesus Christ, and established in the word of God, with full assurance of the Holy Ghost, they went forth proclaiming that the kingdom of God was at hand. And thus preaching through countries and cities, they appointed their first-fruits, having proved them by the Spirit, to be bishops and deacons of those who should afterward believe. Nor was this a new thing; for, indeed, many ages before it was written concerning bishops and deacons. For thus saith the Scripture in a certain place: "I will appoint their bishops in righteousness, and their deacons in faith." [1]

Ch. 44. Our Apostles also knew, through our Lord Jesus Christ, that there would be strife on account of the office of the episcopate.[2] For this cause, therefore, inasmuch as they had obtained a perfect foreknowledge of this, they appointed those already mentioned, and afterward gave instructions that when these should fall asleep other approved men should succeed them in their ministry. We are of the opinion, therefore, that those appointed by them, or afterward by other eminent men, with the consent of the whole Church, and who have blamelessly served the flock of Christ in lowliness of mind, peaceably, and with all modesty, and for a long time have borne a good report with all—these men we consider to be unjustly thrust out of their ministrations.[3] For it will be no light sin for us, if we thrust out those who have offered the gifts of the bishop's office blamelessly and holily. Blessed are those presbyters who have gone before seeing their departure was fruitful and ripe; for they have no fear lest any one should remove them from their appointed place. For we see that ye have displaced certain persons, though they were living honorably, from the ministration which had been honored by them blamelessly.

(b) Didache, 7-15.

The Didache is a very early manual of the instruction for Christian converts. It consists of two quite distinct parts, viz., a brief account of the moral law (chapters 1–6), which appears to be based upon a Jewish original to which the name of The Two Ways has been given, and a

[1] Clement alters the passage slightly; see Is. 60 : 17.
[2] The Greek is ἐπισκοπή (episcopē), meaning primarily "oversight."
[3] This seems to be the occasion for this letter to the Corinthians. As they appear to be several, they correspond to presbyters rather than to bishops, and the use of the term "presbyters" in the passage sustains this interpretation.

somewhat longer account of the various rites of the Church and the regulations governing its organization. Its date is in the first half of the second century and belongs more probably to the first quarter than to the second. It is a document of first-class importance, especially in the part bearing on the organization of the Church, which is here given. The extensive literature on the subject may be found in Krüger, *op. cit.*, § 21.

Ch. 7. But concerning baptism, thus shall ye baptize. Having first recited all these things, baptize in the name of the Father and of the Son and of the Holy Spirit in living [*i. e.*, running] water. But if thou hast not living water, then baptize in any other water; and if thou art not able in cold, in warm. But if thou hast neither, pour water upon the head thrice in the name of the Father and of the Son and of the Holy Spirit. But before baptism let him that baptizeth and him that is baptized fast, and any others also who are able; and thou shalt order him that is baptized to fast a day or two before.

Ch. 8. And let not your fastings be with the hypocrites. For they fast on the second and the fifth days of the week; but do ye keep your fast on the fourth and on the preparation [*i. e.*, the sixth day]. Neither pray ye as the hypocrites, but as the Lord commanded in His Gospel, thus pray ye: Our Father who art in heaven, hallowed be Thy name; Thy kingdom come; Thy will be done, as in heaven, so also on earth; give us this day our daily[1] bread; and forgive us our debt, as we also forgive our debtors; and lead us not into temptation, but deliver us from the Evil One; for Thine is the power and the glory forever.[2] Three times in the day pray ye so.

Ch. 9. But as regards the eucharist [thanksgiving], give ye thanks thus. First, as regards the cup: We give Thee thanks, O our Father, for the holy vine of David, Thy Son, which Thou madest known unto us through Jesus, Thy Son; Thine is the glory forever. Then as regards the breaking

---

[1] The word rendered daily is ἐπιούσιον, the same as that used in Matt. 6:11.

[2] Note the doxology also at the end of the other prayers.

[*i. e.*, of the bread]: We give thanks to Thee, O our Father, for the life and knowledge which thou madest known unto us through Jesus, Thy Son; Thine is the glory forever. As this broken bread was scattered upon the mountains and being gathered together became one, so may Thy Church be gathered together from the ends of the earth into Thy kingdom; for Thine is the glory and the power through Jesus Christ for ever and ever. But let no one eat or drink of this eucharist [thanksgiving] but they that have been baptized into the name of the Lord; for concerning this also the Lord hath said: Give not that which is holy unto the dogs.

Ch. 10. After ye are satisfied give thanks thus: We give Thee thanks, Holy Father, for Thy holy name, which Thou hast made to tabernacle in our hearts, and for the knowledge and faith and immortality, which Thou hast made known unto us through Thy Son Jesus; Thine is the glory forever. Thou, Almighty Master, created all things for Thy name's sake, and gave food and drink unto men for enjoyment, that they might render thanks to Thee; but bestowed upon us spiritual food and drink and eternal life through Thy Son. Before all things we give Thee thanks that Thou art powerful; Thine is the glory forever. Remember, Lord, Thy Church to deliver it from all evil and to perfect it in Thy love; and gather it together from the four winds—even the Church which has been sanctified—into Thy kingdom which Thou hast prepared for it; for Thine is the power and the glory forever. May grace come and may this world pass away. Hosanna to the God of David. If any one is holy, let him come; if any one is not, let him repent. Maran Atha. Amen. But permit the prophets to offer thanksgiving as much as they will.

Ch. 11. Whosoever, therefore, shall come and teach you all these things that have been said receive him; but if the teacher himself be perverted and teach a different doctrine to the destruction thereof, hear him not; but if to the increase of righteousness and knowledge of the Lord, receive him as the Lord.

But concerning the apostles and prophets, so do ye according to the ordinance of the Gospel: Let every apostle coming to you be received as the Lord; but he shall not abide more than a single day, or if there be need, a second likewise; but if he abide three days, he is a false prophet. And when he departs, let not the apostle receive anything save bread until he find shelter; but if he ask money, he is a false prophet. And any prophet speaking in the Spirit ye shall not try, neither discern; for every sin shall be forgiven, but this sin shall not be forgiven. Yet not every one that speaketh in the Spirit is a prophet, but only if he have the ways of the Lord. From his ways, therefore, the false prophet and the [true] prophet shall be recognized. And no prophet when he ordereth a table in the Spirit shall eat of it; otherwise he is a false prophet.[1] And every prophet teaching the truth, if he doeth not what he teacheth, is a false prophet. And every prophet approved and found true, working unto a worldly mystery of the Church,[2] and yet teacheth not to do what he himself doeth, shall not be judged before you; he hath his judgment in the presence of God; for in like manner also did the ancient prophets. And whosoever shall say in the Spirit, Give me silver or anything else, do not listen to him; but if he say to give on behalf of others who are in want, let no one judge him.

Ch. 12. But let every one coming in the name of the Lord be received; and when ye have tested him ye shall know him, for ye shall have understanding on the right hand and on the left. If the comer is a traveller, assist him as ye are able; but let him not stay with you but for two or three days, if it be necessary. But if he wishes to settle with you, being a craftsman, let him work and eat. But if he has no craft, accord-

---

[1] The sense is: If a prophet speaking in the Spirit commands a meal to be prepared for the poor and should himself eat of it, it would be apparent that he ordered it for himself. But if he eats he must be a false prophet.

[2] A most difficult and obscure passage. Various interpretations have been proposed; see the various editions of the Apostolic Fathers, especially Funk's. The rendering here given is strictly literal.

ing to your wisdom provide how without idleness he shall live as a Christian among you. If he will not do this, he is trafficking upon Christ. Beware of such men.

Ch. 13. But every true prophet desiring to settle among you is worthy of his food. In like manner, a true teacher is also worthy, like the workman, of his food. Every first-fruit, then, of the produce of the wine-vat and of the threshing-floor, of thy oxen and of thy sheep, thou shalt take and give as the first-fruit to the prophets; for they are your chief priests. But if ye have not a prophet, give them to the poor. If thou makest bread, take the first-fruit and give according to the commandment. In like manner, when thou openest a jar of wine or oil, take the first-fruit and give to the prophets; yea, and of money and raiment and every possession take the first-fruit, as shall seem good to thee, and give according to the commandment.

Ch. 14. And on the Lord's day gather yourselves together and break bread and give thanks, first confessing your transgressions, that your sacrifice may be pure. And let no man having a dispute with his fellow join your assembly until they have been reconciled, that your sacrifice may not be defiled; for this is the sacrifice spoken of by the Lord: In every place and at every time offer me a pure sacrifice; for I am a great king, saith the Lord, and my name is wonderful among the nations. [Mal. 1 : 11, 14.]

Ch. 15. Appoint [*i. e.*, lay hands on], therefore, for yourselves bishops and deacons worthy of the Lord, men meek, not lovers of money, truthful, and approved; for they also render you the service of prophets and teachers. Despise them not, therefore, for they are your honored ones together with the prophets and teachers.

(c) Ignatius, *Ep. ad Trallianos*, 2, 3.

For Ignatius, see § 8.

Ch. 2. For since ye are subject to the bishop as Jesus Christ, ye appear to me to live not after the manner of men, but

according to Jesus Christ, who died for us, in order that by
believing in His death ye may escape death. It is therefore
necessary that just as ye indeed do, so without the bishop
ye should do nothing, but should also be subject to the presbytery, as to the Apostles of Jesus Christ, our Hope, living
in whom we shall be found [*i. e.*, at the last]. It is right, also,
that the deacons, being [ministers] of the mysteries of Jesus
Christ, should in every respect be well-pleasing to all. For
they are not the ministers of meats and drinks, but servants
of the Church of God. It is necessary, therefore, that they
guard themselves from all grounds of accusation as they would
from fire.

Ch. 3. In like manner, let all reverence the deacons as Jesus
Christ, as also the bishop, who is a type of the Father, and the
presbyters as the sanhedrim of God and the assembly of the
Apostles. Apart from these there is no Church.

(*d*) Ignatius, *Ep. ad Smyrnæos*, 8.

See that ye follow the bishop as Jesus Christ does the
Father, and the presbyters as ye would the Apostles; and reverence the deacons as a commandment of God. Without the
bishop let no one do any of those things connected with the
Church. Let that be deemed a proper eucharist which is
administered either by the bishop or by him to whom he has
intrusted it. Wherever the bishop shall appear there let
also the multitude be, even as wherever Jesus Christ is there
is the Catholic Church. It is not lawful without the bishop
either to baptize or to make an agape. But whatsoever he
shall approve that is also pleasing to God, so that everything
that is done may be secure and valid.

§ 15. Church Discipline

The Church was the company of the saints. How far, then,
could the Church tolerate in its midst those who had committed serious offences against the moral law? A case had
occurred in the Corinthian church about which St. Paul had

given some instructions to the Christians of that city (*cf.* I Cor. 5 : 3-5; II Cor. 13 : 10). There was the idea current that sins after baptism admitted of no pardon and involved permanent exclusion from the Church (*cf.* Heb. 10 : 26). A distinction was also made as to sins whereby some were regarded as "sins unto death" and not admitting of pardon (*cf.* I John 5 : 16). In principle, the exclusion from the Church of those who had committed gross sins was recognized, but as the Church grew it soon became a serious question as to the extent to which this strict discipline could be enforced. We find, therefore, a well-defined movement toward relaxing this rigor of the law. The beginning appears in Hermas, who admits the possibility of one repentance after baptism. A special problem was presented from the first by the difference between the conceptions of marriage held by the Christians and by the heathen. The Church very early took the position that marriage in some sense was indissoluble, that so long as both parties to a marriage lived, neither could marry again, but after the death of one party the surviving spouse could remarry, although this second marriage was looked upon with some disfavor. Both the idea of a second repentance and the idea of the indissolubility of marriage are expressed in the following extract from Hermas:

Hermas, *Pastor*, Man. IV, 1, 3.

Hermas wrotè in the second century. Opinions have varied as to his date, some putting him near the beginning, some near the middle of the century. The weight of opinion seems to be that he lived shortly before 150. His work entitled *The Pastor* is in the form of revelations, and was therefore thought to partake of an inspiration similar to that of Holy Scripture. This naturally gave it a place among Scriptures for a while and accounts for the great popularity of the work in the early Church. It is the best example of an extensive apocalyptic literature which flourished in the Church in the first two centuries.

Ch. 1. If the husband should not take her back [*i. e.*, the penitent wife who has committed adultery] he sins, and brings a great sin upon himself; for he ought to take back her who has sinned and repented; but not frequently; for there is but one repentance to the servants of God [*i. e.*, after becoming the servants of God]. On account of her repentance [*i. e.*, because she may repent, and therefore should be taken back] the husband ought not to marry. This treatment applies to the woman and to the man.

Ch. 3. And I said to him: "I should like to continue my questions." "Speak on," said he. And I said: "I have heard, sir, from some teachers that there is no other repentance than that when we descend into the water and receive remission of our former sins." He said to me: "Thou hast well heard, for so it is. For he who has received remission of his sins ought to sin no more, but to live in purity. Since, however, you inquire diligently into all things, I will point out this also to you, not as giving occasion for error to those who are to believe, or have lately believed, in the Lord. For those who have now believed and those who are to believe have not repentance of their sins, but they have remission of their former sins. For to those who have been called before these days the Lord has set repentance. For the Lord, who knows the heart and foreknows all things, knew the weakness of men and the manifold wiles of the devil, that he would inflict some evil on the servants of God and would act wickedly against them. The Lord, therefore, being merciful, has had mercy on the works of His hands and has set repentance for them; and has intrusted to me the power over this repentance. And therefore I say unto you," he said, "that if after that great and holy calling any one is tempted by the devil and sins, he has one repentance. But if thereupon he should sin and then repent, to such a man his repentance is of no benefit; for with difficulty will he live."[1]

---

[1] This passage is quoted at length by Clement of Alexandria, *Stromata*, II, 12, 13.

MORAL IDEAS 45

§ 16. MORAL IDEAS IN THE POST-APOSTOLIC PERIOD

Christians were convinced that their religion made the highest possible moral demands upon them. They were to live in the world, but remain uncontaminated by it (*cf. supra*, § 11). This belief even candid heathen were sometimes forced to admit (*cf.* Pliny's correspondence with Trajan, *supra*, § 7). The morality of the Christians and the loftiness of their ethical code were common features in the apologies which began to appear in the post-apostolic period (*cf. The Apology of Aristides, infra*, § 20, *a*). Christianity was a revealed code of morals, by the observance of which men might escape the fires of hell and obtain the bliss of immortality (*a*) (*cf. infra*, § 30). At the same time there was developed a tendency toward asceticism, by which a higher excellence might be obtained than the law required of ordinary Christians (*b, c*). This higher morality was not without its compensations; superior merit was recognized by God, and was accordingly rewarded; it might even be applied to offset sins committed (*d, e*). This last idea is to be traced to the book of Tobit (*cf.* also James 5 : 20; I Peter 4 : 8). The fuller development is to be found in the theology of Tertullian and Cyprian (*v. infra*, § 39).

(*a*) Justin Martyr, *Apologia*, I, 10, 12. (MSG, 6 : 339, 342.)

Ch. 10. We have received by tradition that God does not need man's material offerings, since we see that He himself provides all things. And we have been taught, have been convinced, and do believe that He accepts only those who imitate the virtues which reside in Him, temperance and justice and philanthropy, and as many virtues as are peculiar to a God who is called by no given name. And we have been taught that He in the beginning, since He is good, did for man's sake create all things out of unformed matter; and if men by their works show themselves worthy of His design, they are deemed worthy, for so we have received, of reigning

in company with Him, having become incorruptible and incapable of suffering. For as in the beginning He created us
when we were not, so we consider that, in like manner, those
who choose what is pleasing to Him are, on account of their
choice, deemed worthy of incorruption and of fellowship with
Him. For the coming into being at first was not in our power;
and in order that we may follow those things which please Him,
choosing them by means of the rational faculties with which
He has himself endowed us, He both persuades us and leads
us to faith. . . .

Ch. 12. And more than all other men are we your helpers
and allies in promoting peace; for we are of the opinion that
it is impossible for the wicked, or the covetous, or the con-
spirator, or the virtuous to escape the notice of God, and
that each man goes to eternal punishment or salvation
according to the deserts of his actions. For if all men knew
this, no one would choose wickedness, even for a little time,
knowing that he goes to the eternal punishment of fire; but
he would in every respect restrain himself and adorn himself
with virtue, that he might obtain the good gifts of God and
escape punishment. For those who, on account of the laws
and punishments you impose, endeavor when they offend to
escape detection, offend thinking that it is possible to escape
your detection, since you are but men; but if they learned
and were convinced that it is not possible that anything,
whether actually done or only intended, should escape the
notice of God, they would live decently in every respect, on
account of the penalties threatened, as even you yourselves
will admit.

(b) *Didache*, 6. *Cf.* Mirbt, n. 13.

See that no one cause thee to err from this way of the
teaching, since apart from God it teacheth thee. For if thou
art able to bear all the yoke of the Lord, thou wilt be perfect;
but if thou art not able, do what thou art able. And concerning foods, bear what thou art able; but against that which

is sacrificed to idols be exceedingly on thy guard; for it is the service of dead gods.

(c) Hermas, *Pastor*, Man. IV, 4.

And again I asked him, saying: "Sir, since you have been so patient with me, will you show me this also?" "Speak," said he. And I said: "If a wife or husband die, and the widow or widower marry, does he or she commit sin?" "There is no sin in marrying again," said he; "but if they remain un-married, they gain greater honor and glory with the Lord; but if they marry, they do not sin. Guard, therefore, your chastity and purity and you will live to God. What com-mandments I now give you, and what I am to give you, keep from henceforth, yea, from the very day when you were in-trusted to me, and I will dwell in your house. And your former sins will be forgiven, if you keep my commandments. And to all there is forgiveness if they keep these my com-mandments and walk in this chastity."

(d) Clement of Rome, *Ep. ad Corinthios*, II, 4, 16.

Ch. 4. Let us, then, not call Him Lord, for that will not save us. For He saith: "Not every one that saith to me, Lord, Lord, shall be saved, but he that worketh righteousness." Wherefore, brethren, let us confess Him by our works, by lov-ing one another, by not committing adultery, or speaking evil of one another, or cherishing envy; but by being continent, compassionate, and good. We ought also to sympathize with one another, and not be avaricious. By such works let us confess Him, and not by those that are of an opposite kind. And it is not fitting that we should fear men, but rather God. For this reason, if we should do such things, the Lord hath said: "Even though ye were gathered together to me in my very bosom, yet if ye were not to keep my commandments, I would cast you off, and say unto you, Depart from me; I know you not, whence ye are, ye workers of iniquity." [1]

[1] The first part of this quotation has not been identified; the conclusion is Matt. 7 : 23.

Ch. 16. So then, brethren, having received no small occasion to repent, while we have opportunity, let us turn to God,
who called us while we yet have One to receive us. For if
we renounce these indulgences and conquer the soul by not
fulfilling its wicked desires, we shall be partakers of the mercy
of Jesus. Know ye not that the day of judgment draweth
nigh like a burning oven, and certain of the heavens and all
the earth will melt, like lead melting in fire; and then will
appear the hidden and manifest deeds of men? Good, then,
are alms as repentance from sin; better is fasting than prayer,
and alms than both; "charity covereth a multitude of sins,"
and prayer out of a good conscience delivereth from death.
Blessed is every one that shall be found complete in these;
for alms lighten the burden of sin.

(e) Hermas, *Pastor*, Sim. V, 3.

"If you do anything good beyond the commandment of
God, you will gain for yourself more abundant glory, and
will be more honored before God than you would otherwise
be. If, therefore, you keep the commandments of God and
do these services, you will have joy if you observe them according to my commandment." I said unto him: "Sir, whatsoever you command me I will observe; for I know that
you are with me." "I will be with you," he said, "because
you have such a desire for doing good; I will be with all those,"
he said, "who have such a desire. This fasting," he continued, "is very good, provided the commandments of the Lord
be observed. Thus, then, shall you observe the fast which
you intend to keep. First of all, be on your guard against
every evil word and every evil desire, and purify your heart
from all the vanities of this world. If you guard against
these things, your fasting will be perfect. But do thus: having
fulfilled what is written, during the day on which you fast
you will taste nothing but bread and water; and having
reckoned up the price of the dishes of that day which you
intended to have eaten, you will give it to a widow, an orphan,

or to some one in want, and thus you will be humble-minded, so that he who has received benefit from your humility may fill his own soul and pray to the Lord for you. If you observe fasting as I have commanded you, your sacrifice will be acceptable to God, and this fasting will be written down; and the service thus performed is noble and sacred and acceptable to the Lord."

PERIOD III

THE CRITICAL PERIOD: A. D. 140 TO A. D. 200

The interval between the close of the post-apostolic age and the end of the second century, or from about 140 to 200, may be called the Critical Period of Ancient Christianity. In this period there grew up conceptions of Christianity which were felt by the Church, as a whole, to be fundamentally opposed to its essential spirit and to constitute a serious menace to the Christian faith as it had been commonly received. These conceptions, which grew up both alongside of, and within the Church, have been grouped under the term Gnosticism, a generic term including many widely divergent types of teaching and various interpretations of Christian doctrine in the light of Oriental speculation. There were also reactionary and reformatory movements which were generally felt to be out of harmony with the development upon which Christian thought and life had already entered; such were Montanism and Marcionism. To overcome these tendencies and movements the Christian churches in the various parts of the Roman Empire were forced, on the one hand, to develop more completely such ecclesiastical institutions as would defend what was commonly regarded as the received faith, and, on the other hand, to pass from a condition in which the various Christian communities existed in isolated autonomy to some form of organization whereby the spiritual unity of the Church might become visible and better able to strengthen the several members of that Church in dealing with theological and administrative problems. The Church, accordingly, acquired in the Critical Period the

fundamental form of its creed, as an authoritative expression
of belief; the episcopate, as a universally recognized essential
of Church organization and a defence of tradition; and its
canon of Holy Scripture, at least in fundamentals, as the
authoritative primitive witness to the essential teachings of
the Church. It also laid the foundations of the conciliar
system, and the bonds of corporate unity between the scattered communities of the Church were defined and recognized.
At the same time, the Church developed in its conflict with
heathenism an apologetic literature, and in its conflict with
heresy a polemical literature, in which are to be found the
beginnings of its theology or scientific statement of Christian
truth. Of this theology two lines of development are to be
traced: one a utilization of Greek philosophy which arose
from the Logos doctrine of the Apologists, and the other a
realistic doctrine of redemption which grew out of the Asia
Minor type of Christian teaching, traces of which are to be
found in Ignatius of Antioch.

CHAPTER I. THE CHURCH IN RELATION TO THE EM-
PIRE AND HEATHEN CULTURE

In the course of the second century the Church spread
rapidly into all parts of the Empire, and even beyond. It
became so prominent that the relation of the Church to
heathen thought and institutions underwent a marked change.
Persecutions of Christians became more frequent, and thereby
the popular conviction was deepened that Christians were
malefactors. To some extent men of letters began to notice
the new faith and attack it. In opposition to persecution and
criticism, the Church developed an active apologetic or defence of Christianity and Christians against heathen aspersions.

§ 17. The Extension of Christianity.
§ 18. Heathen Religious Feeling and Culture in Relation
to Christianity.

§ 19. Attitude of the Roman Government toward Chris-
       tians, A. D. 138 to A. D. 192.
§ 20. The Literary Defence of Christianity.

§ 17. THE EXTENSION OF CHRISTIANITY

Under the head of Extension of Christianity are to be placed
only such texts as may be regarded as evidence for the presence of the Church in a well-defined locality. It is apparent
that the evidence must be incomplete, for many places must
have received the Christian faith which were unknown to the
writers whose works we have or which they had no occasion
to mention. Rhetorical overstatement of the extension of
the Church was a natural temptation in view of the rapid
spread of Christianity. Each text needs to be scrutinized
and its merits assessed. It should, however, be borne in mind
that the existence of a well-established church in any locality
is in most cases sufficient reason for believing that Christianity
had already been there for some time. In this way valid
historical reasoning carries the date of the extension of the
Church to a locality somewhat further back than does the
date of the appearance of a document which testifies to the
existence of Christianity in a definite place at a definite time.

(a) Tertullian, *Adv. Judæos*, 7. (MSL, 2 : 649.)

Quintus Septimius Florens Tertullianus (circa 160–circa 220 A. D.)
is the most important ante-Nicene Latin ecclesiastical writer. He
has been justly regarded as the founder of Latin theology and the
Christian Latin style. His work is divided into two periods by his
adherence (between 202 and 207 A. D.) to the Montanistic sect.
The treatise *Adversus Judæos* probably belongs to Tertullian's pre-
Montanist period, though formerly placed among his Montanist writings (see Krüger, § 85, 6).   For Geographical references, see W. Smith,
Dictionary of Greek and Roman Geography.

Upon whom else have all nations believed but upon the
Christ who has already come? For whom have the other
nations believed—Parthians, Medes, Elamites, and they who
inhabit Mesopotamia, Armenia, Phrygia, Cappadocia, and

those dwelling in Pontus and Asia, and Pamphylia, sojourners in Egypt, and inhabitants of the region of Africa which is beyond Cyrene, Romans and sojourners, yes, and in Jerusalem, Jews and other nations;[1] as now the varied races of the Gætulians, and manifold confines of the Moors, all the limits of Spain, and the diverse nations of the Gauls, and the places of the Britons inaccessible to the Romans, but subjugated to Christ, and of the Sarmatians and Dacians, and Germans and Scythians, and of many remote nations and provinces and many islands unknown to us and which we can hardly enumerate? In all of these places the name of Christ, who has already come, now reigns.

(b) Tertullian, *Apologeticus adversus Gentes pro Christianis*, 37. (MSL, 1 : 525.)

The date of this work is 197 A. D.

We are but of yesterday, and we have filled every place among you—cities, islands, fortresses, towns, market-places, the very camps, tribes, companies, palace, Senate, and Forum. We have left you only the temples.

(c) Irenæus, *Adv. Hæreses*, I, 10, 3. (MSG, 7 : 551 f.) For text, see Kirch, § 91.

Since the Church has received this preaching and this faith, as we have said, the Church, although it is scattered throughout the whole world, diligently guards it as if it dwelt in one house; and likewise it believes these things as if it had one soul and one heart, and harmoniously it preaches, teaches, and believes these things as if possessing one mouth. For although the languages of the world are dissimilar, yet the import of the tradition is one and the same. For the churches which have been founded in Germany have not believed nor handed down anything different, nor have those among the Iberians, nor those among the Gauls, nor those in the East,

[1] *Cf.* Acts 2 : 9 *ff.*

nor those in Egypt, nor those in Libya, nor those which have been established in the central regions[1] of the world.

(*d*) Bardesanes, *De Fato.* F. Nau, *Bardesane l'astrologue; le livre des lois des pays,* Paris, 1899.

Bardesanes (154-222 A. D.) was the great Christian teacher of Edessa. He lived at the court of Abgar IX (179-214), whom, according to a doubtful tradition, he is said to have converted. The entire book may be found well translated by B. P. Pratten, ANF, VIII, 723-734.

In Syria and Edessa men used to part with their manhood in honor of Tharatha,[2] but when King Abgar became a believer he commanded that every one that did so should have his hand cut off, and from that day until now no one does so in the country of Edessa.

And what shall we say of the new race of us Christians, whom Christ at His advent planted in every country and in every region? For, lo, wherever we are, we are called after the one name of Christ—namely, Christians. On one day, the first day of the week, we assemble ourselves together, and on the days of the readings[3] we abstain from sustenance. The brethren who are in Gaul do not take males for wives, nor those in Parthia two wives; nor do those in Judea circumcise themselves; nor do those of our sisters who are among the Geli consort with strangers; nor do those of our brethren who are in Persia take their daughters for wives; nor do those who are in Media abandon their dead or bury them alive or give them as food to the dogs; nor do those who are in Edessa kill their wives who commit adultery, nor their sisters, but they withdraw from them, and give them over to the judgment of God; nor do those who are in Hatra stone thieves to death; but wherever they are, and in whatever place they are found, the laws of the several countries do not hinder them from obeying the law of their Christ; nor does the Fate of the

[1] Probably Palestine is here meant.
[2] The great Syrian goddess Atargatis.
[3] Reference is obscure.

celestial governors[1] compel them to make use of the things which they regard as impure.

(e) Eusebius, *Hist. Ec.*, V, 10.   (MSG, 20 : 455.)

Missions in the extreme East.

They say that Pantænus displayed such zeal for the divine word that he was appointed a herald of the Gospel of Christ to the nations of the East and was sent as far as India.[2] For indeed there were still many evangelists of the word who sought earnestly to use their inspired zeal, after the example of the Apostles, for the increase and building up of the divine word. Pantænus was one of these, and he is said to have gone to India. The report is that among persons in that country who knew of Christ he found the Gospel according to Matthew, which had anticipated his own arrival. For Bartholomew, one of the Apostles, had preached to them and left them the writing of Matthew in the Hebrew language, and they had preserved it till that time.

§ 18.   HEATHEN RELIGIOUS FEELING AND CULTURE IN
RELATION TO CHRISTIANITY

The Christian religion in the course of the latter part of the second century began to attract the attention of heathen writers; it became an object of literary attack. The principal literary opponent of Christianity was Celsus, who subjected the Christian traditions and customs to a searching criticism to prove that they were absurd, unscientific, and false. Lucian, of Samosata, does not seem to have attacked Christianity from any philosophical or religious interest, but treated it as an object of derision, making sport of it. There

---

[1] A reference to astrological doctrine.

[2] There is good reason for believing that by India is meant what is now understood as India, and not Arabia. There was no little intercourse between India and the West, and we have the direct testimony of Dio Chrysostom, circa 100, that there was intercourse between Alexandria and India, and that Indians came to Alexandria to study in the schools of that city. See DCB, art. " Pantænus."

were also in circulation innumerable heathen calumnies, many of the most abominable character. These have been preserved only by Christian writers. It was chiefly in reference to these calumnies that the Christian apologists wrote. The answer to Celsus made by Origen belongs to a later period, though Celsus represents the best philosophical criticism of Christianity of the latter part of the second century.

(a) Celsus, *The True Word*, in Origen, *Contra Celsum*. (MSG, 11 : 651 *ff.*)

The work of Celsus against Christianity, or *The True Word*, written about 178, is lost, but it has been so incorporated in the elaborate reply of Origen that it can be reconstructed without much difficulty. This Theodor Keim has done. The following extracts from Origen's *Contra Celsum* are quotations from Celsus or references to his criticism of Christianity. For Origen, *v. infra*, § 43, *b*.

I, 1. (MSG, 11 : 651.) Wishing to throw discredit upon Christianity, the first point Celsus brings forward is that the Christians have entered secretly into associations with each other which are forbidden by the laws; saying that "of associations some are public, others again secret; and the former are permitted by the laws; the latter are prohibited by the laws."

I, 4. (MSG, 11 : 661.) Let us notice, also, how he thinks to cast discredit upon our system of morals as neither venerable nor a new branch of instruction, inasmuch as it is common to other philosophers.

I, 9. (MSG, 11 : 672.) He says that "Certain of them do not wish either to give or to receive reasons for those things to which they hold; saying, 'Do not examine, only believe and your faith will save you!'"; and he alleges that such also say: "The wisdom of this life is bad, but foolishness is a good thing."

I, 38. (MSG, 11 : 733.) He admits somehow the miracles which Jesus wrought and by means of which He induced the multitude to follow Him as the Christ. He wishes to throw discredit on them, as having been done not by divine power, but by help of magic, for he says: "That he [Jesus], having been brought up secretly and having served for hire in Egypt, and then coming to the knowledge of certain miraculous powers, returned from thence, and by means of those powers proclaimed himself a god."

II, 55. (MSG, 11 : 884.) "Come, now, let us grant to you that these things [the prediction made by Christ of His resurrection] were said. Yet how many others are there who have used such wonders to deceive their simple hearers, and who made gain of their deception? Such was the case, they say, with Zalmoxis in Scythia, the slave of Pythagoras; and with Pythagoras himself in Italy. . . . But the point to be considered is, whether any one who was really dead ever rose with a veritable body. Or do you imagine the statements of others not only are myths, but appear as such, but you have discovered a becoming and credible termination of your drama, the voice from the cross when he breathed his last, the earthquake and the darkness? that while living he was of no help to himself, but when dead he rose again, and showed the marks of his punishment and his hands as they had been. Who saw this? A frantic woman, as you state, and, if any other, perhaps one of those who were engaged in the same delusion, who, owing to a peculiar state of mind, had either dreamed so, or with a wandering fancy had imagined things in accordance with his own wishes, which has happened in the case of very many; or, which is most probable, there was some one who desired to impress the others with this portent, and by such a falsehood to furnish an occasioh to other jugglers."

II, 63. (MSG, 11 : 896.) "If Jesus desired to show that his power was really divine, he ought to have appeared to those who had ill-treated him, and to him who had condemned him, and to all men universally."

III, 59. (MSG, 11 : 997.) "That I bring no heavier charge than what truth requires, let any one judge from the following. Those who invite to participation in other mysteries make proclamation as follows: 'Every one who has clean hands and

a prudent tongue'; others again thus: 'He who is pure from
every pollution, and whose soul is conscious of no evil, and
who has lived well and justly.' Such is the proclamation made
by those who promise purification from sins. But let us hear
whom the Christians invite. 'Whoever,' they say, 'is a
sinner, whoever is devoid of understanding, whoever is a
child,' and, to speak generally, 'whoever is unfortunate, him
will the kingdom of God receive.' Do you not call him a
sinner, then, who is unjust and a thief and a house-breaker and
a poisoner, a committer of sacrilege and a robber of the dead?
Whom else would a man invite if he were issuing a proclamation for an assembly of robbers?"

VII, 18. (MSG, 11 : 1445.) "Will they not again make this
reflection: If the prophets of the God of the Jews foretold
that he who should come was the son of this same God, how
could he command them through Moses to gather wealth,
to rule, to fill the earth, to put to the sword their enemies from
youth up, and to destroy them utterly, which, indeed, he
himself did in the eyes of the Jews, as Moses says, threatening
them, moreover, that if they did not obey his commands he
would treat them as his open enemies; whilst, on the other
hand, his son, the man of Nazareth, promulgating laws in
opposition to these, declares that no one comes to the Father
who is rich or who loves power or seeks after wisdom or glory;
that men ought to be no more careful in providing food than
the ravens; that they were to be in less concern about their
raiment than the lilies; that to him who has smitten them
once they should offer opportunity to smite again? Is it
Moses or Jesus who lies? Did the Father when he sent Jesus
forget the things he commanded Moses? Or did he change
his mind and, condemning his own laws, send forth a messenger with the opposite instructions?"

V, 14. (MSG, 11 : 1201.) "It is folly for them to suppose
that when God, as if he were a cook, introduces the fire, all
the rest of the human race will be burnt up, while they alone
will remain, not only those who are alive, but also those who

have been dead long since, which latter will arise from the earth clothed with the self-same flesh as during life; the hope, to speak plainly, of worms. For what sort of human soul is it that would still long for a body gone to corruption? For this reason, also, this opinion of yours is not shared by some of the Christians,[1] and they pronounce it exceedingly vile and loathsome and impossible; for what kind of body is that which, after being completely corrupted, can return to its original nature, and to that self-same first condition which it left? Having nothing to reply, they betake themselves to a most absurd refuge—that all things are possible to God. But God cannot do things which are disgraceful, nor does he wish things contrary to his nature; nor, if in accordance with your wickedness you desire something shameful, would God be able to do it; nor must you believe at once that it will be done. For God is the author, not of inordinate desires nor of a nature disordered and confused, but of what is upright and just. For the soul, indeed, he might be able to provide everlasting life; but dead bodies, on the other hand, are, as Heraclitus observes, more worthless than dung. So, then, God neither will nor can declare contrary to reason that the flesh is eternal, which is full of those things which it is not honorable to mention. For he is the reason of all things that exist, and therefore can do nothing either contrary to reason or contrary to himself."

(b) Lucian of Samosata, *De morte Peregrini Prôtei*, §§ 11 *ff.* Preuschen, *Analecta*, I, 20 *ff.*

Ch. 11. About this time he made himself proficient in the marvellous wisdom of the Christians by associating around Palestine with their priests and scribes. And would you believe it? In a short time he convinced them that they were mere children and himself alone a prophet, master of ceremonies, head of the synagogue, and everything. He explained and interpreted some of their books, and he himself also wrote

[1] Probably the Gnostics.

many, so they came to look upon him almost as a God, made him their law-giver and chose him as their patron. . . . At all events, they still worship that enchanter [mage] who was crucified in Palestine for introducing among men this new religious sect.

Ch. 12. Then Proteus was, on this account, seized and thrown into prison, and this very circumstance procured for him during his subsequent career no small renown and the reputation for wonderful powers and the glory which he loved. When, then, he had been put in bonds, the Christians looked upon these things as a misfortune and in their efforts to secure his release did everything in their power. When this proved impracticable, other assistance of every sort was rendered him, not occasionally, but with zeal. From earliest dawn old women, widows, and orphan children were to be seen waiting beside the prison, and men of rank among them slept with him in the prison, having bribed the prison guards. Then they were accustomed to bring in all kinds of viands, and they read their sacred Scriptures together, and the most excellent Peregrinus (for such was still his name) was styled by them a New Socrates.

Ch. 13. Certain came even from the cities of Asia, sent by the Christians at the common charge, to assist and plead for him and comfort him. They exhibit extraordinary activity whenever any such thing occurs affecting their common interest. In short, they are lavish of everything. And what is more, on the pretext of his imprisonment, many contributions of money came from them to Peregrinus at that time, and he made no little income out of it. These poor men have persuaded themselves that they are going to be immortal and live forever; they both despise death and voluntarily devote themselves to it; at least most of them do so. Moreover, their law-giver persuaded them that they were all brethren, and that when once they come out and reject the Greek gods, they should then worship that crucified sophist and live according to his laws. Therefore they despise all things and hold everything in common, having received such ideas from others, without any sufficient basis for their faith. If, then, any impostor or trickster who knows how to manage things came among them, he soon grew rich, imposing on these foolish folk.

Ch. 14. Peregrinus was, however, set at liberty by the governor of Syria at that time, a lover of philosophy, who understood his folly and knew that he would willingly have suffered death that by it he might have acquired glory. Thinking him, however, not worthy of so honorable an end, he let him go. . . .

Ch. 16. A second time he left his country to wander about, having the Christians as a sufficient source of supplies, and he was cared for by them most ungrudgingly. Thus he was supported for some time; at length, having offended them in some way—he was seen, I believe, eating food forbidden among them—he was reduced to want, and he thought that he would have to demand his property back from the city;[1] and having obtained a process in the name of the Emperor, he expected to recover it. But the city sent messengers to him, and nothing was done; but he was to remain where he was, and to this he agreed for once.

(c) Minucius Felix, *Octavius*, VIII, 3–10. (MSL, 3 : 267 *ff*.)

The following passage is taken from an apologetic dialogue entitled *Octavius*. Although it was composed by a Christian, it probably represents the current heathen conceptions of Christianity and its morals, especially its assemblies, where the worst excesses were supposed to take place. In the dialogue the passage is put into the mouth of the disputant who represents the heathen objection to the new faith. The date is difficult to determine, probably it was the last third of the second century.

Ch. 8. . . . Is it not lamentable that men of a reprobate, unlawful, and dangerous faction should rage against the gods? From the lowest dregs, the more ignorant and women, credulous and yielding on account of the heedlessness of their

---

[1] He had given his property to his native place.

sex, gathered and established a vast and wicked conspiracy, bound together by nightly meetings and solemn feasts and inhuman meats—not by any sacred rites, but by such as require expiation. It is a people skulking and shunning the light; in public silent, but in corners loquacious. They despise the temples as charnel-houses; they reject the gods; they deride sacred things. While they are wretched themselves, if allowed they pity the priests; while they are half naked themselves, they despise honors and purple robes. O wonderful folly and incredible effrontery! They despise present torments, but fear those that are uncertain and in the future. While they fear to die after death, for the present life they do not fear to die. In such manner does a deceitful hope soothe their fear with the solace of resuscitation.

Ch. 9. And now, as wickeder things are advancing more successfully and abandoned manners are creeping on day by day, those foul shrines of an impious assembly are increasing throughout the whole world. Assuredly this confederacy should be rooted out and execrated. They know one another by secret marks and signs. They love one another almost before they know one another. Everywhere, also, there is mingled among them a certain religion of lust; and promiscuously they call one another brother and sister, so that even a not unusual debauchery might, by the employment of those sacred names, become incestuous. It is thus that their vain and insane superstition glories in crimes. Nor, concerning these matters, would intelligent report speak of things unless there was the highest degree of truth, and varied crimes of the worst character called, from a sense of decency, for an apology. I hear that they adore the head of an ass, that basest of creatures, consecrated by I know not what silly persuasion—a worthy and appropriate religion for such morals. Some say that they worship the genitalia of their pontiff and priest, and adore the nature, as it were, of their parent. I know not whether these things be false; certainly suspicion has place in the case of secret and nocturnal rites; and he

who explains their ceremonies by reference to a man punished
by extreme suffering for wickedness, and to the deadly wood
of the cross, bestows fitting altars upon reprobate and wicked
men, that they may worship what they deserve. Now the
story of their initiation of young novices is as detestable as
it is well known. An infant covered with meal, so as to deceive
the unwary, is placed before him who is to be defiled with
their rites; this infant is slain with dark and secret wounds
by the young novice, who has been induced to strike harmless
blows, as it were, on the surface of the meal. Thirstily—
O horror! —they lick up its blood; eagerly they divide its
limbs. By this victim they are confederated, with the consciousness of this wickedness they are pledged to a mutual
silence. These sacred rites are more foul than any sort of
sacrilege. And of their banqueting it is well known what
is said everywhere; even the speech of our Cirtensian[1] testifies
to it. On a solemn day they assemble at a banquet with all
their children, their sisters and mothers, people of every sex and
age. There, after much feasting, when the sense of fellowship
has waxed warm and the fervor of incestuous lust has grown
hot with drunkenness, a dog that has been tied to a chandelier
is provoked to rush and spring about by throwing a piece of
offal beyond the length of the line by which he is bound;
and thus the light, as if conscious, is overturned and extinguished in shameless darkness, while unions of abominable
lust involve them by the uncertainty of chance. Although if
all are not in fact, yet all are in their conscience, equally incestuous; since whatever might happen by the act of the individuals is sought for by the will of all.

Ch. 10. I purposely pass over many things, for there are
too many, all of which, or the greater part of them, the
obscurity of their vile religion declares to be true. For why
do they endeavor with such pains to conceal and cloak whatever they worship, since honorable things always rejoice in
publicity, but crimes are kept secret? Why have they no

[1] Fronto. See W. Smith, *Dict. of Greek and Roman Biography.*

altars, no temples, no acknowledged images? Why do they never speak openly, never congregate freely, unless it be for the reason that what they adore and conceal is either worthy of punishment or is something to be ashamed of? Moreover, whence or who is he, or where is the one God, solitary and desolate, whom no free people, no kingdoms, and not even Roman superstition have known? The sole, miserable nationality of the Jews worshipped one God, and one peculiar to itself; but they worshipped him openly, with temples, with altars, with victims, and with ceremonies; and he has so little force or power that he is enslaved together with his own special nation to the Roman deities. But the Christians, moreover, what wonders, what monstrosities, do they feign, that he who is their God, whom they can neither show nor see, inquires diligently into the conduct of all, the acts of all, and even into their words and secret thoughts. They would have him running about everywhere, and everywhere present, troublesome, even shamelessly inquisitive, since he is present at everything that is done, and wanders about in all places. When he is occupied with the whole, he cannot give attention to particulars; or when occupied with particulars, he is not enough for the whole. Is it because they threaten the whole earth, the world itself and all its stars, with a conflagration, that they are meditating its destruction? As if either the natural and eternal order constituted by the divine laws would be disturbed, or, when the league of the elements has been broken up and the heavenly structure dissolved, that fabric in which it is contained and bound together would be overthrown!

§ 19. The Attitude of the Roman Government toward Christians, A. D. 138 to A. D. 192

No general persecution of the Christians was undertaken by the Roman Government during the second century, though Christians were not infrequently put to death under the existing laws. These laws, however, were by no means uniformly carried out. The most sanguinary persecutions were generally occasioned by mob violence and may be compared to modern lynchings. At Lyons and Vienne, in Gaul, there was much suffering in 177. The letter from the churches of these cities to the Christians in Asia and Phrygia, Eusebius, *Hist. Ec.*, V, 1 (PNF, ser. I, vol. I, 211), and the *Martyrdom of Polycarp* (ANF, I, 37) are among the finest pieces of literature in this period and should be read by every student. Under Commodus (180–193), Marcia seems to have aided the Christians suffering persecution. The *Martyrdom of Justin* may be found ANF, I, 303, appended to his works. The doubtful rescript of Hadrian and the certainly spurious rescript of Antoninus Pius may be found in the Appendix to Justin Martyr's works (ANF, I, 186), and in Eusebius, *Hist. Ec.*, IV, 9 and 13. For a discussion of their genuineness, see McGiffert's notes to Eusebius, *Hist. Ec.* The original texts may be found in Preuschen's *Analecta*, I, § 6 f.

(a) Justin Martyr, *Apologia*, II, 2. (MSG, 6:445.)

The martyrdom of Ptolomæus.

A certain woman had been converted to Christianity by Ptolomæus. Her dissolute husband, who had deserted her some time before, was divorced by her on account of his profligacy. In revenge he attempted to injure her, but she sought and obtained the protection of the imperial courts. The husband thereupon turned his attack upon Ptolomæus. According to Ruinart, the martyrdom took place in 166. See DCB, arts. "Ptolomæus" and "Justin Martyr." This and the following martyrdoms illustrate the procedure of the courts in dealing with Christians.

Since he was no longer able to prosecute her, he directed his assaults against a certain Ptolomæus whom Urbicus punished, and who had been the teacher of the woman in the Christian doctrines. And he did this in the following way: He persuaded a centurion, his friend, who had cast Ptolomæus into prison, to take Ptolomæus and interrogate him only as to whether he were a Christian. And Ptolomæus, being a lover of the truth, and not of deceitful or false disposition,

when he confessed himself to be a Christian, was thrown in
chains by the centurion and for a long time was punished in
prison.   At last, when he was brought to Urbicus, he was
asked this one question only: whether he was a Christian.
And again, conscious of the noble things that were his through
the teaching of Christ, he confessed his discipleship in the
divine virtue.   For he who denies anything either denies it
because he condemns the thing itself or he avoids confession
because he knows his own unworthiness or alienation from it;
neither of which cases is that of a true Christian.   And when
Urbicus ordered him to be led away to punishment, a certain
Lucius, who was also himself a Christian, seeing the unreason-
able judgment, said to Urbicus: "What is the ground of this
judgment?   Why have you punished this man: not as an
adulterer, nor fornicator, nor as one guilty of murder, theft, or
robbery, nor convicted of any crime at all, but who has only
confessed that he is called by the name of Christian?   You
do not judge, O Urbicus, as becomes the Emperor Pius, nor
the philosopher, the son of Cæsar, nor the sacred Senate."
And he, replying nothing else to Lucius, said: "You also
seem to me to be such an one."   And when Lucius answered, "Most certainly I am," he then ordered him also
to be led away.   And he professed his thanks, since he knew
that he was going to be delivered from such wicked rulers
and was going to the Father and King of the heavens.
And still a third came forward and was condemned to be
punished.

(b) *Passion of the Scilitan Martyrs.*

Text: J. A. Robinson, *Text and Studies*, I, 2, 112–116,
Cambridge, 1891; reprinted in R. Knopf, *Ausgewählte Märtyreracten*, 34 *ff.*, Tübingen, 1901.

The date of this martyrdom is July 17, 180 A.D.   Scili, the place of
residence of these martyrs, was a small city in northwestern Proconsular Africa.   For an account of ancient martyrologies, see Krüger, §§ 104 *ff.*

When Præsens, for the second time, and Claudianus were consuls, on the seventeenth day of July, and when Speratus, Nartzalus, Cittinus, Donata, Secunda, and Vestia were brought into the judgment-hall at Carthage, the proconsul Saturninus said: Ye can win the indulgence of our lord the Emperor if ye return to a sound mind.

Speratus said: We have never done ill; we have not lent ourselves to wrong; we have never spoken ill; but when we have received ill we have given thanks, because we pay heed to our Emperor.

Saturninus, the proconsul, said: We, too, are religious, and our religion is simple; and we swear by the genius of our lord the Emperor, and pray for his welfare, which also ye, too, ought to do.

Speratus said: If thou wilt peaceably lend me thine ears, I will tell thee the mystery of simplicity.

Saturninus said: I will not lend my ears to thee, when thou beginnest to speak evil things of our sacred rites; but rather do thou swear by the genius of our lord the Emperor.

Speratus said: The empire of this world I know not; but rather I serve that God whom no man hath seen nor with these eyes can see. [I Tim. 6: 16.] I have committed no theft; but if I have bought anything I pay the tax; because I know my Lord, the King of kings and Emperor of all nations.

Saturninus, the proconsul, said to the rest: Cease to be of this persuasion.

Speratus said: It is an ill persuasion to do murder, to bear false witness.

Saturninus, the proconsul, said: Be not partakers of this folly.

Cittinus said: We have none other to fear except only our Lord God, who is in heaven.

Donata said: Honor to Cæsar as Cæsar, but fear to God. [Cf. Rom. 13 : 7.]

Vestia said: I am a Christian.

Secunda said: What I am that I wish to be.

Saturninus, the proconsul, said to Speratus: Dost thou persist in being a Christian?

Speratus said: I am a Christian. And with him they all agreed.

Saturninus, the proconsul, said: Will ye have a space to consider?

Speratus said: In a matter so just there is no considering.

Saturninus, the proconsul, said: What are the things in your chest?

Speratus said: Books and epistles of Paul, a just man.

Saturninus, the proconsul, said: Have a delay of thirty days and bethink yourselves.

Speratus said a second time: I am a Christian. And with him all agreed.

Saturninus, the proconsul, read out the decree from the tablet: Speratus, Nartzalus, Cittinus, Donata, Vestia, Secunda, and the rest who have confessed that they live according to the Christian rite because an opportunity has been offered them of returning to the custom of the Romans and they have obstinately persisted, it is determined shall be put to the sword.

Speratus said: We give thanks to God.

Nartzalus said: To-day we are martyrs in heaven; thanks be to God.

Saturninus, the proconsul, ordered it to be proclaimed by the herald: Speratus, Nartzalus, Cittinus, Veturius, Felix, Aquilinus, Lætatius, Januaria, Generosa, Vestia, Donata, and Secunda I have ordered to be executed.

They all said: Thanks be to God.

And so they all at one time were crowned with martyrdom; and they reign with the Father and the Son and the Holy Ghost, forever and ever.   Amen.

(c) Hippolytus, *Refutatio omnium Hæresium*, X, 7. (MSG, 16 : 3382.)

Hippolytus, a Greek writer of the West, lived at Rome in the time of Zephyrinus (198–217) and until shortly after A. D. 235. He appears to have been consecrated bishop of a schismatical party in Rome. Of his numerous works many have been lost in whole or in part. The *Philosophumena, or the Refutation of All Heresies*, was lost, with the exception of the first book, until 1842, and was then published among the works of Origen. It is of importance as giving much material for the study of Gnosticism. It may be found as a whole translated in ANF, V.

But after a time, when other martyrs were there [*i. e.*, in the mines in Sardinia], Marcia, the pious concubine of Commodus, wishing to perform some good deed, called before her the blessed Victor [193?-202], at that time bishop of the Church, and inquired of him what martyrs were in Sardinia. And he delivered to her the names of all, but did not give the name of Callistus, knowing what things had been attempted by him. Marcia, having obtained her request from Commodus, hands the letter of emancipation to Hyacinthus, a certain eunuch rather advanced in life [or a presbyter], who, receiving it, sailed away to Sardinia. He delivered the letter to the person who at that time was governor of the territory, and he released the martyrs, with the exception of Callistus.

§ 20.   The Literary Defence of Christianity

In reply to the attacks made upon Christianity, the apologists defended their religion along three lines: It was philosophically justified; it was true; it did not favor immorality, but, on the contrary, inculcated virtue. The philosophical defence, or justification, of Christianity was most brilliantly undertaken by Justin Martyr, who employed the current philosophical conception of the Logos. The general proof of Christianity was chiefly based upon the argument from the fulfilment of prophecy. All apologists undertook to show that the heathen calumnies against the Christians were false, that the heathen religions were replete with obscene tales of the gods, and that the worship of idols was absurd.

(*a*) Aristides, *Apology*, 2, 13, 15, 16.   Ed. J. R. Harris and J. A. Robinson, *Texts and Studies*, I, 1, Cambridge, 1891.

The *Apology* of Aristides was long lost, but was found in a Syriac version in 1889. It was then found that much of the Greek original had been incorporated in the *Life of Barlaam and Josaphat*, a popular religious romance of the Middle Ages; see the introduction to the parallel translations by D. H. McKay in ANF, vol. IX, 259–279. This work of Aristides may be as early as 125; if so, it disputes with the similar work of Quadratus the honor of being the first Christian apology.   A large part of it is taken up with a statement of the contradictions and absurdities of the mythology of the Greeks and Barbarians.   Of this statement, ch. 13, quoted below, is the conclusion. Then, after a short passage regarding the Jews, the author passes to an exposition of the faith of Christians and a statement regarding their high morality.

Ch. 2. [Found only in Syriac.] The Christians trace the beginning of their religion to Jesus the Messiah; and He is named the Son of the most high God. And it is said that God came down from heaven and from a Hebrew virgin assumed and clothed Himself with flesh, and that the Son of God lived in a daughter of man. This is taught in that Gospel which, as is related among them, was preached among them a short time ago. And you, also, if you will read therein, may perceive the power that belongs to it. This Jesus, therefore, was born of the race of the Hebrews. He had twelve disciples, that His wonderful plan of salvation might be carried out. But He himself was pierced by the Jews, and He died and He was buried. And they say that after three days He rose and was raised to heaven. Thereupon those twelve disciples went forth into the known parts of the world, and with all modesty and uprightness taught concerning His greatness. And therefore also those at the present time who now believe that preaching are called Christians and they are known.

Ch. 13. When the Greeks made laws they did not perceive that by their laws they condemned their gods. For if their laws are righteous, their gods are unrighteous, because they committed transgressions of the law in that they killed one another, practised sorcery, and committed adultery, robbed, stole, and lay with males, not to mention their other practices. For if their gods have done right in doing all this, as they write, then the laws of the Greeks are unrighteous in not being made according to the will of their gods. And consequently the whole world has gone astray.

Ch. 15. The Christians, O King, in that they go about and seek the truth, have found it and, as we have understood from their writings, they have come much nearer to the truth and correct knowledge than have the other peoples. They know and trust God, the creator of heaven and earth, in whom are all things and from whom are all things, in Him who has no other God beside Him, in Him from whom they have received commandments which they have engraved upon their minds, commandments which they observe in the faith and expectation of the world to come. Wherefore they do not commit adultery or fornication, nor bear false witness, nor covet what is held in pledge, nor covet what is not theirs. They honor father and mother and show kindness to their neighbors. If they are judges, they judge uprightly. They do not worship idols made in human form. And whatsoever they would not that others should do unto them, they do not to others. They do not eat of food offered to idols, because they are pure. And their oppressors they appease and they make friends of them; they do good to their enemies. . . . If they see a stranger, they take him to their dwellings and rejoice over him as over a real brother. For they do not call themselves brethren after the flesh, but after the Spirit and in God. But if one of their poor passes from the world, each one of them who sees him cares for his burial according to his ability. And if they hear that one of them is imprisoned or oppressed on account of the name of their Messiah, all of them care for his necessity, and if it is possible to redeem him, they set him free. And if any one among them is poor and needy, and they have no spare food, they fast two or three days in order to supply him with the needed food.[1] The precepts of their Messiah they observe with great care. They live justly

---

[1] *Cf.* Hermas, *Pastor*, Sim. V, 3. ANF, II, 34.

and soberly, as the Lord their God commanded them. Every morning and every hour they acknowledge and praise God for His lovingkindnesses toward them, and for their food and drink they give thanks to Him. And if any righteous man among them passes from this world, they rejoice and thank God and they escort his body as if he were setting out on a journey from one place to another. . . .

Ch. 16. . . . Their words and precepts, O King, and the glory of their worship and their hope of receiving reward, which they look for in another world, according to the work of each one, you can learn about from their writings. It is enough for us to have informed your Majesty in a few words concerning the conduct and truth of the Christians. For great, indeed, and wonderful is their doctrine for him who will study it and reflect upon it. And verily this is a new people, and there is something divine in it.

(b) Justin Martyr, *Apologia*, I, 46. (MSG, 6:398.)

In the following, Justin Martyr states his argument from the doctrine of the Logos, which was widely accepted in Greek philosophy and found its counterpart in Christianity in the Johannine theology (see below, § 32 a). With Justin should be compared Clement of Alexandria (see below, § 43 a), who develops the same idea in showing the relation of Greek philosophy to the Mosaic dispensation and to the Christian revelation.

We have been taught that Christ is the first-born of God, and we have declared above that He is the Word of whom every race of men partake; and those who lived reasonably were Christians, even though they have been thought atheists; as among the Greeks, Socrates and Heraclitus and those like them; and among the Barbarians, Abraham and Ananias, and Azarias, and Misael, and Elias, and many others whose actions and names we now decline to recount, because we know it would be tedious.

(c) Justin Martyr, *Apologia*, II, 10, 13. (MSG, 6:459, 466.)

Ch. 10. Our doctrines, then, appear to be greater than all human teaching; because Christ who appeared for our sakes, became the whole rational being,[1] body and reason and soul. For whatever either law-givers or philosophers uttered well they elaborated by finding and contemplating some part of the Logos. But since they did not know the whole of the Logos, which is Christ, they often contradicted themselves. And those who by human birth were more ancient than Christ, when they attempted to consider and prove things by reason, were brought before the tribunals as impious persons and busybodies. And Socrates, who was more zealous in this direction than all of them, was accused of the very same crimes as ourselves. For they said that he was introducing new divinities, and did not consider those to be gods whom the State recognized. But he cast out from the State both Homer and the rest of the poets, and taught men to reject the wicked demons and those who did the things which the poets related; and he exhorted them to become acquainted with the God who was unknown to them, by means of the investigation of reason, saying, "That it is not easy to find the Father and Maker of all, nor, having found Him, is it safe to declare Him to all."[2] But these things our Christ did through His own power. For no one trusted in Socrates so as to die for this doctrine, but in Christ, who was partially known even by Socrates (for He was and is the Logos who is in every man, and who foretold the things that were to come to pass both through the prophets and in His own person when He was made of like passions and taught these things), not only philosophers and scholars believed, but also artisans and people entirely uneducated, despising both glory and fear and death; since He is the power of the ineffable Father, and not the mere instrument of human reason.[3]

Ch. 13. . . . I confess that I both boast and with all my strength strive to be found a Christian; not because the teachings of Plato are different from those of Christ, but

---

[1] I. e., the Logos; cf. previous chapter.   [2] See Plato, Timæus, p. 28c.
[3] For a remarkable passage on the moral influence of Christ's teaching as a proof of the truth of His message, see Origen, Contra Celsum, I, 67 f.

because they are not in all respects similar, as neither are those of others, Stoics, poets, and historians. For each man spoke well in proportion to the share he had of the spermatic divine Logos, seeing what was related to it. But they who contradict themselves on the more important points appear not to have possessed the heavenly wisdom and the knowledge which cannot be spoken against. Whatever things were rightly said among all men are the property of us Christians. For next to God we worship and love the Logos, who is from the unbegotten and ineffable God, since also He became man for our sakes, that, becoming a partaker of our sufferings, He might also bring us healing. For all the writers were able to see realities darkly through the sowing of the implanted Logos that was in them. For the seed of anything and a copy imparted according to capacity [*i. e.*, to receive] is one thing, and quite another is the thing itself, of which there is the participation and imitation according to the grace which is from Him.

(*d*) Justin Martyr, *Apologia*, I, 31, 53. (MSG, 6: 375, 406.)
The argument from prophecy.

Ch. 31. There were then among the Jews certain men who were prophets of God, through whom the prophetic Spirit [context shows that the Logos is here meant] published beforehand things that were to come to pass before they happened. And their prophecies, as they were spoken and when they were uttered, the kings who were among the Jews at the several times carefully preserved in their possession, when they had been arranged by the prophets themselves in their own Hebrew language. . . . They are also in possession of all Jews throughout the world. . . . In these books of the prophets we found Jesus our Christ foretold as coming, born of a virgin, growing up to manhood, and healing every disease and every sickness, and raising the dead, and being hated and unrecognized, and crucified, and dying, and rising again, and ascending into heaven, and both being and also called the Son of God, and that certain persons should be sent by Him into every race of men to publish these things, and that rather among the Gentiles [than among the Jews] men should believe on Him.   And He was predicted before He appeared first 5,000 years before, and again 3,000, then 2,000 then 1,000, and yet again 800; for according to the succession of generations prophets after prophets arose.

Ch. 53.   Though we have many other prophecies, we forbear to speak, judging these sufficient for the persuasion of those who have ears capable of hearing and understanding; and considering also that these persons are able to see that we do not make assertions, and are unable to produce proof, like those fables that are told of the reputed sons of Jupiter. For with what reason should we believe of a crucified man that He is the first-born of the unbegotten God, and Himself will pass judgment on the whole human race, unless we found testimonies concerning Him published before He came and was born as a man, and unless we saw that things had happened accordingly?

CHAPTER II. THE INTERNAL CRISIS: THE GNOSTIC AND OTHER HERETICAL SECTS

In the second century the Church passed through an internal crisis even more trying than the great persecutions of the following centuries and with results far more momentous. Of the conditions making possible such a crisis the most important was absence in the Church of norms of faith universally acknowledged as binding.   Then, again, many had embraced Christianity without grasping the spirit of the new religion.   Nearly all interpreted the Christian faith more or less according to their earlier philosophical or religious conceptions; e. g., the apologists within the Church used the philosophical Logos doctrine.   In this way arose numerous interpretations of Christian teaching and perversions of that teaching, some not at all in harmony with the generally received tradition.   These discordant interpretations or perversions are the heretical movements of the second century. They varied in every degree of departure from the generally accepted Christian tradition. Some, like the earlier Gnostics (§ 21), and even the greater Gnostic systems (§ 22), at least in their esoteric teaching, show that their principal inspiration was other than Christian; others, as the Gnosticism of Marcion (§ 23) and the enthusiastic sect of the Montanists (§ 25), seem to have built largely upon exaggerated Christian tenets, contained, indeed, in the New Testament, but not fully appreciated by the majority of Christians; or still others, as the Encratites (§ 24), laid undue stress upon what was generally recognized as an element of Christian morality.

The principal source materials for the history of Gnosticism and other heresies of this chapter may be found collected and provided with commentary in Hilgenfeld, *Ketzergeschichte des Urchristenthums*, Leipsic, 1884.

§ 21. The Earlier Gnostics: Gnosticism in General.
§ 22. The Greater Gnostic Systems.
§ 23. Marcion.
§ 24. The Encratites and Earlier Asceticism.
§ 25. Montanism.

§ 21. THE EARLIER GNOSTICS: GNOSTICISM IN GENERAL

Gnosticism is a generic name for a vast number of syncretistic religious systems prevalent, especially in the East, both before and after the Christian era. For the most part the movement was outside of Christianity, and was already dying out when Christianity appeared. It derived its essential features from Persian and Babylonian sources and was markedly dualistic. As it spread toward the West, it adopted many Western elements, making use of Christian ideas and terms and Greek philosophical concepts. Modified by such new matter, it obtained a renewed lease of life. In proportion as the various schools of Gnosticism became more influenced by Christian elements, they were more easily confused with

Christianity, and accordingly more dangerous to it. Among such were the greater schools of Basilides and Valentinus (see next section). The doctrines of Gnosticism were held by many who were nominally within the Church. The tendency of the Gnostics and their adherents was to form little coteries and to keep much of their teaching secret from those who were attracted by their more popular tenets. The esoteric element seems to have been the so-called "systems" in which the fanciful and mythological element in Gnosticism appears. This, as being the most vulnerable part of the Gnostic teaching, was attacked most bitterly by the opponents of heresy. There are no extant writings of the earlier Gnostics, Simon, Menander, or Cerinthus. They are known only from Christian opponents.

Sources for the history of Gnosticism: The leading sources are the Church Fathers Irenæus, Hippolytus, Tertullian, Clement of Alexandria (all translated in ANF), Origen (in part only translated in ANF), and Epiphanius. The accounts of these bitter enemies must necessarily be used with caution. They contain, however, numerous fragments from Gnostic writings. The fragments in the ante-Nicene Fathers may be found in A. Hilgenfeld, *op. cit.*, in Greek, with commentary. For the literary remains of Gnosticism, see Krüger, §§ 22–31. The more accessible are: *Acts of Thomas* (best Greek text by Bonnet, Leipsic, 1903, German translation with excellent commentary in E. Hennecke, *Neutestamentliche Apokryphen*, Tübingen and Leipsic, 1904); Ptolomæus, *Epistle to Flora* (in Epiphanius, Panarion, Hær. XXXIII); *Hymn of the Soul*, from the *Acts of Thomas* (text and English translation by Bevan in *Text and Studies*, V, 3, Cambridge, 1897, also translated in F. C. Burkitt, *Early Eastern Christianity*, N. Y., 1904).

(*a*) Tertullian, *De Præscriptione Hæreticorum*, 7. (MSL, 2 : 21.)

A wide-spread opinion that Gnosticism was fundamentally a perversion of Christianity finds its most striking expression in the phrase of Harnack that it was "the acute secularizing or Hellenizing of Christianity" (*History of Dogma*, English translation, I, 226). The foundation for this representation is the later Gnosticism, which took over many Christian and Greek elements, and the opinion of Tertullian that Gnosticism and Greek philosophy discussed the same questions and held the same opinions. (*Cf.* the thesis of Hippolytus in his *Philosophumena, or the Refutation of All Heresies;* see the Proemium, ANF, V, 9 *f.*, and especially bk. VII.) Tertullian, although retaining unconsciously the impress of his former Stoicism, was violently opposed to philosophy, and in his denunciation of heresy felt that it was a powerful argument against the Gnostics to show similarities between their teaching and the Greek philosophy he so heartily detested. It is a brilliant work and may be taken as a fair specimen of Tertullian's style.

These are the doctrines of men and of demons born of the spirit of this world's wisdom, for itching ears; and the Lord, calling this foolishness, chose the foolish things of this world to the confusion of philosophy itself. For philosophy is the material of the world's wisdom, the rash interpreter of the nature and dispensation of God. Indeed, heresies themselves are instigated by philosophy. From this source came the eons, and I know not what infinite forms, and the trinity of man in the system of Valentinus; he was of Plato's school. From this source came Marcion's better god with all his tranquillity; he came of the Stoics. Then again the opinion that the soul dies is held by the Epicureans. The denial of the resurrection of the body is taken from the united schools of all philosophers. When matter is made equal to God, you have the teaching of Zeno; and when anything is alleged touching a fiery god, then Heraclitus comes in. The same subject-matter is discussed over and over again by the heretics and the philosophers; the same arguments are involved. Whence and wherefore is evil? Whence and how has come man? Besides these there is the question which Valentinus has very recently proposed, Whence comes God?

(*b*) Irenæus, *Adv. Hær.*, I, 23. (MSG, 7:670.)

Simon Magus. For additional source material, see Justin Martyr, *Apol.* I, 26, 56, *Dial. c. Tryph.*, 120; Hippolytus, *Ref.* VI, 72 *f.* The appearance of Simon in the pseudo-Clementine literature (translated in ANF, VIII), presents an interesting historical problem. The present condition of investigation is given in the article "Clementine Literature" by J. V. Bartlett, in *Encyc. Brit.*, eleventh ed.

Simon the Samaritan, that magician of whom Luke, the disciple and follower of the Apostles, says: "But there was a certain man, Simon by name," etc. [Acts 8 : 9–11, 20, 21, 23.] Since he did not put his faith in God a whit more, he set himself eagerly to contend against the Apostles, in order that he himself might seem to be a wonderful being, and studied with still greater zeal the whole range of magic art, that he might the better bewilder the multitude of men. Such was his procedure in the reign of Claudius Cæsar, by whom also he is said to have been honored with a statue on account of his magic. This man, then, was glorified by many as a god, and he taught that it was he himself who appeared among the Jews as the Son, but descended in Samaria as the Father, while he came to other nations in the character of the Holy Spirit. He represented himself as the loftiest of all powers, that it is he who is over all as the Father, and he allowed himself to be called whatsoever men might name him.

Now this Simon of Samaria, from whom all heresies derive their origin, has as the material for his sect the following: Having redeemed from slavery at Tyre, a city of Phœnicia, a certain woman named Helena,[1] a prostitute, he was in the habit of carrying her about with him, declaring that she was the first conception [*Ennœa*] of his mind, the mother of all, by whom he conceived in his mind to make the angels and archangels. For this Ennœa, leaping forth from him and comprehending the will of her father, descended to the lower regions and generated angels and powers, by whom, also, he declared this world was made. But after she had generated them she was detained by them through jealousy, because they were unwilling that they should be regarded as the progeny of any other being. As to himself, he was wholly unknown to them, but his Ennœa was detained by those powers and

[1] For a discussion of this Helena, see Bousset, *Die Hauptprobleme der Gnosis*, 1907, pp. 77 *ff.*

angels who had been produced by her. She suffered all kinds
of contumely from them, so that she could not return upward
to her father, but was even shut up in a human body and for
ages passed in succession from one female body to another,
as from one vessel to another vessel. She was in that Helen
on whose account the Trojan War was undertaken; wherefore also Stesichorus was struck blind, because he cursed her
in his poems; but afterward, when he had repented and
written those verses which are called palinodes, in which he
sung her praises, he saw once more. Thus passing from
body to body and suffering insults in every one of them, she
at last became a common prostitute; and she it is who was
the lost sheep.

For this purpose he himself had come, that he might win
her first and free her from chains, and confer salvation upon
men by making himself known to them. For since the angels
ruled the world poorly, because each one of them coveted the
principal power, he had come to mend matters and had descended, been transfigured and assimilated to powers and
angels, so that he might appear among men as man, although
he was not a man; and that he was supposed to have suffered
in Judea, although he had not suffered. Moreover, the prophets inspired by the angels, who were the makers of the world,
pronounced their prophecies; for which reason those who place
their trust in him and Helena no longer regard them, but are
free to do what they will; for men are saved according to
his grace, and not according to their righteous works. For
deeds are not righteous in the nature of things, but by mere
accident and just as those angels who made the world have
determined, seeking by such precepts to bring men into bondage. On this account he promised that the world should
be dissolved and that those who are his should be freed from
the rule of them who made the world.

Thus, then, the mystic priests belonging to this sect both
live profligately and practise magical arts, each one to the
extent of his ability. They use exorcisms and incantations,

love-potions, also, and charms, as well as those beings who are called "familiars" [*paredri*] and "dream senders" [*oniropompi*], and whatever other curious arts can be had are eagerly pressed into their service.

(c) Irenæus, *Adv. Hær.*, I, 23. (MSG, 7 : 673.)

The system of Menander. *Cf.* also Eusebius, *Hist. Ec.*, III, 26.

The successor of Simon Magus was Menander, a Samaritan by birth, who also became a perfect adept in magic. He affirms that the first power is unknown to all, but that he himself is the person who has been sent forth by the invisible beings as a saviour for the salvation of men. The world was made by angels, who, as he also, like Simon, says, were produced by the Ennœa. He gives also, as he affirms, by means of the magic which he teaches knowledge, so that one may overcome those angels that made the world. For his disciples obtain the resurrection by the fact that they are baptized into him, and they can die no more, but remain immortal without ever growing old.

(d) Irenæus, *Adv. Hær.*, I, 26. (MSG, 7 : 686.)

The system of Cerinthus. For additional source material, see Irenæus, III, 3, 4; Hippolytus, *Ref.* VII, 33; X, 21; Eusebius, *Hist. Ec.*, III, 28.

Cerinthus, again, taught in Asia that the world was not made by the supreme God, but by a power separated and distant from that Ruler [*principalitate*] who is over the universe, and ignorant of the God who is above all. He represented Jesus as not having been born of a virgin, for this seemed impossible to him, but as having been the son of Joseph and Mary in the same way that all other men are sons, only he was more righteous, prudent, and wise than other men. After his baptism Christ descended upon him in the form of a dove from the Supreme Ruler; and that then he proclaimed the unknown Father and performed miracles. But at last Christ departed from Jesus, and then Jesus suffered and rose again, but Christ remained impassable, since He was a spiritual being.

§ 22. THE GREATER GNOSTIC SYSTEMS: BASILIDES AND VALENTINUS

The Gnostic systems having most influence within the Church and effect upon its development were those of Basilides and Valentinus. Of these teachers and their followers we have not only the accounts of those opponents who attacked principally their esoteric and most characteristically Gnostic tenets, but also fragments and other remains which give a more favorable impression of the religious and moral value of the great schools of Gnosticism. In their "systems" of vast theogonies and cosmologies, in their wild mythological treatment of the most abstract conceptions and their dualism, the Church writers naturally saw at once their most vulnerable and most dangerous element.

(A) *The School of Basilides*

The school of Basilides marks the beginning of the distinctively Hellenistic stadium of Gnosticism. Basilides, its founder, apparently worked first in the East; circa 120–130 he was at Alexandria. He was the first important Gnostic writer. Of his Gospel, Commentary on that Gospel in twenty-four books (*Exegetica*), and his odes only fragments remain of the second, preserved by Clement of Alexandria and in the *Acta Archelai* (collected by Hilgenfeld, *Ketzergeschichte*, 207–213).

Additional source material: Clement of Alexandria, *Strom.*, II, 3, 8, 20; IV, 24, 26 (ANF, II); Hippolytus, *Ref.*, VII, 20–27; X, 14 (= VII, 1–15, X, 10, ANF, V); Eusebius, *Hist. Ec.*, IV, 7. The account of Hippolytus differs markedly from that of Irenæus, and his quotations and references have been the subject of long dispute among scholars.

(a) *Acta Archelai*, 55. (MSG, 10: 1526.)

The *Acta Archelai* purport to be an account of a disputation held in the reign of the Emperor Probus (276–282) by Archelaus, Bishop of Kaskar in Mesopotamia, with Mani, the founder of Manichæanism.

The work is of uncertain authorship; it belongs to the first part of the fourth century. It is the most important source for the Manichæan doctrine (v. infra, § 54). It exists only in a Latin translation probably from a Greek original.

Among the Persians there was also a certain preacher, one Basilides, of more ancient date, not long after the time of our Apostles. Since he was of a shrewd disposition himself, and observed that at that time all other subjects were preoccupied, he determined to affirm that dualism which was maintained also by Scythianus. And so, since he had nothing to advance which he might call his own, he brought the sayings of others before his adversaries. And all his books contain some matters difficult and extremely harsh. The thirteenth book of his Tractates,[1] however, is still extant, which begins thus: "In writing the thirteenth book of our Tractates, the word of salvation furnished us with the necessary and fruitful word. It illustrates[2] under the figure of a rich [principle] and a poor [principle], a nature without root and without place and only supervenes upon things.[3] This is the only topic which the book contains." Does it not, then, contain a strange word, as also certain persons think? Will ye not all be offended with the book itself, of which this is the beginning? But Basilides, returning to the subject, some five hundred lines intervening, more or less, says: "Give up this vain and curious variation, and let us rather find out what inquiries the Barbarians [i. e., the Persians] have instituted concerning good and evil, and to what opinions they have come on all these subjects. For certain among them have said that there are for all things two beginnings [or principles], to which they have referred good and evil, holding these principles are without beginning and ingenerate; that is to say, that in the origins of things there were light and darkness, which existed of themselves, and which were not declared to exist.[4] When these subsisted

[1] Probably to be identified with his Exegetica.
[2] Query: the antagonism between good and evil.
[3] Very obscure; see ANF, and Routh, ad loc., and Neander, Ch. Hist., I, 402.
[4] Routh, loc. cit., proposes as an emendation, "declared to be made."

by themselves, they each led its own proper mode of life as it willed to lead, and such as was competent to it. For in the case of all things, what is proper to it is in amity with it, and nothing seems evil to itself. But after they came to the knowledge of each other, and after the darkness contemplated the light, then, as if fired with a passion for something superior, the darkness rushed to have intercourse with the light."

(b) Clement of Alexandria, *Strom.*, IV, 12. (MSG, 8 : 1289.)

Basilides taught the transmigration of souls as an explanation of human suffering. *Cf.* Origen in *Ep. ad Rom.*, V: "I [Paul], he says, died [Rom. 7 : 9], for now sin began to be reckoned unto me. But Basilides, not noticing that these things ought to be understood of the natural law, according to impious and foolish fables turns this apostolic saying into the Pythagorean dogma, that is, attempts to prove from this word of the Apostle that souls are transferred from one body to another. For he says that the Apostle has said, 'I lived without any law'—*i. e.*, before I came into the body I lived in that sort of body which is not under the law, *i. e.*, of beasts and birds."

Basilides, in the twenty-third book of the Exegetics, respecting those that are punished by martyrdom, expresses himself in the following language: "For I say this, Whosoever fall under the afflictions mentioned, in consequence of unconsciously transgressing in other matters, are brought to this good end by the kindness of Him who brings about all things, though they are accused on other grounds; so that they may not suffer as condemned for what are acknowledged to be iniquities, nor reproached as the adulterer or the murderer, but because they are Christians; which will console them, so that they do not appear to suffer. And if one who has not sinned at all incur suffering (a rare case), yet even he will not suffer aught through the machinations of power, but will suffer as the child which seems not to have sinned would suffer." Then further on he adds: "As, then, the child which has not sinned before, nor actually committed sin, but has in itself that which committed sin, when subjected to suffering is benefited, reaping the advantage of many difficulties; so, also, although a perfect man may not have sinned in act, and yet endures afflictions, he suffers similarly with the child. Having within him the sinful principle, but not embracing the opportunity of committing sin, he does not sin; so that it is to be reckoned to him as not having sinned. For as he who wishes to commit adultery is an adulterer, although he fails to commit adultery, and he who wishes to commit murder is a murderer, although he is unable to kill; so, also, if I see the man without sin, whom I refer to, suffering, though he have done nothing bad, I should call him bad on account of the wish to sin. For I will affirm anything rather than call Providence evil." Then, in continuation, he says expressly concerning the Lord, as concerning man: "If, then, passing from all these observations, you were to proceed to put me to shame by saying, perchance impersonating certain parties, This man has then sinned, for this man has suffered; if you permit, I will say, He has not sinned, but was like a child suffering. If you insist more urgently, I would say, That the man you name is man, but God is righteous, 'for no one is pure,' as one said, 'from pollution.'" But the hypothesis of Basilides says that the soul, having sinned before in another life, endures punishment in this—the elect soul with honor by martyrdom, the other purged by appropriate punishment.

(c) Irenæus, *Adv. Hær.*, I, 24 : 3 ff. (MSG, 7 : 675.)

The system of Basilides, as presented by Irenæus, is dualistic and emanationist; with it is to be compared the presentation of the system by Hippolytus in his *Philosophumena*, where it appears as evolutionary and pantheistic. The trend of present opinion appears to be that the account given by Irenæus is more correct, or, at least, is earlier. The following account has all the appearance of having been taken from an original source (*cf.* Hilgenfeld, *Ketzergeschichte*, 195, 198). It represents the esoteric and more distinctively Gnostic teaching of the school.

Ch. 3. Basilides, to appear to have discovered something more sublime and plausible, gives an immense development to his doctrine. He declares that in the beginning the Nous was born of the unborn Father, that from him in turn was born the Logos, then from the Logos the Phronesis, from the Phronesis Sophia and Dynamis, and from Dynamis and Sophia the powers and principalities and angels, whom he calls the first; and that by these the first heaven was made. Then by emanation from these others were formed, and these created another heaven similar to the first. And in like manner, when still others had been formed by emanations from these, corresponding to those who were over them, they framed another third heaven; and from this third heaven downward there was a fourth succession of descendants; and so on, in the same manner, they say that other and still other princes and angels were formed, and three hundred and sixty-five heavens. Wherefore the year contained the same number of days in conformity with the number of the heavens.

Ch. 4. The angels occupying the lowest heaven, that, namely, which is visible to us, created all those things which are in the world, and made allotments among themselves of the earth, and of those nations which are upon it. The chief of them is he who is thought to be the God of the Jews. Inasmuch as he wished to make the other nations subject to his own people, the Jews, all the other princes resisted and opposed him. Wherefore all other nations were hostile to his nation. But the unbegotten and nameless Father, seeing their ruin, sent his own first-begotten Nous, for he it is who is called Christ, to set free from the power of those who made the world them that believe in him. He therefore appeared on earth as a man to the nations of those powers and wrought miracles. Wherefore he did not himself suffer death, but Simon, a certain Cyrenian, was compelled and bore the cross in his stead; and this latter was transfigured by him that he might be thought to be Jesus and was crucified through ignorance and error; but Jesus himself took the form of Simon and stood by and derided him. For as he is an incorporeal power and the Nous of the unborn Father, he transfigured himself at pleasure, and so ascended to him who had sent him, deriding them, inasmuch as he could not be held, and was invisible to all. Those, then, who know these things have been freed from the princes who made the world; so that it is not necessary to confess him who was crucified, but him who came in the form of a man, and was thought to have been crucified, and was called Jesus, and was sent by the Father, that by this dispensation he might destroy the works of the makers of the world. Therefore, Basilides says that if any one confesses the crucified, he is still a slave, under the power of those who made our bodies; but whoever denies him has been freed from these beings and is acquainted with the dispensation of the unknown Father.

Ch. 5. Salvation is only of the soul, for the body is by nature corruptible. He says, also, that even the prophecies were derived from those princes who made the world, but the law was especially given by their chief, who led the people out of the land of Egypt. He attaches no importance to meats offered to idols, thinks them of no consequence, but makes use of them without hesitation. He holds, also, the use of other things as indifferent, and also every kind of lust. These men, furthermore, use magic, images, incantations, invocations, and every other kind of curious arts. Coining also certain names as if they were those of the angels, they assert that some of these belong to the first, others to the second, heaven; and then they strive to set forth the names, principles, angels, powers, of the three hundred and sixty-five imagined heavens. They also affirm that the name in which the Saviour ascended and descended is Caulacau.[1]

Ch. 6. He, then, who has learned these things, and known all the angels and their causes, is rendered invisible and incomprehensible to the angels and powers, even as Caulacau also was. And as the Son was unknown to all, so must they also be known by no one; but while they know all and pass

---

[1] A mystic name; it is the Hebrew for "line upon line," see Is. 28 : 10. It means norm or rule.

through all, they themselves remain invisible and unknown to all; for "Do thou," they say, "know all, but let nobody know thee." For this reason, persons of such a persuasion are also ready to recant, yea, rather, it is impossible that they should suffer on account of a mere name, since they are alike to all. The multitude, however, cannot understand these matters, but only one out of a thousand, or two out of ten thousand. They declare that they are no longer Jews, and that they are not yet Christians; and that it is not at all fitting to speak openly of their mysteries, but right to keep them secret by preserving silence.

Ch. 7. They make out the local position of the three hundred and sixty-five heavens in the same way as do the mathematicians. For, accepting the theorems of the latter, they have transferred them to their own style of doctrine. They hold that their chief is Abraxas [or Abrasax]; and on this account that the word contains in itself the numbers amounting to three hundred and sixty-five.

(B) *The School of Valentinus*

The Valentinians were the most important of all the Gnostics closely connected with the Church. The school had many adherents scattered throughout the Roman Empire, its leading teachers were men of culture and literary ability, and the sect maintained itself a long time. Valentinus himself was a native of Egypt, and probably educated at Alexandria, where he may have come under the influence of Basilides. He taught his own system chiefly at Rome c. 140–c. 160. The great work of Irenæus against the Gnostics, although having all Gnostics in view, especially deals with the Valentinians in their various forms, because Irenæus was of the opinion that he who refutes their system refutes all (*cf. Adv. Hær.*, IV, *præf.*, 2). It is difficult to reconstruct with certainty the esoteric system of Valentinus as distinguished from possibly later developments of the school, as Irenæus, the principal authority, follows not only Valentinus, but Ptolo-

mæus and others, in describing the system. The following
selection of sources gives fragments of the letters and other
writings of Valentinus himself as preserved by Clement of
Alexandria, passages from Irenæus bringing out distinctive
features of the system, and the important letter of Ptolomæus
to Flora, one of the very few extant writings of the Gnostics
of an early date. It gives a good idea of the character of
the exoteric teaching of the school.

Additional source material: The principal authority for the system
of the Valentinians is Irenæus, *Adv. Hær.*, Lib. I (ANF), see also
Hippolytus, *Refut.*, VI, 24–32 (ANF); "The Hymn of the Soul," from
the *Acts of Thomas*, trans. by A. A. Bevan, *Texts and Studies*, III,
Cambridge, 1897; *The Fragments of Heracleon*, trans. by A. E. Burke,
Text and Studies, I, Cambridge, 1891; see also ANF, IX, index, p. 526,
s. v., Heracleon. The *Excerpta Theodoti* contained in ANF, VIII, are
really the *Excerpta Prophetica*, another collection, identified with the
Excerpta Theodoti by mistake of the editor of the American edition,
A. C. Coxe (on the *Excerpta*, see Zahn, *History of the Canon of the New
Testament*).

(*a*) Clement of Alexandria, *Strom.*, IV, 13. (MSG, 8 : 1296.)

The following passages appear to be taken from the same homily of
Valentinus. The pneumatics are naturally immortal, but have assumed
mortality to overcome it. Death is the work of the imperfect Demiurge. The concluding portion, which is very obscure, does not fit
well into the Valentinian system. *Cf.* Hilgenfeld, *op. cit.*, p. 300.

Valentinian in a homily writes in these words: "Ye are
originally immortal, and ye are children of eternal life, and ye
desired to have death distributed to you, that ye may spend
and lavish it, and that death may die in you and by you; for
when ye dissolve the world, and are not yourselves dissolved,
ye have dominion over creation and all corruption." [1] For
he also, similarly with Basilides, supposes a class saved by
nature [*i. e.*, the pneumatics, *v. infra*], and that this different
race has come hither to us from above for the abolition of
death, and that the origin of death is the work of the Creator

[1] *Cf.* the doctrine of redemption among the Marcosians, a branch of the Valentinians, stated in Irenæus, *Adv. Hær.*, I, 215.

of the world. Wherefore, also, he thus expounds that Scripture, "No one shall see the face of God and live" [Ex. 33 : 20], as if He were the cause of death. Respecting this God, he makes those allusions, when writing, in these expressions: "As much as the image is inferior to the living face, so much is the world inferior to the living Eon. What is, then, the cause of the image? It is the majesty of the face, which exhibits the figure to the painter, to be honored by his name; for the form is not found exactly to the life, but the name supplies what is wanting in that which is formed. The invisibility of God co-operates also for the sake of the faith of that which has been fashioned." For the Demiurge, called God and Father, he designated the image and prophet of the true God, as the Painter, and Wisdom, whose image, which is formed, is to the glory of the invisible One; since the things which proceed from a pair [syzygy] are complements [pleromata], and those which proceed from one are images. But since what is seen is no part of Him, the soul [psyche] comes from what is intermediate, and is different; and this is the inspiration of the different spirit. And generally what is breathed into the soul, which is the image of the spirit [pneuma], and in general, what is said of the Demiurge, who was made according to the image, they say was foretold by a sensible image in the book of Genesis respecting the origin of man; and the likeness they transfer to themselves, teaching that the addition of the different spirit was made, unknown to the Demiurge.

(b) Clement of Alexandria, *Strom.*, II, 20. (MSG, 8 : 1057.)

According to Basilides, the various passions of the soul were no original parts of the soul, but appendages to the soul. "They were in essence certain spirits attached to the rational soul, through some original perturbation and confusion; and that again, other bastard and heterogeneous natures of spirits grow onto them, like that of the wolf, the ape, the lion, and the goat, whose properties, showing themselves around the soul, they say, assimilate the lusts of the soul to the likeness of these animals." See the whole passage immediately preceding the following fragment. The fragment can best be understood by reference to the presentation of the system by W. Bousset in *Encyc. Brit.*, eleventh ed., art. "Basilides."

Valentinus, too, in a letter to certain people, writes in these very words respecting the appendages: "There is One good, by whose presence is the manifestation, which is by the Son, and by Him alone can the heart become pure, by the expulsion of every evil spirit from the heart; for the multitude of spirits dwelling in it do not suffer it to be pure; but each of them performs his own deeds, insulting it oft with unseemly lusts. And the heart seems to be treated somewhat like a caravansary. For the latter has holes and ruts made in it, and is often filled with filthy dung; men living filthily in it, and taking no care for the place as belonging to others. So fares it with the heart as long as there is no thought taken for it, being unclean and the abode of demons many. But when the only good Father visits it, it is sanctified and gleams with light. And he who possesses such a heart is so blessed that he shall see God."

(c) Clement of Alexandria, *Strom.*, II, 8. (MSG, 8 : 972.)

The teaching in the following passage attaches itself to the text, "The fear of God is the beginning of wisdom" (*cf.* Prov. 1 : 7). Compare with it Irenæus, *Adv. Hær.*, I, 30: 6.

Here the followers of Basilides, interpreting this expression [Prov. 1 : 7] say that "the Archon, having heard the speech of the Spirit, who was being ministered to, was struck with amazement both with the voice and the vision, having had glad tidings beyond his hopes announced to him; and that his amazement was called fear, which became the origin of wisdom, which distinguishes classes, and discriminates, and perfects, and restores. For not the world alone, but also the election, He that is over all has set apart and sent forth."

And Valentinus appears also in an epistle to have adopted such views. For he writes in these very words: "And as terror fell on the angels at this creature, because he uttered things greater than proceeds from his formation, by reason

of the being in him who had invisibly communicated a germ
of the supernal essence, and who spoke with free utterance;
so, also, among the tribes of men in the world the works of
men became terrors to those who made them—as, for example, images and statues. And the hands of all fashion things
to bear the image of God; for Adam, formed into the name of
man, inspired the dread attaching to the pre-existing man, as
having his being in him; and they were terror-stricken and
speedily marred the work."

(d) Clement of Alexandria, *Strom.*, III, 7. (MSG, 8 : 1151.)

The Docetism of Valentinus comes out in the following. It is to
be noted that Clement not only does not controvert the position taken
by the Gnostic as to the reality of the bodily functions of Jesus, but
in his own person makes almost the same assertions (*cf. Strom.*, VI, 9).
He might indeed call himself, as he does in this latter passage, a
Gnostic in the sense of the true or Christian Gnostic, but he comes
very close to the position of the non-Christian Gnostic.

Valentinus in an epistle to Agathopous says: "Since He
endured all things, and was continent [*i. e.*, self-controlled],
Jesus, accordingly, obtained for Himself divinity. He ate and
drank in a peculiar manner, not giving forth His food. Such
was the power of His continence [self-control] that the food
was not corrupted in Him, because He himself was without
corruption."

(e) Irenæus, *Adv. Hær.*, I, 7, 15; I, 8, 23. (MSG, 7 : 517,
528.)

The division of mankind into three classes, according to their nature
and consequent capacity for salvation, is characteristic of the Valentinian Gnosticism. The other Gnostics divided mankind into two
classes: those capable of salvation, or the pneumatics, or Gnostics,
and those who perish in the final destruction of material existence, or
the hylics. Valentinus avails himself of the notion of the trichotomy of
human nature, and gives a place for the bulk of Christians, those
who did not embrace Gnosticism; *cf.* Irenæus, *ibid.*, I, 6. Valentinus
remained long within the Church, accommodating his teaching as
far as possible, and in its exoteric side very fully, to the current teaching of the Church. The doctrine as to the psychics, capable of a
limited salvation, appears to be a part of this accommodation.

I, 7, 5. The Valentinians conceive of three kinds of men: the pneumatic [or spiritual], the choic [or material],[1] and the psychic [or animal]; such were Cain, Abel, and Seth. These three natures are no longer in one person, but in the race. The material goes to destruction. The animal, if it chooses the better part, finds repose in an intermediate place; but if it chooses the worse, it, too, goes to the same [destruction]. But they assert that the spiritual principles, whatever Acamoth has sown, being disciplined and nourished here from that time until now in righteous souls, because they were sent forth weak, at last attain perfection and shall be given as brides[2] to the angels of the Saviour, but their animal souls necessarily rest forever with the Demiurge in the intermediate place. And again subdividing the animal souls themselves, they say that some are by nature good and others are by nature evil. The good are those who become capable of receiving the seed; the evil by nature, those who are never able to receive that seed.

I, 8, 23. The parable of the leaven which the woman is said to have hid in three measures of meal they declare manifests the three kinds of men: pneumatic, psychic, and the choic, but the leaven denoted the Saviour himself. Paul also very plainly set forth the choic, the psychic, and the pneumatic, saying in one place: "As is the earthy [choic] such are they also that are earthy" [I Cor. 15 : 48]; and in another place, "He that is spiritual [pneumatic] judgeth all things" [I Cor. 2 : 14]. And the passage, "The animal man receiveth not the things of the spirit" [I Cor. 2 : 15], they affirm was spoken concerning the Demiurge, who, being psychic, knew neither his mother, who was spiritual, nor her seed, nor the Eons in the pleroma.

(f) Irenæus, *Adv. Hær.*, I, 1. (MSG, 7 : 445 f.)

The following passage appears, from the context, to have been written with the teaching of Ptolomæus especially in mind. It should

---

[1] Generally spoken of as hylics.
[2] *Cf.* introductory note to following selection.

be compared with the account further on in the same book, I, 11: 1-3. The syzygies are characteristic of the Valentinian teaching, and the symbolism of marriage plays an important part in the "system" of all the Valentinians. In the words of Duchesne (*Hist. ancienne de l'église*, sixth ed., p. 171): "Valentinian Gnosticism is from one end to the other a 'marriage Gnosticism.' From the most abstract origins of being to their end, there are only syzygies, marriages, and generations." For the connection between these conceptions and antinomianism, see Irenæus, *Adv. Hær.*, I, 6 : 3 *f.* For their sacramental application, *ibid.*, I, 21 : 3. *Cf.* I, 13 : 3, a passage which seems to belong to the sacrament of the bridal chamber.

They [the Valentinians] say that in the invisible and ineffable heights above there exists a certain perfect, pre-existent Eon, and him they call Proarche, Propator, and Bythos; and that he is invisible and that nothing is able to comprehend him. Since he is comprehended by no one, and is invisible, eternal, and unbegotten, he was in silence and profound quiescence in the boundless ages. There existed along with him Ennœa, whom they call Charis and Sige. And at a certain time this Bythos determined to send forth from himself the beginnings of all things, and just as seed he wished to send forth this emanation, and he deposited it in the womb of her who was with him, even of Sige. She then received this seed, and becoming pregnant, generated Nous, who was both similar and equal to him who had sent him forth [1] and alone comprehended his father's greatness. This Nous they also call Monogenes and Father and the Beginning of all Things. Along with him was also sent forth Aletheia; and these four constituted the first and first-begotten Pythagorean Tetrad, which also they denominate the root of all things. For there are first Bythos and Sige, and then Nous and Aletheia. And Monogenes, when he perceived for what purpose he had been sent forth, also himself sent forth Logos and Zoe, being the father of all those who are to come after him, and the beginning and fashioning of the entire

---

[1] The term used for a sending forth is προβολή, or emanation, and is constantly used in Gnosticism; hence the objection on the part of the majority of Christian theologians to the use of the term in describing the relations of the members of the Trinity.

pleroma. From Logos and Zoe were sent forth, by a conjunction, Anthropos and Ecclesia, and thus were formed the first-
begotten Ogdoad, the root and substance of all things, called
among them by four names; namely, Bythos, Nous, Logos,
and Anthropos. For each of these is at once masculine and
feminine, as follows: Propator was united by a conjunction
with his Ennœa, then Monogenes (*i. e.*, Nous) with Aletheia,
Logos with Zoe, Anthropos with Ecclesia.

(*g*) Ptolomæus, *Epistula ad Floram*, ap. Epiphanius, *Panarion, Hær.* XXXIII, 3. Ed. Oehler, 1859. (MSG, 41 : 557.)

Ptolomæus was possibly the most important disciple of Valentinus,
and the one to whom Irenæus is most indebted for his first-hand knowledge of the teaching of the sect of the Valentinians. Of his writings
have been preserved, in addition to numerous brief fragments, a connected passage of some length, apparently from a commentary on the
Prologue or the Gospel of St. John (see Irenæus, *Adv. Hær.*, I, 8: 5),
and the Epistle to Flora. The commentary is distinctly a part of the
esoteric teaching, the epistle is as clearly exoteric.

That many have not [1] received the Law given by Moses,
my dear sister Flora, without recognizing either its fundamental ideas or its precepts, will be perfectly clear to you,
I believe, if you become acquainted with the different views
regarding the same. For some [*i. e.*, the Church] say that
it was commanded by God and the Father; but others [*i. e.*,
the Marcionites], taking the opposite direction, affirm that
it was commanded by an opposing and injurious devil, and
they attribute to him the creation of the world, and say
that he is the Father and Creator. But such as teach such
doctrine are altogether deceived, and each of them strays
from the truth of what lies before him. For it appears not
to have been given by the perfect God and Father, because
it is itself imperfect, and it needs to be completed [*cf.* Matt.
5 : 17], and it has precepts not consonant with the nature and
mind of God; neither is the Law to be attributed to the wick-

---

[1] This negative seems to spoil the sense of the passage, and is omitted in
some editions.

edness of the adversary, whose characteristic is to do wrong. Such do not know what was spoken by the Saviour, that a city or a house divided against itself cannot stand, as our Saviour has shown us. And besides, the Apostle says that the creation of the world was His work (all things were made by Him and without Him nothing was made), refuting the unsubstantial wisdom of lying men, the work not of a god working ruin, but a just one who hates wickedness. This is the opinion of rash men who do not understand the cause of the providence of the Creator [Demiurge] and have lost the eyes not only of their soul, but of their body. How far, therefore, such wander from the way of truth is evident to you from what has been said. But each of these is induced by something peculiar to himself to think thus, some by ignorance of the God of righteousness: others by ignorance of the Father of all, whom the Only One who knew Him alone revealed when He came. To us it has been reserved to be deemed worthy of making manifest to you the ideas of both of these, and to investigate carefully this Law, whence anything is, and the law-giver by whom it was commanded, bringing proofs of what shall be said from the words of our Saviour, by which alone one can be led without error to the knowledge of things.

First of all, it is to be known that the entire Law contained in the Pentateuch of Moses was not given by one—I mean not by God alone; but some of its precepts were given by men, and the words of the Saviour teach us to divide it into three parts. For He attributes some of it to God himself and His law-giving, and some to Moses, not in the sense that God gave laws through him, but in the sense that Moses, impelled by his own spirit, set down some things as laws; and He attributes some things to the elders of the people, who first discovered certain commandments of their own and then inserted them. How this was so you clearly learn from the words of the Saviour. Somewhere the Saviour was conversing with the people, who disputed with Him about divorce, that it was allowed in the Law, and He said to them: Moses, on account of the hardness of your hearts, permitted a man to divorce his wife; but from the beginning it was not so. For God, said He, joined this bond, and what the Lord joined together let not man, He said, put asunder. He therefore pointed out one law that forbids a woman to be separated from her husband, which was of God, and another, which was of Moses, that allows, on account of the hardness of men's hearts, the bond to be dissolved. And accordingly, Moses gives a law opposed to God, for it is opposed to the law forbidding divorce. But if we consider carefully the mind of Moses, according to which he thus legislated, we shall find that he did not do this of his own mere choice, but by constraint because of the weakness of those to whom he was giving the law. For since they were not able to observe that precept of God by which it was not permitted them to cast forth their wives, with whom some of them lived unhappily, and because of this they were in danger of falling still more into unrighteousness, and from that into utter ruin, Moses, intending to avoid this unhappy result, because they were in danger of ruin, gave a certain second law, according to circumstances less evil, in place of the better; and by his own authority gave the law of divorce to them, that if they could not keep that they might keep this, and should not fall into unrighteousness and wickedness by which complete ruin should overtake them. This was his purpose in as far as he is found giving laws contrary to God. That thus the law of Moses is shown to be other than the Law of God is indisputable, if we have shown it in one instance.

And as to there being certain traditions of the elders which have been incorporated in the Law, the Saviour shows this also. For God, said He, commanded: Honor thy father and thy mother, that it may be well with thee. But ye, He said, addressing the elders, have said: It is a gift to God, that by which ye might be profited by me, and ye annul the law of God by the traditions of your elders. And this very thing Isaiah declared when he said: This people honor me with their lips, but their heart is far from me, vainly do they worship me, teaching the doctrines and commandment of men [*cf.* Matt. 15 : 4–9.] Clearly, then, from these things it is shown that this whole Law is to be divided into three parts. And in it we find laws given by Moses, by the elders, and by God; and this division of the whole Law as we have made it, has shown the real truth as to the Law.

But one portion of the Law, that which is from God, is again to be divided into three parts: first, into the genuine precepts, quite untainted with evil, which is properly called the law, and which the Saviour came not to destroy but to complete (for what he completed was not alien to Him, but yet it was not perfect); secondly, the part comprising evil and unrighteous things, which the Saviour did away with as something unfitting His nature; and thirdly, the part which is for types and symbols, which is given as a law, as images of things spiritual and excellent which, from being evident and manifest to the senses, the Saviour changed into the spiritual and unseen. Now the law of God, pure and untainted with anything base, is the Decalogue itself, or those ten precepts distributed in two tables, for the prohibition of things to be avoided and the performance of things to be done. Although they constitute a pure body of laws, yet they are not perfect, but need to be completed by the Saviour. But there is that body of commands which are tainted with unrighteousness; such is the law requiring vengeance and requital of injuries upon those who have first injured us, commanding the smiting out of an eye for an eye and a tooth for a tooth and revenging bloodshed with bloodshed. For one who is second in doing unrighteousness acts no less unrighteously, when the difference is only one of order, doing the self-same work. But such a precept was, and is, in other respects just, because of the infirmity of those to whom the law was given, and it was given in violation of the pure law, and was not consonant with the nature and goodness of the Father of all; it was to a degree appropriate, but yet given under a certain compulsion. For he who forbids the commission of a single murder in that he says, Thou shalt not kill, but commands that he who kills shall in requital be killed, gives a second law and commands a second slaying, when he has forbidden one, and has been compelled to do this by necessity. And therefore the Son, sent by Him, abolishes this portion of the Law, He himself confessing that it is from God, and this, among other things, is to be attributed to an ancient heresy, among which, also, is that God, speaking, says: He that curseth father or mother, let him die the death. But there is that part of the Law which is typical, laying down that which is an image of things spiritual and excellent, which gives laws concerning such matters as offerings, I mean, and circumcision, the Sabbath and fasting, the passover and the unleavened bread, and such like. For all these things, being images and symbols of the truth which had been manifested, have been changed. They were abrogated so far as they were external, visible acts of bodily performance, but they were retained so far as they were spiritual, the names remaining, but the things being changed. For the Saviour commands us to present offerings, though not of irrational animals or of incense, but spiritual offerings—praise, glory, and thanksgiving, and also liberality and good deeds toward the neighbor. He would have us circumcised with a circumcision not of the flesh, but spiritual and of the heart; and have us observe the Sabbath, for he wishes us to rest from wicked actions; and fast, but he does not wish us to observe a bodily fast, but a spiritual, in that we abstain from all that is unworthy. External fasting, however, is observed among our people, since it is capable of benefiting the soul to some degree, if it is practised with reason, when it is neither performed from imitation of any one, nor by custom, nor on account of a day, as if a day were set apart for that purpose; and at the same time it is also for a reminder of true fasting, that they who are not able to fast thus may have a reminder of it from the fast which is external. And that the passover, in the same way, and the unleavened bread are images, the Apostle Paul also makes clear, saying: Christ our Passover is sacrificed for us, and That ye may be unleavened, not having any leaven (for he calls leaven wickedness), but that ye may be a new dough.

This entire Law, therefore, acknowledged to be from God, is divided into three parts: into that part which is fulfilled by the Saviour, such as Thou shalt not kill, thou shalt not commit adultery, thou shalt not forswear thyself, for they are included in this, thou shalt not be angry, thou shalt not lust, thou shalt not swear; into that which is completely abolished, such as an eye for an eye and a tooth for a tooth, being tainted with unrighteousness, and having the same work of unrighteousness, and these are taken away by the Saviour because contradictory (for those things which are contradictory are mutually destructive), "For I say unto you that ye in no wise resist evil, but if any one smite thee turn to him the other cheek also"; and into that part which is changed and converted from that which is bodily into that which is spiritual, as he expounds allegorically a symbol which is commanded as an image of things that are excellent. For these images and symbols, fitted to represent other things, were good so long as the truth was not yet present; but when the truth is present, it is necessary to do the things of truth, not the image of truth. The same thing his disciples and the Apostle Paul teach, inasmuch as in regard to things which are images, as we have already said, they show by the passover and the unleavened bread that they are for our sake, but in regard to the law which is tainted with unrighteousness, they call it the law of commandments and ordinances, that is done away; but as to the law which is untainted with evil, he says that the law is holy and the commandment holy and just and good.

Accordingly, I think that it has been sufficiently shown you, so far as it is possible to discuss the matter briefly, that there are laws of men which have slipped in, and there is the very Law of God which is divided into three parts. There remains, therefore, for us to show, who, then, is that God who gave the Law. But I think that this has been shown you in what has already been said, if you have listened attentively. For if the Law was not given by the perfect God, as we have shown, nor by the devil, which idea merely to mention is unlawful, there is another beside these, one who gave the Law. This one is, therefore, the Demiurge and maker of this whole world and of all things in it, different from the nature of the other two, and placed between them, and who therefore rightly bears the name of the Midst. And if the perfect God is good according to His own nature, as also He is (for that there is only One who is good, namely, God and His Father, the Saviour asserted, the God whom He manifested), there is also one who is of the nature of the adversary, bad and wicked and characterized by unrighteousness. Standing, therefore, between these, and being neither good nor bad nor unjust, he can be called righteous in a sense proper to him, as the judge of the righteousness that corresponds to him, and that god will be lower than the perfect God, and his righteousness lower than His, because he is begotten and not unbegotten. For there is one unbegotten One, the Father, from whom are all things, for all things have been prepared by Him. But He is greater and superior to the adversary, and is of a different essence or nature from the essence of the other. For the essence of the adversary is corruption and darkness, for he is hylic and composite,[1] but the essence of the unbegotten Father of all is incorruptibility, and He is light itself, simple and uniform. But the essence of these[2] brings forth a certain twofold power, and he is the image of the better. Do not let these things disturb you, who wish to learn how from one principle of all things, whom we acknowledge and in whom be believe, namely, the unbegotten and the incorruptible and the good, there exist two other natures, namely, that of corruption and that of the Midst, which are not of

---

[1] Simplicity is always regarded in ancient thought as a characteristic of Deity.
[2] According to another reading, of this one.

the same essence [ἀνομοούσιοι], though the good by nature begets and brings forth what is like itself, and of the same essence [ὁμοούσιος]. For you will learn by God's permission, in due order, both the beginning of this and its generation, since you are deemed worthy of the apostolic tradition, which by a succession we have received, and in due season to test all things by the teaching of the Saviour. The things which in a few words I have said to you, my sister Flora, I have not exhausted, and I have written briefly. At the same time I have sufficiently explained to you the subject proposed, and what I have said will be constantly of use to you, if as a beautiful and good field you have received the seed and will by it produce fruit.

§ 23. MARCION

Recently Marcion has been commonly treated apart from the Gnostics on account of the large use he made of the Pauline writings. By some he has even been regarded as a champion of Pauline ideas which had failed to hold a place in Christian thought. This opinion of Marcion is being modified under the influence of a larger knowledge of Gnosticism. At the bottom Marcion's doctrine was thoroughly Gnostic, though he differed from the vast majority of Gnostics in that his interest seems to have been primarily ethical rather than speculative. His school maintained itself for some centuries after undergoing some minor modifications. Marcion was teaching at Rome, A. D. 140. The aspersions upon his moral character must be taken with caution, as it had already become a common practice to blacken the character of theological opponents, regardless of the truth, a custom which has not yet wholly disappeared.

Additional source material: Justin Martyr, *Apol.*, I, 26, 58; Irenæus, III, 12 : 12 *ff.* The most important source is Tertullian's elaborate *Adversus Marcionem*, especially I, 1 *f.*, 29; III, 8, 11.

(a) Irenæus, *Adv. Hær.*, I, 27 : 1–3. (MSG, 7 : 687.)

The system of Cerdo and Marcion.

Ch. 1. A certain Cerdo, who had taken his fundamental ideas from those who were with Simon [*i. e.*, Simon Magus], and who was in Rome in the time of Hyginus, who held the ninth place from the Apostles in the episcopal succession, taught that the God who was preached by the law and the prophets is not the Father of our Lord Jesus Christ. For the former is known, but the latter is unknown; and the former is righteous, but the other is good.

Ch. 2. And Marcion of Pontus succeeded him and developed a school, blaspheming shamelessly Him who is proclaimed as God by the law and the prophets; saying that He is maker of evils and a lover of wars, inconstant in purpose and inconsistent with Himself. He said, however, that Jesus came from the Father, who is above the God who made the world, into Judea in the time of Pontius Pilate, the procurator of Tiberius Cæsar, and was manifested in the form of a man to those who were in Judea, destroying the prophets and the law, and all the works of that God who made the world and whom he also called Cosmocrator. In addition to this, he mutilated the Gospel which is according to Luke, and removed all that refers to the generation of the Lord, removing also many things from the teaching in the Lord's discourses, in which the Lord is recorded as very plainly confessing that the founder of this universe is His Father; and thus Marcion persuaded his disciples that he himself is truer than the Apostles who delivered the Gospel; delivering to them not the Gospel but a part of the Gospel. But in the same manner he also mutilated the epistles of the Apostle Paul, removing all that is plainly said by the Apostle concerning that God who made the world, to the effect that He is the Father of our Lord Jesus Christ, and all that the Apostle taught by quotation from the prophetical writings which foretold the coming of the Lord.

Ch. 3. He taught that salvation would be only of the souls of those who should receive his doctrine, and that it is impossible for the body to partake of salvation, because it was taken from the earth.

(b) Tertullian, *Adv. Marcion.*, I, 19; IV, 2, 3. (MSL. 2 : 293, 393.)

Tertullian's great work against Marcion is his most important and most carefully written polemical treatise. He revised it three times. The first book of the present revision dates from A. D. 207; the other books cannot be dated except conjecturally. In spite of the openly displayed hostile animus of the writer, it can be used with confidence when controlled by reference to other sources.

I, 19. Marcion's special and principal work is the separation of the law and the Gospel; and his disciples will not be able to deny that in this they have their best means by which they are initiated into, and confirmed in, this heresy. For these are Marcion's antitheses—that is, contradictory propositions; and they aim at putting the Gospel at variance with the law, that from the diversity of the statements of the two documents they may argue for a diversity of gods, also.

IV, 2. With Marcion the mystery of the Christian religion dates from the discipleship of Luke. Since, however, it was under way previously, it must have had its authentic materials by means of which it found its way down to Luke; and by aid of the testimony which it bore Luke himself becomes admissible.

IV, 3. Well, but because Marcion finds the Epistle to the Galatians by Paul, who rebukes even Apostles for "not walking uprightly according to the truth of the Gospel" [Gal. 2 : 14], as well as accuses certain false apostles of being perverters of the Gospel of Christ, he attempts to destroy the standing of those gospels which are published as genuine and under the names of Apostles, or of apostolic men, to secure, forsooth, for his own gospel the credit he takes away from them.

(c) Rhodon, in Eusebius, *Hist. Ec.*, V, 13. (MSG, 20 : 459.)

At this time Rhodon, a native of Asia, who, as he himself states, had been instructed at Rome by Tatian, with whom we have already become acquainted, wrote excellent books, and published among the rest one against the heresy of Marcion which, he says, was in his time divided into various

sects; and he describes those who occasioned the division
and refutes carefully the falsehood devised by each. But hear
what he writes: "Therefore also they have fallen into disagreement among themselves, and maintain inconsistent
opinions. For Apelles, one of their herd, priding himself on
his manner of life and his age, acknowledged one principle
[*i. e.*, source of existence], but says that the prophecies were
from an opposing spirit. And he was persuaded of the truth
of this by the responses of a demoniac maiden named Phi-
lumene. But others hold to two principles, as does the mar-
iner Marcion himself, among these are Potitus and Basiliscus. These, following the wolf of Pontus and, like him,
unable to discover the divisions of things, became reckless,
and without any proof baldly asserted two principles. Again,
others of them drifted into worse error and assumed not only
two, but three, natures. Of these Syneros is the leader
and chief, as those say who defend his teaching."

§ 24. ENCRATITES

Asceticism is a wide-spread phenomenon in nearly all religions. It is to be found in apostolic Christianity. In the early
Church it was regarded as a matter in the option of the Christian who was aiming at the religious life [see above, § 16].
The characteristic of the Encratites was their insistence upon
asceticism as essential to Christian living. They were therefore associated, and with abundant historical justification,
with Gnosticism.

Additional source material: Clement of Alexandria, *Strom.*, III,
passim; Eusebius, *Hist. Ec.*, IV, 29, *cf.* the many references in the
notes to McGiffert's edition, PNF.

(*a*) Hippolytus, VIII, 13. (MSG, 16 : 3368.)

See above, § 19, *c.*

Others, however, styling themselves Encratites, acknowledge some things concerning God and Christ in like manner

with the Church, but in respect to their mode of life they
pass their time inflated with pride; thinking that by meats
they glorify themselves, they abstain from animal food, are
water drinkers, and, forbidding to marry, they devote the rest
of their life to habits of asceticism.

(b) Irenæus, *Adv. Hær.*, I, 28. (MSG, 7 : 690.)

Many offshoots of numerous heresies have already been
formed from those heresies which we have described. . . .
By way of example, let us say there are those springing from
Saturninus and Marcion, who are called Encratites [*i. e.*, self-
controlled], who preached the unmarried state, thus setting
aside the original creation of God, and indirectly condemning Him who made male and female for the propagation of
the human race. Some of those reckoned as belonging to
them have also introduced abstinence from animal food, being
ungrateful to God who created all things. They deny, also,
the salvation of him who was first created. It is but recently
that this opinion has been discovered among them, since a
certain man named Tatian first introduced the blasphemy.
He had been a hearer of Justin's, and as long as he continued
with him he expressed no such views; but after his martyrdom [circa A. D. 165] he separated from the Church, and
having become excited and puffed up by the thought of being
a teacher, as if he were superior to others, he composed his
own peculiar type of doctrine. He invented a system of
certain invisible Eons, like the followers of Valentinus; and,
like Marcion and Saturninus, he declared that marriage was
nothing else than corruption and fornication. But this
denial of Adam's salvation was an opinion due entirely to
himself.

§ 25. MONTANISM

Montanism was, in part at least, an attempt to revive the
enthusiastic prophetic element in the early Christian life. In
its first manifestations, in Asia Minor, Montanism was wild

and fanatical. It soon spread to the West, and in doing so it became, as did other Oriental religious movements (*e. g.*, Gnosticism and Manichæanism, see § 54), far more sober. It even seemed to many serious persons to be nothing more than a praiseworthy attempt to revive or retain certain primitive Christian conditions, both in respect to personal morals and ecclesiastical organization and life. In this way it came to be patronized by not a few (*e. g.*, Tertullian) who, in other respects, deviated in few or no points from the prevailing thought and practice of Christians. See also § 26.

Additional source material: Eusebius, *Hist. Ec.*, V, 16–19, *cf.* literature cited in McGiffert's notes. The sayings of Montanus, Maximilla, and Priscilla are collected in Hilgenfeld, *Ketzergeschichte*, 591 *ff.* See also Hippolytus, *Refut.*, X, 25 *f.* [= X, 21, ANF.]

(*a*) Eusebius, *Hist. Ec.*, V, 16 : 7. (MSG, 20 : 463.)

For Eusebius, see § 3.

There is said to be a certain village named Ardabau, in Mysia, on the borders of Phrygia. There, they say, when Gratus was proconsul of Asia, a recent convert, Montanus by name—who, in his boundless desire for leadership, gave the adversary opportunity against him—first became inspired; and falling into a sort of frenzy and ecstasy raved and began to babble and utter strange sounds, prophesying in a manner contrary to the traditional and constant custom of the Church from the beginning. . . . And he stirred up, besides, two women [Maximilla and Priscilla], and filled them with the false spirit, so that they talked frantically, at unseasonable times, and in a strange manner, like the person already mentioned. . . . And the arrogant spirit taught them to revile the universal and entire Church under heaven, because the spirit of false prophecy received from it neither honor nor entrance into it; for the faithful in Asia met often and in many places throughout Asia to consider this matter and to examine the recent utterances, and they pronounced them profane and rejected the heresy, and thus these persons were expelled from the Church and shut out from the communion.

(b) Apollonius, in Eusebius, *Hist. Ec.*, V, 18. (MSG, 20 : 475.)

Apollonius was possibly bishop of Ephesus. His work against the Montanists, which appears to have been written about 197, was one of the principal sources for Eusebius in his account of the Montanists. Only fragments of his work have been preserved.

This is he who taught the dissolution of marriages; who laid down laws for fasting; who named Pepuza and Tymion (which were small cities in Phrygia) Jerusalem, desiring to gather people to them from everywhere; who appointed collectors of money; who devised the receiving of gifts under the name of offerings; who provided salaries for those who preached his doctrine, so that by gluttony the teaching of his doctrine might prevail.

(c) Hippolytus, *Refut.*, VIII, 19. (MSG, 16 : 3356.)

For Hippolytus, see § 19, c.

But there are others who are themselves in nature more heretical than the Quartodecimans. These are Phrygians by birth and they have been deceived, having been overcome by certain women called Priscilla and Maximilla; and they hold these for prophetesses, saying that in them the Paraclete Spirit dwelt; and they likewise glorify one Montanus before these women as a prophet. So, having endless books of these people, they go astray, and they neither judge their statements by reason nor pay attention to those who are able to judge. But they behave without judgment in the faith they place in them, saying they have learned something more through them than from the law and the prophets and the Gospels. But they glorify these women above the Apostles and every gift, so that some of them presume to say that there was something more in them than in Christ. These confess God the Father of the universe and creator of all things, like the Church, and all that the Gospel witnesses concerning Christ, but invent new fasts and feasts and meals of dry food and meals of radishes, saying that thus they were taught by their women. And some of them agree with the heresy of the Noetians and say that the Father is very Son, and that this One became subject to birth and suffering and death.

CHAPTER III. THE DEFENCE AGAINST HERESY

The Church first met the various dangerous heresies which distracted it in the second century by councils or gatherings of bishops (§ 26). Although it was not difficult to bring about a condemnation of novel and manifestly erroneous doctrine, there was need of fixed norms and definite authorities to which to appeal. This was found in the apostolic tradition, which could be more clearly determined by reference to the continuity of the apostolic office, or the episcopate, and especially to the succession of bishops in the churches founded by Apostles (§ 27), the apostolic witness to the truth, or the more precise determination of what writings should be regarded as apostolic, or the canon of the New Testament (§ 28); and the apostolic faith, which was regarded as summed up in the Apostles' Creed (§ 29). These norms of orthodoxy seem to have been generally established as authoritative somewhat earlier in the West than in the East. The result was that Gnosticism was rapidly expelled from the Church, though in some forms it lingered for centuries (§ 30), and that the Church, becoming organized around the episcopate, assumed by degrees a rigid hierarchical constitution (§ 31).

§ 26. The Beginnings of Councils as a Defence against Heresy.

§ 27. The Apostolic Tradition and the Episcopate.

§ 28. The Canon or the Authoritative New Testament Writings.

§ 29. The Apostles' Creed.

§ 30. Later Gnostics.

§ 31. Results of the Crisis.

§ 26. COUNCILS AS A DEFENCE AGAINST HERESY

Ecclesiastical councils were the first defence against heresy. As the Church had not as yet attained its hierarchical constitution and the autonomy of the local church still persisted, these councils had little more than the combined authority of the several members composing them. They had, as yet, only moral force, and did not speak for the Church officially. With the development of the episcopal constitution, the councils gained rapidly in authority.

Additional source material: See Eusebius, *Hist. Ec.*, V, 16 (given above, § 25, *a*), V, 24; Tertullian, *De Jejun.*, 13.

(*a*) *Libellus Synodicus*, Man. I, 723.

For a discussion of the credibility of the *Libellus Synodicus*, a compilation of the ninth century, see Hefele, *History of the Councils*, § 1.

A holy and provincial synod was held at Hierapolis in Asia by Apollinarius, the most holy bishop of that city, and twenty-six other bishops. In this synod Montanus and Maximilla, the false prophets, and at the same time, Theodotus the tanner, were condemned and expelled. A holy and local synod was gathered under the most holy Bishop Sotas of Anchialus[1] and twelve other bishops, who condemned and rejected Theodotus the tanner and Montanus together with Maximilla.

(*b*) Eusebius, *Hist. Ec.*, V, 18. (MSG, 20:475.)   *Cf.* Mirbt, n. 21.

The following should be connected with the first attempts of the Church to meet the heresy of the Montanists by gatherings of bishops. It also throws some light on the methods of dealing with the new prophets.

Serapion, who, according to report, became bishop of Antioch at that time, after Maximinus, mentions the works

---

[1] A city of Thrace on the Black Sea.

of Apollinarius against the above-mentioned heresy. And he
refers to him in a private letter to Caricus and Pontius, in
which he himself exposes the same heresy, adding as follows:
"That you may see that the doings of this lying band of new
prophecy, as it is called, are an abomination to all the brethren
throughout the world, I have sent you writings of the most
blessed Claudius Apollinarius, bishop of Hierapolis in Asia."
In the same letter of Serapion are found the signatures of
several bishops, of whom one has subscribed himself as follows: "I, Aurelius Cyrenius, a witness, pray for your health."
And another after this manner: "Ælius Publius Julius,
bishop of Debeltum, a colony of Thrace. As God liveth in
the heavens, the blessed Sotas in Anchialus desired to cast
the demon out of Priscilla, but the hypocrites would not
permit him." And the autograph signatures of many other
bishops who agreed with them are contained in the same
letter.

§ 27. The Apostolic Tradition and the Episcopate

The Gnostics claimed apostolic authority for their teaching
and appealed to successions of teachers who had handed
down their teachings. This procedure forced the Church to
lay stress upon the obvious fact that its doctrine was derived
from the Apostles, a matter on which it never had had any
doubt, but was vouched for, not by obscure teachers, but
by the churches which had been founded by the Apostles
themselves in large cities and by the bishops whom the Apostles had instituted in those churches. Those churches,
furthermore, agreed among themselves, but the Gnostic
teachers differed widely. By this appeal the bishop came
to represent the apostolic order (for an earlier conception,
v. supra, § 14, b, c), and to take an increasingly important
place in the church (v. infra, § 31).

Additional source material: For Gnostic references to successions
of teachers, see Tertullian, De Præscr., 25; Clement of Alexandria,
Strom., VII, 17; Hippolytus, Refut., VII, 20. (= VII, 8, ANF.)

(a) Irenæus, *Adv. Hær.*, III, 3: 1–4. (MSG, 7:848.) *Cf.* Mirbt, n. 30.

The first appearance of the appeal to apostolic tradition as pre- served in apostolic sees is the following passage from Irenæus, written about 175. The reference to the church of Rome, beginning, "For with this Church, on account of its more powerful leadership," has been a famous point of discussion. While it is obscure in detail, the application of its general purport to the argument of Irenæus is clear. Since for this passage we have not the original Greek of Irenæus, but only the Latin translation, there seems to be no way of clearing up the obscurities and apparently contradictory statements. The text may be found in Gwatkin, *op. cit.*, and in part in Kirch, *op. cit.*, §§ 110–113.

Ch. 1. The tradition, therefore, of the Apostles, manifested throughout the world, is a thing which all who wish to see the facts can clearly perceive in every church; and we are able to count up those who were appointed bishops by the Apostles, and to show their successors to our own time, who neither taught nor knew anything resembling these men's ravings. For if the Apostles had known hidden mysteries which they used to teach the perfect, apart from and without the knowledge of the rest, they would have delivered them especially to those to whom they were also committing the churches themselves. For they desired them to be very per- fect and blameless in all things, and were also leaving them as their successors, delivering over to them their own proper place of teaching; for if these should act rightly great advan- tage would result, but if they fell away the most disastrous calamity would occur.

Ch. 2. But since it would be very long in such a volume as this to count up the successions [*i. e.*, series of bishops] in all the churches, we confound all those who in any way, whether through self-pleasing or vainglory, or through blindness and evil opinion, gather together otherwise than they ought, by pointing out the tradition derived from the Apostles of the greatest, most ancient, and universally known Church, founded and established by the two most glorious Apostles, Peter and Paul, and also the faith declared to men which through the succession of bishops comes down to our times. For with this Church, on account of its more powerful leadership [*potiorem principalitatem*], every church, that is, the faithful, who are from everywhere, must needs agree; since in it that tradition which is from the Apostles has always been preserved by those who are from everywhere.

Ch. 3. The blessed Apostles having founded and established the Church, intrusted the office of the episcopate to Linus.[1] Paul speaks of this Linus in his Epistles to Timothy. Anacletus succeeded him, and after Anacletus, in the third place from the Apostles, Clement received the episcopate. He had seen and conversed with the blessed Apostles, and their preaching was still sounding in his ears and their tradition was still before his eyes. Nor was he alone in this, for many who had been taught by the Apostles yet survived. In the times of Clement, a serious dissension having arisen among the brethren in Corinth, the Church of Rome sent a suitable letter to the Corinthians, reconciling them in peace, renewing their faith, and proclaiming the doctrine lately received from the Apostles. . . .

Evaristus succeeded Clement, and Alexander Evaristus. Then Sixtus, the sixth from the Apostles, was appointed. After him Telesephorus, who suffered martyrdom gloriously, and then Hyginus; after him Pius, and after Pius Anicetus; Soter succeeded Anicetus, and now, in the twelfth place from the Apostles, Eleutherus [174–189] holds the office of bishop. In the same order and succession the tradition and the preaching of the truth which is from the Apostles have continued unto us.

Ch. 4. But Polycarp, too, was not only instructed by the Apostles, and acquainted with many that had seen Christ, but was also appointed by Apostles in Asia bishop of the church in Smyrna, whom we, too, saw in our early youth (for he lived a long time, and died, when a very old man, a glorious and most illustrious martyr's death); he always

---

[1] See this passage as quoted in Eusebius, *Hist. Ec.*, V, 6, and McGiffert's notes.

taught the things which he had learned from the Apostles, which the Church also hands down, and which alone are true. To these things all the Asiatic churches testify, as do also those who, down to the present time, have succeeded Polycarp, who was a much more trustworthy and certain witness of the truth than Valentinus and Marcion and the rest of the evil-minded. It was he who was also in Rome in the time of Anicetus and caused many to turn away from the above-mentioned heretics to the Church of God, proclaiming that he had received from the Apostles this one and only truth which has been transmitted by the Church. And there are those who heard from him that John, the disciple of the Lord, going to bathe in Ephesus, when he saw Cerinthus within, ran out of the bath-house without bathing, crying: "Let us flee, lest even the bath-house fall, because Cerinthus, the enemy of the truth, is within." And Polycarp himself, when Marcion once met him and said, "Knowest thou us?" replied, "I know the first-born of Satan." Such caution did the Apostles and their disciples exercise that they might not even converse with any of those who perverted the truth; as Paul, also, said: "A man that is a heretic after the first and second admonition, reject; knowing that he that is such subverteth and sinneth, being condemned by himself." There is also a very powerful Epistle of Polycarp written to the Philippians, from which those who wish to, and who are concerned for their own salvation, may learn the character of his faith and the preaching of the truth.

(b) Tertullian, *De Præscriptione*, 20, 21. (MSL, 2 : 38.)

Tertullian worked out in legal fashion the argument of Irenæus from the testimony of the bishops in apostolic churches. He may have obtained the argument from Irenæus, as he was evidently acquainted with his works. From Tertullian's use of the argument it became a permanent element in the thought of the West.

Ch. 20. The Apostles founded in the several cities churches from which the other churches have henceforth borrowed the shoot of faith and seeds of teaching and do daily borrow that they may become churches; and it is from this fact that they also will be counted as apostolic, being the offspring of apostolic churches. Every kind of thing must be judged by reference to its origin. Therefore so many and so great churches are all one, being from that first Church which is from the Apostles. Thus they are all primitive and all apostolic, since they altogether are approved by their unity, and they have the communion of peace, the title of brotherhood, and the interchange of hospitality, and they are governed by no other rule than the single tradition of the same mystery.

Ch. 21. Here, then, we enter our demurrer, that if the Lord Jesus Christ sent Apostles to preach, others than those whom Christ appointed ought not to be received as preachers. For no man knoweth the Father save the Son and he to whom the Son has revealed Him [cf. Luke 10: 22]; nor does it appear that the Son has revealed Him unto any others than the Apostles, whom He sent forth to preach what, of course, He had revealed to them. Now, what they should preach, that is, what Christ revealed to them, can, as I must likewise here enter as a demurrer, properly be proved in no other way than by those very churches which the Apostles themselves founded by preaching to them, both *viva voce*, as the phrase is, and subsequently by epistles. If this is so, it is evident that all doctrine which agrees with those apostolic churches, the wombs and origins of the faith, must be reckoned for truth, as undoubtedly containing what the churches received from the Apostles, the Apostles from Christ, Christ from God. There remains, therefore, for us to show whether our doctrine, the rule of which we have given above [v. infra, § 29, c], agrees with the tradition of the Apostles, and likewise whether the others come from deceit. We hold fast to the apostolic churches, because in none is there a different doctrine; this is the witness of the truth.

(c) Tertullian, *De Præscriptione*, 36. (MSL, 2 : 58.)

It should be noted that the appeal to apostolic churches is to any and all such, and is accordingly just so much the stronger in the

controversy in which it was brought forward. The argument, whenever it occurs, does not turn upon the infallibility of any one see or
church as such. That point is not touched. Such a turn to the
argument would have weakened the force of the appeal in the dispute
with the Gnostics, however powerfully it might be used in other
controversies.

Come, now, you who would indulge a better curiosity, if
you would apply it to the business of your salvation, run
over the apostolic churches, in which the very thrones of
the Apostles are still pre-eminent in their places, in which
their own authentic writings are read, uttering the voice and
representing the face of each of them severally. Achaia is
very near you, in which you find Corinth. Since you are
not far from Macedonia, you have Philippi; there, too,
you have the Thessalonians. Since you are able to cross
to Asia, you get Ephesus. Since, moreover, you are close
upon Italy, you have Rome, from which there comes even
into our own hands the very authority of Apostles themselves.
How happy is that church, on which Apostles poured forth
all their doctrine along with their blood! Where Peter
endures a passion like his Lord's; where Paul wins a crown
in a death like John's; where the Apostle John was first
plunged, unhurt, into boiling oil, and thence remitted to
his island exile! See what she has learned, what taught;
what fellowship she has had with even our churches in Africa!
One Lord God does she acknowledge, the Creator of the
universe, and Christ Jesus born of the Virgin Mary, the Son
of God the Creator; and the resurrection of the flesh; the
law and the prophets she unites in one volume with the
writings of Evangelists and Apostles, from which she drinks
in her faith. This she seals with the water of baptism, arrays
with the Holy Ghost, feeds with the eucharist, cheers with
martyrdom, and against such a discipline thus maintained
she admits no gainsayer.

§ 28. THE CANON OR THE AUTHORITATIVE NEW TESTA-
MENT WRITINGS

The Gnostics used in support of their doctrines writings
which they attributed to the Apostles, thus having a direct
apostolic witness to these doctrines. This they did in imitation of the Church's practice of using apostolic writings for
edification and instruction. Marcion drew up a list of books
which were alone to be regarded as authoritative among his
followers [v. supra, § 23, a]. The point to be made by the
champions of the faith of the great body of Christians was
that only those books could be legitimately used in support
of Christian doctrine which could claim actual apostolic
origin and had been used continuously in the Church. As
a fact, the books to which they appealed had been in use
generation after generation, but the Gnostic works were
unknown until a comparatively recent time and were too
closely connected with only the founders of a sect to deserve
credence. It was a simple literary argument and appeal to
tangible evidence. The list of books regarded as authoritative
constituted the Canon of Scripture. The state of the Canon
in the second half of the second century, especially in the
West, is shown in the following extracts.

Additional source material: See Preuschen, *Analecta*, II, Tübingen,
1910; Tatian, Diatessaron, ANF, IX; The Gospel of Peter, *ibid.*

(a) *The Muratorian Fragment.* Text, B. F. Westcott, *A
General Survey of the History of the Canon of the New Testament*, seventh ed., Cambridge, 1896. Appendix C; Kirch, n.
134; Preuschen, *Analecta*, II, 27. *Cf.* Mirbt, n. 20.

The earliest list of canonical books of the New Testament was
found by L. A. Muratori in 1740 in a MS. of the eighth century.
It lacks beginning and end. It belongs to the middle or the second
half of the second century. It cannot with certainty be attributed
to any known person. The obscure Latin text is probably a translation from the Greek. The fragment begins with what appears to
be an account of St. Mark's Gospel.

. . . but at some he was present, and so he set them down.

The third book of the gospels, that according to Luke. Luke, the physician, compiled it in his own name in order, when, after the ascension of Christ, Paul had taken him to be with him like a student of law. Yet neither did he see the Lord in the flesh; and he, too, as he was able to ascertain events, so set them down. So he began his story from the birth of John.

The fourth of the gospels is John's, one of the disciples. When exhorted by his fellow-disciples and bishops, he said, "Fast with me this day for three days; and what may be revealed to any of us, let us relate to one another." The same night it was revealed to Andrew, one of the Apostles, that John was to write all things in his own name, and they were all to certify.

And therefore, though various elements are taught in the several books of the gospels, yet it makes no difference to the faith of the believers, since by one guiding Spirit all things are declared in all of them concerning the nativity, the passion, the resurrection, the conversation with His disciples, and His two comings, the first in lowliness and contempt, which has come to pass, the second glorious with royal power, which is to come.

What marvel, therefore, if John so firmly sets forth each statement in his epistles, too, saying of himself: "What we have seen with our eyes and heard with our ears and our hands have handled, these things we have written to you"? For so he declares himself to be not an eye-witness and a hearer only, but also a writer of all the marvels of the Lord in order.

The acts, however, of all the Apostles are written in one book. Luke puts it shortly, "to the most excellent Theophilus," that the several things were done in his own presence, as he also plainly shows by leaving out the passion of Peter, and also the departure of Paul from the city [i. e., Rome] on his journey to Spain.

The epistles, however, of Paul make themselves plain to those who wish to understand what epistles were sent by him, and from what place and for what cause. He wrote at some length, first of all, to the Corinthians, forbidding schisms and heresies; next to the Galatians, forbidding circumcision; then to the Romans, impressing on them the plan of the Scriptures, and also that Christ is the first principle of them, concerning which severally it is necessary for us to discuss, since the blessed Apostle Paul himself, following the order of his predecessor John, writes only by name to seven churches in the following order: to the Corinthians a first, to the Ephesians a second, to the Philippians a third, to the Colossians a fourth, to the Galatians a fifth, to the Thessalonians a sixth, to the Romans a seventh; and yet, although for the sake of admonition there is a second to the Corinthians and to the Thessalonians, but one Church is recognized as being spread over the entire world. For John, too, in the Apocalypse, though he writes to seven churches, yet speaks to all. Howbeit to Philemon one, to Titus one, and to Timothy two were put in writing from personal inclination and attachment, to be in honor, however, with the Catholic Church for the ordering of the ecclesiastical mode of life. There is current, also, one to the Laodiceans, another to the Alexandrians, [both] forged in Paul's name to suit a heresy of Marcion, and several others, which cannot be received into the Catholic Church; for it is not fitting that gall be mixed with honey.

The Epistle of Jude, no doubt, and the couple bearing the name of John are accepted in the Catholic [Church], and the Wisdom written by the friends of Solomon in his honor. The Apocalypse, also, of John and of Peter only we receive; which some of us will not have read in the Church. But the Shepherd was written quite lately in our times by Hermas, while his brother Pius, the bishop, was sitting in the chair of the church of the city of Rome; and therefore it ought to be read, indeed, but it cannot to the end of time be publicly read in the Church to the people, either among the prophets, who are complete in number, or among the Apostles.

But of Valentinus, the Arsinoite, and his friends, we receive nothing at all, who have also composed a long new book of Psalms, together with Basilides and the Asiatic founder of the Montanists.

(b) Irenæus, *Adv. Hær.*, III, 11 : 8.   (MSG, 7 : 885.)

The following extract illustrates the allegorical method of exegesis in use throughout the Church, and also the opinion of the author that there were but four gospels, and could be no more than four. It should be noted that the symbolism of the beasts is not that which has become current in ecclesiastical art.

It is not possible that the gospels be either more or fewer than they are. For since there are four regions of the world in which we live, and four principal winds, and the Church is scattered over the whole earth, and the pillar and ground of the Church is the Gospel and the Spirit of Life, it is fitting that she should have four pillars, breathing forth immortality on every side, and giving life to men. From this it is evident that the Word, the Artificer of all, who sitteth upon the cherubim and who contains all things and was manifested to men, has given us the Gospel under four forms, but bound together by one Spirit. As also David says when he prayed for His coming: "Thou that sittest between the cherubim, shine forth" [*cf.* Psalm 80 : 1]. For the cherubim, also, were four-faced, and their faces were images of the dispensation of the Son of God. For he says, "The first living creature was like a lion" [*cf.* Ezek. 1 : 5 *ff.*], symbolizing His effectual working, leadership, and royal power; the second was like a calf, symbolizing His sacrificial and sacerdotal order; but "the third had, as it were, the face of a man," evidently describing His coming as a human being; "the fourth was like a flying eagle," pointing out the gift of the Spirit hovering over the Church. And therefore the gospels are in accord with these things, among which Christ is seated. For that according to John relates His original, effectual, and glorious generation from the Father, thus declaring, "In the beginning was the Word and the Word was with God and the Word was God" [cf. John 1 : 1 ff.], and further, "All things were made by Him and without Him was nothing made." For this reason, also, is that Gospel full of confidence, for such is His person. But that according to Luke, which takes up His priestly character, commenced with Zacharias, the priest, who offers sacrifice to God. For now was made ready the fatted calf, about to be immolated for the recovery of the younger son [Luke 15 : 23]. Matthew, again, relates His generation as a man, saying, "The book of the generation of Jesus Christ, the son of David, the son of Abraham" [Matt. 1 : 1]; and "The birth of Jesus Christ was on this wise" [Matt. 1 : 18]. This, then, is the gospel of His humanity; for which reason the character of a humble and meek man is kept up through the whole gospel. Mark, on the other hand, commences with reference to the prophetical Spirit who comes down from on high to men, saying, "The beginning of the Gospel of Jesus Christ, as it is written in Isaiah the prophet," pointing to the winged aspect of the Gospel, and on this account he makes a compendious and brief narrative, for such is the prophetical character. And the Word of God himself had intercourse with the patriarchs, before Moses, in accordance with His divinity and glory; but for those under the Law He instituted a sacerdotal and liturgical service. Afterward, having been made man for us, He sent the gift of the heavenly Spirit over all the earth, to protect it with 'His wings. Such, then, was the course followed by the Son of God, and such, also, were the forms of the living creatures; and such as was the form of the living creatures, such, also, was the character of the Gospel. For the living creatures are quadriform, and the Gospel is quadriform, as is also the course followed by our Lord. For this reason four principal covenants were given mankind: one prior to the Deluge, under Adam; the second after the Deluge, under Noah; the third was the giving of the law under Moses; the fourth is that which renovates man and sums up all things in itself by means of the Gospel, raising and bearing men upon its wings into the heavenly kingdom.

(c) Tertullian, *Adv. Marcion.*, IV, 5.   (MSL, 2 : 395.)

Tertullian's work against Marcion belongs to the first decade of the third century; see above, § 23, *b*. In the following passage he combines the argument from the apostolic churches with the authority of the apostolic witness. This is the special importance of the reference to the connection of St. Mark's Gospel with St. Peter, and is an application of the principle that the authority of a book in the Church rested upon its apostolic origin.

If it is evidently true that what is earlier is more true, that what is earlier is what is from the beginning, that what is from the beginning is from the Apostles, it will be equally evidently true that what is handed down from the Apostles is what has been a sacred deposit in the churches of the Apostles.   Let us see what milk the Corinthians drank from Paul; to what rule the Galatians were brought for correction; what the Philippians, the Thessalonians, the Ephesians, read; what the Romans near by also say, to whom Peter and Paul bequeathed the Gospel even sealed with their own blood.   We have also John's nursling churches.   For, although Marcion rejects his Apocalypse, the order of bishops, when traced to their origin, will rest on John as their author. Likewise the noble lineage of the other churches is recognized. I say, therefore, that in them, and not only in the apostolic churches, but in all those which are united with them in the fellowship of the mystery [*sacramenti*], that Gospel of Luke, which we are defending with all our might [*cf*. § 23], has stood its ground from its very first publication; whereas Marcion's gospel is not known to most people, and to none whatever is it known without being condemned.   Of course it has its churches, but they are its own; they are as late as they are spurious.   Should you want to know their origins, you will more easily discover apostasy in it than apostolicity, with Marcion, forsooth, as their founder or some one of

Marcion's swarm. Even wasps make combs; so, also, these Marcionites make churches. The same authority of the apostolic churches will afford evidence to other gospels, also, which we possess equally through their means and according to their usage—I mean the Gospel of John and the Gospel of Matthew, but that which Mark published may be affirmed to be Peter's, whose interpreter Mark was. For even the Digest of Luke men usually ascribe to Paul. And it may well seem that the works which disciples publish belong to their masters.

§ 29. THE APOSTLES' CREED

By the middle of the second century there were current in the Church brief confessions of faith which had already been in use from a time in the remoter past as summaries of the apostolic faith. They were naturally attributed to the Apostles themselves, although they seem to have varied in many details. They were used principally in baptism, and were long kept secret from the catechumen until just before that rite was administered. They are preserved only in paraphrase, and can be reconstructed only by a careful comparison of many texts.

Additional source material: See Hahn, *Bibliothek der Symbole und Glaubensregeln der alten Kirche*, third ed., Breslau, 1897; *cf.* Mirbt, n. 16, 16 *a*.

(*a*) Irenæus, *Adv. Hær.*, I, 10. (MSG, 7 : 549 *f.*)

For Irenæus, *v. supra*, § 3, *a.*

The Church, though dispersed through the whole world to the ends of the earth, has received from the Apostles and their disciples the faith: In one God, the Father Almighty, who made the heaven and the earth and the seas, and all that in them is; And in one Christ Jesus, the Son of God, who was incarnate for our salvation; And in the Holy Ghost, who through the prophets preached the dispensations and the advents, and the birth from the Virgin, and the passion, and the resurrection from the dead, and the bodily assumption into the heavens of the beloved Christ Jesus our Lord, and His appearing from the heavens in the glory of the Father, in order to sum up all things under one head [cf. Ephes. 1 : 10], and to raise up all flesh of all mankind, that to Christ Jesus, our Lord and God and Saviour and King, every knee of those that are in heaven and on earth and under the earth should bow [cf. Phil. 2 : 11], according to the good pleasure of the Father invisible, and that every tongue should confess Him, and that He may execute righteous judgment on all; sending into eternal fire the spiritual powers of wickedness and the angels who transgressed and apostatized, and the godless and unrighteous and lawless and blasphemous among men, but granting life and immortality and eternal glory to the righteous and holy, who have both kept the commandments and continued in His love, some from the beginning, some from their conversion.

(b) Irenæus, *Adv. Hær.*, III, 4. (MSG, 7 : 855.)

The following form of the creed more closely resembles the traditional Apostles' Creed. With it compare the paraphrase in Irenæus, *op. cit.*, IV, 33 : 7.

If the Apostles had not left us the Scriptures, would it not be necessary to follow the order of tradition which they handed down to those to whom they committed the churches? To this order many nations of the barbarians gave assent, of those who believe in Christ, having salvation written in their hearts by the Spirit without paper and ink, and guarding diligently the ancient tradition: Believing in one God, Maker of heaven and earth, and all that is in them; through Jesus Christ, the Son of God; who, because of His astounding love toward His creatures, sustained the birth of the Virgin, Himself uniting man to God, and suffered under Pontius Pilate, and rising again was received in brightness, and shall come again in glory as the Saviour of those who are saved and the judge of those who are judged, and sending into eternal fire the perverters of the truth and despisers of His Father and His coming.

(c) Tertullian, *De Virginibus Velandis*, 1.   (MSL, 2 : 937).

Tertullian gives various paraphrases of the creed. The three most important are the following and *d*, *e*. The date of the work *De Virginibus Velandis* is about 211, and belongs to his Montanist period.

The Rule of Faith is altogether one, sole, immovable, and irreformable—namely, of believing in one God the Almighty, the Maker of the world; and His Son, Jesus Christ, born of the Virgin Mary, crucified under Pontius Pilate, on the third day raised again from the dead, received in the heavens, sitting now at the right hand of the Father, coming to judge the quick and the dead, also through the resurrection of the flesh.[1]

(d) Tertullian, *Adv. Praxean*, 2.   (MSL, 2 : 156.)

The work of Tertullian against Praxeas is one of his latest works, and is especially important as developing the doctrine of the Trinity as opposed to the Patripassianism of Praxeas. To this theory of Praxeas, Tertullian refers in the opening sentence of the following extract, quoting the position of Praxeas. See below, § 40, *b*.

"Therefore after a time the Father was born, and the Father suffered, He himself God, the omnipotent Lord, Jesus Christ was preached." But as for us always, and now more, as better instructed by the Paraclete, the Leader into all truth: We believe one God; but under this dispensation which we call the economy there is the Son of the only God, his Word [*Sermo*] who proceeded from Him, through whom all things were made, and without whom nothing was made. This One was sent by the Father into the Virgin, and was born of her, Man and God, the Son of Man and the Son of God, and called Jesus Christ; He suffered, He died and was buried, according to the Scriptures; and raised again by the

---

[1] By a slight change in the order of the words, as suggested by Neander the last two clauses might read more clearly: "To judge the quick and also the dead through the resurrection of the flesh."

Father, and taken up into the heavens, and He sits at the right hand of the Father; He shall come again to judge the quick and the dead: and He thence did send, according to His promise, from the Father, the Holy Ghost, the Paraclete, the Sanctifier of the faith of those who believe in the Father and the Son and the Holy Ghost. That this rule has come down from the beginning, even before any of the earlier heresies, much more before Praxeas, who is of yesterday, the lateness of date of all heresies proves, as also the novelties of Praxeas, a pretender of yesterday.

(e) Tertullian, *De Præscriptione*, 13. (MSL, 2 : 30.)

The Rule of Faith is . . . namely, that by which it is believed: That there is only one God, and no other besides the Maker of the world, who produced the universe out of nothing, through His Word [Verbum], sent forth first of all; that this Word, called His Son, was seen in the name of God in various ways by the patriarchs, and always heard in the prophets, at last was sent down from the Spirit and power of God the Father, into the Virgin Mary, was made flesh in her womb, and born of her, lived as Jesus Christ; that thereupon He preached the new law and the new promise of the kingdom of the heavens; wrought miracles; was fastened to the cross; rose again the third day; was caught up into the heavens; and sat down at the right hand of the Father; He sent in His place the power of the Holy Ghost, to lead the believers; He will come again with glory to take the saints into the enjoyment of eternal life and the celestial promises, and to judge the wicked with perpetual fire, with the restoration of the flesh.

§ 30.   LATER GNOSTICISM

Though Gnosticism was .expelled from the Church as it perfected its organization and institutions on the basis of the episcopate, the Canon of Scripture, and the creeds, outside the Catholic Church, or the Church as thus organized,

Gnosticism existed for centuries, though rapidly declining in the third century. The strength of the movement was still further diminished by loss of many adherents to Manichæanism (*v.* § 54), which had much in common with Gnosticism. The persistence of these sects, together with various later heresies, in spite of the very stringent laws of the Empire against them (*v.* § 73) should prevent any hasty conclusions as to the unity of the faith and the absence of sects in the patristic age. Unity can be found only by overlooking those outside the unity of the largest body of Christians, and agreement by ignoring those who differed from it.

Theodoret of Cyrus, *Epistulæ* 81, 145. (MSG, 83:1259, 1383.)

Ep. 81 was written to the Consul Nonus, A. D. 445. Ep. 145 was written to the monks of Constantinople, A. D. 450.

Ep. 81. To every one else every city lies open, and that not only to the followers of Arius and Eunomius, but to Manichæans and Marcionites, and to those suffering from the disease of Valentinus and Montanus, yes, and even to pagans and Jews; but I, the foremost champion of the teaching of the Gospel, am excluded from every city. . . . I led eight villages of Marcionites with their surrounding country into the way of truth, another full of Eunomians and another of Arians I brought to the light of divine knowledge, and, by God's grace, not a tare of heresy was left among us.

Ep. 145. I do indeed sorrow and lament that I am compelled by the attacks of fever to adduce against men, supposed to be of one and the same faith with myself, the arguments which I have already urged against the victims of the plague of Marcion, of whom, by God's grace, I have converted more than ten thousand and brought them to holy baptism.

§ 31. The Results of the Crisis

The internal crisis, or the conflict with heresy, led the Church to perfect its organization, and, as a result, the foundation was laid for such a development of the episcopate that the Church was recognized as based upon an order of bishops receiving their powers in succession from the Apostles. Just what those powers were and how they were transmitted were matters left to a later age to determine. (*V. infra*, §§ 50, 51.)

(a) Irenæus, *Adv. Hær.*, IV, 26 : 2, 5. (MSG, 7 : 1053.)

That Irenæus, writing about 175, could appeal to the episcopal succession as commonly recognized and admitted, and to use it as a basis of unity for the Church, is generally regarded as evidence of the existence of a wide-spread episcopal organization at an early date in the second century. Possibly the connection of Irenæus with Asia Minor, where the episcopal organization admittedly was earliest, diminishes the force of the argument. The reference to the "charisma of truth," which the bishops were said to possess, was to furnish later a theoretical basis for the authority of bishops assembled in council.

Ch. 2. Wherefore it is incumbent to obey the presbyters who are in the Church, those who, as I have shown, possess the succession from the Apostles; those who together with the succession of the episcopate have received the certain gift [charisma] of the truth according to the good pleasure of the Father; but also to hold in suspicion others who depart from the primitive succession and assemble themselves together in any place whatsoever. . . .

Ch. 5. Such presbyters does the Church nourish, of whom also the prophet says: "I will give thy rulers in peace, and thy bishops in righteousness" [*cf*. Is. 60 : 17]. Of whom also the Lord did declare: "Who, then, shall be a faithful steward, good and wise, whom the Lord sets over His household, to give them their meat in due season? Blessed is that servant whom his Lord when he cometh shall find so doing" [Matt. 24 : 45 *f*.]. Paul, then, teaching us where one may find such, says: "God hath placed in the Church, first, Apostles; secondly, prophets; thirdly, teachers" [I Cor. 12 : 28]. Where, then, the gifts of the Lord have been placed there we are to learn the truth; namely, from those who possess the succession of the Church from the Apostles, and among whom exists that which is sound and blameless in conduct, as well as that which is unadulterated and incorrupt in speech.

(b) Tertullian, *De Præscriptione*, 32. (MSL, 2 : 52.)

In Tertullian's statement as to the necessity of apostolic succession, the language is more precise than in Irenæus's. Bishop and presbyter are not used as interchangeable terms, as would appear in the passage in Irenæus. The whole is given a more legal turn, as was in harmony with the writer's legal mind.

But if there be any heresies bold enough to plant themselves in the midst of the apostolic age, that they may thereby seem to have been handed down from the Apostles, because they were in the time of the Apostles, we can say: Let them produce the originals of their churches; let them unfold the roll of their bishops, running down in due succession from the beginning in such manner that that first bishop of theirs shall be able to show for his ordainer or predecessor some one of the Apostles or of apostolic men—a man, moreover, who continued steadfast with the Apostles. For in this manner the apostolic churches transmit their registers; as the church of Smyrna, which records that Polycarp was placed therein by John; as also the church of Rome, which makes Clement to have been ordained in like manner by Peter. In exactly the same way the other churches likewise exhibit their several worthies, whom, as having been appointed to their episcopal places by the Apostles, they regard as transmitters of the apostolic seed.

CHAPTER IV. THE BEGINNINGS OF CATHOLIC THEOLOGY

The theology of the Church, as distinguished from the current traditional theology, was the statement of the beliefs commonly held by Christians but expressed in the more precise and scientific language of current philosophy, the co-ordination of those beliefs as so stated together with their necessary consequences, and their proof by reference to Holy Scripture and reason. In this attempt to build up a body of reasoned religious ideas there were two lines of thought or interpretation of the common Christianity already distinguished by the middle of the second century, and destined to hold a permanent place in the Church. These were the apologetic conception of Christianity as primarily a revealed philosophy (§ 32), and the so-called Asia Minor school of theology, with its conception of Christianity as primarily salvation from sin and corruptibility (§ 33). In both lines of interpretation the Incarnation played an essential part: in the apologetic as insuring the truth of the revealed philosophy, in the Asia Minor theology as imparting to corruptible man the divine incorruptibility.

§ 32. The Apologetic Conception of Christianity.
§ 33. The Asia Minor Conception of Christianity.

§ 32. THE APOLOGETIC CONCEPTION OF CHRISTIANITY

Christianity was regarded as a revealed philosophy by the apologists. This they considered under three principal aspects: knowledge, or a revelation of the divine nature; a new law, or a code of morals given by Christ; and life, or future rewards for the observance of the new law that had been given. The foundation of all was laid in the doctrine of the Logos (A), which involved, as a consequence, some theory of the relation of the resulting distinctions in the divine nature to the primary conviction of the unity of God, or some doctrine of the Trinity (B). As a result of the new law given, moralism was inevitable, whereby a man by his efforts earned everlasting life (C). The proof that Jesus was the incarnate Logos was drawn from the fulfilment of Hebrew prophecy (D). It should be remembered that the apologists influenced later theology by their actual writings, and not by unexpressed and undeveloped opinions which they held as a part of the common tradition and the Christianity of the Gentile Church. Whatever they might have held in addition to their primary contentions had little or no effect, however valuable it may be for modern students, and the conviction that Christianity was essentially a revealed philosophy became current, especially in the East, finding its most powerful expression in the Alexandrian school. (*V. infra*, § 43.)

(A) *The Logos Doctrine*

As stated by the apologists, the Logos doctrine not only furnished a valuable line of defence for Christianity (*v. supra*, § 20), but also gave theologians a useful formula for stating the relation of the divine element in Christ to God. That divine element was the Divine Word or Reason (Logos). It is characteristic of the doctrine of the Logos as held by the early apologists that, although they make the Word, or Logos, personal and distinguish Him from God the Father, yet that Word does not become personally distinguished from the source of His being until, and in connection with, the creation of the world. Hence there arose the distinction between the *Logos endiathetos*, or as yet within the being of the Father, and the *Logos prophorikos*, or as proceeding forth and becoming a distinct person. Here is, at any rate, a marked advance upon the speculation of Philo, by whom the Logos is not regarded as distinctly personal.

(*a*) Justin Martyr, *Apol.*, I, 46. (MSG, 6 : 398.)

In addition to the following passage from Justin Martyr, see above, § 20, for a longer statement to much the same effect.

We have been taught that Christ is the first-born of God, and we have declared above that He is the Word of whom every race of men were partakers; and those who lived reasonably are Christians even though they have been thought atheists; as among the Greeks, Socrates and Heraclitus, and

men like them; and among the barbarians, Abraham and
Ananias, Azarias, and Missael [the "three holy children,"
companions of Daniel, see LXX, Dan. 3 : 23 *ff*.], and Elias
[*i. e.*, Elijah], and many others whose actions and names we
now decline to recount because we know that it would be
tedious.

(*b*) Theophilus, *Ad Autolycum*, II, 10, 22. (MSG, 6 : 398.)

Theophilus was the sixth bishop of Antioch, from 169 until after
180. His apology, consisting of three books addressed to an otherwise
unknown Autolycus, has alone been preserved of his works. Fragments attributed to him are of very doubtful authenticity. The
date of the third book must be subsequent to the death of Marcus
Aurelius, March 17, 180, which is mentioned. The first and second
books may be somewhat earlier. The distinction made in the following between the *Logos endiathetos* and the *Logos prophorikos* was
subsequently dropped by theologians.

Ch. 10.   God, then, having His own Logos internal [*endiatheton*] within His own bowels, begat Him, emitting Him
along with His own wisdom before all things.

Ch. 22.   What else is this voice but the Word of God,
who is also His Son?   Not as the poets and writers of myths
talk of the sons of the gods begotten from intercourse with
women, but as the Truth expounds, the Word that always
exists, residing within [*endiatheton*] the heart of God.   For
before anything came into existence He had Him for His
counsellor, being His own mind and thought.   But when
God wished to make all that He had determined on, He
begat this Word proceeding forth [*prophorikon*], the first-born
of all creation, not being Himself emptied of the Word [*i. e.*,
being without reason], but having begotten Reason and
always conversing with His reason.

(B)   *The Doctrine of the Trinity*

The doctrine of the Trinity followed naturally from the
doctrine of the Logos.   The fuller discussion belongs to the
Monarchian controversies.   It is considered here as a posi-

tion resulting from the general position taken by the apologists. (*V. infra*, § 40.)

(*a*) Theophilus, *Ad Autolycum*, II, 15. (MSG, 6 : 1078.)

The following passage is probably the earliest in which the word Trinity, or Trias, is applied to the relation of Father, Son, and Holy Ghost. It is usual in Greek theology to use the word Trias as equivalent to the Latin term Trinity. *Cf*. Tertullian, *Adv. Praxean*, 2, for first use of the term Trinity in Latin theology.

In like manner, also, the three days, which were before the luminaries[1] are types of the Trinity (Trias) of God, and His Word, and His Wisdom.

(*b*) Athenagoras, *Supplicatio*, 10, 12. (MSG, 6: 910, 914.)

Athenagoras, one of the ablest of the apologists, was, like Justin Martyr and several others, a philosopher before he became a Christian. His apology, known as *Supplicatio*, or *Legatio pro Christianis*, is his most important work. Its date is probably 177, as it is addressed to the Emperors Marcus Aurelius and Commodus.

Ch. 10. If it occurs to you to inquire what is meant by the Son, I will briefly state that He is the first product of the Father, not as having been brought into existence (for from the beginning God, who is the eternal mind [*Nous*], had the Logos in Himself, being eternally reasonable [λογικός]), but inasmuch as He came forth to be idea and energizing power of all material things, which lay like a nature without attributes, and an inactive earth, the grosser particles being mixed up with the lighter. The prophetic Spirit also agrees with our statements: "The Lord, it says, created me the beginning of His ways to His works." The Holy Spirit himself, also, which operates in the prophets we say is an effluence of God, flowing from Him and returning back again as a beam of the sun.

Ch. 12. Are, then, those who consider life to be this, "Let us eat and drink, for to-morrow we die" [*cf*. I Cor. 15 : 32], and who regard death as a deep sleep and forgetfulness [*cf*. Hom., *Iliad*, XVI, 672], to be regarded as living piously?

[1] Reference to the creation of the sun, moon, and stars on the fourth day of creation.

But men who reckon the present life as of very small worth indeed, and are led by this one thing along—that they know God and with Him His Logos, what is the oneness of the Son with the Father, what the communion of the Father with the Son, what is the Spirit, and what is the unity of these and their distinction, the Spirit, the Son, and the Father—and who know that the life for which we look is far better than can be described in word, provided we arrive at it pure from all wrong-doing, and who, moreover, carry our benevolence to such an extent that we not only love our friends . . . shall we, I say, when such we are and when we thus live that we may escape condemnation, not be regarded as living piously?

(C) *Moralistic Christianity*

The moralistic conception of Christianity, *i. e.*, the view of Christianity as primarily a moral code by the observance of which eternal life was won, remained fixed in Christian thought along with the philosophical conception of the faith as formulated by the apologists. This moralism was the opposite pole to the conceptions of the Asia Minor school, the Augustinian theology, and the whole mystical conception of Christianity.

For additional source material, see above, § 16.

Theophilus, *Ad Autolycum*, II, 27. (MSG, 6 : 27.)

God made man free and with power over himself. That [death], man brought upon himself through carelessness and disobedience, this [life], God vouchsafes to him as a gift through His own love for man and pity when men obey Him. For as man, disobeying, drew death upon himself, so, obeying the will of God, he who desires is able to procure for himself everlasting life. For God has given us a law and holy commandments; and every one who keeps these can be saved, and obtaining the resurrection, can inherit incorruption.

(D) *Argument from Hebrew Prophecy*

The appeal to the fulfilment of Hebrew prophecy was the main argument of the apologists for the divine character of the mission of Christ. The exegesis of the prophetic writings was in the spirit of the times. Hebrew prophecy was also regarded as the source of all knowledge of God outside of Israel. The theory that the Greeks and other nations borrowed was employed to show the connection; in this the apologists followed Philo Judæus. No attempt was made either by them or by Clement of Alexandria to remove the inconsistency of this theory of borrowing with the doctrine of the Logos; see above, under "Logos Doctrine"; also § 20.

Justin Martyr, *Apol.*, I, 30, 44. (MSG, 6 : 374, 394.)

Additional source material: Justin Martyr, *Dial. c. Tryph.*, passim.

Ch. 30. But lest any one should say in opposition to us: What should prevent that He whom we call Christ, being a man born of men, performed what we call His mighty works by magical art, and by this appeared to be the Son of God? We will offer proof, not trusting to mere assertions, but being of necessity persuaded by those who prophesied of Him before these things came to pass.

Ch. 44. Whatever both philosophers and poets have said concerning the immortality of the soul, or punishments after death, or contemplation of things heavenly, or doctrines of the like kind, they have received such suggestions from the prophets as have enabled them to understand and interpret these things. And hence there seem to be seeds of truth among all men.

§ 33. THE ASIA MINOR CONCEPTION OF CHRISTIANITY

The Asia Minor school regarded Christianity primarily as redemption, salvation, the imparting of new power, life, and incorruptibility by union with divinity in the Incarnation. Its leading representative was Irenæus, a native of Asia Minor, but many of his leading ideas had been anticipated by Ignatius of Antioch, and they were shared by many others.

The theology of Irenæus influenced Tertullian to some extent, but its essential points were reproduced by Athanasius, who was directly indebted to Irenæus, and through him it superseded in the Neo-Alexandrian school the tradition derived through Origen and Clement from the apologists. Characteristic features of the Asia Minor theology are the place assigned to the Incarnation as itself effecting redemption or salvation, the idea of recapitulation whereby Christ becomes the head of a new race of redeemed men, a second Adam, and of the eucharist as imparting the incorruptibility of Christ's immortal flesh which is received by the faithful.

(a) Irenæus, *Adv. Hær.*, V, 1. (MSG, 7 : 1119.)

The position of the Incarnation in the system and its relation to redemption.

In no other way could we have learned the things of God, if our Master, existing previously as the Word, had not been made man.   For no one else could have declared to us the truths of the Father than the Father's own Word.   For who else knew the mind of the Lord or who else has been his counsellor? [Rom. 11 : 34].   Nor again in any other way could we have learned except by seeing our Master with our eyes and hearing His voice with our ears; that so as imitators of His acts and doers of His words we might have fellowship with Him and receive of the fulness of Him who is perfect and who was before all creation.   All this we have been made in these latter days by Him who only is supremely good and who has the gift of incorruptibility; inasmuch as we are conformed to His likeness and predestinated to become what we never were before, according to the foreknowledge of the Father, made a first-fruit of His workmanship, we have, therefore, received all this at the foreordained season, according to the dispensation of the Word, who is perfect in all things.   For He, who is the mighty Word and very man, redeeming us by His blood in a reasonable manner, gave

Himself as a ransom for those who had been led into captivity. And since apostasy tyrannized over us unjustly, for though by nature we were God's possession, it yet alienated us contrary to nature, making us its own disciples, the Word of God, powerful in all things and constant in His justice, dealt justly even with apostasy itself, redeeming from it what was His own property. Not by force, the way in which the apostasy had originally gained its mastery over us, greedily grasping at that which was not its own; but by moral force [*secundum suadelam*] as became God, by persuasion and not by force, regaining what He wished; so that justice might not be violated and God's ancient handiwork might not perish. Therefore, since by His own blood the Lord redeemed us and gave His soul for our soul, and His flesh for our flesh, and shed on us His Father's spirit to unite and join us in communion God and man, bringing God down to men by the descent of the Spirit, and raising up man to God by His incarnation, and by a firm and true promise giving us at His advent incorruptibility by communion with Him, and thus all the errors of the heretics are destroyed.

(b) Irenæus, *Adv. Hær.*, III, 18 : 1, 7. (MSG, 6 : 932, 937.)

The following is a statement by Irenæus of his doctrine of recapitulation, which combines the idea of the second Adam of Paul and the Johannine theology.

Ch. 1. Since it has been clearly demonstrated that the Word, who existed in the beginning with God, and by whom all things were made, who also was present with the human race, was in these last days, according to the time appointed by the Father, united to His own workmanship, having been made a man liable to suffering, every objection is set aside of those who say: "If Christ was born at that time, He did not exist before that time." For I have shown that the Son of God did not then begin to be, since He existed with His Father always; but when He was incarnate, and was made man, He commenced afresh [*in seipso recapitulavit*] the long line of human beings, and furnished us in a brief and comprehensive manner with salvation; so that what we had lost in Adam—namely, to be according to the image and likeness of God—that we might recover in Christ Jesus.

Ch. 7. He caused human nature to cleave to and to become one with God, as we have said. For if man had not overcome the adversary of man, the enemy would not have been legitimately overcome. And again, if God had not given salvation, we could not have had it securely. And if man had not been united to God, he could never have become a partaker of incorruptibility. For it was incumbent upon the Mediator between God and man, by His relationship to both, to bring about a friendship and concord, and to present man to God and to reveal God to man. For in what way could we be partakers of the adoption of sons, if we had not received from Him, through the Son, that fellowship which refers to Himself, if the Word, having been made flesh, had not entered into communion with us? Wherefore He passed also through every stage of life restoring to all communion with God.

(c) Irenæus, *Adv. Hær.*, IV, 18 : 5. (MSG, 6 : 1027 *f.*)

The conception of redemption as the imparting of incorruptibility connected itself easily with the doctrine of the eucharist, which had been called by Ignatius of Antioch "the medicine of immortality" (*v. supra*, § 12). With this passage compare Irenæus, *Adv. Hær.*, IV, 17 : 5.

How can they say that the flesh which is nourished with the body of the Lord and with His blood goes to corruption and does not partake of life? Let them, therefore, either alter their opinion or cease from offering the things mentioned. But our opinion is in accordance with the eucharist, and the eucharist, in turn, establishes our opinion. For we offer to Him His own, announcing consistently the fellowship and union of the flesh and the Spirit. For as the bread which is produced from the earth when it receives the invocation of God is no longer common bread, but the eucharist, consisting of two realities, earthly and heavenly, so, also, our bodies, when they receive the eucharist, are no longer corruptible, having the hope of the resurrection unto eternity.

PERIOD IV

THE AGE OF THE CONSOLIDATION OF THE CHURCH: 200 TO 324 A. D.

In the fourth period of the Church under the heathen Empire, or the period of the consolidation of the Church, the number of Christians increased so rapidly that the relation of the Roman State to the Church became a matter of the gravest importance (ch. 1). During a period of comparative peace and prosperity the Church developed its doctrinal system and its constitution (ch. 2). Although the school of Asia Minor became isolated and temporarily ceased to affect the bulk of the Church elsewhere, the school of the apologists was brilliantly continued at Alexandria under Clement and Origen, and later under Origen at Cæsarea in Palestine. Meanwhile the foundations were laid in North Africa for a distinctive type of Western theology, inaugurated by Tertullian and developed by Cyprian. After years of alternating favor and local persecutions, the first general persecution (ch. 3) broke upon the Church, rudely testing its organization and ultimately strengthening and furthering its tendencies toward a strictly hierarchical constitution. In the long period of peace that followed (ch. 4), the discussions that had arisen within the Church as to the relation of the divine unity to the divinity of Christ reached a temporary conclusion, the cultus was elaborated and assumed the essentials of its permanent form, and the episcopate was made supreme over rival authorities within the Church, becoming at once the expression and organ of ecclesiastical unity. At the same time new problems arose; within the

Church there was the appearance of an organized asceticism which appeared for a time to be a rival to the Church's system, and outside the Church the appearance of a hostile rival in the rapidly spreading Manichæan system, in which was revived, in a better organized and therefore more dangerous form, the expelled Gnosticism. The period ends with the last general persecution (ch. 5).

CHAPTER I. THE POLITICAL AND RELIGIOUS CONDITIONS OF THE EMPIRE

The accession of Septimius Severus, A. D. 193, marks a change in the condition of the Empire. It was becoming more harassed by frontier wars, not always waged successfully. Barbarians were gradually settling within the Empire. The emperors themselves were no longer Romans or Italians. Provincials, some not even of the Latin race, assumed the imperial dignity. But it was a period in which the Roman law was in its most flourishing and brilliant stage, under such men as Papinian, Ulpian, and others second only to these masters. Stoic cosmopolitanism made for wider conceptions of law and a deeper sense of human solidarity. The Christian Church, however, profited little by this (§ 34) until, in the religious syncretism which became fashionable in the highest circles, it was favored by even the imperial family along with other Oriental religions (§ 35). The varying fortunes of the emperors necessarily affected the Church (§ 36), though, on the whole, there was little suffering, and the Church spread rapidly, and in many parts of the Empire became a powerful organization (§ 37), with which the State would soon have to reckon.

§ 34. State and Church under Septimius Severus and Caracalla.

§ 35. Religious Syncretism in the Third Century.

§ 36. The Religious Policy of the Emperors from Heliogabalus to Philip the Arabian.

§ 37. The Extension of the Church in the First Half of the Third Century.

§ 34. STATE AND CHURCH UNDER SEPTIMIUS SEVERUS AND CARACALLA

Although Christians were at first favored by Septimius Severus, they were still liable to the severe laws against secret societies, and the policy of Septimius was later to enforce these laws. The Christians tried to escape the penalties prescribed against such societies by taking the form of friendly societies which were expressly tolerated by the law. Nevertheless, numerous cases are to be found in various parts of the Empire in which Christians were put to death under the law. Yet the number of martyrs before the general persecution of Decius in the middle of the century was relatively small. The position of Christians was not materially affected by the constitution of Caracalla conferring Roman citizenship on all free inhabitants of the Empire, and the constitution seems to have been merely a fiscal measure which laid additional burdens upon the provincials.

Additional source material: Eusebius, *Hist. Ec.*, VI, 1–12.

(a) Tertullian, *Ad Scapulam*, 4. (MSL, 1 : 781.)

The account of Tertullian is generally accepted as substantially correct. Scapula was chief magistrate of Carthage and, under the circumstances, the author would not have indulged his tendency to rhetorical embellishment. Furthermore, the book is written with what was for Tertullian great moderation.

How many rulers, men more resolute and more cruel than you, have contrived to get quit of such causes—as Cincius Severus, who himself suggested the remedy at Thysdris, pointing out how Christians should answer that they might be acquitted; as Vespronius Candidus, who acquitted a Christian on the ground that to satisfy his fellow-citizens would create a riot; as Asper, who, in the case of a man who under slight torture had fallen, did not compel him to offer sacrifice, having owned among the advocates and assessors of the court that he was annoyed at having to meddle with such a case! Prudens, too, at once dismissed a Christian brought before him, perceiving from the indictment that it was a case of vexatious accusation; tearing the document in pieces, he refused, according to the imperial command, to hear him without the presence of his accuser. All this might be officially brought under your notice, and by the very advocates, who themselves are under obligations to Christians, although they cry out against us as it suits them. The clerk of one who was liable to be thrown down by an evil spirit was set free; as was also a relative of another, and the little boy of a third. How many men of rank (not to mention common people) have been cured of devils and of diseases! Even Severus himself, the father of Antonine, was mindful of the Christians; for he sought out the Christian Proclus, surnamed Torpacion, the steward of Euhodias, who once had cured him by means of oil, and whom he kept in his palace till his death. Antonine [Caracalla], too, was brought up on Christian milk,[1] was intimately acquainted with this man. But Severus, knowing both men and women of the highest rank to be of this sect, not only did not injure them, but distinguished them with his testimony and restored them to us openly from the raging populace.[2]

(b) Laws Relating to Forbidden Societies.

1. Justinian, *Digest*, XLVII, 23 : 1.

The following is a passage taken from the Institutes of Marcian, Bk. III.

By princely commands it was prescribed to the governors of provinces that they should not permit social clubs and that soldiers should not have societies in the camp. But it is permitted to the poor to collect a monthly contribution, so long as they gather together only once in a month, lest under

---

[1] Probably his wet-nurse was a Christian.
[2] On the occasion of his triumphal entry into Rome.

a pretext of this sort an unlawful society meet. And that this should be allowed not only in the city, but also in Italy and the provinces, the divine Severus ordered. But for the sake of religion they are not forbidden to come together so long as they do nothing contrary to the Senatus-consultum, by which unlawful societies are restrained. It is furthermore not lawful to belong to more than one lawful society, as this was determined by the divine brothers [Caracalla and Geta]; and if any one is in two, it is ordered that it be necessary for him to choose in which he prefers to be, and he shall receive from the society from which he resigns that which belongs to him proportionately of what there is of a common fund.

2. Justinian, *Digest*, I, 12 : 14.

From Ulpian's treatise, *De officio Præfecti Urbi.*

The divine Severus ordered that those who were accused of meeting in forbidden societies should be accused before the prefect of the city.

(c) Persecutions under Severus.

1. Eusebius, *Hist. Ec.*, VI, 1. (MSG, 20 : 522.)

The following extract is important not only as a witness to the fact of the execution of the laws against Christians in Alexandria, but also to the extension of Christianity in the more southern provinces of Egypt.

When Severus began to persecute the churches, glorious testimonies were given everywhere by the athletes of religion. Especially numerous were they in Alexandria, for thither, as to a more prominent theatre, athletes of God were sent from Egypt and all Thebais, according to their merit, and they won crowns from God through their great patience under many tortures and every mode of death. Among these was Leonidas, said to be the father of Origen, who was beheaded while his son was still young.

2. Spartianus, *Vita Severi*, XVII, 1. (*Scriptores Historiæ Augustæ*. Ed. Peter, 1884; Preuschen, *Analecta*, I, 32.)

The date of the following is A. D. 202.

He forbade, under heavy penalties, any to become Jews. He made the same regulation in regard to Christians.

(*d*) Tertullian, *Apol.*, 39. (MSL, 1 : 534.)

In the following, Christian assemblies, or churches, are represented as being a sort of friendly society, similar but superior to those existing all over the Empire, common and tolerated among the poorer members of society. The date of the *Apology* is 197.

Though we have our treasure-chest, it is not made up of purchase money, as if our religion had its price. On the regular day in the month, or when one prefers, each one makes a small donation; but only if it be his pleasure, and only if he be able; for no one is compelled, but gives voluntarily. These gifts are, as it were, piety's deposit fund. For they are taken thence and spent, not on feasts and drinking-bouts, and thankless eating-houses, but to support and bury poor people, to supply the wants of boys and girls destitute of means and parents, and of old persons confined to the house, likewise the shipwrecked, and if there happen to be any in the mines, or banished to the islands, or shut up in the prisons for nothing but their fidelity to the cause of God's Church, they become the nurslings of their confession. But it is mainly for such work of love that many place a brand upon us. See, they say, how they love one another!

(*e*) *The Passion of Perpetua and Felicitas*. (MSL, 3 : 51.) (*Cf.* Knopf, pp. 44–57.)

The date of this martyrdom is A. D. 203. The *Passio SS. Perpetuæ et Felicitatis* has been attributed to Tertullian. It betrays clear evidence of Montanist sympathies. It has even been thought by some that the martyrs themselves were Montanists. At that date probably not a few who sympathized with Montanism were still in good standing in certain parts of the Church. At any rate, the day of their commemoration has been from the middle of the fourth century at Rome March 7. See Kirch, p. 323.

The day of their victory dawned, and they proceeded from the prison into the amphitheatre, as if to happiness, joyous and of brilliant countenances; if, perchance, shrinking, it was with joy and not with fear. Perpetua followed with placid look, and with step and gait as a matron of Christ, beloved of God, casting down the lustre of her eyes from the gaze of all. Likewise Felicitas came, rejoicing that she had safely brought forth, so that she might fight with the beasts. . . . And when they were brought to the gate, and were constrained to put on the clothing—the men that of the priests of Saturn, and the women that of those who were consecrated to Ceres—that noble-minded woman resisted even to the end with constancy. For she said: "We have come thus far of our own accord, that our liberty might not be restrained. For this reason we have yielded our minds, that we might not do any such thing as this; we have agreed on this with you." Injustice acknowledged the justice; the tribune permitted that they be brought in simply as they were. Perpetua sang psalms, already treading under foot the head of the Egyptian [seen in a vision; see preceding chapters]; Revocatus and Saturninus and Saturus uttered threatenings against the gazing people about this martyrdom. When they came within sight of Hilarianus, by gesture and nod they began to say to Hilarianus: "Thou judgest us, but God will judge thee." At this the exasperated people demanded that they should be tormented with scourges as they passed along the rank of the *venatores*. And they, indeed, rejoiced that they should have incurred any one of their Lord's passions.

But He who had said, "Ask and ye shall receive," gave to them, when they asked, that death which each one had desired. For when they had been discoursing among themselves about their wish as to their martyrdom, Saturninus, indeed, had professed that he wished that he might be thrown to all the beasts; doubtless that he might wear a more glorious crown. Therefore, in the beginning of the exhibition he and Revocatus made trial of the leopard, and, moreover, upon the scaffold they were harassed by the bear. Saturus, however, held nothing in greater horror than a bear; but he thought he would be finished by one bite of a leopard. Therefore, when a wild boar was supplied, it was the huntsman who had supplied that boar, and not Saturus, who was gored by that same beast and who died the day after the shows. Saturus only was drawn out; and when he had been bound on the floor near to a bear, the bear would not come forth from his den. And so Saturus for the second time was recalled, unhurt.

Moreover, for the young women the devil, rivalling their sex also in that of the beasts, prepared a very fierce cow, provided especially for that purpose contrary to custom. And so, stripped and clothed with nets, they were led forth. The populace shuddered as they saw one young woman of delicate frame, and another with breasts still dropping from her recent childbirth. So, being recalled, they were unbound. Perpetua was first led in. She was tossed and fell on her loins; and when she saw her tunic torn from her side, she drew it over her as a veil for her thighs, mindful of her modesty rather than of her suffering. Then she was called for again, and bound up her dishevelled hair; for it was not becoming for a martyr to suffer with dishevelled hair, lest she should appear to be mourning in her glory. She rose up, and when she saw Felicitas crushed she approached and gave her her hand and lifted her up. And both of them stood together; and the brutality of the populace being appeased, they were recalled to the Sanavivarian gate. Then Perpetua was received by a certain one who was still a catechumen, Rusticus by name, who kept close to her; and she, as if roused from sleep, so deeply had she been in the Spirit and in an ecstasy, began to look around her and to say to the amazement of all: "I do not know when we are to be led out to that cow." Thus she said, and when she had heard what had already happened, she did not believe it until she had perceived certain signs of injury in her own body and in her dress, and had recognized the catechumen. Afterward, causing that catechumen and the brother to approach, she addressed them, saying: "Stand fast in the faith, and love one another, all of you, and be not offended at our sufferings."

The same Saturus at the other entrance exhorted the soldier Prudens, saying: "Assuredly here I am, as I have promised and foretold, for up to this moment I have felt no beast. And now believe with your whole heart. Lo, I am going forth to the leopard, and I shall be destroyed with one bite." And immediately on the conclusion of the exhibition he was thrown to the leopard; and with one bite by it he was bathed with such a quantity of blood that the people shouted out to him, as he was returning, the testimony of his second baptism: "Saved and washed, saved and washed." Manifestly he was assuredly saved who had been glorified in such a spectacle. Then to the soldier Prudens he said: "Farewell, and be mindful of my faith; and let not these things disturb, but confirm you." And at the same time he asked for a little ring from his finger, and returned it to him bathed in his wound, leaving to him an inherited token and memory of his blood. And then lifeless he was cast down with the rest, to be slaughtered in the usual place. And when the populace called for them into the midst, that as the sword penetrated into their body they might make their eyes partners in the murder, they rose up of their own accord, and transferred themselves whither the people wished; but they first kissed one another, that they might consummate their martyrdom with the rites of peace. The rest, indeed, immovable and in silence, received the sword; and so did Saturus, who had also first ascended the ladder, and first gave up his spirit, for he was waiting for Perpetua. But Perpetua, that she might taste some pain, being pierced between the ribs, cried out loudly and she herself placed the wavering right hand of the youthful gladiator to her throat. Possibly such a woman could not have been slain unless she herself had willed it, because she was feared by the impure spirit. O most brave and blessed martyrs! O truly called and chosen unto the glory of our Lord Jesus Christ! Whoever magnifies, and honors, and adores Him, assuredly ought to read these examples for the edification of the Church, not less than the ancient ones, so that new virtues also may testify that one and the same Holy Spirit is always operating even until now, and God the Father Omnipotent, and his Son Jesus Christ our Lord, whose is glory and infinite power forever and ever. Amen.

(f) Origen, *Contra Celsum*, III, 8. (MSG, 11 : 930.)

Origen is writing just before the first general persecution under Decius about the middle of the century. He points out the relatively small number of those suffering persecution.

With regard to Christians, because they were taught not to avenge themselves upon their enemies, and have thus observed laws of a mild and philanthropic character; and because, although they were able, yet they would not have made war even if they had received authority to do so; for this cause they have obtained this from God: that He has always warred on their behalf, and at times has restrained those who rose up against them and who wished to destroy them. For in order to remind others, that seeing a few engaged in a struggle in behalf of religion, they might also be better fitted to despise death, a few, at various times, and these easily numbered, have endured death for the sake of the Christian religion; God not permitting the whole nation [*i. e.*, the Christians] to be exterminated, but desiring that it should continue, and that the whole world should be filled with this salvation and the doctrines of religion.

(g) Justinian, *Digest*, I, 5 : 17.

The edict of Caracalla (Marcus Aurelius Antoninus) conferring Roman citizenship upon all free inhabitants of the Empire has not been preserved. It is known only from a brief extract from the twenty-second book of Ulpian's work on the Prætorian Edict, contained in the *Digest* of Justinian.

Those who were in the Roman world were made Roman citizens by the constitution of the Emperor Antoninus.

§ 35.   Religious Syncretism in the Third Century

In the third century religious syncretism took two leading forms—the Mithraic worship, which spread rapidly throughout the Empire, and the fashionable interest in novel religions fostered by the imperial court. Mithraism was especially prevalent in the army, and at army posts have been found numerous remains of sanctuaries, inscriptions, etc. It was by far the purest of the religions that invaded the Roman Empire, and drew its leading ideas from Persian sources. The fashionable court interest in novel religions seems not to have amounted to much as a positive religious force, which Mithraism certainly was, though on account of it Christianity was protected and even patronized by the ladies of the imperial household. Among the works produced by this interest was the *Life of Apollonius of Tyana*, written by Philostratus at the command of the Empress Julia Domna. Apollonius was a preacher or teacher of ethics and the Neo-Pythagorean philosophy in the first century, *ob.* A. D. 97.

Additional source material: Philostratus, *Life of Apollonius* (the latest English translation, by F. C. Conybeare, with Greek text in the *Loeb Classical Library*, 1912).

Mithraic Prayer, Albrecht Dietrich, *Eine Mithrasliturgie*, Leipsic, 1903.

The following prayer is the opening invocation of what appears to be a Mithraic liturgy, and may date from a period earlier than the fourth century. It gives, as is natural, no elaborated statement of Mithraic doctrine, but, as in all prayer, much is implied in the forms used and the spirit of the religion breathed through it. The combination has already begun as is shown by the doctrine of the four elements. It should be added that Professor Cumont does not regard it as a Mithraic liturgy at all, but accounts for the distinct mention of the name Mithras, which is to be found in some parts, to a common tendency of semi-magical incantations to employ as many deities as possible.

First Origin of my origin, first Beginning of my beginning, Spirit of Spirit, first of the spirit in me. Fire which to compose me has been given of God, first of the fire in me. Water of water, first of the water in me. Earthy Substance of earthy substance, first of the earthy substance, the entire body of me, N. N. son of N. N., completely formed by an honorable arm and an immortal right hand in the lightless and illuminated world, in the inanimated and the animated. If it seem good to you to restore me to an immortal generation, who am held by my underlying nature, that after this present need which presses sorely upon me I may behold the immortal Beginning with the immortal Spirit, the immortal Water, the Solid and the Air, that I may be born again, by the thought, that I may be consecrated and the holy Spirit may breathe in me, that I may gaze with astonishment at the holy Fire, that I may look upon abysmal and frightful Water of the sun-rising, and the generative Ether poured around may listen to me. For I will to-day look with immortal eyes, I who was begotten a mortal from a mortal womb, exalted by a mighty working power and incorruptible right hand, I may look with an immortal spirit upon the immortal Eon and the Lord of the fiery crowns, purified by holy consecrations, since a little under me stands the human power of mind, which I shall regain after the present bitter, oppressive, and debt-laden need, I, N. N. the son of N. N., according to God's unchangeable decree, for it is not within my power, born mortal, to mount up with the golden light flashes of the immortal illuminator. Stand still, corruptible human nature, and leave me free after the pitiless and crushing necessity.

§ 36. THE RELIGIOUS POLICY OF THE EMPERORS FROM HELIOGABALUS TO PHILIP THE ARABIAN, 217–249

With the brief exception of the reign of Maximinus Thrax (235–238), Christians enjoyed peace from the death of Caracalla to the death of Philip the Arabian. This was not due to disregard of the laws against Christians nor to indifference to suspected dangers to the Empire arising from the new religion, but to the policy of religious syncretism which had come in with the family of Severus. The wife of Septimius Severus was the daughter of Julius Bassianus, priest of the Sun-god of Emesa, and of the rulers of the dynasty of Severus one, Heliogabalus, was himself a priest of the same syncretistic cult, and another, Alexander, was under the influence of the women of the same priestly family.

(a) Lampridius, *Vita Heliogabali*, 3, 6, 7. Preuschen, *Analecta*, I, § 12.

Lampridius is one of the *Scriptores Historiæ Augustæ*, by whom is a series of lives of the Roman emperors. The series dates from the fourth century, and is of importance as containing much information which is not otherwise accessible. The dates of the various lives are difficult to determine. Avitus Bassianus, known as Heliogabalus, a name he assumed, reigned 218–222.

Ch. 3. But when he had once entered the city, he enrolled Heliogabalus among the gods and built a temple to him on the Palatine Hill next the imperial palace, desiring to transfer to that temple the image of Cybele, the fire of Vesta, the Palladium, the sacred shields, and all things venerated by the Romans; and he did this so that no other god than Heliogabalus should be worshipped at Rome. He said, besides, that the religions of the Jews and the Samaritans and the Christian worship should be brought thither, that the priesthood of Heliogabalus should possess the secrets of all religions.

Ch. 6. Not only did he wish to extinguish the Roman religions, but he was eager for one thing thoughout the entire world—that Heliogabalus should everywhere be worshipped as god.

Ch. 7. He asserted, in fact, that all the gods were servants of his god, since some he called his chamber-servants, others slaves, and others servants in various capacities.

(b) Lampridius, *Vita Alexandri Severi*, 29, 43, 49. Preuschen, *Analecta*, I, § 13.

Alexander Severus (222–235) succeeded his cousin Heliogabalus. The mother of Alexander, Julia Mammæa, sister of Julia Soæmias, mother of Heliogabalus, was a granddaughter of Julius Bassianus, whose daughter, Julia Domna, had married Septimius Severus. It was through marriages with the female descendants of Julius, who was priest of the Sun-god at Emesa, that the members of the dynasty of Severus were connected and their attitude toward religion determined. It was in the reign of Alexander that syncretism favorable to Christianity was at its height.

Ch. 29. This was his manner of life: as soon as there was opportunity—that is, if he had not spent the night with his wife—he performed his devotions in the early morning hours in his lararium, in which he had statues of the divine princes and also a select number of the best men and the more holy spirits, among whom he had Apollonius of Tyana, and as a writer of his times says, Christ, Abraham, and Orpheus, and others similar, as well as statues of his ancestors.

Ch. 43. He wished to erect a temple to Christ and to number Him among the gods. Hadrian, also, is said to have thought of doing this, and commanded temples without any images to be erected in all cities, and therefore these temples, because they have no image of the Divinity, are to-day called *Hadriani*, which he is said to have prepared for this end. But Alexander was prevented from doing this by those who, consulting the auspices, learned that if ever this were done all would be Christians, and the other temples would have to be deserted.

Ch. 49. When the Christians took possession of a piece of land which belonged to the public domain and in opposition to them the guild of cooks claimed that it belonged to them, he decreed that it was better that in that place God should be worshipped in some fashion rather than that it be given to the cooks.

(c) Eusebius, *Hist. Ec.*, VI, 21. (MSG, 20 : 574.)

The mother of the Emperor, whose name was Julia Mammæa, was a most pious woman, if ever one was. When the fame of Origen had extended everywhere and had come even to her ears, she desired greatly to see the man, and to make trial of his understanding of divine things, which was admired by all. When she was staying for a time in Antioch, she sent for him with a military escort. Having remained with her for a while and shown her many things which were for the glory of the Lord and of the excellency of divine teaching, he hastened back to his accustomed labors.

(d) Firmilianus, *Ep. ad Cyprianum*, in Cyprian, *Ep.* 75. (MSL, 3 : 1211.) Preuschen, *Analecta*, I, § 14 : 2.

The following epistle is found among the Epistles of Cyprian, to whom it is addressed. It is of importance in connection with the persecution of Maximinus, throwing light on the occasion and extent of the persecution and relating instances of strange fanaticism and exorcism.

But I wish to tell you about an affair connected with this very matter [baptism by heretics, the main subject of the epistle, *v. infra*, § 52] which occurred among us. About twenty years ago, in the time after Emperor Alexander, there happened in these parts many struggles and difficulties, either in common to all men or privately to Christians. There were, furthermore, many and frequent earthquakes, so that many cities throughout Cappadocia and Pontus were thrown down; and some even were dragged down into the abyss and swallowed by the gaping earth. From this, also, there arose a severe persecution against the Christian name. This arose suddenly after the long peace of the previous age. Because of the unexpected and unaccustomed evil, it was rendered more terrible for the disturbance of our people.

Serenianus was at that time governor of our province, a bitter and cruel persecutor. But when the faithful had been thus disturbed and were fleeing hither and thither from fear of persecution and were leaving their native country and crossing over to other regions—for there was opportunity of crossing over, because this persecution was not over the whole world, but was local—there suddenly arose among us a certain woman who in a state of ecstasy announced herself as a prophetess and acted as if filled with the Holy Ghost. And she was so moved by the power of the chief demons that for a long time she disturbed the brethren and deceived them; for she accomplished certain wonderful and portentous things: thus, she promised that she would cause the earth to be shaken, not that the power of the demon was so great that he could shake the earth and disturb the elements, but that sometimes a wicked spirit, foreseeing and understanding that there will be an earthquake, pretends that he will do what he foresees will take place. By these lies and boastings he had so subdued the minds of several that they obeyed him and followed whithersoever he commanded and led. He would also make that woman walk in the bitter cold of winter with bare feet over the frozen snow, and not to be troubled or hurt in any respect by walking in this fashion. Moreover, she said she was hurrying to Judea and Jerusalem, pretending that she had come thence. Here, also, she deceived Rusticus, one of the presbyters, and another one who was a deacon, so that they had intercourse with the same woman. This was shortly after detected. For there suddenly appeared before her one of the exorcists, a man approved and always well versed in matters of religious discipline; he, moved by the exhortation of many of the brethren, also, who were themselves strong in the faith, and praiseworthy, raised himself up against that wicked spirit to overcome it; for the spirit a little while before, by its subtle deceitfulness, had predicted, furthermore, that a certain adverse and unbelieving tempter would come. Yet that exorcist, inspired by God's grace, bravely resisted and showed that he who before was regarded as holy was a most wicked spirit. But that woman, who previously, by the wiles and deceits of the demon, was attempting many things for the deception of the faithful, had among other things by which she deceived many also frequently dared this—to pretend that with an invocation, not to be contemned, she sanctified bread and consecrated the eucharist and offered sacrifice to the Lord without the sacrament as customarily uttered; and to have baptized many, making use of the usual and lawful words of interrogation, that nothing might seem to be different from the ecclesiastical and lawful mode.

(e) Eusebius, *Hist. Ec.*, VI, 34. (MSG, 20 : 595.) Preuschen, *Analecta*, I, § 15, and Kirch, n. 397.

The following tradition that Philip the Arabian was a Christian is commonly regarded as doubtful. That he favored the Christians, and even protected them, may be the basis for such a report.

When Gordianus (238–244) had been Roman Emperor for six years, Philip (244–249) succeeded him. It is reported that he, being a Christian, desired on the day of the last paschal vigil to share with the multitude in the prayers of the Church, but was not permitted by him who then presided to enter until he had made confession and numbered himself among those who were reckoned as transgressors and who occupied the place of penitence. For if he had not done this, he would never have been received by him, on account of the many crimes he had committed, and it is said that he obeyed readily, manifesting in his conduct a genuine and pious fear of God.

§ 37. The Extension of the Church at the Middle of the Third Century

Some approximately correct idea of the extension of the Church by the middle of the third century may be gathered from a precise statement of the organization of the largest church, that at Rome, about the year 250 (a), from the size of provincial synods, of which we have detailed statements for North Africa (b), from references to organized and apparently numerous churches in various places not mentioned in earlier documents (c). That the Church, at least in Egypt and parts adjacent, had ceased to be confined chiefly to the cities and that it was composed of persons of all social ranks is attested by Origen (d).

(a) Cornelius, *Ep. ad Fabium*, in Eusebius, *Hist. Ec.*, VI, 43. (MSG, 20 : 622.) *Cf.* Kirch, n. 222 *ff.*

Cornelius was bishop of Rome 251–253.

This avenger of the Gospel [Novatus] did not then know that there should be one bishop in a Catholic church; yet he was not ignorant (for how could he be) that in it [*i. e.*, the Roman church] there were forty-six presbyters, seven deacons, seven subdeacons, forty-two acolyths, fifty-two exorcists, readers, and janitors, and over fifteen hundred widows and persons in distress, all of whom the grace and kindness of the Master nourished. But not even this great multitude, so necessary in the Church, nor those who through God's providence were rich and full, together with very many, even innumerable, people, could turn him from such desperation and recall him to the Church.

(b) Cyprian, *Epistulæ* 71 [= 70] (MSL, 4 : 424) and 59 : 10 [= 54] (MSL, 3 : 877).

The church in North Africa had grown very rapidly before Cyprian was elevated to the see of Carthage. An evidence of this is the number of councils held in North Africa. That held under Agrippinus, between 218 and 222, was the first known in that part of the Church. Under Cyprian a council was held at Carthage in 258 at which no less than seventy bishops, whose names and opinions have been preserved, are given. See ANF, V, 565 *ff.*

Ep. 71 [= 70]. *Ad Quintum.*

Which thing, indeed, Agrippinus [A. D. 218–222], also a man of worthy memory, with his fellow-bishops, who at that time governed the Lord's Church in the province of Africa and Numidia, decreed, and by the well-weighed examination of the common council established.

Ep. 59 [= 54]: 10. *Ad Cornelium.*

I have also intimated to you, my brother, by Felicianus, that there had come to Carthage Privatus, an old heretic in the colony of Lambesa, many years ago condemned for many and grave crimes by the judgment of ninety bishops, and severely remarked upon in the letters of Fabian and Donatus, also our predecessors, as is not hidden from your knowledge.

(c) Cyprian, *Epistula* 67 [= 68]. (MSL, 3 : 1057, 1065.)

The following extracts from Cyprian's Epistle "To the Clergy and People abiding in Spain, concerning Basilides and Martial," is of importance as bearing upon the development of the appellate jurisdiction of the Roman see, for which see the epistle in its entirety as given in Cyprian's works, ANF, vol. V, for the treatment of the vexed question of discipline in the case of those receiving certificates that they had sacrificed (see below, §§ 45 f.), and as the first definite statements as to localities in Spain where there were Christians and bishops placed over the Church. The mass of martyrdoms that have been preserved refer to still others.

Cyprian . . . to Felix, the presbyter, and to the peoples abiding in Legio [Leon] and Asturica [Astorga], also to Lælius, the deacon, and the people abiding in Emerita [Merida], brethren in the Lord, greeting. When we had come together, dearly beloved brethren, we read your letters, which, according to the integrity of your faith and your fear of God, you wrote to us by Felix and Sabinus, our fellow-bishops, signifying that Basilides and Martial, who had been stained with the certificates of idolatry and bound with the consciousness of wicked crimes, ought not to exercise the episcopal office and administer the priesthood of God. Wherefore, since we have written, dearly beloved brethren, and as Felix and Sabinus, our colleagues, affirm, and as another Felix, of Cæsar-Augusta [Saragossa], a maintainer of the faith and a defender of the truth, signifies in his letter, Basilides and Martial have been contaminated by the abominable certificate of idolatry.

(d) Origen, *Contra Celsum*, III, 9. (MSG, 11 : 951.)

With the following should be compared the statements of Pliny, more than a hundred years earlier, relative to Bithynia. See above, § 7.

Celsus says that "if all men wished to become Christians, the latter would not desire it." That this is false, is evident from this, that Christians do not neglect, as far as they are able, to take care to spread their doctrines throughout the

whole world. Some, accordingly, have made it their business
to go round about not only through cities, but even villages
and country houses, that they may persuade others to become
pious worshippers of God. . . . At present, indeed, when
because of the multitude of those who have embraced the
teaching, not only rich men, but also some persons of rank
and delicate and high-born ladies, receive the teachers of
the Word, there will be some who dare to say that it is for
the sake of a little glory that certain assume the office of
Christian teachers. In the beginning, when there was much
danger, especially to its teachers, this suspicion could have
had no place.

CHAPTER II. THE INTERNAL DEVELOPMENT OF THE
CHURCH IN DOCTRINE, CUSTOM, AND CONSTITUTION

The characteristic Eastern and Western conceptions of
Christianity began to be clearly differentiated in the early
years of the third century. A juristic conception of the
Church as a body at the head of which, and clothed with
authority, appeared the bishop of Rome, had, indeed, become current at Rome in the last decade of the second century on the occasion of the Easter controversy, which had
ended in an estrangement between the previously closely
affiliated churches of Asia Minor and the West, especially
Rome (§ 38). Western theology soon became centred in
North Africa under the legally trained Tertullian, by whom
its leading principles were laid down in harmony with the
bent of the Latin genius (§ 39). In this period numerous
attempts were made to solve the problem arising from the
unity of God and the divinity of Christ, without recourse to
a Logos christology. Some of the more unsuccessful of these
attempts have since been grouped under the heads of Dynamistic and of Modalistic Monarchianism (§ 40). At the same
time Montanism was excluded from the Church (§ 41), as
subversive of the distinction between the clergy and laity

and the established organs of the Church's government, which in the recent rise of a theory of the necessity of the episcopate (see above, § 27) had become important. In the administration of the penitential discipline (§ 42) the position of the clergy and the realization of a hierarchically organized Church was still further advanced, preparatory for the position of Cyprian. At the same time as these constitutional developments were taking place in the West, and especially in North Africa, there occurred in Egypt and Palestine a remarkable advance in doctrinal discussion, whereby the theology of the apologists was developed in the Catechetical School of Alexandria, especially under the leadership of Clement of Alexandria and Origen (§ 43). In this new speculation a vast mass of most fruitful theological ideas was built up, from which subsequent ages drew for the defence of the traditional faith, but some of which served as the basis of new and startling heresies. Corresponding to the intellectual development within the Church was the last phase of Hellenic philosophy, known as Neo-Platonism (§ 44), which subsequently came into bitter conflict with the Church.

§ 38. The Easter Controversy and the Separation of Asia Minor from the West.

§ 39. The Religion of the West: Its Moral and Juristic Character.

§ 40. The Monarchian Controversies.

§ 41. Later Montanism and the Results of Its Exclusion from the Church.

§ 42. The Penitential Discipline.

§ 43. The Catechetical School of Alexandria: Clement and Origen.

§ 44. The End of Ancient Philosophy in Neo-Platonism.

§ 38. The Easter Controversy and the Separation of
the Churches of Asia Minor from
the Western Churches

The Church grew up with only a loose form of organization. Each local congregation was for a while autonomous,
and it was the local constitution that first took a definite and
fixed form. In the first centuries local customs naturally varied, and conflicts were sure to arise when various hitherto
isolated churches came into closer contact and the sense of
solidarity deepened. The first clash of opposing customs occurred over the date of Easter, as to which marked differences existed between the churches of Asia Minor, at that
time the most flourishing part of the Church, and the churches
of the West, especially with the church of Rome, the strongest
local church of all. The course of the controversy is sufficiently stated in the following selection from Eusebius. The
outcome was the practical isolation of the churches of Asia
Minor for many years. The controversy was not settled, and
the churches of Asia Minor did not again play a prominent
part in the Church until the time of Constantine and the
Council of Nicæa, 325 (see § 62, b), although a provisional adjustment of the difficulty, so far as the West was concerned,
took place shortly before, at the Council of Arles (see § 62, a, 2).

Eusebius, *Hist. Ec.*, V, 23, 24. (MSG, 20: 489.) Mirbt,
n. 22, and in Kirch, n. 78 *ff.*

A brief extract from the following may be found above in § 3 in a
somewhat different connection.

Ch. 23. At this time a question of no small importance
arose. For the parishes [*i. e.*, dioceses in the later sense of that
word] of all Asia, as from an older tradition, held that the
fourteenth day of the moon, being the day on which the Jews
were commanded to sacrifice the lamb, should be observed
as the feast of the Saviour's passover, and that it was neces-

sary, therefore, to end their fast on that day, on whatever day of the week it might happen to fall. It was not, however, the custom of the churches elsewhere to end it at this time, but they observed the practice, which from apostolic tradition has prevailed to the present time, of ending the fast on no other day than that of the resurrection of the Saviour. Synods and assemblies of bishops were held on this account, and all with one consent, by means of letters addressed to all, drew up an ecclesiastical decree that the mystery of the resurrection of the Lord from the dead should be celebrated on no other day than on the Lord's Day, and that we should observe the close of the paschal fast on that day only. There is still extant a writing of those who were then assembled in Palestine, over whom Theophilus, bishop of the parish of Cæsarea, and Narcissus, Bishop of Jerusalem, presided; also another of those who were likewise assembled at Rome, on account of the same question, which bears the name of Victor; also of the bishops in Pontus, over whom Palmas, as the oldest, presided; and of the parishes in Gaul, of which Irenæus was bishop; and of those in Osrhoene and the cities there; and a personal letter of Bacchylus, bishop of the church in Corinth, and of a great many others who uttered one and the same opinion and judgment and cast the same vote. Of these, there was one determination of the question which has been stated.

Ch. 24. But the bishops of Asia, led by Polycrates, decided to hold fast to the customs handed down to them. He himself, in a letter addressed to Victor and the church of Rome, set forth the tradition which had come down to him as follows: "We observe the exact day, neither adding nor taking anything away. For in Asia, also, great lights have fallen asleep, which shall rise again on the day of the Lord's coming, when He shall come with glory from heaven and shall seek out all the saints. Of these were Philip, one of the twelve Apostles, who fell asleep at Hierapolis, and his two aged virgin daughters and his other daughter, who, having lived in the Holy

Spirit, rest at Ephesus; and, moreover, John, who reclined on the Lord's bosom, and being a priest wore the sacerdotal mitre, who was both a witness and a teacher; he fell asleep at Ephesus; and, further, Polycarp in Smyrna, both a bishop and a martyr. . . . All these observed the fourteenth day of the passover, according to the Gospel, deviating in no respect, but following the rule of faith. And I, Polycrates, do the same, the least of you all, according to the tradition of my relatives, some of whom I have closely followed. For seven of my relatives were bishops, and I am the eighth. And my relatives always observed the day when the people put away the leaven; I, therefore, am not affrighted by terrifying words. For those greater than I have said, We ought to obey God rather than men." . . . Thereupon[1] Victor, who was over the church of Rome, immediately attempted to cut off from the common unity the parishes of all Asia, with the churches that agreed with them, as being heterodox. And he published letters declaring that all the brethren there were wholly excommunicated. But this did not please all the bishops, and they besought him to consider the things of peace, of neighborly unity and love. Words of theirs are still extant, rather sharply rebuking Victor. Among these were Irenæus, who sent letters in the name of the brethren in Gaul, over whom he presided, and maintained that the mystery of the resurrection of the Lord should be observed only on the Lord's Day, yet he fittingly admonishes Victor that he should not cut off whole churches of God which observed the tradition of an ancient custom, and after many other words he proceeds as follows: "For the controversy is not merely concerning the day, but also concerning the very manner of the fast. For some think that they should fast one day, others two, yet others more; some, moreover, count their days as consisting of forty hours day and night. And this variety of observance has not originated in our times, but long before, in the days of our ancestors. It is likely that they did not

[1] From here text in Kirch, nn. 84 *ff*.

hold to strict accuracy, and thus was formed a custom for their posterity, according to their own simplicity and their peculiar method. Yet all these lived more or less in peace, and we also live in peace with one another; and the disagreement in regard to the fast confirms the agreement in the faith. . . . Among these were the elders [*i. e.*, bishops of earlier date] before Soter, who presided over the church which thou [Victor] now rulest. We mean Anicetus, and Pius, and Hyginus, and Telesphorus, and Sixtus. They neither observed it themselves nor did they permit others after them to do so. And yet, though they did not observe it, they were none the less at peace with those who came to them from the parishes in which it was observed, although this observance was more opposed to those who did not observe it. But none were ever cast out on account of this form, but the elders before thee, who did not observe it, sent the eucharist to those of the other parishes observing it. And when the blessed Polycarp was at Rome in the time of Anicetus, and they disagreed a little about certain other things, they immediately made peace with one another, not caring to quarrel over this point. For neither could Anicetus persuade Polycarp not to observe what he had always observed with John, the disciple of the Lord, and the other Apostles with whom he had associated; neither could Polycarp persuade Anicetus to observe it, as he said that he ought to follow the customs of the elders who had preceded him. But though matters were thus, they nevertheless communed together and Anicetus granted the eucharist in the church to Polycarp, manifestly as a mark of respect.[1] And they parted from each other in peace, maintaining the peace of the whole Church, both of those who observed and those who did not." Thus Irenæus, who was truly well named, became a peace-maker in this matter, exhorting and negotiating in this way for the peace of the churches. And he conferred by letter about this

---

[1] Probably the reference is to the privilege of celebrating the eucharist, and not merely the reception of the sacrament from the hands of Anicetus.

disputed question, not only with Victor, but also with most
of the other rulers of the churches.

§ 39. The Religion of the West : Its Moral and Juristic Character

In the writings of Tertullian a conception of Christianity
is quite fully developed according to which the Gospel was a
new law of life, with its prescribed holy seasons and hours
for prayer; its sacrifices, though as yet only sacrifices of
prayer; its fasts and almsgiving, which had propitiatory
effect, atoning for sins committed and winning merit with
God; its sacred rites, solemnly administered by an established
hierarchy; and all observed for the sake of a reward which
God in justice owed those who kept His commandments.
It is noticeable that already there is the same divided opinion
as to marriage, whereby, on the one hand, it was regarded as
a concession to weakness, a necessary evil, and, on the other,
a high and holy relation, strictly monogamous, and of abiding
worth.   The propitiatory and meritorious character of fasts
and almsgiving as laid down by Tertullian was developed
even further by Cyprian and became a permanent element
in the penitential system of the Church, ultimately affecting
its conception of redemption.

(*a*) Tertullian, *De Oratione*, 23, 25, 28. (MSL, 1 : 1298.)

Ch. 23. As to kneeling, also, prayer is subject to diversity
of observance on account of a few who abstain from kneeling
on the Sabbath.   Since this dissension is particularly on its
trial before the churches, the Lord will give His grace that
the dissentients may either yield or else follow their own
opinion without offence to the others.   We, however, as we
have received, only on the Sunday of the resurrection ought
to guard not only against this kneeling, but every posture and
office of anxiety; deferring even our businesses, lest we give
any place to the devil.   Similarly, too, the period of Pentecost,

is a time which we distinguish by the same solemnity of exultation. But who would hesitate every day to prostrate himself before God, at least in the first prayer with which we enter on the daylight? At fasts, moreover, and stations, no prayer should be made without kneeling and the remaining customary marks of humility. For then we are not only praying, but making supplication, and making satisfaction to our Lord God.

Ch. 25. Touching the time, however, the extrinsic observance of certain hours will not be unprofitable; those common hours, I mean, which mark the intervals of the day—the third, the sixth, the ninth—which we may find in Scripture to have been more solemn than the rest.

Ch. 28. This is the spiritual victim which has abolished the pristine sacrifices. . . . We are the true adorers and true priests, who, praying in the spirit, in the spirit sacrifice prayer, proper and acceptable to God, which, assuredly, He has required, which He has looked forward to for Himself. This victim, devoted from the whole heart, fed on faith, tended by truth, entire in innocence, pure in chastity, garlanded with love [agape], we ought to escort with the pomp of good works, amid psalms and hymns, unto God's altar, to obtain all things from God for us.

(b) Tertullian, *De Jejun.*, 3. (MSL, 2 : 100.)

The following is a characteristic statement of the meritorious and propitiatory character of fasting. See below, *h*, Cyprian.

Since He himself both commands fasting and calls a soul wholly shattered—properly, of course, by straits of diet—a sacrifice (Psalm 51 : 18), who will any longer doubt that of all macerations as to food the rationale has been this: that by a renewed interdiction of food and observance of the precept the primordial sin might now be expiated, so that man may make God satisfaction through the same causative material by which he offended, that is, by interdiction of food; and so, by way of emulation, hunger might rekindle, just as satiety had extinguished, salvation, contemning for the sake of one thing unlawful many things that are lawful?

(c) Tertullian, *De Baptismo*, 17. (MSL, 1 : 1326.)

It remains to put you in mind, also, of the due observance of giving and receiving baptism. The chief priest (*summus sacerdos*), who is the bishop, has the right of giving it; in the second place, the presbyters and deacons, yet not without the bishop's authority, on account of the honor of the Church. When this has been preserved, peace is preserved. Besides these, even laymen have the right; for what is equally received can be equally given. If there are no bishops, priests, or deacons, other disciples are called. The word of the Lord ought not to be hidden away by any. In like manner, also, baptism, which is equally God's property, can be administered by all; but how much more is the rule of reverence and modesty incumbent on laymen, since these things belong to their superiors, lest they assume to themselves the specific functions of the episcopate! Emulation of the episcopal office is the mother of schism.

(d) Tertullian, *De Pœnitentia*, 2. (MSL, 1 : 1340.)

How small is the gain if you do good to a grateful man, or the loss if to an ungrateful man! A good deed has God as its debtor, just as an evil deed has Him also; for the judge is a rewarder of every cause. Now, since God as judge presides over the exacting and maintaining of justice, which is most dear to Him, and since it is for the sake of justice that He appoints the whole sum of His discipline, ought one to doubt that, as in all our acts universally, so, also, in the case of repentance, justice must be rendered to God?

(e) Tertullian, *Scorpiace*, 6. (MSL, 2 : 157.)

If he had put forth faith to suffer martyrdoms, not for the contest's sake, but for its own benefit, ought it not to have had some store of hope, for which it might restrain its own desire and suspend its wish, that it might strive to mount up, seeing that they, also, who strive to discharge earthly functions are eager for promotion? Or how will there be many mansions in the Father's house, if not for a diversity of deserts? How, also, will one star differ from another star in glory, unless in virtue of a disparity of their rays?

(*f*) Tertullian, *Ad Uxorem*, I, 3; II, 8-10. (MSL, 1 : 1390, 1415.) *Cf*. Kirch, n. 181.

I, 3. There is no place at all where we read that marriages are prohibited; of course as a "good thing." What, however, is better than this "good," we learn from the Apostle in that he permits marriage, indeed, but prefers abstinence; the former on account of the insidiousness of temptations, the latter on account of the straits of the times (I Cor. 7 : 26). Now by examining the reason for each statement it is easily seen that the permission to marry is conceded us as a necessity; but whatever necessity grants, she herself deprecates. In fact, inasmuch as it is written, "It is better to marry than to burn" (I Cor. 7 : 9), what sort of "good" is this which is only commended by comparison with "evil," so that the reason why "marrying" is better is merely that "burning" is worse? Nay; but how much better is it neither to marry nor to burn?

II, 8. Whence are we to find adequate words to tell fully of the happiness of that marriage which the Church cements and the oblation[1] confirms, and the benediction seals; which the angels announce, and the Father holds for ratified? For even on earth children do not rightly and lawfully wed without their father's consent. What kind of yoke is that of two believers of one hope, one discipline, and the same service? The two are brethren, the two are fellow-servants; no difference of spirit or flesh; nay, truly, two in one flesh; where there is one flesh the spirit is one.

---

[1] Here, as elsewhere in Tertullian, the oblation, or sacrifice, or offering, is the prayers of the faithful, and not the eucharist.

(g) Tertullian, *De Monogamia*, 9, 10.   (MSL, 2 : 991 *f.*)

This work was written after Tertullian became a Montanist, and with other Montanists repudiated second marriage, to which reference is made in both passages.   But the teaching of the Church regarding remarriage after divorce was as Tertullian here speaks. The reference to offering at the end of ch. 10 does not refer to the eucharist, but to prayers.   See above, *Ad Uxorem*, ch. II, 8.

Ch. 9.   So far is it true that divorce "was not from the beginning" [*cf*. Matt. 19 : 8] that among the Romans it is not till after the six hundredth year after the foundation of the city that this kind of hardness of heart is recorded to have been committed.   But they not only repudiate, but commit promiscuous adultery; to us, even if we do divorce, it will not be lawful to marry.

Ch. 10.   I ask the woman herself, "Tell me, sister, have you sent your husband before in peace?"   What will she answer?   In discord?   In that case she is bound the more to him with whom she has a cause to plead at the bar of God. She is bound to another, she who has not departed from him. But if she say, "In peace," then she must necessarily persevere in that peace with him whom she will be no longer able to divorce; not that she would marry, even if she had been able to divorce him.   Indeed, she prays for his soul, and requests refreshment for him meanwhile, and fellowship in the first resurrection; and she offers on the anniversary of his falling asleep.

(h) Cyprian, *De Opere et Eleemosynis*, 1, 2, 5.   (MSL, 4 : 625.)

Cyprian, Bishop of Carthage (249–258), was the most important theologian and ecclesiastic between Tertullian and Augustine.   He developed the theology of the former especially in its ecclesiastical lines, and his idea of the Church was accepted by the latter as a matter beyond dispute.   His most important contributions to the development of the Church were his hierarchical conceptions, which became generally accepted as the basis of the episcopal organization of the Church (see below, §§ 46, 50, 51).   His writings, which are of great importance in the history of the Church, consist only of epistles and brief tracts.   His influence did much to determine the lines of development of the Western Church, and especially the church of North Africa.   With the following *cf. supra*, § 16.

Ch. 1. Many and great, beloved brethren, are the divine benefits wherewith the large and abundant mercy of God the Father and of Christ both has labored and is always laboring for our salvation: because the Father sent the Son to preserve us and give us life, that He might restore us; and the Son was willing to be sent and to become the son of man, that He might make us the sons of God. He humbled Himself that He might raise up the people who before were prostrate; He was wounded that He might heal our wounds; He served that He might draw to liberty those who were in bondage; He underwent death, that He might set forth immortality to mortals. These are many and great boons of compassion. But, moreover, what a providence, and how great the clemency, that by a plan of salvation it is provided for us that more abundant care should be taken for preserving man who has been redeemed! For when the Lord, coming to us, had cured those wounds which Adam had borne, and had healed the old poisons of the serpent, He gave a law to the sound man, and bade him sin no more lest a worse thing should befall the sinner. We had been limited and shut up in a narrow space by the commandment of innocence. Nor should the infirmity and weakness of human frailty have anything it might do, unless the divine mercy, coming again in aid, should open some way of securing salvation by pointing out works of justice and mercy, so that by almsgiving we may wash away whatever foulness we subsequently contract.

Ch. 2. The Holy Spirit speaks in the sacred Scriptures saying, "By almsgiving and faith sins are purged" [Prov. 16: 6]. Not, of course, those sins which had been previously contracted, for these are purged by the blood and sanctification of Christ. Moreover, He says again, "As water extinguishes fire, so almsgiving quencheth sin" [Eccles. 3 : 30]. Here, also, is shown and proved that as by the laver of the saving water the fire of Gehenna is extinguished, so, also, by almsgiving and works of righteousness the flame of sin is subdued. And because in baptism remission of sins is granted once and for all, constant and ceaseless labor, following the likeness of baptism, once again bestows the mercy of God. . . . The Lord also teaches this in the Gospel. . . . The Merciful One teaches and warns that works of mercy be performed; because He seeks to save those who at great cost He has redeemed, it is proper that those who after the grace of baptism have become foul can once more be cleansed.

Ch. 5. The remedies for propitiating God are given in the words of God himself. The divine instructions have taught sinners what they ought to do; that by works of righteousness God is satisfied, and with the merits of mercy sins are cleansed. . . . He [the angel Raphael, *cf.* Tobit. 12 : 8, 9] shows that our prayers and fastings are of little avail unless they are aided by almsgiving; that entreaties alone are of little force to obtain what they seek, unless they be made sufficient by the addition of deeds and good works. The angel reveals and manifests and certifies that our petitions become efficacious by almsgiving, that life is redeemed from dangers by almsgiving, that souls are delivered from death by almsgiving.

§ 40. THE MONARCHIAN CONTROVERSIES

Monarchianism is a general term used to include all the unsuccessful attempts of teachers within the Church to explain the divine element in Christ without doing violence to the doctrine of the unity of God, and yet without employing the Logos christology. These attempts were made chiefly between the latter part of the second century and the end of the third. They fall into classes accordingly as they regard the divine element in Christ as personal or impersonal. One class makes the divine element to be an impersonal power (Greek, dynamis) sent from God into the man Jesus; hence the term "Dynamistic Monarchians." The other class makes the divine element a person, without, however, making any personal distinction between Father and Son, only a difference in the mode in which the one divine person manifests Himself; hence the term "Modalistic Monarchians." By some the Dynamistic Monarchians have been called Adoptionists, because they generally taught that the man Jesus ultimately became the Son of God, not being such by nature but by "adoption." The name Adoptionist has been so long applied to a heresy of the eighth century, chiefly in Spain, that it leads to confusion to use the term in connection with Monarchianism. Furthermore, to speak of them as Dynamistic Monarchians groups them with other Monarchians, which is desirable. The most important school of Modalistic Monarchians was that of Sabellius, in which the Modalistic principle was developed so as to include the three persons of the Trinity.

The sources may be found collected and annotated in Hilgenfeld, *Ketzergeschichte*.

(A) *Dynamistic Monarchianism*

(*a*) Hippolytus, *Refut.*, VII, 35, 36. (MSG, 16 : 3342.)

Ch. 35. A certain Theodotus, a native of Byzantium, introduced a novel heresy, saying some things concerning the origin of the universe partly in keeping with the doctrines of the true Church, in so far as he admits that all things were created by God. Forcibly appropriating, however, his idea of Christ from the Gnostics and from Cerinthus and Ebion, he alleges that He appeared somewhat as follows: that Jesus was a man, born of a virgin, according to the counsel of the Father, and that after He had lived in a way common to all men, and had become pre-eminently religious, He afterward at His baptism in Jordan received Christ, who came from above and descended upon Him. Therefore miraculous powers did not operate within Him prior to the manifestation of that Spirit which descended and proclaimed Him as the Christ. But some [*i. e.*, among the followers of Theodotus] are disposed to think that this man never was God, even at the descent of the Spirit; whereas others maintain that He was made God after the resurrection from the dead.

Ch. 36. While, however, different questions have arisen among them, a certain one named Theodotus, by trade a money-changer [to be distinguished from the other Theodotus, who is commonly spoken of as Theodotus, the leather-worker], attempted to establish the doctrine that a certain Melchizedek is the greatest power, and that this one is greater than Christ. And they allege that Christ happens to be according to the likeness of this one. And they themselves, similarly with those who have been previously spoken of as adherents of Theodotus, assert that Jesus is a mere man, and that in conformity with the same account, Christ descended upon Him.

(b) *The Little Labyrinth.* in Eusebius, *Hist. Ec.*, V, 28. (MSG, 20 : 511.)

The author of *The Little Labyrinth*, a work from which Eusebius quotes at considerable length, is uncertain. It has been attributed to Hippolytus.

The Artemonites say that all early teachers and the Apostles themselves received and taught what they now declare, and that the truth of the preaching [*i. e.*, the Gospel] was preserved until the time of Victor, who was the thirteenth bishop in Rome after Peter, and that since his successor, Zephyrinus, the truth has been corrupted. What they say might be credible if first of all the divine Scriptures did not contradict them. And there are writings of certain brethren which are older than the times of Victor, and which they wrote in behalf of the truth against the heathen and against heresies of their time. I refer to Justin, Miltiades, Tatian, Clement, and others. In all of their works Christ is spoken of as God. For who does not know the works of Irenæus and of Melito and of others, which teach that Christ is God and man? And how many psalms and hymns, written by the faithful brethren from the beginning, celebrate Christ as the Word of God, speaking of Him as divine? How, then, since the Church's present opinion has been preached for so many years, can its preaching have been delayed, as they affirm, until the times of Victor? And how is it that they are not ashamed to speak thus falsely of Victor, knowing well that he cut off from communion Theodotus, the leather-worker, the leader and father of this God-denying apostasy, and the first to declare that Christ is mere man.

There was a certain confessor, Natalius, not long ago, but in our day. This man was deceived at one time by Asclepiodotus and another Theodotus, a certain money-changer. Both of them were disciples of Theodotus, the leatherworker, who, as I said, was the first person excommunicated by Victor, bishop at that time, on account of this senseless sentiment or, rather, senselessness. Natalius was persuaded by them to allow himself to be chosen bishop of this heresy with a salary, so that he was to receive from them one hundred and fifty *denarii* a month.

They have treated the divine Scriptures recklessly and without fear; they have set aside the rule of ancient faith; and Christ they have not known, not endeavoring to learn what the divine Scriptures declare, but striving laboriously after any form of syllogism which may be found to suit their impiety. And if any one brings before them a passage of divine Scripture, they see whether a conjunctive or a disjunctive form of syllogism can be made from it. And as being of the earth and speaking of the earth and as ignorant of Him that cometh from above, they devote themselves to geometry and forsake the holy writings of God. Euclid is at least laboriously measured by some of them; Aristotle and Theophrastus admired; and Galen, perhaps, by some is even worshipped. But that those who use the arts of unbelievers for their heretical opinion and adulterate the simple faith of the divine Scriptures by the craft of the godless are not near the faith, what need is there to say? Therefore, they have laid their hands boldly upon the divine Scriptures, alleging that they have corrected them. That I am not speaking falsely of them in this matter, whoever wishes can learn. For if any one will collect their respective copies and compare them with one another, he will find that they differ greatly.

(B) *Modalistic Monarchianism*

Additional source material: Hippolytus, *Adversus Noetum, Refutatio*, IX, 7 *ff.*, X, 27; Tertullian, *Adversus Praxean;* Basil, *Ep.* 207, 210. (PNF, ser. II, vol. VIII.)

(a) Hippolytus, *Refut.*, X, 27. (MSG, 16 : 3440.)

The following passages from the great work of Hippolytus give the earlier form of Modalistic Monarchianism. They are also of importance as being a part of the foundation for the statement of Harnack and others, that this heresy was the official Roman doctrine for some years. See also IX, 12, of which the text may be found in Kirch, nn. 201–206. The whole question as to the position of Callistus, or Calixtus, as bishop of Rome and his relations to the Church as a whole is difficult and full of obscurity, due to a large extent to the fact that the principal source for his history is the work of Hippolytus, who, as may easily be seen, was bitterly opposed to him.

Noetus, a Smyrnæan by birth, a reckless babbler and trickster, introduced this heresy, which originated with Epigonus, and was adopted by Cleomenes, and has thus continued to this day among his successors. Noetus asserts that there is one Father and God of the universe, and that He who had made all things was, when He wished, invisible to those who existed, and when He wished He became visible; that He is invisible when He is not seen and visible when He is seen; that the Father is unbegotten when He is not generated, but begotten when He is born of a virgin; that He is not subject to suffering and is immortal when He does not suffer and die, but when His passion came upon Him Noetus admits that the Father suffers and dies. The Noetians think that the Father is called the Son according to events at different times.

Callistus supported the heresy of these Noetians, but we have carefully described his life [see above, § 19, *c*]. And Callistus himself likewise produced a heresy, taking his starting-point from these Noetians. And he acknowledges that there is one Father and God, and that He is the Creator of the universe, and that He is called and regarded as Son by name, yet that in substance He is one.[1] For the Spirit as Deity is not, he says, any being different from the Logos, or the Logos from Deity; therefore, this one person is divided by name, but not according to substance. He supposes this one Logos to be God and he says that He became flesh. He is disposed to maintain that He who was seen in the flesh and crucified is Son, but it is the Father who dwells in Him.

(b) Hippolytus, *Refut.*, IX, 7, 11 f. (MSG, 16 : 3369.)

Ch. 7. There has appeared a certain one, Noetus by name, by birth a Smyrnæan. This person introduced from the tenets of Heraclitus a heresy. Now a certain Epigonus became his minister and pupil, and this person during his sojourn in Rome spread his godless opinion. . . . But Zephyrinus himself was in course of time enticed away and hurried headlong into the same opinion; and he had Callistus as his adviser and fellow-champion of these wicked tenets. . . . The school of these heretics continued in a succession of teachers to acquire strength and to grow because Zephyrinus and Callistus helped them to prevail.

Ch. 11. Now that Noetus affirms that the Son and the Father are the same, no one is ignorant. But he makes a statement as follows: "When, indeed, at the time the Father was not yet born, He was justly styled the Father; and when it pleased Him to undergo generation and to be begotten, He himself became His own Son, not another's." For in this manner he thinks he establishes the Monarchy, alleging that the Father and the Son, so called, are not from one another, but are one and the same, Himself from Himself, and that He is styled by the names Father and Son, according to the changes of times.

---

[1] The word substance as used here in connection with the nature of the Trinity has not taken its later meaning and use.

Ch. 12. Now Callistus brought forward Zephyrinus himself and induced him to avow publicly the following opinions: "I know that there is one God, Jesus Christ; and that excepting Him I do not know another begotten and capable of suffering." When he said, "The Father did not die but the Son," he would in this way continue to keep up ceaseless disturbance among the people. And we [i. e., Hippolytus], becoming aware of his opinions, did not give place to him, but reproved him and withstood him for the truth's sake. He rushed into folly because all consented to his hypocrisy; we, however, did not do so, and he called us worshippers of two gods, disgorging freely the venom lurking within him.

(c) Hippolytus, *Adversus Noetum*. (MSG, 10 : 804.)

The following is from a fragment which seems to be the conclusion of an extended work against various heresies.

Some others are secretly introducing another doctrine who have become the disciples of a certain Noetus, who was a native of Smyrna, and lived not very long ago. This man was greatly puffed up with pride, being inspired by the conceit of a strange spirit. He alleged that Christ was the Father himself, and that the Father himself was born and suffered and died. . . . When the blessed presbyters heard these things they summoned him before the Church and examined him. But he denied at first that he held such opinions. Afterward, taking shelter among some and gathering round him some others who had been deceived in the same way, he wished to maintain his doctrine openly. And the blessed presbyters summoned him and examined him. But he resisted, saying, "What evil, then, do I commit when I glorify Christ?" And the presbyters replied to him, "We, too, know in truth one God; we know Christ; we know that the Son suffered even as He suffered, and died even as He died, and rose again on the third day, and is at the right hand of the Father, and cometh to judge the living and the

dead. And these things which we have learned we assert."
Then, after refuting him, they expelled him from the Church.
And he was carried to such a pitch of pride that he established
a school.

Now they seek to exhibit the foundation of their dogma,
alleging that it is said in the Law, "I am the God of your
fathers; ye shall have no other gods beside me" [*i. e.*, of Moses,
cf. Ex. 3 : 6, 13; 20 : 3]; and again in another passage, "I
am the first and the last and besides me there is none other"
[*cf.* Is. 44 : 6]. Thus they assert that God is one. And then
they answer in this manner: "If therefore I acknowledge
Christ to be God, He is the Father himself, if He is indeed
God; and Christ suffered, being Himself God, and consequently
the Father suffered, for He was the Father himself."

(*d*) Tertullian, *Adv. Praxean*, 1, 2, 27, 29. (MSL, 2 : 177 *f.*,
214.)

Tertullian is especially bitter against Praxeas, because he prevented
the recognition of the Montanists at Rome when it seemed likely that
they would be treated favorably. The work *Adversus Praxean* is
the most important work of Western theology on the Trinity before
the time of Augustine. It was corrected in some important points by
Novatian, but its clear formulæ remained in Western theology permanently. The work belongs to the late Montanistic period of Tertullian.

Ch. 1. In various ways has the devil rivalled the truth.
Sometimes his aim has been to destroy it by defending it.
He maintains that there is one only Lord, the Almighty
Creator of the world, that of this doctrine of the unity he
may fabricate a heresy. He says that the Father himself
came down into the Virgin, was Himself born of her, Himself
suffered, indeed, was Himself Jesus Christ. . . . He [Praxeas]
was the first to import into Rome this sort of perversity, a
man of restless disposition in other respects, and above all
inflated with the pride of martyrdom [confessorship] simply
and solely because of a short annoyance in prison; when,
even if he had given his body to be burned, it would have

profited him nothing, not having the love of God, whose very gifts he resisted and destroyed. For after the Bishop of Rome had acknowledged the prophetic gifts of Montanus, Priscilla, and Maximilla, and in consequence of the acknowledgment had bestowed his peace on the churches of Asia and Phrygia, Praxeas, by importunately urging false accusations against the prophets themselves and their churches, and insisting on the authority of the bishop's predecessors in the see, compelled him to recall the letter of peace which he had issued, as well as to desist from his purpose of acknowledging the said gifts. Thus Praxeas did two pieces of the devil's work in Rome: he drove out prophecy and he brought in heresy; he put to flight the Paraclete and he crucified the Father.

Ch. 2. After a time, then, the Father was born, and the Father suffered—God himself, the Almighty, is preached as Jesus Christ.

Ch. 27. For, confuted on all sides by the distinction between the Father and the Son, which we make while their inseparable union remains as [by the examples] of the sun and the ray, and the fountain and the river—yet by help of their conceit of an indivisible number [with issues] of two and three, they endeavor to interpret this distinction in a way which shall nevertheless agree with their own opinions; so that, all in one person, they distinguish two—Father and Son—understanding the Son to be the flesh, that is the man, that is Jesus; and the Father to be the Spirit, that is God, that is Christ.

Ch. 29. Since we[1] teach in precisely the same terms that the Father died as you say the Son died, we are not guilty of blasphemy against the Lord God, for we do not say that He died after the divine nature, but only after the human. . . . They [the heretics], indeed, fearing to incur blasphemy against the Father, hope to diminish it in this way, admitting that the Father and the Son are two; but if the Son, indeed, suffers, the Father is His fellow-sufferer.

[1] *I. e.*, the followers of Praxeas, who are here introduced as speaking.

(e) *Formula Macrostichos*, in Socrates, *Hist. Ec.*, II, 19. (MSG, 67 : 229.)

In the Arian controversy several councils were held at Antioch in the endeavor to bring about a reconciliation of the parties. At the third council of Antioch, A. D. 345, the elaborate *Formula Macrostichos* was put forth, in which the council attempted to steer a middle course between the Sabellians, who identified the Father and the Son, and the extreme Arians, who made the Son a creature.

Text may also be found in Hahn, *op. cit.*, § 159.

Those who say that the Father, Son, and Holy Spirit are the same person, impiously understanding the three names to refer to one and the same person, we expel with good reason from the Church, because by the incarnation they subject the Father, who is infinite and incapable of suffering, to finitude and suffering in the incarnation. Such are those called Patripassianists by the Romans and Sabellians by us.

(f) Athanasius, *Orationes contra Arianos*, IV, 9, 25. (MSG, 26 : 480, 505.)

For Athanasius, *v. infra*, § 65, c. Of the four *Orations against the Arians*, attributed to Athanasius and placed between the years 356 and 362, doubts have been raised against the genuineness of the fourth. The following quotations are, in any case, valuable as setting forth the Sabellian position. But the case against the fourth oration has not been conclusively proved. In the passage from ch. 25 the statement is that of the Sabellians, not of Athanasius.

Ch. 9. If, again, the One have two names, this is the expedient of Sabellius, who said that Son and Father were the same and did away with both, the Father when there is a Son, and the Son when there is a Father. . . .

Ch. 25. "As there are diversities of gifts but the same Spirit, so also the Father is the same, but is dilated into Son and Spirit."

(g) Athanasius, *Expositio fidei*. (MSG, 25 : 204.)

For the critical questions regarding this little work of uncertain date see PNF, ser. II, vol. VI, p. 83.

For neither do we hold a Son-father, as do the Sabellians, calling Him of one but not of the same essence, and thus destroying the existence of the Son.

(*h*) Basil the Great, *Epistula* 210 : 3. (MSG, 32 : 772, 776.)

Basil the Great, Bishop of Cæsarea in Cappadocia, was one of the more important ecclesiastics of the fourth century, and the leader of the New-Nicene party in the Arian controversy. *V. infra*, § 66, *e*.

Sabellianism is Judaism imported into the preaching of the Gospel under the guise of Christianity. For if a man calls Father, Son, and Holy Spirit one, but manifold as to person [prosopon], and makes one hypostasis of the three, what else does he do than deny the everlasting pre-existence of the Only begotten? . . .

Now Sabellius did not even deprecate the formation of the persons without the hypostasis, saying, as he did, that the same God, being one in substance,[1] was metamorphosed as the need of the moment required and spoken of now as Father, now as the Son, and now as Holy Spirit.

§ 41. LATER MONTANISM AND THE CONSEQUENCES OF ITS EXCLUSION FROM THE CHURCH

In the West Montanism rapidly discarded the extravagant chiliasm of Montanus and his immediate followers; it laid nearly all the stress upon the continued work of the Holy Spirit in the Church and the need of a stricter moral discipline among Christians. This rigoristic discipline or morality was not acceptable to the bulk of Christians, and along with the Montanists was driven out of the Church, except in the case of the clergy, to whom a stricter morality was regarded as applicable. In this way a distinctive morality and mode of life came to be assigned to the clergy, and the separation between clergy and laity, or *ordo* and *plebs*, which was becoming

---

[1] Not οὐσίᾳ, but ὑποκειμένῳ.

established about the time of Tertullian, at least in the West, was permanently fixed. (See § 42, *d*.)

Tertullian, *De Exhortatione Castitatis*, 7. (MSL, 2 : 971.)

As a Montanist, Tertullian rejected second marriage, and in this treatise, addressed to a friend who had recently lost his wife, he treated it as the foulest adultery. This work belongs to the later years of Tertullian's life and incidentally reveals that a sharp distinction between clergy and laity was becoming fixed in the main body of the Church.

We should be foolish if we thought that what is unlawful for priests[1] is lawful for laics. Are not even we laics priests? It is written: "He has made us kings also, and priests to God and his Father." The authority of the Church has made the difference between order [*ordinem*] and the laity [*plebem*], and the honor has been sanctified by the bestowal of the order. Therefore, where there has been no bestowal of ecclesiastical order, you both offer and baptize and are a priest to yourself alone. But where there are three, there is the Church, though they are laics. . . . Therefore, if, when there is necessity, you have the right of a priest in yourself, you ought also to have the discipline of a priest where there is necessity that you have the right of a priest. As a digamist,[2] do you baptize? As a digamist, do you offer? How much more capital a crime it is for a digamist laic to act as a priest, when the priest, if he turn digamist, is deprived of the power of acting as a priest? . . . God wills that at all times we be so conditioned as to be fitted at all times and in all places to undertake His sacraments. There is one God, one faith, one discipline as well. So truly is this the case that unless the laics well observe the rules which are to guide the choice of presbyters, how will there be presbyters at all who are chosen from among the laics?

[1] *Sacerdotes*, and so throughout.
[2] A person married a second time, *i. e.*, after the death of his first wife.

§ 42. THE PENITENTIAL DISCIPLINE

In baptism the convert received remission of all former sins, and, what was equivalent, admission to the Church. If he sinned gravely after baptism, could he again obtain remission? In the first age of the Church the practice as to this question inclined toward rigorism, and the man who sinned after baptism was in many places permanently excluded from the Church (*cf.* Heb. 10 : 26, 27), or the community of those whose sins had been forgiven and were certain of heaven. By the middle of the second century the practice at Rome tended toward permitting one readmission after suitable penance (*a*). After this the penitential discipline developed rapidly and became an important part of the business of the local congregation (*b*). The sinner, by a long course of self-mortification and prayer, obtained the desired readmission (*c*). The Montanists, however, in accord with their general rigorism, would make it extremely hard, if not impossible, to obtain readmission or forgiveness. The body of the Church, and certainly the Roman church under the lead of its bishop, who relied upon Matt. 16 : 18, adopted a more liberal policy and granted forgiveness on relatively easy terms to even the worst offenders (*d*). The discipline grew less severe, because martyrs or confessors, according to Matt. 10 : 20, were regarded as having the Spirit, and therefore competent to speak for God and announce the divine forgiveness. These were accustomed to give "letters of peace," which were commonly regarded as sufficient to procure the immediate readmission of the offender (*e*), a practice which led to great abuse. One of the effects of the development of the penitential discipline was the establishment of a distinction between mortal and venial sins (*f*), the former of which were, in general, acts involving unchastity, shedding of blood, and apostasy, according to the current interpretation of Acts 15 : 29.

(a) Hermas, *Pastor*, Man. IV, 3 : 1.

For Hermas and the *Pastor*, *v. supra*, § 15.

I heard some teachers maintain, sir, that there is no other repentance than that which takes place when we descend into the waters and receive remission of our former sins. He said to me, That was sound doctrine which you heard; for that is really the case. For he who has received remission of his sins ought not to sin any more, but to live in purity. . . . The Lord, therefore, being merciful, has had mercy on the work of His hands, and has set repentance for them; and He has intrusted to me the power over this repentance. And therefore I say unto you that if any one is tempted by the devil, and sins after that great and holy calling in which the Lord has called His people to everlasting life, he has opportunity to repent but once. But if he should sin frequently after this, and then repent, to such a man his repentance will be of no avail, for with difficulty will he live.

(b) Tertullian. *Apology*, 39. (MSL, 1 : 532.)

We meet together as an assembly and congregation that, offering up prayer to God, with united force we may wrestle with Him in our prayers. . . . In the same place, also, exhortations are made, rebukes and sacred censures are administered. For with a great gravity is the work of judging carried on among us, as befits those who feel assured that they are in the sight of God; and you have the most notable example of judgment to come when any one has so sinned as to be severed from common union with us in prayer, in the congregation, and in all sacred intercourse.

(c) Tertullian, *De Pœnitentia*, 4, 9. (MSL, 2 : 1343, 1354.)

According to Bardenhewer, § 50 : 5, this work belongs to the Catholic period of Tertullian's literary activity. Text in part in Kirch, nn. 175 *ff*.

Ch. 4. As I live, saith the Lord, I prefer penance rather than death [*cf.* Ezek. 33 : 11]. Repentance, then, is life, since it is preferred to death. That repentance, O sinner like myself (nay, rather, less a sinner than myself, for I acknowledge my pre-eminence in sins), do you hasten to embrace as a shipwrecked man embraces the protection of some plank. This will draw you forth when sunk in the waves of sin, and it will bear you forward into the port of divine clemency.

Ch. 9. The narrower the sphere of action of this, the second and only remaining repentance, the more laborious is its probation; that it may not be exhibited in the conscience alone, but may likewise be performed in some act. This act, which is more usually expressed and commonly spoken of under the Greek name, exomologesis, whereby we confess our sins to the Lord, not indeed to Him as ignorant of them, but inasmuch as by confession a satisfaction is made; of confession repentance is born; by repentance God is appeased. And thus exomologesis is a discipline for man's prostration and humiliation, enjoining a demeanor calculated to move mercy. With regard, also, to the very dress and food, it commands one to lie in sackcloth and ashes, to cover the body as in mourning, to lay the spirit low in sorrow, to exchange for severe treatment the sins which he has committed; furthermore, to permit as food and drink only what is plain—not for the stomach's sake, but for the soul's; for the most part, however, to feed prayers on fastings, to groan, to weep, and make outcries unto the Lord our God; to fall prostrate before the presbyters and to kneel to God's dear ones; to enjoin on all the brethren to be ambassadors to bear his deprecatory supplication before God. All this exomologesis does, that it may enhance repentance, that it may honor the Lord by fear of danger, may, by itself, in pronouncing against the sinner stand in place of God's indignation, and by temporal mortification (I will not say frustrate, but rather) expunge eternal punishments.

(d) Tertullian, *De Pudicitia*, 1, 21, 22. (MSL, 2 : 1032, 1078.)

Callistus, to whom reference is made in the first chapter, was bishop of Rome 217 to 222. The work, therefore, belongs to the latest period of Tertullian's life.

Ch. 1. I hear that there has been an edict set forth, and, indeed, a peremptory one; namely, that the Pontifex Maximus, the bishop of bishops, issues an edict: "I remit to such as have performed penance, the sins both of adultery and fornication."

Ch. 21. "But," you say, "the Church has the power of forgiving sins." This I acknowledge and adjudge more, I, who have the Paraclete himself in the person of the new prophets, saying: "The Church has the power to forgive sins, but I will not do it, lest they commit still others." . . . I now inquire into your opinion, to discover from what source you usurp this power to the Church.

If, because the Lord said to Peter, "Upon this rock I will build My Church [Matt. 16 : 18] . . . To Thee I have given the keys of the kingdom of heaven," or "Whatsoever thou shalt bind or loose on earth, shall be bound or loosed in heaven," you therefore presume that the power of binding and loosing has descended to you, that is, to every church akin to Peter; what sort of man, then, are you, subverting and wholly changing the manifest intention of the Lord, who conferred the gift personally upon Peter? "On Thee," He says, "I will build my Church," and "I will give thee the keys," not to the Church; and "whatsoever thou shalt have loosed or bound," not what they shall have loosed or bound. For so the result actually teaches. In him (Peter) the Church was reared, that is, through him (Peter) himself; he himself tried the key; you see what key: "Men of Israel, let what I say sink into your ears; Jesus, the Nazarene, a man appointed of God for you,"[1] and so forth. Peter himself, therefore, was the first to unbar, in Christ's baptism, the entrance to the kingdom of heaven, in which are loosed the sins that aforetime were bound. . . .

[1] *Cf.* Acts 2 : 22.

What, now, has this to do with the Church and your Church, indeed, O Psychic? For in accordance with the person of Peter, it is to spiritual men that this power will correspondingly belong, either to an Apostle or else to a prophet. . . . And accordingly the "Church," it is true, will forgive sins; but it will be the Church of the Spirit, by a spiritual man; not the Church which consists of a number of bishops.

Ch. 22. But you go so far as to lavish this power upon martyrs indeed; so that no sooner has any one, acting on a preconceived arrangement, put on soft bonds in the nominal custody now in vogue, than adulterers beset him, fornicators gain access to him; instantly prayers resound about him; instantly pools of tears of the polluted surround him; nor are there any who are more diligent in purchasing entrance to the prison than they who have lost the fellowship of the Church. . . . Whatever authority, whatever reason, restores ecclesiastical peace to the adulterer and the fornicator, the same will be bound to come to the aid of the murderer and the idolater in their repentance.

(e) Tertullian, *Ad Martyres*, 1. (MSL, 1 : 693.)

The following extract from Tertullian's little work addressed to martyrs in prison, written about 197, shows that in his earlier life as a Catholic Christian he did not disapprove of the practice of giving *libelli pacis* by the confessors, a custom which in his more rigoristic period under the influence of Montanism he denounced most vehemently; see preceding extract from *De Pudicitia*, ch. 22. The reference to some discord among the martyrs is not elsewhere explained. For *libelli pacis*, see Cyprian, *Ep.* 10 (=*Ep.* 15), 22 (=21).

O blessed ones, grieve not the Holy Spirit, who has entered with you into the prison; for if He had not gone with you there, you would not be there to-day. Therefore endeavor to cause Him to remain with you there; so that He may lead you thence to the Lord. The prison, truly, is the devil's house as well, wherein he keeps his family. . . . Let him not be successful in his own kingdom by setting you at variance with one another, but let him find you armed and fortified with concord; for your peace is war with him. Some, not able to find peace in the Church, have been accustomed to seek it from the imprisoned martyrs. Therefore you ought to have it dwelling with you, and to cherish it and guard it, that you may be able, perchance, to bestow it upon others.

(f) Tertullian, *De Pudicitia*, 19. (MSL, 2 : 1073.)

The distinction between mortal and venial sins became of great importance in the administration of penance and remained as a feature of ecclesiastical discipline from the time of Tertullian. The origin of the distinction was still earlier. See above, an extract from the same work.

We ourselves do not forget the distinction between sins, which was the starting-point of our discussion. And this, too, for John has sanctioned it [*cf.* I John 5 : 16], because there are some sins of daily committal to which we are all liable; for who is free from the accident of being angry unjustly and after sunset; or even of using bodily violence; or easily speaking evil; or rashly swearing; or forfeiting his plighted word; or lying from bashfulness or necessity? In business, in official duties, in trade, in food, in sight, in hearing, by how great temptations are we assailed! So that if there were no pardon for such simple sins as these, salvation would be unattainable by any. Of these, then, there will be pardon through the successful Intercessor with the Father, Christ. But there are other sins wholly different from these, graver and more destructive, such as are incapable of pardon—murder, idolatry, fraud, apostasy, blasphemy, and, of course, adultery and fornication and whatever other violation of the temple of God there may be. For these Christ will no more be the successful Intercessor; these will not at all be committed by any one who has been born of God, for he will cease to be the son of God if he commit them.

§ 43. The Catechetical School of Alexandria: Clement
and Origen

Three types of theology developed in the ante-Nicene
Church: the Asia Minor school, best represented by Irenæus
(v. § 33); the North African, represented by Tertullian and
Cyprian (v. § 39); and the Alexandrian, in the Catechetical
School of which Clement and Origen were the most distinguished members. In the Alexandrian theology the tradition
of the apologists (v. § 32) that Christianity was a revealed
philosophy was continued, especially by Clement. Origen,
following the bent of his genius, developed other sides of
Christian thought as well, bringing it all into a more systematic form than had ever before been attempted. The
Catechetical School of Alexandria was the most celebrated of
all the educational institutions of Christian antiquity. It
aimed to give a general secular and religious training. It
appears to have been in existence well before the end of the
second century, having been founded, it is thought, by Pantænus. Clement assisted in the instruction from 190, and
from about 200 was head of the school for a few years. In
202 or 203 he was forced by persecution under Septimius
Severus to flee from the city. He died before 215. Of his
works, the most important is his three-part treatise composed
of his *Protrepticus*, an apologetic work addressed to the Greeks;
his *Pædegogus*, a treatise on Christian morality; and his
Stromata, or miscellanies. Origen became head of the Catechetical School in 203, when but eighteen years old, and
remained in that position until 232, when, having been irreg-
ularly ordained priest outside his own diocese and being suspected of heresy, he was deposed. But he removed to Cæsarea
in Palestine, where he continued his work with the greatest
success and was held in the highest honor by the Church in
Palestine and parts other than Egypt. He died 254 or 255 at
Tyre, having previously suffered severely in the Decian perse-

cution. His works are of the highest importance in various fields of theology. *De Principiis* is the first attempt to present in connected form the whole range of Christian theology. His commentaries cover nearly the entire Bible. His *Contra Celsum* is the greatest of all early apologies. The *Hexapla* was the most elaborate piece of text-criticism of antiquity.

Additional source material: Eusebius, *Hist. Ec.*, VI, deals at length with Origen; Gregory Thaumaturgus, *Panegyric on Origen*, in ANF, VI.

(a) Clement of Alexandria, *Stromata*, I, 5. (MSG, 8 : 717.)

Clement's view of the relation of Greek philosophy to Christian revelation is almost identical with that of the apologists, as are also many of his fundamental concepts.

Before the advent of the Lord philosophy was necessary to the Greeks for righteousness. And now it becomes useful to piety, being a kind of preparatory training to those who attain to faith through demonstration. "For thy foot," it is said, "will not stumble" if thou refer what is good, whether belonging to the Greeks or to us, to Providence. For God is the cause of all good things; but of some primarily, as of the Old and the New Testament, and of others by consequence, as philosophy. Perchance, too, philosophy was given to the Greeks directly till the Lord should call the Greeks also. For this was a schoolmaster to bring the Hellenic mind to Christ, as was the law to bring the Hebrews. Philosophy, therefore, was a preparation, paving the way for him who is perfected in Christ.

"Now," says Solomon, "defend wisdom, and it will exalt thee, and it will shield thee with a crown of pleasure." [1] For when thou hast strengthened wisdom with a breastwork by philosophy, and with expenditure, thou wilt preserve her unassailable by sophists. The way of truth is therefore one. But into it, as into a perennial river, streams flow from every side.

[1] Proverbs 4 : 8, 9.

(b) Clement of Alexandria, *Stromata*, VII, 10. (MSG, 9 : 47.)

See Clement of Alexandria, *VIIth Book of the Stromateis*, ed. by Hort and Mayor, London, 1902. In making faith suffice for salvation, Clement clearly distinguishes his position from that of the Gnostics, though he uses the term "gnostic" as applicable to Christians. See next passage.

Knowledge [gnosis], so to speak, is a perfecting of man as man, which is brought about by acquaintance with divine things; in character, life, and word harmonious and consistent with itself and the divine Word. For by it faith is made perfect, inasmuch as it is solely by it that the man of faith becomes perfect. Faith is an internal good, and without searching for God confesses His existence and glorifies Him as existent. Hence by starting with this faith, and being developed by it, through the grace of God, the knowledge respecting Him is to be acquired as far as possible. . . .

But it is not doubting, in reference to God, but believing, that is the foundation of knowledge. But Christ is both the foundation and the superstructure, by whom are both the beginning and the end. And the extreme points, the beginning and the end, I mean faith and love, are not taught. But knowledge, which is conveyed from communication through the grace of God as a deposit, is intrusted to those who show themselves worthy of it; and from it the worth of love beams forth from light to light. For it is said, "To him that hath shall be given" [cf. Matt. 13 : 12]—to faith, knowledge; and to knowledge, love; and to love, the inheritance. . . .

Faith then is, so to speak, a compendious knowledge of the essentials; but knowledge is the sure and firm demonstration of what is received by faith, built upon faith by the Lord's teaching, conveying us on to unshaken conviction and certainty. And, as it seems to me, the first saving change is that from heathenism to faith, as I said before; and the second, that from faith to knowledge. And this latter passing on to love, thereafter gives a mutual friendship between that which knows and that which is known.   And perhaps he who has already arrived at this stage has attained equality with the angels.   At any rate, after he has reached the final ascent in the flesh, he still continues to advance, as is fit, and presses on through the holy Hebdomad into the Father's house, to that which is indeed the Lord's abode.

(c) Clement of Alexandria, *Stromata*, V, 11.   (MSG, 9 : 102, 106.)

The piety of the Christian Gnostic.

The sacrifice acceptable with God is unchanging alienation from the body and its passions.   This is the really true piety. And is not philosophy, therefore, rightly called by Socrates the meditation on death?   For he who neither employs his eyes in the exercise of thought nor draws from his other senses, but with pure mind applies himself to objects, practises the true philosophy. . . .

It is not without reason, therefore, that in the mysteries which are to be found among the Greeks lustrations hold the first place; as also the laver among the barbarians. After these are the minor mysteries, which have some foundation for instruction and preparation for what is to follow. In the great mysteries concerning the universe nothing remains to be learned, but only to contemplate and comprehend with the mind nature and things.   We shall understand the more of purification by confession, and of contemplation by analysis, advancing by analysis to the first notion, beginning with the properties underlying it; abstracting from the body its physical properties, taking away the dimension of depth, then of breadth, and then of length.   For the point which remains is a unit, so to speak, having position; from which, if we abstract position, there is the conception of unity.

If, then, we abstract all that belongs to bodies and things called incorporeal, we cast ourselves into the greatness of Christ, and thence advancing into immensity by holiness, we may reach somehow to the conception of the Almighty, knowing not what He is, but knowing what He is not. And form and motion, or standing, or a throne or place, or right hand or left, are not at all to be conceived as belonging to the Father of the universe, although it is so written. For what each of these signifies will be shown in the proper place. The First Cause is not then in space, but above time and space and name and conception.

(d) Origen, *De Principiis*, I, 2 : 2. (MSG, 11 : 130.)

Origen's doctrine of the "eternal generation of the Son" was of primary importance in all subsequent discussions on the Trinity.

Let no one imagine that we mean anything unsubstantial when we call Him the Wisdom of God; or suppose, for example, that we understand Him to be, not a living being endowed with wisdom, but something which makes men wise, giving itself to, and implanting itself in, the minds of those who are made capable of receiving its virtues and intelligence. If, then, it is once rightly understood that the only begotten Son of God is His Wisdom hypostatically [substantialiter] existing, I know not whether our mind ought to advance beyond this or entertain any suspicion that the hypostasis or substantia contains anything of a bodily nature, since everything corporeal is distinguished either by form, or color, or magnitude. And who in his sound senses ever sought for form, or color, or size, in wisdom, in respect of its being wisdom? And who that is capable of entertaining reverential thoughts or feelings regarding God can suppose or believe that God the Father ever existed, even for a moment of time, without having generated this Wisdom? For in that case he must say either that God was unable to generate Wisdom before He produced her, so that He afterward called into being that which formerly did not exist, or that He could, but—what is impious to say of God—was unwilling to generate; both of which suppositions, it is patent to all, are alike absurd and impious: for they amount to this, either that God advanced from a condition of inability to one of ability, or that, although possessed of the power, He concealed it, and delayed the generation of Wisdom. Therefore we have always held that God is the Father of His only begotten Son, who was born indeed of Him, and derives from Him, what He is, but without any beginning, not only such as may be measured by any divisions of time, but even that which the mind alone contemplates within itself, or beholds, so to speak, with the naked soul and understanding. And therefore we must believe that Wisdom was generated before any beginning that can be either comprehended or expressed.

(e) Origen, *De Principiis*, I, 2 : 10. (MSG, 11 : 138.)

Origen's doctrine of "eternal creation" was based upon reasoning similar to that employed to show the eternal generation of the Son, but it was rejected by the Church, and figures among the heresies known as Origenism. See below, §§ 87, 93.

As no one can be a father without having a son, nor a master without possessing a servant, so even God cannot be called omnipotent[1] unless there exists those over whom He may exercise His power; and therefore, that God may be shown to be almighty it is necessary that all things should exist. For if any one assumes that some ages or portions of time, or whatever else he likes to call them, have passed away, while those things which have been made did not yet exist, he would undoubtedly show that during those ages or periods God was not omnipotent but became omnipotent afterward: viz., from the time that He began to have those over whom He exercised power; and in this way He will appear to have received a certain increase, and to have risen from a lower to a higher condition; since there can be no doubt that it is better for Him to be omnipotent than not to be so. And, now, how can it appear otherwise than absurd, that when God possessed none of those things which it was befitting for Him to possess, He should afterward, by a kind

[1] *I. e.*, having rule over all, not merely able to do all, and so throughout.

of progress, come to have them? But if there never was a time when He was not omnipotent,[1] of necessity those things by which He receives that title must also exist; and He must always have had those over whom He exercised power, and which were governed by Him either as king or prince, of which we shall speak more fully when we come to discuss the subject of creatures.

(*f*) Origen, *De Principiis*, II, 9 : 6. (MSG, 11 : 230.)

The theory of pre-existence and the pretemporal fall of each soul was the basis of Origen's theodicy. It caused great offence in after years when theology became more stereotyped, and it has retained no place in the Church's thought, for the idea ran too clearly counter to the biblical account of the Fall of Adam.

We have frequently shown by those statements which we are able to adduce from the divine Scriptures that God, the Creator of all things, is good, and just, and all-powerful. When in the beginning He created all those beings whom He desired to create, *i. e.*, rational natures, He had no other reason for creating them than on account of Himself, *i. e.*, His goodness. As He himself, then, was the cause of the existence of those things which were to be created, in whom there was neither any variation nor change nor want of power, He created all whom He made equal and alike, because there was no reason for Him to produce variety and diversity. But since those rational creatures themselves, as we have frequently shown and will yet show in the proper place, were endowed with the power of free choice, this freedom of his will incited each one either to progress by imitation of God or induced him to failure through negligence. And this, as we have already stated, is the cause of the diversity among rational creatures, deriving its origin not from the will or judgment of the Creator, but from the freedom of the individual will. God, however, who deemed it just to arrange His creatures according to merit, brought down these differ-

[1] The Greek is preserved here and throws light on the reasoning. The Latin *omnipotens* stands for παντοκράτωρ.

ences of understanding into the harmony of one world, that
He might adorn, as it were, one dwelling, in which there
ought to be not only vessels of gold and silver, but also of
wood and clay and some, indeed, to honor and others to dishonor, with those different vessels, or souls, or understandings.   And these are the causes, in my opinion, why that
world presents the aspect of diversity, while Divine Providence
continues to regulate each individual according to the variety
of his movements or of his feelings and purpose.   On which
account the Creator will neither appear to be unjust in dis-
tributing (for the causes already mentioned) to every one
according to his merits; nor will the happiness or unhappi-
ness of each one's birth, or whatever be the condition that
falls to his lot, be deemed accidental; nor will different cre-
ators, or souls of different natures, be believed to exist.

(g) Origen, *Homil. in Exod.*, VI, 9.   (MSG, 12 : 338.)

In the following passage from Origen's *Commentary on Exodus*
and the four following passages are stated the essential points of
Origen's theory of redemption.   In this theory there are two elements
which have been famous in the history of Christian thought: the relation of the death of Christ to the devil, and the ultimate salvation of
every soul.   The theory that Christ's death was a ransom paid to the
devil was developed by Gregory of Nyssa and Gregory the Great,
and reappeared constantly in theology down to the scholastic period,
when it was overthrown by Anselm and the greater scholastics.
Universal redemption or salvation, especially when it included Satan
himself, was never taken up by Church theologians to any extent,
and was one of the positions condemned as Origenism.   See § 93.

It is certain, they say, that one does not buy that which
is his own.   But the Apostle says: "Ye are bought with a
price."   But hear what the prophet says: "You have been
sold as slaves to your sins, and for your iniquities I have
put away your mother."   Thou seest, therefore, that we are
the creatures of God, but each one has been sold to his sins,
and has fallen from his Creator.   Therefore we belong to God,
inasmuch as we have been created by Him, but we have
become the servants of the devil, inasmuch as we have been

sold to our sins. But Christ came to redeem us when we were servants to that master to whom we had sold ourselves by sinning.

(h) Origen, *Contra Celsum*, VII, 17. (MSG, 11 : 1445.)

If we consider Jesus in relation to the divinity that was in Him, the things which He did in this capacity are holy and do not offend our idea of God; and if we consider Him as a man, distinguished beyond all others by an intimate communion with the very Word, with Absolute Wisdom, He suffered as one who was wise and perfect whatever it behooved Him to suffer, who did all for the good of the human race, yea, even for the good of all intelligent beings. And there is nothing absurd in the fact that a man died, and that his death was not only an example of death endured for the sake of piety, but also the first blow in the conflict which is to overthrow the power of the evil spirit of the devil, who had obtained dominion over the whole world. For there are signs of the destruction of his empire; namely, those who through the coming of Christ are everywhere escaping from the power of demons, and who after their deliverance from this bondage in which they were held consecrate themselves to God, and according to their ability devote themselves day by day to advancement in a life of piety.

(i) Origen, *Homil. in Matt.*, XVI, 8. (MSG, 13 : 1398.)

He did this in service of our salvation so far that He gave His soul a ransom for many who believed on Him. If all had believed on Him, He would have given His soul as a ransom for all. To whom did He give His soul as a ransom for many? Certainly not to God. Then was it not to the Evil One? For that one reigned over us until the soul of Jesus was given as a ransom for us. This he had especially demanded, deceived by the imagination that he could rule over it, and he was not mindful of the fact that he could not endure the torment connected with holding it fast. Therefore death, which appeared to reign over Him, did not reign over Him, since He was "free among the dead" and stronger than the power of death. He is, indeed, so far superior to it that all who from among those overcome by death will follow Him can follow Him, as death is unable to do anything against them. . . . We are therefore redeemed with the precious blood of Jesus. As a ransom for us the soul of the Son of God has been given (not His spirit, for this, according to Luke [cf. Luke 23 : 46] He had previously given to His Father, saying: "Father, into Thy hands I commit my spirit"); also, not His body, for concerning this we find nothing mentioned. And when He had given His soul as a ransom for many, He did not remain in the power of him to whom the ransom was given for many, because it says in the sixteenth psalm [Psalm 16 : 10]: "Thou wilt not leave my soul in hell."

(j) Origen, *De Principiis*, I, 6 : 3.   (MSG, 11 : 168.)

The following states in brief the theory of universal salvation.

It is to be borne in mind, however, that certain beings who fell away from that one beginning of which we have spoken, have given themselves to such wickedness and malice as to be deemed altogether undeserving of that training and instruction by which the human race while in the flesh are trained and instructed with the assistance of the heavenly powers: they continue, on the contrary, in a state of enmity and opposition to those who are receiving this instruction and teaching. And hence it is that the whole life of mortals is full of certain struggles and trials, caused by the opposition and enmity against us of those who fell from a better condition without at all looking back, and who are called the devil and his angels, and other orders of evil, which the Apostle classed among the opposing powers. But whether any of these orders, who act under the government of the devil and obey his wicked commands, will be able in a future world to be converted to righteousness because of their possessing the faculty of freedom of will, or whether persistent and

inveterate wickedness may be changed by habit into a kind
of nature, you, reader, may decide; yet so that neither in
those things which are seen and temporal nor in those which
are unseen and eternal one portion is to differ wholly from
the final unity and fitness of things. But in the meantime,
both in those temporal worlds which are seen, and in those
eternal worlds which are invisible, all those beings are
arranged according to a regular plan, in the order and degree
of merit; so that some of them in the first, others in the
second, some even in the last times, after having undergone
heavier and severer punishments, endured for a lengthened
period and for many ages, so to speak, improved by this stern
method of training, and restored at first by the instruction
of angels and subsequently advanced by powers of a higher
grade, and thus advancing through each stage to a better
condition, reach even to that which is invisible and eternal,
having travelled by a kind of training through every single
office of the heavenly powers. From which, I think, this will
follow as an inference—that every rational nature can, in
passing from one order to another, go through each to all,
and advance from all to each, while made the subject of various
degrees of proficiency and failure, according to its own actions
and endeavors, put forth in the enjoyment of its power of
freedom of will.

(*k*) Origen, *De Principiis*, IV, 9–15. (MSG, 11 : 360, 363,
373.)

Allegorism.
The method of exegesis known as allegorism, whereby the specula-
tions of the Christian theologians were provided with an apparently
scriptural basis, was taken over from the Jewish and Greek philosophers and theologians who employed it in the study of their sacred
books. Origen, it should be added, contributed not a little to a sound
grammatical interpretation as well. For Porphyry's criticism of
Origen's methods of exegesis see Eusebius, *Hist. Ec.*, VI, 19.

Ch. 9. Now the cause, in all the points previously enu-
merated, of the false opinions and of the impious statements

or ignorant assertions about God appears to be nothing else than that the Scriptures are not understood according to their spiritual meaning, but are interpreted according to the mere letter. And therefore to those who believe that the sacred books are not the compositions of men, but were composed by the inspirations of the Holy Spirit, according to the will of the Father of all things through Jesus Christ, and that they have come down to us, we must point out the modes of interpretation which appear correct to us, who cling to the standard of the heavenly Church according to the succession of the Apostles of Jesus Christ. Now that there are certain mystical economies made known in the Holy Scriptures, all, even the most simple of those who adhere to the word, have believed; but what these are, the candid and modest confess they know not. If, then, one were to be perplexed about the incest of Lot with his daughters, and about the two wives of Abraham, and the two sisters married to Jacob, and the two handmaids who bore him children, they can return no other answer than this—that these are mysteries not understood by us. . . .

Ch. 11. The way, then, as it seems to me, in which we ought to deal with the Scriptures and extract from them their meaning is the following, which has been ascertained from the sayings [of the Scriptures] themselves. By Solomon in the Proverbs we find some rule as this enjoined respecting the teaching of the divine writings, "And do thou portray them in a threefold manner, in counsel and knowledge, to answer words of truth to them who propose them to thee" [cf. Prov. 22 : 20 f., LXX]. One ought, then, to portray the ideas of Holy Scripture in a threefold manner upon his soul, in order that the simple man may be edified by the "flesh," as it were, of Scripture, for so we name the obvious sense; while he who has ascended a certain way may be edified by the "soul," as it were. The perfect man, and he who resembles those spoken of by the Apostle, when he says, "We speak wisdom among them that are perfect, but not the wisdom of the world, nor of the rulers of this world, who come to nought; but we speak the wisdom of God in a mystery, the hidden wisdom, which God hath ordained before the ages unto our glory" [I Cor. 2 : 6, 7], may receive edification from the spiritual law, which was a shadow of things to come. For as man consists of body and soul and spirit, so in the same way does the Scripture consist, which has been arranged by God for the salvation of men.

Ch. 12. But as there are certain passages which do not contain at all the "corporeal" sense, as we shall show in the following, there are also places where we must seek only for the "soul," as it were, and "spirit" of Scripture.

Ch. 15. But since, if the usefulness of the legislation and the sequence and beauty of the history were universally evident, we should not believe that any other thing could be understood in the Scriptures save what was obvious, the Word of God has arranged that certain stumbling-blocks, and offences, and impossibilities, should be introduced into the midst of the law and the history, in order that we may not, through being drawn away in all directions by the merely attractive nature of the language, either altogether fall away from the true doctrines, as learning nothing worthy of God, or, by not departing from the letter, come to the knowledge of nothing more divine. And this, also, we must know: that, since the principal aim is to announce the "spiritual" connection in those things that are done and that ought to be done where the Word found that things done according to the history could be adapted to these mystic senses, He made use of them, concealing from the multitude the deeper meaning; but where in the narrative of the development of supersensual things there did not follow the performance of those certain events which was already indicated by the mystical meaning the Scripture interwove in the history the account of some event that did not take place, sometimes what could not have happened; sometimes what could, but did not happen. . . . And at other times impossibilities are recorded for the sake of the more skilful and inquisitive, in order that they may give themselves to the toil of investigation of what is written, and thus attain to a becoming conviction of the manner in which a meaning worthy of God must be sought out in such subjects.

§ 44.   NEO-PLATONISM

The last phase of Hellenic philosophy was religious. It aimed to combine the principles of many schools of the earlier period and to present a metaphysical system that would at once give a theory of being and also furnish a philosophical basis for the new religious life. This final philosophy of the antique world was Neo-Platonism. It was thoroughly eclectic in its treatment of earlier systems, but under Plotinus attained no small degree of consistency. The emphasis was laid especially upon the religious problems, and in the system it may be fairly said that the religious aspirations of heathenism found their highest and purest expression. Because it was in close touch with current culture and in its metaphysical principles was closely akin to the philosophy of the Church teachers, we find Neo-Platonism sometimes a bitter rival of Christianity, at other times a preparation for the Christian faith, as in the case of Augustine and Victorinus.

Additional source material: *Select Works of Plotinus*, translated by Thomas Taylor, ed. G. R. S. Mead, London, 1909 (contains bibliography of other translations of Plotinus, including those in French and German together with a select list of works bearing on Neo-Platonism); *Select Works of Porphyry*, trans. by Thomas Taylor, London, 1823; Taylor translated much from all the Neo-Platonists, but his other books are very scarce. Porphyry's *Epistula ad Marcellam*, trans. by Alice Zimmern, London, 1896.

Porphyry, *Ep. ad Marcellam*, 16–19. *Porphyrii philosophi Platonici opuscula tria*, rec. A. Nauck, Leipsic, 1860.

The letter is addressed to Marcella by her husband, the philosopher Porphyry. It gives a good idea of the religious and ethical character of Neo-Platonism. For the metaphysical aspects see Plotinus, translated by T. Taylor. Porphyry was, after Plotinus, the greatest of the Neo-Platonists, and brought out most clearly those religious elements which were rivals to Christianity. His attack upon Christianity was keen and bitter, and he was consequently especially hated by the Christians. He died at Rome 304.

Ch. 16. You will honor God best when you form your soul to resemble him. This likeness is only by virtue; for only virtue draws the soul upward toward its own kind. There is nothing greater with God than virtue; but God is greater than virtue. But God strengthens him who does what is good; but of evil deeds a wicked demon is the instigator. Therefore the wicked soul flees from God and wishes that the foreknowledge of God did not exist; and from the divine law which punishes all wickedness it shrinks away completely. But a wise man's soul is in harmony with God, ever sees Him, ever is with Him. But if that which rules takes pleasure in that which is ruled, then God cares for the wise and provides for him; and therefore is the wise man blessed, because he is under the protection of God. It is not the discourses of the wise man which are honorable before God, but his works; for the wise man, even when he keeps silence, honors God, but the ignorant man, even in praying and sacrificing, dishonors the Divinity. So the wise man alone is a priest, alone is dear to God, alone knows how to pray.

Ch. 17. He who practises wisdom practises the knowledge of God; though not always in prayer and sacrifice, practising piety toward God by his works. For a man is not rendered agreeable to God by ruling himself according to the prejudices of men and the vain declamations of the sophists. It is the man himself who, by his own works, renders himself agreeable to God, and is deified by the conforming of his own soul to the incorruptible blessed One. And it is he himself who makes himself impious and displeasing to God, not suffering evil from God, for the Divinity does only what is good. It is the man himself who causes his evils by his false beliefs in regard to God. The impious is not so much he who does not honor the statues of the gods as he who mixes up with the idea of God the superstitions of the vulgar. As for thyself, do not hold any unworthy idea of God, of his blessedness or of his incorruptibility.

Ch. 18. The greatest fruit of piety is this—to honor the Deity according to our fatherland; not that He has need of anything, but His holy and happy Majesty invites us to offer Him our homage. Altars consecrated to God do no harm, and when neglected they render no help. But he who honors God as needing anything declares, without knowing it, that he is superior to God. Therefore it is not angering God that harms us, but not knowing God, for wrath is alien to God, because it is the product of the involuntary, and there is nothing involuntary in God. Do not then dishonor the Divinity by human false opinions, for thou wilt not thereby injure the Being enjoying eternal blessedness, from whose incorruptible nature every injury is repelled.

Ch. 19. But thou shouldest not think that I say these things when I exhort to the worship of God; for he who exhorts to this would be ridiculous; as if it were possible to doubt concerning this; and we do not worship Him aright doing this thing or thinking that about God.[1] Neither tears nor supplications turn God from His purpose; nor do sacrifices honor God, nor the multitude of offerings glorify God, but the godlike mind well governed enters into union with God. For like is of necessity joined to like. But the victims of the senseless crowd are food for the flames, and their offerings are the supplies for a licentious life to the plunderers of temples. But, as I have said to thee, let the mind within thee be the temple of God. This must be tended and adorned to become a fit dwelling for God.

[1] *I. e.*, it is not certain rites nor certain beliefs that give merit to our worship.

CHAPTER III.   THE FIRST GENERAL PERSECUTION AND
ITS CONSEQUENCES

On account of various principles of the Roman law, Christians were always liable to severe penalties, and parts of the
Church occasionally suffered fearfully. But it was only in
exceptional cases and sporadically that the laws were enforced. There was, accordingly, no prolonged and systematic
effort made to put down Christianity everywhere until the
reign of Decius (249–251). The renewed interest in heathen
religions and the revived patriotism in some circles occasioned
in 248 by the celebration of the thousandth anniversary of
the founding of Rome may have contributed to a renewal of
hostilities against the Church. Decius undertook the military defence of the frontier. His colleague, Valerian, had
charge of the internal affairs of the Empire and was the
author of the measures against the Christians. Because the
Church included many who had embraced the faith in the
long period when the Church rarely felt the severity of the
laws, many were unable to endure the persecution, and so
apostatized or "fell." The persecution continued only for a
short time in full intensity, but it was not abandoned for a
number of years. It became violent once more when Valerian
became Emperor (253–260). One result of the persecutions
was the rise of serious disputes, and even schisms, from differences regarding the administration of discipline by the bishops.
In the case of the Novatians at Rome, a dissenting Church
which spread rapidly over the Empire came into existence
and lasted for more than two centuries.

For the literature see the following articles:

§ 45. The Decian-Valerian Persecution.
§ 46. The Effects of the Persecution upon the Inner Life
of the Church.

§ 45. THE DECIAN-VALERIAN PERSECUTION

The first persecution which may fairly be said to have been general in purpose and effect was that falling in the reigns of Decius (249–251) and Valerian (253–260). Of the course of the persecution we have information bearing directly upon Carthage, Alexandria, and Asia Minor. But it probably was felt very generally throughout the Church.

Additional source material: Cyprian, *De Lapsis*, Epp. 14, 22, 43; Eusebius, *Hist. Ec.*, VI, 39–45, VII, 11, 15, 30: for original texts see Preuschen, *Analecta*, I, §§ 16, 17; also R. Knopf, *Ausgewählte Märtyreracten* (of these the most reliable are the martyrdom of Pionius and of Cyprian).

(a) Origen, *Contra Celsum*, III, 15. (MSG, 11 : 937.)

Origen, writing about 248, observes the probable approach of a period of persecution for the Church.

That it is not the fear of external enemies which strengthens our union is plain from the fact that this cause, by God's will, has already ceased for a considerable time. And it is probable that the secure existence, so far as this life is concerned, which is enjoyed by believers at present will come to an end, since those who in every way calumniate the Word [*i. e.*, Christianity] are again attributing the frequency of rebellion to the multitude of believers and to their not being persecuted by the authorities, as in former times.

(b) Lactantius, *De Mortibus Persecutorum*, 3, 4. (MSL, 7 : 200.)

Lucius Cælius Firminianus Lactantius was of African birth. Having obtained some local fame as a teacher of rhetoric, he was appointed by Diocletian professor of that subject in his new capital of Nicomedia. This position Lactantius lost during the Diocletian persecution. He was afterward tutor of Crispus, the son of Constantine. His work *On the Death of the Persecutors* is written in a bitter spirit, but excellent style. Although in some circles it has been customary to impeach the veracity of Lactantius, no intentional departure from historical truthfulness, apart from rhetorical coloring, which was inevitable, has been proved against him. Of late there has been some doubt as to the authorship of *De Mortibus Persecutorum*.

Ch. 3. . . . This long peace, however, was afterward interrupted.

Ch. 4. For after many years there appeared in the world an accursed wild beast, Decius by name, who should afflict the Church. And who but a bad man would persecute righteousness? As if for this end he had been raised up to sovereign eminence, he began at once to rage against God, and at once to fall. For having undertaken an expedition against the Carpi, who had then occupied Dacia and Mœsia, he was suddenly surrounded by the barbarians, and slain, together with a great part of his army; nor could he be honored with the rights of sepulture, but, stripped and naked, he lay as food for wild beasts and birds, as became the enemy of God.

(*c*) Eusebius, *Hist. Ec.*, VI, 39. (MSG, 20 : 660.)

The Decian persecution and the sufferings of Origen.

Decius succeeded Philip, who had reigned seven years. On account of his hatred of Philip, Decius commenced a persecution of the churches, in which Fabianus suffered martyrdom at Rome, and Cornelius succeeded him in the episcopate. In Palestine, Alexander, bishop of the church of Jerusalem, was brought again on Christ's account before the governor's judgment seat in Cæsarea, and having acquitted himself nobly in a second confession, was cast into prison, crowned with the hoary locks of venerable age. And after his honorable and illustrious confession at the tribunal of the governor, he fell asleep in prison, and Mazabanes became his successor in the bishopric of Jerusalem. Babylas in Antioch having, like Alexander, passed away in prison after his confession, Fabius presided over that church.

But how many and how great things came upon Origen in the persecution, and what was their final result—as the evil demon marshalled all his forces and fought against the man with his utmost craft and power, assaulting him beyond

all others against whom he contended at that time; and
what and how many things the man endured for the word
of Christ—bonds and bodily tortures and torments under the
iron collar and in the dungeon; and how for many days with
his feet stretched four spaces of the stocks he bore patiently
the threats of fire and whatever other things were inflicted
by his enemies; and how his sufferings terminated, as his
judge strove eagerly with all his might not to end his life;
and what words he left after these things full of comfort to
those needing aid, a great many of his epistles show with
truth and accuracy.

(d) Cyprian, *De Lapsis*, 8–10.   (MSL, 4 : 486.)

The many cases of apostasy in the Decian persecution shocked
the Church inexpressibly.   In peace discipline had been relaxed and
Christian zeal had grown weak.   The same phenomena appeared in
the next great persecution, under Diocletian, after a long period of
peace.   *De Lapsis* was written in the spring of 251, just after the end
of the severity of the Decian persecution and Cyprian's return to
Carthage.   Text in part in Kirch, nn. 227 *ff*.

Ch. 8.   From some, alas, all these things have fallen away,
and have passed from memory.   They indeed did not even
wait, that, having been apprehended, they should go up, or,
having been interrogated, they might deny.   Many were
conquered before the battle, prostrated without an attack.
Nor did they even leave it to be said for them that they seemed
to sacrifice to idols unwillingly.   They ran to the forum of
their own accord; freely they hastened to death, as if they
had formerly wished it, as if they would embrace an opportunity now given which they had always desired.   How
many were put off by the magistrates at that time, when
evening was coming on!   How many even asked that their
destruction might not be delayed!   What violence can such
a one plead, how can he purge his crime, when it was he himself who rather used force that he might perish?   When they
came voluntarily to the capitol—when they freely approached
to the obedience of the terrible wickedness—did not their

tread falter, did not their sight darken, their hearts tremble, their arms fall helplessly down, their senses become dull, their tongues cleave to their mouths, their speech fail? Could the servant of God stand there, he who had already renounced the devil and the world, and speak and renounce Christ? Was not that altar, whither he drew near to die, to him a funeral pile? Ought he not to shudder at, and flee from, the altar of the devil, which he had seen to smoke and to be redolent of a foul stench, as it were, a funeral and sepulchre of his life? Why bring with you, O wretched man, a sacrifice? Why immolate a victim? You yourself have come to the altar an offering, yourself a victim; there you have immolated your salvation, your hope; there you have burned up your faith in those deadly fires.

Ch. 9. But to many their own destruction was not sufficient. With mutual exhortations the people were urged to their ruin; death was pledged by turns in the deadly cup. And that nothing might be wanting to aggravate the crime, infants, also, in the arms of their parents, being either carried or conducted, lost, while yet little ones, what in the very beginning of their nativity they had gained. Will not they, when the day of judgment comes, say: "We have done nothing; nor have we forsaken the Lord's bread and cup to hasten freely to a profane contract. . . ."

Ch. 10. Nor is there, alas, any just and weighty reason which excuses such a crime. One's country was to be left, and loss of one's estate was to be suffered. Yet to whom that is born and dies is there not a necessity at some time to leave his country and to suffer loss of his estate? But let not Christ be forsaken, so that the loss of salvation and of an eternal home should be feared.

(e) Cyprian, *De Lapsis*, 28. (MSL, 4 : 501.)

Those who did not actually sacrifice in the tests that were applied to Christians, but by bribery had procured certificates that they had sacrificed, were known as *libellatici*. It was to the credit of the Christian moral feeling that this subterfuge was not admitted.

Nor let those persons flatter themselves that they need repent the less who, although they have not polluted their hands with abominable sacrifices, yet have defiled their consciences with certificates. That profession of one who denies is the testimony of a Christian disowning what he has been. He says he has done what another has actually committed, and although it is written, "Ye cannot serve two masters" [Matt. 6 : 24], he has served an earthly master in that he has obeyed his edict; he has been more obedient to human authority than to God.

(f) *A Libellus.* From a papyrus found at Fayum.

The text may be found in Kirch, n. 207. This is the actual certificate which a man suspected of being a Christian obtained from the commission appointed to carry out the edict of persecution. It has been preserved these many centuries in the dry Egyptian climate, and is with some others, which are less perfect, among the most interesting relics of the ancient Church.

Presented to the Commission for the Sacrifices in the village of Alexander Island, by Aurelius Diogenes, the son of Satabus, of the village of Alexander Island, about seventy-two years of age, with a scar on the right eyebrow.

I have at other times always offered to the gods as well as also now in your presence, and according to the regulations have offered, sacrificed, and partaken of the sacrificial meal; and I pray you to attest this. Farewell. I, Aurelius Diogenes, have presented this.

[In a second hand.]

I, Aurelius Syrus, testify as being present that Diogenes sacrificed with us.

[First hand.]

First year of the Emperor Cæsar Gaius Messius Quintus Trajanus Decius, pious, happy, Augustus, 2d day of Epiphus. [June 25, 250.]

(g) Cyprian, *Epistula* 80 (=82). (MSL, 4 : 442.)

The date of this epistle is 257–258, at the outbreak of the Valerian persecution, a revival of the Decian. It was therefore shortly before Cyprian's death.

Cyprian to his brother Successus, greeting. The reason why I write to you at once, dearest brother, is that all the clergy are placed in the heat of the contest and are unable in any way to depart hence, for all of them are prepared, in accordance with the devotion of their mind, for divine and heavenly glory. But you should know that those have come back whom I sent to Rome to find out and bring us the truth concerning what had in any manner been decreed respecting us. For many, various, and uncertain things are currently reported. But the truth concerning them is as follows: Valerian has sent a rescript to the Senate, to the effect that bishops, presbyters, and deacons should be immediately punished; but that senators, men of rank, and Roman knights should lose their dignity and be deprived of their property; and if, when their property has been taken away, they should persist in being Christians, that they should then also lose their heads; but that matrons should be deprived of their property and banished. Moreover, people of Cæsar's household, who had either confessed before or should now confess, should have their property confiscated, and be sent in chains and assigned to Cæsar's estates. The Emperor Valerian also added to his address a copy of the letters he prepared for the presidents of the provinces coercing us. These letters we are daily hoping will come, and we are waiting, according to the strength of our faith, for the endurance of suffering and expecting from the help and mercy of the Lord the crown. of eternal life. But know that Sixtus was punished [*i. e.*, martyred] in the cemetery on the eighth day of the ides of August, and with him four deacons. The prefects of the city, furthermore, are daily urging on this persecution; so that if any are presented to them they are punished and their property confiscated.

I beg that these things be made known by you to the rest of our colleagues, that everywhere by their exhortations the brotherhood may be strengthened and prepared for the spiritual conflict, that every one may think less of death than of immortality, and dedicated to the Lord with full faith and courage, they may rejoice rather than fear in this confession, wherein they know that the soldiers of God and Christ are not slain, but crowned. I bid you, dearest brother, ever farewell in the Lord.

§ 46. Effects of the Persecution upon the Inner Life of the Church

The persecution developed the popular opinion of the superior sanctity of martyrdom. This was itself no new idea, having grown up in the Church from the time of Ignatius of Antioch, but it now received new applications and developments (*a, b*). See also § 42, *d*, and below for problems arising from the place the martyrs attempted to take in the organization of the Church and the administration of discipline. This claim of the martyrs was successfully overcome by the bishops, especially under Cyprian's leadership and example. But in the administration of discipline there were sure to arise difficulties and questions, *e. g.*, Was there a distinction to be made in favor of those who had escaped without actually sacrificing? (*c*). No matter what policy was followed by the bishop, there was the liability of the rise of a party in opposition to him. If he was strict, a party advocating laxity appeared, as in the case of Felicissimus at Carthage; if he was milder in policy, a party would call for greater rigor, as in the case of Novatian at Rome (*e*).

Additional source material: Cyprian, *Ep.* 39-45, 51 (ANF, V); Eusebius, *Hist. Ec.*, VI, 43, 45.

(*a*) Origen, *Exhortatio ad Martyrium*, 30, 50. (MSG, 11 : 601, 636.)

An estimate of the importance and value of martyrdom.

The *Exhortation to Martyrdom* was addressed by Origen to his friend and patron Ambrosius, and to Protoctetus, a presbyter of Cæsarea, who were in great danger during the persecution undertaken by Maximinus Thrax (235-238). It was probably written in the reign of that Emperor.

Ch. 30. We must remember that we have sinned and that
it is impossible to obtain forgiveness of sins without baptism,
and that according to the evangelical laws it is impossible
to be baptized a second time with water and the Spirit for
the forgiveness of sins, and therefore the baptism of martyrdom is given us. For thus it has been called, as may be
clearly gathered from the passage: "Can ye drink of the
cup that I drink of, and be baptized with the baptism that
I am baptized with?" [Mark 10 : 38]. And in another place
it is said: "But I have a baptism to be baptized with; and
how am I straightened until it be accomplished!" [Luke 12 :
50]. For be sure that just as the expiation of the cross was
for the whole world, it (the baptism of martyrdom) is for the
cure of many who are thereby cleansed. For as according to
the law of Moses those placed near the altar are seen to
minister forgiveness of sins to others through the blood of
bulls and goats, so the souls of those who have suffered on
account of the testimony of Jesus are not in vain near that
altar in heaven [cf. Rev. 6 : 9 ff.], but minister forgiveness of
sins to those who pray. And at the same time we know that
just as the high priest, Jesus Christ, offered himself as a
sacrifice, so the priests, of whom He is the high priest, offer
themselves as sacrifices, and on account of this sacrifice they
are at the altar as in their proper place.

Ch. 50. Just as we have been redeemed with the precious
blood of Christ, who received the name that is above every
name, so by the precious blood of the martyrs will others be
redeemed.

(b) Origen, *Homil. ad Num.*, X, 2. (MSG, 12 : 658.)

Of Origen's homilies on the Pentateuch only a few fragments of
the Greek text remain. We have them, however, in a Latin translation or paraphrase made by Rufinus. The twenty-eight homilies on
Numbers were written after A. D. 244.

Concerning the martyrs, the Apostle John writes in the
Apocalypse that the souls of those who have been slain for

the name of the Lord Jesus are present at the altar; but he who is present at the altar is shown to perform the duties of priest. But the duty of a priest is to make intercession for the sins of the people. Wherefore I fear, lest, perchance, inasmuch as there are made no martyrs, and sacrifices of saints are not offered for our sins, we will not receive remission of our sins. And therefore I fear, lest our sins remaining in us, it may happen to us what the Jews said of themselves, that not having an altar, nor a temple, nor priesthood, and therefore not offering sacrifices, our sins remain in us, and so no forgiveness is obtained. . . . And therefore the devil, knowing that remission of sins is obtained by the passion of martyrdom, is not willing to raise public persecutions against us by the heathen.

(c) Cyprian, *Epistula* 55, 14 (=51). (MSL, 3 : 805.)

The opinion of the Church as to the *libellatici*. The date is 251 or 252.

Since there is much difference between those who have sacrificed, what a want of mercy it is, and how bitter is the hardship, to associate those who have received certificates with those who have sacrificed, when he who has received the certificate may say, "I had previously read and had been informed by the discourse of the bishop that we ought not to sacrifice to idols, that the servant of God ought not to worship images; and therefore that I might not do this which is not lawful, when the opportunity of receiving a certificate was offered (and I would not have received it, if the opportunity had not been offered) I either went or charged some one other person going to the magistrate to say that I am a Christian, that I am not allowed to sacrifice, that I cannot come to the devil's altars, and that I will pay a price for this purpose, that I may not do what is not lawful for me to do"! Now, however, even he who is stained by a certificate, after he has learned from our admonitions that he ought not to have done even this, and though his hand is pure, and no contact of deadly food has polluted his lips, yet his conscience is nevertheless polluted, weeps when he hears us, and laments, and is now admonished for the things wherein he has sinned, and having been deceived, not so much by guilt as by error, bears witness that for another time he is instructed and prepared.

(d) *Epistula pacis*, Cyprian, *Epistula* 16. (MSL, 4 : 268.) *Cf.* Kirch, n. 241.

This brief Letter of Peace is a specimen of the forms that were being issued by the confessors, and which a party in the Church regarded as mandatory upon the bishops. These Cyprian strenuously and successfully resisted. See also Cyprian, *Ep.* 21, in ANF, V, 299.

All the confessors to Cyprian, pope,[1] greeting. Know that we all have given peace to those concerning whom an account has been rendered you as to what they have done since they committed their sin; and we wish to make this rescript known through you to the other bishops. We desire you to have peace with the holy martyrs. Lucianus has written this, there being present of the clergy an exorcist and a lector.

(e) Cyprian, *Epistula* 43, 2, 3. (MSL, 4 : 342.)

The schism of Felicissimus was occasioned by the position taken by Cyprian in regard to the admission of the *lapsi* in the Decian persecution. But it was at the same time the outcome of an opposition to Cyprian of longer standing, on account of jealousy, as he had only recently become a Christian when he was made bishop of Carthage.

Ch. 2. It has appeared whence came the faction of Felicissimus, on what root and by what strength it stood. These men supplied in a former time encouragements and exhortations to confessors, not to agree with their bishop, not to maintain the ecclesiastical discipline faithfully and quietly, according to the Lord's precepts, not to keep the glory of their confession with an uncorrupt and unspotted mode of life. And lest it should have been too little to have corrupted

---

[1] The term *papa* is applied to Cyprian several times in the extant epistles addressed to him.

the minds of certain confessors and to have wished to arm a
portion of our broken fraternity against God's priesthood,
they have now applied themselves with their envenomed
deceitfulness to the ruin of the lapsed, to turn away from
the healing of their wound the sick and the wounded, and
those who, by the misfortune of their fall, are less fit and less
able to take stronger counsels; and having left off prayers and
supplications, whereby with long and continued satisfaction
the Lord is to be appeased, they invite them by the deceit of
a fallacious peace to a fatal rashness.

Ch. 3. But I pray you, brethren, watch against the snares
of the devil, and being careful for your own salvation, guard
diligently against this deadly deceit.   This is another persecution and another temptation.   Those five presbyters are
none other than the five leaders who were lately associated
with the magistrates in an edict that they might overthrow
our faith, that they might turn away the feeble hearts of the
brethren to their deadly nets by the perversion of the truth.
Now the same scheme, the same overturning, is again brought
about by the five presbyters, linked with Felicissimus, to the
destruction of salvation, that God should not be besought,
and that he who has denied Christ should not appeal for
mercy to the same Christ whom he has denied; that after
the fault of the crime repentance also should be taken away;
and that satisfaction should not be made through bishops
and priests, but, the Lord's priests being forsaken, a new
tradition of sacrilegious appointment should arise contrary
to the evangelical discipline.   And although it was once arranged as well by us as by the confessors and the clergy of
the city,[1] likewise by all the bishops located either in our
province or beyond the sea [i. e., Italy], that there should be
no innovations regarding the case of the lapsed unless we all
assembled in one place, and when our counsels had been
compared we should then decide upon some moderate sen-

[1] I. e., Rome.   There was a vacancy at that time, A. D. 250, in the episcopate
of Rome and the clergy administered the affairs of that church *sede vacante*.

tence, tempered alike with discipline and with mercy; against this, our counsel, they have rebelled and all priestly authority has been destroyed by factious conspiracies.

(f) Eusebius, *Hist. Ec.*, VI, 43. (MSG, 20 : 616.)

The schism of Novatian at Rome was occasioned by the question of discipline of the lapsed. While the schism of Felicissimus was in favor of more lenient treatment of those who had fallen, the schism of Novatian was in favor of greater strictness. The sect of Novatians, named after the founder, Novatus or Novatianus, lasted for more than two centuries.

Novatus [Novatianus], a presbyter at Rome, being lifted up with arrogance against these persons, as if there was no longer for them a hope of salvation, not even if they should do all things pertaining to a pure and genuine conversion, became the leader of the heresy of those who in the pride of their imagination style themselves Cathari.[1] Thereupon a very large synod assembled at Rome, of bishops in number sixty, and a great many more presbyters and deacons; and likewise the pastors of the remaining provinces deliberated in their places by themselves concerning what ought to be done. A decree, accordingly, was confirmed by all that Novatus and those who joined with him, and those who adopted his brother-hating and inhuman opinion, should be considered by the Church as strangers; but that they should heal such of the brethren as had fallen into misfortune, and should minister to them with the medicines of repentance. There have come down to us epistles of Cornelius, bishop of Rome, to Fabius, of the church at Antioch, which show what was done at the synod at Rome, and what seemed best to all those in Italy and Africa and the regions thereabout. Also other epistles, written in the Latin language, of Cyprian and those with him in Africa, by which it is shown that they agreed as to the necessity of succoring those who had been tempted, and of cutting off from the Catholic Church the leader of the heresy and all that joined him.

[1] *I. e.*, the pure ones.

CHAPTER IV. THE PERIOD OF PEACE FOR THE
CHURCH: A. D. 260 TO A. D. 303

After the Decian-Valerian persecution (250–260) the Church enjoyed a long peace, rarely interrupted anywhere by hostile measures, until the outbreak of the second great general persecution, under Diocletian (303–313), a space of over forty years. In this period the Church cast off the chiliasm which had lingered as a part of a primitive Jewish conception of Christianity (§ 47), and adapted itself to the actual condition of this present world. Under the influence of scientific theology, especially that of the Alexandrian school, the earlier forms of Monarchianism disappeared from the Church, and the discussion began to narrow down to the position which it eventually assumed in the Arian controversy (§ 48). Corresponding to the development of the theology went that of the cultus of the Church, and already in the West abiding characteristics appeared (§ 49). The cultus and the disciplinary work of the bishops advanced in turn the hierarchical organization of the Church and the place of the bishops (§ 50), but the theory of local episcopal autonomy and the universalistic tendencies of the see of Rome soon came into sharp conflict (§ 51), especially over the validity of baptism administered by heretics (§ 52). In this discussion the North African Church assumed a position which subsequently became the occasion of the most serious schism of the ancient Church, or Donatism. In this period, also, is to be set the rise of Christian Monasticism as distinguished from ordinary Christian asceticism (§ 53). At the same time, a dangerous rival of Christianity appeared in the East, in the form of Manichæanism, in which were absorbed nearly all the remnants of earlier Gnosticism (§ 54).

§ 47. The Chiliastic Controversy.

§ 48. Theology of the Second Half of the Third Century under the Influence of Origen.

§ 49. The Development of the Cultus.
§ 50. The Episcopate.
§ 51. The Unity of the Church and the See of Rome.
§ 52. Controversy on the Baptism of Heretics.
§ 53. Beginnings of Christian Monasticism.
§ 54. Manichæanism.

§ 47. The Chiliastic Controversy

During the third century the belief in chiliasm as a part
of the Church's faith died out in nearly all parts of the
Church. It did not seem called for by the condition of the
Church, which was rapidly adjusting itself to the world in
which it found itself. The scientific theology, especially that
of Alexandria, found no place in its system for such an article as chiliasm. The belief lingered, however, in country
places, and with it went no little opposition to the "scientific"
exegesis which by means of allegory explained away the promises of a millennial kingdom. The only account we have of
this so-called "Chiliastic Controversy" is found in connection
with the history of the schism of Nepos in Egypt given by
Eusebius. But it may be safely assumed that the condition
of things here described was not peculiar to any one part of
the Church, though an open schism resulting from the conflict of the old and new ideas is not found elsewhere.

Additional source material: Origen, *De Principiis*, II, 11 (ANF, IV);
Lactantius, *Divinæ Institutiones*, VII, 14–26 (ANF, VII); Methodius,
Symposium, IX, 5 (ANF, VI); *v. infra*, § 48.

Eusebius, *Hist. Ec.*, VII, 24.   (MSG, 20 : 693.)

Dionysius was bishop of Alexandria 248–265, after serving as the
head of the Catechetical School, a position which he does not seem
to have resigned on being advanced to the episcopate. His work
On the Promises has, with the exception of fragments preserved by
Eusebius, perished, as has also the work of Nepos, *Against the Allegorists*. The date of the work of Nepos is not known. That of the
work of Dionysius is placed conjecturally at 255. The "Allegorists,"
against whom Nepos wrote, were probably Origen and his school, who
developed more consistently and scientifically the allegorical method
of exegesis; see above, § 43, *k*.

Besides all these, the two books *On the Promises* were prepared by him [Dionysius]. The occasion of these was Nepos, a bishop in Egypt, who taught that the promises made to the holy men in the divine Scriptures should be understood in a more Jewish manner, and that there would be a certain millennium of bodily luxury upon this earth. As he thought that he could establish his private opinion by the Revelation of John, he wrote a book on this subject, entitled *Refutation of Allegorists*. Dionysius opposes this in his books *On the Promises*. In the first he gives his own opinion of the dogma; and in the second he treats of the Revelation of John,[1] and, mentioning Nepos at the beginning, writes of him as follows:

"But since they bring forward a certain work of Nepos, on which they rely confidently, as if it proved beyond dispute that there will be a reign of Christ upon earth, I confess that in many other respects I approve and love Nepos for his faith and industry and his diligence in the Scriptures, and for his extensive psalmody with which many of the brethren are still delighted; and I hold the man in the more reverence because he has gone before us to rest. . . . But as some think his work very plausible, and as certain teachers regard the law and the prophets as of no consequence, and do not follow the Gospels, and treat lightly the apostolic epistles, while they make promises as to the teaching of this work as if it were some great hidden mystery, and do not permit our simpler brethren to have any sublime and lofty thoughts concerning the glorious and truly divine appearing of our Lord and our resurrection from the dead, and our being gathered together unto Him, and made like Him, but, on the contrary, lead them to a hope for small things and mortal things in the kingdom of God, and for things such as exist now—since this is the case, it is necessary that we should

---

[1] In the next chapter of Eusebius (=VII, 25) there are the critical reasons against the apostolic authorship of the Revelation of St. John, based upon a critical comparison with the Fourth Gospel and the Epistles of St. John, reasons which are still current in radical critical circles.

dispute with our brother Nepos as if he were present." Farther on he says:

"When I was in the district of Arsinoe, where, as you know, this doctrine has prevailed for a long time, so that schisms and apostasies of entire churches have resulted, I called together the presbyters and teachers of the brethren in the villages—such brethren as wished being present—and I exhorted them to make a public examination of this question. Accordingly when they brought me this book, as if it were a weapon and fortress impregnable, sitting with them from morning till evening for three successive days, I endeavored to correct what was written in it. . . . And finally the author and mover of this teaching, who was called Coracion, in the hearing of all the brethren present acknowledged and testified to us that he would no longer hold this opinion, nor discuss it, nor mention it, nor teach it, as he was fully convinced by the arguments against it."

§ 48. THEOLOGY OF THE SECOND HALF OF THE THIRD CENTURY UNDER THE INFLUENCE OF ORIGEN

By the second half of the third century theology had become a speculative and highly technical science (a), and under the influence of Origen, the Logos theology, as opposed to various forms of Monarchianism (b), had become universal. Under this influence, Paul of Samosata, reviving Dynamistic Monarchianism, modified it by combining with it elements of the Logos theology (c–e). At the same time there was in various parts of the Church a continuation of the Asia Minor theological tradition, such as had found expression in Irenæus. A representative of this theology was Methodius of Olympus (f).

Additional source material: Athanasius, *De Sent. Dionysii* (PNF, ser. II, vol. IV).

(a) Gregory Thaumaturgus, *Confession of Faith.* (MSG, 46 : 912.)

Gregory Thaumaturgus, or the Wonder-worker, was born about 213 in Neo-Cæsarea in Pontus. He studied under Origen at Cæsarea in Palestine from 233 to 238, and became one of the leading representatives of the Origenistic theology, representing the orthodox development of that school, as distinguished from Paul of Samosata and Lucian.

The following Confession of Faith is found only in the *Life of Gregory Thaumaturgus*, by Gregory of Nyssa. (MSG, 46 : 909 *f.*) Its genuineness is now generally admitted; see Hahn, *op. cit.*, § 185. According to a legend, it was communicated to Gregory in a vision by St. John on the request of the Blessed Virgin. It represents the speculative tendency of Origenism and current theology after the rise of the Alexandrian school. It should be noted that it differs markedly from other confessions of faith in not employing biblical language.

There is one God, the Father of the living Word, His substantive Wisdom, Power, and Eternal Image, the perfect Begetter of the perfect One, the Father of the Only begotten Son.

There is one Lord, only One from only One, God from God, the image and likeness of the Godhead, the active Word, The Wisdom which comprehends the constitution of all things, and the Power which produced all creation; the true Son of the true Father, Invisible of Invisible, and Incorruptible of Incorruptible, and Immortal of Immortal, and Everlasting of Everlasting.

And there is one Holy Spirit having His existence from God, and manifested by the Son [namely, to men], [1] the perfect likeness of the perfect Son, Life and Cause of the living [the sacred Fount], Sanctity, Leader of sanctification, in whom is revealed God the Father, who is over all and in all, and God the Son, who is through all; a perfect Trinity [2] not divided nor differing in glory and eternity and sovereignty.

There is, therefore, nothing created or subservient in the Trinity, nor introduced as if not there before, but coming afterward; for there never was a time when the Son was lacking to the Father, nor the Spirit to the Son, but the same Trinity is ever unvarying and unchangeable.

[1] The bracketed phrases are doubtful.
[2] Gregory uses the term Trias for Trinity here and throughout.

(b) Athanasius, *De Sent. Dionysii*, 4, 5, 6, 13–15. (MSG, 25 : 484 *f.*, 497 *f.*)

What has been called the "Controversy of the two Dionysii" was in reality no controversy. Dionysius of Alexandria [*v. supra*, § 48] wrote a letter to the Sabellians near Cyrene, pointing out the distinction of the Father and the Son. In it he used language which was, to say the least, indiscreet. Complaint was made to Dionysius, bishop of Rome, that the bishop of Alexandria did not hold the right view of the relation of the Son to the Father and of the divinity of the Son. Thereupon, Dionysius of Rome wrote to Dionysius of Alexandria. In reply, Dionysius of Alexandria pointed out at length, in a *Refutation and Defence*, his actual opinion on the matter as a whole, rather than as merely opposed to Modalistic Monarchianism or Sabellianism. The course of the discussion is sufficiently clear from the extracts. Athanasius is writing in answer to the Arians, who had appealed to the letter of Dionysius in support of their opinion that the Son was a creature, and that there was when He was not [*v. infra*, § 63]. His work, from which the following extracts are taken, was written between 350 and 354.

Ch. 4. They (the Arians) say, then, that in a letter the blessed Dionysius has said: "The Son of God is a creature and made, and not His own by nature, but in essence alien from the Father, just as the husbandman is from the vine, or the shipbuilder is from the boat; for that, being a creature, He was not before He came to be." Yes. He wrote it, and we, too, admit that such was his letter. But as he wrote this, so also he wrote very many other epistles, which ought to be read by them, so that from all and not from one merely the faith of the man might be discovered.

Ch. 5. At that time [*i. e.*, when Dionysius wrote against the Sabellians] certain of the bishops of Pentapolis in Upper Libya were of the opinion of Sabellius. And they were so successful with their opinion that the Son of God was scarcely preached any longer in the churches. Dionysius heard of this, as he had charge of those churches (*cf.* Canon 6, Nicæa, 325; see below, § 72), and sent men to counsel the guilty ones to cease from their false doctrine. As they did not cease but waxed more shameless in their impiety, he was compelled to meet their shameless conduct by writing the said letter and to define from the Gospels the human nature of the Saviour, in order that, since those men waxed bolder in denying the Son and in ascribing His human actions to the Father, he accordingly, by demonstrating that it was not the Father but the Son that was made man for us, might persuade the ignorant persons that the Father is not the Son, and so by degrees lead them to the true godhead of the Son and the knowledge of the Father.

Ch. 6. . . . If in his writings he is inconsistent, let them [*i. e.*, the Arians] not draw him to their side, for on this assumption he is not worthy of credit. But if, when he had written his letter to Ammonius, and fallen under suspicion, he made his defence, bettering what he had said previously, defending himself, but not changing, it must be evident that he wrote what fell under suspicion by way of "accommodation."

Ch. 13. The following is the occasion of his writing the other letters. When Bishop Dionysius had heard of the affairs in Pentapolis and had written in zeal for religion, as I have said, his letter to Euphranor and Ammonius against the heresy of Sabellius, some of the brethren belonging to the Church, who held a right opinion, but did not ask him so as to learn from himself what he had written, went up to Rome and spake against him in the presence of his namesake, Dionysius, bishop of Rome. And the latter, upon hearing it, wrote simultaneously against the adherents of Sabellius and against those who held the same opinions for uttering which Arius was cast out of the Church; and he called it an equal and opposite impiety to hold with Sabellius or with those who say that the Word of God is a creature, framed and originated. And he wrote also to Dionysius [*i. e.*, of Alexandria] to inform him of what they had said about him. And the latter straightway wrote back and inscribed a book entitled *A Refutation and a Defence*.

Ch. 14. . . . In answer to these charges he writes, after certain prefatory matter in the first book of the work entitled *A Refutation and a Defence*, in the following terms:

Ch. 15. "For never was there a time when God was not a Father." And this he acknowledges in what follows, "that Christ is forever, being Word and Wisdom and Power. For it is not to be supposed that God, having at first no issue, afterward begat a Son. But the Son has his being not of Himself, but of the Father."

(c) Eusebius, *Hist. Ec.*, VII, 27, 29, 30. (MSG, 25 : 705.)

The deposition of Paul of Samosata.

The controversy concerning Paul's doctrinal views is sufficiently set forth in the extract from Eusebius given below. Paul was bishop of Antioch from about 260 to 268. His works have perished, with the exception of a few fragments. The importance of Paul is that in his teaching is to be found an attempt to combine the Logos theology of Origen with Dynamistic Monarchianism, with results that appeared later in Arianism, on the one hand, and Nestorianism, it is thought, on the other.

Ch. 27. After Sixtus had presided over the church of Rome eleven years, Dionysius, namesake of him of Alexandria, succeeded him. About that time Demetrianus died in Antioch, and Paul of Samosata received that episcopate. As he held low and degraded views of Christ, contrary to the teaching of the Church, namely, that in his nature He was a common man, Dionysius of Alexandria was entreated to come to the synod. But being unable to come on account of age and physical weakness, he gave his opinion on the subject under consideration by a letter. But the other pastors of the churches assembled from all directions, as against a despoiler of the flock of Christ, all making haste to reach Antioch.

Ch. 29. During his [Aurelian's, 270–275] reign a final synod composed of a great many bishops was held, and the leader of heresy in Antioch was detected and his false doctrine clearly shown before all, and he was excommunicated from the Catholic Church under heaven. Malchion especially drew him out from his hiding-place and refuted him. He was a man learned also in other matters, and principal of the sophist school of Grecian learning in Antioch; yet on account of the superior nobility of his faith in Christ he had been made a presbyter of that parish [*i. e.*, diocese]. This man, having conducted a discussion with him, which was taken down by stenographers, and which we know is still extant, was alone able to detect the man who dissembled and deceived others.

Ch. 30. The pastors who had assembled about this matter prepared by common consent an epistle addressed to Dionysius, bishop of Rome, and Maximus of Alexandria, and sent it to all the provinces. . . .

After other things they describe as follows the manner of life which he led: "Whereas he has departed from the rule [*i. e.*, of faith], and has turned aside after base and spurious teachings, it is not necessary—since he is without—that we should pass judgment upon his practices: as for instance . . . in that he is haughty and is puffed up, and assumes worldly dignities, preferring to be called ducenarius rather than bishop; and struts in the market-places, reading letters and reciting them as he walks in public, attended by a body-guard, with a multitude preceding and following him, so that the faith is envied and hated on account of his pride and haughtiness of heart, . . . or that he violently and coarsely assails in public the expounders of the Word that have departed this life, and magnifies himself, not as bishop, but as a sophist and juggler, and stops the psalms to our Lord Jesus Christ as being novelties and the productions of modern men, and trains women to sing psalms to himself in the midst of the church on the great day of the passover. . . . He is unwilling to acknowledge that the Son of God came down from heaven. (And this is no mere assertion, but is abundantly proved from the records which we have sent you; and not least where he says, 'Jesus Christ is from below'.) . . . And there are the women, the '*subintroductæ*,' as the people of Antioch call them, belonging to him and to the presbyters and deacons with him. Although he knows and has convicted these men, yet he connives at this and their incurable sins, in order that they may be bound to him, and through fear for themselves may not dare to accuse him for his wicked words and deeds. . . ."

As Paul had fallen from the episcopate, as well as from the orthodox faith, Domnus, as has been said, succeeded to the service of the church at Antioch [*i. e.*, became bishop]. But as Paul refused to surrender the church building, the Emperor Aurelian was petitioned; and he decided the matter most equitably, ordering the building to be given to those to whom the bishops of Italy and of the city of Rome should adjudge it. Thus this man was driven out of the Church, with extreme disgrace, by the worldly power.

Such was Aurelian's attitude toward us at that time; but in the course of time he changed his mind in regard to us, and was moved by certain advisers to institute a persecution against us. And there was great talk about it everywhere. But as he was about to do it, and was, so to speak, in the very act of signing the decrees against us, the divine judgment came upon him and restrained him at the very verge of his undertaking.

(*d*) Malchion of Antioch, *Disputation with Paul.* (MSG, 10 : 247–260.)

The doctrine of Paul of Samosata,
The following fragments are from the disputation of Malchion with Paul at the Council of Antioch, 268 [see extract from Eusebius, *Hist. Ec.*, VII, 27, 29, 30; see above (*c*)], which Malchion is said to have revised and published. The passages may be found also in Routh, *Reliquiæ Sacræ*, second ed., III, 300 *ff.* Fragments I–III are from the work of the Emperor Justinian, *Contra Monophysitas;* fragment IV is from the work of Leontius of Byzantium, *Adversus Nestorianos et Eutychianos.*

I. The Logos became united with Him who was born of David, who is Jesus, who was begotten of the Holy Ghost. And Him the Virgin bore by the Holy Spirit; but God generated that Logos without the Virgin or any one else than God, and thus the Logos exists.

II. The Logos was greater than Christ. Christ became

greater through Wisdom, that we might not overthrow the dignity of Wisdom.

III. In order that the Anointed, who was from David, might not be a stranger to Wisdom, and that Wisdom might not dwell so largely in another. For it was in the prophets, and more in Moses, and in many the Lord was, but more also in Christ as in a temple. For Jesus Christ was one and the Logos was another.

IV. He who appeared was not Wisdom, for He could not be found in an outward form, neither in the appearance of a man; for He is greater than all things visible.

(e) Paul of Samosata, *Orationes ad Sabinum*, Routh, *op. cit.*, III, 329.

The doctrine of Paul.
Paul's work addressed to Sabinus has perished with the exception of a few fragments. See Routh, *op. cit.*

I. Thou shouldest not wonder that the Saviour had one will with God; for just as nature shows us a substance becoming one and the same out of many things, so the nature of love makes one and the same will out of many through a manifest preference.

II. He who was born holy and righteous, having by His struggle and sufferings overcome the sin of our progenitors, and having succeeded in all things, was united in character to God, since He had preserved one and the same effort and aim as He for the promotion of things that are good; and since He has preserved this inviolate, His name is called that above every name, the prize of love having been freely bestowed upon Him.

(f) Epiphanius, *Panarion*, *Hær.* LXV. (MSG, 42 : 12.)

The doctrine of Paul of Samosata.
Epiphanius was bishop of Salamis, 367–403. His works are chiefly polemical and devoted to the refutation of all heresies, of which he gives accounts at some length. He is a valuable, though not always

reliable, source for many otherwise unknown heresies. In the present case we have passages from Paul's own writings that confirm and supplement the statements of the hereseologist.

He [Paul of Samosata] says that God the Father and the Son and the Holy Spirit are one God, that in God is always His Word and His Spirit, as in a man's heart is his own reason; that the Son of God does not exist in a hypostasis, but in God himself. . . . That the Logos came and dwelt in Jesus, who was a man. And thus he says God is one, neither is the Father the Father, nor the Son the Son, nor the Holy Spirit the Holy Spirit, but rather the one God is Father and in Him is his Son, as the reason is in a man. . . . But he did not say with Noetus that the Father suffered, but only, said he, the Logos came and energized and went back to the Father.

(g) Methodius of Olympus, *Symposium*, III, 4, 8. (MSG, 18 : 65, 73.)

The theology of Origen was not suffered to go without being challenged by those who could not accept some of his extreme statements. Among those opposed to him were Peter, bishop of Alexandria, and Methodius, bishop of Olympus. Both were strongly influenced by Origen, but the denial of a bodily resurrection and the eternity of the creation were too offensive. The more important of the two is Methodius, who combined a strong anti-Origenistic position on these two points with that "recapitulation" theory of redemption which has been called the Asia Minor type of theology and is represented also by Irenæus; see above, § 27. He has been called the author of the "theology of the future," with reference to his relation to Athanasius, in that he laid the foundation for a doctrine of redemption which superseded that of the old Alexandrian school, and became established in the East under the lead of Athanasius and the Nicene divines generally.

Methodius was bishop of Olympus, in Lycia. The statements that he also held other sees are unreliable. He died in 311 as a martyr. Nothing else is known with certainty as to his life. Of his numerous and well-written works, only one, *The Banquet, or Symposium*, has been preserved entire. His work *On the Resurrection* is most strongly opposed to Origen and his denial of the bodily resurrection.

Ch. 4. For let us consider how rightly he [Paul] compared Adam to Christ, not only considering him to be the type and image, but also that Christ Himself became the very same thing, because the Eternal Word fell upon Him. For it was fitting that the first-born of God, the first shoot, the Only begotten, even the Wisdom [of God], should be joined to the first-formed man, and first and first-born of men, and should become incarnate. And this was Christ, a man filled with the pure and perfect Godhead, and God received into man. For it was most suitable that the oldest of the Æons and the first of the archangels, when about to hold communion with men, should dwell in the oldest and first of men, even Adam. And thus, renovating those things which were from the beginning, and forming them again of the Virgin by the Spirit, He frames the same just as at the beginning.

Ch. 8.   The Church could not conceive believers and give them new birth by the laver of regeneration unless Christ, emptying Himself for their sakes, that He might be contained by them, as I said, through the recapitulation of His passion, should die again, coming down from heaven, and, being "joined to His wife," the Church, should provide that a certain power be taken from His side, so that all who are built up in Him should grow up, even those who are born again by the laver, receiving of His bones and of His flesh; that is, of His holiness and of His glory. For he who says that the bones and flesh of Wisdom are understanding and virtue, says most rightly; and that the side [rib] is the Spirit of truth, the Paraclete, of whom the illuminated [*i. e.*, baptized], receiving, are fitly born again to incorruption.

(*h*) Methodius of Olympus, *De Resurrect.*, I, 13.   (MSG, 18 : 284.)

De Resur., I, 13.[1]   If any one were to think that the earthly image is the flesh itself, but the heavenly image is some other spiritual body besides the flesh, let him first consider that Christ, the heavenly man, when He appeared, bore the same form of limbs and the same image of flesh as ours, through

[1] On the whole passage, *cf.* I Cor. 15 : 42 *ff.*

which, also, He, who was not man, became man, that, "as in Adam all die, even so in Christ shall all be made alive." For if it was not that he might set the flesh free and raise it up that He bore flesh, why did He bear flesh superfluously, as He purposed neither to save it nor to raise it up? But the Son of God does nothing superfluous. He did not take, then, the form of a servant uselessly, but to raise it up and save it. For He was truly made man, and died, and not in appearance, but that He might truly be shown to be the first begotten from the dead, changing the earthly into the heavenly, and the mortal into the immortal.

§ 49. THE DEVELOPMENT OF THE CULTUS

The Church's cultus and sacramental system developed rapidly in the third century. The beginnings of the administration of the sacraments according to prescribed forms are to be traced to the Didache and Justin Martyr (see above, §§ 13, 14). At the beginning of the third century baptism was already accompanied by a series of subsidiary rites, and the eucharist was regarded as a sacrifice, the benefit of which might be directed toward specific ends. The further development was chiefly in connection with the eucharist, which effected in turn the conception of the hierarchy (see below, § 50). Baptism was regarded as conferring complete remission of previous sins; subsequent sins were atoned for in the penitential discipline (see above, § 42). As for the eucharist, the conception of the sacrifice which appears in the Didache, an offering of praise and thanksgiving, gradually gives place to a sacrifice which in some way partakes of the nature of Christ's sacrificial death upon the cross. At the same time, the elements are more and more completely identified with the body and blood of Christ, and the nature of the presence of Christ is conceived under quasi-physical categories. As representatives of the lines of development, Tertullian, at the beginning of the century, and Cyprian, at the middle, may be taken. That a similar development took place in the East is evident, not only from the references to thc same in the writings of Origen and others, but also from the appearance in the next century of elaborate services, or liturgies, as well as the doctrinal statements of writers generally.

(*a*) Tertullian, *De Corona*, 3. (MSL, 2 : 98.)

The ceremonies connected with baptism.

And how long shall we draw the saw to and fro through this line when we have an ancient practice which by anticipation has settled the state of the question? If no passage of Scripture has prescribed it, assuredly custom, which without doubt flowed from tradition, has confirmed it. For how can anything come into use if it has not first been handed down? Even in pleading tradition written authority, you say, must be demanded. Lèt us inquire, therefore, whether tradition, unless it be written, should not be admitted. Certainly we shall say that it ought not to be admitted if no cases of other practices which, without any written instrument, we maintain on the ground of tradition alone, and the countenance thereafter of custom, affords us any precedent. To deal with this matter briefly, I shall begin with baptism. When we are going to enter the water, but a little before, in the church and under the hand of the president, we solemnly profess that we renounce the devil, and his pomp, and his angels. Hereupon we are thrice immersed, making a somewhat ampler pledge than the Lord has appointed in the Gospel. Then, when we are taken up (as new-born children), we taste first of all a mixture of milk and honey; and from that day we refrain from the daily bath for a whole week. We take also in congregations, before daybreak, and from the hands of none but the presidents, the sacrament of the eucharist, which the Lord both commanded to be eaten at meal-times, and by all. On the anniversary day we make offerings for the dead as birthday honors. We consider fasting on the Lord's Day to be unlawful, as also to worship kneeling. We rejoice in the same privilege from Easter to Pentecost. We feel pained should any wine or bread, even though our own, be cast upon the ground. At every forward step and movement, at every going in and going out, when we put on our shoes, at the bath, at table, on lighting the lamps, on couch, on seat, in all the ordinary actions of daily life, we trace upon the forehead the sign [*i. e.*, of the cross].

(*b*) Tertullian, *De Baptismo*, 5–8. (MSL, 1 : 1314.)

The whole passage should be read as showing clearly that Tertullian recognized the similarity between Christian baptism and heathen purifying washings, but referred the effects of the heathen rites to evil powers, quite in harmony with the Christian admission of· the reality of heathen divinities as evil powers and heathen exorcisms as wrought by the aid of evil spirits.

Ch. 5. . . . Thus man will be restored by God to His likeness, for he formerly had been after the image of God; the image is counted being in His form [*in effigie*], the likeness in His eternity [*in æternitate*]. For he receives that Spirit of God which he had then received from His afflatus, but afterward lost through sin.

Ch. 6. Not that in the waters we obtain the Holy Spirit, but in the water, under (the witness of angels) we are cleansed and prepared for the Holy Spirit. . . .

Ch. 7. After this, when we have issued from the font, we are thoroughly anointed with a blessed unction according to the ancient discipline, wherein on entering the priesthood men were accustomed to be anointed with oil from a horn, wherefore Aaron was anointed by Moses. . . . Thus, too, in our case the unction runs carnally, but profits spiritually; in the same way as the act of baptism itself is carnal, in that we are plunged in the water, but the effect spiritual, in that we are freed from sins.

Ch. 8. In the next place, the hand is laid upon us, invoking and inviting the Holy Spirit through benediction. . . . But this, as well as the former, is derived from the old sacramental rite in which Jacob blessed his grandsons born of Joseph,

Ephraim, and Manasses; with his hands laid on them and interchanged, and indeed so transversely slanted the one over the other that, by delineating Christ, they even portended the future benediction in Christ. [*Cf.* Gen. 48 : 13 *f.*]

(c) Cyprian, *Ep. ad Cæcilium, Ep.* 63, 13–17. (MSL, 4 : 395.)

The eucharist.

Thascius Cæcilius Cyprianus, bishop of Carthage, was born about 200, and became bishop in 248 or 249. His doctrinal position is a development of that of Tertullian, beside whom he may be placed as one of the founders of the characteristic theology of North Africa. His discussion of the place and authority of the bishop in the ecclesiastical system was of fundamental importance in the development of the theory of the hierarchy, though it may be questioned whether his particular theory of the relation of the bishops to each other ever was realized in the Church. For his course during the Decian persecution see §§ 45, 46. He died about 258, in the persecution under Valerian.

In the epistle from which the following extract is taken Cyprian writes to Cæcilius to point out that it is wrong to use merely water in the eucharist, and that wine mixed with water should be used, for in all respects we do exactly what Christ did at the Last Supper when he instituted the eucharist. In the course of the letter, which is of some length, Cyprian takes occasion to set forth his conception of the eucharistic sacrifice, which is a distinct advance upon Tertullian. The date of the letter is about 253.

Ch. 13. Because Christ bore us all, in that He also bore our sins, we see that in the water is understood the people, but in the wine is showed the blood of Christ. But when in the cup the water is mingled with the wine the people is made one with Christ, and the assembly of believers is associated and conjoined with Him on whom it believes; which association and conjunction of water and wine is so mingled in the Lord's cup that that mixture cannot be separated any more. Whence, moreover, nothing can separate the Church—that is, the people established in the Church, faithfully and firmly continuing in that in which they have believed—from Christ in such a way as to prevent their undivided love from always abiding and adhering. Thus, therefore, in consecrating the cup water alone should not be offered to the Lord, even as wine alone should not be offered. For if wine only is offered, the blood of Christ begins to be without us.[1] But if the water alone be offered, the people begin to be without Christ, but when both are mingled and are joined to each other by an intermixed union, then the spiritual and heavenly sacrament is completed. Thus the cup of the Lord is not, indeed, water alone, nor wine alone, nor unless each be mingled with the other; just as, on the other hand, the body of the Lord cannot be flour alone or water alone, nor unless both should be united and joined together and compacted into the mass of one bread: in which sacrament our people are shown to be one; so that in like manner as many grains are collected and ground and mixed together into one mass and made one bread, so in Christ, who is the heavenly bread, we may know that there is one body with which our number is joined and united.

Ch. 14. There is, then, no reason, dearest brother, for any one to think that the custom of certain persons is to be followed, who in times past have thought that water alone should be offered in the cup of the Lord. For we must inquire whom they themselves have followed. For if in the sacrifice which Christ offered none is to be followed but Christ, we ought certainly to obey and do what Christ did, and what He commanded to be done, since He himself says in the Gospel: "If ye do whatsoever I command you, henceforth I call you not servants, but friends" [John 15 : 14 f.]. . . . If Jesus Christ, our Lord and God, is Himself the chief priest of God the Father, and has first offered Himself a sacrifice to the Father, and has commanded this to be done in commemoration of Himself, certainly that priest truly acts in the place of Christ who imitates what Christ did; and he then offers a true and full sacrifice in the Church of God to God the Father

---

[1] *Sanguis Christi incipit esse sine nobis.* Paschasius Radbertus quotes this, *De corpore et sanguine Domini*, ch. 11, MSL, 120 : 1308.

when he proceeds to offer it according to what he sees Christ himself to have offered.

Ch. 15. But the discipline of all religion and truth is overturned unless what is spiritually prescribed be faithfully observed; unless, indeed, any one should fear in the morning sacrifices lest the taste of wine should be redolent of the blood of Christ.[1] Therefore, thus the brotherhood is beginning to be kept back from the passion of Christ in persecutions by learning in the offerings to be disturbed concerning His blood and His blood-shedding. . . . But how can we shed our blood for Christ who blush to drink the blood of Christ?

Ch. 16. Does any one perchance flatter himself with this reflection—that, although in the morning water alone is seen to be offered, yet when we come to supper we offer the mingled cup? But when we sup, we cannot call the people together for our banquet that we may celebrate the truth of the sacrament in the presence of the entire brotherhood. But still it was not in the morning, but after supper that the Lord offered the mingled cup. Ought we, then, to celebrate the Lord's cup after supper, that so by continual repetition of the Lord's Supper we may offer the mingled cup? It was necessary that Christ should offer about the evening of the day, that the very hour of sacrifice might show the setting and the evening of the world as it is written in Exodus: "And all the people of the synagogue of the children of Israel shall kill it in the evening." [2] And again in the Psalms: "Let the lifting up of my hands be an evening sacrifice." [3] But we celebrate the resurrection of the Lord in the morning.

Ch. 17. And because we make mention of His passion in all sacrifices (for the Lord's passion is the sacrifice which we offer), we ought to do nothing else than what He did. For the Scripture says: "For as often as ye eat this bread and

[1] Reference to the possibility of detecting Christians in times of persecution by the odor of wine which they had received in the eucharist early in the morning.

[2] Ex. 12 : 6.   [3] Psalm. 141 : 2.

drink this cup, ye do show forth the Lord's death till He come."[1] As often, therefore, as we offer the cup in commemoration of the Lord and His passion, let us do what it is known the Lord did.

§ 50. THE EPISCOPATE IN THE CHURCH

The greatest name connected with the development of the hierarchical conception of the Church in the third century is without question Cyprian (see § 49). He developed the conception of the episcopate beyond the point it had reached in the hands of Tertullian, to whom the institution was important primarily as a guardian of the deposit of faith and a pledge of the continuity of the Church. In the hands of Cyprian the episcopate became the essential foundation of the Church. According to his theory of the office, every bishop was the peer of every other bishop and had the same duties to his diocese and to the Church as a whole as every other bishop. No bishop had any more than a moral authority over any other. Only the whole body of bishops, or the council, could bring anything more than moral authority to bear upon an offending prelate. The constitution of the council was not as yet defined. In several points the ecclesiastical theories of Cyprian were not followed by the Church as a whole, notably his opinion regarding heretical baptism (see § 47), but his main contention as to the importance of the episcopate for the very existence (*esse*), and not the mere welfare (*bene esse*), of the Church was universally accepted. His theory of the equality of all bishops was a survival of an earlier period, and represented little more than his personal ideal. The following sections should also be consulted in this connection.

Additional source material: Cyprian deals with the hierarchical constitution in almost every epistle; see, however, especially the following: 26 : 1 [33 : 1], 51 : 24 [55 : 24], 54 : 5 [59 : 5], 64 : 3 [3 : 3],

[1] I Cor. 11 : 26.

72 : 21 [73 : 21], 74 : 16 [75 : 16] (important for the testimony of Firmilian as to the hierarchical ideas in the East). *Serapion's Prayer Book*, trans. by J. Wordsworth, 1899.

(a) Cyprian, *Epistula* 68, 8 [=66].   (MSL, 4 : 418.)

Although a rebellious and arrogant multitude of those who will not obey depart, yet the Church does not depart from Christ; and they are the Church who are a people united to the priest, and the flock which adheres to its pastor.   Whence you ought to know that the bishop is in the Church and the Church in the bishop; and that if any one be not with the bishop, he is not in the Church, and that those flatter themselves in vain who creep in, not having peace with God's priests, and think that they communicate secretly with some; while the Church, which is Catholic and one, is not cut nor divided, but is indeed connected and bound together by the cement of the priests who cohere with one another.

(b) Council of Carthage, A. D. 256.   (MSL, 3 : 1092.)

The council of Carthage, in 256, was held, under the presidency of Cyprian, to act on the question of baptism by heretics.   See § 52. Eighty-seven bishops were present.   The full report of proceedings is to be found in the works of Cyprian.   See ANF, V, 565, and Hefele, § 6.   The theory of Cyprian which is here expressed is that all bishops are equal and independent, as opposed to the Roman position taken by Stephen, and that the individual bishop is responsible only to God.

Cyprian said: . . . It remains that upon this matter each of us should bring forward what he thinks, judging no man, nor rejecting from the right of communion, if he should think differently.   For neither does any one of us set himself up as a bishop of bishops, nor by tyrannical terrors does any one compel his colleagues to the necessity of obedience; since every bishop, according to the allowance of his liberty and power, has his own proper right of judgment, and can no more be judged by another than he himself can judge another. But let us all wait for the judgment of our Lord Jesus Christ, who alone has the power of advancing us in the government of His Church, and of judging us in our conduct here.

(c) Cyprian, *Epistula* 67 : 5. (MSL, 3 : 1064.)

The following epistle was written to clergy and people in Spain, *i. e.*, at Leon, Astorga, and Merida, in regard to the ordination of two bishops, Sabinus and Felix, in place of Basilides and Martial, who had lapsed in the persecution and had been deprived of their sees. The passage illustrates the methods of election and ordination of bishops, and the failure of Cyprian, with his theory of the episcopate, to recognize in the see of Rome any jurisdiction over other bishops. Its date appears to be about 257.

You must diligently observe and keep the practice delivered from divine tradition and apostolic observance, which is also maintained among us, and throughout almost all the provinces: that for the proper celebration of ordinations all the neighboring bishops of the same province should assemble with that people for which a prelate is ordained. And the bishops should be chosen in the presence of the people, who have most fully known the life of each one, and have looked into the doings of each one as respects his manner of life. And this also, we see, was done by you in the ordination of our colleague Sabinus; so that, by the suffrage of the whole brotherhood, and by the sentence of the bishops who had assembled in their presence, and who had written letters to you concerning him, the episcopate was conferred upon him, and hands were imposed on him in the place of Basilides. Neither can an ordination properly completed be annulled, so that Basilides, after his crimes had been discovered and his conscience made bare, even by his own confession, might go to Rome and deceive Stephen, our colleague, who was placed at a distance and was ignorant of what had been done, so as to bring it about that he might be replaced unjustly in the episcopate from which he had been justly deposed.

§ 51. The Unity of the Church and the See of Rome

In the middle of the third century there were in sharp conflict two distinct and opposed theories of Church unity: the theory that the unity was based upon adherence to and comformity with the see of Peter; and the theory that the episcopate was itself one, and that each bishop shared equally in it. The unity was either in one see or in the less tangible unity of an order of the hierarchy. The former was the theory of the Roman bishops; the latter, the theory of Cyprian of Carthage, and possibly of a number of other ecclesiastics in North Africa and Asia Minor. Formerly polemical theology made the study of this point difficult, at least with anything like impartiality. In the passage given below from Cyprian's treatise *On the Unity of the Catholic Church* the text of the Jesuit Father Kirch is followed in the most difficult and interpolated chapter 4. As Father Kirch gives the text it is perfectly consistent with the theory of Cyprian as he has elsewhere stated it, and that the interpolated text is not. See, however, P. Battifol, *Primitive Catholicism*, Lond., 1911, Excursus E.

Additional source material: *V. supra*, § 27; also Mirbt, §§ 56–69. The little treatise *De Aleatoribus* (MSL, 4 : 827), from which Mirbt gives an extract (n. 71), might be cited in this connection, but its force depends upon its origin. It is wholly uncertain that it was written either by a bishop of Rome or in Italy. *Cf.* Bardenhewer. Kirch also gives the text in part, n. 276; for other references, see Kirch.

(*a*) Cyprian, *De Catholicæ Ecclesiæ Unitate*, 4, 5. (MSL, 4 : 513.)

The tract entitled *On the Unity of the Catholic Church* is the most famous of Cyprian's works. As the theory there developed is opposed to that which became dominant, and as Cyprian was regarded as the great upholder of the Church's constitution, interpolations were early made in the text which seriously distort the sense. These interpolations are to-day abandoned by all scholars. The best critical edition of the works of Cyprian is by W. von Hartel in the CSEL, but critical texts of the following passage with references to literature and indication of interpolations may be found in Mirbt (Prot.), n. 52, and in Kirch (R. C.), n. 234 (chapter 4 only).

Ch. 4. The Lord speaks to Peter, saying: "I say unto thee, that thou art Peter; and upon this rock I will build my Church and the gates of hell shall not prevail against it. I will give thee the keys of the Kingdom of Heaven; and whatsoever thou shalt bind on earth shall be bound also in heaven; and whatsoever thou shalt loose on earth shall be loosed also in heaven" (Matt. 16 : 18, 19). [To the same He says after His resurrection: "Feed my sheep" (John 21 : 15). Upon him He builds His Church, and to him He commits His sheep to be fed, and although. *Interpolation.*] Upon one he builds the Church, although also to all the Apostles after His resurrection He gives an equal power and says, "As the Father has sent me, I also send you: receive ye the Holy Ghost: whosesoever sins ye retain, they shall be retained" (John 20 : 21); yet, that He might show the unity, [He founded one see. *Interpolation.*] He arranged by His authority the origin of that unity as beginning from one. Assuredly the rest of the Apostles were also what Peter was, with a like partnership both of honor and power; but the beginning proceeds from unity [and the primacy is given to Peter. *Interpolation*], that there might be shown to be one Church of Christ [and one see. And they are all shepherds, but the flock is shown to be one which is fed by the Apostles with unanimous consent. *Interpolation*]. Which one Church the Holy Spirit also in the Song of Songs designates in the person of the Lord and says: "My dove, my spotless one, is but one. She is the only one of her mother, chosen of her that bare her" (Cant. 6 : 9). Does he who does not hold this unity of the Church [unity of Peter. *Corrupt reading*] think that he holds the faith? Does he who strives against and resists the Church [who deserts the chair of Peter. *Interpolation*] trust that he is in the Church, when, moreover, the blessed Apostle Paul teaches the same things and sets forth the sacrament of unity, saying, "There is one body and one spirit, one hope of your calling, one Lord, one faith, one baptism, one God"? (Eph. 4 : 4.)

Ch. 5. And this unity we ought to hold firmly and assert, especially we bishops who preside in the Church, that we may prove the episcopate itself to be one and undivided. Let no one deceive the brotherhood by a falsehood; let no one corrupt the truth by a perfidious prevarication. The episcopate is one, each part of which is held by each one in its entirety. The Church, also, is one which is spread abroad far and wide into a multitude by an increase of fruitfulness. As there are many rays of the sun, but one light, and many branches of a tree, but one strength based upon its tenacious root, and since from one spring flow many streams, although the multiplicity seems diffused in the liberality of an overflowing abundance, yet the unity is still preserved in its source.

(b) Firmilian of Cæsarea, *Ep. ad Cyprianum*, in Cyprian, *Ep.* 74 [=75]. (MSL, 3 : 1024.)

The matter in dispute was the rebaptism of those heretics who had received baptism before they conformed to the Church. See § 52. It was the burning question after the rise of the Novatian sect. Stephen, bishop of Rome (254–257), had excommunicated a number of churches and bishops, among them probably Cyprian himself. See the epistle of Dionysius to Sixtus of Rome, the successor of Stephen, in Eusebius, *Hist. Ec.*, VII, 5. "He" (Stephen) therefore had written previously concerning Helenus and Firmilianus and all those in Cilicia, Cappadocia, Galatia, and the neighboring countries, saying that he would not communicate with them for this same cause: namely, that they rebaptized heretics. This attitude of Stephen roused no little resentment in the East, as is shown by the indignant tone of Firmilian, who recognizes no authority in Rome. The text may be found in Mirbt, n. 74, and in part in Kirch, n. 274. The epistle of Firmilian is to be found among the epistles of Cyprian, to whom it was written.

Ch. 2. We may in this matter give thanks to Stephen that it has now happened through his unkindness [inhumanity] that we receive proof of your faith and wisdom.

Ch. 3. But let these things which were done by Stephen be passed by for the present, lest, while we remember his audacity and pride, we bring a more lasting sadness on ourselves from the things he has wickedly done.

Ch. 6. That they who are at Rome do not observe those things in all cases which have been handed down from the beginning, and vainly pretend the authority of the Apostles, any one may know; also, from the fact that concerning the celebration of the day of Easter, and concerning many other sacraments of divine matters, one may see that there are some diversities among them, and that all things are not observed there alike which are observed at Jerusalem; just as in very many other provinces also many things are varied because of the difference of places and names, yet on this account there is no departure at all from the peace and unity of the Catholic Church. And this departure Stephen has now dared to make; breaking the peace against you, which his predecessors have always kept with you in mutual love and honor, even herein defaming Peter and Paul, the blessed Apostles, as if the very men delivered this who in their epistles execrated heretics and warned us to avoid them. Whence it appears that this tradition is human which maintains heretics, and asserts that they have baptism, which belongs to the Church alone.

Ch. 17. And in this respect I am justly indignant at this so open and manifest folly of Stephen, that he who so boasts of the place of his episcopate and contends that he holds the succession of Peter, on whom the foundation of the Church was laid, should introduce many other rocks and establish new buildings of many churches, maintaining that there is a baptism in them by his authority; for those who are baptized, without doubt, make up the number of the Church. . . . Stephen, who announces that he holds by succession the throne of Peter, is stirred with no zeal against heretics, when he concedes to them, not a moderate, but the very greatest power of grace.

Ch. 19. This, indeed, you Africans are able to say against Stephen, that when you knew the truth you forsook the error of custom. But we join custom to truth, and to the Romans' custom we oppose custom, but the custom of truth, holding from the beginning that which was delivered by Christ and the Apostles. Nor do we remember that this at any time began among us, since it has always been observed here, that we have known none but one Church of God, and have accounted no baptism holy except that of the holy Church.

Ch. 24. Consider with what want of judgment you dare to blame those who strive for the truth against falsehood.[1] . . . For how many strifes and dissensions have you stirred up throughout the churches of the whole world! Moreover, how great sin have you heaped up for yourself, when you cut yourself off from so many flocks! For it is yourself that you have cut off. Do not deceive yourself, since he is really the schismatic who has made himself an apostate from the communion of ecclesiastical unity. For while you think that all may be excommunicated by you, you have alone excommunicated yourself from all; and not even the precepts of an Apostle have been able to mould you to the rule of truth and peace.[2]

Ch. 25. How carefully has Stephen fulfilled these salutary commands and warnings of the Apostle, keeping in the first place lowliness of mind and meekness! For what is more lowly or meek than to have disagreed with so many bishops throughout the whole world, breaking peace with each one of them in various kinds of discord: at one time with the Easterns, as we are sure is not unknown to you; at another time with you who are in the south, from whom he received bishops as messengers sufficiently patiently and meekly as not to receive them even to the speech of common conference; and, even more, so unmindful of love and charity as to command the whole brotherhood that no one should receive them into his house, so that not only peace and communion, but also a shelter and entertainment were denied to them when they came. This is to have kept the unity of the Spirit

---

[1] This whole passage is supposed to be addressed to Stephen. *Cf.* the opening words of § 25.

[2] Eph. 4: 1–6 follows.

in the bond of peace, to cut himself off from the unity of love,
and to make himself a stranger in all things to his brethren,
and to rebel against the sacrament and the faith with the madness of contumacious discord. . . . Stephen is not ashamed
to afford patronage to such a position in the Church, and for
the sake of maintaining heretics to divide the brotherhood;
and, in addition, to call Cyprian a false Christ, and a false
Apostle, and a deceitful worker, and he, conscious that all
these characters are for himself, has been in advance of you
by falsely objecting to another those things which he himself ought to bear.

§ 52.   CONTROVERSY OVER BAPTISM BY HERETICS

In the great persecutions schisms arose in connection with
the administration of discipline (*cf.* § 46).   The schismatics
held in general the same faith as the main body of Christians.
Were the sacraments, then, they administered to be regarded
as valid in such a sense that when they conformed to the
Catholic Church, which they frequently did, they need not
be baptized, having once been validly baptized; or should
their schismatic baptism be regarded as invalid and they be
required to receive baptism on conforming if they had not
previously been baptized within the Church?   Was baptism
outside the unity of the Church valid?   Rome answered in
the affirmative, admitting conforming schismatics without
distinguishing as to where they had been baptized; North
Africa answered in the negative and required not, indeed, a
second baptism, but claimed that the Church's baptism was
alone valid, and that if the person conforming had been baptized in schism he had not been baptized at all.   This view
was shared by at least some churches in Asia Minor (*cf.*
§ 51, *b*), and possibly elsewhere.   It became the basis of the
Donatist position (*cf.* § 62), which schism shared with the
Novatian schism the opinion, generally rejected by the
Church, that the validity of a sacrament depended upon the

spiritual condition of the minister of the sacrament, *e. g.*, whether he was in schism or no.

Additional source material: Seventh Council of Carthage (ANF, vol. V); Eusebius, *Hist. Ec.*, VII, 7 : 4–6; Augustine, *De Baptismo contra Donatistas*, Bk. III (PNF, ser. I, vol. IV).

(*a*) Cyprian, *Ep. ad Jubianum, Ep.* 73, 7 [=72]. (MSL, 3 : 1159, 168.)

A portion of this epistle may be found in Mirbt, n. 70.

Ch. 7.   It is manifest where and by whom the remission of sins can be given, *i. e.*, that remission which is given by baptism.   For first of all the Lord gave the power to Peter, upon whom He built the Church, and whence he appointed and showed the source of unity, the power, namely, that that should be loosed in heaven which he loosed on earth [John 20 : 21 quoted].   When we perceive that only they who are set over the Church and established in the Gospel law and in the ordinance of the Lord are allowed to baptize and to give remission of sins, we see that outside of the Church nothing can be bound or loosed, for there there is no one who can either bind or loose anything.

Ch. 21.   Can the power of baptism be greater or of more avail than confession, than suffering when one confesses Christ before men, and is baptized in his own blood?   And yet, even this baptism does not benefit a heretic, although he has confessed Christ and been put to death outside the Church, unless the patrons and advocates of heretics [*i. e.*, those whom Cyprian is opposing] declare that the heretics who are slain in a false confession of Christ are martyrs, and assign to them the glory and the crown of martyrdom contrary to the testimony of the Apostle, who says that it will profit them nothing although they are burned and slain.   But if not even the baptism of a public confession and blood can profit a heretic to salvation, because there is no salvation outside of the Church, how much less shall it benefit him if, in a hiding-place and a cave of robbers stained with the contagion of adulterous waters, he has not only not put off his old sins, but rather heaped up still newer and greater ones! Wherefore baptism cannot be common to us and to heretics, to whom neither God the Father nor Christ the Son, nor the Holy Ghost, nor the faith, nor the Church itself is common. And wherefore they ought to be baptized who come from heresy to the Church, so that they who are prepared and receive the lawful and true and only baptism of the holy Church, by divine regeneration for the kingdom of God may be born of both sacraments, because it is written: "Except a man be born of water and of the Spirit, he cannot enter the kingdom of God" [John 3 : 5].

Ch. 26. These things, dearest brother, we have briefly written to you according to our modest abilities, prescribing to none and prejudging none, so as to prevent any one of the bishops doing what he thinks well, and having the free exercise of his judgment.

(b) Cyprian, *Ep. ad Magnum, Ep.* 75 [=69]. (MSL, 3 : 1183.) *Cf.* Mirbt, n. 67.

With your usual diligence you have consulted my poor intelligence, dearest son, as to whether, among other heretics, they also who come from Novatian ought, after his profane washing, to be baptized and sanctified in the Catholic Church, with the lawful, true, and only baptism of the Church. In answer to this question, as much as the capacity of my faith and the sanctity and truth of the divine Scriptures suggest, I say that no heretics and schismatics at all have any right to power. For which reason Novatian, since he is without the Church and is acting in opposition to the peace and love of Christ, neither ought to be, nor can be, omitted from being counted among the adversaries and antichrists. For our Lord Jesus Christ, when He declared in His Gospel that those who were not with Him were His adversaries, did not point out any species of heresy, but showed that all who were not with Him, and who were not gathering with Him, were scattering His flock, and were His adversaries, saying: "He that is not with me is against me, and he that gathereth not with me scattereth" [Luke 11 : 23]. Moreover, the blessed Apostle John distinguished no heresy or schism, neither did he set down any specially separated, but he called all who had gone out from the Church, and who acted in opposition to the Church, antichrists, saying, "Ye have heard that Antichrist cometh, and even now are come many antichrists; wherefore we know that this is the last time. They went out from us, but they were not of us, for if they had been of us, they would have continued with us" [I John 2 : 18 f.]. Whence it appears that all are adversaries of the Lord and are antichrists who are known to have departed from the charity and from the unity of the Catholic Church.

§ 53. The Beginnings of Monasticism

Asceticism in some form is common to almost all religions. It was practised extensively in early Christianity and ascetics of both sexes were numerous. This asceticism, in addition to a life largely devoted to prayer and fasting, was marked by refraining from marriage. But these ascetics lived in close relations with those who were non-ascetics. Monasticism is an advance upon this earlier asceticism in that it attempts to create, apart from non-ascetics, a social order composed only of ascetics in which the ascetic ideals may be more successfully realized. The transition was made by the hermit life in which the ascetic lived alone in deserts and other solitudes. This became monasticism by the union of ascetics for mutual spiritual aid. This advance is associated with St. Anthony. See also Pachomius, in § 77.

Additional source material: Pseudo-Clement, *De Virginitate* (ANF, VIII, 53); Methodius, *Symposium* (ANF, VI, 309); the *Lausiac History of Palladius*, E. C. Butler, *Texts and Studies*, Cambridge, 1898; *Paradise, or Garden of the Holy Fathers*, trans. by E. A. W. Budge, London, 1907.

Athanasius, *Vita S. Antonii*, 2–4, 44.   (MSG, 26 : 844, 908.)

Anthony, although not the first hermit, gave such an impetus to the ascetic life and did so much to bring about some union of ascetics that he has been popularly regarded as the founder of monasticism. He died 356, at the age of one hundred and five. His *Life*, by St. Athanasius, although formerly attacked, is a genuine, and, on the whole, trustworthy account of this remarkable man. It was written either 357 or 365, and was translated into Latin by Evagrius of Antioch (died 393). Everywhere it roused the greatest enthusiasm for monasticism. The *Life of St. Paul of Thebes*, by St. Jerome, is of very different character, and of no historical value.

Ch. 2. After the death of his parents, Anthony was left alone with one little sister. He was about eighteen or twenty years old, and on him rested the care of both the home and his sister. Now it happened not six months after the death of his parents, and when he was going, according to custom, into the Lord's house, and was communing with himself, that he reflected as he walked how the Apostles left all and followed the Saviour, and how, in the Acts, men sold their possessions and brought and laid them at the Apostles' feet for distribution to the needy, and what and how great a hope was laid up for them in heaven. While he was reflecting on these things he entered the church, and it happened that at that time the Gospel was being read, and he heard the Lord say to the rich man: "If thou wouldest be perfect, go and sell that thou hast and give to the poor; and come and follow me and thou shalt have treasure in heaven." Anthony, as though God had put him in mind of the saints and the passage had been read on his account, went out straightway from the Lord's house, and gave the possessions which he had from his forefathers to the villagers—they were three hundred acres, productive and very fair—that they should be no more a clog upon himself and his sister. And all the rest that was movable he sold, and, having got together much money, he gave it to the poor, reserving a little, however, for his sister's sake.

Ch. 3. And again as he went into the Lord's house, and hearing the Lord say in the Gospel, "Be not anxious for the morrow," he could stay no longer, but went and gave also those things to the poor. He then committed his sister to known and faithful virgins, putting her in a convent [*parthenon*], to be brought up, and henceforth he devoted himself outside his house to ascetic discipline, taking heed to himself and training himself patiently. For there were not yet many monasteries in Egypt, and no monk at all knew of the distant desert; but every one of those who wished to give heed to themselves practised the ascetic discipline in solitude near his own village. Now there was in the next village an old man who had lived from his youth the life of a hermit. Anthony, after he had seen this man, imitated him in piety. And at first he began to abide in places outside the village. Then, if he heard of any good man anywhere, like the prudent bee, he went forth and sought him, nor did he turn back to his own place until he had seen him; and he returned, having got from the good man supplies, as it were, for his journey in the way of virtue. So dwelling there at first, he steadfastly held to his purpose not to return to the abode of his parents or to the remembrance of his kinsfolk; but to keep all his desire and energy for the perfecting of his discipline. He worked, however, with his hands, having heard that "he who is idle, let him not eat," and part he spent on bread and part he gave to the needy. And he prayed constantly, because he had learned that a man ought to pray in secret unceasingly. For he had given such heed to what was read that none of those things that were written fell from him to the ground; for he remembered all, and afterward his memory served him for books.

Ch. 4. Thus conducting himself, Anthony was beloved by all. He subjected himself in sincerity to the good men he visited, and learned thoroughly wherein each surpassed him in zeal and discipline. He observed the graciousness of one, the unceasing prayer of another; he took knowledge of one's freedom from anger, and another's kindliness; he gave heed to one as he watched, to another as he studied; one he admired for his endurance, another for his fasting and sleeping on the ground; he watched the meekness of one, and the long-suffering of another; and at the same time he noted the piety toward Christ and the mutual love which animated all.

Athanasius describes Anthony's removal to the desert and the coming of disciples to him, and weaves into his narrative, in the form of a speech, a long account of the discipline laid down, probably by Anthony himself, chs. 16–43. It is to this long speech that the opening words of the following section refers.

Ch. 44. While Anthony was thus speaking all rejoiced; in some the love of virtue increased, in others carelessness was thrown aside, the self-conceit of others was stopped; and all were persuaded to despise the assaults of the Evil One, and marvelled at the grace given Anthony from the Lord for the discerning of spirits. So their cells were in the mountains, like tabernacles filled with holy bands of men who sang psalms, loved reading, fasted, prayed, rejoiced in the hope of things to come, labored in almsgiving, and maintained love and harmony with one another. And truly it was possible to behold a land, as it were, set by itself, filled with piety and justice. For then there was neither the evil-doer nor the injured, nor the reproaches of the tax-gatherer; but instead a multitude of ascetics, and the one purpose of all was to aim at virtue. So that one beholding the cells again and seeing such good order among the monks would lift up his voice and say: "How goodly are thy dwellings, O Jacob, and thy tents, O Israel; as shady glens and as a garden by a river; as tents which the Lord has pitched, and like cedars near the waters" [Num. 24 : 5, 6].

Ch. 45. Anthony, however, returned, according to his custom, alone to his cell, increased his discipline, and sighed daily as he thought of the mansions of heaven, having his desire fixed on them and pondering over the shortness of man's life.

§ 54.   MANICHÆANISM

The last great rival religion to Christianity was Manichæan-ism, the last of the important syncretistic religions which drew from Persian and allied sources. Its connection with Christianity was at first slight and its affinities were with Eastern Gnosticism. After 280 it began to spread within the Empire, and was soon opposed by the Roman authorities. Yet it flourished, and, like other Gnostic religions, with which it is to be classed, it assimilated more and more of Christianity, until in the time of Augustine it seemed to many as merely a form of Christianity. On account of its general character, it absorbed for the most part what remained of the earlier Gnostic systems and schools.

Additional source material: The most important accessible works are the so-called *Acta Archelai* (ANF, V, 175–235), the anti-Mani-chæan writings of Augustine (PNF, ser. I, vol. IV), and Alexander of Lycopolis, *On the Manichæans* (ANF, VI, 239). On Alexander of Lycopolis, see DCB. In the opinion of Bardenhewer, Alexander was probably neither a bishop nor a Christian at all, but a heathen and a Platonist.   Roman edict against Manichæanism in Kirch, n. 294.

An Nadim, *Fihrist*. (Translation after Kessler, *Mani*, 1889.)

The *Fihrist, i. e.*, Catalogue, is a sort of history of literature made in the eleventh century by the Moslem historian An Nadim.   In spite of its late date, it is the most important authority for the original doctrines of Mani and the facts of his life, as it is largely made up from citations from ancient authors and writings of Mani and his original disciples.

(*a*) The Life of Mani.

Mohammed ibn Isak says: Mani was the son of Fatak,[1] of the family of the Chaskanier. Ecbatana is said to have been the original home of his father, from which he emigrated to the province of Babylon. He took up his residence in Al Madain, in a portion of the city known as Ctesiphon. In that place was an idol's temple, and Fatak was accustomed to go into it, as did also the other people of the place. It happened one

[1] Or, Fonnak.

day that a voice sounded forth from the sacred interior of the temple, saying to him: "Fatak, eat no flesh, drink no wine and refrain from carnal intercourse." This was repeated to him several times on three days. When Fatak perceived this, he joined a society of people in the neighborhood of Dastumaisan which were known under the name of Al-Mogtasilah, *i. e.*, those who wash themselves, baptists, and of whom remnants are to be found in these parts and in the marshy districts at the present time. These belonged to that mode of life which Fatak had been commanded to follow. His wife was at that time pregnant with Mani, and when she had given him birth she had, as they say, glorious visions regarding him, and even when she was awake she saw him taken by some one unseen, who bore him aloft into the air, and then brought him down again; sometimes he remained even a day or two before he came down again. Thereupon his father sent for him and had him brought to the place where he was, and so he was brought up with him in his religion. Mani, in spite of his youthful age, spake words of wisdom. After he had completed his twelfth year there came to him, according to his statement, a revelation from the King of the Paradise of Light, who is God the Exalted, as he said. The angel which brought him the revelation was called Eltawan; this name means "the Companion." He spoke to Mani, and said: "Separate thyself from this sort of faith, for thou belongest not among its adherents, and it is obligatory upon you to practise continence and to forsake the fleshly desires, yet on account of thy youth the time has not come for thee to take up thy public work." But when he was twenty-four years old, Eltawan appeared to him and said: "Hail, Mani, from me and from the Lord who has sent me to thee and has chosen thee to be his prophet. He commands thee now to proclaim thy truth and on my announcement to proclaim the truth which is from him and to throw thyself into this calling with all thy zeal."

The Manichæans say: He first openly entered upon his

work on the day when Sapor, the son of Ardaschir, entered upon his reign, and placed the crown upon his head; and this was Sunday, the first day of Nisan (March 20, 241), when the sun stood in the sign Aries. He was accompanied by two men, who had already attached themselves to his religion; one was called Simeon, the other Zakwa; besides these, his father accompanied him, to see how his affairs would turn out.

Mani said he was the Paraclete, whom Jesus, of blessed memory,[1] had previously announced. Mani took the elements of his doctrine from the religion of the Magi and Christianity. . . . Before he met Sapor Mani had spent about forty years in foreign lands.[2] Afterward he converted Peroz, the brother of Sapor, and Peroz procured him an audience with his brother Sapor. The Manichæans relate: He thereupon entered where he was and on his shoulders were shining, as it were, two candles. When Sapor perceived him, he was filled with reverence for him, and he appeared great in his eyes; although he previously had determined to seize him and put him to death. After he had met him, therefore, the fear of him filled him, he rejoiced over him and asked him why he had come and promised to become his disciple. Mani requested of him a number of things, among them that his followers might be unmolested in the capital and in the other territories of the Persian Empire, and that they might extend themselves whither they wished in the provinces. Sapor granted him all he asked.

Mani had already preached in India, China, and among the inhabitants of Turkestan, and in every land he left behind him disciples.[3]

[1] The author is a Moslem, and therefore speaks of Jesus with great respect; Mani regarded Jesus as evil.

[2] This is undoubtedly a mistake.

[3] Important material has been recently recovered from Turfan in Chinese Turkestan, reported by Messrs. Stein, Le Coq, and F. K. W. Müller, in *Sitzungsberichte der Berliner Academie*, for 1904, p. 348; for 1905, p. 1077; for 1908, p. 398; for 1909, p. 1202; for 1910, pp. 293, 307.

(*b*) The Teaching of Mani.

The following extract from the same work gives but the beginning of an extended statement of Mani's teaching. But it is hoped that enough is given to show the mythological character of his speculation. The bulk of his doctrine was Persian and late Babylonian, and the Christian element was very slight. It is clear from the writings of St. Augustine that the doctrine changed much in later years in the West.

The doctrine of Mani, especially his dogmas of the Eternal, to whom be praise and glory, of the creation of the world and the contest between Light and Darkness: Mani put at the beginning of the world two eternal principles. Of these one is Light, the other Darkness. They are separated from each other. As to the Light, this is the First, the Mighty One, and the Infinite. He is the Deity, the King of the Paradise of Light. He has five members or attributes, namely, gentleness, wisdom, understanding, discretion, and insight; and further five members or attributes, namely, love, faith, truth, bravery, and wisdom. He asserts that God was from all eternity with these attributes. Together with the Light-God there are two other things from eternity, the air and the earth.

Mani teaches further: The members of the air, or the Light-Ether, are five: gentleness, wisdom, understanding, discretion, and insight. The members of the Light-Earth are the soft gentle breath, the wind, the light, the water, and the fire. As to the other Original Being, the Darkness, its members are also five: the vapor, the burning heat, the fiery wind, the poison, and the darkness.

This bright shining Primal Being was in immediate proximity with the dark Primal Being, so that no wall of partition was between them and the Light touched the Darkness on its broad side. The Light is unlimited in its height, and also to the right hand and to the left; the Darkness, however, is unlimited in its depth, and also to the right hand and to the left.

From this Dark-Earth rose Satan, not so that he himself was without beginning, although his parts were in their ele-

ments without beginning.   These parts joined themselves
together from the elements and formed themselves into Satan.
His head was like that of a lion, his trunk like that of a dragon,
his wings as those of a bird, his tail like that of a great fish,
and his four feet like the feet of creeping things.   When this
Satan had been formed from the Darkness—his name is the
First Devil—then he began to devour and to swallow up and
to ruin, to move about to the right and to the left, and to get
down into the deep, so that he continually brought ruin and
destruction to every one who attempted to overmaster him.
Next he hastened up on high and perceived the rays of light,
but felt an aversion to them.   Then when he saw how these
rays by reciprocal influence and contact were increased in
brilliancy, he became afraid and crept together into himself,
member by member, and withdrew for union and strengthening back to his original constituent parts.   Now once more
he hastened back into the height, and the Light-Earth noticed
the action of Satan and his purpose to seize and to attack and
to destroy.   But when she perceived this thereupon the world
æon of Insight perceived it, then the æon of Wisdom, the
æon of Discretion, the æon of the Understanding, and then
the æon of Gentleness.   Thereupon the King of the Paradise
of Light perceived it and reflected on means to gain the mastery over him.   His armies were indeed mighty enough to
overcome him; he had the wish, however, to accomplish this
himself.   Therefore he begat with the spirit of his right hand,
with the five æons, and with his twelve elements a creature,
and that was the Primal Man, and him he sent to the conquest of Darkness.[1]

CHAPTER V. THE LAST GREAT PERSECUTION

The last of the persecutions was closely connected with the
increased efficiency of the imperial administration after a

[1] By primal man is not meant the first of mankind on earth, but a super-
natural being.

period of anarchy, and was more effective because of the greater centralization of the government which Diocletian had introduced (§ 55). It was preceded by a number of minor persecuting regulations, but broke forth in its full fury in 303, raging for nearly ten years (§ 56). It was by far the most severe of all persecutions, in extent and duration and severity surpassing that of Decius and Valerian. As in that persecution, very many suffered severely, still more lapsed, unprepared for suffering, as many were in the previous persecution, and the Church was again rent with dissensions and schisms arising over the question of the administration of discipline.

§ 55. The Reorganization of the Empire by Diocletian.
§ 56. The Diocletian Persecution.
§ 57. The Rise of Schisms in Consequence of the Diocletian Persecution.

§ 55. The Reorganization of the Empire by Diocletian

After a period of anarchy Diocletian (284–305) undertook a reorganization of the Empire for the sake of greater efficiency. Following a precedent of earlier successful emperors, he shared (285) the imperial authority with a colleague, Maximianus, who in 286 became Augustus of the West. As the greatest danger seemed to lie in the East, Diocletian retained the Eastern part of the Empire, and having already abandoned Rome as the imperial residence (284), he settled in Nicomedia in Bithynia. To provide for a succession to the throne more efficient than the chance succession of natural heirs, two Cæsars were appointed in 293, Constantius Chlorus for the West, and Galerius, the son-in-law of Diocletian, for the East. Constantius at once became the son-in-law of Maximianus. These Cæsars were to ascend the throne when the *Augusti* resigned after twenty years' reign. The scheme worked temporarily for greater efficiency, but ended in civil war as the claims of natural heirs were set aside in favor of an artificial dynasty. At the same time the system bore heavily upon the people and the prosperity of the Empire rapidly declined.

Bibliography in *Cambridge Medieval History*, London and New York, 1911, vol. I.

Lactantius, *De Mortibus Persecutorum*, 7.   (MSL, 7 : 204.)

When Diocletian, the author of crimes and deviser of evils, was ruining all things, not even from against God could he withhold his hand. This man, partly by avarice and partly by timidity, overturned the world. For he made three persons sharers with him in the government. The Empire was divided into four parts, and armies were multiplied, since each of the four princes strove to have a much larger military force than any emperor had had when one emperor alone carried on the government. There began to be a greater number of those who received taxes than of those who paid them; so that the means of the husbandmen were exhausted by enormous impositions, the fields were abandoned, and cultivated grounds became woodlands, and universal dismay prevailed. Besides, the provinces were divided into minute portions and many presidents and prefects lay heavy on each territory, and almost on every city. There were many stewards and masters and deputy presidents, before whom very few civil causes came, but only condemnations and frequent forfeitures, and exactions of numberless commodities, and I will not say often repeated, but perpetual and intolerable, wrongs in the exacting of them.

§ 56. The Diocletian Persecution

The last great persecution was preceded by a number of laws aimed to annoy the Christians. On March 12, 295, all soldiers in the army were ordered to offer sacrifice. In 296 sacred books of the Christians were sought for and burnt at Alexandria. In 297 or 298 Christian persecutions began in the army, but the great persecution itself broke out in 303, as described below. Among other reasons for energetic

measures in which Galerius took the lead, appears to have
been that prince's desire to establish the unity of the Empire
upon a religious basis, which is borne out by his attempts to
reorganize the heathen worship immediately after the cessa-
tion of the persecution. In April, 311, the edict of Galerius,
known as the Edict of the Three Emperors, put an official
end to the persecution. In parts of the Empire, however,
small persecutions took place and the authorities attempted
to attack Christianity without actually carrying on persecutions, as in the wide-spread dissemination of the infamous
"Acts of Pilate," which were posted on walls and spread
through the schools. In the territories of Constantius Chlorus the persecution had been very light, and there was none
under Constantine who favored Christians from the first.

Additional source material: Eusebius, *Hist. Ec.*, VIII, and IX,
9; his little work *On the Martyrs of Palestine* will be found after the
eighth book. Lactantius, *De Mortibus Persecutorum*. The principal
texts will be found in Preuschen's *Analecta*, I, §§ 20, 21; see also R.
Knopf, *Ausgewählte Märtyreracten*.

(a) Lactantius, *De Mortibus Persecutorum*, 12 ff. (MSL,
7 : 213.)

The outbreak of the persecution.

A fit and auspicious day was sought for the accomplishment of this undertaking [*i. e.*, the persecution of the Chris-
tians]; and the festival of the great god Terminus, celebrated
on the seventh calends of March [Feb. 23], was chosen, to
put an end, as it were, to this religion,

"That day the first of death, was first of evil's cause" (Vergil),

and cause of evils which befell not only the Christians but
the whole world. When that day dawned, in the eighth
consulship of Diocletian and seventh of Maximianus, suddenly, while it was hardly light, the prefect, together with
the chief commanders, tribunes, and officers of the treasury,
came to the church [in Nicomedia], and when the gates had

been forced open they sought for an image of God. The books of the Holy Scriptures were found and burnt; the spoil was given to all. Rapine, confusion, and tumult reigned. Since the church was situated on rising ground, and was visible from the palace, Diocletian and Galerius stood there as if on a watch-tower and disputed long together whether it ought to be set on fire. The opinion of Diocletian prevailed, for he feared lest, when so great a fire should once be started, the city might be burnt; for many and large buildings surrounded the church on all sides. Then the prætorian guard, in battle array, came with axes and other iron instruments, and having been let loose everywhere, in a few hours they levelled that very lofty building to the ground.

Ch. 13. Next day the edict was published ordaining that men of the Christian religion should be deprived of all honors and dignities; and also that they should be subjected to torture, of whatsoever rank or position they might be; and that every suit of law should be entertained against them; but they, on the other hand, could not bring any suit for any wrong, adultery, or theft; and finally, that they should have neither freedom nor the right of suffrage. A certain person, although not properly, yet with a brave soul, tore down this edict and cut it up, saying in derision: "These are the triumphs of Goths and Samaritans." Having been brought to judgment, he was not only tortured, but was burnt in the legal manner, and with admirable patience he was consumed to ashes.

Ch. 14. But Galerius was not satisfied with the terms of the edict, and sought another way to gain over the Emperor. That he might urge him to excess of cruelty in persecution, he employed private agents to set the palace on fire; and when some part of it had been burnt the Christians were accused as public enemies, and the very appellation of Christian grew odious on account of its connection with the fire in the palace. It was said that the Christians, in concert with the eunuchs, had plotted to destroy the princes, and that both the emperors had well-nigh been burnt alive in their own palace. Diocletian, who always wanted to appear shrewd and intelligent, suspecting nothing of the deception, but inflamed with anger, began immediately to torture all his domestics.

(b) Eusebius, *Hist. Ec.*, VIII, 2; 6 : 8. (MSG, 20 : 753.)

The edicts of Diocletian.
The first passage occurs, with slight variations, in the introduction to the work, *On the Martyrs of Palestine.*

Ch. 2. It was in the nineteenth year of the reign of Diocletian, in the month Dystus; called March by the Romans, when the feast of the Saviour's passion was near at hand, that royal edicts were published everywhere commanding that the churches be levelled to the ground, the Scriptures be destroyed by fire, and all holding places of honor be branded with infamy, and that the household servants, if they persisted in the profession of Christianity, be deprived of their freedom.

Such was the original edict against us. But not long after other decrees were issued, commanding that all the rulers of the churches everywhere should be first thrown into prison, and afterward compelled by every means to sacrifice.

Ch. 6 : 8. Such things occurred in Nicomedia at the beginning of the persecution. But not long after, as persons in the country called Melitina and others throughout Syria attempted to usurp the government, a royal edict commanded that the rulers of the churches everywhere be thrown into prison and bonds. What was to be seen after this exceeds all description. A vast multitude were imprisoned in every place; and the prisons everywhere, which had long before been prepared for murderers and grave-robbers, were filled with bishops, presbyters and deacons, readers and exorcists, so that room was no longer left in them for those condemned for crimes. And as other decrees followed the first, directing that those in prison, if they sacrificed, should be permitted to depart from the prison in freedom, but that those who refused should be harassed with many tortures, how could any one again number the multitude of martyrs in every province, and especially those in Africa and Mauretania, and Thebais and Egypt ?

(c) Edict of Galerius, A. D. 311.   Eusebius, *Hist. Ec.*, VIII, 17.   (MSG, 20 : 792.)   *Cf.* Preuschen, *Analecta*, I, § 21: 5.

This may also be found in Lactantius, *De Mortibus Persecutorum*, ch. 34.   It is known as the "Edict of Three Emperors," as it was issued from Nicomedia in the name of Galerius, Constantine, and Licinius. The date is April 30, 311.   By it the persecution was not wholly ended. Galerius died in the next month, but Maximinus Daza resumed the persecution.   There was for six months, however, some mitigation of the persecutions in the East, granted at the request of Constantine.

Amongst our other measures, which we are always making for the use and profit of the commonwealth, we have hitherto endeavored to bring all things into conformity with the ancient laws and public order of the Romans, and to bring it about also that the Christians, who have abandoned the religion of their ancestors, should return to sound reason. For in some way such wilfulness has seized the Christians and such folly possessed them that they do not follow those constitutions of the ancients, which peradventure their own ancestors first established, but entirely according to their own judgment and as it pleased them they were making such laws for themselves as they would observe, and in different places were assembling various sorts of people.   In short, when our command was issued that they were to betake themselves to the institutions of the ancients, many of them were subdued by danger, many also were ruined.   Yet when great numbers of them held to their determination, and we saw that they neither gave worship and due reverence to the gods nor yet regarded the God of the Christians, we therefore, mindful of our most mild clemency and of the unbroken custom whereby we are accustomed to grant pardon to all men, have thought that in this case also speediest indulgence

ought to be granted to them, that the Christians might exist
again and might establish their gatherings, yet so that they
do nothing contrary to good order. By another letter we
shall signify to magistrates how they are to proceed. Wherefore, in accordance with this our indulgence, they ought to
pray their God for our good estate, for that of the commonwealth, and for their own, that the commonwealth may endure
on every side unharmed and that they may be able to live
securely in their own homes.

(d) Constantine, *Edict of Milan*, A. D. 313, in Lactantius,
De Mortibus Persecutorum, 48. (MSL, 7 : 267.) See also
Eusebius. *Hist. Ec.*, X, 5 : 2. (MSG, 20 : 880.)

The so-called Edict of Milan, granting toleration to the Christians,
is not the actual edict, but a letter addressed to a prefect and referring
to the edict, which probably was much briefer. The following passage is translated from the emended text of Lactantius, as given in
Preuschen, *op. cit.*, I, § 22 : 4.

When I, Constantine Augustus, and I, Licinius Augustus,
had happily met together at Milan, and were having under
consideration all things which concern the advantage and
security of the State, we thought that, among other things
which seemed likely to profit men generally, we ought, in the
very first place, to set in order the conditions of the reverence paid to the Divinity by giving to the Christians and all
others full permission to follow whatever worship any man
had chosen; whereby whatever divinity there is in heaven
may be benevolent and propitious to us, and to all placed
under our authority. Therefore we thought we ought, with
sound counsel and very right reason, to lay down this law,
that we should in no way refuse to any man any legal right
who has given up his mind either to the observance of Christianity or to that worship which he personally feels best suited
to himself; to the end that the Supreme Divinity, whose
worship we freely follow, may continue in all things to grant
us his accustomed favor and good-will. Wherefore your
devotion should know that it is our pleasure that all pro-

visions whatsoever which have appeared in documents hitherto
directed to your office regarding Christians and which appeared utterly improper and opposed to our clemency should
be abolished, and that every one of those men who have the
same wish to observe Christian worship may now freely and
unconditionally endeavor to observe the same without any
annoyance or molestation.   These things we thought it well
to signify in the fullest manner to your carefulness, that you
might know that we have given free and absolute permission
to the said Christians to practise their worship.   And when
you perceive that we have granted this to the said Christians,
your devotion understands that to others also a similarly
full and free permission for their own worship and observance
is granted, for the quiet of our times, so that every man may
have freedom in the practice of whatever worship he has
chosen.   And these things were done by us that nothing be
taken away from any honor or form of worship.   Moreover,
in regard to the Christians, we have thought fit to ordain
this also, that if any appear to have bought, either from our
exchequer or from others, the places in which they were
accustomed formerly to assemble, and concerning which definite orders have been given before now, and that by letters
sent to your office, the same be restored to the Christians,
setting aside all delay and dispute, without payment or demand of price.   Those also who have obtained them by gift
shall restore them in like manner without delay to the said
Christians; and those, moreover, who have bought them,
as well as those who have obtained them by gift, if they
request anything of our benevolence, they shall apply to the
deputy that order may be taken for them too by our clemency.
All these must be delivered over at once and without delay
by your intervention to the corporation of the Christians.
And since the same Christians are known to have possessed
not only the places where they are accustomed to assemble,
but also others belonging to their corporation, namely, to the
churches and not to individuals, all these by the law which

we have described above you will order to be restored without
any doubtfulness or dispute to the said Christians—that is, to
their said corporations and assemblies; provided always, as
aforesaid, that those who restore them without price, as we
said, shall expect a compensation from our benevolence. In
all these things you must give the aforesaid Christians your
most effective intervention, that our command may be fulfilled as soon as may be, and that in this matter also order
may be taken by our clemency for the public quiet. And
may it be, as already said, that the divine favor which we
have already experienced in so many affairs, shall continue
for all time to give us prosperity and successes, together with
happiness for the State. But that it may be possible for
the nature of this decree and of our benevolence to come
to the knowledge of all men, it will be your duty by a proclamation of your own to publish everywhere and bring to
the notice of all men this present document when it reaches
you, that the decree of this our benevolence may not be
hidden.

§ 57. Rise of Schisms in Consequence of the Diocle-
tian Persecution

The Diocletian persecution and its various continuations,
on account of the severity of the persecution and its great
extent, seriously strained the organization of the Church for
a time, and in at least three important Church centres gave
rise to schisms, of which two were of some duration. The
causes for these schisms, as in the case of the schisms connected with the Decian persecution, are to be found in the
confusion caused by the enforced absence of bishops from
their sees and in the administration of discipline. In the
latter point the activity of the confessors no longer plays
any part, as the authority of the bishops in the various communities is now undisputed by rival. It was a question of
greater or less rigor in readmitting the lapsed to the com-

munion of the Church.   For the canons of discipline in force
in Alexandria, see the *Canonical Epistle of Peter of Alexandria*,
ANF, VI, 269 *ff*.   (MSG, 18 : 467.)   They were regarded
by the rigorist party in Alexandria as too lax.   Of the three
schisms known to have arisen from the Diocletian persecution, that in Alexandria is known as the Meletian schism,
and three selections are given bearing on it.   For the proposals of the Council of Nicæa to bring about a settlement
and union, see the *Epistle of the Synod of Nicæa*, Socrates,
Hist. Ec., I, 9 (given below, § 61, *II*, *b*).   The schism continued
until the fifth century.   The schism at Rome, known as the
schism of Heraclius, was much less important.   It was caused
by the party advocating greater laxity in discipline, and was
for a time difficult to deal with on account of long vacancies
in the Roman episcopate.   The duration of the schism could
not have been long, but the solution of the questions raised
by it is unknown.   In fact, the history of the Roman church
is exceedingly obscure in the half-century preceding the
Council of Nicæa.   The third schism, that of the Donatists
in North Africa, which broke out in Carthage, was the most
considerable in the Church before the schisms arising from
the christological controversies.   For the Donatist schism,
see §§ 61, 67, 72.

(*a*) *Epistle of Hesychius, Pachomius, Theodorus, and Phileas
to Meletius.*   (MSG, 10 : 1565.)

The Meletian schism.

The following epistle was written in the name of these four bishops,
probably by Phileas, bishop of Thmuis, one of the number, to Meletius,
bishop of Lycopolis.   The four were in prison when it was written.
It is the most important document bearing on the schism, and is
important as setting forth the generally accepted legal opinion of the
time regarding ordination and the authority of bishops.   The document exists only in a Latin translation from a Greek original, and
appears to form, with the two following fragments, a continuous narrative, possibly a history of the Church, but nothing further is known
of it.   For an account of the Meletian schism see Socrates, *Hist. Ec.*,
1, 6 *ff*.   The text of these selections bearing on the Meletian schism is
to be found in Routh, *op. cit.*, IV, 91 *ff*.

Hesychius, Pachomius, Theodorus, and Phileas to Meletius, our friend and fellow-minister in the Lord, greeting. In simple faith, regarding as uncertain the things which have been heard concerning thee, since some have come to us and certain things are reported foreign to divine order and ecclesiastical rule which are being attempted, yea, rather, which are being done by thee, we were not willing to credit them when we thought of the audacity implied by their magnitude, and we thought that they were uncertain attempts. But since so many coming to us at the present time have lent some credibility to these reports, and have not hesitated to attest them as facts, we, greatly astonished, have been compelled to write this letter to thee. And what agitation and sadness have been caused to us all in common and to each of us individually by the ordination performed by thee in parishes not pertaining to thee, we are unable sufficiently to express. We have not delayed, however, by a short statement, to prove thy practice wrong.

In the law of our fathers and forefathers, of which thou also are not thyself ignorant, it is established, according to the divine and ecclesiastical order (for it is all for the good pleasure of God and the zealous regard for better things), that it has been determined and settled by them that it is not lawful for any bishop to perform ordinations in other parishes than his own. This law is exceedingly important and wisely devised. For, in the first place, it is but right that the conversation and life of those who are ordained should be examined with great care; and, in the second place, that all confusion and turbulence should be done away with. For every one shall have enough to do in managing his own parish, and in finding, with great care and many anxieties, suitable subordinates among those with whom he has passed his whole life, and who have been trained under his hands. But thou, considering none of these things, nor regarding the future, nor considering the law of our holy Fathers and those who have put on Christ in long succession, nor the honor of our great bishop and father, Peter,[1] on whom we all depend in the hope which we have in the Lord Jesus Christ, nor softened by our imprisonments and trials, and daily and multiplied reproaches, nor the oppressions and distress of all, hast ventured on subverting all things at once. And what means will be left for thee for justifying thyself with respect to these things?

But perhaps thou wilt say, I did this to prevent many from being drawn away with the unbelief of many, because the flocks were in need and forsaken, there being no pastor with them. Well, but it is most certain that they were in no such destitution; in the first place, because there were many going among them and able to visit them; and, in the second place, even if there were some things neglected by them, representation should have come from the people, and we should have duly considered the matter. But they knew that they were in no want of ministers, and therefore they did not come to seek thee. They knew that either we were wont to warn them from such complaint or there was done, with all carefulness, what seemed profitable; for it was done under correction and all was considered with well-approved honesty. Thou, however, giving such careful attention to the deceits of certain men and their vain words,[2] hast, as it were, stealthily leaped forward to the performance of ordinations. For if, indeed, those accompanying thee constrained thee to this and compelled thee and were ignorant of the ecclesiastical order, thou oughtest to have followed the rule and have informed us by letter; and in that way what seemed expedient would have been done. And if perchance some persuaded thee to credit their story, who said to thee that it was all over with us—a matter which could not have been unknown to thee, because there were many passing and repassing by us who might visit thee—even if this had been so, yet oughtest thou to have waited for the judgment of the superior father and his allowance of this thing. But thinking nothing of

---

[1] Bishop of Alexandria.   [2] See next selection.

these matters, and hoping something different, or rather
having no care for us, thou hast provided certain rulers for
the people. For now we learn that there are also divisions,
because thy unwarrantable ordination displeased many.

And thou wert not readily persuaded to delay such procedure or restrain thy purpose, no, not even by the word of
the Apostle Paul, the most blessed seer and the man who put
on Christ, the Apostle of us all; for he, in writing to his dearly
loved Timothy, says: "Lay hands suddenly on no man,
neither be partaker of other men's sins." [I Tim. 5 : 22.]
And thus he at once shows his own consideration of him, and
gives his example and exhibits the law according to which,
with all carefulnesss and caution, candidates are chosen for
the honor of ordination. We make this declaration to thee,
that in the future thou mayest study to keep within the safe
and salutary limits of the law.

(*b*) *Fragment on the Meletian Schism.* (MSG, 10 : 1567.)

For the connection of the Meletians with Arianism, see Socrates,
Hist. Ec., I, 6. Text in Routh, *op. cit.*, IV, 94.

Meletius received and read this epistle, and he neither
wrote a reply, nor repaired to them in prison, nor went to the
blessed Peter [bishop of Alexandria]. But when all these
bishops, presbyters, and deacons had suffered in the prison,[1]
he at once entered Alexandria. Now in that city there
was a certain person, Isidorus by name, turbulent in character, and possessed with the ambition of being a teacher.
And there was also a certain Arius, who wore the habit of
piety and was in like manner possessed with the ambition
of being a teacher. And when they discovered the object of
Meletius's passion and what it was he sought, hastening to
him and regarding with malice the episcopal authority of the
blessed Peter, that the aim and desire of Meletius might be
made manifest, they discovered to Meletius certain presbyters, then in hiding, to whom the blessed Peter had given

[1] Diocletian persecution, A. D. 306.

authority to act as diocesan visitors for Alexandria. And Meletius, recommending them to improve the opportunity given them for rectifying their error, suspended them for a time, and by his authority ordained two persons in their places, one of whom was in prison and the other in the mines. On learning these things, the blessed Peter, with much endurance, wrote to the people of Alexandria in the following terms. [See next selection.]

(c) Peter of Alexandria. *Epistle to the Church in Alexandria.* (MSG, 18 : 510.)

For Peter of Alexandria, see DCB. Peter was in hiding when he wrote the following to the Alexandrian church in 306. He died 312 as a martyr.

Peter to the brethren in the Lord, beloved and established in the faith of God, peace. Since I have discovered that Meletius acts in no way for the common good, for he does not approve the letter of the most holy bishops and martyrs, and invading my parish, has assumed so much to himself as to endeavor to separate from my authority the priests and those who had been intrusted with visiting the needy, and, giving proof of his desire for pre-eminence, has ordained in the prison several unto himself; now take ye heed to this and hold no communion with him, until I meet him in company with some wise men, and see what designs they are which he has thought upon. Fare ye well.

(d) *Epitaph of Eusebius, Bishop of Rome.* Cf. Kirch, n. 534.

Schism of Heraclius.
The following epitaph was placed on the tomb of Eusebius, bishop of Rome (April 18 to August 17, 310 A. D.), by Damasus, bishop of Rome (366–384.)

I, Damasus, have made this:
Heraclius forbade the fallen to lament their sin,
Eusebius taught the wretched ones to weep for their crimes.
The people was divided into parties by the increasing madness.

Sedition, bloodshed, war, discord, strife arose.
At once they were equally smitten by the ferocity of the
        tyrant.[1]
Although the guide of the Church[2] maintained intact the
        bonds of peace.
He endured exile joyful under the Lord as judge,
And gave up this earthly life on the Trinacrian shore.[3]

[1] Maxentius.   [2] Eusebius.   [3] Sicily.

THE SECOND DIVISION OF ANCIENT CHRISTIANITY

THE CHURCH UNDER THE CHRISTIAN EMPIRE: FROM 312 TO CIRCA 750

The second division of the history of ancient Christianity, or Christianity under the influence of the Græco-Roman type of culture, begins with the sole rule of Constantine, A. D. 324, or his sole reign in the West, A. D. 312, and extends to the beginning of the Middle Ages, or that period in which the Germanic nations assumed the leading rôle in the political life of western Europe. The end of this division of Church history may be placed, at the latest, about the middle of the eighth century, as the time when the authority of the Eastern Empire ceased to affect materially the fortunes of the West. But it is impossible to name any year or reign or political event as of such outstanding importance as to make it a *terminus ad quem* for the division which will command the suffrages of all as the boundary between the ancient and the mediæval epochs of history.

The second division of ancient Christianity may be subdivided into three periods:

I. The Imperial State Church of the Undivided Empire, or until the Death of Theodosius the Great, or to 395.

II. The Church in the Divided Empire until the Collapse of the Western Empire and the Schism between the East and the West arising out of the Monophysite Controversies, or to circa 500.

III. The Dissolution of the Imperial Church of the West and the Transition to the Middle Ages.

In the third period is to be placed the beginnings of the Middle Ages, as the German invaders had long before 500 established their kingdoms and had begun to dominate the affairs of the West. But the connection of the Church of the West, or rather of Italy, with the East was long so close that the condition of the Church is more that of a dissolution of the ancient imperial State Church than of a building up of the mediæval Church. At the same time, the transition to the Middle Ages, so far as the Church is concerned at least, takes place under the influence of the ancient tradition, and institutions are established in which the leading elements, taken from ancient life, are not yet transformed by Germanic ideas. The East knew no Middle Age. For a history of the Eastern Church other divisions would have to be made, but in a history in which, for practical reasons, the development is traced in Western Christianity, the affairs of the Eastern Church must be treated as subordinate to those of Western Christianity.

For the second division of the history of ancient Christianity, the principal sources available in English are the translations in *A Select Library of the Nicene and Post-Nicene Fathers of the Christian Church*. Edited by Ph. Schaff and H. Wace. The *First Series* of this collection (PNF, ser. I) contains the principal works of Augustine and Chrysostom. The *Second Series* (PNF, ser. II) is for historical study even more valuable, and gives, generally with very able introductions and excellent bibliographies, the most important works of many of the leading patristic writers, including the principal ecclesiastical historians, as well as Athanasius, Gregory of Nazianzus, Gregory of Nyssa, Basil the Great, Cyril of Jerusalem, Hilary of Poitiers, Jerome, Rufinus, Cassian, Vincent of Lérins, Leo the Great, Gregory the Great, and others. These translations are in part fresh versions, and in part older versions but slightly, if at all, revised, taken from the *Library of the Fathers of the Holy Catholic Church anterior to the Division of the East and West*, Oxford, 1838, *et seq.*

For the period before the outbreak of the great christological controversies, the ecclesiastical historians are of great value. There are no less than four continuations of the *Ecclesiastical History* of Eusebius accessible: the ecclesiastical histories of Socrates, 324-439 (ed. R. Hussey, Oxford, 1853); of Sozomen, 324-425 (ed. R. Hussey, Oxford, 1860); of Rufinus, 324-395, which is appended to a Latin version or rather revised and "edited" Latin version of Eusebius; of Theodoret, 323-428 (ed. Gaisford, Oxford, 1854). Fragments of the *Ecclesiastical History* of the Arian Philostorgius, from the appearance of Arius as a teacher until 423, have been translated and are to be found in Bohn's *Ecclesiastical Library*. For the period after the Council of Ephesus, A. D. 431, there is no such abundance, but Evagrius, of whose history (ed. Parmentier and Bidez, London, 1898) there is a translation in Bohn's *Ecclesiastical Library*, though not in PNF, is of great value as he gives many original documents; and a portion of the *Ecclesiastical History* of John of Ephesus (trans. by R. P. Smith, Oxford, 1860) carries the history to about 600. There are also works devoted to the history of the West by Gregory of Tours, the Venerable Bede, and Paulus Diaconus, and others of the greatest value for the third period of this division. They will be mentioned in their place.

As the series of the great church councils begins with the Christian Empire, the *History of the Councils*, by Hefele, becomes indispensable to the student of ecclesiastical history, not only for its narrative but for the sources epitomized or given in full. It has been translated into English as far as the close of the eighth century, or well into the beginnings of the history of the mediæval Church. The new French translation should be used if possible as it contains valuable additional notes. In connection with Hefele may be used:

Percival, *The Seven Ecumenical Councils*, in PNF, ser. II, vol. XIV.

Wm. Bright, *Notes on the Canons of the First Four General*

Councils, 1882, should be consulted for this period. Bruns, *op. cit.*, and Lauchert, *op. cit.*, give texts only.

The two great collections of secular laws are:

Codex Theodosianus, ed. Mommsen and Meyer, Berlin, 1905.

Corpus Juris Civilis, ed. Krüger, Mommsen, Schoell, and Knoll, Berlin, 1899–1902.

The Cambridge Medieval History, vol. I, 1912, covers the period beginning with Constantine and extending to the beginning of the fifth century. It contains valuable bibliographies of a more discriminating character than those in the *Cambridge Modern History*, and render bibliographical references unnecessary. To this the student is accordingly referred for such matters. The second volume of this work will cover the period 500–850.

PERIOD I

THE IMPERIAL STATE CHURCH OF THE UNDIVIDED EMPIRE, OR UNTIL THE DEATH OF THEODOSIUS THE GREAT, 395

The history of the Church in the first period of the second division of the history of ancient Christianity has to deal primarily with three lines of development, viz.: first, the relation of the Church to the imperial authority and the religious forces of the times, whereby the Church became established as the sole authorized religion of the Empire, and heathenism and heresy were prohibited by law; secondly, the development of the doctrinal system of the Church until the end of the Arian controversy, whereby the full and eternal deity of the Son was established as the Catholic faith; thirdly, the development of the constitution, the fixation of the leading ecclesiastical conceptions, and the adaptation of the system of the Church to the practical needs of the times. The entire period may be divided into two main parts by the reign of Julian the Apostate (361–363); and the reign of Constantine as Emperor of the West (312–324) may be regarded as a prelude to the main part of the history. On the death of Theodosius the Great in 395, the Empire became permanently divided, and though in the second period the courses of the Church in the East and in the West may be treated to some extent together, yet the fortunes, interests, and problems of the two divisions of the Church begin to diverge.

CHAPTER I. THE CHURCH AND EMPIRE UNDER CONSTANTINE

Constantine was the heir to the political system of Diocletian. The same line of development was followed by him and his sons, and with increasing severity the burden pressed upon the people. But the Church, which had been fiercely persecuted by Diocletian and Galerius, became the object of imperial favor under Constantine. At the same time in many parts of the Empire, especially in the West, the heathen religion was rooted in the affections of the people and everywhere it was bound up with the forms of state. The new problems that confronted Constantine on his accession to sole authority in the West, and still more when he became sole Emperor, were of an ecclesiastical rather than a civil character. In the administration of the Empire he followed the lines laid down by Diocletian (§ 58). But in favoring the Church he had to avoid alienating the heathen majority. This he did by gradually and cautiously extending to the Church privileges which the heathen religion had enjoyed (§ 59), and with the utmost caution repressing those elements in heathenism which might be plausibly construed as inimical to the new order in the state (§ 60). At the same time, Constantine found in the application of his policy to actual conditions that he could not favor every religious sect that assumed the name of Christian. He must distinguish between claimants of his bounty. He must also bring about a unity in the Church where it had been threatened (§ 61), and repress what might lead to schism. Accordingly he found himself, immediately after his accession to sole authority, engaged in ecclesiastical discussions and adjudicating by councils ecclesiastical cases (§ 62).

§ 58. The Empire under Constantine and His Sons

Constantine became sole Emperor of the West, 312, and by the defeat of Licinius, July 23, 324, sole ruler of the entire Roman Empire. On his death, May 22, 337, his three sons divided between them the imperial dignity: Constantine II (337–340), taking Gaul, Spain, and Britain; Constans (337–350), Italy, Africa, and Illyria, and in 340 receiving the share of Constantine II; Constantius (337–361), taking the East, including Egypt. Of these three the ablest was Constantius who, after the renewed Persian war (337–350), became, on the death of Constans, sole Emperor. Although the imperial authority was divided and the ecclesiastical policy of each Emperor followed the religious condition and theological complexion of his respective portion of the Empire, the social conditions were everywhere much the same. There were under Constantine and also under his sons the continuation of that centralization which had already been carried far by Diocletian, the same court ceremonial and all that went with it, and the development of the bureaucratic system of administration. The economic conditions steadily declined as the imperial system became constantly more burdensome (*v. supra*, § 55), and the changes in the distribution of wealth and the administration of landed property affected disastrously large sections of the populace. A characteristic feature of Roman society, which affected the position of the Church not a little, was the tendency to regard callings and trades as hereditary, and by the fourth century this was enforced by law. The aim of this legislation was to provide workmen to care for the great public undertakings for the support of the populace of the cities and for the maintenance of the public business. This policy affected both the humble artisan and the citizen of curial rank. The former, although given various privileges, was crushed down by being obliged to continue in what was often an unprofitable occupation; the latter was made responsible for the taxes and various public burdens which custom, gradually becoming law, laid upon him. Constant attempt was made by great numbers to escape these burdens and disabilities by recourse to other occupations, and especially to the Christian ministry with its immunities (see § 59, *c*). Constant legislation endeavored to prevent this and restore men to their hereditary places. The following extracts from the Theodosian Code are enactments of Constantine, and are intended to illustrate the condition, under that Emperor, of the law as to hereditary occupations and guilds, and the position of the curiales, so as to explain the law as to admission to the priesthood.

(a) *Codex Theodosianus*, XIII, 5, 1; A. D. 314.

The Theodosian Code was a collection of law made at the command of Theodosius II, A. D. 438. See § 80. It was intended to comprise all the laws of general application made since the accession of Constantine and arranged under appropriate titles.

If a shipman shall have been originally a lighterman, none the less he shall remain permanently among those among whom it shall appear that his parents had been.

(b) *Codex Theodosianus*, XIII, 5, 3; A. D. 319.

If any shipman shall have obtained surreptitiously or in any other way immunity, it is our will that he be not at all admitted to plead any exemption. But also if any one possess a patrimony liable to the duties of a shipman, although he may be of higher dignity, the privileges of honor shall be of no avail to him in this matter, but let him be held to this duty either by the whole or in proportion. For it is not just that when a patrimony liable to this public duty has been excused all should not bear the common burden in proportion to ability.

(c) *Codex Theodosianus*, XIV, 4, 1; A. D. 334.

Because the guild of swineherds has fallen off to but few, we command that they plead in the presence of the Roman people, for the defence should be made to them for whom the burden was established. . . . Therefore let them know that the personal property of the swineherds is liable to public burdens and let them choose one of two courses: either let them retain the property which is liable to the functions of swineherd, and let themselves be held to the duty of swineherd, or let them name some suitable person whom they will, who shall satisfy the same requirement. For we suffer no one to be exempt from the obligation of this thing, but whether they have advanced in honors, or by some fraud have escaped, we command that they be brought back and the same thing performed, the Roman people being present and witnessing, and we are to be consulted, that we may take note of those who make use of these shifts; as for further avoidance of public duties, it is by no means to be granted any, but he who shall have been able to escape shall run danger of his safety, the privilege having been taken away from him.

(d) *Codex Theodosianus*, XII, 1, 11; A. D. 325.

The following laws illustrate the attempts of the curiales to escape their burdens.

Because some have forsaken the curiæ and have fled to the camps of the soldiery, we prescribe that all who shall be found not yet indebted to the chief centurion, are to be dismissed from the soldiery and returned to the same curiæ; those only are to remain among the soldiery who are retained on account of the necessities of the place or the troop.

(e) *Codex Theodosianus*, XII, 1, 12; A. D. 325.

If any one belongs in a larger or smaller town and desiring to avoid the same, betakes himself to another for the sake of dwelling there, and shall have attempted to make petitions concerning this or shall have relied upon any sort of fraud that he may escape the birth from his own city, let him bear the burden of the decurionate of both cities, of one because it was his choice, of the other because of his birth.

(f) *Codex Theodosianus*, XVI, 2, 3, *cf.* XVI, 2, 6; A. D. 326.

Since a constitution that has been issued prescribes that thereafter no decurion nor child of a decurion or person with suitable wealth and able to support the public burdens shall have recourse to the name and duties of the clergy, but only those shall be called to the place of the deceased who are of small fortune and are not held liable to civil burdens, we have learned that some have been molested, who before the promulgation of the said law had joined themselves to the company of the priests. Therefore we decree that these shall be free from all annoyance, but those who after the promulgation of the law, to avoid their public duties took recourse to the number of the clergy, shall be separated from that body and restored to their curial rank and made liable for their civil duties.

§ 59. Favor Shown the Church by Constantine

Neither on his conversion nor on his attainment of the sole rule of the Empire did Constantine establish the Church as the one official religion of the State. The ruler himself professed the Christian religion and neither abolished the former religion of the State nor disestablished it. But he granted to his own religion favors similar to those enjoyed by the heathen religious systems (*a–d*), though these privileges were only for the Catholic Church, and not for heretics (*e*); and he passed such laws as would make it possible for Christians to carry out their religious practices, *e. g.*, that Christians should not be compelled to sacrifice when the laws prescribed sacrifices (*f*), that Sunday be observed (*g*), and that celibacy might be practised (*h*).

Additional source material: Eusebius, *Vita Constantini* (PNF, ser. II, vol. I), II, 24–42, 46; IV, 18–28. Sozomen, *Hist. Ec.* (PNF, ser. II, vol. II), I, 9.

(*a*) Constantine, *Ep. ad Cæcilianum*, in Eusebius, *Hist. Ec.*, X, 6. (MSG, 20 : 892.)

The probable date of this epistle is A. D. 313, though there is uncertainty. Text in Kirch, nn. 323 *f*.

Constantine Augustus to Cæcilianus, Bishop of Carthage. Since it is our pleasure that something should be granted in all the provinces, namely, Africa and Numidia and Mauritania, to certain ministers of the legitimate and most holy Catholic religion, to defray their expenses, I have given written instructions to Ursus, the illustrious finance minister of Africa, and have directed him to make provision to pay to thy firmness three thousand folles.[1] Do thou, therefore, when thou hast received the above sum of money, command that it be distributed among all those mentioned above, according to the brief sent unto thee by Hosius. But if thou shouldest find that anything is wanting for the fulfilment of this my purpose in regard to all of them, thou shalt demand without hesitation from Heracleides, our treasurer, whatever thou findest to be necessary. For I commanded him, when he was present, that if thy firmness should ask him for any money, he should see to it that it be paid without any delay. And since I have learned that some men of unsettled mind wish to turn the people from the most holy and Catholic Church by a certain method of shameful corruption, do thou know that I gave command to Anulinus, the proconsul, and also to Patricius, vicar of the prefects, when they were present, that they should give proper attention not only to other matters, but also, above all, to this, and that they should not overlook such a thing when it happened. Wherefore if thou shouldest see any such men continuing in this madness, do thou without delay go to the above-mentioned judges and report the matter to them; that they may correct them as I commanded them when they were present. The divinity of the great God preserve thee many years.

(*b*) Constantine, *Ep. ad Anulinum*, in Eusebius, *Hist. Ec.*, X, 7. (MSG, 20 : 893.)

The following epistle, of the same year as the preceding to Cæcilianus, is the basis of exemptions from the clergy from public duties. The extension of these exemptions was made by the decree of 319, given below. Text in Kirch, n. 325.

Greeting to thee, our most esteemed Anulinus. Since it appears from many circumstances that when that religion is despised in which is preserved the chief reverence for the most

[1] A folle was a sum of money, possibly 208 denarii.

celestial Power, great dangers are brought upon public affairs; but that when legally adopted and observed it affords most signal prosperity to the Roman name and remarkable felicity to all the affairs of men, through the divine beneficence, it seemed good to me, most esteemed Anulinus, that those men who give their services with due sanctity and with constant observance of this law to the worship of the divine religion should receive recompense for their labors. Wherefore it is my will that those within the province intrusted to thee, in the Catholic Church over which Cæcilianus presides, who give their services to this holy religion, and who are commonly called clergymen, be entirely exempted from all public duties, that by any error or sacrilegious negligence they may not be drawn away from the service due to the Deity, but may devote themselves without any hindrance to their own law. For it seems that when they show greatest reverence to the Deity the greatest benefits accrue to the State. Farewell, our most esteemed and beloved Anulinus.

(c) *Codex Theodosianus*, XVI, 2, 2; A. D. 319.

By the following law the exemption of the clergy from public burdens was made universal. As many availed themselves of the clerical immunities to escape their burdens as curiales, a law was soon afterward passed limiting access to the ministry to those in humbler social position. *V. supra*, 58 *f.*

Those who in divine worship perform the services of religion—that is, those who are called clergy—are altogether exempt from public obligations, so that they may not be called away from their sacred duties by the sacrilegious malice of certain persons.

(d) *Codex Theodosianus*, XVI, 2, 4; A. D. 321.

The Church is hereby permitted to receive legacies. This was a recognition of its corporate character in the law, and indirectly its act of incorporation.

Every one has permission to leave when he is dying whatsoever goods he wishes to the most holy Catholic Church. . . .

(e) Codex Theodosianus, XVI, 5, 1; A. D. 326.

Privileges were granted only to the clergy of the Catholic or great Church as distinguished from heretics and schismatics. The State was, accordingly, forced by its exemptions and privileges granted the Church to take up a position as to heresy and schism. See for Constantine's policy toward heresy, Eusebius, *Vita Constantini*, III, 64 *ff.* (PNF, ser. II, vol. I.)

Privileges which have been bestowed in consideration of religion ought to be of advantage only to those who observe the Catholic law. It is our will that heathen and schismatics be not only without the privileges but bound by, and subject to, various political burdens.

(f) Codex Theodosianus, XVI, 2, 5; A. D. 323.

This and the following laws were passed to enable the Christians to escape from disadvantages in the carrying out of their religion. This law, that Christians should not be compelled to sacrifice, was enacted just before the final encounter with Licinius.

Because we have heard that ecclesiastics and others belonging to the Catholic religion are compelled by men of different religions to celebrate the sacrifices of the lustrum, we, by this decree, do ordain that if any one believes that those who observe the most sacred law ought to be compelled to take part in the rites of a strange superstition, let him, if his condition permits, be beaten with staves, but if his rank exempts him from such rigor, let him endure the condemnation of a very heavy fine, which shall fall to the State.

(g) Codex Justinianus, III, 12, 3; A. D. 321. Cf. Kirch, n. 748.

Sunday is to be observed.
For the Justinian Code see below, § 94, Introduction.

All judges and city people and the craftsmen shall rest upon the venerable Day of the Sun. Country people, however, may freely attend to the cultivation of the fields, because it frequently happens that no other days are better adapted for planting the grain in the furrows or the vines in trenches. So that the advantage given by heavenly providence may not for the occasion of a short time perish.

(h) *Codex Theodosianus*, VIII, 16, 1. *Cf.* Kirch, n. 750.

Celibacy was favored by the Church. By the *Lex Julia et Papia Poppea* it had been forbidden under a fine and loss of rights under wills. Childless marriages also rendered the parties liable to disabilities.

Those who are held as celibates by the ancient law are freed from the threatened terrors of the laws, and let them so live as if by the compact of marriage they were among the number of married men, and let all have an equal standing as to taking what each one deserves. Neither let any one be held childless; and let them not suffer the penalties set for this. The same thing we hold regarding women, and freely to all we loose from their necks the commands which the law placed upon them as a certain yoke. But there is no application of this benefit to husbands and wives as regards each other, whose deceitful wiles are often scarcely restrained by the appointed rigor of the law, but let the pristine authority of the law continue between such persons.

§ 60. THE REPRESSION OF HEATHENISM UNDER CONSTANTINE

Constantine's religious policy in respect to heathenism may have been from the first to establish Christianity as the sole religion of the Empire and to put down heathenism. If so, in the execution of that policy he proceeded with great caution, especially in the period before his victory over Licinius. It looks at times as if for a while he aimed at a parity of religions. Certain is the fact that only as conditions became more favorable to active measures of repression he increased the severity of his laws against what was of doubtful legality in heathenism, though he was statesman enough to recognize the difference in the religious conditions between the East and the West, especially as to the hold which Christianity had upon the mass of the people. While his measures in the East became constantly harsher, in the West he tolerated heathenism. The commonly received theory is that Constantine changed his policy. All the facts can be as easily understood on the hypothesis that as a statesman he had constant regard to the advisability of drastic execution of a policy which he in theory accepted and would have carried out in its entirety everywhere if he had been able.

Additional source material: Eusebius, *Vita Constantini* (PNF), II, 44 *f.*, 47 *f.*, 54 *ff.*

(*a*) *Codex Theodosianus*, IX, 16, 2; A. D. 319.

Private sacrifices forbidden.

Haruspices and priests and those accustomed to serve this rite we forbid to enter any private house, or under the pretence of friendship to cross the threshold of another, under the penalty established against them if they contemn the law.[1] But those of you who regard this rite, approach the public altars and shrines and celebrate the solemnities of your custom; for we do not indeed prohibit the duties of the old usage to be performed in broad daylight.

(*b*) *Codex Theodosianus*, XVI, 10, 1; A. D. 320–321.

Haruspicia in certain circumstances to be observed.

If any part of our palace or other public buildings should be struck by lightning let the custom be retained of the ancient observance as to what it signifies, and let it be examined by the haruspices and very carefully written down, collected, and brought to our attention; to others also the permission of practising this custom is conceded, provided they refrain from domestic sacrifices, which are expressly forbidden.

(*c*) *Codex Theodosianus*, XV, 1, 3; A. D. 326.

Unfinished heathen temples need not be completed.

We direct that the judges of the provinces be warned not to give orders for any new work before they complete the build-

[1] *I. e.*, as to offering sacrifices.

ings left incomplete by their predecessors, the erection of temples only being excepted.

§ 61. THE DONATIST SCHISM UNDER CONSTANTINE

The Donatist schism arose in connection with the Diocletian persecution, in part over the policy of Mensurius of Carthage regarding the fanatical desire for martyrdom and the delivery of the sacred books according to the edict of persecution. Combined with this were the personal ambitions of the Archdeacon Cæcilianus, the offended dignity of the Primas of Numidia, Bishop Secundus of Tigisi, and the pique of a wealthy female devotee, Lucilla. It was mixed up with the customs of the North African church, whereby the Primas of Numidia exercised a leading authority in the conduct of the election of the bishop of Carthage, and also with the notion prevalent in the same church, for which also Cyprian contended in the controversy on the baptism of heretics [see § 52], that the validity of a sacrament depended in some way upon the personal character of the minister of that sacrament. It was asserted by the partisans of Secundus, who elected Majorinus bishop of Carthage, that Felix of Aptunga, the consecrator of Cæcilianus, who had been elected by the other party, had delivered the sacred books to the heathen officials, and was therefore guilty as a traditor. A schism, accordingly, arose in Carthage which spread rapidly throughout North Africa. The party of Majorinus soon came under the lead of Donatus the Great, his successor in the schismatical see of Carthage. The Donatist schism became of importance almost at once, and as it was inconsistent with Constantine's religious policy, which called for Church unity,[1] it presented an immediate difficulty in the execution of laws granting favors to the Catholic Church.[2] On account of the interests involved, the schism was of long duration, lasting after the conquest of North Africa by the Vandals, and

[1] *V. infra*, § 62, Introduction.   [2] *V. supra*, §§ 59 *f.*

even to the Saracen conquest, though long since of no importance.

Anulinus, *Ep. ad Constantinum*, in Augustine, *Ep.* 88. (MSG, 33 : 303.)

To Constantine Augustus from Anulinus, a man of proconsular rank, proconsul of Africa.

The welcome and adored celestial writings sent by your Majesty to Cæcilianus, and those who act under him and are called clergy, I have devoutly taken care to record in the archives of my humility, and have exhorted those parties that when unity has been made by the consent of all, since they are seen to be exempt from all other burdens by your Majesty's clemency, and having preserved the Catholic unity, they should devote themselves to their duties with the reverence due the sanctity of the law and to divine things. After a few days, however, there arose some, to whom a crowd of people joined themselves, who thought that proceedings should be taken against Cæcilianus and presented me a sealed packet wrapped in leather and a small document without seal, and earnestly requested that I should transmit them to the sacred and venerable court of your divinity, which your Majesty's most humble servant has taken care to do, Cæcilianus continuing meanwhile as he was. The acts pertaining to the case have been subjoined, in order that your Majesty may be able to make a decision concerning the whole matter. I have sent two documents, one in a leathern envelope entitled "A Document of the Catholic Church, the Charges against Cæcilianus, Furnished by the Party of Majorinus"; the other attached without a seal to the same leathern envelope. Given on the 17th day before the calends of May, in the third consulship of our Lord Constantine Augustus [April 15, 313].

§ 62. Constantine's Endeavors to Bring about the Unity of the Church by Means of General Synods: The Councils of Arles and Nicæa

One of the intentions of Constantine in his support of Christianity seems to have been the employment of the Christian religion as a basis for imperial unity. The policy of several earlier emperors in reviving heathenism, and Galerius in his persecution of the Christians, seems likewise to have been to use religion as a basis of unity. One of the first tasks Constantine encountered after he became sole ruler of the West was to restore the unity of the Church in Africa, which had been endangered by the disputes culminating in the Donatist schism; and when he became sole ruler of the Empire a new task of a similar character was to restore unity to the Church of the East, endangered by the Meletian schism in Egypt [*v. supra*, § 57, *a*], the Arian controversy in its first stage [*v. infra*, § 63], and the estrangement of the Asia Minor churches, due to the Easter controversy [*v. supra*, § 38]. It was a masterstroke of policy on the part of Constantine to use the Church's conciliar system on an enlarged scale to bring about this unity. The Church was made to feel that the decision was its own and to be obeyed for religious reasons; at the same time the Emperor was able to direct the thought and action of the assembly in matters of consequence and to give to conciliar action legal and coercive effect. The two great assemblies summoned to meet the problems of the West and of the East were respectively the Councils of Arles, A. D. 314, and of Nicæa, A. D. 325.

I.   The Council of Arles A. D. 314

(*a*) Constantine, *Convocatio concilii Arelatensis*, in Eusebius, *Hist. Ec.*, X, 5. (MSG, 20 : 888.) *Cf.* Kirch, nn. 321 *f.;* Mirbt, nn. 89, 93–97.

For the Council of Arles, see Hefele, §§ 14, 15.

Constantine Augustus to Chrestus, Bishop of Syracuse. When some began wickedly and perversely to disagree among themselves in regard to the holy worship and the celestial power and Catholic doctrine, I, wishing to put an end to such disputes among them, formerly gave command that certain bishops should be sent from Gaul, and that the opposing parties, who were contending persistently and incessantly with each other, should be summoned from Africa; that in their presence and in the presence of the bishop of Rome the matter which appeared to be causing the disturbance might be examined and decided with all care. But since, as it happens, some, forgetful both of their own salvation and of the reverence due to the most holy religion, do not even yet bring hostilities to an end, and are unwilling to conform to the judgment already passed, and assert that those who expressed their opinions and decisions were few, or that they had been too hasty and precipitate in giving judgment, before all the things which ought to have been accurately investigated had been examined—on account of all this it has happened that those very ones who ought to hold brotherly and harmonious relations toward each other are shamefully, or rather abominably, divided among themselves, and give occasion for ridicule to those men whose souls are alien as to this most holy religion. Wherefore it has seemed necessary to me to provide that this dissension, which ought to have ceased after the judgment had been already given, by their own voluntary agreement, should now, if possible, be brought to an end by the presence of many. Since, therefore, we have commanded a number of bishops from a great many different places to assemble in the city of Arles, before the calends of August, we have thought proper to write to thee also that thou shouldest secure from the most illustrious Latronianus, Corrector of Sicily, a public vehicle, and that thou shouldest take with thee two others of the second rank whom thou thyself shalt choose, together with three servants, who may serve you on the way, and betake thyself to the above-mentioned place before the appointed day; that by thy firmness and by the

wise unanimity and harmony of the others present, this dispute, which has disgracefully continued until the present
time, in consequence of certain shameful strifes, after all has
been heard, which those have to say who are now at variance
with one another, and whom we have likewise commanded
to be present, may be settled in accordance with the proper
faith, and that brotherly harmony, though it be but gradual,
may be restored. May Almighty God preserve thee in
health many years.

(*b*) *Synodal Epistle addressed to Sylvester, Bishop of Rome,*
Bruns, II, 107. *Cf.* Kirch, nn. 330–337.

The following extracts give the canons of most importance in the
history of the times.   The exact wording of the canons has not been
retained in the letter, which is the only record extant of the action of
the council.   The text from which the following is translated is that
given by the monks of St. Maur in their *Collectio Conciliorum Galliæ*,
reprinted by Hefele, § 15, and Bruns, *Canones Apostolorum et Conciliorum*, II, 107 *ff.*   It is to be preferred to the text of Mansi and the
older collections.
The first canon settled for the West the long-standing question as
to the date of Easter.   The Roman custom as to the day of the week
and computation of the time of year should be followed everywhere;
the same decision was reached at Nicæa for the East (*v.* § 62, *II, a*).
As a matter of fact, however, the computation customary at Alexandria eventually prevailed as the more accurate.
The eighth and thirteenth canons touch upon North African disputes.   The former overrules the contention of Cyprian and his colleagues, that heretical or schismatical baptisms were invalid.   It also
laid down a principle by which Novatianism stood condemned.   The
thirteenth applied a similar principle to ordination; the crimes of the
bishop who gave the ordination should not invalidate the ordination
of a suitable person, as was claimed in the case of the ordination of
Cæcilianus by Felix of Aptunga, accused as a *traditor;* further it ruled
out the complaints against Felix until more substantial proof be
brought, the official documents that he had made the tradition required
by the edict of persecution.

Marinus and the assembly of bishops, who have come
together in the town of Arles, to the most holy lord and brother
Sylvester.   What we have decreed with general consent we
signify to your charity that all may know what ought to be
observed in the future.

1. In the first place, concerning the observation of the Lord's Easter, we have determined that it be observed on one day and at one time throughout the world by us, and that you send letters according to custom to all.

8. Concerning the Africans, because they make use of their own law, to the effect that they rebaptize, we have determined that if any one should come from heresy to the Church they should ask him the creed; and if they should perceive that he had been baptized in the name of the Father and of the Son and of the Holy Ghost, hands only should be laid upon him that he might receive the Holy Ghost. That if when asked he should not reply this Trinity, let him be baptized.

9. Concerning those who bring letters of the confessors, it pleased us that these letters having been taken away, they should receive other letters of communion.

13. Concerning those who are said to have given up the Holy Scriptures or the vessels of the Lord or the name of their brethren, it has pleased us whoever of them shall have been convicted by public documents and not by mere words, should be removed from the clerical order; though if the same have been found to have ordained any, and those whom they have ordained are worthy, it shall not render their ordination invalid. And because there are many who are seen to oppose the law of the Church and think that they ought to be admitted to bring accusation by hired witnesses, they are by no means to be admitted, except, as we have said above, they can prove their accusations by public documents.

II. The Council of Nicæa

For the Council of Nicæa, see Hefele, §§ 18–44. All church histories give large space to the Council of Nicæa. *V. infra*, §§ 63 *ff.*, 72, *a.*

(*a*) Council of Nicæa, 325, *Synodical Letter*, Socrates, *Hist. Ec.* I, 9. (MSG, 67 : 77.) Text in Kirch, nn. 369 *ff.*; Mirbt, n. 107.

To the holy and, by the grace of God, great Church of the Alexandrians, and to our beloved brethren throughout Egypt, Libya, and Pentapolis, the bishops assembled at Nicæa constituting the great and holy synod, send greetings in the Lord.

Since by the grace of God, a great and holy synod has been convened at Nicæa, our most pious sovereign Constantine having summoned us out of various cities and provinces for that purpose, it appeared to us indispensably necessary that a letter should be written also to you on the part of the sacred synod; in order that you may know what subjects were brought under consideration, what rigidly investigated, and also what was eventually determined on and decreed. In the first place, the impiety and guilt of Arius and his adherents were examined into, in the presence of our most pious Emperor Constantine: and it was unanimously decided that his impious opinion be anathematized, with all the blasphemous expressions and terms he has blasphemously uttered, affirming that the Son of God sprang from nothing, and that there was a time when He was not; saying, moreover, that the Son of God was possessed of a free will, so as to be capable either of vice or virtue; and calling Him a creature and a work. All these the holy synod has anathematized, having scarcely patience to endure the hearing of such an impious or, rather, bewildered opinion, and such abominable blasphemies. But the conclusion of our proceedings against him you must either have heard or will hear; for we would not seem to trample on a man who has received the chastisement which his crime deserved. Yet so strong is his impiety as to involve Theonas, Bishop of Marmarica, and Secundus of Ptolemais; for they have suffered the same condemnation as himself. But the grace of God freed us from this false doctrine, impiety, and blasphemy, and from those persons who have dared to cause discord and division among the people previously at peace; and there still remained the contumacy of Meletius to be dealt with, and those who had been ordained by him; and we shall now state to you, beloved brethren, what resolution the synod came to on this point. Acting with more clemency toward Meletius, although, strictly speaking, he was wholly undeserving of favor, the council permitted him to remain in his own city, but decreed that he should exercise no authority either to ordain or nominate for ordination; and that he should appear in no other district or city on this pretence, but simply retain a nominal dignity; that those who had received appointments from him, after having been confirmed by a more legitimate ordination, should be admitted to communion on these conditions: that they should continue to hold their rank and ministry, but regard themselves as inferior in every respect to all those who had been previously ordained and established in each place and church by our most honored fellow-minister Alexander. In addition to these things, they shall have no authority to propose or nominate whom they please, or to do anything at all without the concurrence of a bishop of the Catholic Church, who is one of Alexander's suffragans. Let such as by the grace of God and your prayers have been found in no schism, but have continued in the Catholic Church blameless, have authority to nominate and ordain those who are worthy of the sacred office, and to act in all things according to ecclesiastical law and usage. Whenever it may happen that any of those placed in the Church die, then let such as have been recently admitted into orders be advanced to the dignity of the deceased, provided that they appear worthy, and that the people should elect them, and the bishop of Alexandria confirm their choice. This is conceded to all the others, indeed, but as for Meletius personally we by no means grant the same, on account of his formerly disorderly conduct; and because of the rashness and levity of his character he is deprived of all authority and jurisdiction, as a man liable again to create similar disturbances. These are things which specially affect Egypt and the most holy Church of the Alexandrians; and if any other canon or ordinance should be established, our lord and most honored fellow-minister and brother Alexander being present with us, will on his return to you enter into more minute details, inasmuch as he is not only a participator in whatever is transacted, but has the principal direction of it. We have also to announce the good news to you concerning the unanimity as to the holy feast of Easter: that this by your prayers has been settled so that all the brethren in the East, who have hitherto kept this festival with the Jews, will henceforth conform to the Romans and to us, and to all who from the earliest times have observed our period of celebrating Easter. Rejoicing, therefore, on account of a favorable termination of matters and in the extirpation of all heresy, receive with the greater honor and more abundant love our fellow-minister and your bishop, Alexander, who has greatly delighted us by his presence, and even at his advanced age has undergone extraordinary exertions in order that peace might be re-established among you. Pray on behalf of us all, that the decisions to which we have so justly come may be inviolably maintained through Almighty God and our Lord Jesus Christ, together with the Holy Spirit to whom be glory forever. Amen.

(b) Council of Nicæa, Canon 8, *On the Novatians*, Bruns, I, 8.

The Church recognized the substantial orthodoxy of the Novatians, and according to the principles laid down at Arles (cc. 8, 13, § 62 *I*, *b*) the ordination of the Novatians was regarded as valid. The following canon, although a generous concession on the part of the Church, did not bring about a healing of the schism which lasted several centuries. The last mention of the Novatians is contained in the 95th canon of the second Trullan Council, known as the Quinisext, A. D. 692.

Canon 8. Concerning those who call themselves Cathari, who come over to the Catholic and Apostolic Church, the great and holy synod decrees that they who are ordained shall continue as they are among the clergy. But before all things it is necessary that they should profess in writing that they will observe and follow the teachings of the Catholic and Apostolic Church; that is, that they will communicate with those who have been twice married and with those who have lapsed during the persecution, and upon whom a period of penance has been laid and a time for restoration fixed; so that in all things they will follow the teachings of the Catholic Church. Wheresoever, then, whether in villages or in cities, only these are found who have been ordained, let them remain as found among the clergy and in the same rank. But if any come over where there is a bishop or presbyter of the Catholic Church, it is manifest that the bishop of the Church must have the dignity of a bishop, and he who was named bishop by those who are called Cathari shall have the honor of a presbyter, unless it seem fit to the bishop to share with him the honor of the title. But if this should not seem good to him, then shall the bishop provide for him a place as chorepiscopus, or as presbyter, in order that he may be evidently seen to be of the clergy, and that in one city there may not be two bishops.

(c) *Codex Theodosianus*, XVI, 5, 2; A. D. 326.

With the generous treatment of the Novatians by the Council of Nicæa should be compared the mild and generous treatment of Constantine, who distinguished them from other heretics.

We have not learned that the Novatians have been so condemned that we believe that to them should not be granted what they claim. Therefore we prescribe as to the buildings of their churches and places suitable for burial that they are to possess, without any molestation, those buildings and lands, namely, which on ground of long possession or from purchase or claim for any sound reason they may have. It will be well looked out for that they attempt to claim nothing for themselves of those things which before their secession belonged evidently to the churches of perpetual sanctity.

CHAPTER II. THE ARIAN CONTROVERSY UNTIL THE
EXTINCTION OF THE DYNASTY OF CONSTANTINE

The Arian controversy may be divided into four periods
or stadia:

1. From the outbreak of the Arian controversy to the
Council of Nicæa (318–325). In this stadium the positions
of the parties are defined, and the position of the West, in
substantial agreement with that of Alexander and Athanasius, forced through by Constantine and Hosius at Nicæa
(§ 63).

2. From the Council of Nicæa to the death of Constantine
(325–337). In this stadium, without the setting aside of the
formula of Nicæa, an attempt is made to reconcile those who
in fact dissented. In this period Constantine, now living in
the East, inclines toward a position more in harmony with
Arianism and more acceptable in the East than was the doctrine of Athanasius. This is the period of the Eusebian
reaction (§ 64).

3. From the death of Constantine to the death of Constantius (337–361). In this stadium the anti-Nicæan party
is victorious in the East (§ 65), but as it included all those
who for any reason were opposed to the definition of Nicæa,
it fell apart on attaining the annulment of the decision of
Nicæa. There arose, on the one hand, an extreme Arian
party and, on the other, a homoiousian party which approx-
imated closely to the Athanasian position but feared the
Nicene terminology.

4. From the accession of Julian to the council of Constantinople (361–381). Under the pressure brought against
Christianity by Julian (§ 68), parties but little removed from
each other came closer together (§ 70). A new generation
of theologians took the lead, with an interpretation of the
Nicene formula which made it acceptable to those who had
previously regarded it as Sabellian. And under the lead of
these men, backed by the Emperor Theodosius, the reaf-

firmation of the Nicene formula at Constantinople, 381, was accepted by the East (§ 71).

In the period in which the Arian controversy is by far the most important series of events in Church history, the attitude of the sons of Constantine toward heathenism and Donatism was of secondary importance, but it should be noticed as throwing light on the ecclesiastical policy which made the Arian controversy so momentous. In their policy toward heathenism and dissent, the policy of Constantine was carried to its logical completion in the establishment of Christianity as the only lawful religion of the Empire (§ 67).

Arianism may be regarded as the last attempt of Dynamistic Monarchianism (*v. supra*, § 40) to explain the divinity of Jesus Christ without admitting His eternity. It was derived in part from the teaching of Paul of Samosata through Lucian of Antioch. Paul of Samosata had admitted the existence of an eternal but impersonal Logos in God which dwelt in the man Jesus. Arianism distinguished between a Logos uncreated, an eternal impersonal reason in God, and a personal Logos created in time, making the latter, the personal Logos, only in a secondary sense God. This latter Logos, neither eternal nor uncreated, became incarnate in Jesus, taking the place in the human personality of the rational soul or logos. To guard against the worship of a being created and temporal, and to avoid the assertion of two eternal existences, the anti-Arian or Athanasian position, already formulated by Alexander, made the personal Logos of one essence or substance with the Father, eternal as the Father, and thereby distinguishing between begetting, or the imparting of subsistence, and creating, or the calling into being from nothing, a distinction which Arianism failed to make; and thus allowing for the eternity and deity of the Son without detracting from the monotheism which was universally regarded as the fundamental doctrine of Christianity as a body of theology. In this controversy the party of Alexander and Athanasius was animated, at least in the earlier stages of the controversy, not so much by speculative interests as by religious motives, the relation of Jesus to redemption, and they were strongly influenced by Irenæus. The party of Arius, on the other hand, was influenced by metaphysical interests as to the relation of being to creation and the contrast between the finite and the infinite. It may be said, in general, that until the council of Chalcedon, and possibly even after that, the main interest that kept alive theological discussion was intimately connected with vital problems of religious life of the times. After that the scholastic period began to set in and metaphysical discussions were based upon the formulæ of the councils.

§ 63. The Outbreak of the Arian Controversy and the Council of Nicæa A. D. 325

The Arian controversy began in Alexandria about 318, as related by Socrates (a). The positions of the two parties were defined from the beginning both by Alexander, bishop of Constantinople (b), and Arius himself (c), who by appealing to Eusebius of Nicomedia, his fellow-student in the school of Lucian of Antioch, enlisted the support of that able ecclesiastical politician and courtier and at once extended the area of the controversy throughout the East. By means of poems of a somewhat popular character entitled the Thalia, about 322 (d), Arius spread his doctrines still further, involving others than the trained professional theologian. In the meanwhile Arius and some other clergy sympathizing with him in Egypt were deposed about 320 (e). Constantine endeavored to end the dispute by a letter, and, failing in this, sent Hosius of Cordova, his adviser in ecclesiastical matters, to Alexandria in 324. On the advice of Hosius, a synod was called to meet at Nicæa in the next year, after the pattern of the earlier synod for the West at Arles in 314. Here the basis for a definition of faith was a non-committal creed presented by Eusebius of Cæsarea, the Church historian (f). This

was modified, probably under the influence of Hosius, so as
to be in harmony at once with the tenets of the party of
Alexander and Athanasius, and with the characteristic theology of the West (g).

Additional source material: J. Chrystal, *Authoritative Christianity*,
Jersey City, 1891, vol. I; *The Council of Nicæa: The Genuine Remains;*
H. R. Percival, *The Seven Ecumenical Councils* (PNF, ser. II, vol. XIV);
Athanasius, *On the Incarnation* (PNF, ser. II, vol. IV).

(a) Socrates, *Hist. Ec.*, I, 5.　(MSG, 67 : 41.)

The outbreak of the controversy at Alexandria circa 318.

After Peter, who was bishop of Alexandria, had suffered
martyrdom under Diocletian, Achillas succeeded to the episcopal office, and after Achillas, Alexander succeeded in the
period of peace above referred to.　Conducting himself fear-
lessly, he united the Church.　By chance, one day, in the presence of the presbyters and the rest of his clergy, he was discussing too ambitiously the doctrine of the Holy Trinity,
teaching that there was a unity in the Trinity.　But Arius,
one of the presbyters under his jurisdiction, a man of no
inconsiderable logical acumen, imagining that the bishop was
subtly introducing the doctrine of Sabellius the Libyan, from
the love of controversy took the opposite opinion to that of
the Libyan, and, as he thought, vigorously responded to the
things said by the bishop.　"If," said he, "the Father begat
the Son, He that was begotton had a beginning of existence;
and from this it is evident that there was a time when the
Son was not.　It follows necessarily that He had His subsistence [hypostasis] from nothing."

(b) Alexander of Alexandria, *Ep. ad Alexandrum*, in Theodoret, *Hist. Ec.*, I, 3.　(MSG, 88 : 904.)

A statement of the position of Alexander made to Alexander, bishop
of Constantinople.
This extract is to be found at the end of the letter; it is evidently
based upon the creed which is reproduced with somewhat free glosses.
The omissions in the extract are of the less important glosses and proof-

texts. For the position of Alexander the letter of Arius to Eusebius of Nicomedia given below (c) should also be examined.

We believe as the Apostolic Church teaches, In one unbegotten Father, who of His being has no cause, immutable and invariable, and who subsists always in one state of being, admitting neither of progression nor diminution; who gave the law and the prophets and the Gospel; of patriarchs and Apostles and all saints, Lord; and in one Lord Jesus Christ, the only begotten Son of God, begotten not out of that which is not, but of the Father, who is; yet not after the manner of material bodies, by severance or emanation, as Sabellius and Valentinus taught, but in an inexpressible and inexplicable manner. . . . We have learned that the Son is immutable and unchangeable, all-sufficient and perfect, like the Father, lacking only His "unbegottenness." He is the exact and precisely similar image of His Father. . . . And in accordance with this we believe that the Son always existed of the Father. . . . Therefore His own individual dignity must be reserved to the Father as the Unbegotten One, no one being called the cause of His existence: to the Son, likewise, must be given the honor which befits Him, there being to Him a generation from the Father which has no beginning. . . . And in addition to this pious belief respecting the Father and the Son, we confess as the sacred Scriptures teach us, one Holy Spirit, who moved the saints of the Old Testament, and the divine teachers of that which is called the New. We believe in one and only Catholic and Apostolic Church, which can never be destroyed even though all the world were to take counsel to fight against it, and which gains the victory over all the impious attacks of the heterodox. . . . After this we receive the resurrection from the dead, of which Jesus Christ our Lord became the first-fruits; who bore a body, in truth, not in semblance, derived from Mary, the mother of God [theotokos] in the fulness of time sojourning among the race, for the remission of sins: who was crucified and died, yet for all this suffered no diminution of His Godhead. He rose from the dead, was taken into heaven, and sat down on the right hand of the Majesty on high.

(c) Arius, *Ep. ad Eusebium*, in Theodoret, *Hist. Ec.*, I, 4. (MSG, 88 : 909.)

A statement in the words of Arius of his own position and that of Alexander addressed to Eusebius of Nicomedia.

To his very dear lord, the man of God, the faithful and orthodox Eusebius, Arius unjustly persecuted by Alexander the Pope, on account of that all-conquering truth of which you are also the champion, sendeth greeting in the Lord.

. . . Alexander has driven us out of the city as atheists, because we do not concur in what he publicly preaches; namely, "God is always, the Son is always; as the Father so the Son; the Son coexists unbegotten with God; He is everlastingly begotten; He is the unbegotten begotten; neither by thought nor by any interval does God precede the Son; always God, always the Son; the Son is of God himself."

. . . To these impieties we cannot listen even though heretics threaten us with a thousand deaths. But we say and believe and have taught and do teach, that the Son is not unbegotten, nor in any way part of the Unbegotten; nor from any substance [hypokeimenon],[1] but that of His own will and counsel He has subsisted before time and before ages, as perfect God only begotten and unchangeable, and that before He was begotten or created or purposed or established He was not. For He was not unbegotten. We are persecuted because we say that the Son has a beginning, but that God is without beginning. This is the cause of our persecution, and likewise because we say that He is of that which is not.[2] And this we say because He is neither part of God, nor of any substance [hypokeimenon]. For this we are persecuted; the rest you know. I bid thee farewell in the Lord, remem-

---

[1] ὑποκείμενον.

[2] ἐξ οὐκ ὄντων, the phrase which was afterward the foundation of the Arian sect of the Exoukontians.

bering our afflictions, my fellow-Lucianist and true Eusebius [*i. e.*, pious].

(*d*) Arius, *Thalia*, in Athanasius, *Orat. contra Arianos*, I, 2. (MSG, 26 : 21.)

The following extracts from the *Thalia*, although given by Athanasius, the opponent of Arius, are so in harmony with what Arius and his followers asserted repeatedly that they may be regarded as correctly representing the work from which they profess to be taken.

God was not always Father; but there was when God was alone and was not yet Father; afterward He became a Father. The Son was not always; for since all things have come into existence from nothing, and all things are creatures and have been made, so also the Logos of God himself came into existence from nothing and there was a time when He was not; and that before He came into existence He was not; but He also had a beginning of His being created. For God, he says, was alone and not yet was there the Logos and Wisdom. Afterward He willed to create us, then He made a certain one and named Him Logos and Wisdom and Son, in order that by Him He might create us. He says, therefore, that there are two wisdoms, one proper to, and existing together with, God; but the Son came into existence by that wisdom, and was made a partaker of it and was only named Wisdom and Logos. For Wisdom existed by wisdom and the will of God's wisdom. So, he says, that there is another Logos besides the Son in God, and the Son partaking of that Logos is again named Logos and Son by grace. . . . There are many powers; and there is one which is by nature proper to God and eternal; but Christ, again, is not the true power of God, but is one of those which are called powers, of whom also the locust and the caterpillar are called not only a power but a great power [Joel 2 : 2], and there are many other things like to the Son, concerning whom David says in the Psalms: "The Lord of Powers";[1] likewise the Logos is mutable, as are all

───────────

[1] Psalm 24 : 10; Hebrew, The Lord of Hosts ; LXX, The Lord of Powers.

things, and by His own free choice, so far as He wills, remains good; because when He wills He is able to change, as also we are, since His nature is subject to change. Then, says he, God foreseeing that He would be good, gave by antici- pation to Him that glory, which as a man He afterward had from His virtue; so that on account of His works, which God foresaw, God made Him to become such as He is now.

(e) Council of Alexandria, A. D. 320, *Epistula encyclica*, in Socrates, *Hist. Ec.*, I, 6. (MSG, 67 : 45.) *Cf.* Kirch, nn. 353 *ff.*

The encyclical of the Council of Alexandria under Alexander, in which Arius and his sympathizers were deposed, was possibly composed by Athanasius. It is commonly found in his works, entitled *Depositio Arii*. It is also found in the *Ecclesiastical History* of Socrates. For council, see Hefele, § 20.

Those who became apostates were Arius, Achillas, Æithales, Carpones, another Arius, and Sarmates, who were then pres- byters; Euzoius, Lucius, Julianus, Menas, Helladius, and Gaius, who were then deacons; and with them Secundus and Theonas, then called bishops. And the novelties which they have invented and put forth contrary to the Scriptures are the following: God was not always a Father, but there was a time when He was not a Father. The Logos of God was not always, but came into existence from things that were not; wherefore there was a time when He was not; for the Son is a creature and a work. Neither is He like in essence to the Father. Neither is He truly by nature the Logos of the Father; neither is He His true Wisdom; but He is one of the things made and created, and is called the Logos and Wisdom by an abuse of terms, since He himself originated by God's own logos and by the wisdom that is in God, by which God has made not only all things but Him also. Wherefore He is in His nature subject to change and variation as are all rational creatures. And the Logos is foreign, is alien and separated from the being [*ousia*] of God. And the Father cannot be[1]

---

[1] Some texts insert "seen nor."

described by the Son, for the Logos does not know the Father perfectly and accurately, neither can He see Him perfectly. Moreover, the Son knows not His own essence as it really is; for He was made on account of us, that God might create us by Him as by an instrument; and He would not have existed had not God willed to create us. Accordingly some one asked them whether the Logos of God is able to change as the devil changed, and they were not afraid to say that He can change; for being something made and created, His nature is subject to change.

(*f*) Eusebius of Cæsarea, *Creed*, in Socrates, *Hist. Ec.*, I, 8. (MSG, 67 : 69.) *Cf.* Hahn, § 188.

This creed was presented at the Council of Nicæa by the historian Eusebius, who took the lead of the middle party at the council. He stated that it had long been in use in his church.

We believe in one God, Father Almighty, the maker of all things visible and invisible; and in one Lord Jesus Christ, the Logos of God, God of God, Light of Light, Life of Life, only begotten Son, the first-born of all creation, begotten of His Father before all ages, by whom, also, all things were made, who for our salvation became flesh, who lived among men, and suffered and rose again on the third day, and ascended to the Father, and will come again in glory to judge the living and the dead. We believe also in one Holy Spirit. We believe that each of these [*i. e.*, three] is and subsists;[1] the Father truly Father, the Son truly Son; the Holy Spirit truly Holy Spirit; as our Lord also said, when He sent His disciples to preach: "Go teach all nations, baptizing them in the name of the Father and of the Son and of the Holy Spirit" [Matt. 28 : 19].

(*g*) Council of Nicæa A. D. 325, *Creed*, in Socrates, *Hist. Ec.*, I, 8. (MSG, 67 : 68.) *Cf.* Hahn, § 142.

The creed of Nicæa is to be carefully distinguished from what is commonly called the Nicene creed. The actual creed put forth at the

[1] ὑπάρχειν.

council is as follows. The discussion by Loofs, *Dogmengeschichte*, § 32, is brief but especially important, as he shows that the creed was drawn up under the influence of the Western formulæ.

We believe in one God, Father Almighty, maker of all things visible and invisible; and in one Lord Jesus Christ, the Son of God, begotten of His Father, only begotten, that is of the *ousia* of the Father, God of God, Light of Light, true God of true God; begotten, not made, of one substance[1] with the Father, by whom all things were made, both things in heaven and things in earth, who for us men and for our salvation, came down from heaven and was made [became] flesh and was made [became] man, suffered and rose again on the third day, ascended into the heavens and comes to judge living and dead.

But those who say there was when He was not, and before being begotten He was not, and He was made out of things that were not[2] or those who say that the Son of God was from a different substance [hypostasis] or being [*ousia*] or a creature, or capable of change or alteration, these the Catholic Church anathematizes.

§ 64. The Beginnings of the Eusebian Reaction under Constantine

Shortly after the Council of Nicæa, Constantine seems to have become aware of the fact that the decision at that council was not acceptable in the East as a whole, representing, as it did, what was generally felt to be an extreme position. In coming to this opinion he was much influenced by Eusebius of Nicomedia who, by powerful court interest, was soon recalled from exile and even became the leading ecclesiastical adviser of Constantine. The policy of this bishop was to prepare the way for the revocation of the decree of Nicæa by a preliminary rehabilitation of Arius (*a*), and by attacking the leaders of the opposite party (*b*). Constantine, however, never consented to the abrogation of the creed of Nicæa.

---

[1] Homoousios.   [2] ἐξ οὐκ ὄντων.

Additional source material: Socrates, *Hist. Ec.*, I, 8 (letter of Eusebius to his diocese), 14, 28 *ff*. Eusebius, *Vita Constantini*, III, 23; Athanasius, *Historia Arianorum*, §§ 4–7.

(*a*) Arius, *Confession of Faith*, in Socrates, *Hist. Ec.*, I, 26. (MSG, 67 : 149.)

As a part of the process whereby Arius should be rehabilitated by being received back into the Church he was invited by Constantine to appear at the court. He was there presented to the Emperor and produced a confession of faith purposely vague and general in statement, but intended to give the impression that he held the essentials of the received orthodoxy. The text is that given by Hahn, § 187.

Arius and Euzoius to our most religious and pious Lord, the Emperor Constantine.

In accordance with the command of your devout piety, sovereign lord, we declare our faith, and before God we profess in writing that we and our adherents believe as follows:

We believe in one God, the Father Almighty; and in the Lord Jesus Christ His Son, who was made by Him before all ages, God the Word, through whom all things were made, both those which are in heaven and those upon earth; who descended, and became incarnate, and suffered, and rose again, ascended into the heavens, and will again come to judge the living and the dead. Also in the Holy Spirit, and in the resurrection of the flesh, and in the life of the coming age, and in the kingdom of the heavens, and in one Catholic Church of God, extending from one end of the earth to the other.

This faith we have received from the holy gospels, the Lord therein saying to His disciples: "Go teach all nations, baptizing them in the name of the Father, and of the Son, and of the Holy Spirit." If we do not so believe and truly receive the Father, Son, and Holy Spirit, as the whole Catholic Church and the Holy Scriptures teach (in which we believe in every respect) God is our judge both now and in the coming judgment. Wherefore we beseech your piety, most devout Emperor, that we who are persons consecrated to the ministry, and holding the faith and sentiments of the Church and of the Holy Scriptures, may by your pacific and devoted piety be reunited to our mother, the Church, all superfluous questions and disputings being avoided; that so both we and the whole Church may be at peace and in common offer our accustomed prayers for your tranquil reign and on behalf of your whole family.

(*b*) Socrates, *Hist. Ec.*, I, 23.   (MSG, 67 : 140.)

The attack of the Arians upon Athanasius and his party.

The partisans of Eusebius and Theognis having returned from their exile, they received again their churches, having expelled, as we observed, those who had been ordained in their stead. Moreover they came into great consideration with the Emperor, who honored them exceedingly, as those who had returned from error to the orthodox faith. They, however, abused the license granted them by exciting commotions in the world greater than before; being instigated to this by two causes—on the one hand, the Arian heresy with which they had been previously infected, and on the other hand, by animosity against Athanasius because in the synod he had so vigorously withstood them in the discussion of the articles of the faith. And in the first place they objected to the ordination of Athanasius, not only as of one unworthy of the episcopate, but also as of one not elected by qualified persons. But when he had shown himself superior to this calumny (for having assumed direction of the Church of the Alexandrians, he ardently contended for the Nicene creed), then the adherents of Eusebius exerted themselves to cause the removal of Athanasius and to bring Arius back to Alexandria; for thus only did they think they should be able to cast out the doctrine of consubstantiality and introduce Arianism. Eusebius therefore wrote to Athanasius to receive Arius and his adherents; and when he wrote he not only entreated him, but he openly threatened him. When Athanasius would by no means accede to this he endeavored to persuade the Emperor to receive Arius in audience and then permit him to return to Alexandria; and how he accomplished these things I shall tell in its proper place.

Meanwhile, before this, another commotion was raised in the Church. In fact those of the household of the Church again disturbed her peace. Eusebius Pamphilius says that immediately after the synod Egypt became agitated by intestine divisions; but he does not give the reason for this. From this he has gained the reputation of being disingenuous and of avoiding the specification of the causes of these dissensions from a determination on his part not to give his sanction to the proceedings at Nicæa. Yet as we ourselves have discovered from various letters which the bishops wrote to one another after the synod, the term homoousios troubled some of them. So that while they occupied themselves about it, investigating it very minutely, they roused the strife against each other. It seemed not unlike a contest in the dark; for neither party appeared to understand distinctly the grounds on which they calumniated one another. Those who objected to the word homoousios conceived that those who approved it favored the opinion of Sabellius and Montanus; they therefore called them blasphemers, as subverting the existence of the Son of God. And again those who defended the term, charging their opponents with polytheism, inveighed against them as introducers of heathen superstitions. Eustathius, bishop of Antioch, accuses Eusebius Pamphilius of perverting the Nicene creed; Eusebius again denies that he violates that exposition of the faith, and accuses Eustathius of introducing the opinion of Sabellius. Therefore each of them wrote as if contending against adversaries; but both sides admitted that the Son of God has a distinct person and existence, confessing that there is one God in three persons (hypostases) yet they were unable to agree, for what cause I do not know, and could in no way be at peace.

§ 65. The Victory of the Anti-Nicene Party in the East

When Constantine died in 337 the party of Eusebius of Nicomedia was completely in the ascendant in the East. A council at Antioch, 339, deposed Athanasius, and he was expelled from Alexandria, and Gregory of Cappadocia was consecrated in his place. Athanasius, with Marcellus of Ancyra and other supporters of the Nicene faith, repaired to Rome where they were supported by Julius, bishop of Rome, at a well-attended local council in 340 (*a, b*). In the East numerous attempts were made to formulate a confession of faith which might take the place of the Nicene creed and prove acceptable to all parties. The most important of these were produced at the Council of Antioch, 341, at which no less than four creeds were formulated (*c, d*).

Additional source material: Percival, *The Seven Ecumenical Councils* (PNF, ser. II, vol. XIV); Socrates, *Hist. Ec.* (PNF, ser. II, vol. II), II, 19 (Formula Macrostichos); Athanasius, *De Synodis* (PNF, ser. II, vol. IV).

(*a*) Athanasius, *Apologia contra Arianos*, 20. (MSG, 25 : 280.)

Athanasius and his allies in exile in the West are exonerated at Rome.

The Eusebians wrote also to Julius, thinking to frighten me, requesting him to call a council, and Julius himself to be the judge if he pleased. When, therefore, I went up to Rome, Julius wrote to the Eusebians, as was suitable, and sent moreover two of his presbyters, Elpidius and Philoxenus. But when they heard of me they became confused, because they did not expect that we would come up; and they declined, alleging absurd reasons for so doing, but in truth fearing lest the things should be proved against them which Valens and Ursacius afterward confessed. However, more than fifty bishops assembled in the place where the presbyter Vito held his congregation, and they acknowledged my defence and gave me the confirmation both of their communion and their love. On the other hand, they expressed great indignation against the Eusebians and requested that Julius write to the following effect to them who had written to him. And he wrote and sent it by Count Gabienus.

(b) Julius of Rome, *Epistula*, in Athanasius, *Apologia contra Arianos*, §§ 26 ff. (MSG, 25 : 292.)

Julius to his dearly beloved brethren, Danius, Flacillus, Narcissus, Eusebius, and Matis, Macedonius, Theodorus, and their friends, who have written him from Antioch, sends health in the Lord.

§ 26. . . . It is necessary for me to inform you that although I alone wrote, yet it was not my opinion only, but of all the bishops throughout Italy and in these parts. I, indeed, was unwilling to cause them all to write, lest they might have weight by mere numbers. The bishops, however, assembled on the appointed day, and agreed in these opinions, which I again write to signify to you; so that, dearly beloved, although I alone address you, yet you may know it is the opinion of all. . . .

§ 27. That we have not admitted to our communion our fellow-bishops Athanasius and Marcellus either hastily or unjustly, although sufficiently shown above, it is but fair to set briefly before you. The Eusebians first wrote against Athanasius and his fellows, and you have also written now; but many bishops out of Egypt and other provinces wrote in his favor. Now in the first place, your letters against him contradict each other, and the second have no sort of agreement with the first, but in many instances the former are refuted by the latter, and the latter are impeached by the former. . . .

§ 29. Now when these things were thus represented, and so many witnesses appeared in his behalf, and so much advanced by him in his own justification, what did it become

us to do?   Or what did the rule of the Church require except
that we should not condemn the man, but rather receive him
and hold him as a bishop as we have done. . . .

§ 32.   With respect to Marcellus, forasmuch as you have
written concerning him also as impious in respect to Christ,
I am anxious to inform you that, when he was here, he positively declared that what you had written concerning him
was not true; but, being nevertheless requested by us to give
an account of his faith, he answered in his own person with
the utmost boldness, so that we recognize that he maintains
nothing outside of the truth.   He confessed that he piously
held the same doctrine concerning our Lord and Saviour
Jesus Christ as the Catholic Church holds; and he affirmed
that he had held these opinions not merely now but for a very
long time since; as indeed our presbyters, who were at a
former time at the Council of Nicæa, testified to his orthodoxy, for he maintained both then and now his opposition to
the heresy of Arius; on which point it is right to admonish
you, that none of you admit such heresy, but instead abom-
inate it as alien from the wholesome doctrine.   Since he professed orthodox opinions and offered testimony to his orthodoxy, what again ought we in his case to have done except
to treat him as a bishop, as we did, and not reject him from
our communion? . . .

§ 33.   For not only the bishops Athanasius and Marcellus
and their fellows came here and complained of the injustice
that had been done them, but many other bishops, also, from
Thrace, from Cœle-Syria, from Phœnicia, and Palestine; and
presbyters, not a few, and others from Alexandria and from
other parts were present at the council here and, in addition
to their own statements, lamented bitterly before all the
assembled bishops the violence and injustice which the
churches had suffered; and they affirmed that outrages similar to those which had been committed in Alexandria had
occurred not in word only but in deed in their own churches
and in others also.

(c) *Second Creed of Antioch*, A. D. 341, in Athanasius, *De Synodis Arimini et Seleuciæ*, ch. 23. (MSG, 26 : 721.) Also in Socrates, *Hist. Ec.*, II, 10. (MSG, 67 : 201.) *Cf.* Hahn, § 154.

The Council of Antioch in 341 was gathered ostensibly to dedicate the great church of that city, in reality to act against the Nicene party. It was attended by ninety or more bishops of whom thirty-six were Arians. The others seem to have been chiefly members of the middle party. The dogmatic definitions of this council have never been accepted by the Church; on the other hand, the canons on discipline have always enjoyed a very high place in the esteem of later generations. The following creed, the second of the Antiochian creeds, is traditionally regarded as having been composed originally by Lucian of Antioch, the master of Arius. Hence it is known as the creed of Lucian.

We believe in accordance with evangelic and apostolic tradition in one God the Father Almighty, the creator, the maker and provider of all things. And in one Lord Jesus Christ, His only begotten Son, God, through whom are all things, who was begotten of His Father before all ages, God of God, whole of whole, only one of only one, perfect of perfect, king of king, lord of lord, the living word, living wisdom, true light, way, truth, resurrection, shepherd, door, unchangeable, unalterable, and immutable, the unchangeable likeness of the Godhead, both of the substance, and will and power and glory of the Father, the first-born of all creation, who was in the beginning with God, God Logos, according to what is said in the Gospel: "and the word was God," through whom all things were made, and "in whom all things consist," who in the last days came down from above, and was born of a virgin, according to the Scriptures, and became man, the mediator between God and man, and the apostle of our faith, and the prince of life; as He says, "I have come down from heaven, not to do mine own will, but the will of Him that sent me"; who suffered for us, and rose the third day and ascended into heaven and sitteth on the right hand of the Father, and comes again with glory and power to judge the

living and the dead.   And in the Holy Spirit given for consolation and sanctification and perfection to those who believe; as also our Lord Jesus Christ commanded his disciples,
saying, "Go ye, teach all nations, baptizing them in the name
of the Father and of the Son and of the Holy Spirit," clearly
of the Father who is really a Father, and of the Son who is
really a Son, and of the Holy Spirit who is really a Holy
Spirit; these names being assigned not vaguely nor idly, but
indicating accurately the special subsistence [hypostasis],
order, glory of those named, so that in subsistence they are
three, but in harmony one.

Having then this faith from the beginning and holding it
to the end, before God and Christ we anathematize all heretical false doctrines.   And if any one contrary to the right
faith of the Holy Scriptures, teaches and says that there has
been a time, a season, or age, or being or becoming, before
the Son of God was begotten, let him be accursed.   And if
any one says that the Son is a creature as one of the creatures,
or generated as one of the things generated, or made as one
of the things made, and not as the divine Scriptures have
handed down each of the forenamed statements; or if a man
teaches or preaches anything else contrary to what we have
received, let him be accursed.   For we truly and clearly both
believe and follow all things from the Holy Scriptures that
have been transmitted to us by the prophets and Apostles.

(d) *Fourth Creed of Antioch*, Socrates, *Hist. Ec.*, II, 18.
(MSG, 67 : 221.)   *Cf.* Hahn, § 156.

This creed is an approximation to the Nicene creed but without the
use of the word of especial importance, homoousios.   Valuable critical
notes on the text of this and the preceding creed are to be found in
Hahn; as these creeds are to be found both in the work of Athanasius
on the councils of synods of Ariminum and Seleucia, in the ecclesiastical
history of Socrates and elsewhere, there is a variety of readings, but
of minor significance so far as the essential features are concerned.

We believe in one God, Father Almighty, the creator and
maker of all things, of whom the whole family in heaven and

upon earth is named; and in his only begotten Son, our Lord
Jesus Christ, who was begotten of the Father before all ages;
God of God, light of light, through whom all things in the
heavens and upon earth, both visible and invisible were
made: who is the word, and wisdom, and power, and life,
and true light: who in the last days for our sake was made
[became] man, and was born of the holy Virgin; was crucified,
and died; was buried, arose again from the dead on the third
day, and ascended into heaven, is seated at the right hand
of the Father, and is coming at the consummation of the age
to judge the living and the dead, and to render to each according to his works: whose kingdom, being perpetual, shall continue to infinite ages (for He shall sit at the right hand of the
Father, not only in this age, but also in that which is to come).
And in the Holy Spirit; that is, in the comforter, whom the
Lord, according to His promise, sent to His Apostles after
His ascension into the heavens, to teach and bring all things
to their remembrance: by whom, also, the souls of those who
have sincerely believed in Him shall be sanctified; and those
who assert that the Son was made of things which are not,
or of another subsistence [hypostasis], and not of God, or that
there was a time or age when He did not exist the holy Catholic Church accounts as aliens.

§ 66. COLLAPSE OF THE ANTI-NICENE MIDDLE PARTY; THE RENEWAL OF ARIANISM; THE RISE OF THE HO-MOOUSIAN PARTY

When Constantius became sole Emperor, on the death of
his brother Constans in 350, there was no further need of
considering the interests of the Nicene party. Only the
necessity of establishing his authority in the West against
usurpers engaged his attention until 356, when a series of
councils began, designed to put an end to the Nicene faith.
Of the numerous confessions of faith put forth, the second
creed of Sirmium of 357 is important as attempting to abol-

ish in connection with the discussion the use of the term *ousia* and likewise *homoousios* and *homoiousios* (*a*). At Nice in Thrace a still greater departure from Nicæa was attempted in 359, and a creed was put forth (*b*), which is of special significance as containing the first reference in a creed to the *desensus ad inferos* and to the fact that it was subscribed by the deputies of the West including Bishop Liberius of Rome. For the discussion of this act of Liberius, see J. Barmby, art. "Liberius" in DCB; see also *Catholic Encyclopædia*, art. "Liberius." It was also received in the synod of Seleucia in the East. On these councils see Athanasius, *De Synodis* (PNF). It was in reference to this acceptance of the creed of Nice that Jerome wrote "The whole world groaned and was astonished that it was Arian." See Jerome, *Contra Luciferianos*, §§ 18 *ff*. (PNF, ser. II, vol. VI).

Inasmuch as the anti-Nicene opposition party was a coalition of all parties opposed to the wording of the Nicene creed, as soon as that creed was abolished the bond that held them together was broken. At once there arose an extreme Arianism which had remained in the background. On the other hand, those who were opposed to Arianism sought to draw nearer the Nicene party. These were the Homoiousians, who objected to the term homoousios as savoring of Sabellianism, and yet admitted the essential point implied by it. That this was so was pointed out by Hilary of Poitiers (*c*) who contended that what the West meant by homoousios the East meant by homoiousios. The Homoiousian party of the East split on the question of the deity of the Holy Spirit. Those of them who denied the deity of the Spirit remained Semi-Arians.

(*a*) *Second Creed of Sirmium*, in Hilary of Poitiers, *De Synodis*, ch. 11. (MSL, 10 : 487.) *Cf.* Hahn, § 161.

The Council of Sirmium in 357 was the second in that city. It was attended entirely by bishops from the West. But among them were Ursacius, Valens, and Germinius, leaders of the opposition to the Nicene creed. Hosius under compulsion signed the following; see Hilary, *loc cit*. The Latin original is given by Hilary.

It is evident that there is one God, the Father Almighty, according as it is believed throughout the whole world; and His only Son Jesus Christ our Saviour, begotten of Him before the ages. But we cannot and ought not to say there are two Gods. . . .

But since some or many persons were disturbed by questions as to substance, called in Greek *ousia*, that is, to make it understood more exactly, as to *homoousios* or what is called *homoiousios*, there ought to be no mention of these at all, nor ought any one to state them; for the reason and consideration that they are not contained in the divine Scriptures, and that they are above man's understanding, nor can any man declare the birth of the Son, of whom it is written: "Who shall declare His generation?" For it is plain that only the Father knows how He begat the Son, and the Son how He was begotten of the Father. There is no question that the Father is greater. No one can doubt that the Father is greater than the Son, in honor, dignity, splendor, majesty and in the very name Father, the Son himself testifying, He that sent Me is greater than I. And no one is ignorant that it is Catholic doctrine that there are two persons of Father and Son; and that the Father is greater, and that the Son is subordinated to the Father, together with all things which the Father hath subordinated to Him; and that the Father has no beginning and is invisible, immortal, and impassible, but that the Son has been begotten of the Father, God of God, light of light, and of this Son the generation, as is aforesaid, no one knows but His Father. And that the Son of God himself, our Lord and God, as we read, took flesh or a body, that is, man of the womb of the Virgin Mary, as the angel announced. And as all the Scriptures teach, and especially the doctor of the Gentiles himself, He took of Mary the Virgin, man, through whom He suffered. And the whole faith is summed up and secured in this, that the Trinity must always be preserved, as we read in the Gospel: "Go ye and baptize all nations in the name of the

Father, and of the Son, and of the Holy Ghost." Complete and perfect is the number of the Trinity. Now the Paraclete, or the Spirit, is through the Son: who was sent and came according to His promise in order to instruct, teach, and sanctify the Apostles and all believers.

(b) *Creed of Nice* A. D. 359, Theodoret, *Hist. Ec.*, II, 16. (MSG, 82 : 1049.) *Cf.* Hahn, § 164.

The deputies from the Council of Ariminum were sent to Nice, a small town in Thrace, where they met the heads of the Arian party. A creed, strongly Arian in tendency, was given them and they were sent back to Ariminum to have it accepted. See Theodoret, *loc. cit.*, and Athanasius, *De Synodis.*

We believe in one and only true God, Father Almighty, of whom are all things. And in the only begotten Son of God, who before all ages and before every beginning was begotten of God, through whom all things were made, both visible and invisible; begotten, only begotten, alone of the Father alone, God of God, like the Father that begat Him, according to the Scriptures, whose generation no one knoweth except only the Father that begat Him. This only begotten Son of God, sent by His Father, we know to have come down from heaven, as it is written, for the destruction of sin and death; begotten of the Holy Ghost and the Virgin Mary, as it is written, according to the flesh. Who companied with His disciples, and when the whole dispensation was fulfilled, according to the Father's will, was crucified, dead and buried, and descended to the world below, at whom hell itself trembled; on the third day He rose from the dead and companied with His disciples, and when forty days were completed He was taken up into the heavens, and sitteth on the right hand of His Father, and is coming at the last day of the resurrection, in His Father's glory, to render to every one according to his works. And in the Holy Ghost, which the only begotten Son of God, Jesus Christ, both God and Lord, promised to send to the race of men, the comforter, as it is written, the spirit of truth, and this Spirit He himself sent after He had ascended into the heavens and sat at the right hand of the Father, from thence He is coming to judge both the quick and the dead.

But the word "substance," which was simply inserted by the Fathers and not being understood was a cause of scandal to the people because it was not found in the Scriptures, it hath seemed good to us to remove, and that for the future no mention whatever be permitted of "substance," because the sacred Scriptures nowhere make any mention of the "substance" of the Father and the Son. Nor must one "subsistence" [hypostasis] be named in relation to the person [prosopon] of Father, Son, and Holy Ghost. And we call the Son like the Father, as the Holy Scriptures call Him and teach. But all heresies, both those already condemned, and any, if such there be, which have arisen against the document thus put forth, let them be anathema.

(c) Hilary of Poitiers, *De Synodis*, §§ 88, 89, 91. (MSL, 10 : 540.)

That the Homoiousian party meant substantially the same by their term homoiousios as did the Homoousians or the Nicene party, by their term homoousios.

Hilary was of great importance in the Arian controversy in bringing the Homoiousian party of the East and the Nicene party of the West to an agreement. The Eastern theologians, who hesitated to accept the Nicene term, were eventually induced to accept, understanding by the term homoousios the same as homoiousios. See below, § 70.

§ 88. Holy brethren, I understand by homoousios God of God, not of an unlike essence, not divided, but born; and that the Son has a birth that is unique, of the substance of the unknown God, that He is begotten yet co-eternal and wholly like the Father. The word homoousios greatly helped me already believing this. Why do you condemn my faith in the homoousios, which you cannot disapprove by the confession of the homoiousios? For you condemn my faith, or rather your own, when you condemn its verbal equivalent. Does somebody else misunderstand it? Let us together condemn the misunderstanding, but not take away the security of your faith. Do you think that one must subscribe to the Samosetene Council, so that no one may make use of homoousios in the sense of Paul of Samosata? Then let us subscribe to the Council of Nicæa, so that the Arians may not impugn the word homoousios. Have we to fear that homoiousios does not imply the same belief as homoousios? Let us decree that there is no difference between being of one and being of a similar substance. But may not the word homoousios be understood in a wrong sense? Let it be proved that it can be understood in a good sense. We hold one and the same sacred truth. I beseech you that the one and the same truth which we hold, we should regard as sacred among us. Forgive me, brethren, as I have so often asked you to do. You are not Arians; why, then, by denying the homoousios, should you be thought to be Arians?

§ 89. . . . True likeness belongs to a true natural connection. But when the true natural connection exists, the homoousios is implied. It is likeness according to essence when one piece of metal is like another and not plated. . . . Nothing can be like gold but gold, or like milk that does not belong to that species.

§ 91. I do not know the word homoousios or understand it unless it confesses a similarity of essence. I call God of heaven and earth to witness, that when I heard neither word, my belief was always such that I should have interpreted homoiousios by homoousios. That is, I believed that nothing could be similar according to nature unless it was of the same nature.

§ 67. THE POLICY OF THE SONS OF CONSTANTINE TOWARD HEATHENISM AND DONATISM

Under the sons of Constantine a harsher policy toward heathenism was adopted. Laws were passed forbidding heathen sacrifices (a, b), and although these were not carried out vigorously in the West, where there were many heathen members of the leading families, they were more generally enforced in the East, and heathenism was thereby much reduced, at least in outward manifestations. As to heresy, the action of the emperors and especially Constantius in his constant endeavor to set aside the Nicene faith involved harsh measures against all who differed from the approved theology of the court. Donatism called for special treatment. A policy of conciliation was attempted, but on account of the failure to win over the Donatists and their alliance with fierce revolutionary fanatics, the Circumcellions, violent measures were taken against them which nearly extirpated the sect.

(a) *Codex Theodosianus*, XVI, 10, 2; A. D. 341.

This edict of Constantius is of importance here as it seems to imply that Constantine did more toward repressing heathen sacrifices than to forbid those celebrated in private. It is, however, the only evidence of his prohibiting sacrifice, and it might have been due to misunderstanding that his example is here cited.

Let superstition cease; let the madness of sacrifices be abolished. For whoever, against the law of the divine prince, our parent [Constantine] and this command of our clemency, shall celebrate sacrifices, let a punishment appropriate to him and this present decision be issued.

(b) *Codex Theodosianus*, XVI, 10, 3; A. D. 342.

In the West Constans did not enforce the law against sacrifices with great severity, but tolerated the existence and even use of certain temples without the walls.

Although all superstition is to be entirely destroyed, yet we will that the temple buildings, which are situated without the walls, remain intact and uninjured. For since from some have arisen various sports, races, and contests, it is not proper that they should be destroyed, from which the solemnity of ancient enjoyments are furnished to the Roman people.

(c) *Codex Theodosianus*, XVI, 10, 4; A. D. 346.

It is our pleasure that in all places and in all cities the temples be henceforth closed, and access having been forbidden to all, freedom to sin be denied the wicked. We will that all abstain from sacrifices; that if any one should commit any such act, let him fall before the vengeance of the sword. Their goods, we decree, shall be taken away entirely and recovered to the fisc, and likewise rectors of provinces are to be punished if they neglect to punish for these crimes.

(*d*) Optatus, *De schismate Donatistarum*, III, §§ 3, 4. (MSL, 11 : 999.)

The principal historical writer treating the schism of the Donatists is Optatus, Bishop of Mileve. His work on this sect was written about 370 and revised and enlarged in 385. It is of primary importance not merely for the history but for the dogmatic discussions on the doctrine of the Church, Bk. II, the doctrine of the sacraments, the idea of *opus operatum* as applied to them, Bk. V; in all of which he laid the foundation upon which Augustine built. In addition to the passage from Optatus given here, Epistles 88 and 185 by Augustine are accessible in translations and will be found of assistance in filling in the account of the Circumcellions. The latter is known as *De correctione Donatistarum* and is published in the anti-Donatist writings of Augustine in PNF, ser. I, vol. IV; the most important passages are §§ 15 and 25. It is probable that the party of the Circumcellions was originally due to a revolt against intolerable agrarian conditions and that their association with the Donatists was at first slight.

§ 3. . . . The Emperor Constans did not send Paulus and Macarius primarily to bring about unity, but with alms, that, assisted by them, the poor of the various churches might be relieved, clothed, and fed. When they came to Donatus, your father, and showed him why they had come, he was seized with his accustomed furious anger and broke forth with these words: "What has the Emperor to do with the Church." . . .

§ 4. If anything, therefore, has been done harshly in bringing about unity,[1] you see, brother Parmenianus, to whom it ought to be attributed. Do you say that the military was sought by us Catholics; if so, then why did no one

———
[1] *I. e.*, in forcing the Donatists to return to the Church.

see the military in arms in the proconsular province?   Paulus
and Macarius came, everywhere to consider the poor and to
exhort individuals to unity; and when they approached
Bagaja, then another Donatus, bishop of that city, desiring
to place an obstacle in the way of unity and hinder the work
of those coming, whom we have mentioned, sent messengers
throughout the neighboring places and all markets, and summoned the Circumcellions, calling them Agonistici, to come
to the said place.   And at that time the gathering of these
was desired, whose madness a little before had been seen by
the bishops themselves to have been impiously inspired.   For
when men of this sort before the unity[1] wandered through
various places, when Axido and Fasir were called by the same
mad ones the leaders of the saints, no one could be secure in
his possessions; written evidences of indebtedness lost their
force; no creditor was at liberty at that time to demand anything.   All were terrified by the letters of those who boasted
that they were the leaders of the saints, and if there was any
delay in fulfilling their commands, suddenly a furious multitude hurried up and, terror going on before, creditors were
surrounded with a wall of dangers, so that those who ought
to have been asked for their protection were by fear of death
compelled to use humble prayers.   Each one hastened to
abandon his most important duties; and profit was thought
to have come from these outrages.   Even the roads were no
longer at all safe, because masters, turned out of their carriages, ran humbly before their slaves sitting in the places of
their masters.   By the judgment and rule of these the order
of rank between masters and servants was changed.   Therefore when there arose complaint against the bishops of your
party, they are said to have written to Count Taurinus, that
such men could not be corrected in the Church, and they
demanded that they should receive discipline from the said
count.   Then Taurinus, in response to their letters, com-

---

[1] The temporary defeat of the Donatist party which was celebrated at the
Council of Carthage in 348–349.   See Hefele, § 70.

manded an armed body of soldiers to go through the markets
where the Circumcellions were accustomed to wander. In
Octavum very many were killed, many were beheaded and
their bodies, even to the present day, can be counted by the
white altars or tables.[1] When first some of their number
were buried in the basilicas, Clarus, a presbyter in Subbulum,
was compelled by his bishop to disinter those buried. Whence
it is reported that what was done had been commanded to be
done, when it is admitted that sepulture in the house of
God is not granted. Afterward the multitude of these people increased. In this way Donatus of Bagaja found whence
he might lead against Macarius a raging mob. Of that sort
were those who were to their own ruin murderers of themselves in their desire for a false martyrdom. Of these, also,
were those who rushed headlong and threw themselves down
from the summits of lofty mountains. Behold from what
numbers the second Bishop Donatus formed his cohorts!
Those who were bearing treasure which they had obtained
for the poor were held back by fear. They decided in so
great a predicament to demand from Count Sylvester armed
soldiery, not that by these they should do violence to any one,
but that they might stop the force drawn up by the aforesaid
Bishop Donatus. Thus it happened that an armed soldiery
was seen. Now, as to what followed, see to whom it ought or
can be ascribed. They had there an infinite number of those
summoned, and it is certain that a supply of provisions for a
year had been provided. Of the basilicas they made a sort
of public granary, and awaited the coming of those against
whom they might expend their fury, if the presence of armed
soldiery had not prevented them. For when, before the
soldiers came, the metatores,[2] as was the custom, were sent,
they were not properly received, contrary to the apostolic precept, "honor to whom honor, custom to whom custom, tribute to whom tribute, owe no man anything." For those who

[1] Tombs built in the shape of altars which were table-shaped.
[2] The metatores were those who were sent ahead of a troop of soldiers to provide for quartering them upon the inhabitants.

had been sent with their horses were smitten by those whose names you have made public with malicious intent. They were the authors of their own wrong; and what they could suffer they themselves taught by these outrages. The soldiers who had been maltreated returned to their fellows, and for what two or three suffered, all grieved. All were roused, and their officers could not restrain the angered soldiers.

§ 68. JULIAN THE APOSTATE

The reign of Julian the Apostate (361–363) is important in the history of the Christian Church, in the first place, as indicating the slight hold which heathenism had retained as a system upon the bulk of the people and the impossibility of reviving it in any form in which it might compete with the Church. Julian attempted to inject into a purified heathenism those elements in the Christian Church which he was forced to admire. The result was a fantastic mixture of rites and measures with which the heathen would have nothing to do. In the second place, in the development of the Church's doctrinal system, and especially in the Arian controversy, the reign of Julian gave the contestants, who were obliged to stand together against a common enemy, reason for examining in a new way the points they had in common, and enabled them to see that some at least differed more over the expression than over the content of their faith. The character of Julian has long been a favorite subject of study and especially the motives that induced him to abandon Christianity for the Neo-Platonic revival of heathenism.

Additional source material: Socrates, *Hist. Ec.*, III; Ammianus Marcellinus, *Roman History*, XVI–XXV, translated by C. D. Yonge (Bohn's Classical Library); *Select Works of Julian*, translated by C. W. King (Bohn).

(a) Socrates, *Hist. Ec.*, III, 1. (MSG, 67 : 368.)

The Emperor Julian.
The account of the Emperor Julian as given by Socrates is probably the best we have. It is, on the whole, a model of a fair statement,

such as is characteristic of the history of Socrates in nearly all its parts. In spite of its length it is worthy of a place in its entirety, as it explains the antecedents of a character which the world has had difficulty in understanding.

Constantine, who gave Byzantium his own name, had two brothers born of the same father but by a different mother, of these one was named Dalmatius, the other Constantius. Dalmatius had a son of the same name as his own; Constantius had two sons, Gallus and Julian. Now, as on the death of Constantine, the founder of Constantinople, the soldiery had put the younger brother Constantius to death, the lives of his two orphaned children were also endangered; but a disease, apparently fatal, preserved Gallus from the violence of his father's murderers; and as to Julian, his age—for he was only eight years old at the time—protected him. The Emperor's jealousy toward them having been subdued, Gallus attended schools at Ephesus in Ionia, in which country considerable possessions had been left them by their parents. Julian, however, when he was grown up pursued his studies at Constantinople, going constantly to the palace, where the schools then were, in simple attire and under the care of the eunuch Mardonius. In grammar, Nicocles, the Lacedæmonian, was his instructor; and Ecbolius, the sophist, who was at that time a Christian, taught him rhetoric; for the Emperor Constantius had made provision that he should have no pagan masters, lest he should be seduced to pagan superstitions; for Julian was a Christian at the beginning. Since he made great progress in literature, the report began to spread that he was capable of ruling the Roman Empire; and this popular rumor becoming generally spread abroad, greatly disquieted the Emperor. Therefore he removed him from the great city to Nicomedia, forbidding him at the same time to frequent the school of Libanius the Syrian sophist. For Libanius, having been driven away by the teachers of Constantinople, had opened a school at Nicomedia. Here he gave vent to his indignation against the teachers in his treatise composed against them. Julian, however, was interdicted from being his auditor, because Libanius was a pagan in religion; nevertheless because he admired his orations, he procured them and read them secretly and diligently. As he was becoming very expert in the rhetorical art, Maximus the philosopher arrived in Nicomedia, not the Byzantine, Euclid's father, but the Ephesian whom the Emperor Valentinian afterward caused to be executed as a practicer of magic. This took place later; at that time the only thing that attracted him to Nicomedia was the fame of Julian. Having obtained from him a taste for the principles of philosophy, Julian began to imitate the religion of his teacher, who had instilled into his mind a desire for the Empire. When these things reached the ears of the Emperor, wavering between hope and fear, Julian became very anxious to lull the suspicion that had been awakened, and he who was at first truly a Christian then became one in pretence. Shaved to the very skin, he pretended to live the monastic life; and while in private he pursued philosophical studies, in public he read the sacred writings of the Christian Church. Moreover, he was appointed reader of the church in Nicomedia. Thus by these pretexts he escaped the Emperor's displeasure. Now he did all this from fear, but he by no means abandoned his hope; telling many of his friends that times would be happier when he should possess all. While his affairs were in this condition his brother Gallus, who had been created Cæsar, when he was on his way to the East came to Nicomedia to see him. But when Gallus was slain shortly after, Julian was immediately suspected by the Emperor; therefore the latter directed that he should be kept under guard; he soon found means, however, of escaping from his guards, and fleeing from place to place he managed to be in safety. At last Eusebia, the wife of the Emperor, having discovered him in his retreat, persuaded the Emperor to do him no harm, and to permit him to go to Athens to study philosophy. From thence—to be brief—the Emperor recalled him and afterward created him Cæsar, and having given him his own sister Helen in marriage, he sent him to Gaul against the barbarians. For the barbarians whom the Emperor Constantius had hired as auxiliary forces against Magnentius, being of no use against that usurper, were pillaging the Roman cities. Inasmuch as he was young he ordered him to undertake nothing without consulting the other military chiefs. . . . Julian's complaint to the Emperor of the inertness of his military officers procured for him a coadjutor in the command more in sympathy with his ardor; and by their combined efforts an assault was made upon the barbarians. But they sent him an embassy, assuring him that they had been ordered by letters of the Emperor to march into Roman territories, and they showed him the letters. But he cast the ambassadors into prison, vigorously attacked the forces of the enemy and totally defeated them; and having taken their king prisoner, he sent him to Constantius. After these successes he was proclaimed Emperor by the soldiers; and inasmuch as there was no imperial crown at hand, one of the guards took the chain which he wore around his own neck and placed it upon Julian's head. Thus Julian became Emperor; but whether he subsequently conducted himself as a philosopher, let my readers determine. For he neither sent an embassy to Constantius, nor paid him the least homage in acknowledgment of past favors; but conducted everything just as it pleased him. He changed the rulers of the provinces, and he sought to bring Constantius into contempt by reciting publicly in every city the letters which Constantius had written to the barbarians. For this reason the cities revolted from Constantius and attached themselves to him. Then he openly put off the pretence of being a Christian; going about to the various cities, he opened the pagan temples, offering sacrifices to the idols, and designating himself "Pontifex Maximus"; and the heathen celebrated their pagan festivals with pagan rites. By doing these things he excited a civil war against Constantius; and thus as far as he was concerned all the evils involved in war happened. For this philosopher's desire could not have been fulfilled without much bloodshed. But God, who is the judge of His own counsels, checked the fury of these antagonists without detriment to the State by the removal of one of them. For when Julian arrived among the Thracians, it was announced that Constantius was dead. And thus did the Roman Empire at that time escape the intestine strife. Julian entered Constantinople and at once considered how he might conciliate the masses and secure popular favor. Accordingly, he had recourse to the following measures: he knew that Constantius was hated by all the people who held the homoousian faith and had driven them from the churches and had proscribed and exiled their bishops. He was aware, also, that the pagans were extremely discontented because they had been forbidden to sacrifice to their gods, and were anxious to get their temples opened and to be at liberty to offer sacrifices to their idols. Thus he knew that both classes secretly entertained hostile feelings toward his predecessor, and at the same time the people in general were exceedingly exasperated by the violence of the eunuchs, and especially by the rapacity of Eusebius, the chief officer of the imperial bed-chamber. Therefore he treated all with craftiness. With some he dissembled; others he attached to himself by conferring obligations upon them, led by a desire for vainglory;' but to all he manifested how he stood toward the heathen religion. And first, in order to slander Constantius and condemn him as cruel toward his subjects among the people generally, he recalled the exiled bishops and restored to them their confiscated estates. He next commanded suitable agents to open the pagan temples without delay. Then he directed that those who had been treated unjustly by the eunuchs should receive back the property of which they had been plundered. Eusebius, the chief officer of the imperial bed-chamber, he punished with death, not only on account of the injuries he had inflicted on others, but because he was assured that it was through his machinations his brother Gallus had been killed. The body of Constantius he honored with an imperial funeral, but he expelled the eunuchs, the barbers, and cooks from the palace. . . . At night, remaining awake, he wrote orations which he afterward delivered in the Senate, going thither from the palace, though in fact he was the first and only Emperor since the time of Julius Cæsar who made speeches in that assembly. He honored those who were eminent for literary attainments, and especially those who taught philosophy; in consequence of which an abundance of pretenders to learning of this sort resorted to the palace from all quarters, men who wore their palliums and were more conspicuous for their costume than for their erudition. These impostors, who invariably adopted the religious sentiments of their prince, were inimical to the welfare of the Christians; but since Julian himself was overcome by excessive vanity he derided all his predecessors in a book which he wrote, entitled "The Cæsars." Led by the same haughty disposition, he composed treatises against the Christians as well.

(b) Sozomenus, *Hist. Ec.*, V, 3.   (MSG, 67 : 1217.)

Julian's restoration of heathenism.

When Julian was placed in sole possession of the Empire he commanded all the temples throughout the East to be reopened; and he also commanded that those which had been neglected to be repaired, those which had fallen into ruins to be rebuilt, and the altars to be restored. He assigned considerable money for this purpose. He restored the customs of antiquity and the ancestral ceremonies in the cities and the sacrifices. He himself offered libations openly and sacrificed publicly; and held in honor those who were zealous in these things. He restored to their ancient privileges the initiators and the priests, the hierophants and the servants of the temples, and confirmed the legislation of former emperors in their favor. He granted them exemption from duties and other burdens as they had previously had had such exemption.

He restored to the temple guardians the provisions which had been abolished. He commanded them to be pure from meats, and to abstain from whatever, according to pagan opinion, was not befitting him who had announced his purpose of leading a pure life.

(c) Sozomenus, *Hist. Ec.*, V, 5. (MSG, 67 : 1225.)

Julian's measures against the Christians.

Among those who benefited by the recall of those who had been banished for their religious beliefs were not only the orthodox Christians who suffered under Constantius, but also the Donatists and others who had been expelled from their homes by the previous emperors.

Julian recalled all who, during the reign of Constantius, had been banished on account of their religious beliefs, and restored to them their property which had been confiscated by law. He charged the people not to commit any act of injustice against any of the Christians, not to insult them and not to constrain them to sacrifice unwillingly. . . . He deprived the clergy, however, of their immunities, honors, and provisions which Constantine had conferred, repealed the laws which had been enacted in their favor, and reinforced their statutory liabilities. He even compelled the virgins and widows, who on account of their poverty were reckoned among the clergy, to refund the provision which had been assigned them from the public treasury. . . . In the intensity 'of his hatred of the faith, he seized every opportunity to ruin the Church. He deprived it of its property, votive offerings, and sacred vessels, and condemned those who had demolished temples during the reign of Constantine and Constantius to rebuild them or to defray the expense of re-erection. On this ground, since they were unable to repay the sum and also on account of the search after sacred money, many of the priests, clergy, and other Christians were cruelly tortured and cast into prison. . . . He recalled the priests who had been banished by the Emperor Constantius; but it is said that he issued this order in their behalf, not out of mercy, but that through contention among themselves the churches might be involved in fraternal strife and might fall away from their law, or because he wished to asperse the memory of Constantius.

(d) Julian, *Ep.* 49, *ad Arsacium;* Julian, Imp., *Epistulæ*, ed. Hertlein, Leipsic, 1875 *f.;* also in Sozomenus, *Hist. Ec.,* V, 16. (MSG, 67 : 1260.)

To Arsacius, High Priest of Galatia. Hellenism[1] does not flourish as we would have it, because of its votaries. The worship of the gods, however, is grand and magnificent beyond all our prayers and hopes. Let our Adrastea be propitious to these words. No one a little while ago could have dared to look for such and so great a change in a short time. But do we think that these things are enough, and not rather consider that humanity shown strangers, the reverent diligence shown in burying the dead, and the false holiness as to their lives have principally advanced atheism?[2] Each of these things is needful, I think, to be faithfully practised among us. It is not sufficient that you alone should be such, but in general all the priests, as many as there are throughout Galatia, whom you must either shame or persuade to be zealous, or else deprive them of their priestly office, if they do not come with their wives, children, and servants to the temples of the gods, or if they support servants, sons, or wives who are impious toward the gods and prefer atheism to piety. Then exhort the priests not to frequent the theatres, not to drink in taverns, nor to practise any art or business which is shameful or menial. Honor those who comply, expel those who disobey. Establish hostelries in every city, so that strangers, or whoever has need of money, may enjoy our philanthropy, not merely those of our own, but also those of other religions. I have meanwhile made plans by which you will be able to meet the expense. I have commanded that throughout the whole of Galatia annually thirty thousand bushels of corn and sixty thousand measures of wine be given,

[1] The religion of the pagans.   [2] *I. e.*, Christianity.

of which the fifth part I order to be devoted to the support of the poor who attend upon the priests; and the rest is to be distributed by us among strangers and beggars. For if there is not one among the Jews who begs, and even the impious Galileans, in addition to their own, support also ours, it is shameful that our poor should be wanting our aid.

(e) Sozomenus, *Hist. Ec.*, V, 16. (MSG, 67 : 1260.)

Measures taken by Julian for the restoration of heathenism.

The Emperor, who had long since been eager that Hellenism should prevail through the Empire, was bitterly grieved seeing it excelled by Christianity. The temples, however, were kept open; the sacrifices and the ancient festivals appeared to him in all the cities to come from his will. He grieved that when he considered that if they should be deprived of his care they would experience a speedy change. He was particularly chagrined on discovering that the wives, children, and servants of many pagan priests professed Christianity. On reflecting that the Christian religion had a support in the life and behavior of those professing it, he determined to introduce into the pagan temples everywhere the order and discipline of the Christian religion: by orders and degrees of the ministry, by teachers and readers to give instruction in pagan doctrines and exhortations, by appointed prayers on certain days and at stated hours, by monasteries both for men and for women who desired to live in philosophical retirement, likewise hospitals for the relief of strangers and of the poor, and by other philanthropy toward the poor to glorify the Hellenic doctrine. He commanded that a suitable correction be appointed by way of penance after the Christian tradition for voluntary and involuntary transgressions. He is said to have admired especially the letters of recommendation of the bishops by which they commended travellers to other bishops, so that coming from anywhere they might go to any one and be hospitably received as known and as friends, and be cared for kindly on the evidence of these testimonials.

Considering also these things, he endeavored to accustom the pagans to Christian practices.

(*f*) Sozomenus, *Hist. Ec.*, V, 18.   (MSG, 67 : 1269.)

Cf. Socrates, *Hist. Ec.*, III, 16.

Julian forbade the children of Christians to be instructed in the writings of the Greek poets and authors, and to frequent the public schools. . . . He did not permit Christians to be educated in the learning of the Greeks, since he considered that only from them the power of persuasion was gained. Apollinaris,[1] therefore, at that time employed his great learning and ingenuity in the production of a heroic epic on the antiquities of the Hebrews to the reign of Saul as a substitute for the poem of Homer. . . . He also wrote comedies in imitation of Menander, and imitated the tragedies of Euripides and the odes of Pindar. . . . Were it not that men were accustomed to venerate antiquity and to love that to which they are accustomed, the works of Apollinaris would be equally praised and taught.

(*g*) Julian, *Epistula* 42.

Edict against Christian teachers of the classics.
This is the famous decree prohibiting Christians from teaching the Greek classics, and was quite generally understood by Christians as preventing them from studying the same.

I think true culture consists not in proficiency in words and speech, but in a condition of mind which has sound intentions and right opinions concerning good and evil, the honorable and the base. Whoever, therefore, thinks one thing and teaches those about him another appears to be as wanting in culture as in honor. If in trifles there is a difference between thought and speech, it is nevertheless an evil in some way to be endured; but if in important matters any one thinks one thing and teaches in opposition to what he thinks, this is the trick of charlatans, the act not of good men, but of

---

[1] See DCB, art. "Apollinaris the Elder."

those who are thoroughly depraved, especially in the case of those who teach what they regard as most worthless, deceiving and enticing by flattery into evil those whom they wish to use for their own purposes. All those who undertake to teach anything should be upright in life and not cherish in their minds ideas which are in opposition to those commonly received; most of all I think that such they ought to be who converse with the young on learning, or who explain the writings of the ancients, whether they are teachers of eloquence or of rhetoric, and still more if they are sophists. For they aim to be not merely teachers of words but of morals as well, and claim instruction in political science as belonging to their field. Whether this be true, I will leave undetermined. But praising them as those who thus strive for fine professions, I would praise them still more if they neither lied nor contradicted themselves, thinking one thing and teaching their pupils another. Homer, Hesiod, Demosthenes, Herodotus, Thucydides, Isocrates, and Lysias were indebted to the gods for all their science. Did they not think that they were under the protection of Hermes and of the Muses? It seems to me, therefore, absurd that those who explain their writings should despise the gods they honored. But when I think it is absurd, I do not say that, on account of their pupils, they should alter their opinions; but I give them the choice, either not to teach what they do not hold as good, or, if they prefer to teach, first to convince their pupils that Homer, Hesiod, or any of those whom they explain and condemn, is not so godless and foolish in respect to the gods as they represent him to be. For since they draw their support and make gain from what these have written, they confess themselves most sordidly greedy of gain, willing to do anything for a few drachmas. Hitherto there were many causes for the lack of attendance upon the temples, and overhanging fear gave an excuse for keeping secret the right teaching concerning the gods. Now, however, since the gods have granted us freedom, it seems to me absurd that men should teach what they do not regard as good. If they believe that all those men are wise whose writings they expound and as whose prophets they sit, let them first imitate their piety toward the gods; but if they think that these writers erred concerning the most honored gods, let them go into the churches of the Galileans and expound Matthew and Luke, believing whom you forbid attendance upon the sacrifices. I would that your ears and tongues were born again, as you would say, of those things in which I always take part, and whoever loves me thinks and does. This law is to apply to teachers and instructors generally. Whoever among the youth wishes to make use of their instruction is not forbidden. For it would not be fair in the case of those who are yet youths and do not know which way to turn, to forbid the best way, and through fear to compel them to remain unwillingly by their ancestral institutions. Although it would be right to cure such people against their wills as being insane, yet it is permitted all to suffer under this disease. For it is my opinion that the ignorant should be instructed, not punished.

CHAPTER III. THE TRIUMPH OF THE NEW NICENE ORTHODOXY OVER HETERODOXY AND HEATHENISM

The Arian controversy was the most important series of events in the internal history of the Christian Church in the fourth century, without reference to the truth or error of the positions taken or the rightful place of dogma within the Church. It roused more difficulties, problems, and disputes, led to more persecutions, ended in greater party triumphs than any other ecclesiastical or religious movement. It entered upon its last important phase about the time of the accession of the Emperor Julian. From that time the parties began to recognize their real affiliations and sought a basis of union in a common principle. The effect was that on the accession of Christian emperors the Church was able to advance rapidly toward a definitive statement. Of the

emperors that followed Julian, Valentinian I (364–375), who
ruled in the West, took a moderate and tolerant position in
the question regarding the existence of heathenism alongside
of the Church and heretical parties within the Church, though
afterward harsher measures were taken by his son and successor (§ 69). In the East his colleague Valens (364–368)
supported the extreme Arian party and persecuted the other
parties, at the same time tolerating heathenism. This only
brought the anti-Arians more closely together as a new party
on the basis of a new interpretation of the Nicene formula
(§ 70, cf. § 66, c). On the death of Valens at Adrianople,
378, an opportunity was given this new party, which it has
become customary to call the New Nicene party, to support
Theodosius (379–395) in his work of putting through the
orthodox formula at the Council of Constantinople, 381 (§ 71).

§ 69. The Emperors from Jovian to Theodosius and
Their Policy toward Heathenism and Arianism.
§ 70. The Dogmatic Parties and Their Mutual Relations.
§ 71. The Emperor Theodosius and the Triumph of the
New Nicene Orthodoxy at the Council of Constantinople, A. D. 381.

§ 69. THE EMPERORS FROM JOVIAN TO THEODOSIUS AND
THEIR POLICY TOWARD HEATHENISM AND ARIANISM

The reign of Jovian lasted so short a time, June, 363, to
February, 364, that he had no time to develop a policy, and
the assertion of Theodoret that he extinguished the heathen
sacrificial fires is doubtful. On the death of Jovian, Valentinian was elected Emperor, who soon associated with himself his brother Valens as his colleague for the East. The
two were tolerant toward heathenism, but Valens took an
active part in favor of Arianism, while Valentinian held aloof
from doctrinal controversy. On the death of Valentinian I,
his sons Gratian (murdered at Lyons, 383) and Valentinian
II (murdered at Vienne by Arbogast, 392), succeeded to

the Empire. Under them the policy of toleration ceased, heathenism was proscribed. In the East under Theodosius, appointed colleague of Gratian in 379, the same policy was enforced. Arianism was now put down with a strong hand in both parts of the Empire.

(a) Ammianus Marcellinus, *Roman History*, XXX, 9, § 5.

The religious policy of Valentinian I.
Ammianus Marcellinus is probably the best of the later Roman historians, and is the chief authority for much of the secular history from 353 to 378, in which period he is a source of the first rank, writing from personal observation and first-hand information. Ammianus was himself a heathen, but he seems not to have been embittered by the persecution to which his faith had been subjected. He was a man of a calm and judicial mind, and his judgment is rarely biassed, even when he touches upon ecclesiastical matters which, however, he rarely does.

Valentinian was especially remarkable during his reign for his moderation in this particular—that he kept a middle course between the different sects of religion, and never troubled any one, nor issued any orders in favor of one kind of worship rather than another; nor did he promulgate any threatening edicts to bow down the necks of his subjects to the form of worship to which he himself was inclined; but he left these parties just as he found them, without making any alterations.

(b) *Codex Theodosianus*, XII, 1, 75; A. D. 371.

In this edict Valentinian I confirms the immunities of the heathen priesthood which had been restored by Julian. The heathen priesthood is here shown to continue as still open to aspirants after political honors and conferring immunities upon those who attained it. The curial had to pass through the various offices in fixed order before he attained release from burdens which had been laid upon him by the State's system of taxation.

Let those be held as enjoying immunity who, advancing by the various grades and in due order, have performed their various obligations and have attained by their labor and approved actions to the priesthood of a province or to the honor of a chief magistracy, gaining this position not by favor and votes obtained by begging for them, but with the favorable report of the citizens and commendation of the public as a whole, and let them enjoy the repose which they shall have deserved by their long labor, and let them not be subject to those acts of bodily severity in punishment which it is not seemly that *honorati* should undergo.

(c) Theodoret, *Hist. Ec.*, IV, 21; V, 20. (MSG, 82 : 1181.)

The following statement of Theodoret might seem to have been inspired by the general hatred which was felt for the violent persecutor and pronounced Arian, Valens. Nevertheless the statement is supported by references to the conditions under Valens made by Libanius in his *Oratio pro Templis*, addressed to the Emperor Theodosius.

IV, 21. At Antioch Valens spent considerable time, and gave complete license to all who under cover of the Christian name, pagans, Jews, and the rest preached doctrines contrary to those of the Gospel. The slaves of this error even went so far as to perform pagan rites, and thus the deceitful fire which after Julian had been quenched by Jovian, was now rekindled by permission of Valens. The rites of the Jews, of Dionysus and Demeter were no longer performed in a corner as they would have been in a pious reign, but by revellers running wild in the forum. Valens was a foe to none but to them that held the apostolic doctrine.

V, 20. Against the champions of the apostolic decrees alone he persisted in waging war. Accordingly, during the whole period of his reign the altar fire was lit, libations and sacrifices were offered to idols, public feasts were celebrated in the forum, and votaries initiated in the orgies of Dionysus ran about in goatskins, mangling dogs in Bacchic frenzy.

(d) Symmachus, *Memorial to Valentinian II;* Ambrose, *Epistula* 17. (MSL, 16 : 1007.)

A petition for the restoration of the altar of Victory in the Senate House at Rome.

Symmachus, prefect of the city, had previously appealed to Gratian to restore the altar which had been removed. The following petition, of which the more impressive parts are given, was made in 384, two years after the first petition. The opening paragraph refers to the former petition. The memorial is found among the Epistles of Ambrose, who replies to it.

1. As soon as the most honorable Senate, always devoted to you, knew what crimes were made amenable to law, and saw that the reputation of late times was being purified by pious princes, following the example of a favorable time, it gave utterance to its long-suppressed grief and bade me be once again the delegate to utter its complaints. But through wicked men audience was refused me by the divine Emperor, otherwise justice would not have been wanting, my lords and emperors of great renown, Valentinian, Theodosius, and Arcadius, victorious, triumphant, and ever august.

3. It is our task to watch on behalf of your clemency. For by what is it more suitable that we defend the institutions of our ancestors, and the rights and destiny of our country, than by the glory of these times, which is all the greater when you understand that you may not do anything contrary to the custom of your ancestors? We request, then, the restoration of that condition of religious affairs which was so long of advantage to the State. Let the rulers of each sect and of each opinion be counted up; a late one [Julian] practised the ceremonies of his ancestors, a later [Valentinian I], did not abolish them. If the religion of old times does not make a precedent, let the connivance of the last [Valentinian and Valens] do so.

4. Who is so friendly with the barbarians as not to require an altar of Victory? . .

5. But even if the avoidance of such an omen[1] were not sufficient, it would at least have been seemly to abstain from injuring the ornaments of the Senate House. Allow us, we beseech you, as old men to leave to posterity what we received as boys. The love of custom is great. Justly did the act of

_____
[1] As the destruction of the altar of Victory.

the divine Constantius last for a short time. All precedents
ought to be avoided by you, which you know were soon
abolished.[1] . . .

6. Where shall we swear to obey your laws and commands? By what religious sanctions shall the false mind be
terrified, so as not to lie in bearing witness? All things are,
indeed, filled with God, and no place is safe for the perjured,
but to be bound in the very presence of religious forms has
great power in producing a fear of sinning. That altar preserves the concord of all; that altar appeals to the good faith
of each; and nothing gives more authority to our decrees than
that our order issues every decree as if we were under the
sanction of an oath. So that a place will be opened to perjury, and my illustrious princes, who are defended by a public oath, will deem this to be such.

7. But the divine Constantius is said to have done the
same. Let us rather imitate the other actions of that prince
[Valentinian I], who would have undertaken nothing of the
kind, if any one else had committed such an error before him.
For the fall of the earlier sets his successor right, and amend-
ment results from the censure of a previous example. It was
pardonable for your clemency's ancestor in so novel a matter
not to guard against blame. Can the same excuse avail us,
if we imitate what we know to have been disapproved?

8. Will your majesties listen to other actions of this same
prince, which you may more worthily imitate? He diminished none of the privileges of the sacred virgins, he filled the
priestly offices with nobles. He did not refuse the cost of
the Roman ceremonies, and following the rejoicing Senate
through all the streets of the Eternal City, he beheld the
shrines with unmoved countenance, he read the names of the
gods inscribed on the pediments, he inquired about the origin
of the temples, and expressed admiration for their founders.
Although he himself followed another religion, he maintained
these for the Empire, for every one has his own customs,

---

[1] *I. e.*, by Julian and Valentinian.

every one his own rites. The divine Mind has distributed different guardians and different cults to different cities. As souls are separately given to infants as they are born, so to a people is given the genius of its destiny. Here comes in the proof from advantage, which most of all vouches to man for the gods. For, since our reason is wholly clouded, whence does the knowledge of the gods more rightly come to us, than from the memory and records of successful affairs? Now if a long period gives authority to religious customs, faith ought to be kept with so many centuries, and our ancestors ought to be followed by us as they happily followed theirs.

9. Let us now suppose that we are present at Rome and that she addresses you in these words: "Excellent princes, fathers of your country, respect my years to which pious rites have brought me. Let me use the ancestral ceremonies, for I do not repent of them. Let me live after my own fashion, for I am free. This worship subdued the world to my laws, these sacred rites repelled Hannibal from the walls, and the Senones from the capitol. Have I been reserved for this, that when aged I should be blamed? I will consider what it is thought should be set in order, but tardy and discreditable is the reformation of old age."

10. We ask, therefore, peace for the gods of our fathers and of our country. It is just that what all worship be considered one. We look on the same stars, the sky is common, the same world surrounds us. What difference does it make by what paths each seeks the truth? We cannot attain to so great a secret by one road; but this discussion is rather for persons at ease; we offer now prayers, not conflict.[1]

(e) Ambrose, *Epistula* 18. (MSL, 16 : 1013.)

Reply of Ambrose to the Memorial of Symmachus.

Immediately after the receipt of the Memorial of Symmachus by Valentinian II, a copy was sent to Ambrose, who wrote a reply or letter of advice to Valentinian, which might be regarded as a counter-

---

[1] The rest of the petition is taken up chiefly with a protest against the confiscation of the endowments for the vestal virgins.

petition. In it he enters upon the arguments of Symmachus. Although he could not present the same pathetic figure of an old man pleading for the religion of his ancestors, his arguments are not unjust, and dispose satisfactorily of the leading points made by Symmachus. The line of reasoning represents the best Christian opinion of the times on the matter of the relation of the State to heathenism.

3. The illustrious prefect of the city has in a memorial set forth three propositions which he considers of force—that Rome, he says, asks for her rites again, that pay be given to her priests and vestal virgins, and that a general famine followed upon the refusal of the priests' stipends. . . .

7. Let the invidious complaints of the Roman people come to an end. Rome has given no such charge. She speaks other words. "Why do you daily stain me with the useless blood of the harmless herd? Trophies of victory depend not upon the entrails of the flock, but on the strength of those who fight. I subdued the world by a different discipline. Camillus was my soldier who slew those who had taken the Tarpeian rock, and brought back to the capitol the standards taken away; valor laid low those whom religion had not driven off. . . . Why do you bring forward the rites of our ancestors? I hate the rites of Neros. Why should I speak of emperors of two months,[1] and the ends of rulers closely joined to their commencements. Or is it, perchance, a new thing for barbarians to cross their boundaries? Were they, too, Christians whose wretched and unprecedented cases, the one a captive emperor[2] and under the other[3] the captive world,[4] made manifest that their rites which promised victory were false? Was there then no altar of Victory? . . .

8. By one road, says he, one cannot attain to so great a secret. What you know not, that we know by the voice of God. And what you seek by fancies we have found out from

[1] Allusion to the very brief reign of several.
[2] Valerian taken captive by Sapor.   [3] Galienus.
[4] Reference to the " thirty tyrants."

the very wisdom and truth of God. Your ways, therefore, do not agree with ours. You implore peace for your gods from the Emperor, we ask peace for our emperors themselves from Christ. . . .

10. But, says he, let the ancient altars be restored to their images, and their ornaments to the shrines. Let this demand be made of one who shares in their superstitions; a Christian emperor has learned to honor the altar of Christ alone. . . . Has any heathen emperor raised an altar to Christ? While they demand the restoration of things which have been, by their own example they show us how great reverence Christian emperors ought to pay to the religion which they follow, since heathen ones offered all to their superstitions.

We began long since, and now they follow those whom they excluded. We glory in yielding our blood, an expense moves them. . . . We have increased through loss, through want, through punishment; they do not believe that their rites can continue without contribution.

11. Let the vestal virgins, he says, retain their privileges. Let those speak thus who are unable to believe that virginity can exist without reward, let those who do not trust virtue, encourage it by gain. But how many virgins have their promised rewards gained for them? Hardly are seven vestal virgins received. See the whole number whom the fillet and chaplets for the head, the robes of purple dye, the pomp of the litter surrounded by a company of attendants, the greatest privileges, immense profits, and a prescribed time for virginity have gathered together.

12. Let them lift up the eyes of soul and body, let tnem look upon a people of modesty, a people of purity, an assembly of virginity. Not fillets are the ornament of their heads, but a veil common in use but ennobled by chastity; the enticement of beauty not sought out, but laid aside; none of those purple insignia, no delicious luxuries, but the practice of fasts; no privileges, no gains; all other things, in fine, of such a kind that one would think them restrained from desire

whilst practising their duties. But whilst the duty is being practised the desire for it is aroused. Chastity is increased by its own sacrifice. That is not virginity which is bought with a price, and not kept through a desire for virtue; that is not purity which is bought by auction for money or which is bid for a time.

16. No one has denied gifts to shrines and legacies to soothsayers; their land only has been taken away, because they did not use religiously that which they claimed in right of religion. Why did not they who allege our example practise what we did? The Church has no possessions of her own except the faith. Hence are her returns, her increase. The possessions of the Church are the maintenance of the poor. Let them count up how many captives the temples have ransomed, what food they have contributed for the poor, to what exiles they have supplied the means of living. Their lands, then, have been taken away, but not their rights.

23. He says the rites of our ancestors ought to be retained. But why, seeing that all things have made a progress toward what is better? . . . The day shines not at the beginning, but as time proceeds it is bright with increase of light and grows warm with increase of heat.

27. We, too, inexperienced in age, have an infancy of our senses, but, changing as years go by, lay aside the rudimentary conditions of our faculties.

28. Let them say, then, that all things ought to have remained in their first dark beginnings; that the world covered with darkness is now displeasing because it has brightened with the rising of the sun. And how much more pleasant is it to have dispelled the darkness of the mind than that of the body, and that the rays of faith should have shone than that of the sun. So, then, the primeval state of the world, as of all things, has passed away that the venerable old age of hoary faith might follow. . . .

30. If the old rites pleased, why did Rome also take up foreign ones? I pass over the ground hidden with costly

buildings, and shepherds' cottages glittering with degenerate gold. Why, that I may reply to the very matter which they complain of, have they eagerly received the images of captured cities, and conquered gods, and the foreign rites of alien superstition? Whence, then, is the pattern of Cybele washing her chariots in a stream counterfeiting the Almo? Whence were the Phrygian prophets and the deities of unjust Carthage, always hateful to the Romans? And he whom the Africans worship as Celestis, the Persians as Mithra, and the greater number as Venus, according to a difference of name, not a variety of deities?

31. They ask to have her altar erected in the Senate House of the city of Rome, that is where the majority who meet together are Christians! There are altars in all the temples, and an altar also in the Temple of Victory. Since they delight in numbers, they celebrate their sacrifices everywhere. To claim a sacrifice on this one altar, what is it but to insult the faith? Is it to be borne that a heathen should sacrifice and a Christian be present? . . . Shall there not be a common lot in that common assembly? The faithful portion of the Senate will be bound by the voices of those who call upon the gods, by the oaths of those who swear by them. If they oppose they will seem to exhibit their falsehood, if they acquiesce, to acknowledge what is a sacrilege.

(f) *Codex Theodosianus*, XVI, 10, 12; A. D. 392.

Decree of Theodosius prohibiting heathen worship as a crime of the same character as treason.

The following decree may be said to have permanently forbidden heathenism, at least in the East, though as a matter of fact many heathen not only continued to practise their rites in defiance of the law or with the connivance of the authorities, but also received appointments at the court and elsewhere. The law was never repealed. In course of time heathenism disappeared as a religious system.

XVI, 10, 12. Hereafter no one of whatever race or dignity, whether placed in office or discharged therefrom with honor, powerful by birth or humble in condition and fortune, shall in any place or in any city sacrifice an innocent victim to a senseless image, venerate with fire the household deity by a more private offering, as it were the genius of the house, or the Penates, and burn lights, place incense, or hang up garlands. If any one undertakes by way of sacrifice to slay a victim or to consult the smoking entrails, let him, as guilty of lese-majesty, receive the appropriate sentence, having been accused by a lawful indictment, even though he shall not have sought anything against the safety of the princes or concerning their welfare. It constitutes a crime of this nature to wish to repeal the laws, to spy into unlawful things, to reveal secrets, or to attempt things forbidden, to seek the end of another's welfare, or to promise the hope of another's ruin. If any one by placing incense venerates either images made by mortal labor, or those which are enduring, or if any one in ridiculous fashion forthwith venerates what he has represented, either by a tree encircled with garlands or an altar of cut turfs, though the advantage of such service is small, the injury to religion is complete, let him as guilty of sacrilege be punished by the loss of that house or possession in which he worshipped according to the heathen superstition. For all places which shall smoke with incense, if they shall be proved to belong to those who burn the incense, shall be confiscated. But if in temples or public sanctuaries or buildings and fields belonging to another, any one should venture this sort of sacrifice, if it shall appear that the acts were performed without the knowledge of the owner, let him be compelled to pay a fine of twenty-five pounds of gold, and let the same penalty apply to those who connive at this crime as well as those who sacrifice. We will, also, that this command be observed by judges, defensors, and curials of each and every city, to the effect that those things noted by them be reported to the court, and by them the acts charged may be punished. But if they believe anything is to be overlooked by favor or allowed to pass through negligence, they will lie under a judicial warning. And when they have been warned, if by any neg-

ligence they fail to punish they will be fined thirty pounds
of gold, and the members of their court are to be subjected to
a like punishment.

§ 70. The Dogmatic Parties and Their Mutual Relations

The parties in the Arian controversy became greatly divided
in the course of the conflict. Speaking broadly, there were
still two groups, of which one was composed of all those who
regarded the Son as a creature and so not eternal and not
truly God; and the other, of those who regarded Him as uncreated and in some real sense eternal and truly God, yet
without denying the unity of God. The former were the
various Arian parties tending to constant division. The latter can hardly yet be comprised under one common name,
and might be called the anti-Arian parties, were it not that
there was a positive content to their faith which was in far
better harmony with the prevailing religious sentiment of
the East and was constantly receiving accessions. In the
second generation after Nicæa, a new group of theologians
came to the front, of whom the most important were Eustathius of Sebaste, Cyril of Jerusalem, and the three Cappadocians, Basil, Gregory of Nazianus, and Gregory of Nyssa, most
of whom had at least sympathized with the Homoiousian
party. Already at the synod of Ancyra, in 358, an approach
was made toward a reconciliation of the anti-Arian factions,
in that, by a more careful definition, homoousios was rejected
only in the sense of identity of being, and homoiousios was
asserted only in the sense of equality of attributes in the not
identical subjects which, however, shared in the same essence.
Homoiousios did not mean mere similarity of being. (Anathemas in Hahn, § 162; Hefele, § 80.) The line of development ultimately taken was by a precise distinction between
hypostasis and *ousia*, whereby *hypostasis*, which never meant
person in the modern sense, which later is represented by the

Greek *prosopon*, was that which subsists and shares with other *hypostases* in a common essence or *ousia*.

Additional source material: Athanasius, *De Synodis* (PNF); Basil, *Epp.* 38, 52, 69, 125 (PNF, ser. II, vol. VIII); Hilary of Poitiers, *De Synodis*, cc. 87–91 (PNF, ser. II, vol. IX); Socrates, *Hist. Ec.*, III, 25.

Council of Alexandria A. D. 362. *Tomus ad Antiochenos.* (MSG, 26 : 797.)

The Council of Alexandria, A. D. 362, was held by Athanasius in the short time he was allowed to be in his see city at the beginning of the reign of Julian. In the synodal letter or tome addressed to the Nicene Christians at Antioch we have the foundation of the ultimate formula of the Church as opposing Arianism, one substance and three persons, one *ousia* and three *hypostases*. The occasion of the letter was an attempt to win over the Meletian party in the schism among the anti-Arians of Antioch. Meletius and his followers appear to have been Homoiousians who were strongly inclined to accept the Nicene confession. Their church was in the Old Town, a portion of Antioch. Opposed to them was Paulinus with his party, which held firmly to the Nicene confession. The difficulty in the way of a full recognition of the Nicene statement by Meletius and his followers was that it savored of Sabellianism. The difficulty of the party of Paulinus in recognizing the orthodoxy of the Meletians was their practice of speaking of the three hypostases or subsistences, which was condemned by the words of the Nicene definition.[1] The outcome of the Alexandrian Council in the matter was that a distinction could be made between *ousia* and *hypostasis*, that the difference between the parties was largely a matter of terminology, that those who could use the Nicene symbol with the understanding that the Holy Ghost was not a creature and was not separate from the essence of Christ should be regarded as orthodox. Out of this understanding came the "New Nicene" party, of which the first might be said to have been Meletius, who accepted *homoousios* in the sense of *homoiousios*, and of which the "three great Cappadocians" became the recognized leaders.

The Council of Alexandria, in addition to condemning the Macedonian heresy, in advance of Constantinople, also anticipated that assembly by condemning Apollinarianism without mentioning the teacher by whom the heresy was taught. It is condemned in the seventh section of the tome.

§ 3. As many, then, as desire peace with us, and especially those who assemble in the Old Town, and those again who are seceding from the Arians, do ye call to yourselves, and

[1] *V. supra*, § 63.

receive them as parents their sons, and as tutors and guardians
welcome them; and unite them to our beloved Paulinus and
his people, without requiring more from them than to anathematize the Arian heresy and confess the faith confessed by the
holy Fathers at Nicæa and to anathematize also those who
say that the Holy Ghost is a creature and separate from the
essence of Christ. For this is in truth a complete renunciation
of the abominable heresy of the Arians, to refuse to divide
the Holy Trinity, or to say that any part of it is a creature.

§ 5. . . . As to those whom some were blaming for speaking of three subsistences (hypostases), on the ground that the
phrase is unscriptural and therefore suspicious, we thought
it right, indeed, to require nothing beyond the confession of
Nicæa, but on account of the contention we made inquiry of
them, whether they meant, like the Arian madmen, subsistences foreign and strange and alien in essence from one
another, and that each subsistence was divided apart by itself, as is the case with other creatures in general and those
begotten of men, or like substances, such as gold, silver, or
brass; or whether, like other heretics, they meant three beginnings and three Gods, by speaking of three subsistences.

They assured us in reply that they neither meant this nor
had ever held it. But upon our asking them "what, then,
do you mean by it, or why do you use such expressions?" they
replied: Because they believe in a Holy Trinity, not a trinity
in name only, but existing and subsisting in truth, both
Father truly existing and subsisting, and a Son, truly substantial and subsisting, and a Holy Ghost subsisting and
really existing do we acknowledge, said they, and that neither
had they said there were three Gods or three beginnings,
nor would they at all tolerate such as said or held so, but that
they acknowledged a Holy Trinity, but one Godhead and one
beginning, and that the Son is co-essential with the Father,
as the Fathers said; and the Holy Ghost not a creature,
nor external, but proper to, and inseparable from, the essence
of the Father and the Son.

§ 6. Having accepted, then, these men's interpretation of their language and their defence, we made inquiry of those blamed by them for speaking of one subsistence, whether they use the expression in the sense of Sabellius, to the negation of the Son and Holy Ghost, or as though the Son was non-substantial, or the Holy Ghost without subsistence. But they in their turn assured us that they neither said this nor had ever held it, but, "we use the word subsistence thinking it the same thing to say subsistence or essence." [1] But we hold there is One, because the Son is of the essence of the Father and because of the identity of nature. For we believe that there is one Godhead, and that the nature of it is one, and not that there is one nature of the Father, from which that of the Son and of the Holy Ghost are distinct. Well, thereupon, they who had been blamed for saying that there were three subsistences agreed with the others, while those who had spoken of one essence, also confessed the doctrine of the former as interpreted by them. And by both sides Arius was anathematized as an adversary of Christ, and Sabellius, and Paul of Samosata as impious men, and Valentinus and Basilides as aliens from the truth, and Manichæus as an inventor of mischief. And all, by God's grace, and after the above explanations, agreed together that the faith confessed by the Fathers at Nicæa is better and more accurate than the said phrases, and that for the future they would prefer to be content to use its language.

§ 7. But since, also, certain seemed to be contending together concerning the fleshly economy of the Saviour, we inquired of both parties. And what the one confessed the others also agreed to: that not as when the word of the Lord came to the prophets, did it dwell in a holy man at the consummation of the ages, but that the Word himself was made flesh; and being in the form of God, He took the form of a servant, and from Mary after the flesh became man for us, and that thus in Him the human race is perfectly and wholly

[1] Hypostasis or ousia; *cf.* the Nicene definition, § 63, g.

delivered from sin and made alive from the dead, and led into the kingdom of heaven. For they also confess that the Saviour had not a body without a soul, nor without sense or intelligence;[1] for it was not possible, when the Lord had become man for us, that His body should be without intelligence; nor was the salvation, effected in the Word himself, a salvation of the body only, but of the soul also. And being Son of God in truth, He became also Son of Man; and being God's only begotten Son, He became also at the same time "first-born among many brethren." Wherefore neither was there one Son of God before Abraham, another after Abraham: nor was there one that raised up Lazarus, another that asked concerning him; but the same it was that said as man, "Where does Lazarus lie?" and as God raised him up; the same that as man and in the body spat, but divinely as Son of God opened the eyes of the man blind from his birth; and while, as Peter says, in the flesh He suffered, as God He opened the tomb and raised the dead. For which reasons, thus understanding all that is said in the Gospel, they assured us that they held the same truth about the Word's incarnation and becoming man.

§ 71. THE EMPEROR THEODOSIUS AND THE TRIUMPH OF THE NEW NICENE ORTHODOXY AT THE COUNCIL OF CONSTANTINOPLE A. D. 381

The Emperor Theodosius was appointed colleague of Gratian and Valentinian II, 378. He issued in conjunction with these emperors an edict (*Cod. Theod.*, XVI, 1, 2; *cf. Cod. Just.*, I, 1, 1, *v. infra*, § 72, *B, e*), requiring all subjects of the Empire to hold the orthodox faith in the Trinity. He then called a council of Eastern bishops to meet at Constantinople in 381 to settle the question as to the succession to the see of that city and to confirm the creed of Nicæa as the faith of the Eastern half of the Church. Gregory of Nazianus

[1] The Apollinarian heresy.

was appointed bishop of Constantinople, but was forced to resign, having formerly been bishop of Sasima, from which he had been translated in violation of the Nicene canons. As soon as it was apparent that the bishops would have to accept the Nicene faith the thirty-six Macedonians withdrew. Their opinion as to the Holy Spirit, that He was not divine in the same sense that the Son was divine, was condemned, without express statement of the point condemned, as was also the teaching of Apollinaris as to the nature of Christ. The council was not intended to be an ecumenical or general council, and it was not regarded as such even in the East until after the Council of Chalcedon, A. D. 451, and then probably on account of the creed which was then falsely attributed to the Fathers of Constantinople. In the West the council was not recognized as an ecumenical council until well into the sixth century. (See Hefele, § 100.) The council issued no creed and made no additions to the Nicene creed. It published a tome, since lost, setting forth the faith in the Trinity. It enacted four canons, of which only the first three are of general application.

Additional source material: Percival, *Seven Ecumenical Councils* (PNF); Theodoret, *Hist. Ec.*, V, 6–9; Socrates, *Hist. Ec.*, V, 8; Basil, *De Spiritu Sancto* (PNF), Hefele, §§ 95–100.

(*a*) Council of Constantinople, A. D. 381, *Canons*, Bruns, I, 20. *Cf.* Kirch, nn. 583 *ff.*

The text of the canons of the council may be found in Hefele, § 98, and also in Bruns. The *Translations and Reprints* of the University of Pennsylvania give translations. For the address of the council to Theodosius, see § 72, *B.* The fourth canon is of a merely temporary importance.

Canon 1. The faith of the three hundred and eighteen Fathers who were assembled at Nicæa in Bithynia shall not be set aside but shall remain dominant. And every heresy shall be anathematized, especially that of the Eunomians or Anomœans, the Arians or Eudoxians, the semi-Arians or

Pneumatomachians, the Sabellians, Marcellians, Photinians, and Apollinarians.

Canon 2. The bishops are not to go beyond their dioceses to churches lying outside of their bounds, nor bring confusion on churches; but let the bishop of Alexandria, according to the canons, alone administer the affairs of Egypt; and let the bishops of the East manage the East alone, the privileges of the church in Antioch, which are mentioned in the canons of Nicæa, being preserved; and let the bishops of the Asian diocese administer the Asian affairs only; and the Pontic bishops only Pontic matters; and the Thracian bishops only Thracian matters. And let not the bishops go beyond their dioceses for ordination or any other ecclesiastical ministrations, unless they be invited. And the aforesaid canon concerning dioceses being observed, it is evident that the synod of each province will administer the affairs of that particular province as was decreed at Nicæa. But the churches of God in heathen nations must be governed according to the custom which has prevailed from the time of the Fathers.

Canon 3. The bishop of Constantinople, however, shall have the prerogative of honor after[1] the bishop of Rome; because Constantinople is New Rome.

(b) Cyril of Jerusalem, *Creed*. (*Cf*. MSG, 33 : 533.) *Cf*. Hahn, § 124.

The clauses which are here given are the headings of the sixth to the eighteenth *Catechetical Lectures* of Cyril of Jerusalem in which the writer expounded the baptismal creed of Jerusalem. This creed is approximately reconstructed by bringing together the headings. Its date is circa 345. It should be compared with the creed of the church of Salamis, in the next selection. They are the precursors of what is now known as the Nicene creed, incorrectly attributed to the Council of Constantinople A. D. 381.

We believe in one God, the Father Almighty, maker of heaven and earth, and of all things visible and invisible.

And in one Lord Jesus Christ, the Son of God, the only

---

[1] *I. e.*, following.

begotten, begotten of the Father, true God, before all the ages, through whom all things were made;

Incarnate and made man; crucified and buried;

And rose again the third day;

And ascended into heaven;

And sat on the right hand of the Father;

And shall come again in glory to judge the quick and the dead, of whose kingdom there shall be no end.

And in one Holy Ghost, the Paraclete, who spake by the prophets;

And in one baptism of repentance for remission of sins;

And in one holy Catholic Church;

And in the resurrection of the flesh;

And in the life eternal.

(c) Epiphanius, *Ancoratus*, chs. 119 *f.* (MSG, 43 : 252.) *Cf.* Hahn, § 125.

Epiphanius, bishop of Salamis, was the most important of the hereseologists of the Fathers, gathering to form his work on heresies some scores of heterodox systems of teachings. His passion for orthodoxy was taken advantage of by Theophilus of Antioch to cause trouble for Chrysostom and others; see Origenistic controversy, § 87. The *Ancoratus*, from which the following creed is taken, is a statement of the Catholic faith which, amidst the storms of the Arian controversy, should serve as an anchor of salvation for the Christians. The date of the following creed, which has come to be known as the Salaminium, is 374. It is evidently based upon that of Jerusalem given by Cyril.

We believe in one God the Father Almighty, maker of heaven and earth and of all things visible and invisible.

And in one Lord Jesus Christ, the only begotten Son of God, begotten of the Father before all worlds, that is, of the substance of the Father, light of light, very God of very God, begotten, not made, being of one substance [homoousios] with the Father; by whom all things were made, both those in heaven and those on earth; who for us men and for our salvation came down from heaven and was incarnate by the Holy Ghost and the Virgin Mary, and was made man; He was crucified for us under Pontius Pilate, and suffered and was buried; and the third day He rose again, according to the Scriptures; and ascended into heaven, and sitteth on the right hand of the Father; and He shall come again in glory to judge the quick and the dead; of whose kingdom there shall be no end.

And in the Holy Ghost, the Lord and giver of life, who proceedeth from the Father, who with the Father and the Son together is worshipped and glorified, who spake by the prophets; and in one holy Catholic and Apostolic Church; we acknowledge one baptism for the remission of sins; and we look for the resurrection of the dead and the life of the world to come.

But those who say there was a time when He was not, and He was not before He was begotten, or He was made of nothing, or of another substance or essence [hypostasis or ousia], saying that the Son of God is effluent or variable— these the Catholic and Apostolic Church anathematizes.

CHAPTER IV. THE EMPIRE AND THE IMPERIAL STATE CHURCH

In the period extending from the accession of Constantine (311 or 324) to the death of Theodosius the Great (395), the characteristic features of the Church's organization took definite form, and its relations to the secular authorities and the social order of the Empire were defined. Its constitution with its hierarchical organization of clergy, of courts, and synods, together with its intimate union, at least in the East, with the imperial authority, became fixed (§ 72). As the Church of the Empire, it was under the control and patronage of the State; all other forms of religion, whether pagan or Christian, schismatical or heretical, were severely repressed (§ 73). The Christian clergy, as officials in this State Church, became a class by themselves in the society of the Empire, not only as the recipients of privileges, but as having special functions in the administration of justice, and eventually in the superintendence of secular officials and secular business (§ 74). By degrees the Christian spirit influenced the spirit of the laws and the popular customs, though less than at first sight might have been expected; the rigors of slavery were mitigated and cruel gladiatorial sports abandoned (§ 75). Meanwhile popular piety was by no means raised by the influx of vast numbers of heathen into the Church; bringing with them no little of their previous modes of thought and feeling, and lacking the testing of faith and character furnished by the persecutions, they lowered the general moral tone of the Church, so that Christians everywhere were affected by these alien ideas and feelings (§ 76). The Church, however, endeavored to raise the moral tone and ideals and to work effectively in society by care for the poor and other works of benevolence, and in its regulation of marriage, which began in this period to be a favorite subject of legislation for the Church's councils (§ 76). In monasticism this striving against the lowering forces in Christian society and for a higher type of life most clearly manifested itself, and, beginning in Egypt, organized forms of asceticism spread throughout the East and toward the end of the period to the West as well (§ 78). But monasticism was not confined to the private ascetic. The priesthood, as necessarily presenting an example of higher moral life, began to be touched by the ascetic spirit, and in the West this took the form of enforced clerical celibacy, though the custom of the East remained far less rigorous (§ 79). In presenting these lines of development, it is at times convenient to pass beyond the exact bounds of the period, so that the whole subject may be brought together at this point of the history.

§ 72. The Constitution of the State Church.
§ 73. The Sole Authority of the State Church.
§ 74. The Position of the Church in the Social Order of the Empire.
§ 75. The Social Significance of the State Church.
§ 76. Popular Piety and the Reception of Heathenism in the Church.

§ 77. The Extension of Monasticism throughout the Empire.

§ 78. Influence of Ascetic Ideals within the Church: Clerical Celibacy.

§ 72. The Constitution of the State Church

The Church's constitution received its permanent form in this period. The conciliar system was carried to its logical completion in the ecumenical council representing the entire Church and standing at the head of a system which included the provincial and patriarchal councils, at least in theory. The clergy were organized into a hierarchy which rested upon the basis of the single bishop in his diocese, who had under him his clergy, and culminated in the patriarchs placed over the great divisions of the State Church, corresponding to the primary divisions of the Empire. The Emperor assumed the supreme authority in the Church, and the foundation was laid for what became under Justininian Cæsaropapism. By the institution of the hierarchical gradation of authority and jurisdiction, for the most part corresponding to the political and administrative divisions of the Empire, the Church both assumed a rigidly organized form and came more easily under the control of the secular authority.

(A) *The Ecumenical Council*

The Council of Nicæa was held before there was any definition of the place of an ecumenical council. Many councils were held during the Arian controversy that were quite as representative. It was taken for granted that the councils were arranged in a scale of authority corresponding to the extent of the Church represented. The first clear statement of this principle is at the Council of Constantinople A. D. 382.

Council of Constantinople, A. D. 382, *Canon* 2.   Text, Hefele, § 98.

The so-called second general council was held in 381, but in the next year nearly the same bishops were called together by Theodosius (*cf.* Theodoret, *Hist. Ec.*, V, 9). In a letter addressed to the Western bishops at a council at Rome this council speaks of their previous meeting at Constantinople in 381 as being an ecumenical council. The query suggests itself whether, considering the fact that it actually only represented the East and did represent more than one patriarchate, "ecumenical" might not be understood as being used in a sense similar to that in which the African bishops spoke of their councils as *universalis*. See Hefele, § 100, note.

The following canon is printed as the sixth canon of Constantinople, A. D. 381, in Hefele and the other collections, *e. g.*, Bruns and Percival.

. . . If persons who are neither heretics, nor excommunicated, nor condemned, nor charged with crime claim to have a complaint in matters ecclesiastical against the bishop,[1] the holy synod commands such to bring their charges first before all the bishops of the province, and to prove before them the charges against the accused bishop. But should it happen that the comprovincials be unable to settle the charges alleged against the bishop, the complainants shall have recourse then to the larger synod of the bishops of that diocese,[2] who shall be called together on account of the complaint; and the complainants may not bring their complaint until they have agreed in writing to take upon themselves the same punishment which would have fallen upon the accused, in case the complainants in the course of the matter should be proved to have brought a false charge against the bishop. But if any one, holding in contempt these directions, venture to burden the ear of the Emperor, or the tribunals of the secular judges, or disturb an ecumenical synod,[3] dishonoring the bishops of their patriarchal province, such shall not be admitted to make complaint, because he despises the canons and violates the Church's order.

[1] *I. e.*, of their diocese.

[2] In the sense of patriarchal province, following the use of the word "diocese" in the administrative system of the Empire. It should be noted that the patriarchal council seems not to have become well defined in the Church's system and never to have come into actual use.

[3] For the development of the ecumenical council, see below, § 91, *a*. This scheme of nicely adjusted appeals never took permanent place in the Church owing to obvious difficulties.

(B) *The Hierarchical Organization*

(*a*) Council of Nicæa, A. D. 325, *Canons*. Text, Hefele, § 42. *Cf.* Kirch, nn. 364–368.

Canons of organization.
Canon 4 regulates the ordinations of bishops; Canon 5 orders that excommunications in one diocese shall hold good everywhere; Canon 6 defines the larger provincial organization which eventually resulted in the patriarchates; Canon 7 defines the position of the bishopric of Jerusalem; Canons 15 and 16 place the bishops permanently in their sees and the clergy under their own proper bishop.

Canon 4.   It is by all means proper that a bishop should be appointed by all the bishops in the province; but should this be difficult, either on account of urgent necessity or because of distance, three at least should assemble, and the suffrages of the absent should also be given and communicated in writing, and then the ordination should take place. But in every province the ratification of what is done should be left to the metropolitan.

Canon 5.   Concerning those, whether of the clergy or of the laity, who have been excommunicated in the several provinces, let the provisions of the canon be observed by the bishops which provides that persons cast out by some be not readmitted by others. . . . Nevertheless, inquiry should be made whether they have been excommunicated through captiousness, or contentiousness, or any such like ungracious disposition in the bishops. And that this matter may have due investigation, it is decreed that in every province synods shall be held twice a year, in order that when all the bishops of the province are assembled together, such questions may be thoroughly examined by them, that so those who have confessedly offended against their bishop may be seen by all to be for just causes excommunicated, until it shall appear fit to a general meeting of the bishops to pronounce a milder sentence upon them. And let these synods be held, the one before Lent (that the pure gift may be offered to God after all bitterness has been put away) and let the second be held about autumn.

Canon 6. Let the ancient customs in Egypt, Libya, and Pentapolis prevail, that the bishop of Alexandria shall have jurisdiction in all these, since the like is customary for the bishop of Rome also.[1] Likewise in Antioch and the other provinces, let the churches retain their privileges. And this is to be universally understood, that if any one be made bishop without the consent of his metropolitan, the great synod has declared that such a man ought not to be bishop. If, however, two or three bishops shall, from natural love of contradiction, oppose the common suffrage of the rest, it being reasonable and in accordance with the ecclesiastical law, then let the choice of the majority prevail.

Canon 7. Since custom and ancient tradition have prevailed that the bishop of Ælia [i. e., Jerusalem] should be honored, let him, saving its due dignity to the metropolis, have the next place of honor.

Canon 15. On account of the great disturbance and discords that occur, it is decreed that the custom prevailing in certain places contrary to the canon must wholly be done away; so that neither bishop, presbyter, nor deacon shall pass from city to city. And if any one, after this decree of the holy and great synod, shall attempt any such thing or continue in such course, his proceedings shall be utterly void, and he shall be restored to the church for which he was ordained bishop or presbyter.

Canon 16. Neither presbyters, nor deacons, nor any others enrolled among the clergy, who, not having the fear of God before their eyes, nor regarding the ecclesiastical canon, shall recklessly remove from their own church, ought by any means to be received by another church; but every constraint should

---

[1] This sixth canon of Nicæa very early received the title: "Concerning the Primacy of the Roman Church," and had this addition placed as its first clause: "The Roman Church has always had the primacy." In this form the canon was cited by the Roman legates at the Council of Chalcedon in 451, but they were immediately confuted by the Eastern theologians.

be applied to restore them to their own parishes;[1] and, if they will not go, they must be excommunicated. And if one shall dare surreptitiously to carry off and in his own church ordain a man belonging to another, without the consent of his own proper bishop from whom, although he was enrolled in the clergy list, he has seceded, let the ordination be void.

(*b*) Synod of Antioch, A. D. 341, *Canons*, Bruns, I, 80 *f*. *Cf*. Kirch, nn. 439 *ff*.

For the Council of Antioch, see § 65, *c*. These canons on discipline were held in highest authority in the Church, although enacted by Arians whose creed was rejected. They obtained this position in the law of the Church because they carried further the natural line of development long since taken in the ecclesiastical system. *Cf*. Hefele, § 56.

Canon 2. All who enter the Church of God and hear the Holy Scriptures, but do not communicate with the people in prayers, or who turn away, by reason of some disorder, from the holy partaking of the eucharist, are to be cast out of the Church until, after they shall have made confession, have brought forth fruits of penance, and have made earnest entreaty, they shall have obtained forgiveness; and it is unlawful to communicate with excommunicated persons, or to assemble in private houses and pray with those who do not pray in the Church; or to receive in one church those who do not assemble with another church. And if any one of the bishops, presbyters, or deacons, or any one in the canon shall be found communicating with excommunicated persons, let him also be excommunicated, as one who brings confusion on the order of the Church.

Canon 3. If any presbyter or deacon or any one whatever belonging to the priesthood shall forsake his own parish and shall depart, and, having wholly changed his residence, shall set himself to remain for a long time in another parish, let him no longer officiate; especially if his own bishop shall summon and urge him to return to his own parish, and he

---

[1] Here, as generally, parish means diocese.

shall disobey. And if he persist in his disorder, let him be wholly deposed from his ministry, so that no further room be left for his restoration. And if another bishop shall receive a man deposed for this cause, let him be punished by the common synod as one who nullifies the ecclesiastical laws.

Canon 4. If any bishop be deposed by a synod, or any presbyter or deacon, who has been deposed by his bishop, shall presume to execute any part of the ministry, whether it be a bishop according to his former function, or a presbyter, or a deacon, he shall no longer have any prospect of restoration in another synod, nor any opportunity of making his defence; but they who communicate with him shall be cast out of the Church, and particularly if they have presumed to communicate with the persons aforementioned, knowing the sentence pronounced against them.

Canon 6. If any one has been excommunicated by his own bishop, let him not be received by others until he has either been restored by his own bishop, or until, when a synod is held, he shall have appeared and made his defence, and, having convinced the synod, shall have received a different sentence. And let this decree apply to the laity, and to the presbyters and deacons, and all who are enrolled in the clergy list.

Canon 9. It behooves the bishops in each province to acknowledge the bishop who presides in the metropolis, and who has to take thought of the whole province; because all men of business come together from every quarter to the metropolis. Wherefore it is decreed that he have precedence in rank, and that the other bishops do nothing extraordinary without him, according to the ancient canon which prevailed from the time of our fathers, or such things only as pertain to their own particular parishes and the districts subject to them. For each bishop has authority over his own parish, both to manage it with piety, which is incumbent on every one, and to make provision for the whole district which is dependent upon his city; to ordain presbyters and deacons;

and to settle everything with judgment. But let him not undertake anything further without the bishop of the metropolis; neither the latter without the consent of the others.

Canon 10. The holy synod decrees that those [bishops] living in village and country districts, or those who are called chorepiscopi, even though they have received ordination to the episcopate, shall regard their own limits and manage the churches subject to them, and be content with the care and administration of these; but they may ordain readers, subdeacons, and exorcists, and shall be content with promoting these; but they shall not presume to ordain either a presbyter or a deacon, without the consent of the bishop of the city to which he and his district are subject. And if he shall dare to transgress these decrees, he shall be deposed from the rank which he enjoys. And a chorepiscopus is to be appointed by the bishop of the city to which he is subject.

(c) Council of Sardica, A. D. 343 or 344, *Canons*, Bruns, I, 88. *Cf.* Mirbt, n. 113, and Kirch, nn. 448 *ff.*

The Council of Sardica was intended to be composed of representatives from the entire Empire who might be able to settle once and for all the Arian question. It met at Sardica on the boundary between the two divisions of the Empire as they were then defined. The Eastern ecclesiastics, strongly Arian, found themselves outnumbered by the Western bishops who supported Athanasius and the Nicene definition of faith. The Eastern representatives withdrew to Philippopolis near by, and held their own council. The following canons were intended to provide a system of appeal for cases like that of Athanasius, and although they do not seem to have been acted upon enough to have become a part of the Church's system, yet they were of great importance inasmuch as subsequently they were used as late as the ninth century for a support to a wholly different system of appeals. These canons were very early attributed to the Council of Nicæa A. D. 325.

Canon 3. Bishop Hosius said: This, also, it is necessary to add—that bishops shall not pass from their own province to another province in which there are bishops, unless perchance they are invited by their brethren, that we seem not to close the door to charity. But if in any province a bishop have an action against his brother bishop, neither shall call in as judge a bishop from another province. But if judgment shall have gone against any bishop in a case, and he think that he has a good case, in order that the question may be heard, let us, if it be your pleasure, honor the memory of St. Peter the Apostle, and let those who have tried the case write to Julius, the bishop of Rome, and if he shall decide that the case should be retried, let it be retried, and let him appoint judges; but if he shall be satisfied that the case is such that what has been done should not be disturbed, what has been decreed shall be confirmed.

Is this the pleasure of all? The synod answered: It is our pleasure.

Canon 4. Bishop Gaudentius said: If it please you, it is necessary to add to this sentence, which full of sincere charity thou hast pronounced, that if any bishop has been deposed by the judgment of those bishops who happened to be in the vicinity, and he asserts that he has fresh matter in defence, a new bishop is not to be settled in his see, unless the bishop of Rome judge and render a decision as to this.

Latin Version of Canon 4. Bishop Gaudentius said: If it please you, there ought to be added to this sentence, which full of holiness thou hast pronounced, that if any bishop has been deposed by the judgment of those bishops who dwell in the vicinity, and he asserts that the business ought to be conducted by him in the city of Rome, another bishop should in nowise be ordained in his see after the appellation of him who appears to have been deposed, unless the cause shall have been determined by the judgment of the bishop of Rome.

Canon 5.[1] Bishop Hosius said: Let it be decreed that if a bishop shall have been accused and the assembled bishops of the same region shall have deposed him from his office, and he, so to speak, appeals and takes refuge with the bishop of the Roman Church and wishes to be heard by him, if he[2] think it right to renew the examination of his case, let him be

---

[1] This is the seventh canon of the Latin version of the canons.
[2] *I. e.*, Bishop of Rome.

pleased to write to those of fellow-bishops who are nearest the province that they may examine the particulars with care and accuracy and give their votes on the matter in accordance with the word of truth.   And if any one demand that his case be heard yet again, and at his request it seems good to the bishop of Rome to send presbyters from his own side, let it be in the power of that bishop, according as he judges it to be good and decides it to be right, that some be sent to be judges with the bishops and invested with his authority by whom they were sent.   And be this also ordained.   But if he thinks that they [the bishops] are sufficient for the hearing and determining of the matter of the bishop, let him do what shall seem good in his most prudent judgment.

The bishops answered: What has been said is approved.

(d) Gratian and Valentinian, *Rescript;* A. D. 378.   (MSG, 13: 586.)   Mirbt, nn. 118 *f.*

This rescript was sent in answer to a petition addressed to the emperors by a Roman council under Damasus.   It is, therefore, found connected with an epistle in the works of Damasus.   It does not seem to have been the foundation of any claim or to have played any considerable part in the development of the Roman primacy.   It is of importance in the present connection as illustrating the part emperors took in the internal affairs of the Church.   For Damasus and the disturbances in connection with his election, *v. infra*, § 74, *a.* The rescript may be found in Mansi, III, 624; Hardouin, I, 842; and in Gieseler, I, 380.

6. If any one shall have been condemned by the judgment of Damasus, which he shall have delivered with the council of five or seven bishops, or by the judgment or council of those who are Catholics, and if he shall unlawfully attempt to retain his church,[1] in order that such a one, who has been called to the priestly judgment, shall not escape by his contumacy, it is our will that such a one be remitted by the illustrious prefects of Gaul and Italy, either by the proconsul or the vicars, use having been made of due authority, to the episcopal judgment, and shall come to the city of Rome under

[1] *I. e.*, ecclesiastical position.

an escort; or if such insolence of any one shall appear in parts very far distant, the entire pleading of his case shall be brought to the examination of the metropolitan of the province in which the bishop is, or if he himself is the metropolitan, then of necessity he shall hasten without delay to Rome, or to those whom the Roman bishop shall assign as judges, so that whoever shall have been deposed shall be removed from the confines of the city in which they were priests. For we punish those who deserve punishment less severely than they deserve, and we take vengeance upon their sacrilegious stubbornness more gently than it merits. And if the unfairness or partiality of any metropolitan, bishop, or priest is suspected, it is allowed to appeal to the Roman bishop or to a council gathered of fifteen neighboring bishops, but so that after the examination of the case shall have been concluded what was settled shall not be begun over again.

(*e*) *Codex Theodosianus*, XVI, 1, 2; Feb. 27, A. D. 380. *Cf.* Kirch, n. 755.

The following edict was issued by Gratian, Valentinian and Theodosius, requiring the acceptance of the orthodox faith by all subjects. In other words, the emperors, following the example of Constantius and Valens in enforcing Arianism, are now enforcing the Nicene theology. Sozomenus, *Hist. Ec.*, VII, 4, gives the circumstances under which this edict was issued.

It is our will that all the peoples whom the government of our clemency rules shall follow that religion which a pious belief from Peter to the present declares the holy Peter delivered to the Romans, and which it is evident the pontiff Damasus and Peter, bishop of Alexandria, a man of apostolic sanctity, follow; that is, that according to the apostolic discipline and evangelical doctrine we believe in the deity of the Father and the Son and the Holy Ghost of equal majesty, in a holy trinity. Those who follow this law we command shall be comprised under the name of Catholic Christians; but others, indeed, we require, as insane and raving, to bear the infamy of heretical teaching; their gatherings shall not re-

ceive the name of churches; they are to be smitten first with
the divine punishment and after that by the vengeance of our
indignation, which has the divine approval.

(f) *Codex Theodosianus*, XVI, 1, 3.

Gratian, Valentinian, and Theodosius to Auxonius, proconsul of
Asia.

To enforce still further the principles of Nicene orthodoxy certain
bishops were named as teachers of the true faith, communion with
whom was a test of orthodoxy.

We command that all churches be forthwith delivered up
to the bishops who confess the Father, the Son, and the Holy
Ghost to be of one majesty and power; of the same glory
and of one splendor, making no distinction by any profane
division, but rather harmony by the assertion of the trinity
of the persons and the unity of the Godhead, to the bishops
who are associated in communion with Nectarius, bishop of
the Church of Constantinople, and with Timotheus in Egypt,
bishop of the city of Alexandria; in the parts of the Orient,
who are in communion with Pelagius, bishop of Laodicæa
and Diodorus, bishop of Tarsus; in proconsular Asia and in
the diocese of Asia, who are in communion with Amphilochius,
bishop of Iconium, and Optimus, bishop of Antioch; in the
diocese of Pontus, who are in communion with Helladius,
bishop of Cæsarea, and Otreius, bishop of Melitina, and
Gregory, bishop of Nyssa, Terennius, bishop of Scythia, Mar-
marius, bishop of Marcianopolis. Those who are of the communion and fellowship of approved priests[1] ought to be admitted to possess the Catholic churches; but all who dissent
from the communion of the faith of those whom the special
list has named ought to be expelled from the churches as
manifest heretics; and no opportunity whatsoever ought to
be allowed them henceforth of obtaining episcopal churches[2]
that the priestly orders of the true and Nicene faith may
remain pure and no place be given to evil cunning, according
to the evident form of our precept.

[1] *I. e.*, bishops.   [2] *I. e.*, episcopal sees.

(g) Council of Constantinople, A. D. 381, *Address to Theodosius*. See Mansi, III, 557.

The following letter illustrates the relation of the councils in the East to the imperial authority. The emperors called the various general councils, directed their discussions and confirmed the results. In this way their findings were given the force of laws and authority throughout the Church. *V. infra,* §§ 90, 91.

To the most religious Emperor Theodosius, the holy synod of bishops assembled in Constantinople out of different provinces.

We begin our letter to your Piety with thanks to God, who has established the Empire of your Piety for the common peace of the churches and for the support of the true faith. And, after rendering due thanks unto God, as in duty bound, we lay before your Piety the things which have been done in the holy synod. When, then, we had assembled in Constantinople, according to the letter of your Piety, we first of all renewed our unity of heart each with the other, and then we pronounced some concise definitions, ratifying the faith of the Nicene Fathers, and anathematizing the heresies which have sprung up contrary thereto. Besides these things, we also framed certain canons for the better ordering of the churches, all which we have subjoined to this our letter. We therefore beseech your Piety that the decree of the synod may be ratified, to the end that as you have honored the Church by your letter of citation, so you should set your seal to the conclusion of what has been decreed. May the Lord establish your Empire in peace and righteousness, and prolong it from generation to generation; and may He add unto your earthly powers the fruition of the heavenly kingdom also. May God, by the prayers of the saints, show favor to the world, that you may be strong and eminent in all good things as an Emperor most truly pious and beloved of God.

(h) Synod of Antioch, A. D. 341, *Canons*, Bruns, I, 80.

The following canons passed at Antioch are the first touching a habit which they did little to correct. The so-called sixth canon of

Constantinople, 381, in reality a canon of the council of the next year, took up the matter again. All through the great controversies appeals were constantly made to the emperors because, after all, they alone had the authority. *Cf.* Hefele, § 56.

Canon 11. If any bishop, or presbyter, or any one whatever of the canon shall presume to betake himself to the Emperor without the consent and letters of his bishop of the province and particularly of the bishop of the metropolis, such a one shall be publicly deposed and cast out, not only from the communion, but also from the rank which he happens to have had; inasmuch as he dares to trouble the ears of our Emperor, beloved of God, contrary to the law of the Church. But, if necessary business shall require any one to go to the Emperor, let him do it with the advice and consent of the metropolitan and other bishops in the province, and let him undertake his journey with the letters from them.

Canon 12. If any presbyter or deacon deposed by his own bishop, or any bishop deposed by a synod, shall dare trouble the ears of the Emperor, when it is his duty to submit his case to a greater synod of bishops, and to refer to more bishops the things which he thinks right, and to abide by the examination and decision made by them; if, despising these, he shall trouble the Emperor, he shall be entitled to no pardon, neither shall he have opportunity of defence, nor any hope of future restoration.

§ 73. SOLE AUTHORITY OF THE STATE CHURCH

When Theodosius had successfully forced upon the East the theology of Nicæa, his policy as to religious matters was manifest. No longer was heresy to be allowed. Laws were to control opinion in the same way that they did conduct. The old plea of the persecuted Christians under the heathen Roman Empire, *religio non cogi potest*, was completely forgotten. As Christianity was the one sole religion of divine character, based upon the unique divine act of the incarnation, it was folly to allow men to continue in heathenism—it might even be dangerous to the State to allow them, as it might bring down the just vengeance of God. With this policy the populace was completely in accord, especially when it led to the plunder and destruction of heathen sanctuaries, and many of the more zealous of the clergy were willing to lead in the assault. In these ways the State Church obtained a two-fold exclusive authority: as regards heathenism, and as regards heresy.

(a) *Codex Theodosianus.*
Laws regarding heathenism.
XVI, 10, 14; A. D. 399.

Whatever privileges were conceded by the ancient laws to the priests, ministers, prefects, hierophants of sacred things, or by whatsoever name they may be designated, are to be abolished henceforth, and let them not think that they are protected by a granted privilege when their religious confession is known to have been condemned by the law.

XVI, 10, 16; A. D. 399.

If there are temples in the fields, let them be destroyed without crowd or tumult. For when these have been thrown down and carried away, the support of superstition will be consumed.

XVI, 10, 15; A. D. 399.

This law appears again in the *Cod. Just.*, I, 13, 3, for it appears to have been necessary even as late as the sixth century to prevent unauthorized destructions of temples which were in the cities and might be fairly regarded as ornaments to the city.

We prohibit sacrifices yet so that we wish that the ornaments of public works to be preserved. And that those who attempt to overthrow them may not flatter themselves that it is with some authority, if any rescript or, perchance, law is alleged, let these documents be taken from their hands and referred to our knowledge.

XVI, 10, 21; A. D. 416.

Those who are polluted by the error or crime of pagan rites are not to be admitted to the army nor to receive the distinction and honor of administrator or judge.

XVI, 10, 23; A. D. 423.

Although the pagans that remain ought to be subjected to capital punishment if at any time they are detected in the abominable sacrifices of demons, let exile and confiscation of goods be their punishment.

XVI, 10, 24; A. D. 423. (Retained in *Cod. Just.*, I, 11, 16.)

The Manichæans and those who are called Pepyzitæ [Montanists] and also those who by this one opinion are worse than all heretics, in that they dissent from all as to the venerable day of the Easter festival, we subject to the same punishment, viz.: confiscation of goods and exile, if they persist in the same unreason. But this we especially demand of Christians, both those who are really such and those who are called such, that they presume not, by an abuse of religion, to lay hands upon the Jews and pagans who live peaceably and who attempt nothing riotous or contrary to the laws. For if they should do violence to them living securely and take away their goods, let them be compelled to restore not merely what they have taken away but threefold and fourfold. Let the rectors of provinces, officials, and provincials know that if they permit these things to be done, they themselves will be punished, as well as those who do them.

(*b*) Theodoret, *Hist. Ec.*, V, 29. (MSG, 82 : 1256.)

The destruction of temples.
The following passage is illustrative of the temper of those who took part in the destruction of heathen sanctuaries. The imperial edicts for these acts were obtained in 399. Chrysostom, the leader in the movement, fairly represents the best thought and temper of the Church.

On receiving information that Phœnicia was still suffering from the madness of the demons' rites, he [John Chrysostom] got together some monks fired with divine zeal and despatched them, armed with imperial edicts, against the idols' shrines. He did not draw from the imperial treasury the money to pay the craftsmen and their assistants who were engaged in the work of destruction, but he persuaded certain faithful and wealthy women to make liberal contributions, pointing out to them how great would be the blessing their generosity would win. Thus the remaining shrines of the demons were utterly destroyed.

(c) Socrates, *Hist. Ec.*, VII, 15. (MSG, 67 : 768.)

The murder of Hypatia.

The fearful murder of Hypatia represents another aspect of the opposition to heathenism, in which the populace seconded the efforts of the authorities in a policy of extirpating paganism.

There was a woman in Alexandria named Hypatia. She was the daughter of the philosopher Theon, and she had attained such a proficiency in literature and science as to surpass by far all the philosophers of her own time. Having succeeded to the Platonic school, which had come down from Plotinus, she explained all the principles of philosophy to her auditors. Therefore many from all sides, wishing to study philosophy, came to her. On account of the self-possession and ease of manner which she had acquired by her study, she not infrequently appeared with modesty in the presence of magistrates. Neither did she feel abashed in entering an assembly of men. For all men, on account of her extraordinary dignity and virtue, admired her the more. Against her envious hostility arose at that time. For as she had frequent interviews with Orestes [governor of Alexandria] it was calumniously reported among the Christian populace that it was she who prevented Orestes from being reconciled to the bishop [Cyril]. Some men of this opinion and of a hotheaded disposition, whose leader was a reader named Peter, waylaid her returning home. Dragging her from her carriage they took her to the church called Cæsareum. There they completely stripped her and murdered her with tiles. When they had torn her in pieces, they took her mangled limbs to a place called Cinaron, and there they burnt them. This affair brought no little opprobrium, not only upon Cyril but also upon the whole Alexandrian Church. And surely murders, fights, and actions of that sort are altogether alien to those who hold the things of Christ. These things happened in the fourth year of the episcopate of Cyril [415].

(d) Socrates, Hist. Ec., VII, 11. (MSG, 67 : 757.)

Novatians and the Church at the beginning of the fifth century.
Socrates is the principal authority for the later history of the Novatians. It is probable that his interest in them and evident sympathy for them were due to some connection with the sect, perhaps in his early years, and he gives many incidents in their history, otherwise unknown.

After Innocent [401–417], Zosimus [417–418] governed the Roman Church for two years, and after him Boniface [418–422] presided over it for three years. Celestinus [422–432] succeeded him, and this Celestinus took away the churches from the Novatians at Rome and obliged Rusticula, their bishop, to hold his meetings secretly in private houses. Until this time the Novatians had flourished exceedingly in Rome, having many churches there and gathering large congregations. But envy attacked them there, also, as soon as the Roman episcopate, like that of Alexandria, extended itself beyond the limits of ecclesiastical jurisdiction, and degenerated into its present state of secular domination. And for this cause the bishops would not suffer even those who agreed with them in matters of faith to enjoy the privileges of assembling in peace, but stripping them of all they possessed, praised them merely for these agreements in faith. The bishops of Constantinople kept themselves free from this sort of conduct; in so much as in addition to tolerating them and permitting them to hold their assemblies within the city, as I have already stated,[1] they treated them with every mark of Christian regard.

[1] See Socrates, Hist. Ec., V, 10.

(*e*) *Codex Theodosianus*, XVI, 5, 40; A. D. 407.

Edict of Arcadius and Honorius against the Manichæans and other heretics. (Retained in *Cod. Just.*, I, 5, 4.)   *Cf.* Mirbt, n. 155.

What we have thought concerning the Donatists we have recently set forth. Especially do we pursue, with well-merited severity, the Manichæans, the Phrygians, and the Priscillianists,[1] since men of this sort have nothing in common with others, neither in custom nor laws. And first we declare that their crime is against the State, because what is committed against the divine religion is held an injury of all. And we will take vengeance upon them by the confiscation of their goods, which, however, we command shall fall to whomsoever is nearest of their kindred, in ascending or descending lines or cognates of collateral branches to the second degree, as the order is in succession to goods. Yet it shall be so that we suffer the right to receive the goods to belong to them, only if they themselves are not in the same way polluted in their conscience. And it is our will that they be deprived of every grant or succession from whatever title derived. In addition, we do not leave to any one convicted of this crime the right of giving, buying, selling, or finally of making a contract. The prosecution shall continue till death. For if in the case of the crime of treason it is lawful to attack the memory of the deceased, not without desert ought he to endure condemnation. Therefore let his last will and testament be invalid, whether he leave property by testament, codicil, epistle, or by any sort of will, if ever he has been convicted of being a Manichæan, Phrygian, or Priscillianist, and in this case the same order is to be followed as in the grades above stated; and we do not permit sons to succeed as heirs unless they forsake the paternal depravity; for we grant forgiveness of the offence to those repenting. We will that slaves be without harm if, rejecting their sacrilegious master, they pass over to the Catholic Church by a

---

[1] In the code of Justinian this reads " Manichæans and Donatists."

more faithful service. Property on which a congregation of men of this sort assemble, in case the owner, although not a participator in the crime, is aware of the meeting and does not forbid it, is to be annexed to our patrimony; if the owner is ignorant, let the agent or steward of the property, having been punished with scourging, be sent to labor in the mines, and the one who hires the property, if he be a person liable to such sort of punishment, be deported. Let the rectors of provinces, if by fraud or force they delay the punishment of these crimes when they have been reported, or if conviction have been obtained neglect punishment, know that they will be subject to the fine of twenty pounds of gold. As for defensors and heads of the various cities and the provincial officials, a penalty of ten pounds is to compel them to do their duty, unless performing those things which have been laid down by the judges in this matter, they give the most intelligent care and the most ready help.

(f) Leo the Great, *Epistula* 7. (MSL, 54 : 620.)

Manichæanism in Rome.
This epistle, addressed to the bishops throughout Italy, shows the way in which zealous bishops could, and were expected to, co-operate with the secular authorities in putting down heresy.
Leo the Great [440–461], the greatest of the popes before Gregory the Great, was equally great as an ecclesiastical statesman, as theologian, and universally acknowledged leader of the Roman people in the times of the invasions of Attila and Genseric. Without being the creator of the papal idea, he was able so to gather up the elements that had been developed by Siricius, Innocent, and others, as to give it a classical expression that almost warrants one in describing him as the first of the popes in the later sense of that term. His literary remains consist of sermons, of which ninety-six are genuine, in which, among other matters, he sets forth his conception of the Petrine prerogative (see below, § 87, b), and letters in which he deals with the largest questions of ecclesiastical politics, especially in the matter of the condemnation of Monophysitism at the Council of Chalcedon. See below, § 91.

Our search has discovered in the city a great many followers and teachers of the Manichæan impiety, our watchfulness has proclaimed them, and our authority and censure have checked them: those whom we could reform we have corrected and driven to condemn Manichæus with his preachings and teachings, by public confession in the Church, and by the subscription of their own hands; and thus we have lifted those who have acknowledged their fault from the pit of their impiety, by granting them opportunity for repentance. But some who had so deeply involved themselves that no remedy could assist them have been subjected to the laws, in accordance with the constitutions of our Christian princes, and lest they should pollute the holy flock by their contagion, have been banished into perpetual exile by the public judges. And all the profane and disgraceful things which are found, as well in their writings as in their secret traditions, we have disclosed and clearly proved to the eyes of Christian laity, that the people might know what to shrink from or avoid; so that he that was called their bishop was himself tried by us and betrayed the criminal views which he held in his mystic religion, as the record of our proceedings can show you. For this, too, we have sent you for instruction; and after reading them you will be able to understand all the discoveries we have made.

And because we know that some of those who are involved here in too close an accusation for them to clear themselves have fled, we have sent this letter to you, beloved, by our acolyte; that your holiness, dear brothers, may be informed of this, and see fit to act more diligently and cautiously, lest the men of Manichæan error be able to find opportunity of hurting your people and of teaching these impious doctrines. For we cannot otherwise rule those intrusted to us unless we pursue, with the zeal of faith in the Lord, those who are destroyers and destroyed; and with what severity we can bring to bear, cut them off from intercourse with sound minds, lest this pestilence spread much wider. Wherefore I exhort you, beloved, I beseech and warn you to use such watchful diligence as you ought and can employ in tracking them out lest they find opportunity of concealment anywhere.

(g) Leo the Great, *Epistula* 15. (MSL, 54 : 680.)

An account of the tenets of the Priscillianists. Leo is answering a letter sent him by Bishop Turribius of Asturia, in which that bishop had given him statements about the faith of these sectaries. It appears that these statements which Leo quotes and refutes in brief are not wholly correct and that the Priscillianists were far from being as heretical as they have been commonly represented. See articles in the recent encyclopædias, *e. g.*, New Schaff-Herzog, and Encyclopædia Britannica, 11th ed. The change in opinion is due to the discovery of writings of Priscillian himself. Nevertheless, these statements, defective as they may be, represent the opinion of the times as to these heretics and the general attitude toward what was regarded as heretical and savoring of Manichæanism.[1]

1. And so under the first head is shown what impious views they hold about the divine Trinity; they affirm that the person of the Father, the Son, and the Holy Ghost is one and the same, as if the same God were named now Father, now Son, now Holy Ghost; and as if He who begat were not one, He who was begotten another, and He who proceedeth from both yet another; but an undivided unity must be understood, spoken of under three names, but not consisting of three persons. . . .

2. Under the second head is displayed their foolish and empty fancy about the issue of certain virtues from God which He began to possess, and which were posterior to God in His own essence. . . .

3. Again the language of the third head shows that these same impious persons assert that the Son of God is called "only begotten" for this reason that He alone was born of a virgin. . . .

4. The fourth head deals with the fact that the birthday of Christ, which the Catholic Church venerates as His taking on Him the true man, because "the Word became flesh and dwelt among us," is not truly honored by these men, but they pretend that they honor it, for they fast on that day, as they do also on the Lord's Day, which is the day of Christ's

[1] For further detail of the history of the Priscillianists, see Sulpicius Severus, *Sacred History*, II, 46–51. (PNF, ser. II, vol. XI.)

resurrection. No doubt they do this because they do not believe that Christ the Lord was truly born in man's nature, but maintain that by a sort of illusion there was an appearance of what was not a reality.

5. Their fifth head refers to their assertion that man's soul is a part of the divine substance, and that the nature of our human state does not differ from its Creator's nature. . . .

6. The sixth points out that they say that the devil never was good and that his nature is not God's handiwork, but that he came forth of chaos and darkness. . . .

7. In the seventh place follows that they condemn marriage and are horrified at begetting children, in which, as in nearly all things, they agree with the profanity of the Manichæans.

8. Their eighth point is that the formation of men's bodies is the device of the devil and that the seed of conception is shaped by the aid of demons in the womb. . . .

9. The ninth notice declares that they say that the sons of promise are born, indeed, of women, conceived by the Holy Spirit; lest the offspring that is born of carnal seed should seem to share in God's estate. . . .

10. Under the tenth head they are reported as asserting that the souls which are placed in men's bodies have previously been without a body and have sinned in their heavenly habitation and for this reason have fallen from their high estate to a lower one alighting upon ruling spirits of divers qualities, and after passing through a succession of powers of the air and stars, some fiercer, some milder, are enclosed in bodies of different sorts and conditions, so that whatever variety and inequality is meted out to us in this life, seems the result of previous causes. . . .

11. Their eleventh blasphemy is that in which they suppose that both the souls and bodies of men are under the influence of fatal stars. . . .

12. The twelfth of these points is this: that they map out the parts of the soul under certain powers and the limbs under

others; and they suggest the characters of the inner powers that rule the soul by giving them the names of the patriarchs; and on the other hand, they attribute the signs of the stars to those under which they put the body.

§ 74. The Position of the State Church in the Social Order of the Empire

The elevation of the Church exposed the Church to worldliness whereby selfish men, or men carried away with partisan zeal, took advantages of its privileges or contended fiercely for important appointments. The clergy all too frequently ingratiated themselves with wealthy members of their flocks that they might receive from them valuable legacies, an abuse which had to be corrected by civil law; factional spirit occasionally led to bloodshed in episcopal elections. But on the other hand the Church was employed by the State in an important work which properly belonged to the secular administration, viz., the administration of justice in the episcopal courts of arbitration, for which see *Cod. Just.*, I, tit. 3, *de Episcopali Audientia; cf.* E. Loening, *Geschichte des deutschen Kirchenrechts*, vol. I; and in the supervision of civil officials in the expenditures of funds for public improvements. These are but instances of their large public activity according to law.

(*a*) Ammianus Marcellinus, *Hist. Rom.*, XXVII, 3, §§ 12 *ff.* *Cf.* Kirch, nn. 607 *ff.*

Damasus and Ursinus.
The strife which attained shocking proportions in connection with the election of Damasus seems to have been connected with the schism at Rome occasioned by the attitude of Liberius in the Arian controversy. Damasus proved one of the ablest bishops that Rome ever had in the ancient Church. For aid in overcoming the partisans of Ursinus a Roman council appealed to the Emperor Gratian, whose answer is given in part above, § 72, *e.*

12. Damasus and Ursinus, being both immoderately eager to obtain the bishopric, formed parties and carried on the

conflict with great asperity, the partisans of each carrying their violence to actual battle, in which men were wounded and killed. And as Juventius, prefect of the city, was unable to put an end to it, or even to soften these disorders, he was at last by their violence compelled to withdraw to the suburbs.

13. Ultimately Damasus got the best of the strife by the strenuous efforts of his partisans. It is certain that on one day one hundred and thirty-seven dead bodies were found in the Basilica of Sicinus, which is a Christian church. And the populace who had thus been roused to a state of ferocity were with great difficulty restored to order.

14. I do not deny, when I consider the ostentation that reigns at Rome, that those who desire such rank and power may be justified in laboring with all possible exertion and vehemence to obtain their wishes; since after they have succeeded, they will be secure for the future, being enriched by offerings of matrons, riding in carriages, dressing splendidly, and feasting luxuriously, so that their entertainments surpass even royal banquets.

15. And they might be really happy if, despising the vastness of the city which they excite against themselves by their vices, they were to live in imitation of some of the priests in the provinces, whom the most rigid abstinence in eating and drinking, and plainness of apparel, and eyes always cast on the ground, recommend to the everlasting Deity and His true worshippers as pure and sober-minded men.

(b) *Codex Theodosianus*, XVI, 2, 20; A. D. 370. *Cf.* Kirch, n. 759.

The following law is only one of several designed to correct what threatened to become an intolerable abuse.

Ecclesiastics and those who wish to be known by the name of the continent [1] are not to come into possession of the houses of widows and orphan girls, but are to be put aside by public

---

[1] *I. e.,* ascetics and monks.

courts if afterward the affines and near relatives of such think that they ought to be put away. Also we decree that the aforesaid may acquire nothing whatsoever from the liberality of that woman to whom privately, under the cloak of religion, they have attached themselves, or from her last will; and all shall be of no effect which has been left by one of these to them, they shall not be able to receive anything by way of donation or testament from a person in subjection. But if, by chance, after the warning of our law, these women shall think something is to be left to them by way of donation or in their last will, let it be seized by the fisc. But if they should receive anything by the will of those women in succession to whom or to whose goods they have the support of the *jus civile* or the benefit of the edict, let them take it as relatives.

(c) *Codex Theodosianus*, I, 27, 2; A. D. 408.

Edict of Arcadius, Honorius, and Theodosius II concerning the *Audientia Episcopalis*.
According to Roman law many cases were frequently decided by an arbitrator, according to an agreement between the litigants. The bishops had long acted as such in many cases among Christians. As they did not always decide suits on authorization by the courts, their decisions did not have binding authority in all cases. But after Constantine's recognition of the Church they were given authority to decide cases, and according to an edict of 333 their decisions were binding even if only one litigant appealed to his judgment. But this was reduced to cases in which there was an agreement between the parties. The following law, the earliest extant, though probably not the earliest, may be found, curtailed by the omission of the second sentence, in *Cod. Just.*, I, 4, 8.

An episcopal judgment shall be binding upon all who chose to be heard by the priests.[1] For since private persons may hear cases between those who consent, even without the knowledge of the judges, we suffer it to be permitted them. That respect is to be shown their decisions which is required to be shown your authority,[2] from which there is no

---

[1] Priest, *sacerdos*, is here used, as so often, not for presbyter but for bishop.
[2] As this was addressed to Theodorus, the prætorian prefect, the authority of the decision is rendered of the highest character.

appeal. By the court and the officials execution is to be given the sentence, so that the episcopal judicial examination may not be rendered void.

(d) *Codex Theodosianus*, II, 1, 10; A. D. 398.

Law of Arcadius and Honorius.
The following law is cited to show that in the legalization of the *Audientia Episcopalis* the legislation followed a principle that was not peculiar to the position of the Church as the State Church. The Jews had a similar privilege. The conditions under which their religious authorities could act as arbitrators were similar to that in which the bishops acted. This edict can also be found in *Cod. Just.*, I, 9, 8.

Jews living at Rome, according to common right, are in those cases which do not pertain to their superstition, their court, laws, and rights, to attend the courts of justice, and are to bring and defend legal actions according to the Roman laws; hereafter let them be under our laws. If, indeed, any by agreement similar to that for the appointment of arbitrators, decide that the litigation be before the Jews or the patriarchs by the consent of both parties and in business of a purely civil character, they are not forbidden by public law to choose their courts of justice; and let the provincial judges execute their decisions as if the arbitrators had been assigned them by the sentence of a judge.

(e) *Codex Justinianus*, I, 4, 26.

The following law of the Emperor Justinian, A. D. 530, is one of many showing the way in which the bishops were employed in many duties of the State which hardly fell.to their part as ecclesiastics.

With respect to the yearly affairs of cities, whether they concern the ordinary revenues of the city, either from funds derived from the property of the city, or from legacies and private gifts, or given or received from other sources, whether for public works, or for provisions, or public aqueducts, or the maintenance of baths or ports, or the construction of walls and towers, or the repairing of bridges and roads, or for trials in which the city may be engaged in reference to public or private interests, we decree as follows: The very pious bishop and three men of good reputation, in every respect the first men of the city, shall meet and each year not only examine the work done, but take care that those who conduct them or have been conducting them, shall manage them with exactness, shall render their accounts, and show by the production of the public records that they have duly performed their engagements in the administration of the sums appropriated for provisions, or baths, or for the expenses involved in the maintenance of roads, aqueducts, or any other work.

§ 75. Social Significance of the State Church

The Church at no time degenerated into a mere department of the State. In spite of the worldly passions that invaded it and the dissensions that distracted it, the Church remained mindful of its duty as not merely a guardian of the deposit of faith but as a school of Christian morality. This was the principle of the penitential discipline of the ante-Nicene period. It was saved from becoming a mere form, or lost altogether by the custom which became general after 400, of having the confession of sin made in private. In matters of great moral concern, such as the treatment of slaves, marriage, and divorce, and the cruel sports of the arena, the Church was able to exert its influence and eventually bring about a change in the law. And in standing for righteousness, instances were not lacking when the highest were rebuked by the Church, as in the great case of Ambrose and Theodosius.

(a) Leo the Great, *Epistula* 168, ch. 2. (MSL, 54 : 1210.) *Cf.* Denziger, n. 145.

Confession should no longer be public, but only private. From the tone of the letter it would appear that private confession had been customary for some time and that public confession had so far gone out of use as to appear as a novelty. *V. supra*, § 42.

I direct that that presumptuous violation of the apostolic rule be entirely done away, which we have recently learned has been without warrant committed by some; namely, concerning penance, which is demanded of the faithful, that a written confession in a schedule concerning the nature of each particular sin be not recited publicly, since it suffices that the guilt of conscience be made known by a secret confession to the priests alone. Although that fulness of faith appears to be laudable which on account of the fear of God is not afraid to blush before men, yet because the sins of all are not such that those who demand penance would not be afraid to publish them, let a custom so objectionable be done away; that many may not be deterred from the remedies of penitence, since they are ashamed or are afraid to disclose their deed to their enemies, by which they might be ruined by the requirements of the laws. For that confession suffices which is first offered to God, then further to the priest, who intervenes as with intercessions for the sins of the penitent. In this way many can be brought to penitence if the bad conscience of the one making the confession is not published in the ears of the people.

(b) *Codex Theodosianus*, IV, 7, 1; A. D. 321. *Cf.* Kirch, n. 749.

Edict of Constantine granting the privilege of manumission to take place in churches.

The Church does not seem to have been opposed to slavery as an institution. It recognized it as a part of the social order, following the advice of St. Paul. But, at the same time, also following his advice, it endeavored to inculcate Christian love in the treatment of slaves, and legislated frequently on the matter. The edict of Constantine was in favor of this humane teaching of the Church to the extent that it enabled it to forward the tendency toward manumission of slaves, which the Church taught as a pious act. This edict is to be found in *Cod. Just.*, I, 13, 2.

Those who from the motives of religion shall give deserved liberty to their slaves in the midst of the Church shall be regarded as having given the same with the same legal force as that by which Roman citizenship has been customarily given with the traditional solemn rites. But this is permitted only to those who give this liberty in the presence of the priest. But to the clergy we concede more, so that, when they give liberty to their slaves, they may be said to have granted a full enjoyment of liberty, not merely in the face of the Church and the religious people, but also, when in their last disposition of their effects they shall have given liberty or shall direct by any words whatsoever that it be given, on the day of the publication of their will liberty, without any witness or intervention of the law, shall belong to them immediately.

(c) Canons bearing on Slavery:

Synod of Elvira, A. D. 309, *Canon* 5, Bruns, II, 1.

If a mistress seized with furious passion beat her female slave with whips so that within three days she gives up her soul in suffering, inasmuch as it is uncertain whether she killed her wilfully or by chance, let her, if it was done wilfully, be readmitted after seven years, when the lawful penance has been accomplished; or after the space of five years if it was by chance; but if she should become ill during the appointed time, let her receive the communion.

Synod of Gangra, A. D. 343, *Canon* 3, Bruns, I, 107.

If any one, under the pretence of piety, advises a slave to despise his master and run away from his service and not with good will and full respect serve his master, let him be anathema.

Synod of Agde, A. D. 509, *Canon* 7, Bruns, II, 147.

As slaves were a valuable possession, bishops could no more alienate them than any other property, or only under the same conditions. This canon lays down principles generally followed in the relation of the Church toward the unfree of every sort on lands belonging to the endowments of the Church.

The bishops should possess the houses and slaves of the Church in a faithful manner and without diminishing the right of the Church, as the primitive authorities direct, and also the vessels of their ministry as intrusted to them. That is, they should not presume to sell nor alienate by any contracts those things from which the poor live. If necessity requires that something should be disposed of either as a usufruct[1] or in direct sale, let the case be first shown before two or three bishops of the same province or neighborhood, as to why it is necessary to sell; and after the priestly discussion has taken place, let the sale which was made be confirmed by their subscription; otherwise the sale or transaction made shall not have validity. If the bishop bestows upon any deserving slaves of the Church their liberty, let the liberty that has been conferred be respected by his successors, together with that which the manumitter gave them when they were freed; and we command them to hold twenty solidi in value in fields, vineyards, and dwellings; what shall have been given more the Church shall reclaim after the death of the one who manumitted.[2] But little things and things of less utility to the Church we permit to be given to strangers and clergy for their usufruct, the right of the Church being maintained.

(d) *Apostolic Constitutions*, IV, 6.   (MSG, 1 : 812.)

Cruelty to slaves was placed upon the same moral level as cruelty and oppression of other weak and defenceless people.

The Apostolic Constitutions form an elaborate treatise upon the Church and its organization in eight books, which appear, according to the consensus of modern scholars, to belong to the early part of the fifth century. The Apostolic Canons are eighty-five canons appended to the eighth book.

Now the bishop ought to know whose oblations he ought to receive, and whose he ought not. For he is to avoid corrupt dealers and not receive their gifts. . . . He is also to avoid those that oppress the widow and overbear the orphan, and

---

[1] In a usufruct the title remained with the grantor, and the grantee merely had the use or enjoyment of the land.

[2] On the principle that one who had a life interest in property (and only such the bishop had) could alienate for a period not extending beyond his natural life.

fill the prisons with the innocent, and abuse their own slaves wickedly, I mean with stripes and hunger and hard service.

(e) *Apostolic Canons, Canon* 81, Bruns, I, 12.

This deals with the question of the ordination of a slave. Later, if a slave was ordained without his master's consent, the ordination held, but the bishop was obliged to pay the price of the slave to his master. *Cf.* Council of Orleans, A. D. 511, *Can.* 8.

We do not permit slaves to be ordained to the clergy without their masters' consent; for this would wrong those that owned them. For such a practice would occasion the subversion of families. But if at any time a servant appears worthy to be ordained to a high office, such as Onesimus appears to have been, and if his master allows it, and gives him his freedom, and dismisses him free from his house, let him be ordained.

(f) Gregory the Great, *Ep. ad Montanam et Thomam.* (MSL, 77 : 803.)

Gregory and others approved of manumission of slaves as an act of self-denial, for therein a man surrendered what belonged to him, as in almsgiving; but he and others also justified the practice of manumission upon lines that recall Stoic ideas of man's natural freedom. Yet, at the same time, Gregory could insist upon the strict discipline of slaves in the administration of the Church property.

The following is a letter of manumission addressed apparently to a man and his wife.

Since our Redeemer, the Maker of every creature, vouchsafed to assume human flesh for this end, that when by the grace of His divinity the chain of slavery wherewith we were held had been broken He might restore us to our pristine liberty, it is a salutary deed if men, whom nature originally produced free, and whom the law of nations has subjected to the yoke of slavery, be restored by the benefit of manumission to the liberty in which they were born. And so moved by loving-kindness and consideration of the case, we make you Montana and Thomas, slaves of the holy Roman Church, which with the help of God we serve, free from this day and

Roman citizens, and we release to you all your private property.[1]

(g) *Codex Theodosianus*, XV, 12, 1; A. D. 325. *Cf.* Kirch, n. 754.

Constitution of Constantine regarding gladiatorial shows.
This edict was by no means enforced everywhere. In a shorter form it passed into the *Cod. Just.* (XI, 44, 1), but only after the edict of Honorius had stopped these shows.

Bloody spectacles are not pleasing in civil rest and domestic tranquillity. Wherefore we altogether prohibit them to be gladiators[2] who, it may be, for their crimes have been accustomed to receive this penalty and sentence, and you shall cause them rather to serve in the mines, that without blood they may pay the penalty of their crimes.

(h) Theodoret, *Hist. Ec.*, V, 26. (MSG, 82 : 1256.)

Honorius, who had inherited the Empire of Europe, put a stop to gladiatorial combats, which had long been held in Rome, and he did this under the following circumstances. There was a certain man named Telemachus who had embraced the ascetic life. He had set out for the East and for this reason had repaired to Rome. There, when the abominable spectacle was being exhibited, he went himself into the stadium, and stepping down into the arena endeavored to stop the men who were wielding their weapons against one another. The spectators of the slaughter were indignant and, inspired by the mad fury of the demon who delights in these bloody deeds, stoned the peacemaker to death. When the admirable Emperor was informed of this he numbered Telemachus in the army of the victorious martyrs, and put an end to that impious practice.

(i) Ambrose, *Ep.* 51. (MSL, 16 : 1210.) *Cf.* Kirch, nn. 754 ff.

---

[1] The peculium of the slave, property which he was allowed to possess but only by the sufferance of the master.

[2] The Constitution ends here in Justinian's collection.

Letter to the Emperor Theodosius after the massacre at Thessalonica in 390.

The Emperor had ordered a general massacre of the inhabitants of Thessalonica because of a sedition there. Ambrose wrote to him the following letter after having pleaded in vain with him before the massacre to deal mercifully with the people. (The well-known story of the penitence of Theodosius may be found in Theodoret, *Hist. Ec.*, V, 17.) His residence at the seat of the imperial government at that time, Milan, made him the chief adviser to the court in spite of the fact that the Arian influence was strong at court, as the empress mother Justina was an Arian, *cf.* Ambrose, *Ep.* 20, 21. (PNF, ser. II, vol. X.)

4. Listen, august Emperor, I cannot deny that you have a zeal for the faith; I confess that you have the fear of God. But you have a natural vehemence, which, if any one endeavors to soothe it, you quickly turn to mercy; and if any one stirs it up, you allow it to be roused so much that you can scarcely restrain it. Would that it might be that, if no one soothed it, at least no one inflamed it. To yourself I willingly intrust it, restrain yourself and overcome your natural vehemence by the love of piety. . . .

6. There took place in the city of the Thessalonians that of which no memory recalls the like, which I was not able to prevent taking place; which, indeed, I had before said, would be most atrocious when I so often petitioned concerning it[1] and which as you yourself show, by revoking it too late, you consider to be grave, and this I could not extenuate when committed. . . .

After citing from the Bible several cases of kings exhibiting penance for sins, Ambrose continues:

11. I have written this, not to confound you, but that the examples of kings may stir you up to put away this sin from your kingdom, for you will put it away by humbling your soul before God. You are a man, temptation has come to you; conquer it. Sin is not done away but by tears and penitence. Neither angel can do it, nor archangel. The Lord himself,

---

[1] *Cf.* Paulinus, *Vita Ambros.* MSL. 14 : 37.

who alone can say "I am with you," if we have sinned, does not forgive any but those who do penance.

12. I urge, I beg, I exhort, I warn; for it is grief to me that you who were an example of unheard-of piety, who were conspicuous for clemency, who would not suffer single offenders to be put in peril, should not mourn that so many innocent persons have perished. Though you have waged war most successfully, though in other matters too you are worthy of praise, yet piety was ever the crown of your actions. The devil envied that which you had as a most excellent possession. Conquer him whilst you still possess that wherewith you can conquer. Do not add another sin to your sin by a course of action which has injured many.

13. I, indeed, though a debtor to your kindness, for which I cannot be ungrateful, that kindness which I regard as surpassing that of many emperors, and has been equalled by one only, I have no cause, I say, for a charge of contumacy against you, but have cause for fear. I dare not offer the sacrifice if you intend to be present. Is that which is not allowed after the shedding of the blood of one innocent person allowed after the shedding of the blood of many? I think not.

(j) *Codex Theodosianus*, III, 16, 2; A. D. 421.

The later Roman law of divorce.
The Roman law under the Empire was extremely favorable to divorce, making it easy for either party to become rid of the other for any cause that seemed sufficient. The Christian Church from the first, following the teaching of Christ, opposed divorce. Marriage was an indissoluble relation; see § 39 f, g. It was only by degrees that much change could be introduced into the civil law. The following law of Theodosius II gives the condition of the law in the fifth century. It shows that to some extent the Christian principles regarding marriage had affected legislation.

If a woman leave her husband by a repudiation made by her and prove no cause for her divorcing him, the gifts which she received as bride shall be taken away and she shall likewise be deprived of her dowry, and be subjected to the pun-

ishment of deportation; and to her we deny not only the right
of marriage with another man, but also the right of post-
liminium.[1]   But if the woman opposed to the marriage prove
faults of morals and vices, though of no great gravity, let
her lose her dowry and pay back to her husband her marriage
gift, and let her never join herself in marriage with another;
that she may not stain her widowhood with the impudence
of unchastity we give the repudiated husband the right of
bringing an accusation by law.   Hereafter if she who abandons
her husband prove grave causes and a guilt involving great
crimes, let her obtain a control of her dowry and marriage
gifts, and five years after the day of repudiation she shall
receive the right of remarrying; for it would then appear that
she had acted rather out of detestation of her husband than
from desire after another.   Likewise, if the husband bring
a divorce and charge grave crimes against the woman, let
him bring action against the accused under the laws and let
him both have the dowry (sentence having been obtained)
and let him receive his gifts to her and let the free choice of
marrying another be granted him immediately.   But if it
is an offence of manners and not of a criminal nature, let him
receive the donations, relinquish the dowry, and marry after
two years.   But if he merely wishes to dissolve the marriage
by dissent, and she who is put away is charged with no fault
or sin, let the man lose the donation and the dowry, and in
perpetual celibacy let him bear as a penalty for his wrongful
divorce the pain of solitude; to the woman, however, is conceded after a year the right to remarry.   Regarding the re-
tention of the dowry on account of the children we command
that the directions of the old law shall be observed.

(k) Jerome, *Epistula* 78, *ad Oceanum*. (MSL, 22 : 691.)

Divorce and remarriage.

The principle here laid down by Jerome was that which ultimately
prevailed in the Church of the West, that after divorce there could be
no remarriage, inasmuch as the marriage bond was indissoluble, though
the parties might be separated by the law. But another principle

---

[1] *I. e.*, of returning to her former home and condition.

was also made a part of the code of Christian morality, that what was forbidden a woman was also forbidden a man, *i. e.*, the moral code as to chastity was the same for both sexes.

§ 3. The Lord hath commanded that a wife should not be put away except for fornication; and that when she has been put away, she ought to remain unmarried [Matt. 19 : 9; I Cor. 7 : 11]. Whatever is given as a commandment to men logically applies to women also. For it cannot be that while an adulterous wife is to be put away, an incontinent husband must be retained. . . . The laws of Cæsar are different, it is true, from the laws of Christ. Papinian commands one thing; our Paul another.[1] Among them the bridles are loosened for immodesty in the case of men. But with us what is unlawful for women is equally unlawful for men; and both are bound by the same conditions of service. She[2] then put away, as they report, a husband that was a sinner; she put away one who was guilty of this and that crime. . . . She was a young woman; she could not preserve her widowhood. . . . She persuaded herself and thought that her husband had been lawfully put away from her. She did not know, that the strictness of the Gospel takes away from women all pretexts for remarriage, so long as their former husbands are alive.

    (*l*) Jerome, *Adversus Jovinianum*, I, 7. (MSL, 23 : 229.)

The inferiority of marriage to virginity.
While the Church teachers insisted on the indissolubility of marriage and its sanctity, in not a few cases they depreciated marriage. Of those who did this Jerome may be regarded as the most characteristic and representative of a tendency which had set in, largely in connection with the increase of monasticism, regarded as the only form of Christian perfection.

"It is good for a man not to touch a woman."[3] If it is good not to touch a woman, it is bad to touch one; for noth-

---

[1] *I. e.*, in distinction from Paulus the eminent Roman lawyer, a contemporary of Papinian.
[2] Fabiola (*cf.* DCB), on whose death Jerome is here writing to her husband Oceanus.
[3] See I Cor. 7 : 1 *ff.*

ing is opposed to goodness but the bad. But if it be bad and the evil is pardoned, it is conceded that a worse evil may not happen. But what sort of good is that which is allowed only because there may be something worse? He would have never added, "Let each man have his own wife," unless he had previously said, "But because of fornication." . . . "Defraud ye not one another, except it be by consent for a season, that ye may give yourselves unto prayer." What, I pray, is the quality of that good thing which hinders prayer, which does not allow the body of Christ to be received? So long as I do a husband's part, I fail in continency. The same Apostle in another place commands us to pray always.[1]

9. "It is better to marry than to burn." If marriage itself be good, do not compare it with fire, but simply say, "It is good to marry." I suspect the goodness of that thing which must be only the lesser of two evils. What I want is not the smaller evil, but a thing that is absolutely good.

(m) Chrysostom, *Hom*. 66 *in Matth*. (XX, 30). (MSG, 58 : 630.)

The Church took the lead in philanthropy and not only organized relief of poor but constantly exhorted people to contribute to the cause. See above, § 68, *d*.

If both the wealthy and those next to them in wealth were to distribute among themselves those in need of bread and raiment, scarcely would one poor person fall to the share of fifty men, or even a hundred. Yet, nevertheless, though in such great abundance of persons able to assist them, they are wailing every day. And that thou mayest learn their inhumanity, recall that the Church[2] has a revenue of one of the lowest among the wealthy, and not of the very rich; and consider how many widows it succors every day, how many

[1] *Cf*. Council of Carthage, A. D. 398, *Can*. 13. "When the bridegroom and bride are to be blessed by the priest they are to be presented by their parents and paranymphs. And let them when they have received the benediction remain in virginity the same night out of reverence for the benediction."

[2] *I. e.*, of Antioch, where Chrysostom was a presbyter and delivered these homilies.

virgins; for indeed the list of them amounts to the number of three thousand. Together with these she succors them that dwell in prison, the sick in the caravansaries, the healthy, those that are absent from their homes, those that are maimed in their bodies, those that wait upon the altar; and with respect to food and raiment, those that casually come every day; and her substance is in no respect diminished. So that if ten men only were thus willing to spend, there would be no poor.

(*n*) Gregory of Nazianzus, *Panegyric on Basil*, ch. 63. (MSG, 36 : 577.)

Gregory of Nazianzus was the friend and schoolmate of Basil. The action of Basil in forcing upon him the bishopric of Sasima led to an estrangement and brought about the tragedy of Gregory's ecclesiastical career, his forced resignation of the archiepiscopal see of Constantinople. See Gregory's oration, "The Last Farewell" (PNF, ser. II, vol. VII, 385). Nevertheless, the death of Basil was an occasion for him to deliver his greatest oration. It was probably composed and delivered several years after Basil's decease and after Gregory had retired from Constantinople to his home at Nazianzus.

Go forth a little way from the city, behold the New City,[1] the storehouse of piety . . . where disease is regarded in a philosophic light, and disaster is thought to be a blessing in disguise, and sympathy is tested. Why should I compare with this work Thebes having the seven gates, and the Egyptian Thebes and the walls of Babylon . . . and all other objects of men's wonder and of historic record, from all of which, except for some slight glory, there was no advantage to their founders? My subject is the most wonderful of all, the short road to salvation, the easiest ascent to heaven.[2] There is no longer before our eyes that terrible and piteous spectacle of men dead before their death, in many members of their body already dead, driven away from their cities and homes and public places and fountains, ay and from their

---

[1] The name given to the extensive charitable institutions founded by Basil.
[2] For this conception of the value to the giver to be found in almsgiving, see above, § 39, *h*.

dearest ones, recognizable by their names rather than by their features. . . . He, however, it was who most of all persuaded us men, as being men, not to despise men nor to dishonor Christ, the head of all, by inhuman treatment of them; but in the misfortune of others to establish well our own lot and to lend to God that mercy, since we ourselves need mercy. He did not therefore disdain to honor disease with his lips; he was noble and of noble ancestry and of brilliant reputation, but he saluted them as brethren, not out of vainglory, as some might suppose (for who was so far removed from this feeling?), but taking the lead in approaching to tend them in consequence of his philosophy, and so giving not only a speaking but also a silent instruction. Not only the city, but the country and parts beyond behave in like manner; and even the leaders of society have vied with one another in their philanthropy and magnanimity toward them.

§ 76. Popular Piety and the Reception of Heathenism in the Church

When vast numbers poured into the Church in the fourth century and the profession of Christianity no longer involved danger, morals became less austere, and the type of piety became adapted to the religious condition of those with whom the Church had now to deal. This is shown in the new place that the intercession of saints and the veneration of their relics take in the religious life of the times. Yet these and similar forms of devotion in popular piety were not new and cannot be attributed in principle to any wholesale importation of heathenism into the Church, as was charged at the time and often since. In principle, and to some extent in practice, they can be traced to times of persecution and danger. But, on the other hand, no little heathenism was brought into the Church by those who came into it without any adequate preparation or real change of religious feeling. With this heathenism the Church had to struggle, either casting it out in whole or in part, or rendering it as innocuous as possible. In spite of all, many heathen superstitions remained everywhere in Christendom, though playing for the most part such an inferior rôle as to be negligible in the total effect.

Additional source material: Eusebius, *Vita Constantini* (PNF); III, 21, 28; IV, 38, 39, 54.

(*a*) Ambrose, *De Viduis*, ch. 9. (MSL, 16 : 264.)

The importance and value of calling upon the saints for their intercessions.

When Simon's mother-in-law was lying sick with violent fever, Peter and Andrew besought the Lord for her: "And He stood over her and commanded the fever and it left her, and immediately she arose and ministered unto them." . . .

So Peter and Andrew prayed for the widow. Would that there were some one who could so quickly pray for us, or better still, they who prayed for the mother-in-law—Peter and Andrew his brother. Then they could pray for one related to them, now they are able to pray for us and for all. For you see that one bound by great sin is less fit to pray for herself, certainly less likely to obtain for herself. Let her then make use of others to pray for her to the Physician. For the sick, unless the Physician be called to them by the prayers of others, cannot pray for themselves. The flesh is weak, the soul is sick and hindered by the chains of sins, and cannot direct its feeble steps to the throne of that great Physician. The angels must be entreated for us, who have been to us as guardians; the martyrs must be entreated whose patronage we seem to claim by a sort of pledge, the possession of their body. They can entreat for our sins, who, if they had any sins, washed them in their own blood; for they are the martyrs of God, our leaders, the beholders of our life and of our actions. Let us not be ashamed to take them as intercessors for our weakness, for they themselves knew the weakness of the body, even when they overcame.

(*b*) Jerome, *Contra Vigilantium*, chs. 4 *ff*. (MSL, 23 : 357.)

A defence of the worship and practice of the Church, especially in regard to veneration of relics against the criticism of Vigilantius.

Jerome's attack on Vigilantius is in many respects a masterpiece of scurrility, and unworthy of the ability of the man. But it is invaluable as a statement of the opinions of the times regarding such matters as the veneration of relics, the attitude toward the departed saints and martyrs, and many other elements of the popular religion which have been commonly attributed to a much later period.

Ch. 4. Among other words of blasphemy he [Vigilantius] may be heard to say: "What need is there for you not only to reverence with so great honor but even to adore I know not what, which you carry about in a little vessel and worship?" And again in the same book, "Why do you adore by kissing a bit of powder wrapped up in a cloth?" and further on, "Under the cloak of religion we see really a heathen ceremony introduced into the churches; while the sun is shining heaps of tapers are lighted, and everywhere I know not what paltry bit of powder wrapped in a costly cloth is kissed and worshipped. Great honor do men of this sort pay to the blessed martyrs, who, as they think, are to be glorified by trumpery tapers, but to whom the Lamb who is in the midst of the throne, with all the brightness of His majesty gives light."

Ch. 5. . . . Is the Emperor Arcadius guilty of sacrilege, who, after so long a time, conveyed the bones of the blessed Samuel from Judæa to Thrace? Are all the bishops to be considered not only sacrilegious but silly as well, who carried that most worthless thing, dust and ashes, wrapped in silk and in a golden vessel? Are the people of all the churches fools, who went to meet the sacred relics, and received them with as much joy as if they beheld the living prophet in the midst of them, so that there was one great swarm of people from Palestine to Chalcedon and with one voice the praises of Christ resounded? . . .

Ch. 6. For you say that the souls of the Apostles and martyrs have their abode either in the bosom of Abraham, or in some place of refreshment, or under the altar of God, and that they cannot leave their own tombs and be present

where they will.   They are, it seems, of senatorial rank and
are not in the worst sort of prison and among murderers, but
are kept apart in liberal and honorable custody in the isles of
the blessed and the Elysian fields.   Do you lay down laws for
God?   Will you throw the Apostles in chains?   So that to the
day of judgment they are to be kept in confinement and are
not with the Lord, although it is written concerning them,
"They follow the Lamb whithersoever He goeth."   If the Lamb
is present everywhere, then they who are with the Lamb, it
must be believed, are everywhere.   And while the devil and
the demons wander through the whole world, and with only
too great speed are present everywhere, the martyrs after shedding their blood are to be kept out of sight shut up in a cof-
fin[1] from whence they cannot go forth?   You say in your
pamphlet that so long as we are alive we can pray for one
another; but after we are dead the prayer of no person for
another can be heard, and especially because the martyrs,
though they cry for the avenging of their blood, have never
been able to obtain their request.   If Apostles and martyrs,
while still in the body, can pray for others, when they ought
still to be anxious for themselves, how much more must they
do so after they have their crowns and victories and triumphs?
A single man, Moses, won pardon from God for six hundred
thousand armed men; and Stephen, the follower of his Lord
and the first martyr for Christ, entreats pardon for his persecutors; and after they have entered on their life with Christ,
shall they have less power?   The Apostle Paul says that
two hundred and seventy-six souls were given him in the ship;
and after his dissolution, when he began to be with Christ,
must he then shut up his mouth and be unable to say a word
for those who throughout the whole world have believed in
his Gospel?   Shall Vigilantius the live dog be better than Paul
the dead lion?

(c) Council of Laodicæa, A. D. 343–381, *Canons* 35 *f.*,
Bruns, I, 77.

[1] "Shut up in the altar" is another reading.

The Council of Laodicæa is of uncertain date, but its earliest possible date is 343 and the latest 381, *i. e.*, between the Councils of Sardica and Constantinople. See Hefele, § 93. It owes its importance not to any immediate effect it had upon the course of the Church's development, but to the fact that its canons were incorporated in collections and received approval, possibly at Chalcedon, A. D. 451, though not mentioned by name in Canon 1, and certainly at the Quinisext, A. D. 692, Canon 2. In the West the canons were of importance as having been used by Dionysius Exiguus in his collection. That the Canon of Holy Scripture was settled at this council is a traditional commonplace in theology, but hardly borne out by the facts. The council only drew up one of the several imperfect lists of sacred books which appeared in antiquity. The following canons show the influx of heathenism into the Church, resulting from the changed status of the Church.

Canon 35. Christians must not forsake the Church of God and go away and invoke angels and gather assemblies, which things are forbidden. If, therefore, any one shall be found engaged in secret idolatry, let him be anathema; for he has forsaken our Lord Jesus Christ and gone over to idolatry.

Canon 36. They who are of the priesthood and of the lower clergy shall not be magicians, enchanters, mathematicians[1] nor astrologers; nor shall they make amulets, which are chains for their own souls. And those who wear such we command to be cast out of the Church.

(*d*) Augustine, *Epistula* 29. (MSL, 33 : 117.)

Heathenism in the Church.
An Epistle of Augustine, written when Augustine was still a presbyter of Hippo, concerning the birthday of Leontius, formerly bishop of Hippo. In it he tells Alypius that he had at length put an end to the custom among the Catholics of Hippo of taking part in splendid banquets on the birthday of saints, as was then the custom in the African churches.

Ch. 8. When the day dawned on which they were accustomed to prepare themselves for excess in eating and drinking, I received notice that some, even of those who were present at my sermon, had not yet ceased complaining, and that so great was the power of detestable custom among them that,

---

[1] *Cf.* Suetonius, *Vita Tiberii*, c. 36, *expulsit et mathematicos*. Probably they were a sort of fortune-tellers, computers of nativities, etc. *Cf.* Hefele, *loc. cit.*

using no other argument, they asked: "Wherefore is this now prohibited? Were they not Christians who in former times did not interfere with this practice?" . . .

Ch. 9. Lest, however, any slight should seem to be put by us upon those who before our time either tolerated or dared not put down such manifest wrong-doings of an undisciplined multitude, I explained to them the necessity by which this custom seems to have arisen in the Church; namely, that when, in the peace which came after such numerous and violent persecutions, crowds of heathen who wished to assume the Christian religion were kept back because, having been accustomed to celebrate the feasts connected with idols in revelling and drunkenness, they could not easily refrain from these pleasures so hurtful and so habitual; and it seemed good to our ancestors that for a time a concession should be made to this infirmity, that after they had renounced the former festivals they might celebrate other feasts, in honor of the holy martyrs, which were observed, not with the same profane design, although with similar indulgence. Now upon them as persons bound together in the name of Christ, and submissive to the yoke of His august authority, the wholesome restraints of sobriety were laid; and these restraints, on account of the honor and fear of Him who appointed them they might not resist; and that therefore it was now time that those who did not dare to deny that they were Christians should begin to live according to Christ's will; being now Christians they should reject those things conceded that they might become Christians.

§ 77. The Extension of Monasticism Throughout the Empire

Asceticism arose within the Christian Church partly as the practical expression of the conviction of the worthlessness of things transitory and partly as a reaction against the moral laxity of the times. As this laxity could not be kept entirely out of the Church, and Christians everywhere were exposed to it, those who sought the higher life felt the necessity of retirement. From the life of the isolated hermit, asceticism advanced naturally to the community type of the ascetic life. There were forerunners in non-Christian religions of the solitary ascetic and the cenobite in Egypt, Palestine, India, and elsewhere, but all the essentials of Christian monasticism can be adequately explained without employing the theory of borrowing or imitation. For the principal points of development, *v.* §§ 53, 78, 104. When monasticism had once made itself a strong factor in the Christian religious life of Egypt, it was quickly taken up by other parts of the Church as it satisfied a widely felt want. In Asia Minor Basil of Cæsarea was the great promoter and organizer of the ascetic life; and his rule still obtains throughout the East. In the West Athanasius appears to have introduced monastic ideas during his early exiles. Ambrose was a patron of the movement. Martin of Tours, Severinus, and John Cassian did much to extend it in Gaul. Augustine organized his clergy according to a monastic rule which ultimately played a large part in later monasticism.

(a) Palladius, *Historia Lausiaca*, ch. 38. (MSG, 34 : 1099.)

The Rule of Pachomius.

Palladius, the author of the history of monasticism, known as the *Historia Lausiaca*, was an Origenist, pupil of Evagrius Ponticus, and later bishop in Asia Minor. He is not to be confused with Palladius of Helenopolis, who lived about the same time, in the first part of the fifth century. The work of Palladius receives its name from the fact that it is dedicated to a high official, Lausus by name. Palladius made a careful study of monasticism, travelling extensively in making researches for his work. He also used what written material was available. It is probable that the text is largely interpolated, but on the whole it is a trustworthy account of the early monasticism. It was written about A. D. 420, and the following account of Pachomius should be compared with that of Sozomenus, *Hist. Ec.*, III, 14, written some years later. Text in Kirch, nn. 712 *ff.*

There is a place in the Thebaid called Tabenna, in which lived a certain monk Pachomius, one of those men who have attained the highest form of life, so that he was granted predictions of the future and angelic visions. He was a great lover of the poor, and had great love to men. When, therefore, he was sitting in a cave an angel of the Lord came in and appeared to him and said: Pachomius you have done well those things which pertain to your own affairs; therefore sit no longer idle in this cave. Up, therefore, go forth and gather all the younger monks and dwell with them and give them laws according to the form which I give thee. And he gave him a brass tablet on which the following things were written:

1. Give to each to eat and drink according to his strength; and give labors according to the powers of those eating, and forbid neither fasting nor eating. Thus appoint difficult labors to the stronger and those who eat, but the lighter and easy tasks to those who discipline themselves more and are weaker.

2. Make separate cells in the same place; and let three remain in a cell. But let the food of all be prepared in one house.

3. They may not sleep lying down, but having made seats built inclining backward let them place their bedding on them and sleep seated.

4. But by night let them wear linen tunics, being girded about. Let each of them have a shaggy goatskin, made white. Without this let them neither eat nor sleep. When they go in unto the communion of the mysteries of Christ every Sabbath and Lord's Day, let them loose their girdles and put off the goatskin, and enter with only their cuculla [cf. DCA]. But he made the cuculla for them without any fleece, as for boys; and he commanded to place upon them certain branding marks of a purple cross.

5. He commanded that there be twenty-four groups of the brethren, according to the number of the twenty-four letters. And he prescribed that to each group should be given as a name a letter of the Greek alphabet, from Alpha and Beta, one after another, to Omega, in order that when the archi-

mandrite asked for any one in so great a company, that one may be asked who is the second in each, how group Alpha is, or how the group Beta; again let him salute the group Rho; the name of the letters following its own proper sign. And upon the simpler and more guileless place the name Iota; and upon those who are more ill-tempered and less righteous the letter Xi. And thus in harmony with the principles and the life and manners of them arrange the names of the letters, only the spiritual understanding the meaning.

6. There was written on the tablet that if there come a stranger of another monastery, having a different form of life, he shall not eat nor drink with them, nor go in with them into the monastery, unless he shall be found in the way outside of the monastery.

7. But do not receive for three years into the contest of proficients him who has entered once for all to remain with them; but when he has performed the more difficult tasks, then let him after a period of three years enter the stadium.

8. When they eat let them veil their faces, that one brother may not see another brother eating. They are not to speak while they eat; nor outside of their dish or off the table shall they turn their eyes toward anything else.

9. And he made it a rule that during the whole day they should offer twelve prayers; and at the time of lighting the lamps, twelve; and in the course of the night, twelve; and at the ninth hour, three; but when it seemed good for the whole company to eat, he directed that each group should first sing a psalm at each prayer.

But when the great Pachomius replied to the angel that the prayers were few, the angel said to him: I have appointed these that the little ones may advance and fulfil the law and not be distressed; but the perfect do not need to have laws given to them. For being by themselves in their cells, they have dedicated their entire life to contemplation on God. But to these, as many as do not have an intelligent mind, I will give a law that as saucy servants out of fear for the

Master they may fulfil the whole order of life and direct it properly. When the angel had given these directions and fulfilled his ministry he departed from the great Pachomius. There are monasteries observing this rule, composed of seven thousand men, but the first and great monastery, wherein the blessed Pachomius dwelt, and which gave birth to the other places of asceticism, has one thousand three hundred men.

(b) Basil the Great, *Regula fusius tractata*, Questio 7. (MSG, 31 : 927.)

The Rule of St. Basil is composed in the form of question and answer, and in place of setting down a simple, clearly stated law, with perhaps some little exhortation, goes into much detailed argument, even in the briefer Rule. In the following passage Basil points out the advantages of the cenobitic life over the solitary or hermit life. It is condensed as indicated.

Questio VII. Since your words have given us full assurance that the life [*i. e.*, the cenobitic life] is dangerous with those who despise the commandments of the Lord, we wish accordingly to learn whether it is necessary that he who withdraws should remain alone or live with brothers of like mind who have placed before themselves the same goal of piety.

Responsio 1. I think that the life of several in the same place is much more profitable. First, because for bodily wants no one of us is sufficient for himself, but we need each other in providing what is necessary. For just as the foot has one ability, but is wanting another, and without the help of the other members it would find neither its own power strong nor sufficient of itself to continue, nor any supply for what it lacks, so it is in the case of the solitary life: what is of use to us and what is wanting we cannot provide for ourselves, for God who created the world has so ordered all things that we are dependent upon each other, as it is written that we may join ourselves to one another [*cf.* Wis. 13: 20]. But in addition to this, reverence to the love of Christ does not permit each one to have regard only to his own affairs, for love, he says, seeks not her own [I Cor. 13: 5]. The solitary life has only one goal, the service of its own interests. That clearly is opposed to the law of love, which the Apostle fulfilled, when he did not in his eyes seek his own advantage but the advantage of many, that they might be saved [*cf.* I Cor. 10 : 33]. Further, no one in solitude recognizes his own defects, since he has no one to correct him and in gentleness and mercy direct him on his way. For even if correction is from an enemy, it may often in the case of those who are well disposed rouse the desire for healing; but the healing of sin by him who sincerely loves is wisely accomplished. . . . Also the commands may be better fulfilled by a larger community, but not by one alone; for while this thing is being done another will be neglected; for example, by attendance upon the sick the reception of strangers is neglected; and in the bestowal and distribution of the necessities of life (especially when in these services much time is consumed) the care of the work is neglected, so that by this the greatest commandment and the one most helpful to salvation is neglected; neither the hungry are fed nor the naked clothed. Who would therefore value higher the idle, useless life than the fruitful which fulfils the commandments of God?

3. . . . Also in the preservation of the gifts bestowed by God the cenobitic life is preferable. . . . For him who falls into sin, the recovery of the right path is so much easier, for he is ashamed at the blame expressed by so many in common, so that it happens to him as it is written: It is enough that the same therefore be punished by many [II Cor. 2 : 6]. . . . There are still other dangers which we say accompany the solitary life, the first and greatest is that of self-satisfaction. For he who has no one to test his work easily believes that he has completely fulfilled the commandments. . . .

4. For how shall he manifest his humility, when he has no one to whom he can show himself the inferior? How shall he manifest compassion, cut off from the society of many? How will he exercise himself in patience, if no one opposes his wishes?

(c) Council of Chalcedon, A. D. 451, *Canon* 4.   Bruns, I, 26.

The subjection of the monastery and the monks to the bishop.

Asceticism of the solitary life was apart from the organization of the Church; when this form of life had developed in cenobitism it still remained for a time, at least, outside the ecclesiastical organization. Athanasius, who was a patron of the monastic life and often found support and refuge among the monks, did much to bring Egyptian monasticism back to the Church, and in the fifth century monks became a great power in ecclesiastical affairs, *cf.* the Origenistic controversy, *v. infra*, § 88. Basil, at once archbishop of Cæsarea and leading exponent of monastic ideas, brought the two to some extent together. But always the episcopal control was only with difficulty brought to bear on the monastic life, and in the West this opposition of the two religious forces ultimately became embodied in the principle of monastic exemption. The Council of Chalcedon, in 451, aimed to correct the early abuse by placing the monasteries under the control of the bishop.

They who lead a true and worthy monastic life shall enjoy the honor that belongs to them. But since there are some who assume the monastic condition only as a pretence, and will upset the ecclesiastical and civil regulations and affairs, and run about without distinction in the cities and want to found cloisters for themselves, the synod therefore has decreed that no one shall build a cloister or house of prayer or erect anywhere without the consent of the bishop of the city; and further, that also the monks of every district and city shall be subject to the bishop, that they shall love peace and quiet and observe the fasts and prayers in the places where they are assigned continually; that they shall not cumber themselves with ecclesiastical and secular business and shall not take part in such; they shall not leave their cloisters except when in cases of necessity they may be commissioned by the bishop of the city with such; that no slave shall be admitted into the cloister in order to become a monk without the permission of his master. Whoever violates this our order shall be excommunicated, that the name of God be not blasphemed. The bishop of the city must keep a careful oversight of the cloisters.

(d) Jerome, *Epistula* 127, *ad Principiam*. (MSL, 22 : 1087.)

The introduction of monasticism into the West during the Arian controversy.

5. At that time no high-born lady at Rome knew of the profession of the monastic life, neither would she have dared, on account of the novelty, publicly to assume a name that was regarded as ignominious and vile. It was from some priests of Alexandria and from Pope Athanasius[1] and subsequently from Peter,[2] who, to escape the persecution of the Arian heretics, had fled for refuge to Rome as the safest haven of their communion—it was from these that she [Marcella] learned of the life of the blessed Anthony, then still living, and of the monasteries in the Thebaid, founded by Pachomius, and of the discipline of virgins and widows. Nor was she ashamed to profess what she knew was pleasing to Christ. Many years after her example was followed first by Sophronia and then by others. . . . The revered Paula enjoyed Marcella's friendship, and it was in her cell that Eustochium, that ornament of virginity, was trained.

(e) Augustine, *Confessiones*, VIII, ch. 6.   (MSL, 32 : 755.)

The extension of monasticism in the West.

Upon a certain day . . . there came to the house to see Alypius and me, Pontitianus, a countryman of ours, in so far as he was an African, who held high office in the Emperor's court. What he wanted with us I know not. We sat down to talk together, and upon the table before us, used for games, he noticed by chance a book; he took it up, opened it, and, contrary to his expectations, found it to be the Apostle Paul, for he imagined it to be one of those books the teaching of which was wearing me out. At this he looked up at me smilingly, and expressed his delight and wonder that he so unexpectedly found this book, and this only, before my eyes. For he was both a Christian and baptized, and in constant and

---

[1] The title of pope which was not yet restricted even by Latins to the bishop of Rome was in general use as the title of the bishop of Alexandria.

[2] Successor of Athanasius in the see of Alexandria.

daily prayers he often prostrated himself before Thee our God in the Church. When, then, I had told him that I bestowed much pains upon these writings, a conversation ensued on his speaking of Anthony, the Egyptian monk, whose name was in high repute among Thy servants, though up to that time unfamiliar to us. When he came to know this he lingered on that topic, imparting to us who were ignorant a knowledge of this man so eminent, and marvelling at our ignorance. But we were amazed, hearing Thy wonderful works most fully manifested in times so recent, and almost in our own, wrought in the true faith and the Catholic Church. We all wondered—we that they were so great, and he that we had never heard of them.

From this his conversation turned to the companies in the monasteries, and their manners so fragrant unto Thee, and of the fruitful deserts of the wilderness, of which we knew nothing. And there was a monastery at Milan full of good brethren, without the walls of the city, under the care of Ambrose, and we were ignorant of it. He went on with his relation, and we listened intently and in silence. He then related to us how on a certain afternoon, at Treves, when the Emperor was taken up with seeing the Circensian games, he and three others, his comrades, went out for a walk in the gardens close to the city walls, and there, as they chanced to walk two and two, one strolled away with him, while the other two went by themselves; and these in their ramblings came upon a certain cottage where dwelt some of Thy servants, "poor in spirit," of whom "is the kingdom of heaven," and they found there a book in which was written the life of Anthony. This one of them began to read, marvel at, and be inflamed by it; and in the reading to meditate on embracing such a life, and giving up his worldly employments to serve Thee. . . . Then Pontitianus, and he that had walked with him through other parts of the garden, came in search of them to the same place, and, having found them, advised them to return as the day had declined. . . . But the other two, setting their affections upon heavenly things, remained in the cottage. And both of them had affianced brides who also, when they heard of this, dedicated their virginity to God.

(*f*) Sulpicius Severus, *Life of St. Martin of Tours*, ch. 10. (MSL, 20 : 166.)

Monasticism in Gaul.
St. Martin, bishop of Tours, was born 316, became bishop of Tours in 371, and died 396. He was the most considerable figure in the Church life of Gaul at that time. Sulpicius Severus was his disciple and enthusiastic biographer. For John Cassian and his works on monasticism, see PNF, ser. II, vol. XI.

And now having entered upon the episcopal office, it is beyond my power to set forth how well and how much he [Martin] performed. For he remained with the utmost constancy the same as he had been before. In his heart there was the same humility and in his garments the same simplicity; and so full of dignity and courtesy, he maintained the dignity of a bishop, yet so as not to lay aside the objects and virtues of a monk. Accordingly he made use for some time of the cell connected with the church; but afterward, when he felt it impossible to tolerate the disturbance of the numbers of those visiting it, he established a monastery for himself about two miles outside the city. This spot was so secret and retired that he did not desire the solitude of a hermit. For, on one side, it was surrounded by a precipitous rock of a lofty mountain; while the river Loire has shut in the rest of the plain by a bend extending back for a distance. The place could be approached by only one passage, and that very narrow. Here, then, he possessed a cell constructed of wood; many also of the brethren had, in the same manner, fashioned retreats for themselves, but most of them had formed these out of the rock of the overhanging mountain, hollowed out into caves. There were altogether eighty disciples, who were being disciplined after the example of the saintly master. No one there had anything which was called his own; all things were possessed in common. It was not allowed either to buy or sell anything, as is the custom amongst most monks. No art was practised there except that of transcribers, and even to this the more youthful were assigned, while the elders spent their time in prayer. Rarely did any of them go beyond the cell unless when they assembled at the place of prayer. They all took their food together after the hour of fasting was past. No one used wine except when illness compelled him. Most of them were dressed in garments of camel's hair. Any dress approaching softness was there deemed criminal, and this must be thought the more remarkable because many among them were such as are deemed of noble rank, who though very differently brought up had forced themselves down to this degree of humility and patience, and we have seen many of these afterward as bishops. For what city or church could there be that would not desire to have its priest from the monastery of Martin?

§ 78. CELIBACY OF THE CLERGY AND THE REGULATION OF CLERICAL MARRIAGE

The insistence upon clerical celibacy and even the mere regulation of the marriage of the clergy contributed not a little to making a clear distinction between the clergy and the laity which became a marked feature in the constitution of the Church. The East and the West have always differed as to clerical marriage. In the East the parish clergy have always been married; the bishops formerly married have long since been exclusively of the unmarried clergy. The clergy who do not marry become monks. This seems to have been the solution of practical difficulties which were found to arise in that part of the Church in connection with general clerical celibacy. In the West the celibacy of the clergy as a body was an ideal from the beginning of the fourth century, and became an established principle by the middle of the fifth century under Leo the Great, though as a matter of fact it was not enforced as a universal obligation of the clerical order until the reforms of Gregory VII. In the following canons and documents the division is made between the East and the West, and the selected documents are arranged chronologically so as to show the progress in legislation toward the condition that afterward became dominant in the respective divisions of the Empire and the Church.

(A)   *Clerical Marriage in the East*

(*a*) Council of Ancyra, A. D. 314, *Canon* 10. Bruns, I, 68. *Cf.* Mirbt, n. 90.

The following canon is important as being the first Eastern regulation of a council bearing on the subject and having been generally followed long before the canons of this council were adopted as binding by the Council of Constantinople known as the Quinisext in 692, Canon 2; *cf.* Hefele, § 327. For the Council of Ancyra, see Hefele, § 16.

Canon 10.   Those who have been made deacons, declaring when they were ordained that they must marry, because they were not able to abide as they were, and who afterward married, shall continue in the ministry because it was conceded to them by the bishop.   But if they were silent on the matter, undertaking at their ordination to abide as they were, and afterward proceeded to marry, they shall cease from the diaconate.

(*b*) Council of Nicæa, A. D. 325, *Canon* 3. Bruns, I, 15. *Cf.* Mirbt, n. 101, Kirch, n. 363.

The meaning of the following canon is open to question because of the term *subintroducta* and the concluding clause. Hefele contends that every woman is excluded except certain specified persons. But the custom of the East was not to treat the rule as meaning such. See E. Venables, art. "Subintroductæ," in DCB; and Achelis, art. "Subintroductæ," in PRE. Hefele's discussion may be found in his *History of the Councils*, §§ 42 and 43; in the latter he discusses the question as to the position of the council as to the matter of clerical celibacy.

Canon 3.   The great synod has stringently forbidden any bishop, presbyter, deacon, or any one of the clergy whatever, to have a *subintroducta* (συνείσακτος) dwelling with him, except only a mother, sister, or aunt, or such persons only as are beyond all suspicion.

(c) Council of Gangra, A. D. 355–381, *Canon* 4. Bruns, I, 107.

The canons of this council were approved at the Quinisext together with those of Ancyra and Laodicæa and others. This canon is directed against the fanaticism of the Eustathians.

Canon 4. If any one shall maintain, concerning a married presbyter, that it is not lawful to partake of the oblation that he offers, let him be anathema.

(d) Socrates, *Hist. Ec.*, V, 22. (MSG, 67 : 640.)

That the custom of clerical celibacy grew up without much regard to conciliar action, and that canons only later regulated what had been established and modified by custom, is illustrated by the variation in the matter of clerical marriage noted by Socrates.

I myself learned of another custom in Thessaly. If a clergyman in that country should, after taking orders, cohabit with his wife, whom he had legally married before ordination, he would be degraded.[1] In the East, indeed, all clergymen and even bishops abstain from their wives; but this they do of their own accord and not by the necessity of law; for many of them have had children by their lawful wives during their episcopate. The author of the usage which obtains in Thessaly was Heliodorus, bishop of Tricca in that country, under whose name it is said that erotic books are extant, entitled *Ethiopica*, which he composed in his youth. The same custom prevails in Thessalonica and in Macedonia and Achaia.

(e) Quinisext Council, A. D. 692, *Canons* 6, 12, 13, 48. Bruns, I, 39 *ff.*

Canons on celibacy.

The Trullan Council fixed the practice of the Eastern churches regarding the celibacy of the clergy. In general it may be said that the clergyman was not allowed to marry after ordination. But if he married before ordination he did not, except in the case of the bishops, separate from his wife, but lived with her in lawful marital relations.

---

[1] *Cf.* Apostolic Canons, 6, 27; also Council of Neo-Cæsarea, Can. 1.

Canon 6. Since it is declared in the Apostolic Canons that of those who are advanced to the clergy unmarried, only lectors and cantors are able to marry, we also, maintaining t is, determine that henceforth it is in nowise lawful for any subdeacon, deacon, or presbyter after his ordination to contract matrimony; but if he shall have dared to do so, let him be deposed. And if any of those who enter the clergy wishes to be joined to a wife in lawful marriage before he is ordained subdeacon, deacon, or presbyter, let it be done.

Canon 12. Moreover, it has also come to our knowledge that in Africa and Libya and in other places the most God-beloved bishops in those parts do not refuse to live with their wives, even after consecration, thereby giving scandal and offence to the people. Since, therefore, it is our particular care that all things tend to the good of the flock placed in our hands and committed to us, it has seemed good that henceforth nothing of the kind shall in any way occur. . . . But if any shall have been observed to do such a thing, let him be deposed.

Canon 13. [Text in Kirch, nn. 985 ff.] Since we know it to be handed down as a rule of the Roman Church that those who are deemed worthy to be advanced to the diaconate and presbyterate should promise no longer to cohabit with their wives, we, preserving the ancient rule and apostolic perfection and order, will that lawful marriage of men who are in holy orders be from this time forward firm, by no means dissolving their union with their wives nor depriving them of their mutual intercourse at a convenient season. . . . For it is meet that they who assist at the divine altar should be absolutely continent when they are handling holy things, in order that they may be able to obtain from God what they ask in sincerity.

Canon 48. The wife of him who is advanced to the episcopal dignity shall be separated from her husband by mutual consent, and after his ordination and consecration to the episcopate she shall enter a monastery situated at a distance from the abode of the bishop, and there let her enjoy the bishop's provision. And if she is deemed worthy she may be advanced to the dignity of a deaconess.

(B)   *Clerical Celibacy in the West*

(*a*) Council of Elvira, A. D. 306, *Canon* 33. **Bruns, II,** 6. *Cf*. Mirbt, n. 90, and Kirch, n. 305.

This is the earliest canon of any council requiring clerical celibacy. For the Council of Elvira, see Hefele, § 13; A. W. W. Dale, *The Synod of Elvira*, London, 1882. For discussion of reasons for assigning a later date, see E. Hennecke, art. "Elvira, Synode um 313," in PRE, and the literature there cited. The council was a provincial synod of southern Spain.

Canon 33. It was voted that it be entirely forbidden[1] bishops, presbyters, and deacons, and all clergy placed in the ministry to abstain from their wives and not to beget sons: whoever does this, let him be deprived of the honor of the clergy.

(*b*) Siricius, *Decretal*, A. D. 385.   (MSL, 13 : 1138.)   Mirbt, nn. 122 *f.; cf*. Denziger, nn. 87 *ff*.

Clerical celibacy: the force of decretals.
In the following passages from the first authentic decretal, the celibacy of the clergy is laid down as of divine authority in the Church, and the rule remains characteristic of the Western Church. See Canon 13 of the Quinisext Council, above, § 78, *e*. The binding authority of the decretals of the bishop of Rome is also asserted, and this, too, becomes characteristic of the jurisprudence of the Western Church.

Ch. 7 (§ 8). Why did He admonish them to whom the holy of holies was committed, Be ye holy, because I the Lord your God am holy? [Lev. 20 : 7.] Why were they commanded to dwell in the temple in the year of their turn to officiate, afar from their own homes? Evidently it was for the reason that they might not be able to maintain their

---

[1] Note the extraordinary form in which the clergy are apparently forbidden to do what in reality the council commands; namely, that they should abandon marital relations with their wives. *Cf*. Hefele, *loc. cit*. Can. 80 of Elvira uses the same uncouth phraseology.

marital relations with their wives, so that, adorned with a pure conscience, they might offer to God an acceptable sacrifice. After the time of their service was accomplished they were permitted to resume their marital relations for the sake of continuing the succession, because only from the tribe of Levi was it ordained that any one should be admitted to the priesthood. . . . Wherefore also our Lord Jesus, when by His coming He brought us light, solemnly affirmed in the Gospel that He came not to destroy but to fulfil the law. And therefore He who is the bridegroom of the Church wished that its form should be resplendent with chastity, so that in the day of Judgment, when He should come again, He might find it without spot or blemish, as He taught by His Apostle. And by the rule of its ordinances which may not be gainsaid, we who are priests and Levites are bound from the day of our ordination to keep our bodies in soberness and modesty, so that in those sacrifices which we offer daily to our God we may please Him in all things.

Ch. 15 (§ 20). To each of the cases, which by our son Bassanius you have referred to the Roman Church as the head of your body, we have returned, as I think, a sufficient answer. Now we exhort your brotherly mind more and more to obey the canons and to observe the decretals that have been drawn up, that those things which we have written to your inquiries you may cause to be brought to the attention of all our fellow-bishops, and not only of those who are placed in your diocese, but also of the Carthaginians, the Bætici, the Lusitani, and the Gauls, and those who in neighboring provinces border upon you, those things which by us have been helpfully decreed may be sent accompanied by your letters. And although no priest of the Lord is free to ignore the statutes of the Apostolic See and the venerable definitions of the canons, yet it would be more useful and, on account of the long time you have been in holy orders, exceedingly glorious for you, beloved, if those things which have been written you especially by name, might through your agreement with us be brought to the notice of all our brethren, and that, seeing that they have not been drawn up inconsiderately but prudently and with very great care, they should remain inviolate, and that, for the future, opportunity for any excuse might be cut off, which is now open to no one among us.

(c) Council of Carthage, A. D. 390, *Canon* 2. Bruns, I, 117.
See also Canon 1 of the same council.

Canon 2. Bishop Aurelius said: "When in a previous council the matter of the maintenance of continence and chastity was discussed, these three orders were joined by a certain agreement of chastity through their ordination, bishops, I say, presbyters, and deacons; as it was agreed that it was seemly that they, as most holy pontiffs and priests of God, and as Levites who serve divine things, should be continent in all things whereby they may be able to obtain from God what they ask sincerely, so that what the Apostles taught and antiquity observed, we also keep." By all the bishops it was said: "It is the pleasure of all that bishops, presbyters, and deacons, or those who handle the sacraments, should be guardians of modesty, and refrain themselves from their wives." By all it was said: "It is our pleasure that in all things, and by all, modesty should be preserved, who serve the altar."

(d) Leo the Great, *Ep.* 14, *ad Anastasium; Ep.* 167, *ad Rusticum.* (MSL, 54 : 672, 1204.)

The final form of the Western rule, that the clergy, from subdeacon to bishop, both inclusive, should be bound to celibacy, was expressed in its permanent form by Leo the Great in his letters to Anastasius and Rusticus. From each of these letters the passage bearing on the subject is quoted. By thus following up the ideas of the Council of Elvira and the Council of Carthage as well as the decretal of Siricius, the subdeacon was included among those who were vowed to celibacy, for he, too, served at the altar, and came to be counted as one of the major orders of the ministry.

Ep. 14, Ch. 5. Although they who are not within the ranks of the clergy are free to take pleasure in the companionship of wedlock and the procreation of children, yet, for the sake of exhibiting the purity of complete continence, even subdeacons are not allowed carnal marriage; that "both they that have wives be as though they had none" [I Cor. 7 : 29], and they that have not may remain single. But if in this order, which is the fourth from the head, this is worthy to be observed, how much more is it to be kept in the first, the second, and the third, lest any one be reckoned fit for either the deacon's duties or the presbyter's honorable position, or the bishop's pre-eminence, who is discovered as not yet having bridled his uxorious desires.

Ep. 167, Quest. 3. Concerning those who minister at the altar and have wives, whether they may cohabit with them.

Reply. The same law of continence is for the ministers of the altar as for the bishops and priests who, when they were laymen, could lawfully marry and procreate children. But when they attained to the said ranks, what was before lawful became unlawful for them. And therefore in order that their wedlock may become spiritual instead of carnal, it is necessary that they do not put away their wives[1] but to have them "as though they had them not," whereby both the affection of their married life may be retained and the marriage functions cease.

[1] This last point was considerably modified by the subsequent canon law.

PERIOD II

THE CHURCH FROM THE PERMANENT DIVISION OF THE EMPIRE UNTIL THE COLLAPSE OF THE WESTERN EMPIRE AND THE FIRST SCHISM BETWEEN THE EAST AND THE WEST, OR UNTIL ABOUT A. D. 500

In the second period of the history of the Church under the Christian Empire, the Church, although existing in two divisions of the Empire and experiencing very different political fortunes, may still be regarded as forming a whole. The theological controversies distracting the Church, although different in the two halves of the Græco-Roman world, were felt to some extent in both divisions of the Empire and not merely in the one in which they were principally fought out; and in the condemnation of heresy, each half of the Church assisted the other. Though already marked lines of cleavage are clearly perceptible, and in the West the dominating personality of Augustine forwarded the development of the characteristic theology of the West, setting aside the Greek influences exerted through Hilary, Ambrose, Rufinus, and Jerome, and adding much that was never appreciated in the East —yet the opponent of Augustine was condemned at the general council of Ephesus, 431, held by Eastern bishops in the East; and at the same time in the East the controversies regarding the union of the divine and human natures in Christ, although of interest almost entirely in the East and fought out by men of the East, found their preliminary solution at Chalcedon in 451 upon a basis proposed by the West. On the other hand, the attitudes of the two halves of the Church toward many profound problems were radically different, and the emergence of the Roman See as the great centre of the West amid the overturn of the Roman world by the barbarians, and the steadily increasing ascendency of the State over the Church in the East tended inevitably to separate ecclesiastically as well as politically the two divisions of the Empire. As the emperors of the East attempted to use dogmatic parties in the support of a political policy, the differences between the Church of the East, under the Roman Emperor, and the Church of the West, where the imperial authority had ceased to be a reality, became manifest in a schism resulting from the Monophysite controversy and the attempt to reconcile the Monophysites.

CHAPTER I.   THE CHURCH AT THE BEGINNING OF THE
   PERMANENT SEPARATION OF THE TWO PARTS OF
   THE ROMAN EMPIRE

Although Theodosius the Great had been the dominating power in the government of the Empire almost from his accession in 379, he was sole ruler of the united Roman Empire for only a few months before his death in 395.   The East and the West became henceforth permanently divided after having been united, since the reorganization of the Empire under Diocletian in 285, for only three periods aggregating twenty-eight years in all.   The imperial authority was divided between the sons of Theodosius, Arcadius taking the sovereignty of the East and Honorius that of the West.   Stilicho, a Vandal, directed the fortunes of the West until his death in 408, but the Empire of the East soon began to take a leading part, especially after the barbarians commenced to invade the West about 405, and to establish independent kingdoms within the boundaries of the Empire.   The German tribes that settled within the Empire were either Arians when they entered or became such almost immediately after; this Arianism had been introduced among the West Goths from Constantinople during the dominance of that creed.   The Franks alone of all the Germanic tribes were heathen when they settled within the Empire.

§ 79.   The Empire of the Dynasty of Theodosius.
§ 80.   The Extension of the Church about the Beginning of the Fifth Century.

§ 79.   THE EMPIRE OF THE DYNASTY OF THEODOSIUS
Emperors of the West:
   Honorius; born 384, Emperor 395–423.
   Valentinian III; born 419, Emperor 425–455; son of Galla Placidia, the daughter of Theodosius the Great, and the Empress of the West 419–450.
Emperors of the East:
   Arcadius: born 377, Emperor 395–408.
   Theodosius II: born 401, Emperor 408–450.
   Marcianus: Emperor 450–457; husband of Pulcheria (born 399, died 453), daughter of Arcadius.

The greatest event in the first half of the fifth century, the period in which the degenerate descendants of Theodosius still retained the imperial title, was the Barbarian Invasion, a truly epoch-making event.   In 405 the Vandals, Alans, and Suevi crossed the Rhine, followed later by the Burgundians.   August 24, 410, Alarich, the king of the West Goths, captured Rome.   In 419 the West Gothic kingdom was established with Toulouse as a capital.   In 429 the Vandals began to establish themselves in North Africa, and about 450 the Saxons began to invade Britain, abandoned by the Romans about 409.   Although the West was thus falling to pieces, the theory of the unity of the Empire was maintained and is expressed in the provision of the new Theodosian Code of 439 for the uniformity of law throughout the two parts of the Empire.   This theory of unity was not lost for centuries and was influential even into the eighth century.

   (a) Jerome, *Ep.* 123, *ad Ageruchiam.*   (MSL, 22 : 1057.)

The Barbarian Invasions in the opening years of the fifth century.

Jerome's letters are not to be considered a primary source for the barbarian invasion, but they are an admirable source for the way the invasion appeared to a man of culture and some patriotic feeling. With this passage should be compared his *Ep.* 60, *ad Heliodorum,* § 16, written in 396, in which he expresses his belief that Rome was falling and describes the barbarian invaders. The following letter was written 409.

§ 16. Innumerable savage tribes have overrun all parts of Gaul. The whole country between the Alps and the Pyrenees, between the Rhine and the ocean, have been laid waste by Quadi, Vandals, Sarmatians, Alans, Gepidi, Herules,[1] Saxons, Bergundians, Allemans and, alas for the common weal—even the hordes of the Pannonians. For Asshur is joined with them (Psalm 83 : 8). The once noble city of Mainz has been captured and destroyed. In its church many thousands have been massacred. The people of Worms have been extirpated after a long siege. The powerful city of Rheims, the Ambiani [a tribe near Amiens], the Altrabtæ [a tribe near Arras], the Belgians on the outskirts of the world, Tournay, Speyer, and Strassburg have fallen to Germany. The provinces of Aquitaine and of the Nine Nations, of Lyons and Narbonne, with the exception of a few cities, all have been laid waste. Those whom the sword spares without, famine ravages within. I cannot speak of Toulouse without tears; it has been kept hitherto from falling by the merits of its revered bishop, Exuperius. Even the Spains are about to perish and tremble daily as they recall the invasion of the Cymri; and what others have suffered once they suffer continually in fear.

§ 17. I am silent about other places, that I may not seem to despair of God's mercy. From the Pontic Sea to the Julian Alps, what was once ours is ours no longer. When for thirty years the barrier of the Danube had been broken there was war in the central provinces of the Roman Empire. Long use dried our tears. For all, except a few old people,

---

[1] See Putzger, *Historischer Schul-Atlas,* 1905.

had been born either in captivity or during a blockade, and they did not long for a liberty which they had never known. Who will believe it? What histories will seriously discuss it, that Rome has to fight within her borders, not for glory but for bare life; and that she does not fight even, but buys the right to exist by giving gold and sacrificing all her substance? This humiliation has been brought upon her, not by the fault of her emperors, both of them most religious men [Arcadius and Honorius], but by the crime of a half-barbarian traitor,[1] who with our money has armed our foes against us.

(b) Jerome, *Prefaces to Commentary on Ezekiel.* (MSL, 25. 15 : 75.)

The fall of Rome.
Jerome's account of the capture of Rome by Alarich is greatly exaggerated (see his *Ep.* 127, *ad Principiam*). By his very exaggeration, however, one gains some impression of the shock the event must have occasioned in the Roman world.

Preface to Book I.   Intelligence has suddenly been brought to me of the death of Pammachus and Marcella, the siege of Rome [A. D. 408], and the falling asleep of many of my brethren and sisters. I was so stupefied and dismayed that day and night I could think of nothing but the welfare of all. . . . But when the bright light of all the world was put out,[2] or, rather, when the Roman Empire was decapitated, and, to speak more correctly, the whole world perished in one city, "I became dumb and humbled myself, and kept silence from good words, but my grief broke out afresh, my heart was hot within me, and while I was musing the fire was kindled" [Psalm 39 : 3, 4].

Preface to Book III.   Who would believe that Rome, built up by the conquest of the whole world, had collapsed; that she had become both the mother of nations and their tomb; that all the shores of the East, of Egypt, of Africa, which had once

---

[1] Stilicho, on whose advice the Senate granted a subsidy to Alarich, in 408, of four thousand pounds of gold.
[2] Capture of Rome, A. D. 410, by Alarich.

belonged to the imperial city should be filled with the hosts of her men-servants and maid-servants; that every day holy Bethlehem should be receiving as mendicants men and women who were once noble and abounding in every kind of wealth?

(c) Theodosius II, *Novella I, de Theodosiani Codicis Auctoritate;* Feb. 15, 439.

The Emperors Theodosius and Valentinian, Augusti, to Florentius, Prætorian Prefect of the East.

Our clemency has often been at a loss to understand the cause of the fact that, although so many rewards are held out for the maintenance of arts and studies, so few and rare are they who are fully endowed with a knowledge of the civil law, and that although so many have grown pale from late studies, scarcely one or two have gained a sound and complete learning. When we consider the enormous multitude of books, the diversity in the forms of process, and the difficulty of legal cases, and, further, the huge mass of imperial constitutions which, hidden as it were under a veil of gross mist and darkness, precludes man's intellect from gaining a knowledge of them, we have performed a task needful for our age, and, the darkness having been dispelled, we have given light to the laws by a brief compendium. Noble men of approved faithfulness were selected, men of well-known learning, to whom the matter was intrusted. We have published the constitutions of former princes, cleared by interpretation of difficulties so that men may no longer have to wait formidable responses from expert lawyers as from a shrine, since it is quite plain what is the value of a donation, by what action an inheritance is to be sued for, with what words a contract is to be made. . . . Thus having wiped out the cloud of volumes, on which many wasted their lives and explained nothing in the end, we establish a compendious knowledge of the imperial constitutions since the time of the divine Constantine, and permit no one after the first day of next January to use in courts and daily practice of law the imperial law, or to draw up pleadings except from these books which bear our name and are kept in the sacred archives. . . .

To this we add that henceforward no constitution can be passed in the West or in any other place by the unconquerable Emperor, the son of our clemency, the everlasting Augustus Valentinian, or possess any legal validity, except the same by a divine pragmatica be communicated to us.   The same rule is to be observed in the acts which are promulgated by us in the East; and those are to be condemned as spurious which are not recorded in the Theodosian Code [certain documents excepted which were kept in the registers of bureaux].

§ 80.   THE EXTENSION OF THE CHURCH ABOUT THE BEGIN-NING OF THE FIFTH CENTURY

The most important missionary work in the early part of the fifth century was the extension of the work of Ulfilas among the German tribes and the work of the missionaries of the West in Gaul and western Germany.   Of the latter the most important was Martin of Tours.

(a) Socrates, *Hist. Ec.*, II, 41.   (MSG, 67 : 349.)

Ulfilas.

Additional material for the life of Ulfilas may be found in the *Ecclesiastical History* of Philostorgius, fragments of which, as preserved, may be found appended to the Bohn translation of Sozomen's *Ecclesiastical History*.

After giving a list of creeds put forth by various councils, from Nicæa down to the Arian creed of Constantinople, 360 (text may be found in Hahn, § 167), Socrates continues:

The last creed was that put forth at Constantinople [A. D. 360], with the appendix.   For to this was added the prohibition respecting the mention of substance [ousia], or subsistence [hypostasis], in relation to God.   To this creed Ulfilas, bishop of the Goths, then first gave his assent.   For before that time he had adhered to the faith of Nicæa; for he was a disciple of Theophilus, bishop of the Goths, who was present at the Nicene Council, and subscribed what was there determined.

(b) Ulfilas, *Confession of Faith.*   Hahn, § 198.

This confession of faith, which Ulfilas describes as his testament, is found at the conclusion of a letter of Auxentius, his pupil, an Arian bishop of Silistria, in Mœsia Inferior; see note of Hahn.   It should be compared with that of Constantinople of 360.

I, Ulfilas, bishop and confessor, have always thus believed, and in this sole and true faith I make my testament before my Lord: I believe that there is one God the Father, alone unbegotten and invisible; and in His only begotten Son, our Lord and God, the fashioner and maker of all creation, not having any one like him—therefore there is one God of all, who, in our opinion, is God—and there is one Holy Spirit, the illuminating and sanctifying power—as Christ said to his apostles for correction, "Behold I send the promise of my Father to you, but remain ye in the city of Jerusalem until ye be indued with power from on high"; and again, "And ye shall receive power coming upon you from the Holy Spirit" —neither God nor Lord, but a minister of Christ in all things; not ruler, but a subject, and obedient in all things to the Son, and the Son himself subject and obedient in all things to his Father . . . through Christ . . . with the Holy Spirit. . . .[1]

(c) Socrates, *Hist. Ec.*, IV, 23.   (MSG, 67 : 551.)

The barbarians dwelling beyond the Danube, who are called Goths, having been engaged in a civil war among themselves, were divided into two parties; of one of these Fritigernus was the leader, of the other Athanaric.   When Athanaric had obtained an evident advantage over his rival, Fritigernus had recourse to the Romans and implored their assistance against his adversary.   When these things were reported to the Emperor Valens [364–378], he ordered the troops garrisoned in Thrace to assist those barbarians against the barbarians fighting against them.   They won a complete victory over Athanaric beyond the Danube, totally routing the enemy. This was the reason why many of the barbarians became

---

[1] The termination is fragmentary.

Christians: for Fritigernus, to show his gratitude to the Emperor for the kindness shown him, embraced the religion of the Emperor, and urged those under him to do the same. Therefore it is that even to this present time so many of the Goths are infected with the religion of Arianism, because the emperors at that time gave themselves to that faith.   Ulfilas, the bishop of the Goths at that time, invented the Gothic letters and, translating the Holy Scriptures into their own language, undertook to instruct these barbarians in the divine oracles.   But when Ulfilas taught the Christian religion not only to the subjects of Fritigernus but to the subjects of Athanaric also, Athanaric, regarding this as a violation of the privileges of the religion of his ancestors, subjected many of the Christians to severe punishments, so that many of the Arian Goths of that time became martyrs.   Arius, indeed, failing to refute the opinion of Sabellius the Libyan, fell from the true faith and asserted that the Son of God was a new God; but the barbarians, embracing Christianity with greater simplicity, despised this present life for the faith of Christ.

(*d*) Sulpicius Severus, *Vita S. Martini*, 13.   (MSL, 20 : 167.)

Sulpicius Severus was a pupil of Martin of Tours, and wrote the life of his master during the latter's lifetime (died 397), but published it after his death.   He wrote also other works on Martin.   The astounding miracles they contain present curious problems for the student of ethics as well as of history.   As St. Martin was one of the most popular saints of Gaul, and in this case the merits of the man and his reputation as a saint were in accord, the works of Sulpicius became the basis of many popular lives of the saint.   The following passage illustrates the embellishment which soon became attached to all the lives of religious heroes.   It is, however, one of the least astounding of the many miracles the author relates in apparent good faith.   Whatever may be the judgment regarding the miracle, the story contains several characteristic touches met with in the history of missions in the following centuries: *e. g.*, the destruction of heathen temples and objects of worship.   This sacred tree also finds its duplicate in other attacks upon heathen sanctuaries.

Ch. 13.   When in a certain village he had demolished a very ancient temple, and had set about cutting down a pine-tree,

which stood close to the temple, the chief priest of that place
and a crowd of other heathen began to oppose him. And
though these people, under the influence of the Lord, had
been quiet while the temple was being overthrown, they could
not patiently allow the tree to be cut down. Martin carefully instructed them that there was nothing sacred in the
trunk of a tree; let them rather follow God, whom he himself
served. He added that it was necessary that that tree be cut
down, because it had been dedicated to a demon [i. e., to a
heathen deity]. Then one of them, who was bolder than the
others, said: "If you have any trust in the God whom you
say you worship, we ourselves will cut down this tree, you shall
receive it when it falls; for if, as you declare, your Lord is
with you, you will escape all injury." Then Martin, courageously trusting in the Lord, promised that he would do this.
Thereupon all that crowd of heathen agreed to the condition;
for they held the loss of their tree a small matter, if only they
got the enemy of their religion buried beneath its fall. Accordingly when that pine-tree was hanging over in one direction, so that there was no doubt as to what side it would fall
on being cut, Martin, having been bound, was, in accordance
with the decision of these pagans, placed in that spot where,
as no one doubted, the tree was about to fall. They began,
therefore, to cut down their own tree with great joy and
mirth. At some distance there was a great multitude of
wondering spectators. And now the pine-tree began to totter
and to threaten its own ruin by falling. The monks at a distance grew pale and, terrified by the danger ever coming
nearer, had lost all hope and confidence, expecting only the
death of Martin. But he, trusting in the Lord, and waiting
courageously, when now the falling pine had uttered its expir-
ing crash, while it was now falling, while it was just rushing
upon him, with raised hand put in its way the sign of salvation [i. e., the sign of the cross]. Then, indeed, after the
manner of a spinning top (one might have thought it driven
back) it fell on the opposite side, so that it almost crushed the

rustics, who had been standing in a safe spot. Then truly a shout was raised to heaven; the heathen were amazed by the miracle; the monks wept for joy; and the name of Christ was extolled by all in common. ·The well-known result was that on that day salvation came to that region. For there was hardly one of that immense multitude of heathen who did not desire the imposition of hands, and, abandoning his impious errors, believe in the Lord Jesus. Certainly, before the times of Martin, very few, nay, almost none, in those regions had received the name of Christ; but through his virtues and example it has prevailed to such an extent that now there is no place there which is not filled with either very crowded churches or monasteries. For wherever he destroyed heathen temples, there he was accustomed to build, immediately, either churches or monasteries.

CHAPTER II. THE CHURCH OF THE WESTERN EMPIRE
IN THE FIFTH CENTURY

The period between the closing years of the fourth century, in which the struggle was still going on between heathenism and Christianity (§ 81), and the end of the Roman Empire of the West is of fundamental importance in the study of the history of the Christian Church of the West. In this period were laid the foundations for its characteristic theology and its ecclesiastical organization. The former was the work of St. Augustine, the most powerful religious personality of the Western Church. In this he built partly upon the traditions of the West, but also, largely, upon his own religious experience (§ 82). These elements were developed and modified by the two great controversies in which, by discussion, he formulated more completely than ever had been done before the idea of the Church and its sacraments in opposition to the Donatists (§ 83), and the doctrines of sin and grace in opposition to a moralistic Christianity, represented by Pelagius (§ 84). The leading ideas of Augustine, however, could be appropriated only as they were modified and brought into conformity with the dominant ecclesiastical and sacramental system of the Church, in the semi-Pelagian controversy, which found a tardy termination in the sixth century (§ 85). In the meanwhile the inroads of the barbarians with all the horrors of the invasions, the confusion in the political, social, and ecclesiastical organization, threatened the overthrow of all established institutions. In the midst of this anarchy, the Roman See, in the work of Innocent I, and still more clearly in the work of Leo the Great, enunciated its ideals and became the centre, not merely of ecclesiastical unity, in which it had often to contest its claims with the divided Church organizations of the West, but still more as the ideal centre of unity for all those that held to the old order of the Empire with its culture and social life (§ 86).

§ 81.   The Western Church toward the End of the Fourth
        Century.
§ 82.   Augustine's Life and Place in Western Thought.
§ 83.   Augustine and the Donatist Schism.
§ 84.   The Pelagian Controversy.
§ 85.   The semi-Pelagian Controversy.
§ 86.   The Roman Church as the Centre of the Catholic
        Roman Element of the West.

§ 81.   The Western Church Toward the End of the
        Fourth Century

Heathenism lingered as a force in society longer in the West than in the East, not merely among the peasantry, but among the higher classes. This was partly due to the conservatism of the aristocratic classes and the superior form in which the religious philosophy of Neo-Platonism had been presented to the West. This presentation was due, in no small part, to the work of such philosophers as Victorinus, who translated the earlier works of the Neo-Platonists so that it escaped the tendencies, represented by Jamblichus, toward theurgy and magic, and an alliance with polytheism and popular superstition. Victorinus himself became a Christian, passing by an easy transition from Neo-Platonism to Christianity; a course in which he was followed by Augustine, and, no doubt, by others as well.

Augustine, *Confessiones*, VIII, 2. (MSL, 32 : 79.)

The conversion of Victorinus.

To Simplicianus then I went—the father of Ambrose,[1] in receiving Thy grace,[2] and whom he truly loved as a father. To him I narrated the windings of my error. But when I mentioned to him that I had read certain books of the Platonists, which Victorinus, formerly professor of rhetoric at Rome (who died a Christian, as I had heard), had translated into Latin, he congratulated me that I had not fallen upon the writings of other philosophers, which were full of fallacies and deceit, "after the rudiments of this world" [Col. 2 : 8], whereas they, in many respects, led to the belief in God and His word. Then to exhort me to the humility of Christ, hidden from the wise and revealed to babes, he spoke of Victorinus himself, whom, while he was in Rome, he had known intimately; and of him he related that about which I will not be silent. For it contained great praise of Thy grace, which ought to be confessed unto Thee, how that most learned old man, highly skilled in all the liberal sciences, who had read, criticised, and explained so many works of the philosophers; the teacher of so many noble senators, who, also, as a mark of his excellent discharge of his duties, had both merited and obtained a statue in the Roman Forum (something men of this world esteem a great honor), he, who had been, even to that age, a worshipper of idols and a participator in the sacrilegious rites to which almost all the nobility of Rome were addicted, and had inspired the people with the love of "monster gods of every sort, and the barking Anubis, who hold their weapons against Neptune and Venus and Minerva" [Vergil, *Æneid*, VIII, 736 *ff.*], and those whom Rome once conquered, she now worshipped, all of which Victorinus, now

---

[1] At the time a bishop.   [2] *I. e.*, Simplicianus had baptized Ambrose.

old, had defended so many years with vain language,[1] he now blushed not to be a child of Thy Christ, and an infant at Thy fountain, submitting his neck to the yoke of humility, and subduing his forehead to the reproach of the cross.

O Lord, Lord, who hast bowed the heavens and come down, touched the mountains and they smoked [Psalm 144 : 5], by what means didst Thou convey Thyself into that bosom? He used to read, Simplicianus said, the Holy Scriptures and most studiously sought after and searched out all the Christian writings, and he said to Simplicianus, not openly, but secretly and as a friend: "Knowest thou that I am now a Christian?" To which he replied: "I will not believe it, nor will I rank you among the Christians unless I see you in the Church of Christ." Whereupon he replied derisively: "Do walls then make Christians?" And this he often said, that already he was a Christian; and Simplicianus used as often to make the same answer, and as often the conceit of the walls was repeated. For he was fearful of offending his friends, proud demon worshippers, from the height of whose Babylonian pride, as from the cedars of Lebanon, which the Lord had not yet broken [Psalm 29 : 5], he seriously thought a storm of enmity would descend upon him. But after that he had derived strength from reading and inquiry, and feared lest he should be denied by Christ before the holy angels if he was now afraid to confess Him before men [Matt. 10 : 33], and appeared to himself to be guilty of a great fault in being ashamed of the sacraments of the humility of Thy word, and not being ashamed of the sacrilegious rites of those proud demons, which as a proud imitator he had accepted, he became bold-faced against vanity and shamefaced toward the truth, and suddenly and unexpectedly said to Simplicianus, as he himself informed me: "Let us go to the Church; I wish to be made a Christian." And he, unable to contain himself for joy, went with him. When he had been admitted to the first sacrament of instruction [i. e., the Catechumenate], he, not long after, gave in his

---

[1] This is hardly fair to Victorinus and his pre-Christian religious views.

name that he might be regenerated by baptism. Meanwhile Rome marvelled and the Church rejoiced; the proud saw and were enraged; they gnashed with their teeth and melted away [Psalm 92 : 9]. But the Lord God was the hope of Thy servant, and He regarded not vanities and lying madness [Psalm 40 : 4].

Finally the hour arrived when he should make profession of his faith, which, at Rome, they, who are about to approach Thy grace, are accustomed to deliver from an elevated place, in view of the faithful people, in a set form of words learnt by heart. But the presbyters, he said, offered Victorinus the privilege of making his profession more privately, as was the custom to do to those who were likely, on account of bashfulness, to be afraid; but he chose, rather, to profess his salvation in the presence of the holy assembly. For it was not salvation that he had taught in rhetoric and yet he had publicly professed that. How much less, therefore, ought he, when pronouncing Thy word, to dread Thy meek flock, who, in the delivery of his own words, had not feared the mad multitudes! So then, when he ascended to make his profession, and all recognized him, they whispered his name one to the other, with a tone of congratulation. And who was there among them that did not know him? And there ran through the mouths of all the rejoicing multitude a low murmur: "Victorinus! Victorinus!" Sudden was the burst of exultation at the sight of him, and as sudden the hush of attention that they might hear him. He pronounced the true faith with an excellent confidence, and all desired to take him to their hearts, and by their love and joy they did take him to them; such were the hands with which they took him.

§ 82. Augustine's Life and Place in the Western Church

Aurelius Augustinus, the greatest of the Latin fathers, was born 354, at Tagaste, in Numidia. He was educated to be a teacher of rhetoric, and practised his profession at Carthage,

Rome, and Milan. From 374 to 383, he was a Manichæan catechumen, for although his mother, Monnica, was a Christian, his religious education had been very meagre, and he was repelled by the literary character of the Scriptures as commonly interpreted. In 387, after a long struggle, and passing through various schools of thought, he, with his son Adeodatus, were baptized at Milan by Ambrose. In 391 he became a presbyter, and in 394 bishop of Hippo Regius, a small town in North Africa. He died 430, during the Vandal invasion. Of his works, the *Confessions* are the most widely known, as they have become a Christian classic of edification of the first rank. They give an account of his early life and conversion, but are more useful as showing his type of piety than as a biography. From them is learned the secret of his influence upon the Western world. The literary activity of Augustine was especially developed in connection with the prolonged controversies, in which he was engaged throughout his episcopate (see §§ 83, 84), but he wrote much in addition to controversial treatises. The group of characteristic doctrines known as "Augustinianism," viz.: Original Sin, Predestination, and Grace and the doctrines connected with them, were, to a large extent, the outcome of his own religious experience. He had known the power and depth of sin. He had discovered the hand of God leading him in spite of himself. He knew that his conversion was due, not to his own effort or merit, but to God's grace.

The works of Augustine have been translated in part in PNF, ser. I, vols. I–VIII. There are many translations of the *Confessions;* among others, one by E. B. Pusey, in "Library of the Fathers of the Holy Catholic Church," reprinted in "Everyman's Library."

(*a*) Augustine, *Confessiones*, VIII, 12. (MSL, 32 : 761.)

The conversion of Augustine.

This is, perhaps, the most famous passage in the *Confessions*. It came at the end of a long series of attempts to find peace in various forms of philosophy and religion. Augustine regarded it as miraculous, the crown and proof of the work of grace in him. The scene was in Milan, 387, in the garden of the villa he occupied with his friend Alypius. The principal obstacle to his embracing Christianity was his reluctance to abandon his licentious life. To this the reference is made in the passage from Scripture which he read, *i. e.*, Rom. 13 : 13, 14.

When a profound reflection had, from the depths of my soul, drawn together and heaped up all my misery before the sight of my heart, there arose a mighty storm, accompanied by as mighty a shower of tears. That I might pour it all forth in its own words I arose from beside Alypius; for solitude suggested itself to me as fitter for the business of weeping. So I retired to such a distance that even his presence could not be oppressive to me. Thus it was with me at that time, and he perceived it; for something, I believe, I had spoken, wherein the sound of my voice appeared choked with weeping, and thus I had risen up. He then remained where we had been sitting, very greatly astonished. I flung myself down, I know not how, under a certain fig-tree, giving free course to my tears, and the streams of my eyes gushed out, an acceptable sacrifice unto Thee. And not indeed in these words, yet to this effect, spake I much unto Thee—"But Thou, O Lord, how long?" [Psalm 13 : 1]. "How long, Lord? Wilt Thou be angry forever? Oh, remember not against us former iniquities" [Psalm 79 : 5, 8]; for I felt that I was held fast by them. I sent up these sorrowful cries: "How long, how long? To-morrow, and to-morrow? Why not now? Why is there not this hour an end to my uncleanness?"

I was saying these things and was weeping in the most bitter contrition of my heart, when, lo, I hear the voice as of a boy or girl, I know not which, coming from a neighboring house, chanting and oft repeating: "Take up and read; take up and read." Immediately my countenance was changed, and I began most earnestly to consider whether it was usual for children in any kind of game to sing such words; nor could I remember ever to have heard the like anywhere. So, restraining the torrent of my tears, I rose up, interpreting it in no other way than as a command to me from Heaven to

open the book and read the first chapter I should light upon.
For I had heard of Anthony [see also § 77, *e*], that accidentally
coming in whilst the Gospel was being read, he received the
admonition as if what was read was addressed to him: "Go
and sell that thou hast, and give to the poor, and thou shalt
have treasure in heaven; and come and follow me" [Matt.
19 : 21]. And by such oracle was he forthwith converted unto
Thee. So quickly I returned to the place where Alypius was
sitting; for there had I put down the volume of the Apostles,
when I rose thence. I seized, I opened, and in silence I read
that paragraph on which my eye first fell: "Not in rioting
and drunkenness, not in chambering and wantonness, not in
strife and envying; but put ye on the Lord Jesus Christ, and
make not provision for the flesh to fulfil the lusts thereof"
[Rom. 13 : 13, 14]. No further would I read; there was no
need; for instantly, as the sentence ended, by a light, as it
were, of security infused into my heart, all the gloom of doubt
vanished away.

Closing the book, then, and putting either my finger between, or some other mark, I now with a tranquil countenance
made it known to Alypius. And he thus disclosed to me what
was wrong in him, which I knew not. He asked to look at
what I had read. I showed him; and he looked even further
than I had read, and I knew not what followed. This, in
fact, followed: "Him that is weak in the faith, receive ye"
[Rom. 14 : 1]; which he applied to himself, and discovered
to me. By this admonition was he strengthened; and by a
good resolution and purpose, very much in accord with his
character (wherein, for the better, he was always far different
from me), without any restless delay he joined me. Thence
we go to my mother. We tell her—she rejoices. We relate
how it came to pass—she exults and triumphs, and she blesses
Thee, who art "able to do exceeding abundantly above all
that we ask or think" [Eph. 3 : 20]; for she perceived Thee to
have given her more for me than she used to ask by her pitiful
and most doleful groanings. For Thou didst so convert me

unto Thyself, that I sought neither a wife, nor any other hope of this world—standing in that rule of faith in which Thou, so many years before, had showed me unto her. And thou didst turn her grief unto gladness [Psalm 30 : 11], much more plentiful than she had desired, and much dearer and chaster than she used to crave, by having grandchildren of my flesh.

(b) Augustine, *Confessiones*, X, 27, 29, 43. (MSL, 32 : 795, 796, 808.)

The following passages from the *Confessions* are intended to illustrate Augustine's type of piety.

Ch. 29. My whole hope is only in Thy exceeding great mercy. Give what Thou commandest and command what Thou wilt.[1] Thou imposest continency upon us. "And when I perceived," saith one, "that no one could be continent except God gave it; and this was a point of wisdom also to know whose this gift was" [Wis. 8 : 21]. For by continency are we bound up and brought into one, whence we were scattered abroad into many. For he loves Thee too little, who besides Thee loves aught which he loves not for Thee. O love, who ever burnest and art never quenched! O charity, my God, kindle me! Thou commandest continency; give what Thou commandest, and command what Thou wilt.

Ch. 27. Too late have I loved Thee, O fairness, so ancient, yet so new! Too late have I loved Thee. For behold Thou wast within and I was without, and I was seeking Thee there; I, without love, rushed heedlessly among the things of beauty Thou madest. Thou wast with me, but I was not with Thee. Those things kept me far from Thee, which, unless they were in Thee, were not. Thou didst call and cry aloud, and Thou broke through my deafness. Thou didst gleam and shine and¦chase away my blindness. Thou didst exhale fragrance and I drew in my breath and I panted for Thee. I tasted, and

---

[1] This is the phrase which so deeply offended Pelagius; *Da quod jubes, et jube quod vis.*

did hunger and thirst. Thou didst touch me, and I burned for Thy peace.

Ch. 43. O how Thou hast loved us, O good Father, who sparedst not thine only Son, but didst deliver Him up for us wicked ones! [Rom. 8 : 32.] O how Thou hast loved us, for whom He, who thought it not robbery to be equal with Thee, "became obedient unto death, even the death of the cross" [Phil. 2 : 8]. He alone, "free among the dead" [Psalm 88 : 5], that had power to lay down His life, and power to take it again [John 10 : 18]; for us was He unto Thee both victor and the victim, and the victor became the victim; for He was unto Thee both priest and sacrifice, and priest because sacrifice; making us from being slaves to become Thy sons, by being born of Thee, and by serving us. Rightly, then, is my strong hope in Him, because Thou didst cure all my diseases by Him who sitteth at Thy right hand and maketh intercession for us [Rom. 8 : 34]; else should I utterly despair. For numerous and great are my infirmities, yea numerous and great are they; but Thy medicine is greater. We might think that Thy word was removed from union with man and despair of ourselves had not He been "made flesh and dwelt among us" [John 1 : 14].

(c) Augustine, *De Civitate Dei*, XIII, 3, 14. (MSL, 41 : 378; 86.)

The Fall of Man and Original Sin.

The *City of God* is Augustine's great theodicy, apology, and philosophy of universal history. It was begun shortly after the capture of Rome, and the author was engaged upon it from 413 to 426. It was the source whence the mediæval ecclesiastics drew their theoretical justification for the curialistic principles of the relation of State and Church, and at the same time the one work of St. Augustine that Gibbon the historian regarded highly. For an analysis see Presensée, art. "Augustine" in DCB.

Compare the position of Augustine with the following passage from St. Ambrose, *On the Death of Satyrus*, II, 6, "Death is alike to all, without difference for the poor, without exception for the rich. And so although through the sin of one alone, yet it passed upon all; . . . In Adam I fell, in Adam I was cast out of paradise. In Adam I died;

how shall the Lord call me back, except He find me in Adam; guilty as I was in him, so now justified in Christ." [MSL, 16 : 1374.]

The first men would not have suffered death if they had not sinned. . . . But having become sinners they were so punished with death, that whatsoever sprang from their stock should also be punished with the same death. For nothing else could be born of them than what they themselves had been. The condemnation changed their nature for the worse in proportion to the greatness of their sin, so that what was before as punishment in the man who had first sinned, followed as of nature in others who were born. . . . In the first man, therefore, the whole human nature was to be transmitted by the woman to posterity when that conjugal union received the divine sentence of its own condemnation; and what man was made, not when he was created but when he sinned, and was punished, this he propagated, so far as the origin of sin and death are concerned.

Ch. 14. For God, the author of natures, not of vices, created man upright; but man, being by his own will corrupt and justly condemned, begot corrupted and condemned children. For we were all in that one man when we were all that one man, who fell into sin by the woman who had been made from him before the sin. For not yet was the particular form created and distributed to us, in which we as individuals were to live; but already the seminal nature was there from which we were to be propagated; and this being vitiated by sin, and bound by the chain of death, and justly condemned, man could not be born of man in any other state. And thus from the bad use of free will, there originated a whole series of evils, which with its train of miseries conducts the human race from its depraved origin, as from a corrupt root, on to the destruction of the second death, which has no end, those only being excepted who are freed by the grace of God.

(d) Augustine, *De Correptione et Gratia*, 2. (MSL, 44 : 917.)

Grace and Free Will.

Now the Lord not only shows us what evil we should shun, and what good we should do, which is all the letter of the law can do; but moreover He helps us that we may shun evil and do good [Psalm 37 : 27], which none can do without the spirit of grace; and if this be wanting, the law is present merely to make us guilty and to slay us. It is on this account that the Apostle says: "The letter killeth, but the spirit giveth life" [II Cor. 3 : 6]. He, then, who lawfully uses the law, learns therein evil and good, and not trusting in his own strength, flees to grace, by the help of which he may shun evil and do good. But who flees to grace except when "the steps of a man are ordered by the Lord, and He wills his ways"? [Psalm 37 : 23.] And thus also to desire the help of grace is the beginning of grace. . . . It is to be confessed, therefore, that we have free choice to do both evil and good; but in doing evil every one is free from righteousness and is a servant of sin, while in doing good no one can be free, unless he have been made free by Him who said: "If the Son shall make you free, then you shall be free indeed" [John 8 : 36]. Neither is it thus, that when any one shall have been made free from the dominion of sin, he no longer needs the help of his Deliverer; but rather thus, that hearing from Him, "Without me ye can do nothing" [John 15 : 5], he himself also says to Him: "Be Thou my helper! Forsake me not!"

(e) Augustine, *De Civitate Dei*, XV, 1.   (MSL, 41 : 437.)

Predestination.
Inasmuch as all men are born condemned, and of themselves have not the power to turn to grace, which alone can save them, it follows that the bestowal of grace whereby they may turn is not dependent upon the man but upon God's sovereign good pleasure. This is expressed in the doctrine of Predestination. For a discussion of the position of Augustine respecting Predestination and his other doctrines as connected with it, see J. B. Mozley, *A Treatise on the Augustinian Doctrine of Predestination*, 1873, a book of great ability. *Cf.* also Tixeront, *History of Dogmas*, vol. II.

I trust that we have already done justice to these great and difficult questions regarding the beginning of the world, of the soul, and of the human race itself. This race we have distributed into two parts: the one consisting of those who live according to man, the other of those who live according to God. And these we have also mystically called the two cities, or the two communities of men, of which one is predestined to reign eternally with God, and the other to suffer eternal punishment with the devil. . . .

Each man, because born of condemned stock, is first of all born from Adam, evil and carnal, and when he has been grafted into Christ by regeneration he afterward becomes good and spiritual. So in the human race, as a whole, when these two cities began to run their course by a series of births and deaths, the citizen of this world was born first, and after him the stranger of this world, and belonging to the City of God,[1] predestined by grace, elected by grace, by grace a stranger here below, and by grace a citizen above. For so far as regards himself he is sprung from the same mass, all of which is condemned in its origin; but God like a potter (for this comparison is introduced by the Apostle judiciously and not without thought) of the same lump made one vessel to honor and another to dishonor [Rom. 9 : 21].

(f) Augustine, *De Correptione et Gratia*, chs. 23 (9), 39 (13). (MSL, 44 : 930, 940.)

Ch. 23 (9). Whosoever, therefore, in God's most providential ordering are foreknown [*præsciti*] and predestinated, called justified, glorified—I say not, even though not yet born again, but even though not yet born at all—are already children of God, and absolutely cannot perish. . . . From Him, therefore, is given also perseverance in good even to the end; for it is not given except to those who will not perish, since they who do not persevere will perish.[2]

Ch. 39 (13). I speak of those who are predestinated to the

---

[1] This figure of the two cities is the motif of the whole work, in which the idea is developed in the greatest detail.

[2] See Augustine's treatise *On the Gift of Perseverance*, PNF, ser. I, vol. V.

kingdom of God, whose number is so certain that no one can
either be added to them or taken from them; not of those who
when He had announced and spoken, were multiplied beyond
number [Psalm 40 : 6].   For these may be said to be called
[*vocati*] but not chosen [*electi*], because they are not called
according to purpose.[1]

(g) Augustine, *Enchiridion*, 100.   (MSL, 40 : 279.)

Twofold Predestination.
Augustine does not commonly speak of predestination of the wicked,
i. e., those who are not among the elect and consequently predestinated
to grace and salvation.   As a rule he speaks of predestination in connection with the saints, those who are saved.   But that he, with perfect consistency, regarded the wicked as also predestinated is shown by
the following, as also other passages in his works, e. g., *City of God*, XV, 1
(*v. supra*), XXII, ch. 24 : 5.   This point has a bearing in connection
with the controversy on predestination in the ninth century, in which
Gottschalk reasserted the theory of a double predestination.

These are the great works of the Lord, sought out according to all His good pleasure [Psalm 111 : 2], and wisely sought
out, that when the angelic and the human creature sinned,
that is, did not do what He willed but what the creature itself willed, so by the will of the creature, by which was done
what the Creator did not will, He carried out what He himself
willed; the supremely Good thus turning to account even
what is evil; to the condemnation of those whom He has
justly predestinated to punishment and to the salvation of
those whom He has mercifully predestinated to grace.

(h) Augustine, *De Civitate Dei*, XVI, 2.   (MSL, 41 : 479.)

Augustine's theory of allegorical interpretation.
Augustine had been repelled by the literal interpretation of the
Scriptures and turned to the Manichæans who rejected the Old Testa-
ment.   *Confessions*, III, 5.   From Ambrose he learned the "mystical"
or allegorical method of interpreting the Old Testament, cf. *Confessions*,
VI, 4.   With Augustine's theory, treated at length, especially in his
De Doctrina Christiana, Bk. 3, should be compared Origen's in *De Prin-
cipiis*, IV, 9–15.   See above, § 43, B.

[1] This distinction is of importance in Augustine's theory of the Church.

These secrets of the divine Scriptures we investigate as we can;[1] some in more, some in less agreement, but all faithfully holding it as certain that these things were neither done nor recorded without some foreshadowing of future events, and that they are to be referred only to Christ and His Church, which is the City of God, the proclamation of which has not ceased since the beginning of the human race; and we now see it everywhere accomplished. From the blessing of the two sons of Noah and from the cursing of the middle son, down to Abraham, for more than a thousand years, there is no mention of any righteous person who worshipped God. I would not, therefore, believe that there were none, but to mention every one would have been very long, and there would have been historical accuracy rather than prophetic foresight. The writer of these sacred books, or rather the Spirit of God through him, sought for those things by which not only the past might be narrated, but the future foretold, which pertained to the City of God; for whatever is said of these men who are not its citizens is given either that it may profit or be made glorious by a comparison with what is different. Yet it is not to be supposed that all that is recorded has some signification; but those things which have no signification of their own are interwoven for the sake of the things which are significant. Only by the ploughshare is the earth cut in furrows; but that this may be, other parts of the plough are necessary. Only the strings of the harp and other musical instruments are fitted to give forth a melody; but that they may do so, there are other parts of the instrument which are not, indeed, struck by those who sing, but with them are connected the strings which are struck and produce musical notes. So in prophetic history some things are narrated which have no significance, but are, as it were, the framework to which the significant things are attached.

(i) Augustine, *Enchiridion*, 109, 110. (MSL, 40 : 283.)

[1] He has been explaining the significance of the references to the three sons of Noah.

Augustine in his teaching combined a number of different theological tendencies, without working them into a consistent system. His doctrines of Original Sin, Predestination, Grace are by no means harmonized with his position regarding the Church and the sacraments in which he builds upon the foundation laid in the West, especially by Optatus. See below, § 83. There is also a no small remnant of what might be called pre-Augustinian Western piety, which comes down from Tertullian and of which the following is an illustration, a passage which is of significance in the development of the doctrine of purgatory. Cf. Tertullian, De Monogamia, ch. 10. See above, § 39.

§ 109. The time, moreover, which intervenes between a man's death and the final resurrection, keeps the soul in a hidden retreat, as each is deserving of rest or affliction, according to what its lot was when it lived in the flesh.

§ 110. Nor can it be denied that the souls of the dead are benefited by the piety of their living friends, when the sacrifice of the Mediator is offered, or alms given in the Church in their behalf. But these services are of advantage only to those who during their lives merited that services of this kind could help them. For there is a manner of life which is neither so good as not to require these services after death, nor so bad that these services are of no avail after death. There is, on the other hand, a kind of life so good as not to require them; and again one so bad that when they depart this life they render no help. Therefore it is here that all the merit and demerit is acquired, by which one can either be relieved or oppressed after death. No one, then, need hope that after he is dead he shall obtain the merit with God which he had neglected here. And, accordingly, those services which the Church celebrates for the commendation of the dead are not opposed to the Apostle's words: "For we must all appear before the judgment-seat of Christ, that every one may receive the things done in his body, according to that he hath done, whether it be good or bad" [Rom. 14 : 10; II Cor. 5 : 10]. For that merit that renders services profitable to a man, each one has acquired while he lives in the body. For it is not to every one that these services are profitable. And why are they not profitable to all, except it be because of the different kinds of lives that men lead in the body? When, therefore, sacrifices either of the altar or of alms of any sort are offered on behalf of the dead who have been baptized, they are thanksgivings for the very good; they are propitiations [*propitiationes*] for the not very bad; and for the case of the very bad, even though they do not assist the dead, they are a species of consolation to the living. And to those to whom they are profitable, their benefit consists either in full remission of sins, or at least in making the condemnation more tolerable.

§ 83. AUGUSTINE AND THE DONATIST SCHISM

After the recall of the Donatists by the Emperor Julian, the sect rapidly increased, though soon numerous divisions appeared in the body. The more liberal opinions of the Donatist grammarian Tychonius about 370 were adopted by many of the less fanatical. The connection of the party with the Circumcellions alienated others. The contest for rigorism led by Maximianus about 394 occasioned a schism within the Donatist body.

Augustine's activity in the Donatist troubles began as soon as he was made bishop of Hippo, as his town was made up largely of Donatists, who probably constituted more than a half of the population. The books written by him after 400 have alone survived.

The turning-point in the history of Donatism was the Collatio, or conference, held at Carthage in 411. Two hundred and seventy-nine Donatist, and two hundred and eighty-six Catholic, bishops were present. Augustine was one of those who represented the Catholic position. The victory was adjudged by the imperial commissioners to the Catholic party. After this the laws against the sect were enforced relentlessly, and Donatism rapidly lost its importance. The Vandal invasion in 429 changed the condition of things for a time.   The last traces of Donatism disappear only with the Moslem invasion in the seventh century.

The importance of the Donatist controversy is that in it were defined the doctrines of the Church and of the sacraments, definitions which, with some modifications, controlled the theology of the Church for centuries.

(*a*) Optatus, *De Schismate Donatistarum*, II, 1–3.   (MSL, 11 : 941.)

The unity of the Catholic Church.

Ch. 1. The next thing to do . . . is to show that there is one Church which Christ called a dove and a bride.   Therefore the Church is one, the sanctity of which is derived from the sacraments; and it is not valued according to the pride of persons.   Therefore this one dove Christ also calls his beloved bride.   This cannot be among heretics and schismatics. . . . You have said, brother Parmenianus, that it is with you alone . . . among you in a small part of Africa, in the corner of a small region, but among us in another part of Africa will it not be?   In Spain, in Gaul, in Italy, where you are not, will it not be? . . . And through so many innumerable islands and other provinces, which can scarcely be numbered, will it not be?   Wherein then will be the propriety of the Catholic name, since it is called Catholic, because it is reasonable[1] and everywhere diffused?

Ch. 2. I have proved that that is the Catholic Church, which spread throughout the whole world, and now are its ornaments to be recalled; and it is to be seen where the first five gifts [*i. e.*, notes of the Church] are, which you say are six.   Among these the first is the cathedra, and unless a bishop, who is the angel [the second gift or note according to the Donatists], sit in it, no other gift can be joined.   It is to be seen who first placed a see and where. . . . You cannot deny that in the

---

[1] Dupin in his edition of Optatus, *ad. loc.*, points out that there were current two etymologies of Catholic; according to one κατὰ λόγον it meant reasonable, and according to the other, κατὰ ὅλον general or universal.

city of Rome the episcopal cathedra was first placed by Peter, and in it sat Peter, the head of all the Apostles, wherefore he is called Cephas, so that in that one cathedra unity is preserved by all, that the other Apostles might not claim each one for himself a cathedra; so that he is a schismatic and a sinner who against that one cathedra sets up another.

Ch. 3. Therefore Peter first sat in that single cathedra, which is the first gift of the Church, to him succeeded Linus . . . to Damasus, Siricius, who is our contemporary, with whom the world together with us agree in one fellowship of communion by the interchange of letters. Recite the origin of your cathedra, you who would claim for yourself the Holy Church [*cf.* Tertullian, *De Præscriptione*, c. 32].

(*b*) Optatus, *De Schismate Donatistarum*, V, 4. (MSL, 11 : 1051.)

The validity of sacraments is not dependent on the character of those who minister them. With this should be compared Augustine, *Contra litteras Petiliani Donatistæ*, II, 38–91, and the treatise *De Baptismo contra Donatistas libri septem*, which is little more than a working out in a thousand variations of this theme.

In celebrating this sacrament of baptism there are three things which you can neither increase, diminish, nor omit. The first is the Trinity, the second the believer, and the third the minister. . . . The first two remain ever immutable and unmoved. The Trinity is always the same, the faith in each is one. But the person of him who ministers is clearly not equal to the first two points, in that it alone is mutable. . . . For it is not one man who always and everywhere baptizes. In this work there were formerly others, and now others still, and again there will be others; those who minister may be changed, the sacraments cannot be changed. Since therefore you see that they who baptize are ministers and are not lords, and the sacraments are holy in themselves, not on account of men, why is it that you claim so much for yourselves? Why is it that you endeavor to exclude God from His gifts? Permit God to be over the things which are His. For that gift cannot be performed by a man because it is divine. If you think it can be so bestowed, you render void the words of the prophets and the promises of God, by which it is proved that God washes, not man.

(c) Augustine, *De Baptismo contra Donatistas*, IV, 17 (§ 24).   (MSL, 43 : 169.)

Baptism without the Church valid but unprofitable.
Augustine, as opposing the Donatists and agreeing with the Catholic Church, asserted the validity of baptism when conferred by one outside the communion of the Church. It was notorious that Cyprian and the Council of Carthage, A. D. 258 [see ANF, vol. V., pp. 565 *ff.*; *cf.* Hefele, § 6], had held an opposite opinion. As Cyprian was the great teacher of North Africa, and in the highest place in the esteem of all, Augustine was forced to make "distinctions." This he did in his theory as to the validity of baptism as in the following passage. The Sixth Book of the same treatise is composed of a statement of the bishops at the Council of Carthage, and Augustine's answer to each statement.

"Can the power of baptism," says Cyprian, "be greater than confession, than martyrdom, that a man should confess Christ before men, and be baptized in his own blood, and yet," he says, "neither does this baptism profit the heretic, even though for confessing Christ he be put to death outside the Church." This is most true; for by being put to death outside the Church, he is proved not to have had that charity of which the Apostle says: "Though I give my body to be burned and have not charity, it profiteth me nothing" [I Cor. 13 : 3]. But if martyrdom is of no avail for the reason that charity is lacking, neither does it profit those who, as Paul says, and Cyprian further sets forth, are living within the Church without charity, in envy and malice; and yet they can both receive and transmit true baptism. "Salvation," he says, "is not without the Church." Who denies this? And therefore whatever men have that belongs to the Church, outside the Church it profits them nothing toward salvation. But it is one thing not to have, another to have it but to no use. He who has it not must be baptized that he may have it; he who has to no use must be corrected, that what he has he may have to some use. Nor is the water in baptism "adulterous," because neither is the creature itself, which God made, evil, nor is the fault to be found in the words of the Gospel in the mouths of any who are astray; but the fault is theirs in whom there is an adulterous spirit, even though it may receive the adornment of the sacrament from a lawful spouse. It therefore can be true that baptism is "common to us and to the heretics," since the Gospel can be common to us, although their error differs from our faith; whether they think otherwise than the truth about the Father or Son or the Holy Spirit; or, being cut away from unity, do not gather with Christ, but scatter abroad, because it is possible that the sacrament of baptism can be common to us if we are the wheat of the Lord with the covetous within the Church and with robbers and drunkards and other pestilent persons, of whom it is said, "They shall not inherit the kingdom of God," and yet the vices by which they are separated from the kingdom of God are not shared by us.

(d) Augustine, *Ep.* 98, *ad Bonifatium.* (MSL, 33 : 363.)

Relation of the sacrament to that of which it is the sign. Sacraments are effective if no hinderance is placed to their working.

On Easter Sunday we say, "This day the Lord rose from the dead," although so many years have passed since His resurrection. . . . The event itself being said to take place on that day, because, although it really took place long before, it is on that day sacramentally celebrated. Was not Christ once for all offered up in His own person as a sacrifice? And yet, is He not likewise offered up in the sacrament as a sacrifice, not only in the special solemnities of Easter, but also daily among our congregations; so that when a man is questioned and answers that He is offered as a sacrifice in that ordinance, does he not declare what is strictly true? For if sacraments had not some points of real resemblance to the things of which they are the sacraments, they would not be

450 THE CHURCH TO ABOUT A. D. 500

sacraments at all. [Augustine's general definition of a sacrament is that it is a sign of a sacred thing.] In most cases, moreover, they do, in virtue of this likeness, bear the names of the realities which they resemble. As therefore in a certain manner the sacrament of the body of Christ is the body of Christ, the sacrament of the blood of Christ is the blood of Christ, so the sacrament of faith is faith. . . . Now, believing is nothing else than having faith; and accordingly, when on behalf of an infant as yet incapable of exercising faith, the answer is given that he believes, this answer means that he has faith because of the sacrament of faith, and in like manner the answer is made that he turns himself toward God because of the sacrament of conversion, since the answer itself belongs to the celebration of the sacrament. Thus the Apostle says, in regard to this sacrament of baptism: "We are buried with Christ by baptism into death." He does not say, "We have signified our being buried with Him," but: "We have been buried with Him." He has therefore given to the sacrament pertaining to so great a transaction no other name than the word describing the transaction itself.

10. Therefore an infant, although he is not yet a believer in the sense of having that faith which includes the consenting will of those who exercise it, nevertheless becomes a believer through the sacrament of that faith. . . . The infant, though not yet possessing a faith helped by the understanding, is not obstructing[1] faith by an antagonism of the understanding, and therefore receives with profit the sacrament of faith.

(e) Augustine, *De Correctione Donatistarum*, §§ 22 ff. (MSL, 33 : 802.)

The argument in favor of using force to compel the Donatists to return to the Church.

[1] The expression *opponere obicem* became in scholastic theology of great importance in connection with the *ex opere operato* nature of the sacraments of the New Law. On this whole matter of the sacraments in the Fathers, see Schwanne, *Dogmengeschichte*, § 93, which is very clear and helpful, especially as showing the basis of scholastic theory of the sacraments in the patristic period, and that, too, without doing violence to his authorities.

The indelible character of sacraments, *i. e.*, baptism. For other references, see Mirbt, n. 137.

Augustine in the early part of the Donatist controversy was not in favor of using force. Like the others, *e. g.*, Optatus, he denied that force had been employed by the Church. About 404 the situation changed, and his opinion did likewise. This work, known also as Epistle CLXXXV, was written circa 417. Compare Augustine's position with the statement of Jerome, "Piety for God is not cruelty," *cf.* Hagenbach, *History of Christian Doctrines,* § 135 : 7. The Donatists had much injured their position by their treatment of a party which had produced a schism in their own body, the Maximianists.

§ 22. Who can love us more than Christ who laid down His life for the sheep? And yet, after calling Peter and the other Apostles by His word alone, in the case of Paul, formerly Saul, the great builder of His Church, but previously its cruel persecutor, He not only constrained him with His voice, but even dashed him to the earth with His power. . . . Where is what they [the Donatists] are accustomed to cry: "To believe or not to believe is a matter that is free"? Toward whom did Christ use violence? Whom did He compel? Here they have the Apostle Paul. Let them recognize in his case Christ's first compelling and afterward teaching; first striking and afterward consoling. For it is wonderful how he who had been compelled by bodily punishment entered into the Gospel and afterward labored more in the Gospel than all they who were called by word only; and the greater fear compelled him toward love, that perfect love which casts out fear.

§ 23. Why, therefore, should not the Church compel her lost sons to return if the lost sons compelled others to perish? Although even men whom they have not compelled but only led astray, their loving mother embraces with more affection if they are recalled to her bosom through the enforcement of terrible but salutary laws, and are the objects of far more deep congratulation than those whom she has never lost. Is it not a part of the care of the shepherd, when any sheep have left the flock, even though not violently forced away, but led astray by soft words and by coaxings, and they have begun to be possessed by strangers, to bring them back to the

fold of his master when he has found them, by the terrors or
even the pains of the whip, if they wish to resist; especially
since, if they multiply abundantly among the fugitive slaves
and robbers, he has the more right in that the mark of the
master is recognized on them, which is not outraged in those
whom we receive but do not baptize?[1]   So indeed is the error
of the sheep to be corrected that the sign of the Redeemer
shall not be marred.   For if any one is marked with the royal
stamp by a deserter, who has himself been marked with it, and
they receive forgiveness, and the one returns to his service,
and the other begins to be in the service in which he had not
yet been, that mark is not effaced in either of them, but rather
it is recognized in both, and approved with due honor because
it is the king's.   Since they cannot show that that is bad to
which they are compelled,[2] they maintained that they ought
not to be compelled to the good.   But we have shown that
Paul was compelled by Christ; therefore the Church in compelling the Donatists is following the example of her Lord,
though in the first instance she waited in hopes of not having
to compel any, that the prediction might be fulfilled concerning the faith of kings and peoples.

§ 24.   For in this sense also we may interpret without
absurdity the apostolic declaration when the blessed Apostle
Paul says: "Being ready to revenge all disobedience, when
your obedience is fulfilled" [II Cor. 10 : 6].   Whence also
the Lord himself bids the guests to be brought first to His
great supper, and afterward compelled; for when His servants
answered Him, "Lord, it is done as thou hast commanded,
and yet there is room," He said to them: "Go out into the
highways and hedges and compel them to come in" [Luke
14 : 22, 23].   In those, therefore, who were first brought in

---

[1] The basis of the doctrine of the indelible character of baptism. *Cf.* Augustine, *Contra epist. Parm.*, II, 13, 28.   "Each [baptism and the right of
giving baptism] is indeed a sacrament, and by a certain consecration each is
given to a man, this when he is baptized, that when he is ordained; therefore
in the Catholic Church it is not lawful to repeat either."   *Cf.* next passage.

[2] This was written after the conference with the Donatists in 411, in which
victory was adjudged to the Catholics.

with gentleness the former obedience is fulfilled, but in those who were compelled the disobedience is avenged. For what else is the meaning of "Compel them to come in," after it had previously been said, "Bring in," and the answer was: "Lord, it is done as Thou commandest, and yet there is room"? Wherefore if by the power which the Church has received by divine appointment in its due season, through the religious character and faith of kings, those who are found in the highways and hedges—that is, in heresies and schisms— are compelled to come in, then let them not find fault because they are compelled, but consider to what they are so compelled. The supper of the Lord, the unity, is of the body of Christ, not only in the sacrament of the altar but also in the bond of peace.

(f) Augustine, *Contra epistulam Parmeniani*, II, 13 (29). (MSL, 43 : 71.)

Indelibility of baptism.

Parmenianus was the Donatist bishop who succeeded Donatus in the see of Carthage. The letter here answered was written to Tychonius, a leading Donatist. In it Parmenianus calls the Church defiled because it contained unworthy members. The answer of Augustine was written in 400, many years later.

If any one, either a deserter or one who has never served as a soldier, signs any private person with the military mark, would not he who has signed be punished as a deserter, when he has been arrested, and so much the more severely as it could be proved that he had never at all served as a soldier, and at the same time along with him would not the most impudent giver of the sign, be punished if he have surrendered him? Or perchance he takes no military service, but is afraid of the military mark [*character*] in his body, and he betakes himself to the clemency of the Emperor, and when he has poured forth prayers and obtained forgiveness, he then begins to undertake military service, when the man has been liberated and corrected is that mark [*character*] ever repeated, and not rather is he not recognized and approved? Would

the Christian sacraments by chance be less enduring than this
bodily mark, since we see that apostates do not lack baptism,
and to them it is never given again when they return by
means of penitence, and therefore it is judged not possible to
lose it.

(g) Augustine, *Contra epistulam Manichæi*, ch. 4 (5). (MSL,
42 : 175.)   *Cf.* Mirbt, n. 132.

Authority of the Catholic Church.
This work, written in 396 or 397, is important in this connection as
showing the place the Catholic Church took in the mind of Augustine
as an authority and the nature of that authority.

Not to speak of that wisdom which you [the Manichæans]
do not believe to be in the Catholic Church, there are many
other things which most justly keep me in her bosom.   The
consent of people and nations keeps me in the Church; so
does her authority, inaugurated by miracles, nourished by
hope, enlarged by love, established by age.   The succession
of priests keeps me, beginning from the very seat of Peter
the Apostle, to whom the Lord after His resurrection gave it
in charge to feed His sheep down to the present episcopate.
And so lastly does the name itself of Catholic, which not
without reason, amid so many heresies, that Church alone
has so retained that, though all heretics wish to be called
Catholics, yet when a stranger asks where the Catholic
Church meets no heretic will venture to point to his own
basilica or house.   Since then so many and so great are the
very precious ties belonging to the Christian name which
rightly keep a man who is a believer in the Catholic Church
. . . no one shall move me from the faith which binds my
mind with ties so many and so strong to the Christian religion.

Let us see what Manichæus teaches us; and in particular
let us examine that treatise which you call the Fundamental
Epistle in which almost all that you believe is contained.   For
in that unhappy time when we read it, we were called by you

enlightened.   The epistle begins: "Manichæus, an apostle of Jesus Christ, by the providence of God the Father.   These are wholesome words from the perennial and living fountain."   Now, if you please, patiently give heed to my inquiry.   I do not believe that he is an apostle of Christ.   Do not, I beg of you, be enraged and begin to curse.   You know that it is my rule not to believe without consideration anything offered by you.   "Wherefore I ask, who is this Manichæus?"   You reply, "An apostle of Christ."   1 do not believe it.   Now you are at a loss what to say or do; for you promised to give me knowledge of the truth, and you force me to believe something I do not know.   Perhaps you will read the Gospel to me, and from it you will attempt to defend the person of Manichæus.   But should you meet with a person not yet believing the Gospel, what could you reply to him if he said to you: "I do not believe"?   For my part I should not believe the Gospel except the authority of the Catholic Church moved me.   So then I have assented to them when they say to me, "Believe the Gospel"; why should I not assent to them saying to me: "Do not believe the Manichæans"?

§ 84.   The Pelagian Controversy

The Pelagian controversy, in which the characteristic teaching of Augustine found its best expression, may be divided into three periods.   In the first period, beginning about 411, Pelagius and Cælestius, who had been teaching at Rome unmolested since 400 and had come to Carthage, probably on account of the barbarian attack upon Rome, are opposed at Carthage, and six propositions attributed to Cælestius are condemned at a council there, where he attempted to be ordained.   Cælestius leaves for the East and is ordained at Ephesus, 412, and Pelagius soon after follows him.   In the second period, 415-417, the controversy is in the East as well as in the West, as Augustine by letters to Jerome gave warn-

ing about Pelagius, and councils are held at Jerusalem and
Diospolis, where Pelagius is acquitted of heresy. This was
probably due as much to the general sympathy of the Eastern
theologians with his doctrine as to any alleged misrepresenta-
tion by Pelagius. But in North Africa synods are also held
condemning Pelagius, and their findings are approved by
Innocent of Rome. But Pelagius and Cælestius send confessions of faith to Zosimus (417–418), Innocent's successor,
who reproves the Africans and acquits Pelagius and Cælestius
as entirely sound. In the third period, 417–431, the attack
on Pelagius is taken up at Rome itself by some of the clergy,
and an imperial edict is obtained against the Pelagians.
Zosimus changes his opinion and approves the findings of a
general council called at Carthage in 418, in which the doctrines of original sin and the need of grace are asserted. The
last act of the controversy in its earlier form, after the deposition of the leading Pelagians, among them Julian, of
Eclanum, their theologian, is the condemnation of Pelagius at
the Council of Ephesus, in 431. *V. infra*, § 89.

Additional source material: See A. Bruckner, *Quellen zur Geschichte
des pelagianischen Streites* (in Latin), in Krüger's *Quellenschriften*,
Freiburg-im-Breisgau, 1906. The principal works of Augustine bearing on the Pelagian controversy may be found in PNF. ser. I, vol. V.

(a) Augustine, *Ep.* 146, *ad Pelagium*. (MSL, 33 : 596.)

This was probably written before the controversy. As to its use
later, see Augustine, *De gestis Pelagii*, chs. 51 (26) *f.* (PNF).

I thank you very much that you have been so kind as to
make me glad by your letter informing me of your welfare.
May the Lord recompense you with those blessings that you
forever be good and may live eternally with Him who is eternal, my lord greatly beloved and brother greatly longed for.
Although I do not acknowledge that anything in me deserves
the eulogies which the letter of your benevolence contains
about me, I cannot, however, be ungrateful for the good-will
therein manifested toward one so insignificant, while suggest-

ing at the same time that you should rather pray for me that I may be made by the Lord such as you suppose me already to be.

(*b*) Augustine. *De Peccatorum Meritis et Remissione et de Baptismo Parvulorum.* (MSL, 44 : 185, 188.)

Augustine's testimony as to the character of Pelagius.

This work was written in 412, after the condemnation of Cælestius at Carthage. It was the first in the series of polemical writings against the teaching of Pelagius. The first book is especially important as a statement of Augustine's position as to the nature of justifying grace.

It should be recalled that Pelagius was a monk of exemplary life, and a zealous preacher of morality. It may be said that in him the older moralistic tendency in theology was embodied in opposition to the new religious spirit of Augustine. *Cf.* Bruckner, *op. cit.*, n. 4.

III. 1. However, within the last few days I have read some writings of Pelagius, a holy man, as I hear, who has made no small progress in the Christian life, and these writings contain very brief expositions of the Epistles of Paul the Apostle.[1]

III. 3. But we must not omit that this good and praiseworthy man (as they who know him describe him as being) has not advanced this argument against the natural transmission of sin in his own person.

(*c*) Pelagius, *Fragments*, in Augustine's *De Gratia Christi et de Peccato Originali.* (MSL, 44 : 364, 379.)

The teaching of Pelagius can be studied not only in his opponent's statements but in his own words. These are to be found in his commentary (see note to previous selection), and also in fragments found in Augustine's writings and several minor pieces (see below).

I. 7. Very ignorant persons think that we do wrong in this matter to divine grace, because we say that it by no means perfects sanctity in us without our will: as if God could impose any commands upon His grace and would not supply also the help of His grace to those to whom He has given commands, so that men might more easily accomplish through grace what they are required to do by their free will. And

---

[1] These commentaries were falsely published under the name of Jerome and may be found in his works. (MSL, 30 : 670.)

this grace we do not for our part, as you suppose, allow to consist merely in the law, but also in the help of God.   God helps us by His teaching and revelation when He opens the eyes of our heart; when He points out to us the future, that we may not be absorbed in the present; when He discovers to us the snares of the devil; when He enlightens us with manifold and ineffable gifts of heavenly grace.   Does the man who says this appear to you to be a denier of grace?   Does he not acknowledge both man's free will and God's grace?

I. 39.

Speaking of the text Rom. 7 : 23: "But I see another law in my members, warring against the law of my mind, and bringing me into captivity to the law of sin which is in my members."

Now what you [*i. e.*, Augustine, whom he is addressing] wish us to understand of the Apostle himself, all Church writers assert that he spoke in the person of the sinner, and of one still under the law, who by reason of very long custom of vice was held bound, as it were, by a certain necessity of sinning, and who, although he desired good with his will in practice, indeed, was driven into evil.   In the person, however, of one man the Apostle designates the people who sinned still under the ancient law, and this people, he declares, are to be delivered from this evil of custom through Christ, who first of all remits all sins in baptism, to those who believe on Him, and then by an imitation of Himself incites them to perfect holiness, and by the example of virtues overcomes the evil custom of sins.

(*d*) Pelagius, *Epistula ad Demetriadem*. (MSL, 33 : 1100 *ff*.)

This epistle, from which selections are given, was written probably about 412 or 413.   As it gives a statement of the teaching of Pelagius in his own words, it is of especial historical interest.   Demetrias was a virgin, and probably under the spiritual direction of Pelagius, though little is known of her.   Text in Bruckner, *op. cit.*, n. 56.

Ch. 2.   As often as I have to speak of the principles of virtue and a holy life, I am accustomed first of all to call attention to the capacity and character of human nature, and to show what it is able to accomplish; then from this to arouse the feelings of the hearer, that he may strive after different kinds of virtue, that he may permit himself to be roused to acts which perhaps he had regarded as impossible. For we are quite unable to travel the way of virtue if hope does not accompany us. For all attempts to accomplish anything cease if one is in doubt whether he will attain the goal. This order of exhortation I follow in other minor writings and in this case also. I believe it must be kept especially in mind where the good of nature needs to be set forth the more in detail as the life is to be more perfectly formed, that the spirit may not be more neglectful and slow in its striving after virtue, as it believes itself to have the less ability, and when it is ignorant of what is within it, think that it does not possess it.

Ch. 3. One must be careful to see to it that . . . one does not think that a man is not made good because he can do evil and is not compelled to an immutable necessity of doing good through the might of nature. For if you diligently consider it and turn your mind to the subtler understanding of the matter, the better and superior position of man will appear in that from which his inferior condition was inferred. But just in this freedom in either direction, in this liberty toward either side, is placed the glory of our rational nature. Therein, I say, consists the entire honor of our nature, therein its dignity; from this the very good merit praise, from this their reward. For there would be for those who always remain good no virtue if they had not been able to have chosen the evil. For since God wished to present to the rational creature the gift of voluntary goodness and the power of the free will, by planting in man the possibility of turning himself toward either side, He made His special gift the ability to be what he would be in order that he, being capable of good and evil, could do either and could turn his will to either of them.

Ch. 8. We defend the advantage of nature not in the sense

that we say it cannot do evil, since we declare that it is capable of good and evil; we only protect it from reproach.   It should not appear as if we were driven to evil by a disease of nature, we who do neither good nor bad without our will, and to whom there is always freedom to do one of two things, since always we are able to do both. . . . Nothing else makes it difficult for us to do good than long custom of sinning which has infected us since we were children, and has gradually corrupted us for many years, so that afterward it holds us bound to it and delivered over to it, so that it almost seems as if it had the same force as nature.

If before the Law, as we are told, and long before the appearance of the Redeemer, various persons can be named who lived just and holy lives, how much more after His appearance must we believe that we are able to do the same, we who have been taught through Christ's grace, and born again to be better men; and we who by His blood have been reconciled and purified, and by His example incited to more perfect righteousness, ought to be better than they who were before the Law, better than they who were under the law.

(e) Marius Mercator, *Commonitorium super nomine Cælestii*, ch. 1.   (MSL, 48 : 67.)   *Cf.* Kirch, nn. 737 *ff*.

The Council of Carthage and the opinions of Cælestius condemned at that council, 411.

Marius Mercator, a friend and supporter of Augustine, was one of the most determined opponents of Pelagianism, as also of Nestorianism. His dates are not well determined.   In 418 he sent works to Augustine to be examined by the latter, and he seems to have lived until after the Council of Chalcedon, 451.   The work from which the selection is taken was written, 429, in Greek, and translated and republished in Latin, 431 or 432.   With the following should be compared Augustine's *De Gratia Christi et Peccato Originali*, II, 2 *f*., and *Ep.* 175 : 6; 157 : 3, 22.

A certain Cælestius, a eunuch from his mother's womb, a disciple and auditor of Pelagius, left Rome about twenty years ago and came to Carthage, the metropolis of all Africa, and there he was accused of the following heads before Aurelius, bishop of that city, by a complaint from a certain Paulinus, a deacon of Bishop Ambrose of Milan, of sacred memory, as the record of the acts stands in which the same complaint is inserted (a copy of the acts of the council we have in our hands) that he not only taught this himself, but also sent in different directions throughout the provinces those who agreed with him to disseminate among the people these things, that is:

1. Adam was made mortal and would have died whether he had sinned or had not sinned.

2. The sin of Adam injured himself alone, and not the human race.

3. New-born children are in that state in which Adam was before his fall.

4. Neither by the death and sin of Adam does the whole race die, nor by the resurrection of Christ does the whole race rise.

5. The Law leads to the kingdom of heaven as well as the Gospel.

6. Even before the coming of the Lord there were men without sin.

(f) Pelagius, *Confessio fidei*. (MSL, 45 : 1716 f.) Hahn, § 209.

The confession of faith addressed to Innocent of Rome, but actually laid before Zosimus, in 417, consists of an admirably orthodox statement of the doctrine of the Trinity and of the incarnation, an expansion of the Nicene formula with feference to perversions of the faith by various heretics, and in conclusion a statement of Pelagius's own opinions regarding free will, grace, and sin. It is due to the irony of history that it should have been found among the works of both Jerome and Augustine, long passed current as a composition of Augustine, *Sermo CCXXXVI*, and should have been actually quoted by the Sorbonne, in 1521, in its articles against Luther. It also appears in the *Libri Carolini*, III, 1, as an orthodox exposition of the faith. The passages which bear upon the characteristic Pelagian doctrine are here given. Fragments of the confessions of other Pelagians, *e. g.*, Cælestius, and Julius of Eclanum, are found in Hahn, §§ 210 and 211. For the proceedings in the East, see Hefele, § 118.

We hold that there is one baptism, which we assert is to be administered to children in the same words of the sacrament as it is administered to adults. . . .

We execrate also the blasphemy of those who say that anything impossible to do is commanded man by God, and the commands of God can be observed, not by individuals but by all in common, also those who with the Manichæans condemn first marriages or with the Cataphrygians condemn second marriages. . . . We so confess the will is free that we say that we always need the aid of God, and they err who with the Manichæans assert that man cannot avoid sins as well as those who with Jovinan say that man cannot sin; for both take away the liberty of the will.   But we say that man can both sin and not sin, so that we confess that we always have free will.

(g) Augustine, *Sermo* 131.   (MSL, 38 : 734.)   *Cf.* Kirch, n. 672.

Causa finita est.
Late in 416 synods were held in Carthage and Milcoe condemning Pelagianism.   On January 27, 417, Innocent wrote to the Africans, approving their councils and condemning Pelagianism, incidentally stating the supreme authority of the Roman See and requiring that nothing should ever be definitively settled without consulting the Apostolic See (text of passage in Denziger, ed. 1911, n. 100).   September 23 of the same year, about the time when Pelagius and Cælestius were at Rome with Zosimus seeking to rehabilitate themselves in the West, Augustine delivered a sermon in which he made the following statement.   It is the basis of the famous phrase *Roma locuta, causa finita est,* a saying which is apocryphal, however, and not found in the works of Augustine.

What, therefore, is said concerning the Jews, that we see in them [*i. e.,* the Pelagians].   They have the zeal for God; I bear witness, that they have a zeal for God, but not according to knowledge.   Why is it not according to knowledge? Because, being ignorant of the justice of God and wishing to establish their own, they are not subject to the righteousness of God [Rom. 10 : 2 *f.*].   My brethren, have patience with me.

When you find such, do not conceal them, let there be not false mercy in you. Most certainly when you find such, do not conceal them. Refute those contradicting, and those resisting bring to me. For already two councils about this case have been sent to the Apostolic See, whence also rescripts have come. The case has been ended; would that the error might some time end! Therefore let us warn them that they pay attention; let us teach them that they may be instructed; let us pray that they may be changed.

(*h*) Zosimus, III *Ep. ad Episcopos Africæ de causa Cælestii* A. D. 417. (MSL, 45 : 1721.)   *Cf.* Bruckner, *op. cit.*, n. 28.

Fragments of his later *Epistula tractoria* together with other letters may be found in Bruckner, *op. cit.*

Likewise Pelagius sent letters also containing an extended justification of himself, to which he added a profession of his faith, what he condemned and what he followed, without any dissimulation, so that all subtilities of interpretation might be avoided. There was a public recitation of these. They contained all things like those which Cælestius had previously presented and expressed in the same sense and drawn up in the same thoughts. Would that some of you, dearest brethren, could have been present at the reading of the letters. What was the joy of the holy men who were present; what was the admiration of each of them! Some of them could scarcely restrain themselves from tears and weeping, that such men of absolutely correct faith could have been suspected. Was there a single place in which the grace of God or his aid was omitted?

(*i*) Council of Carthage, A. D. 418, *Canons*.   Bruns, I, 188.

These canons of the Council of Carthage, A. D. 418, were incorporated in the *Codex Canon Ecclesiæ Africanæ* adopted at the· Council of Carthage A. D. 419.   The numbers given in brackets are the numbers in that Codex.   Interprovincial councils were known in North Africa as "general councils."

In the consulate of the most glorious emperors, Honorius for the twelfth time and Theodosius for the eighth, on the calends of May, at Carthage in the Secretarium of the Basilica of Faustus, when Bishop Aurelius presided over the general council, the deacons standing by, it pleased all the bishops, whose names and subscriptions are indicated, met together in the holy synod of the church of Carthage:

1 [109]. That whosoever should say that Adam, the first man, was created mortal, so that whether he had sinned or not, he would have died in the body—that is, he would have gone forth of the body, not because of the desert [or merit] of sin, but by natural necessity, let him be anathema.

2 [110]. Likewise that whosoever denies that infants newly from their mother's womb should be baptized, or says that baptism is for remission of sins, but that they derive from Adam no original sin, which is removed by the laver of regeneration, whence the conclusion follows that in them the form of baptism for the remission of sins is to be understood as false and not true, let him be anathema.

For not otherwise can be understood what the Apostle says, "By one man sin has come into the world,[1] and so it passed upon all men in that all have sinned," than as the Catholic Church everywhere diffused has always understood it. For on account of this rule of faith, even infants, who could have committed no sin themselves, therefore are truly baptized for the remission of sins, in order that what in them is the result of generation may be cleansed by regeneration.

3 [111]. Likewise, that whoever should say that the grace of God, by which a man is justified through Jesus Christ our Lord, avails only for the remission of past sins, and not for assistance against committing sins in the future, let him be anathema.

4 [112]. Also, whoever shall say that the same grace of God through Jesus Christ our Lord helps us not to sin only in that by it are revealed to us and opened to our understand-

---

[1] Some manuscripts add "and death through sin."

ing the commandments, so that we may know what to seek, what we ought to avoid, and also that we should love to do so, but that through it we are not helped so that we are able to do what we know we should do, let him be anathema. For when the Apostle says, "Wisdom puffeth up, but charity edifieth," it were truly infamous were we to believe that we have the grace of Christ for that which puffeth us up, but have it not for that which edifieth, since each is the gift of God, both to know what we ought to do, and to love it so as to do it; so that wisdom cannot puff us up while charity is edifying us. For as it is written of God, "Who teacheth man knowledge," so also it is written, "Love is of God."

5 [113]. It seemed good that whosoever should say that the grace of justification is given to us only that we might be able more readily by grace to perform what we were commanded to do through our free will; as if when grace was not given, although not easily, yet nevertheless we could even without grace fulfil the divine commandments, let him be anathema. For the Lord spake concerning the fruits of the commandments, when he said, "Without me ye can do nothing," and not "Without me ye can do it but with difficulty."

6 [114]. It seemed also good that as St. John the Apostle says, "If ye shall say that we have no sin, we deceive ourselves and the truth is not in us"; whosoever thinks that this should be so understood as to mean that out of humility we ought to say that we have sin, and not because it is really so, let him be anathema. For the Apostle goes on to add, "But if we confess our sins, he is faithful and just to forgive us our sins and to cleanse us from all iniquity," where it is sufficiently clear that this is said not only in humility but also in truth. For the Apostle might have said, "If we shall say we have no sins we shall extol ourselves, and humility is not in us"; but when he says, "we deceive ourselves and the truth is not in us," he sufficiently intimates that he who affirmed that he had no sin would speak not that which is true but that which is false.

7 [115]. It has seemed good that whosoever should say that when in the Lord's Prayer, the saints say, "Forgive us our trespasses," they say this not for themselves, because they have no need of this petition, but for the rest who are sinners of the people; and that therefore none of the saints can say, "Forgive me my trespasses," but "Forgive us our trespasses"; so that the just is understood to seek this for others rather than for himself, let him be anathema.

8 [116]. Likewise it seemed good, that whosoever asserts that these words of the Lord's Prayer when they say, "Forgive us our trespasses," are said by the saints out of humility and not in truth, let them be anathema.

The following canon, although it seems to have been enacted for the case of Apiarius, is nevertheless often cited in the same connection as the eight against Pelagius, and is therefore given here for the sake of convenience.

18 [125]. Likewise, it seemed good that presbyters, deacons, or other of the lower clergy who are to be tried, if they question the decision of their bishops, the neighboring bishops having been invited by them with the consent of their bishops shall hear them and determine whatever separates them. But should they think that an appeal should be carried from them, let them not carry the appeal except to African councils or to the primates of their provinces. But whoso shall think of carrying an appeal across the seas, shall be admitted to communion by no one in Africa.[1]

§ 85. Semi-Pelagian Controversy

With the condemnation of Pelagianism the doctrine of Augustine in its logically worked out details was not necessarily approved. The necessity of baptism for the remission of sins in all cases was approved as well as the necessity of grace. The doctrine of predestination, an essential feature in the Augustinian system, was not only not accepted but was

[1] For the discussion on appeals across the sea, i. e., to Rome, see Hefele, § 119; A. W. Haddan, art. "Appeal" in DCA.

vigorously opposed by many who heartily condemned Pelagianism. The ensuing discussion, known as the Semi-Pelagian controversy (427–529), was largely carried on in Gaul, which after the Vandal occupation of North Africa, became the intellectual centre of the Church in the West. The leading opponent of Augustine was John Cassian (ob. 435), abbot of a monastery at Marseilles, hence the term Massilians applied to his party, and his pupil, Vincent of Lerins, author of *Commonitorium*, written 434. The chief Augustinians were Hilary and Prosper of Aquitaine. The discussion was not continuous. About 475 it broke out again when Lucidus was condemned at a council at Lyons and forced to retract his predestinarian views; and again about 520. The matter received what is regarded as its solution in the Council of Orange, 529, confirmed by Boniface II in 531. By the decrees of this council so much of the Augustinian system as could be combined with the teaching and practice of the Church as to the sacraments was formally approved.

(a) John Cassian, *Collationes*, XIII, 7 *ff*. (MSL, 49 : 908.)

John Cassian, born about 360, was by birth and education a man of the East, and does not appear in the West until 405, when he went to Rome on some business connected with the exile of Chrysostom, his friend and patron. In 415 he established two monasteries at Marseilles, one for men and the other for women. He had himself been educated as a monk and made a careful study of monasticism in Egypt and Palestine. Western monasticism is much indebted to him for his writings, *De Institutis Cœnobiorum* and the *Collationes*. In the former, he describes the monastic system of Palestine and Egypt and the principal vices to which the monastic life is liable; in the latter, divided into three parts, Cassian gives reports or what purports to be reports of conversations he and his friend Germanus had with Egyptian ascetics. These books were very popular during the Middle Ages and exerted a wide influence.

Ch. 7. When His [God's] kindness sees in us even the very smallest spark of good-will shining forth or which He himself has, as it were, struck out from the hard flints of our hearts, He fans it and fosters it and nurses it with His breath, as He "will have all men to be saved and to come unto the knowledge of the truth" [I Tim. 2 : 4]. . . . For He is true and lieth not when He lays down with an oath: "As I live, saith the Lord, I will not the death of a sinner, but that he should turn from his way and live" [Ezek. 33 : 11]. For if He willeth not that one of His little ones should perish, how can we think without grievous blasphemy that He willeth not all men universally, but only some instead of all to be saved. Those then who perish, perish against His will, as He testifieth against each of them day by day: "Turn from your evil ways, for why will ye die, O house of Israel?" [Ezek. 33 : 11.] . . . The grace of Christ is then at hand every day, which, while it "willeth all men to be saved and come to the knowledge of the truth," calleth all without exception, saying: "Come unto me all ye that labor and are heavy laden and I will give you rest" [Matt. 11 : 28]. But if he calls not all generally but only some, it follows that not all are heavy laden with either original sin or actual sin, and that this saying is not a true one: "For all have sinned and come short of the glory of God" [Rom. 3 : 23]; nor can we believe that "death passed on all men" [Rom. 5 : 12]. And so far do all who perish, perish against the will of God, that God cannot be said to have made death, as the Scripture itself testifieth: "For God made not death, neither hath He pleasure in the destruction of the living" [Wisdom 1 : 13].

Ch. 8.   When He sees anything of a good-will arisen in us He at once enlightens it and strengthens it and urges it on to salvation, giving increase to that which He himself implanted or He sees to have arisen by our own effort.

Ch. 9. . . . But that it may be still more evident that through the good of nature, which is bestowed by the kindness of the Creator, sometimes the beginnings of a good-will arise, yet cannot come to the completion of virtue unless they are directed by the Lord, the Apostle is a witness, saying: "For to will is present with me, but to perform what is good I find not" [Rom. 7 : 18].

Ch. 11. . . . If we say that the beginnings of a good-will

are always inspired in us by the grace of God, what shall we say about the faith of Zacchæus, or of the piety of that thief upon the cross, who by their own desire brought violence to bear upon the Kingdom of Heaven, and so anticipated the special leadings of their callings? . . .

Ch. 12. We should not hold that God made man such that he neither wills nor is able to do good. Otherwise He has not granted him a free will, if He has suffered him only to will or be capable of evil, but of himself neither to will nor be capable of what is good. . . . It cannot, therefore, be doubted that there are by nature seeds of goodness implanted in every soul by the kindness of the Creator; but unless these are quickened by the assistance of God, they will not be able to attain to an increase of perfection; for, as the blessed Apostle says: "Neither is he that planteth anything nor he that watereth, but God that giveth the increase" [I Cor. 3 : 7]. But that freedom of will is to some degree in a man's power is very clearly taught in the book called *The Pastor*,[1] where two angels are said to be attached to each one of us, *i. e.*, a good and a bad one, while it lies in a man's own option to choose which to follow. And, therefore, the will always remains free in man, and it can either neglect or delight in the grace of God. For the Apostle would not have commanded, saying, "Work out your own salvation with fear and trembling" [Phil. 2 : 12], had he not known that it could be advanced or neglected by us. . . . But that they should not think that they did not need divine aid he adds: "For it is God who worketh in you both to will and accomplish His good pleasure" [Phil. 2 : 13]. The mercy of the Lord, therefore, goes before the will of man, for it is said, "My God will prevent me with His mercy" [Psalm 59 : 10], and again, that He may put our desire to the test, our will goes before God who waits, and for our good delays.

(*b*) Vincent of Lerins, *Commonitorium*, chs. 2, 23, 26. (MSL, 50 : 659.)

---

[1] Hermas, *Pastor*, Man. VI. (ANF, vol. II.)

The rule of Catholic verity.

Vincent of Lerins wrote his *Commonitorium* in 434, three years after the death of Augustine, who had been commended in 432 to the clergy of Gaul by Celestine of Rome [*Ep.* 21; Denziger, nn. 128–142; Mansi IV, 454 *ff.*]. Vincent attacked Augustine in his *Commonitorium*, not openly, but, so far as the work has been preserved, covertly, under the pseudonym of Peregrinus. The work consists of two books, of which the second is lost with the exception of what appear to be some concluding chapters, or a summary taking the place of the book. In the first book he lays down the general principle as to the tests of Catholic truth. In doing so he is careful to point out several cases of very great teachers, renowned for learning, ability, and influence, who, nevertheless, erred against the test of Catholic truth, and brought forward opinions which, on account of their novelty, were false. It is a working out in detail of the principles of the idea of Tertullian in his *De Præscriptione* [*v. supra*, § 27]. The Augustinian doctrines of predestination and grace could not stand the test of the appeal to antiquity. After laying down his test of truth it appears to have been the author's intention to prove thereby the doctrine of Augustine false. The so-called "Vincentian rule" is often quoted without a thought that it was intended, primarily, as an attack upon Augustine. The *Commonitorium* may be found translated in PNF, ser. II, vol. XI.

Ch. 2 [4]. I have often inquired earnestly and attentively of very many men eminent for sanctity and learning, how and by what sure and, so to speak, universal rule I might be able to distinguish the truth of the Catholic faith from the falsehood of heretical pravity, and I have always, and from nearly all, received an answer to this effect: That whether I or any one else should wish to detect the frauds of heretics as they arise, or to avoid their snares, and to continue sound and complete in the faith, we must, the Lord helping, fortify our faith in two ways: first, by the authority of the divine Law, and then, by the tradition of the Catholic Church.

But here some one, perhaps, will ask: Since the canon of Scripture is complete and sufficient for everything, and more than sufficient, what need is there to add to it the authority of the Church's interpretation? For this reason: because, owing to the depth of Holy Scripture, all do not accept it in one and the same sense, but one understands its words one way, another in another way; so that almost as many opinions may be drawn from it as there are men. . . . Therefore it is very necessary, on account of so great intricacies, and of such various errors, that the rule of a right understanding of the prophets and Apostles should be framed in accordance with the standard of ecclesiastical and Catholic interpretation.

Moreover, in the Catholic Church itself all possible care should be taken that we hold that faith which has been believed everywhere, always, and by all. For that is truly and properly "Catholic" which, as the name implies and the reason of the thing declares, comprehends all universally. This will be the case if we follow universality, antiquity, and consent. We shall follow universality in this way, if we confess that one faith to be true which the whole Church throughout the world confesses; antiquity, if we in nowise depart from those interpretations which it is manifest were notoriously held by our holy ancestors and fathers; consent in like manner, if in antiquity itself we adhere to the consentient definitions and determinations of all, or at least almost all, priests and doctors.

Ch. 23 [59]. The Church of Christ, the careful and watchful guardian of the doctrines deposited in her charge, never changes anything in them, never diminishes, never adds; does not cut off what is necessary, does not add what is superfluous, does not lose her own, does not appropriate what is another's, but, while dealing faithfully and judiciously with ancient doctrine, keeps this one object carefully in view—if there be anything which antiquity has left shapeless and rudimentary, to fashion and to polish it; if anything already reduced to shape and developed, to consolidate and strengthen it; if any already ratified and defined, to keep and guard it. Finally, what other objects have councils ever aimed at in their decrees, than to provide that what was before believed in simplicity, should in the future be believed intelligently; that what was before preached coldly, should in the future be

preached earnestly; that what before was practised negligent-
ly, should henceforth be practised with double solicitude?

Passage referring especially to Augustine.

Ch. 26 [69]. But what do they say? "If thou be the Son
of God, cast thyself down"; that is, "If thou wouldest be
a son of God, and wouldest receive the inheritance of the Kingdom of Heaven, cast thyself down; that is, cast thyself down
from the doctrine and tradition of that sublime Church, which
is imagined to be nothing less than the very temple of God."
And if one should ask one of the heretics who gives this advice:
How do you prove it? What ground have you for saying
that I ought to cast away the universal and ancient faith of
the Catholic Church? he has only the answer ready: "For it
is written"; and forthwith he produces a thousand testimonies, a thousand examples, a thousand authorities from the
Law, from the Psalms, from the Apostles, from the prophets,
by means of which, interpreted on a new and wrong principle,
the unhappy soul is precipitated from the height of Catholic
truth to the lowest abyss of heresy. Then with the accompanying promises, the heretics are wont marvellously to be-
guile the incautious. For they dare to teach and promise
that in their church, that is, in the conventicle of their communion, there is a certain great and special and altogether
personal grace of God, so that whosoever pertain to their
number, without any labor, without any effort, without any
industry, even though they neither ask, nor seek, nor knock,[1]
have such a dispensation from God, that borne up of angel
hands, that is, preserved by the protection of angels, it is impossible they should ever dash their feet against a stone, that
is, that they should ever be offended.

(c) Council of Orange, A. D. 529, *Canons*. Bruns II, 176.
Cf. Denziger, n. 174.

[1] The references are to Augustine, *De Dono Perseverantiæ*, ch. 23 [64], and
to Prosper of Aquitaine's epistle to Augustine, see Augustine, *Ep.* 225. Citations
from both in PNF, ser. II, vol. XI, p. 158.

The end of the Semi-Pelagian controversy.

The Council of Orange, A. D. 529, was made up of several bishops and some lay notables who had gathered for the dedication of a church at Orange. Cæsarius of Arles had received from Felix IV of Rome eight statements against the Semi-Pelagian teaching. He added some more of his own to them, and had them passed as canons by the company gathered for the dedication. It is noteworthy that the lay notables signed along with the bishops. Boniface II, to whom the canons were sent, confirmed them in 532: "We approve your above written confession as agreeable to the Catholic rule of the Fathers." Cf. Hefele, § 242. For the sources of the canons, see Seeberg, *History of Doctrines*, Eng. trans., I, 380, note 3. For the sake of brevity the scriptural quotations are not given, merely indicated by references to the Bible.

Canon 1. Whoever says that by the offence of the disobedience of Adam not the entire man, that is, in body and soul, was changed for the worse, but that the freedom of his soul remained uninjured, and his body only was subject to corruption, has been deceived by the error of Pelagius and opposes Scripture [Ezek. 18:20; Rom. 6:16; II Peter 2:19].

Canon 2. Whoever asserts that the transgression of Adam injured himself only, and not his offspring, or that death only of the body, which is the penalty of sin, but not also sin, which is the death of the soul, passed by one man to the entire human race, wrongs God and contradicts the Apostle [Rom. 5:12].

Canon 3. Whoever says that the grace of God can be bestowed in reply to human petition, but not that the grace brings it about so that it is asked for by us, contradicts Isaiah the prophet and the Apostle [Is. 65:1; Rom. 10:20].

Canon 4. Whoever contends that our will, to be set free from sin, may anticipate God's action, and shall not confess that it is brought about by the infusion of the Holy Spirit and his operation in us, that we wish to be set free, resists that same Holy Spirit speaking through Solomon: " The will is prepared by the Lord" [Proverbs 8:35, *cf.* LXX; not so in Vulgate or Heb.], and the Apostle [Phil. 2:13].

Canon 5. Whoever says the increase, as also the beginning of faith and the desire of believing, by which we believe in

Him who justifies the impious, and we come to the birth of
holy baptism, is not by the free gift of grace, that is, by the
inspiration of the Holy Spirit turning our will from unbelief
to belief, from impiety to piety, but belongs naturally to us,
is declared an adversary of the apostolic preaching [Phil.
1 : 6; Ephes. 2 : 8]. For they say that faith by which we
believe in God is natural, and they declare that all those who
are strangers to the Church of Christ in some way are believing.

Canon 6. Whoever says that to us who, without the grace
of God, believe, will, desire, attempt, struggle for, watch,
strive for, demand, ask, knock, mercy is divinely bestowed,
and does not rather confess that it is brought about by the
infusion and inspiration of the Holy Spirit in us that believe,
will, and do all these other things as we ought, and annexes
the help of grace to human humility and obedience, and does
not admit that it is the gift of that same grace that we are
obedient and humble, opposes the Apostle [I Cor. 4 : 7].

Canon 7. Whoever asserts that by the force of nature we
can rightly think or choose anything good, which pertains to
eternal life, or be saved, that is, assent to the evangelical
preaching, without the illumination of the Holy Spirit, who
gives to all grace to assent to and believe the truth, is deceived by an heretical spirit, not understanding the voice of
the Lord [John 15 : 5], and of the Apostle [II Cor. 3 : 5].

Canon 8. Whoever asserts that some by mercy, others by
free will, which in all who have been born since the transgression of the first man is evidently corrupt, are able to come
to the grace of baptism, is proved an alien from the faith.
For he asserts that the free will of all has not been weakened
by the sin of the first man, or he evidently thinks that it has
been so injured that some, however, are able without the
revelation of God to attain, by their own power, to the
mystery of eternal salvation. Because the Lord himself
shows how false this is, who declares that not some, but no
one was able to come to Him unless the Father drew him

[John 6 : 4], and said so to Peter [Matt. 16 : 17] and the Apostle [I Cor. 12 : 3].

The canons that follow are less important. The whole concludes with a brief statement regarding the points at issue, as follows:

And so according to the above sentences of the Holy Scriptures and definitions of ancient Fathers, by God's aid, we believe that we ought to believe and preach:

That by the sin of the first man, free will was so turned aside and weakened that afterward no one is able to love God as he ought, or believe in God, or do anything for God, which is good, except the grace of divine mercy comes first to him [Phil. 1 : 6, 29; Ephes. 2 : 8; I Cor. 4 : 7, 7 : 25; James 1 : 17; John 3 : 27]. . . .

We also believe this to be according to the Catholic faith, that grace having been received in baptism, all who have been baptized, can and ought, by the aid and support of Christ, to perform those things which belong to the salvation of the soul, if they labor faithfully.

But not only do we not believe that some have been predestinated to evil by the divine power, but also, if there are any who wish to believe so evil a thing, we say to them, with all detestation, anathema.

Also this we profitably confess and believe, that in every good we do not begin and afterward are assisted by the mercy of God, but without any good desert preceding, He first inspires in us faith and love in Him, so that we both faithfully seek the sacrament of baptism, and after baptism with His help are able to perform those things which are pleasing to Him. Whence it is most certainly to be believed that in the case of that thief, whom the Lord called to the fatherland of paradise, and Cornelius the Centurion, to whom an angel of the Lord was sent, and Zacchæus, who was worthy of receiving the Lord himself, their so wonderful faith was not of nature, but was the gift of the divine bounty.

And because we desire and wish our definition of the ancient

Fathers, written above, to be a medicine not only for the clergy but also for the laity, it has been decided that the illustrious and noble men, who have assembled with us at the aforesaid festival, shall subscribe it with their own hand.

§ 86. The Roman Church as the Centre of the Catholic Roman Element of the West

In the confusion of the fifth century, when the provinces of the Roman Empire were being lopped off one by one, Italy invaded, and the larger political institutions disappearing, the Church was the one institution that maintained itself. In not a few places among the barbarians the bishops became the acknowledged heads of the Roman element of the communities. In meeting the threatened invasion of Italy by Attila, Leo was the representative of the Roman people, the head of the embassy sent to induce the Hun to recross the Danube. Under such circumstances the see of Rome constantly gained in importance politically and ecclesiastically. As a centre of unity it was far more powerful than a feeble emperor at Ravenna or puppets set up by barbarians. It was the one and only great link between the provinces and the representative of the ancient order. It represented Rome, an efficient and generally gratefully recognized authority. In the development of the papal idea the first stadium was completed with the pontificate of Leo the Great (440–461), who, fully conscious of the inherited Petrine prerogatives, expressed them the most clearly, persistently, and, on the whole, most successfully of any pontiff before Gregory the Great. Leo, therefore, stands at the end of a development marked by the utterances of Victor, Cornelius, Siricius, Innocent I, Zosimus, Boniface I, and Celestine. For their statements of the authority of the Roman see, see Denziger, under their names, also Kirch and Mirbt. The whole may be found combined in one statement in Schwanne, *Dogmengeschichte*, I, 413 *f.;* II, 661–698.

Additional source material: In English there is comparatively little except the writings of Leo, see especially *Sermones* 2, 82, 84; *Epistulæ* 4, 6, 10, 12, 13, 14, 17, 105, 167; Jerome, *Ep.* 146, *ad Evangelum*. Kirch, Mirbt, and Denziger give many references to original texts and citations.

(*a*) Leo the Great, *Sermo* 3. (MSL, 55 : 145 *f*.)

On the prerogatives of Peter and his see.

Ch. 2. . . . . From His overruling and eternal providence we have received also the support of the Apostle's aid, which assuredly does not cease from its operation; and the strength of the foundation, on which the whole lofty building of the Church is reared, is not weakened by the weight of the temple that rests upon it. For the solidity of that faith which was praised in the chief of the Apostles is perpetual; and, as that remains which Peter believed in Christ, so that remains which Christ instituted in Peter. For when, as has been read in the Gospel lesson [*i. e.*, for the day], the Lord has asked the disciples whom they believed Him to be, amid the various opinions that were held, the blessed Peter replied, saying: "Thou art the Christ," etc. [Matt. 16 : 16-19].

Ch. 3. The dispensation of the truth therefore abides, and the blessed Peter, persevering in the strength of the rock which he has received, has not abandoned the helm of the Church which he undertook. For he was ordained before the rest in such a way that since he is called the rock, since he is pronounced the foundation, since he is constituted the doorkeeper of the kingdom of heaven, since he is set up as the judge to bind and to loose, whose judgments shall retain their validity in heaven, from all these mystical titles we might know the nature of his association with Christ. And still to-day he more fully and effectually performs what is intrusted to him, and carries out every part of his duty and charge in Him and with Him, through whom he has been glorified. And so if anything is rightly done or rightly decreed by us, if anything is obtained from the mercy of God by daily supplications, it is his work and merits whose power lives in his see and whose authority excels. For this, dearly beloved, that confession gained, that confession which, inspired in the Apostle's heart by God the Father, transcends all the uncertainty of human opinions, and was endued with the firmness of a rock, which no assaults could shake. For throughout the Church Peter daily says, "Thou art the Christ, the Son of the living God," and every tongue which confesses the Lord is inspired by the instruction [*magisterio*] of that voice.

(*b*) Leo the Great, *Ep.* 104, *ad Marcianum Augustum*, A. D. 452. (MSL, 54 : 993.)

Condemnation of the twenty-eighth canon of Chalcedon.

This and the two following epistles upon the twenty-eighth canon of the Council of Chalcedon define the relation of the Roman see to councils, canons, and patriarchal sees.   Apostolic sees may not be constituted by mere canon; political importance of a place does not regulate its ecclesiastical position; the see of Rome can reject the canons of councils even though general; apostolic sees connected with Peter may not have their authority diminished.   For the twenty-eighth canon of Chalcedon, *v. infra*, § 90, *d*.

Ch. 3. Let the city of Constantinople have, as we desire, its glory, and may it, under the protection of God's right hand, long enjoy the rule of your clemency. Yet the basis of things secular is one, and the basis of things divine another; and there can be no sure building save on that rock which the Lord laid as a foundation.   He that covets what is not his due, loses what is his own.   Let it be enough for the aforesaid [Anatolius, bishop of Constantinople] that by the aid of your piety and by my favorable assent he has obtained the bishopric of so great a city.   Let him not disdain a royal city, which he cannot make an apostolic see; and let him on no account hope to be able to rise by injury to others.   For the privileges of the churches, determined by the canons of the holy Fathers, and fixed by the decrees of the Nicene synod, cannot be overthrown by an unscrupulous act, nor disturbed by an innovation.   And in the faithful execution of this task by the aid of Christ, it is necessary that I show an unflinching devotion;

for it is a charge intrusted to me, and it tends to condemnation if the rules sanctioned by the Fathers and laid down under the guidance of God's spirit at the synod of Nicæa for the government of the whole Church are violated with my connivance (which God forbid) and if the wishes of a single brother have more weight with me than the common word of the Lord's whole house.

(c) Leo the Great, *Ep.* 105, *ad Pulcheriam Augustam* A. D. 452. (MSL, 54 : 997.)

Condemnation of all canons contravening those of Nicæa.

§ 3. Let him [Anatolius] know to what sort of man he has succeeded, and, expelling all the spirit of pride, let him imitate the faith of Flavian, his modesty and his humility, which raised him up even to a confessor's glory. If he will shine with his virtues, he will be praiseworthy and everywhere he will win an abundance of love, not by seeking human things, but divine favor. And by this careful course I promise that my heart will also be bound to him, and the love of this apostolic see which we have ever bestowed upon the church of Constantinople shall never be violated by any change. Because, if rulers, lacking self-restraint, fall into errors, yet the purity of the churches of Christ continues. As for the assents of bishops which are in contradiction with the regulations of the holy canons composed at Nicæa, in conjunction with your faithful race we do not recognize them, and by the authority of the blessed Apostle Peter we absolutely disannul in comprehensive terms in all cases ecclesiastical, following those laws which the Holy Ghost set forth by three hundred and eighteen bishops for the pacific observance of all priests, so that, even if a much greater number were to pass a different decree from theirs, whatever was opposed to their constitution would have to be held in no respect.

(d) Leo the Great, *Ep.* 106, *ad Anatolium* A. D. 452. (MSL, 54 : 1005.)

The relation of the apostolic sees to Peter.

Your purpose is in no way whatever supported by the written assent of certain bishops, given, as you allege, sixty years ago,[1] and never brought to the knowledge of the Apostolic See by your predecessors; under this project[2] which from its outset was tottering and has already collapsed, you now wish to place too late and useless props. . . . The rights of provincial primates may not be overthrown, nor metropolitan bishops be defrauded of privileges based on antiquity. The see of Alexandria may not lose any of that dignity which it merited through St. Mark, the evangelist and disciple of the blessed Peter, nor may the splendor of so great a church be obscured by another's clouds, when Dioscurus fell through his persistence in impiety. The church of Antioch, too, in which first, at the preaching of the blessed Apostle Peter, the Christian name arose, must continue in the position assigned to it by the Fathers, and, being set in the third place [Can. 6, Nicæa, 325, v. supra, § 72], must never be lowered therefrom. For the see is one thing, and those who preside in it something different; and an individual's great honor is his own integrity.

(e) Leo the Great, *Ep.* 6, *ad Anastasium* A. D. 444. (MSL, 54 : 616.) *Cf.* Kirch, nn. 814 *ff.*

The policy of centralization. The primates are representatives of the bishop of Rome. Anastasius was bishop of Thessalonica.

Ch. 2. Inasmuch, dear brother, as your request has been made known to us through our son Nicholas, the priest, that you also, like your predecessors, might receive from us in your turn authority over Illyricum for the observance of the rules, we give our consent, and earnestly exhort that no concealment and no negligence may be allowed in the management of the churches situated throughout Illyricum, which we commit to

---

[1] Reference to the Council of Constantinople, 381, known as the Second General Council, but not yet acknowledged as such; see above, § 71.

[2] The elevation of the see at Constantinople to supremacy in the East.

you in our stead, following the precedent of Siricius, of blessed memory, who then, for the first time acting on a fixed method, intrusted them to your last predecessor but one, Anysius, of holy memory, who had at the time well deserved of the Apostolic See, and was approved by after events, that he might render assistance to the churches situated in that province, whom he wished to keep up to the discipline. . . .

Ch. 5. Those of the brethren who have been summoned to a synod should attend, and not deny themselves to the holy congregation. . . . But if any more important question spring up, such as cannot be settled there under your presidency, brother, send your report and consult us, so that we may write back under the revelation of the Lord, of whose mercy it is that we can do aught, because He has breathed favorably upon us; that by our decision we may vindicate our right of cognizance in accordance with old-established tradition, and the respect which is due the Apostolic See; for as we wish you to exercise your authority in our stead, so we reserve to ourselves points which cannot be decided on the spot and persons who have appealed to us.[1]

CHAPTER III. THE CHURCH IN THE EASTERN EMPIRE

At the beginning of the permanent division of the Empire, the church life of the East was disturbed by a series of closely connected disputes known as the First Origenistic Controversy (§ 87), in which were comprised a conflict between a rationalistic tendency, connected with the religious philosophy of Origen, and a traditionalism that eschewed speculation, a bitter rivalry between the great sees of Alexandria, the relig-

[1] *Cf. Ep.* 14, *ad Anastasium,* written somewhat later: "From which model [the difference in the rank and order of the Apostles] has arisen a distinction between bishops also, and by an important ordinance it has been provided that every one should not claim everything for himself; but that there should be in each province one whose opinion should have priority among the brethren; and again, that certain whose appointment is in the greater cities should undertake fuller responsibility, through whom the care of the universal Church should converge toward Peter's one seat, and nothing anywhere should be separated from its head."

ious and intellectual capital of the East, and Constantinople, the church of the new imperial city, and personal disputes. But more serious controversies were already beginning. While the Church of the West was laying the foundations of the papal system, the Church of the East was falling more and more under the dominance of the secular authority; while the West was developing its anthropology, with its doctrines of Original Sin, Grace, and Election, the East was entering upon the long discussion of the topic which had been left by the Arian controversy—granted that the incarnate Son of God is truly eternal God, in what way are the divine and human natures related to the one personality of the incarnate God (§ 88)?   The controversies that arose over this topic involved the entire Church of the East, and found in the general councils of Ephesus, A. D. 431 (§ 89), and Chalcedon, A. D. 451 (§ 90), partial solutions.   In the case of each council, permament schisms resulted, and large portions of the Church of the East broke away from the previous unity (§ 91,); and on account of the intimate connection between the affairs of the Church and the secular policy of the Empire, a schism was caused between the see of Rome and the churches in communion with the see of Constantinople.

§ 87.   The First Origenistic Controversy and the Victory of Traditionalism.

§ 88.   The Christological Problem and the Theological Tendencies.

§ 89.   The Nestorian Controversy and the Council of Ephesus, 431.

§ 90.   The Eutychian Controversy and the Council of Chalcedon, 451.

§ 91.   The Results of Chalcedon and the Rise of Schism from the Monophysite Controversy.

§ 92.   The Church of Italy under the Ostrogoths and during the first Schism between Rome and the Eastern Church.

§ 87. The First Origenistic Controversy and the Triumph of Traditionalism

In the East the leading theologians of the fourth century were educated under the influence of Origenism; among these were Basil of Cæsarea, Gregory of Nyssa, and Gregory of Nazianzus. In the West the feeling regarding Origen was not so favorable, but the Western theologians, Jerome and Rufinus, who were then living in Palestine, shared in the general admiration of Origen. But a series of brief controversies broke out in which the standing of Origen as an orthodox theologian was seriously attacked, as well as the whole tendency for which he stood. The result was a wide-spread condemnation of the spiritualizing teaching of the great Alexandrian, and the rise of what might be called an anthropomorphic traditionalism. The first of the three controversies took place in Palestine, 395–399, and was occasioned by Epiphanius of Salamis, a zealous opponent of heresy. He denounced Origen and induced Jerome to abandon Origen; and Rufinus was soon in bitter enmity with Jerome. The second controversy took place in Egypt about the same time, when a group of monks in the Scetic desert, who were violently opposed to Origenism, compelled Theophilus, bishop of Alexandria and an admirer of Origen, to abandon that theologian and to side with them against the monks of the Nitrian desert, who were Origenists, and to condemn Origen at a council at Alexandria, 399. The third controversy involved John Chrysostom, bishop of Constantinople, who had protected four Nitrian monks who had fled to his protection. Theophilus seized the opportunity and, with the assistance for a time of Epiphanius, ultimately brought about the downfall of Chrysostom, who died deposed and in exile, 404. No controversies of the ancient Church are less attractive than the Origenistic, in which so much personal rancor, selfish ambition, mean intrigue, and so little profound thought were involved. The literature, therefore, is scanty.

Additional source material: Jerome, *Ep.* 86–99 (PNF); Rufinus and
Jerome, controversial writings bearing on Origenism in PNF, ser.
II, vol. III, pp. 417–541; Socrates, *Hist. Ec.*, VI, 2–21; Sozomen, *Hist.
Ec.*, VIII, 2–28.

(a) Basil, *De Spiritu Sancto*, 27.   (MSG, 32 : 187.)

The force of unwritten tradition.
The following is the most important and authoritative statement of
the force of unwritten tradition in the Eastern Church.   It is referred
to by John of Damascus in his defence of images (*De Fide Orthod.*, IV,
16), *cf.* § 109.   It is placed in the present section as illustrating the
principle of traditionalism which, in a fanatical form, brought about
the Origenistic controversies.

Of the beliefs and public teachings preserved in the Church,
some we have from written tradition, others we have received as delivered to us "in a mystery" by the tradition of
the Apostles; and both of these have in relation to true piety
the same binding force.   And these no one will gainsay, at
least no one who is versed even moderately in the institutions
of the Church.   For were we to reject such customs as are
unwritten as having no great force, we should unintentionally
injure the gospels in their very vitals; or, rather, reduce our
public definition to a mere name and nothing more.   For
example, to take the first and most general instance, who is
there who has taught us in writing to sign with the cross those
who have trusted in the name of our Lord Jesus Christ?
What writing has taught us to turn to the East in our prayers?
Which of the saints has left us in writing the words at the
invocation and at the displaying of the bread in the eucharist and the cup of blessing?   For we are not, as is well known,
content with what the Apostle or the Gospel has recorded;
but, both before and after, we say other words as having great
importance for the mystery, and these we derive from unwritten teaching.   Moreover, we bless the water of baptism
and the oil of chrism, and, besides this, him who is baptized.
From what writings?   Is it not from the silent and mystical
tradition?   What written word teaches the anointing of oil
itself?   And whence is it that a man is baptized three times?

And as to other customs of baptism, from what Scripture comes the renunciation of Satan and his angels? Does not this come from the unpublished and secret teaching which our fathers guarded in silence, averse from curious meddling and inquisitive investigation, having learned the lesson that the reverence of the mysteries is best preserved in silence? How was it proper to parade in public the teaching of those things which it was not permitted the uninitiated to look at?

(b) Jerome, *Preface to the Vulgate Translation of the New Testament.* (MSL, 29 : 557.)

Jerome's free critical attitude in his work in his earlier life.
This preface is addressed to Bishop Damasus of Rome and is dated 383.

You urge me to make a new work out of an old and, as it were, to sit in judgment on the copies of the Scriptures already scattered throughout the whole world; and, inasmuch as they differ among themselves, I am to decide which of them agree with the Greek original. A pious labor, but a perilous presumption; to judge others, myself to be judged of all; to change the language of the aged, and to carry back the world already grown gray, back to the beginnings of its infancy! Is there a man, learned or unlearned, who will not, when he takes the volume into his hands and perceives that what he reads differs from the flavor which once he tasted, break out immediately into violent language and call me a forger and a profane person for having the audacity to add anything to the ancient books or to change or correct anything? I am consoled in two ways in bearing this odium: in the first place, that you, the supreme bishop, command it to be done; and secondly, even on the testimony of those reviling us, what varies cannot be true. For if we put faith in the Latin texts, let them tell us which; for there are almost as many texts as copies. But if the truth is to be sought from many, why should we not go back to the orignal Greek and correct the mistakes introduced by inaccurate translators, and the blundering alterations of confident and ignorant men, and further, all that has been added or altered by sleepy copyists? I am not discussing the Old Testament, which was turned into Greek by the Seventy Elders, and has reached us by a descent of three steps. I do not ask what Aquila and Symmachus think, or why Theodotion takes a middle course between the ancients and the moderns. I am willing to let that be a true translation which had apostolic approval [*i. e.*, the LXX]. I am now speaking of the New Testament. This was undoubtedly composed in Greek, with the exception of the work of the Apostle Matthew, who first published the gospel of Christ in Judea and in Hebrew. This [*i. e.*, the New Testament], as it is in our language, is certainly marked by discrepancies, and the stream flows in different channels; it must be sought in one fountainhead. I pass over those manuscripts bearing the names of Lucian and Hesychius, which a few contentious persons perversely support. It was not permitted these writers to amend anything in the Old Testament after the labor of the Seventy; and it was useless to make corrections in the New, for translations of the Scriptures already made in the language of many nations show that they are additions and false. Therefore this short preface promises only the four gospels, of which the order is Matthew, Mark, Luke, and John, revised by a comparison of the Greek manuscripts and only of the ancient manuscripts. And that they might not depart far from the Latin customarily read, I have used my pen with some restraint, so that having corrected only the passages which seemed to change the meaning, I have allowed the rest to remain as it was.

(*c*) Jerome, *Ep.* 7, *ad Pammachium.*   (MSL, 23 : 376.)

The principal errors of Origen according to Jerome.

This is the most important work of Jerome in the controversy known as the Origenistic controversy. Jerome attacks in this work John, bishop of Jerusalem, and writes as a result of the work of Epiphanius in Palestine three years before. The following were addressed to John to reject, as a test of that bishop's orthodoxy. See above, § 43.

First, in the book περὶ ἀρχῶν it is said [I, 1 : 8]: "For as it is unfitting to say that the Son can see the Father, so it is not meet to think that the Holy Spirit can see the Son."

Secondly, that souls are bound in this body as in a prison; and that before man was made in paradise they dwelt among rational creatures in the heavens. Wherefore, afterward, to console itself, the soul says in the Psalms, "Before I was humbled I went wrong," and "Return, my soul, unto thy rest," and "Lead my soul out of prison," and similarly elsewhere.

Thirdly, that he says that both the devil and the demons will some time or other repent and ultimately reign with the saints.

Fourthly, that he interprets the coats of skins, with which Adam and Eve were clothed after their fall and ejection from paradise, to be human bodies, and no doubt they were previously in paradise without flesh, sinews, or bones.

Fifthly, he most openly denies the resurrection of the flesh, the bodily structure, and the distinction of sexes by which we men are distinguished from women, both in his explanation of the first psalm and in many other treatises.

Sixthly, he so allegorizes paradise as to destroy the truth of history, understanding angels instead of trees, heavenly virtues instead of rivers; and he overthrows all that is contained in the history of paradise by his tropological interpretation.

Seventhly, he thinks that the waters which in the Scriptures are said to be above the heavens are holy and supernal powers; while those which are upon the earth and beneath the earth are, on the contrary, demoniacal powers.

Eighthly, that the image and likeness of God, in which man was created, was lost and was no longer in man after he was expelled from paradise.

(d) Anastasius, *Ep. ad Simplicianum*, in Jerome, *Ep.* 95. (MSL, 22 : 772.)

Condemnation of Origen by Anastasius, bishop of Rome, A. D. 400.

To his lord and brother, Simplicianus, Anastasius.

It is felt right that a shepherd have great care and watchfulness over his flock.   In like manner, also, the careful watchman from his lofty tower keeps a lookout day and night on behalf of the city.   In the hour of tempest and peril the prudent shipmaster suffers great distress of mind lest by the tempest and the violent waves his vessel be dashed upon the rocks.   With similar feelings that reverend and honorable man Theophilus, our brother and fellow-bishop, ceases not to watch over the things which make for salvation, that God's people in the different churches may not by reading Origen run into awful blasphemies.

Having been informed, then, by the letter of the aforesaid, we inform your holiness that just as we are set in the city of Rome, in which the prince of the Apostles, the glorious Peter, founded the Church and then by his faith strengthened it; to the end that no man contrary to the commandment read these books which we have mentioned and the same we have condemned; and with earnest prayers we have urged that the precepts of the Evangelists which God and Christ have inspired the Evangelists to teach ought not to be forsaken; but that is to be remembered which the venerable Apostle Paul preached by way of warning: "If any one preach a gospel unto you other than that which was preached unto you, let him be anathema" [Gal. 1:8]. Holding fast, therefore, this precept, we have intimated that everything written in days past by Origen that is contrary to our faith is even by us rejected and condemned.

We have written these things to your holiness by the hand of the presbyter Eusebius, who, being a man filled with a glowing faith and having the love of the Lord, has shown me some blasphemous chapters at which we shuddered and which we condemned, but if any other things have been put forth by Origen, you should know that with their author they are alike condemned by me.   The Lord have you in safe-keeping, my lord and brother deservedly held in honor.

(e) Rufinus, *Preface to Translation of Origen's "De Principiis."* (MSL, 22 : 733 and also MSG, 11 : 111.)

In this preface Rufinus refers, without mentioning names, to Jerome. Inasmuch as it was perfectly clear to whom the allusion was made, as the translator and admirer of Origen, Jerome felt himself personally attacked and retorted furiously upon Rufinus.

I know that a great many of the brethren, incited by their desire for a knowledge of the Scriptures, have requested various men versed in Greek letters to make Origen a Roman and give him to Latin ears. Among these was our brother and associate [*i. e.*, Jerome], who was so requested by Bishop Damasus, when he translated the two homilies on the Song of Songs from Greek into Latin, prefixed to the work a preface so full of beauty and so magnificent that he awoke in every one the desire of reading Origen and of eagerly examining his works, and he said that to the soul of that man the words might well be applied, "The King has brought me into his chamber" [Cant. 2 : 4], and he declared that Origen in his other books surpassed all other men, but in this had surpassed himself. What he promised in his preface is, indeed, that he would give to Roman ears not only these books on the Song of Songs, but many others of Origen. But, as I perceive, he is so pleased with his own style that he pursues an object bringing him more glory, viz., to be the father of a book rather than a translator. I am therefore following out a task begun by him and commended by him. . . . In translation, I follow as far as possible the method of my predecessors, and especially of him whom I have already mentioned, who, after he had translated into Latin above seventy of the books of Origen, which he called Homilies, and also a certain number of the tomes written on the Apostle [the Epistles of St. Paul], since a number of offensive passages are to be found in the Greek, eliminated and purged, in his translation, all of them, so that the Latin reader will find nothing in these which jar on our faith. Him, therefore, we follow, not indeed with the power of his eloquence, but as far as we can in his rules and methods;

that is, taking care not to promulgate those things which in
the books of Origen are found to be discrepant and contradictory one to the other.   The cause of these variations I
have set forth fully in the apology which Pamphilus wrote
for the books of Origen, to which is appended a short treatise
showing how proofs which, as I judge, are quite clear in his
books have in many cases been falsified by heretical and evil-
disposed persons.

(f) Augustine, *Ep.* 73, Ch. 8.   (MSL, 33 : 249.)

The attempt of Augustine to bring about a reconciliation between
Rufinus and Jerome.   Jerome had written some affectionate words to
Augustine to which he alludes in the beginning of the following passage:

When, by these words, now not only yours but also mine,
I am gladdened and refreshed, and when I am comforted not
a little by the desire of both of us for mutual fellowship, which
has been suspended and is not satisfied, suddenly I am pierced
through by the darts of keenest sorrow when I consider that
between you [*i. e.*, Rufinus and Jerome] (to whom God granted
in fullest measure and for a long time that which both of us
have longed for, that in closest and most intimate fellowship
you tasted together the honey of Holy Scriptures) such a
blight of bitterness has broken out, when, where, and in whom
it was not to be feared, since it has befallen you at the very
time when, unencumbered, having cast away secular burdens, you were following the Lord, were living together in
that land in which the Lord walked with human feet, when
He said, "Peace I leave with you, My peace I give unto you";
being, moreover, men of mature age, whose life was devoted
to the study of the word of God.   Truly, "man's life on earth
is a period of trial" [Job 7 : 1].   Alas, that I cannot meet
you both together, perchance that in agitation, grief, and fear
I might cast myself at your feet, weep till I could weep no
more, and appeal as I love you, first to each of you for his
own sake, and then for the sake of those, especially the weak,
"for whom Christ died" [I Cor. 8 : 11], who to their great

peril look on you as on the stage of time, imploring you not
to scatter abroad, in writing, those things about each other
which when reconciled, you, who are now unwilling to be
reconciled, could not then destroy, and which when reconciled
you would not dare to read lest you should quarrel anew.

(g) Socrates, *Hist. Ec.*, VI, 15. (MSG, 67 : 708.)

The fall of Chrysostom.
Epiphanius had gone to Constantinople on the suggestion of Theophilus, and there, in his zeal, had violated the canons of ordination
as generally received. In this case he had ordained priests in the
diocese of Chrysostom and without his permission. Other troubles
had arisen. On being called to account for his conduct by Chrysostom,
Epiphanius hastily left the city, and died on the voyage back to his
diocese, Salamis, in Cyprus.

When Epiphanius had gone John was informed by some
person that the Empress Eudoxia had set Epiphanius
against him. Being of a fiery temperament and of ready
utterance, he soon after pronounced to the public an invective
against women in general. The people readily took this as
uttered indirectly against the Empress, and so the speech,
laid hold of by evil-disposed persons, was brought to the
knowledge of those in authority. At length the Empress,
having been informed of it, immediately complained to her
husband of the insult offered her, saying that the insult
offered her was an insult to him. He therefore gave orders
that Theophilus should speedily convoke a synod against John;
Severianus also co-operated in promoting this, for he still
retained his grudge [*i. e.*, against Chrysostom. See DCB,
art. "Severianus, bishop of Gabala."]. No great length of
time, accordingly, intervened before Theophilus arrived, having stirred up many bishops from different cities; but this,
also, the summons of the Emperor had commanded. Especially did they assemble who had one cause or another of complaint against John, and there were present besides those
whom John had deposed, for John had deposed many bishops
in Asia when he went to Ephesus for the ordination of Hera-

clides. Accordingly they all, by previous agreement, assembled at Chalcedon in Bithynia. . . . Now none of the clergy [*i. e.*, of Constantinople] would go forth to meet Theophilus or pay him the customary honors because he was openly known as John's enemy. But the Alexandrian sailors—for it happened that at that time the grain-transport ships were there—on meeting him, greeted him with joyful acclamations. He excused himself from entering the church, and took up his abode at one of the imperial mansions called "The Placidian." Then, in consequence of this, many accusations began to be poured forth against John, and no longer was there any mention of the books of Origen, but all were intent on pressing a variety of absurd accusations. When these preliminary matters were settled the bishops were convened in one of the suburbs of Chalcedon, which is called "The Oak," and immediately cited John to answer charges which were brought against him. . . . And since John, taking exception to those who cited him, on the ground that they were his enemies, demanded a general council, without delay they repeated their citation four times; and as he persisted in his refusal to answer, always giving the same reply, they condemned him, and deposed him without giving any other cause for his deposition than that he refused to obey when summoned. This, being announced toward evening, incited the people to a very great sedition, insomuch that they kept watch all night and would by no means suffer him to be removed from the church, but cried out that the charges against him ought to be determined by a larger assembly. A decree of the Emperor, however, commanded that he should be immediately expelled and sent into exile. When John knew this he voluntarily surrendered himself about noon, unknown to the populace, on the third day after his condemnation; for he dreaded any insurrectionary movement on his account, and he was accordingly led away.

(*h*) Theophilus of Alexandria, *Ep. ad Hieronymum*, in Jerome, *Ep.* 113. (MSL, 22 : 932.)

Theophilus on the fall of Chrysostom.

To the well-beloved and most loving brother Jerome, Theophilus sends greeting in the Lord.

At the outset the verdict of truth satisfies but few; but the Lord, speaking by the prophet, says, "My judgment goeth forth as the light," and they who are surrounded with a horror of darkness do not with clear mind perceive the nature of things, and they are covered with eternal shame and know by their outcome that their efforts have been in vain. Wherefore we also have always desired that John [Chrysostom], who for a time ruled the church of Constantinople, might please God, and we have been unwilling to accept as facts the cause of his ruin in which he behaved himself rashly. But not to speak of his other misdeed, he has by taking the Origenists into his confidences,[1] by advancing many of them to the priesthood, and by this crime saddening with no slight grief that man of God, Epiphanius, of blessed memory, who has shone throughout all the world a bright star among bishops, deserved to hear the words, "Babylon is fallen, is fallen."

§ 88. THE CHRISTOLOGICAL PROBLEM AND THE THEOLOGICAL TENDENCIES

The Arian controversy in bringing about the affirmation of the true deity of the Son, or Logos, left the Church with the problem of the unity of the divine and human natures in the personality of Jesus. It seemed to not a few that to combine perfect deity with perfect humanity would result in two personalities. Holding fast, therefore, to the reality of the human nature, a solution was attempted by Apollinarius, or Apollinaris, by making the divine Logos take the place of the human logos or reason. Mankind consisted of three parts: a body, an animal soul, and a rational spirit. The Logos was thus united to humanity by substituting the divine for

[1] This probably refers to "the four long brothers."

the human logos. But this did violence to the integrity of the human nature of Christ. This attempt on the part of Apollinaris was rejected at Constantinople, but also by the Church generally. The human natures must be complete if human nature was deified by the assumption of man in the incarnation. On this basis two tendencies showed themselves quite early: the human nature might be lost in the divinity, or the human and the divine natures might be kept distinct and parallel or in such a way that certain acts might be assigned to the divine and certain to the human nature. The former line of thought, adopted by the Cappadocians, tended toward the position assumed by Cyril of Alexandria and in a more extreme form by the Monophysites. The latter line of thought tended toward what was regarded as the position of Nestorius. In this position there was such a sharp cleavage between the divine and the human natures as apparently to create a double personality in the incarnate Son. This divergence of theological statement gave rise to the christological controversies which continued in various forms through several centuries in the East, and have reappeared in various disguises in the course of the Church's theological development.

Additional source material: There are several exegetical works of Cyril of Alexandria available in English, see Bardenhewer, § 77, also a German translation of three treatises bearing on christology in the Kempten *Bibliothek der Kirchenväter*, 1879. For the general point of view of the Cappadocians and the relation of the incarnation to redemption, see Gregory of Nyssa, *The Great Catechism* (PNF, ser. II, vol. V), *v. infra*, § 89 and references in Seeberg, § 23.

(a) Apollinaris, *Fragments*. Ed. H. Lietzmann.

His Christology.
The following fragments of the teaching of Apollinaris are from H. Lietzmann, *Apollinaris von Laodicea und seine Schule. Texte und Untersuchungen*, 1904. Many fragments are to be found in the *Dialogues* which Theodoret wrote against Eutychianism, which he traced to the teaching of Apollinaris. The first condemnation of Apollinaris was at Rome, 377, see Hefele, § 91; Theodoret, *Hist. Ec.*, V, 10, gives the letter of Damasus issued in the name of the synod.

P. 224 [81].   If God had been joined with a man, one complete being with another complete being, there would be two sons of God, one Son of God by nature, another through adoption.

P. 247 [150].   They who assume a twofold spirit in Christ pull a stone out with their finger.   For if each is independent and impelled by its own natural will, it is impossible that in one and the same subject the two can be together, who will what is opposed to each other; for each works what is willed by it according to its own proper and personal motives.

P. 248 [152].   They who speak of one Christ, and assert that there are two independent spiritual natures in Him, do not know Him as the Logos made flesh, who has remained in His natural unity, for they represent Him as divided into two unlike natures and modes of operation.

P. 239 [129].   If a man has soul and body, and both remain distinguished in unity, how much more has Christ, who joins His divine being with a body, both as a permanent possession without any commingling one with the other?

P. 209 [21, 22].   The Logos became flesh, but the flesh was not without a soul, for it is said that it strives against the spirit and opposes the law of the understanding.   [In this Apollinaris takes up the trichotomy of human nature, a view which he did not apparently hold at the beginning of his teaching.]

P. 240 [137].   John [John 2 : 19] spoke of the destroyed temple, that is, of the body of Him who would raise it up again.   The body is altogether one with Him.   But if the body of the Lord has become one with the Lord, then the characteristics of the body are proved to be characteristics of Him on account of the body.

(b) Apollinaris, *Letter to the Emperor Jovian*.   Lietzmann, 250 *ff.*

We confess the Son of God who was begotten eternally before all times, but in the last times was for our salvation

born of Mary according to the flesh; . . . and we confess that
the same is the Son of God and God according to the spirit,
Son of man according to the flesh; we do not speak of two
natures in the one Son, of which one is to be worshipped and
one is not to be worshipped, but of only one nature of the
Logos of God, which has become flesh and with His flesh is
worshipped with one worship; and we confess not two sons,
one who is truly God's Son to be worshipped and another the
man—who is of Mary and is not to be worshipped, who by the
power of grace had become the Son of God, as is also the case
with men, but one Son of God who at the same time was born
of Mary according to the flesh in the last days, as the angel
answered the Theotokos Mary who asked, "How shall this
be?"—"The Holy Ghost will come upon thee." He, accordingly, who was born of the Virgin Mary was Son of God by
nature and truly God . . . only according to the flesh from
Mary was He man, but at the same time, according to the
spirit, Son of God; and God has in His own flesh suffered our
sorrows.

(c) Gregory of Nazianzus, *Ep. I ad Cledonium*. (MSG,
37 : 181.)

In this epistle Gregory attacks Apollinaris, basing his argument on
the notion of salvation by incarnation, which formed the foundation
of the most characteristic piety of the East, had been used as a major
premise by Athanasius in opposition to Arianism, and runs back to
Irenæus and the Asia Minor school; see above, § 33.

If any one trusted in a man without a human mind, he is
himself really bereft of mind and quite unworthy of salvation. For what has not been assumed has not been healed;
but what has been united to God is saved. If only half of
Adam fell, then that which is assumed and saved may be half
also; but if the whole, it must be united to the whole of Him
that was begotten and be saved as a whole. Let them not,
then, begrudge us our complete salvation, or clothe the Saviour only with bones and nerves and the semblance of humanity. For if His manhood is without soul [ἄψυχος], even

the Arians admit this, that they may attribute His passion to the godhead, as that which gives motion to the body is also that which suffers. But if He had a soul and yet is without a mind, how is He a man, for man is not a mindless [ἄνουν] animal? And this would necessarily involve that His form was human, and also His tabernacle, but His soul was that of a horse, or an ox, or some other creature without mind. This, then, would be what is saved, and I have been deceived in the Truth, and have been boasting an honor when it was another who was honored. But if His manhood is intellectual and not without mind, let them cease to be thus really mindless.

But, says some one, the godhead was sufficient in place of the human intellect. What, then, is this to me? For godhead with flesh alone is not man, nor with soul alone, nor with both apart from mind, which is the most essential part of man. Keep, then, the whole man, and mingle godhead therewith, that you may benefit me in my completeness. But, as he asserts [i. e., Apollinaris], He could not contain two perfect natures. Not if you only regard Him in a bodily fashion. For a bushel measure will not hold two bushels, nor will the space of one body hold two or more bodies. But if you will look at what is mental and incorporeal, remember that I myself can contain soul and reason and mind and the Holy Spirit; and before me this world, by which I mean the system of things visible and invisible, contained Father, Son, and Holy Ghost. For such is the nature of intellectual existences that they can mingle with one another and with bodies, incorporeally and invisibly. . . .

Further, let us see what is their account of the assumption of the manhood, or the assumption of the flesh, as they call it. If it was in order that God, otherwise incomprehensible, might be comprehended, and might converse with men through His flesh as through a veil, their mask is a pretty one, a hypocritical fable; for it was open to Him to converse with us in many other ways, as in the burning bush [Ex. 3 : 2] and in the appearance of a man [Gen. 18 : 5]. But if it was that He might destroy the condemnation of sin by sanctifying like by like, then as He needed flesh for the sake of the condemned flesh and soul for the sake of the soul, so also He needed mind for the sake of mind, which not only fell in Adam but was first to be affected, as physicians say, of the illness. For that which received the commandment was that which failed to observe the commandment, and that which failed to observe the commandment was that also which dared to transgress, and that which transgressed was that which stood most in need of salvation, and that which needed salvation was that which also was assumed. Therefore mind was taken upon Him.

(*d*) Council of Constantinople, A. D. 382, *Epistula Synodica.* Hefele, § 98.

Condemnation of Apollinarianism.

At the Council of Constantinople held the year after that which is known as the Second General Council, and attended by nearly the same bishops, there was an express condemnation of Apollinaris and his doctrine, for though Apollinaris had been condemned in 381, the point of doctrine was not stated. The synodical letter of the council of 382 is preserved only in part in Theodoret, *Hist. Ec.*, V, 9, who concludes his account with these words:

Similarly they openly condemn the innovation of Apollinarius [so Theodoret writes the name] in the phrase, "And we preserve the doctrine of the incarnation of the Lord, holding the tradition that the dispensation of the flesh is neither soulless, nor mindless, nor imperfect."

(*e*) Theodore of Mopsuestia, *Creed.* Hahn, § 215.

The position of the Nestorians.

The following extracts are from the creed which was presented at the Council of Ephesus, 431, and was written by Theodore of Mopsuestia, the greatest theologian of the party which stood with Nestorius. Although it does not state the whole doctrine of Theodore, yet its historical position is so important that its characteristic passages belong in the present connection. Bibliographical and critical notes in Hahn, *loc. cit.*

Concerning the dispensation which the Lord God accomplished for our salvation in the dispensation according to the

Lord Christ, it is necessary for us to know that the Lord God the Logos assumed a complete man, who was of the seed of Abraham and David, according to the statement of the divine Scriptures, and was according to nature whatsoever they were of whose seed He was, a perfect man according to nature, consisting of reasonable soul and human flesh, and the man who was as to nature as we are, formed by the power of the Holy Spirit in the womb of the Virgin, born of a woman, born under the law, that he might redeem us all from the bondage of the law [Gal. 4 : 4] who receive the adoption of sonship which was long before ordained, that man He joined to himself in an ineffable manner. . . .

And we do not say that there are two Sons or two Lords, because there is one God [Son?] according to substance, God the Word, the only begotten Son of the Father, and He who has been joined with Him is a participator in His deity and shares in the name and honor of the Son; and the Lord according to essence is God the Word, with whom that which is joined shares in honor. And therefore we say neither two Sons nor two Lords, because one is He who has an inseparable conjunction with Himself of Him who according to essence is Lord and Son, who, having been assumed for our salvation, is with Him received as well in the name as in the honor of both Son and Lord, not as each one of us individually is a son of God (wherefore also we are called many sons of God, according to the blessed Paul), but He alone in an unique manner having this, namely, in that He was joined to God the Word, participating in the Sonship and dignity, takes away every thought of two Sons or two Lords, and offers indeed to us in conjunction with the God the Word, to have all faith in Him and all understanding and contemplation, on account of which things also He receives from every creature the worship and sacrifice of God. Therefore we say that there is one Lord, namely, the Lord Jesus Christ, by whom all things were made, understanding principally God the Word, who according to substance is Son of God and

Lord, equally regarding that which was assumed, Jesus of Nazareth, who God anointed with the Spirit and power, as in conjunction with God the Lord, and participating in sonship and dignity, who also is called the second Adam, according to the blessed Apostle Paul, as being of the same nature as Adam.

(*f*) Theodore of Mopsuestia, *Fragments*. Swete, *Theodori epis. Mops. in epistulas b. Pauli commentarii*, Cambridge, 1880, 1882.

In the appendix to the second volume of this work by Theodore there are many fragments of Theodore's principal dogmatic work, *On the Incarnation*, directed against Eunomius. The work as a whole has not been preserved. In the same appendix there are also other important fragments. The references are to this edition.

P. 299.   If we distinguish the two natures, we speak of one complete nature of God the Word and a complete person (πρόσωπον). But we name complete also the nature of the man and also the person. If we think on the conjunction (συνάφεια) then we speak of one person.

P. 312.   In the moment in which He [Jesus] was formed [in the womb of the Virgin] He received the destination of being a temple of God. For we should not believe that God was born of the Virgin unless we are willing to assume that one and the same is that which is born and what is in that which is born, the temple, and God the Logos in the temple. . . . If God had become flesh, how could He who was born be named God from God [*cf*. Nicene Creed], and of one being with the Father? for the flesh does not admit of such a designation.

P. 314.   The Logos was always in Jesus, also by His birth and when He was in the womb, at the first moment of his beginning; to His development He gave the rule and measure, and led Him from step to step to perfection.

P. 310.   If it is asked, did Mary bear a man, or is she the bearer of God [Theotokos], we can say that both statements are true. One is true according to the nature of the case;

the other only relatively. She bore a man according to nature, for He was a man who was in the womb of Mary. . . . She is Theotokos, since God was in the man who was born; not enclosed in Him according to nature, but was in Him according to the relation of His will.

(g) Nestorius, *Fragments*. Loofs, *Nestoriana*.

The fragments of Nestorius have been collected by Loofs, *Nestoriana*, Halle, 1905; to this work the references are made. It now appears that what was condemned as Nestorianism was a perversion of his teaching and that Nestorius was himself in harmony with the definition which was put forth at Chalcedon, a council which he survived and regarded as a vindication of his position after the wrong done him at Ephesus by Cyril; cf. Bethune-Baker, *Nestorius and His Teaching*, Cambridge, 1908.

P. 252. Is Paul a liar when he speaks of the godhead of Christ and says: "Without father, without mother, without genealogy"? My good friend, Mary has not born the godhead, for that which is born of the flesh is flesh. . . . A creature has not born the Creator, but she bore a man, the organ of divinity; the Holy Ghost did not create God the Word, but with that which was born of the Virgin He prepared for God the Word, a temple, in which He should dwell.

P. 177. Whenever the Holy Scriptures make mention of the works of salvation prepared by the Lord, they speak of the birth and suffering, not of the divinity but of the humanity of Christ; therefore, according to a more exact expression the holy Virgin is named the bearer of Christ [Christotokos].

P. 167. If any one will bring forward the designation, "Theotokos," because the humanity that was born was conjoined with the Word, not because of her who bore, so we say that, although the name is not appropriate to her who bore, for the actual mother must be of the same substance as her child, yet it can be endured in consideration of the fact that the temple, which is inseparably united with God the Word, comes of her.

P. 196. Each nature must retain its peculiar attributes,

and so we must, in regard to the union, wonderful and exalted far above all understanding, think of one honor and confess one Son. . . . With the one name Christ we designate at the same time two natures. . . . The essential characteristics in the nature of the divinity and in the humanity are from all eternity distinguished.

P. 275. God the Word is also named Christ because He has always conjunction with Christ. And it is impossible for God the Word to do anything without the humanity, for all is planned upon an intimate conjunction, not on the deification of the humanity.

(*h*) Gregory of Nyssa, *Contra Eunomium*, V, 5. (MSG, 45 : 705.)

The Christology of the Cappadocians.
The Cappadocians use language which was afterward condemned when given its extreme Alexandrian interpretation. Hefele, § 127, may be consulted with profit.

The flesh is not identical with the godhead before this is transformed into the godhead, so that necessarily some things are appropriate to God the Word, other things to the form of a servant. If, then, he [Eunomius] does not reproach himself with a duality of Words, on account of such confusion, why are we slanderously charged with dividing the faith into two Christs, we who say that He who was highly exalted after His passion, was made Lord and Christ by His union with Him who is verily Lord and Christ, knowing by what we have learned that the divine nature is always one and the same mode of existence, while the flesh in itself is that which reason and sense apprehend concerning it, but when mixed with the divine it no longer remains in its own limitations and properties, but is taken up to that which is overwhelming and transcendent. Our contemplation, however, of the respective properties of the flesh and of the godhead remains free from confusion, so long as each of these is considered in itself, as, for example, "The Word was before the ages, but

flesh came into being in the last times." . . . It is not the
human nature that raises up Lazarus, nor is it the power that
cannot suffer that weeps for him when he lies in the grave;
the tear proceeds from the man, the life from the true Life.
. . . So much as this is clear . . . that the blows belong to
the servant in whom the Lord was, the honors to the Lord,
whom the servant compassed about, so that by reason of
contact and the union of natures the proper attributes of each
belong to both, as the Lord receives the stripes of the servant,
while the servant is glorified with the honor of the Lord.

The godhead "empties" itself that it may come within the
capacity of the human nature, and the human nature is renewed by becoming divine through its commixture with the
divine. . . . As fire that lies in wood, hidden often below the
surface, and is unobserved by the senses of those who see or
even touch it, is manifest, however, when it blazes up, so
too, at His death (which He brought about at His will, who
separated His soul from His body, who said to His own Father
"Into Thy hands I commend My spirit" [Luke 23 : 46],
"who," as He says, "had power to lay it down and had
power to take it again"), He who, because He is the Lord of
glory, despised that which is shame among men, having concealed, as it were, the flame of His life in His bodily nature,
by the dispensation of His death, kindled and inflamed it
once more by the power of His own godhead, warming into
life that which had been made dead, having infused with the
infinity of His divine power those humble first-fruits of our
nature; made it also to be that which He himself was, the
servile form to be the Lord, and the man born of Mary to
be Christ, and Him, who was crucified through weakness, to
be life and power, and making all such things as are piously
conceived to be in God the Word to be also in that which the
Word assumed; so that these attributes no longer seem to be
in either nature, being, by commixture with the divine, made
anew in conformity with the nature that overwhelms it; par-
ticipates in the power of the godhead, as if one were to say

that a mixture makes a drop of vinegar mingled in the deep to be sea, for the reason that the natural quality of this liquid does not continue in the infinity of that which overwhelms it.

§ 89. THE NESTORIAN CONTROVERSY; THE COUNCIL OF EPHESUS A. D. 431.

The Council of Ephesus was called to settle the dispute which had arisen between Cyril and the Alexandrians and Nestorius, archbishop of Constantinople, and the Antiochians. Several councils had been held previously, and much acrimonious debate. Both parties desired a council to adjust the dispute. The Emperor Theodosius II, in an edict of November 19, 430, called a council to be held on the following Whitsunday at Ephesus. The council was opened by Cyril and Memnon, bishop of Ephesus, June 22, a few days after the date assigned. This opening of the synod was opposed by the imperial commissioner and the party of Nestorius, because many of the Antiochians had not yet arrived. Cyril and Memnon, who had undertaken to bring about the condemnation and deposition of Nestorius, forced through their programme. On June 26 or 27 the Antiochians arrived, and, under the presidency of John of Antioch, and with the approval of the imperial commissioner, they held a council attended by about fifty bishops, while two hundred attended the rival council under Cyril. This smaller council deposed Cyril and Memnon. Both synods appealed to the Emperor and were confirmed by him. But shortly after Cyril and Memnon were restored. The Antiochians now violently attacked the successful Alexandrians but, having abandoned Nestorius, patched up a union with the Alexandrians, by which Cyril subscribed in 433 to a creed drawn up by the Antiochians, probably by Theodoret of Cyrus. Accordingly, the council of Cyril was now recognized by the Antiochians, as well as by the imperial authority, and became known as the Council of Ephesus, A. D. 431.

Additional source material: Socrates, *Hist. Ec.*, VII, 29–34; Theodoret, *Epistulæ* in PNF, ser. II, vol. III, and his counter propositions to the Anathemas of Cyril, *ibid.*, pp. 27–31; Percival, *The Seven Ecumenical Councils* (PNF).

(a) Cyril of Alexandria, *Anathematisms*. Hahn, § 219.

Condemnation of the position of Nestorius.

Cyril held a council at Alexandria in 430, in which he set forth the teaching of Nestorius, as he understood it, in the form of anathemas against any who held the opinions which he set forth in order. Nestorius immediately replied by corresponding anathematisms. They may be found translated PNF, ser. II, vol. XIV, p. 206, where they are placed alongside of Cyril's. In the meantime, Celestine of Rome had called upon Nestorius to retract, though as a matter of fact the Nestorian or Antiochian position was more in harmony with the position held in Rome, *e. g.*, compare Anath. IV with the language of Nestorius and Leo, see *Tome* of Leo in § 90. A Greek text of these Anathematisms of Cyril may be found also in Denziger, n. 113, as they were described in the Fifth General Council as part of the acts of the Council of Ephesus A. D. 431; the Latin version (the Greek is lost) of the Anathematisms of Nestorius, as given by Marius Mercator are in Kirch, nn. 724–736.

I. If any one shall not confess that the Emmanuel is in truth God, and that therefore the holy Virgin is Theotokos, inasmuch as according to the flesh she bore the Word of God made flesh; let him be anathema.

II. If any one shall not confess that the Word of God the Father is united according to hypostasis to flesh, and that with the flesh of His own He is one Christ, the same manifestly God and man at the same time; let him be anathema.

III. If any one after the union divide the hypostases in the one Christ, joining them by a connection only, which is according to worthiness, or even authority and power, and not rather by a coming together, which is made by a union according to nature; let him be anathema.

IV. If any one divide between the two persons or hypostases the expressions in the evangelical and apostolic writings, or which have been said concerning Christ by the saints, or by Himself concerning Himself, and shall apply some to Him as to a man regarded separately apart from the Word of

God, and shall apply others, as appropriate to God only, to the Word of God the Father; let him be anathema.

V. If any one dare to say that the Christ is a god-bearing man, and not rather that He is in truth God, as an only Son by nature, because "The Word was made flesh," and hath share in flesh and blood as we have; let him be anathema.

VI. If any one shall dare to say that the Word of God the Father is the God of Christ or the Lord of Christ, and shall not rather confess Him as at the same time both God and man, since according to the Scriptures the Word became flesh; let him be anathema.

VII. If any one say that Jesus is, as a man, energized by the Word of God, and that the glory of the Only begotten is attributed to Him as being something else than His own; let him be anathema.

VIII. If any one say that the man assumed ought to be worshipped together with God the Word, and glorified together with Him, and recognized together with Him as God, as one being with another (for this phrase "together with" is added to convey this meaning) and shall not rather with one adoration worship the Emmanuel and pay Him one glorification, because "the Word was made flesh"; let him be anathema.

IX. If any man shall say that the one Lord Jesus Christ was glorified by the Spirit, so that He used through Him a power not His own, and from Him received power against unclean spirits, and power to perform divine signs before men, and shall not rather confess that it was His own spirit, through which He worked these divine signs; let him be anathema.

X. The divine Scriptures say that Christ was made the high priest and apostle of our confession [Heb. 3 : 1], and that for our sakes He offered Himself as a sweet odor to God the Father. If then any one say that it is not the divine Word himself, when He was made flesh and had become man as we are, but another than He, a man born of a woman, yet different from Him who has become our high priest and apostle; or if any one say that He offered Himself as an offering for Himself, and not rather for us, whereas, being without sin, He had no need of offering; let him be anathema.

XI. If any one shall not confess that the flesh of the Lord is life-giving, and belongs to the Word of God the Father as His very own, but shall pretend that it belongs to another who is united to Him according to worthiness, and who has served as only a dwelling for the Divinity; and shall not rather confess that that flesh is life-giving, as we say, because it has been made the possession of the Word who is able to give life to all; let him be anathema.

XII. If any one shall not confess that the Word of God suffered in the flesh, and that He was crucified in the flesh, and that likewise He tasted death in the flesh, and that He is become the first-born from the dead [Col. 1 : 18], for as God He is the life and life-giving; let him be anathema.

(b) Council of Ephesus, A. D. 431, *Condemnation of Nestorius*. Mansi, IV, 1211.

The text may also be found in Hefele, § 134, under the First Session of the Council.

The holy synod says: Since in addition to other things the impious Nestorius has not obeyed our Citation and did not receive the most holy and God-fearing bishops who were sent to him by us, we were compelled to proceed to the examination of his impieties. And, discovering from his letters and treatises and from the discourses recently delivered by him in this metropolis, which have been testified to, that he has held and published impious doctrines, and being compelled thereto by the canons and by the letter of our most holy father and fellow-servant Celestine, the Roman bishop, we have come, with many tears, to this sorrowful sentence against him: Our Lord Jesus Christ whom he has blasphemed, decrees through the present most holy synod that Nestorius be excluded from the episcopal dignity and from all priestly communion.

(c) Council of Ephesus, A. D. 431, *Ep. ad Celestinum.*
Mansi, IV, 1330–1338.

The letter is very long and gives an almost complete history of the
council. It may be found complete in PNF, *loc. cit.*, p. 237. It is of
special importance in connection with the Pelagian controversy, as it
states that the Council of Ephesus had confirmed the Western deposition of the Pelagians.

The letters were read which were written to him [Nestorius]
by the most holy and reverend bishop of the church of Alexandria, Cyril, which the holy synod approved as being orthodox and without fault, and in no point out of agreement,
either with the divinely inspired Scriptures, or with the faith
handed down and set forth in the great synod by the holy
Fathers who were assembled some time ago at Nicæa, as
your holiness, also rightly having examined this, has given
witness. . . .

When there had been read in the holy synod what had been
done touching the deposition of the irreligious Pelagians and
Celestinians, of Celestius, Pelagius, Julianus, Præsidius,
Florus, Marcellinus, and Orontius, and those inclined to like
errors, we also deemed it right that the determinations of
your holiness concerning them should stand strong and firm.
And we all were of the same mind, holding them deposed.

(d) Council of Ephesus, A. D. 431, *Canons*, Bruns, I, 24.

The text may be found also in Hefele, § 141.

Whereas it is needful that they who were detained from the
holy synod and remained in their own district or city for any
reason, ecclesiastical or personal, should not be ignorant of
the matters which were decreed by the synod; we therefore
notify your holiness and charity that——

I. If any metropolitan of a province, forsaking the holy
and ecumenical synod, has joined the assembly of apostasy
[the council under John of Antioch], or shall join the same
hereafter; or if he has adopted, or shall adopt, the doctrines

of Celestius,[1] he has no power in any way to do anything in opposition to the bishops of the province because he is already cast forth by the synod from all ecclesiastical communion, and is without authority; but he shall be subjected to the same bishops of the province and to the neighboring bishops who hold the orthodox doctrines, to be degraded completely from his episcopal rank.

II. If any provincial bishops were not present at the holy synod, and have joined or attempted to join the apostasy; or if, after subscribing to the deposition of Nestorius, they went back to the assembly of apostasy, these, according to the decree of the holy synod, are to be deposed completely from the priesthood and degraded from their rank.

(e) Council of Ephesus, A. D. 431, *Manifesto of John of Antioch and his council against Cyril and his council*. Mansi, IV, 1271.

The holy synod assembled in Ephesus, by the grace of God and at the command of the pious emperors, declares: We should indeed have wished to be able to hold a synod in peace, according to the canons of the holy Fathers and the letters of our most pious and Christ-loving emperors; but because you held a separate assembly from a heretical, insolent, and obstinate disposition, although, according to the letters of our most pious emperors, we were in the neighborhood, and because you have filled both the city and the holy synod with every sort of confusion, in order to prevent the examination of points agreeing with the Apollinarian, Arian, and Eunomian heresies and impieties, and have not waited for the arrival of the most religious bishops summoned from all regions by our pious emperors, and when the most magnificent Count Candidianus warned you and admonished you in writing and verbally that you should not hear such a matter, but await

---

[1] The friendly treatment Nestorius had given the exiled Pelagians, when they came to Constantinople, had led the men of the West to connect Nestorianism with Pelagianism and to condemn the two as if there was some necessary connection between them.

the common judgment of all the most holy bishops; therefore know thou, O Cyril, bishop of Alexandria, and thou, O
Memnon, bishop of this city, that ye are dismissed and deposed from all sacerdotal functions as the originators and
leaders of all this disorder and lawlessness, and those who
have violated the canons of the Fathers and the imperial
decrees. And all ye others who seditiously and wickedly,
and contrary to all ecclesiastical sanctions and the royal decrees, gave your consent are excommunicated until you acknowledge your fault and reform and accept anew the faith
set forth by the holy Fathers at Nicæa, adding to it nothing
foreign or different, and until ye anathematize the heretical
propositions of Cyril, which are plainly repugnant to evangelical and apostolic doctrine, and in all things comply with
the letters of our most pious and Christ-loving emperors, who
require a peaceful and accurate consideration of the dogma.

(f) Creed of Antioch A. D. 433.   Hahn, § 170.

This creed was probably composed by Theodoret of Cyrus, and was
sent by Count Johannes to the Emperor Theodosius in 431 as expressing the teaching of the Antiochian party.   The bitterest period of the
Nestorian controversy was after the council which is commonly regarded as having settled it.   The Antiochians and the Alexandrians
attacked each other vigorously.   At last, in 433, John, bishop of Antioch, sent the creed given below to Cyril of Alexandria, who signed it.
The creed expresses accurately the position of Nestorius.   In this way
a union was patched up between the contending parties.   But the
irreconcilable Nestorians left the Church permanently.   This creed
in the form in which it had been presented to the Emperor was at the
beginning and the end worded somewhat differently, cf. Hahn, loc. cit.,
note.

We therefore acknowledge our Lord Jesus Christ, the Son
of God, the only begotten, complete God and complete man,
of a rational soul and body; begotten of the Father before the
ages according to His godhead, but in the last days for us and
for our salvation, of the Virgin Mary, according to the manhood; that He is of the same nature as the Father according
to His godhead, and of the same nature with us according to

His manhood; for a union of the two natures has been made; therefore we confess one Christ, one Son, one Lord. According to this conception of the unconfused union, we confess that the holy Virgin is Theotokos, because God the Word was made flesh and became man, and from her conception united with Himself the temple received from her. We recognize the evangelical and apostolic utterances concerning the Lord, making common, as in one person, the divine and the human characteristics, but distinguishing them as in two natures; and teaching that the godlike traits are according to the godhead of Christ, and the humble traits according to His manhood.

§ 90. THE EUTYCHIAN CONTROVERSY AND THE COUNCIL OF CHALCEDON A. D. 451

What is known as the Eutychian controversy is less a dogmatic controversy than a struggle between the patriarchs of the East for supremacy, using party theological differences as a support. Few passages in the history of the Church are more painful. The union made in 433 between the Antiochian and Alexandrian parties lasted fifteen years, or until after the death of those who entered into it. At Antioch Domnus became bishop in 442, at Alexandria Dioscurus in 444, and at Constantinople Flavian in 446. Early in 448 Dioscurus, who aimed at the domination of the East, began to attack the Antiochians as Nestorians. In this he was supported at Constantinople by Chrysaphius, the all-powerful minister of the weak Theodosius II, and the archimandrite Eutyches, the godfather of the minister. Eusebius of Dorylæum thereupon accused Eutyches, who held the Alexandrian position in an extreme form, of being heretical on the doctrine of the Incarnation. Eutyches was condemned by Flavian at an endemic synod [cf. DCA, I, 474], November 22, 448. Both Eutyches and Flavian [cf. Leo the Great, Ep. 21, 22] thereupon turned to Leo, bishop of Rome. Leo, abandoning the traditional Roman alliance with Alexandria, on which Dioscurus had counted, supported Flavian, sending him June 13, 449, a dogmatic epistle (the *Tome, Ep.* 28) defining, in the terms of Western theology, the point at issue. A synod was now called by Theodosius at Ephesus, August, 449, in which Dioscurus with the support of the court triumphed. Eutyches was restored, and the leaders of the Antiochian party, Flavian, Eusebius, Ibas, Theodoret, and others deposed. Flavian [*cf.* Kirch, nn. 804*ff.*], Eusebius, and Theodoret appealed to Leo, who vigorously denounced the synod as a council of robbers (Latrocinium Ephesinum). At the same time the situation at the court, upon which Dioscurus depended, was completely changed by the fall of Chrysaphius and the death of Theodosius. Pulcheria, his sister, and Marcian, her husband, succeeded to the throne, both adherents of the Antiochian party, and opposed to the ecclesiastical aspirations of Dioscurus. A new synod was now called by Marcian at Chalcedon, a suburb of Constantinople. Dioscurus was deposed, as well as Eutyches, but Ibas and Theodoret were restored after an examination of their teaching. A definition was drawn up in harmony with the *Tome* of Leo. It was a triumph for Leo, which was somewhat lessened by the passage of canon 28, based upon the third canon of Constantinople, A. D. 381, a council which was henceforth recognized as the "Second General Council." Leo refused to approve this canon, which remained in force in the East and was renewed at the Quinisext Council A. D. 692.

Additional source material: W. Bright, *Select Sermons of S. Leo the Great on the Incarnation; with his twenty-eighth Epistle called the "Tome,"* Second ed., London, 1886; Percival, *The Seven Ecumenical Councils* (PNF); Evagrius, *Hist. Ec.,* II, 1–5, 18, Eng. trans., London, 1846 (also in Bohn's *Ecclesiastical Library*); also much material in Hefele, §§ 170–208.

(a) Council of Constantinople, A. D. 448, *Acts.* Mansi, VI, 741 *ff.*

The position of Eutyches and his condemnation.
Inasmuch as Eutyches was no theologian and no man of letters, he

has left no worked-out statement of his position. What he taught can be gathered only from the acts of the Council of Constantinople A. D. 448. These were incorporated in the acts of the Council of Ephesus, A. D. 449, and as his friends were there they may be regarded as trustworthy. The acts of the Council of Ephesus, A. D. 449 were read in the Council of Chalcedon, A. D. 451, and in this way the matter is known.

The following passages are taken from the seventh sitting of the Council of Constantinople, November 22, 448.

Archbishop Flavian said: Do you confess that the one and the same Son, our Lord Jesus Christ, is consubstantial with His Father as to His divinity, and consubstantial with His mother as to His humanity?

Eutyches said: When I intrusted myself to your holiness I said that you should not ask me further what I thought concerning the Father, Son, and Holy Ghost.

The archbishop said: Do you confess Christ to be of two natures?

Eutyches said: I have never yet presumed to speculate concerning the nature of my God, the Lord of heaven and earth; I confess that I have never said that He is consubstantial with us. Up to the present day I have not said that the body of our Lord and God was consubstantial with us; I confess that the holy Virgin is consubstantial with us, and that of her our God was incarnate. . . .

Florentius, the patrician, said: Since the mother is consubstantial with us, doubtless the Son is consubstantial with us.

Eutyches said: I have not said, you will notice, that the body of a man became the body of God, but the body was human, and the Lord was incarnate of the Virgin. If you wish that I should add to this that His body is consubstantial with us, I will do this; but I do not understand the term consubstantial in such a way that I do not deny that he is the Son of God. Formerly I spoke in general not of a consubstantiality according to the flesh; now I will do so, because your Holiness demands it. . . .

Florentius said: Do you or do you not confess that our

Lord, who is of the Virgin, is consubstantial and of two natures after the incarnation?

Eutyches said: I confess that our Lord was of two natures before the union [*i. e.*, the union of divinity and humanity in the incarnation], but after the union one nature. . . . I follow the teaching of the blessed Cyril and the holy Fathers and the holy Athanasius, because they speak of two natures before the union, but after the union and incarnation they speak not of two natures but of one nature.

Condemnation of Eutyches.

Eutyches, formerly presbyter and archimandrite, has been shown, by what has taken place and by his own confession, to be infected with the heresy of Valentinus and Apollinaris, and to follow stubbornly their blasphemies, and rejecting our arguments and teaching, is unwilling to consent to true doctrines. Therefore, weeping and mourning his complete perversity, we have decreed through our Lord Jesus Christ, who has been blasphemed by him, that he be deprived of every sacerdotal office, that he be put out of our communion, and deprived of his position over a monastery. All who hereafter speak with him or associate with him, are to know that they also are fallen into the same penalty of excommunication.

(*b*) Leo the Great, *Epistola Dogmatica* or the *Tome.* Hahn, § 176. (MSL, 54 : 763.)

This letter was written to Flavian on the subject which had been raised by the condemnation of Eutyches in 448. It is of the first importance, not merely in the history of the Church, but also in the history of doctrine. Yet it cannot be said that Leo advanced beyond the traditional formulæ of the West, or struck out new thoughts [*cf.* Augustine, *Ep.* 187, text and translation of most important part in Norris, *Rudiments of Theology*, 1894, pp. 262–266]. It was to be read at the Council of Ephesus, 449 A. D., but was not. It soon became widely known, however, and was approved at the endemic Council of Constantinople, A. D. 450, and when read at Chalcedon, the Fathers of the council cried out: "Peter has spoken by the mouth of Leo."

It may be found translated in PNF, ser II, vol. XII, p. 38, and again vol. XIV, p. 254. The best critical text is given in Hahn, § 224. A

translation with valuable notes may be found in Wm. Bright, *op. cit.*
Hefele, § 176, gives a paraphrase and text with useful notes. The most
significant passages, which are here translated, may be found in Denziger, nn. 143 *f.*

Ch. 3. Without detracting from the properties of either
nature and substance, which came together in one person,
majesty took on humility; strength, weakness; eternity, mortality; and to pay off the debt of our condition inviolable
nature was united to passible nature, so that as proper
remedy for us, one and the same mediator between God and
man, the man Jesus Christ, could both die with the one and
not die with the other.   Thus in the whole and perfect nature
of true man was true God born, complete in what was His
and complete in what was ours. . . .
Ch. 4. There enters, therefore, these lower parts of the
world the Son of God, descending from His heavenly seat, and
not quitting the glory of His Father, begotten in a new order
by a new nativity.   In a new order: because He who was invisible in His own nature, was made visible in ours; He who
was incomprehensible [could not be contained], became com-
prehensible in ours;   remaining before all times, He began to
be in time;   the Lord of all, He took upon Him the form of a
servant, having obscured His immeasurable majesty.   He who
was God, incapable of suffering, did not disdain to be man,
capable of suffering, and the immortal to subject Himself to
the laws of death.   Born by a new nativity: because the inviolate virginity knew not concupiscence, it ministered the
material of the flesh.   The nature of the Lord was assumed
from the mother, not sin; and in the Lord Jesus Christ, born
of the womb of the Virgin, because His nativity is wonderful,
yet is His nature not dissimilar to ours.   For He who is true
God, is likewise true man, and there is no fraud[1] since both
the humility of the man and the loftiness of God meet.[2]   For

[1] *I. e.*, not mere appearance without reality, as in Docetism and Monophysitism.
[2] Hefele, *loc. cit.*, interprets the phrase, *invicem sunt* as a mutual interpene-
tration.

as God is not changed by the manifestation of pity, so the man is not consumed [absorbed] by the dignity. For each form [*i. e.*, nature] does in communion with the other what is proper to it [*agit enim utraque forma cum alterius communione quod proprium est*]; namely, by the action of the Word what is of the Word, and by the flesh carrying out what is of the flesh. One of these is brilliant with miracles, the other succumbs to injuries. And as the Word does not depart from equality with the paternal glory, so the flesh does not forsake the nature of our race.[1]

(*c*) Council of Chalcedon, A. D. 451, *Definition.* Mansi, VII, 107.

The definition of Chalcedon lays down the fundamental principles upon which rests the doctrine of the incarnation, both in Eastern and Western theology. It is the necessary complement and result of the discussion that led to the definition of Nicæa, and is theologically second only to that in importance. At Nicæa the true and eternal deity of the Son who became incarnate was defined; at Chalcedon the true, complete, and abiding humanity of manhood of the incarnate Son of God. In this way two natures were asserted to be in the incarnate Logos. According to Chalcedon, which came after the Nestorian and the Eutychian controversies, these natures are neither to be confused so that the divine nature suffers or the human nature is lost in the divine, nor to be separated so as to constitute two persons. The definition was, however, not preceded by any clear understanding of what was to be understood by nature in relation to hypostasis. This was left for later discussion. There was even then left open the question as to the relation of the will to the nature, and this gave rise to the Monothelete controversy (see § 110). But the definition of Chalcedon is important not merely for the history of doctrine but also for the general history of the Church. The course of Christianity in the East depends upon the great controversies, and in Monophysitism the Church of the East was split into permanent divisions. The divisions of the Eastern Church prepared the way for the Moslem conquests. The attempts made to set aside the definition of Chalcedon as a po-

---

[1] In explanation of this Leo adds further on: To be hungry and thirsty, to be weary and to sleep, is clearly human; but to satisfy five thousand men with five loaves, and to bestow on the woman of Samaria living water . . . is, without doubt, divine. . . . It is not the part of the same nature to be moved to pity for a dead friend, and when the stone that closed that four days' grave was removed, to raise that same friend to life with a voice of command.

litical move led to a temporary schism between the East and the West.

In this definition, it should be noted, the Council of Constantinople, A. D. 381, for the first time takes its place alongside of Nicæa and Ephesus, A. D. 431, and the so-called creed of Constantinople is placed on the same level as the creed put forth at Nicæa. The creed of Constantinople eventually took the place of the creed of Nicæa even in the East.

The text of the definition may be found in its most important dogmatic part in Hefele, § 193; Hahn, § 146; Denziger, n. 148. For a general description of the council, see Evagrius, *Hist. Ec.*, II, 3, 4. Extracts from the acts in PNF, ser. II, vol. XIV, 243 *ff*.

The holy, great, and ecumenical synod, assembled by the grace of God and the command of our most religious and Christian Emperors Marcian and Valentinian, Augusti, at Chalcedon, the metropolis of the province of Bithynia, in the martyry of the holy and victorious martyr Euphemia, has decreed as follows:

Our Lord and Saviour Jesus Christ, when strengthening the knowledge of the faith in his disciples, to the end that no one might disagree with his neighbor concerning the doctrines of religion, and that the proclamation of the truth might be set forth equally to all men, said: "My peace I leave with you, my peace I give unto you." But since the Evil One does not desist from sowing tares among the seeds of godliness, but ever invents something new against the truth, therefore the Lord, providing, as He ever does, for the human race, has raised up this pious, faithful, and zealous sovereign, and He has called together unto Himself from all parts the chief rulers of the priesthood, so that, with the grace of Christ, our common Lord, inspiring us, we may cast off every plague of falsehood from the sheep of Christ and feed them with the tender leaves of truth. And this we have done, with unanimous consent driving away erroneous doctrine and renewing the unerring faith of the Fathers, publishing to all the creed of the three hundred and eighteen [*i. e.*, the creed of Nicæa], and to their number adding as Fathers those who have received the same summary of religion. Such are the one hundred and fifty who afterward assembled in great Constantinople and ratified the same faith. Moreover, observing the order and every form relating to the faith which was observed by the holy synod formerly held in Ephesus, of which Celestine of Rome and Cyril of Alexandria, of holy memory, were the leaders [*i. e.*, Ephesus A. D. 431], we do declare that the exposition of the right and blameless faith made by the three hundred and eighteen holy and blessed Fathers, assembled at Nicæa in the reign of Constantine, of pious memory, shall be pre-eminent, and that those things shall be of force also which were decreed by the one hundred and fifty holy Fathers at Constantinople for the uprooting of the heresies which had then sprung up and for the confirmation of the same Catholic and apostolic faith of ours.

Then follow:

"The Creed of the Three Hundred and Eighteen Fathers at Nicæa." The so-called Constantinopolitan creed, without the "filioque."

This wise and salutary formula of divine grace sufficed for the perfect knowledge and confirmation of religion; for it teaches the perfect doctrine concerning Father, Son, and Holy Ghost, and sets forth the incarnation of the Lord to them that faithfully receive it. But forasmuch as persons undertaking to make void the preaching of the truth have through their individual heresies given rise to empty babblings, some of them daring to corrupt the mystery of the Lord's incarnation for us and refusing to use the name Theotokos in reference to the Virgin, while others bringing in a confusion and mixture, and idly conceiving that there is one nature of the flesh and the godhead, maintaining that the divine nature of the Only begotten is by mixture capable of suffering; therefore this present, great, and ecumenical synod, desiring to exclude from them every device against the truth and teaching that which is unchanged from the beginning, has at the very outset decreed that the faith of the three hundred and eighteen Fathers shall be preserved inviolate. And on account of them that contend against the Holy Ghost, it confirms the doctrine afterward delivered concerning the substance of the Spirit by the one hundred and fifty holy Fathers assembled in the imperial city, which doctrine they declare unto all men, not as though they were introducing anything that had been lacking in their predecessors, but in order to explain through written documents their faith concerning the Holy Ghost against those who were seeking to destroy His sovereignty. And on account of those who are attempting to corrupt the mystery of the dispensation [*i. e.,* the incarnation], and who shamelessly pretend that He who was born of the holy Virgin Mary was a mere man, it receives the synodical letters of the blessed Cyril, pastor of the church of Alexandria, addressed to Nestorius and to the Easterns,[1] judging them suitable for the refutation of the frenzied folly of Nestorius and for the instruction of those who long with holy ardor for a knowledge of the saving symbol. And to these it has rightly added for the confirmation of the orthodox doctrines the letter of the president of the great and old Rome, the most blessed and holy Archbishop Leo, which was addressed to Archbishop Flavian, of blessed memory,[2] for the removal of the false doctrines of Eutyches, judging them to be agreeable to the confession of the great Peter and to be a common pillar against misbelievers. For it opposes those who would rend the mystery of the dispensation into a duad of Sons; it repels from the sacred assembly those who dare to say that the godhead of the Only begotten is capable of suffering; it resists those who imagine there is a mixture or confusion in the two natures of Christ; it drives away those who fancy His form as a servant is of an heavenly or of some substance other than that which was taken of us,[3] and it anathematizes those who foolishly talk of two natures of our Lord before

---

[1] See PNF, ser. II, vol. XIV; To Nestorius, p. 197; To the Easterns, *i. e.,* to John of Antioch (Cyril, *Ep.* 39), p. 251.

[2] See above, the *Tome* of Leo.

[3] It was charged against Eutyches that he taught that the Son brought His body with Him from heaven. This Eutyches denied.

the union,[1] conceiving that after the union there was only one.[2]

Following the holy Fathers,[3] we all with one voice teach men to confess that the Son and our Lord Jesus Christ is one and the same, that He is perfect in godhead and perfect in manhood, truly God and truly man, of a reasonable soul and body, consubstantial with His Father as touching His godhead, and consubstantial with us as to His manhood,[4] in all things like unto us, without sin; begotten of His Father before all worlds according to His godhead; but in these last days for us and for our salvation of the Virgin Mary, the Theotokos, according to His manhood, one and the same Christ, Son, Lord, only begotten Son,[5] in[6] two natures, unconfusedly, immutably, indivisibly, inseparably; the distinction of natures being preserved and concurring in one person and hypostasis,[7] not separated or divided into two persons, but one and the same Son and Only begotten, God the Word, the Lord Jesus Christ, as the prophets from the beginning have spoken concerning Him, and as the Lord Jesus Christ himself has taught us, and as the creed of the Fathers has delivered us.

These things having been expressed by us with great accuracy and attention, the holy ecumenical synod decrees that no one shall be permitted to bring forward another

[1] This is the position of Eutyches. Cyril of Alexandria also taught the same; cf. Loofs, *Leitfaden zum Studium der Dogmengeschichte*, 1906, § 37, 2.

[2] Cyril's phrase was "The one nature of the incarnate Logos"; cf. Ottley, *The Doctrine of the Incarnation*, 1896, II, 93.

[3] The text of this passage, the most important dogmatically, may be found in all the references given above.

[4] Against Eutyches, who denied this point, and also against Apollinaris, *v. supra*, § 88, *a*.

[5] The Nestorians were accused of dividing the person of Christ into two Sons.

[6] The present Greek text reads "of two natures," but "in two natures" was the original reading. For the evidence, see Hefele, § 193 (Eng. trans., III, p. 348, note); see also Hahn, § 146, n. 34. "Of" appears to be an early forgery. On the other side, see Dorner, *History of the Doctrine of the Person of Christ*, Eng. trans., div. II, vol. I, p. 411; Baur, *Dreieinigkeit*, I, 820*f*.

[7] Πρόσωπον and ὑπόστασις are here used as probably not distinguishable; see Hatch, *Hibbert Lectures*, pp. 275*ff*; Loofs in PRE, V, 637, l. 12.

faith,[1] nor to write, nor to compose, nor to excogitate, nor to teach such to others. But such as dare to compose another faith, or to bring forward, or to teach, or to deliver another creed to such as wish to be converted to the knowledge of the truth from among the Gentiles or the Jews, or any heresy whatever; if they be bishops or clerics, let them be deposed, the bishops from the episcopate, the clerics from the clerical rank; but if they be monks or laymen, let them be anathematized.

(d) Council of Chalcedon, A. D. 451, *Canon* 28. Bruns, I, 32.

The rank of the see of Constantinople.
This canon is closely connected with Canon 3 of Constantinople, A. D. 381, but goes beyond that in extending the authority of Constantinople. With this canon should be compared Canons 9 and 17 of Chalcedon, which, taken with Canon 28, make Constantinople supreme in the East. For the circumstances in which the Canon was passed, see Hefele, § 200. The letter of the council submitting its decrees to Leo for approval and explaining this canon is among the Epistles of Leo, *Ep.* 98. (PNF, ser. II, vol. XII, p. 72.) For Leo's criticism, *v. supra*, § 86. See W. Bright, *Notes on the Canons of the First Four General Councils*, 1882. A valuable discussion of the canon in its historical setting is in Hergenröther, *Photius, Patriarch von Constantinopel*, 1867, I, 74–89.
Texts of the canon may be found in Kirch, n. 868, and Hefele, *loc. cit.*

Following in all things the decisions of the holy Fathers, and acknowledging the canon, which has just been read, of the one hundred and fifty bishops, beloved of God, we also do enact and decree the same things concerning the privileges of the most holy Church of Constantinople or New Rome. For the Fathers rightly granted privileges to the throne of Old Rome, because it was the royal city, and the one hundred and fifty most religious bishops, moved by the same considerations, gave equal privileges to the most holy throne of New Rome, judging with good reason that the city which is honored with the sovereignty and the Senate, and also enjoys equal privileges with old imperial Rome, should in ecclesias-

---

[1] *I. e.*, teaching as to these points in the form of a definition.

tical matters also be magnified as she is, and rank next after her; so that in the dioceses of Pontus, Asia, and Thrace the metropolitans, and such bishops also of the dioceses afore-said as are among the barbarians, should be ordained only by the aforesaid most holy throne of the most holy Church of Constantinople; every metropolitan of the aforesaid dioceses together with the bishops of his province ordaining bishops of the province, as has been declared by the divine canons; but that, as has been said above, the metropolitans of the aforesaid dioceses shall be ordained by the archbishop of Constantinople, after the proper elections have been held ac-cording to custom and have been reported to him.

(e) Council of Chalcedon, A. D. 451, *Protests of the Legates of Leo against Canon* 28.   Mansi, VII, 446.

Lucentius, the bishop [legate of Leo], said: The Apostolic See gave orders that all things should be done in our presence [Latin text: The Apostolic See ought not to be humiliated in our presence], and therefore whatever was done yesterday during our absence, to the prejudice of the canons, we pray your highnesses [*i. e.*, the royal commissioners who directed the affairs of the council] to command to be rescinded.   But if not, let our protest be placed in these acts [*i. e.*, the minutes of the council then being approved], so that we may know clearly what we are to report to that apostolic and chief bishop of the whole Church [Latin text: to that apostolic man and Pope of the universal Church], so that he may be able to take action with regard either to the indignity done to his see or to the setting at naught of the canons.

§ 91.   Results of the Decision of Chalcedon: the Rise of Schisms from the Monophysite Controversy

The definition of the Council of Chalcedon, in spite of its condemnation of Nestorius and its approval of the letters of Cyril, was a triumph of the Antiochian school and a condem-

nation of Alexandrian theology. At Chalcedon no more than
at Nicæa was a controversy settled. So far from being settled
at the council, Monophysitism began with it its long career
in the Eastern Church only to end in permanent schisms.
As soon as the results of Chalcedon were known the Church
was in an uproar. Riots broke out in Jerusalem against the
patriarch. At Alexandria, Timothy Ælurus, a Monophysite,
was able to drive out the orthodox patriarch. In Antioch,
Petrus Fullo did the same and added to the liturgical Trisagion [Is. 6 : 3] the Theopaschite phrase: "God who was
crucified for us." The Emperor Marcian died 457 and was
succeeded by Leo I (457–474). His grandson Leo II (474)
was succeeded by his father Zeno (474–475, 477–491). Zeno
was temporarily deposed by Basiliscus (475–477), who, basing
his authority upon the Monophysite faction, issued an
Encyclion condemning Chalcedon and Leo's Epistle, and making Monophysitism the religion of the Empire. Zeno was
restored by a Dyophysite faction under the lead of Acacius,
patriarch of Constantinople. Zeno, to win back the Monophysites, issued in 482 the *Henoticon*, setting aside Chalcedon and making only the definition of Nicæa authoritative.
Dissatisfaction arose on both sides, and minor schisms in the
East took place. With Rome a schism arose lasting 484–519.

Additional source material: Evagrius, *Hist. Ec.*, lib. III.

(*a*) Basiliscus, *Encyclion;* A. D. 476; in Evagrius, *Hist.
Ec.*, III, 4. (MSG, 86, II : 2600.) *Cf.* Kirch. nn. 879 *f.*

Although an anti-encyclion was issued in 477 condemning Eutyches
as well as Nestorius, the attempts of Basiliscus were in vain.

The Emperor Cæsar Basiliscus, pious, victorious, triumphant, supreme, ever-worshipful Augustus, and Marcus, the
most noble Cæsar, to Timotheus, archbishop of the great city
of the Alexandrians, most reverend and beloved of God.

Whatever laws the pious emperors before us, who worshipped the blessed and immortal and life-giving Trinity, have
decreed in behalf of the true and apostolic faith, these laws,

we say, as always beneficial for the whole world, we will at
no time to be inoperative, but rather we promulgate them as
our own. We, preferring piety and zeal in the cause of our
God and Saviour, Jesus Christ, who created and has made us
glorious before all diligence in human affairs, and also believing that concord among the flocks of Christ is the preservation
of ourselves and our subjects, the firm foundation and unshaken bulwark of our Empire, and, accordingly, being rightly
moved with godly zeal and offering to God and our Saviour,
Jesus Christ, the unity of the holy Church as the first-fruits of
our reign, do ordain as the basis and confirmation of human
felicity, namely, the symbol of the three hundred and eighteen
holy Fathers who were in time past assembled with the Holy
Ghost at Nicæa, into which both ourselves and all our believing subjects were baptized; that this alone should have reception and authority with the orthodox people in all the most
holy churches of God as the only formulary of the right faith,
and sufficient for the utter destruction of all heresy and for
the complete unity of the holy churches of God; the acts of
the one hundred and fifty holy Fathers assembled in this
imperial city, in confirmation of the sacred symbol itself and
in condemnation of those who blasphemed against the Holy
Ghost, retaining their own force; as well as of all done in the
metropolitan city of the Ephesians against the impious Nestorius and those who subsequently favored his opinions.[1] But
the proceedings which have disturbed the unity and good
order of the holy churches of God, and the peace of the whole
world, that is to say, the so-called *Tome* of Leo, and all things
done at Chalcedon in innovation upon the before-mentioned
holy symbol of the three hundred and eighteen holy Fathers,
whether by way of definition of the faith or setting forth of
symbols, or interpretation, or instruction, or discourse; we
decree that these shall be anathematized both here and everywhere by all the most holy bishops in every church and shall
be given to the flames by whomsoever they shall be found,

[1] It is to be noted that condemnation of Eutyches is not confirmed.

insomuch as it was so enjoined respecting all heretical doctrines by our predecessors of pious and blessed memory,
Constantine and Theodosius the younger [*v. supra*, § 73],
and that, having thus been rendered null, they shall be utterly
cast out from the one and only Catholic and Apostolic Orthodox Church, as superseding the everlasting and saving definitions of the three hundred and eighteen Fathers, and those of
the blessed Fathers who, by the Holy Ghost, decreed at Ephesus [it is possible that there is a fault in the text here; the
expected reading of the passage would be: and of the one
hundred and fifty bishops who decreed concerning the Holy
Spirit; and of those who were assembled at Ephesus] that
no one, either of the priesthood or laity, be allowed to
deviate in any respect from that most sacred constitution
of the holy symbol, and we decree that these be anathematized together with all the innovations upon the sacred symbol which were made at Chalcedon and the heresy of those
who do not confess that the only begotten Son of God was
truly incarnate and made man of the Holy Ghost and of the
holy and ever-virgin Mary, Theotokos, but falsely allege that
either from heaven or in mere phantasy and seeming He took
flesh; and, in short, every heresy and whatever else at any
time in any manner or place in the whole world, in either
thought or word, has been devised as an innovation upon
and in derogation of the sacred symbol.   And inasmuch as it
belongs especially to imperial providence to furnish to their
subjects, with forecasting deliberation, security not only for
the present but for the future, we decree that everywhere
the most holy bishops shall subscribe to this our sacred circular letter when exhibited to them, and shall distinctly declare that they submit to the sacred symbol of the three hundred and eighteen holy Fathers alone, which the one hundred
and fifty holy Fathers confirmed, as it was also defined by the
most holy Fathers who subsequently assembled in the metropolitan city of the Ephesians, that they should submit to the
sacred symbol of the three hundred and eighteen holy Fathers,

as the definition of faith, and shall anathematize everything
done at Chalcedon as an offence to the orthodox people and
utterly cast it out of the churches as an impediment to the
general happiness and our own.[1] Those, moreover, who after
the issuing of this our sacred letter, which we trust has been
issued according to God, in an endeavor to bring about that
unity which all desire for the holy churches of God, shall attempt to bring forward or so much as to name the innovation upon the faith made at Chalcedon, either in discourse,
instruction, or writing, in whatsoever manner or place—
those persons, as the cause of confusion and tumult in the
churches of God and among the whole body of our subjects,
and as enemies of God and to our safety, we command
(in accordance with the laws ordained by our predecessor
Theodosius, of blessed and pious memory, against such sorts
of evil designs, which laws are subjoined to this our sacred
circular) that, if they be bishops or clergy, they be deposed;
if monks or laymen, that they be subjected to banishment
and every mode of confiscation and the severest penalties.
For so the holy and homoousian Trinity, the Creator and
Life-giver of the universe, which has ever been adored by us
in piety, now also is served by us in the destruction of the
before-mentioned tares and the confirmation of the true and
apostolic traditions of the holy symbol, becoming favorable
and gracious both to our souls and to every one of our subjects, shall ever aid us and preserve in peace human affairs.

(b) Zeno, *Henoticon;* in Evagrius, *Hist. Ec.*, III, 14. (MSG,
86, II : 2620.) *Cf.* Kirch, nn. 883 *f.*

Zeno published his *Henoticon* in 482 as an attempt to win back the
Monophysites. Evagrius says, in a note to the document: "When
these things were read, those who were in Alexandria were joined to the
holy Catholic and Apostolic Church." The effect so far as the West
went was just the opposite. Felix III protested and threatened. But
Acacius, bishop of Constantinople, who was chiefly responsible for the
document, refused to listen. Felix (*cf.* Evagrius, III, 18) and Acacius

---

[1] This left the theological situation precisely as it was after the "Latrocinium Ephesinum" of 449.

thereupon issued mutual excommunications. On the accession of the Emperor Anastasius [491–518] the *Henoticon* continued in force, as his sympathies were with the Monophysites. It will be noted that the *Henoticon* not merely sets aside Chalcedon but introduces phrases which make it appear that the same moral subject is present in every act, whether of humility or majesty, and that it is God who suffers. These are characteristic Monophysite positions.

The Emperor Cæsar Zeno, pious, victorious, triumphant, supreme, ever-worshipful Augustus, to the most reverend bishops and clergy, and to the monks and laity throughout Alexandria, Egypt, Libya, and Pentapolis.

Being assured that the origin and constitution, the might and invincible shield of our sovereignty, is the only right and true faith, which the three hundred and eighteen holy Fathers assembled at Nicæa set forth by divine inspiration, and the one hundred and fifty holy Fathers who in like manner met at Constantinople, confirmed; we night and day employ every means of prayer, of zealous care, and of laws, that the holy Catholic and Apostolic Church of God in every place may be multiplied, which is the incorruptible and immortal mother of our sceptre; and that the pious laity, continuing in peace and unanimity in respect to God, may, together with the bishops, highly beloved of God, the most pious clergy, the archimandrites, and monks, offer up acceptably their supplications in behalf of our sovereignty. So long as our great God and Saviour, Jesus Christ, who was made man and brought forth of Mary, the holy Virgin and Theotokos, approves and readily accepts the praise we render by concord and our service, the power of enemies will be crushed and swept away, and all will bend their necks to our power, which is according to God, and peace and its blessings, kindly temperature, abundant produce, and whatever else is beneficial will be liberally bestowed upon men. Since, then, the irreprehensible faith is the preserver of both ourselves and Roman affairs, petitions have been offered to us from pious archimandrites and hermits and other venerable persons, imploring with tears that there be unity for the most holy churches, and the parts should be joined to parts which the enemy of all good has of old time attempted to keep apart, knowing that, if he assails the body of the Church sound and complete, he will be defeated. For, since it happens that of unnumbered generations which during the lapse of so many years in time have withdrawn from life, some have departed deprived of the laver of regeneration, and others have been borne away on the inevitable journey of man without having partaken of the divine communion; and innumerable murders have also been committed; and not only the earth, but the very air has been filled by a multitude of blood-sheddings, who would not pray that this state of things might be transformed into good? For this reason we were anxious that you should know that neither we nor the churches everywhere have ever held or shall hold, nor are we aware of any persons who hold, any other symbol or teaching or definition of faith or creed than the aforementioned holy symbol of the three hundred and eighteen holy Fathers, which the aforesaid one hundred and fifty holy Fathers confirmed. If any person should hold such, we regard him as an alien; for we are confident that this symbol alone is, as we said, the preserver of our sovereignty. And all the people desiring the saving illumination were baptized, receiving this faith only, and this the holy Fathers assembled at Ephesus also followed; who deposed the impious Nestorius and those who subsequently held his sentiments. And this Nestorius we also anathematize, together with Eutyches and all who entertain opinions contrary to the above-mentioned, receiving at the same time the twelve chapters of Cyril, of holy memory, formerly archbishop of the holy Catholic Church of the Alexandrians. We confess, moreover, that the only begotten Son of God, himself God, who truly became man, namely, our Lord Jesus Christ, is consubstantial with the Father as to his godhead, and the same consubstantial with ourselves as respects his manhood; that having descended and become flesh of the Holy Ghost and Mary, the Virgin and Theotokos, He is one and not two;

for we affirm that both His miracles and the sufferings which
He voluntarily endured in the flesh, are of one; for we do
not in any degree admit those who either make a division
or a confusion or introduce a phantom; inasmuch as His
truly sinless incarnation from the Theotokos did not produce
an addition of a son, because the Trinity continued as a
Trinity, even when one of the Trinity, God the Word, did
become incarnate. Knowing, then, that neither the holy
orthodox churches of God in all places nor the priests, highly
beloved of God, who are at their head, nor our own sovereignty, have allowed or do allow any other symbol or definition of faith than the before-mentioned holy teaching, we
have united ourselves thereunto without hesitation. And
these things we write, not as making an innovation upon the
faith, but to satisfy you; and every one who has held or
holds any other opinion, either at the present or at another
time, whether at Chalcedon or in any synod whatever, we
anathematize; and specially the aforementioned Nestorius
and Eutyches, and those who maintain their doctrines. Link
yourselves, therefore, to the spiritual mother, the Church, and
in her enjoy divine communion with us, according to the
aforesaid one and only definition of the faith of the three
hundred and eighteen holy Fathers. For your all-holy
mother, the Church, waits to embrace you as true children,
and longs to hear your gentle voice so long withheld. Speed
yourselves, therefore, for by so doing you will both draw
toward yourselves the favor of our Master and Saviour and
God, Jesus Christ, and be commended by our sovereignty.

§ 92. THE CHURCH OF ITALY UNDER THE OSTROGOTHS AND
DURING THE FIRST SCHISM BETWEEN ROME AND THE
EASTERN CHURCH

The schism between New and Old Rome lasted from 484 to
517, but attempts were made on both sides to end the de-
plorable situation. The two successors of Acacius were will-

ing to resume communion with Rome and restore the name of
the bishop of Rome to the diptychs, but refused to take the
names of their predecessors from the same, as required by the
latter. Gelasius (492–496), Anastasius II (496–498), and
Symmachus (498–514) held firmly but unavailingly to the
Roman contention that, before any communion was possible,
the name of Acacius must be struck from the diptychs—in
the case of the dead an act as condemnatory as excommunication in the case of the living. Meanwhile the Roman see
boldly asserted the independence of the Church, and protested
against the action of the Emperor in setting aside the decree
of Chalcedon as usurpation and tyranny. This is most clearly
set forth by Gelasius, in his epistle to the Emperor Anastasius.
The schism finally came to an end in 519, in accordance with
the ecclesiastical policy of Justinian, and at that time the
Formula of Hormisdas (514–523) was accepted by the heads
of the Eastern Church by an act constituting a complete surrender of the claims of the Orientals.

While the schism was still existing and Rome was treating
with the East upon an independent footing, the situation
in Italy was far less brilliant. The Arian king, the Ostro-
goth Theodoric (489, 493–526) ruled Italy, and the attitude
of the Roman see was far less authoritative toward the local
ruler. It was, however, a period of great importance for the
future of the Church; Boethius, Cassiodorus, Dionysius Exiguus, and Benedict of Nursia (*v. infra*, §§ 104, 105) all
belong to this period and the decree of Gelasius, *De Recipiendis Libris*, was of permanent influence upon the theological science of the West.

Additional source material: Cassiodorus, *Varia*, Eng. trans. (condensed), by T. Hodgkin (*The Letters of Cassiodorus*), London, 1886.

(*a*) Gelasius, *Ep. ad Imp. Anastasium.* (MSL, 59 : 42.)

A definition of the relation between the secular and religious authority.

The date of this epistle is 494. The period is not dealt with at any
length in English works on ecclesiastical history; see, however, T.

Greenwood, *Cathedra Petri*, II, pp. 41–84, the chapter entitled "Papal Prerogative under Popes Gelasius and Symmachus."

After Gelasius has alluded to the circumstances in which he is writing and excused his not writing, he mentions his natural devotion to the Roman Emperor—being himself by birth a Roman citizen—his desire as a Christian to share with him the right faith, and as vicar of the Apostolic See his constant anxiety to maintain the true faith; he then proceeds:

I beseech your piety not to regard as arrogance duty in divine affairs. Far be it from a Roman prince, I pray, to regard as injury truth that has been intimated to him. For, indeed, there are, O Emperor Augustus, two by whom principally this world is ruled: the sacred authority of the pontiffs and the royal power. Of these the importance of the priests is so much the greater, as even for kings of men they will have to give an account in the divine judgment. Know, indeed, most clement son, that although you worthily rule over the human race, yet as a man of devotion in divine matters you submit your neck to the prelates, and also from them you await the matters of your salvation, and in making use of the celestial sacraments and in administering those things you know that you ought, as is right, to be subjected to the order of religion rather than preside over it; know likewise that in regard to these things you are dependent upon their judgment and you should not bend them to your will. For if, so far as it pertains to the order of public discipline, the priests of religion, knowing that the imperial power has been bestowed upon you by divine providence, obey your laws, lest in affairs of exclusively mundane determination they might seem to resist, with how much more gladness, I ask, does it become you to obey them who have been assigned to the duty of performing the divine mysteries. Just as there is no light risk for the pontiffs to be silent about those things which belong to the service of the divinity, so there is no small peril (which God forbid) to those who, when they ought to obey, refuse to do so. And if it is right that the hearts of the faithful be submitted to all priests generally who treat

rightly divine things, how much more is obedience to be shown
to the prelate of that see which the highest divinity wished
to be pre-eminent over all priests and which the devotion of
the whole Church continually honors?

(b) Gelasius, *Epist. de Recipiendis et non Recipiendis Libris.*
Mansi, VIII, 153 *ff.*

This decretal is evidently made of matter of different dates, as has
been shown by Hefele, § 217, and probably contains matter which may
be later than Gelasius.   In the first section of the decretal is a list of
the canonical books of the Bible, as in the Vulgate; the decretal
then sets forth the claims of the Roman see (§ 2), the books to be received (§ 3), and the books which the Roman Church rejects (§ 4).
In respect to several there are various comments added, but these
have in several cases been omitted for the sake of brevity, where they
are of less importance.   Portions of the decretal in Denziger, nn. 162–
164; the full text of the decretal may be found in Mansi VIII, 153 *ff.*
Preuschen, *Analecta*, vol. II, pp. 52 *ff.;* Mirbt, n. 168.

II. Although the one dwelling of the universal Catholic
Church spread through the world is of Christ, the holy Roman
Church, however, has been placed before the other churches
by no synodical decrees, but has obtained the primacy by
the evangelic voice of our Lord and Saviour, saying, "Thou
art Peter, and upon this rock I will build my Church," etc.[1]
To it was given the fellowship of the most blessed Apostle
Paul, that chosen vessel who not at a different time, as heretics prate, but at one time and on one and the same day by
a glorious death, was crowned together with Peter in agony
in the city of Rome under the Emperor Nero.   And they
equally consecrated the said holy Roman Church to Christ
and placed it over all the others in the whole world by their
presence and venerable triumph.

III.   Therefore the first see of Peter the Apostle is the
Roman Church, not having any spot or wrinkle or any such
thing.   The second see was consecrated at Alexandria in the
name of the blessed Peter by Mark, his disciple and the evangelist.   He himself, having been directed by the Apostle Peter

[1] Matt. 16 : 18 *f.*

to Egypt, preached the word of truth and consummated a glorious martyrdom. But as the third see of the same most blessed Apostle Peter is held the see of Antioch, since he held that before he came to Rome, and there the name of the new people, the name of Christians, arose.

IV, 1. And although no other foundation can be laid than that which has been laid, which is Christ Jesus, yet after the writings of the Old and New Testaments,[1] which we receive regularly, the same holy Roman Church does not prohibit these following writings to be received for the purposes of edification:

2. The holy synod of Nicæa, according to the three hundred and eighteen Fathers, under the Emperor Constantine.

3. The holy synod of Ephesus, in which Nestorius was condemned with the consent of the most blessed Pope [*papa*] Celestine, held under Cyril, the prelate of the see of Alexandria, and Acadius, a bishop sent from Italy.

4. The holy synod of Chalcedon, which was held under the Emperor Marcian and Anatolius, bishop of Constantinople, and in which Nestorius, Eutyches, and Dioscurus were condemned.

V, 1. Likewise the works of the blessed Cæcilius Cyprianus, martyr, and bishop of Carthage; 2. . . . of Gregory the bishop of Nazianzus; 3. . . . of Basil, bishop of Cappadocia; 4. . . . of Athanasius, bishop of Alexandria; 5. . . . of John [Chrysostom], bishop of Constantinople; 6. . . . of Theophilus, bishop of Alexandria; 7. . . . of Cyril, bishop of Alexandria; 8. . . . of Hilary, bishop of Poitiers; 9. . . . of Ambrose, bishop of Milan; 10. . . . of Augustine, bishop of Hippo; 11. . . . of Jerome, the presbyter; 12. . . . of Prosper; 13. . . . likewise the Epistle of the blessed Pope Leo to Flavian, bishop of Constantinople, against Eutyches and other heretics; and if any one dispute even so much as an

---

[1] The list is given in the early part of the epistle not here given; see Preuschen, *loc. cit.*

iota of the text of the epistle, and will not reverently receive it in all points, let him be anathema.

14. Likewise the works and treatises of the orthodox Fathers are to be read, who in no respect have deviated from the union with the holy Roman Church, nor have separated from its faith and teaching; but, by the grace of God, have shared in communion with it even to the last days of their life.

15. Likewise the decretal epistles which the most blessed Popes at different times have given from the city of Rome, in reply to consultations of various fathers, are to be reverently received.

16. Likewise the acts of the holy martyrs. . . . But, according to an ancient custom and singular caution, they are not to be read in the holy Roman Church, because the names of those who wrote them are not known. . . .

17. Likewise the lives of the fathers Paul, Antony, Hilarion, and all hermits which the most blessed Jerome has described, we receive in honor.

18. Likewise the acts of the blessed Sylvester, prelate of the Apostolic See, although the name of the writer is unknown; however, we know that it is read by many Catholics in the city of Rome, and on account of its ancient use many churches have copied it.

19. Likewise the writing concerning the discovery of the cross and another concerning the discovery of the head of the blessed John the Baptist. . . .

20. Rufinus, a most religious man, has published many books on ecclesiastical affairs and has also translated several writings. But because the venerable Jerome has criticised him in various points for his freedom in judgment, we are of the same opinion as we know Jerome is, and not only concerning Rufinus but all others whom, out of zeal toward God and devotion to the faith, Jerome has condemned.

21. Likewise several works of Origen which the blessed Jerome does not reject we receive as to be read; the remaining works along with their author we declare are to be rejected.

22. Likewise the chronicles of Eusebius of Cæsarea and the books of his *Ecclesiastical History*, although in the first book of his narrative he has been a little warm and afterward he wrote one book in praise and defence of Origen, the schismatic, yet on account of the mention of several things, which pertain to instruction, we say that they are to that extent not to be rejected. . . .

23. Likewise we approve Orosius; 24. . . . the works of Sedulius; 25. . . . the works of Juvencus. . . .

VI. Other works which have been written by heretics or schismatics the Catholic and Apostolic Roman Church in no respect receives, and these, although they are not received and are to be avoided by Catholics, we believe ought to be added below.

There follow a list of thirty-five apocryphal gospels, acts, and similar documents. The epistle continues:

36. The book which is called *The Canons of the Apostles;* 37. the book called *Physiologus*, written by heretics and ascribed to Ambrose; 38. the history of Eusebius Pamphilius; 39. the works of Tertullian; 40. . . . of Lactantius or Firminianus; 41. . . . of Africanus; 42. . . . Postumianus and Gallus; 43. . . . of Montanus, Priscilla, and Maximilla; 44. . . . all the works of Faustus the Manichæan; 45. the works of Commodus; 46. the works of another Clement of Alexandria; 47. the works of Thascius Cyprianus; 48. of Arnobius; 49. of Tichonius; 50. of Cassianus a presbyter of Gaul; 51. Victorinus of Pettau; 52. of Frumentius the blind; 53. of Faustus of Reiz; 54. the Epistle of Jesus to Abgar; 55. Passion of St. Cyricus and Julitta; 56. Passion of St. Georgius; 57. the writings which are called the "Curse of Solomon"; 58. all phylacteries which have been written not with the names of angels, as they pretend, but rather of demons; 59. these works and all similar to them which Simon Magus [a list of heretics down to] Peter [Fullo] and another Peter [Mongus], of whom one defiled

Alexandria and the other Antioch, Acacius of Constantinople with his adherents, as also all heretics or disciples of heretics or schismatics have taught or written, whose names we do not remember are not only repudiated by the entire Roman Catholic Church, but we declare are bound forever with an indissoluble anathema together with their authors and followers of their authors.

(c) Hormisdas, *Formula*. Mansi, VIII, 407. *Cf.* Denziger, nn. 171 *f.*

The formula which Hormisdas of Rome (514–523) proposed in 515, and which was accepted Easter 519 by the patriarch John II of Constantinople and many other Orientals, and which ended the schism between Rome and Constantinople occasioned by Acacius. As soon as this formula was accepted the leading Monophysites fled to Egypt.

The beginning of salvation is to preserve the rule of a correct faith and to deviate in no respect from the constitutions of the fathers. And because the teaching of our Lord Jesus Christ cannot be allowed to fail, who said, "Thou art Peter, and upon this rock I will build my Church," etc. [Matt. 16 : 18], these things which were said are proved by the effects of things, because in the Apostolic See religion has always been preserved without spot or blemish. Desiring in no respect to be separated from this hope and faith, and following the constitutions of the Fathers, we anathematize all heretics, and especially the heretic Nestorius, who was once bishop of the city of Constantinople, and condemned in the Council of Ephesus by Pope Celestine and by the holy Cyril, prelate of the city of Alexandria. Likewise we anathematize Eutyches and Dioscurus of Alexandria, condemned in the holy synod of Chalcedon which we follow and embrace; adding to these Timotheus the parricide, known as Ælurus, and also his disciple and follower Peter [Mongus], also Acacius, who remained in the society of their communion; because he mixed himself with their communion he deserves the same sentence of condemnation as they; no less condemning Peter [Fullo] of Antioch with his followers and the followers of all those above named. We receive and approve, therefore, all the universal Epistles of Pope Leo which he wrote concerning the Christian religion. And therefore, as we have said, following in all things the Apostolic See and approving all of its constitutions, I trust that I may be deemed worthy to be in the communion with you, in which as the Apostolic See declares there is, complete and true, the totality of the Christian religion.

PERIOD III

THE DISSOLUTION OF THE IMPERIAL STATE CHURCH AND THE TRANSITION TO THE MIDDLE AGES: FROM THE BEGINNING OF THE SIXTH CENTURY TO THE LATTER PART OF THE EIGHTH

The third period of the ancient Church under the Christian Empire begins with the accession of Justin I (518–527), and the end of the first schism between Rome and Constantinople (519). The termination of the period is not so clearly marked. By the middle and latter part of the eighth century, however, the imperial Church has ceased to exist in its original conception. The Church in the East has become, in great part, a group of national schismatic churches under Moslem rulers, and only the largest fragment of the Church of the East is the State Church of the greatly reduced Eastern empire. In the West, the imperial influence has ceased, and the Roman see has allied its fortunes with the rising Frankish power, and the rise of a Western empire is already foreshadowed.

In this period, the imperial ecclesiastical system, which had begun with Constantine, found its completion in the Cæsaropapism which was definitively established by Justinian as the constitution of the Eastern Church. But at the same time the Monophysite churches seceded and became permanent national churches. The long Christological controversy found, at least as regards Monophysitism, its settlement on a basis derived from the revived Aristotelian philosophy; and the mystical piety of the East, with its apparatus of hierarchy and sacraments, found its characteristic expression in the works of Dionysius the Areopagite.

While in the East the Church was assuming its permanent form, in the West the condition of the Church was being profoundly influenced by the completely changed political organization of what had been the Roman Empire of the West, but was now parcelled out among new Germanic nationalities. The Church in the various kingdoms, in spite of its adherence to the see of Rome as the centre of Catholic unity, came, to no small extent, under the secular authority, and Christianity in Ireland, in Spain, among the Franks, Anglo-Saxons, and even among the Lombards in Italy assumed a national character, coming largely under the control and subject to the laws and customs of the nation. In this period were laid the foundations of the leading ecclesiastical institutions of the Middle Ages, as the Church, although still under the influence of antiquity, adapted itself and its institutions to the changed condition due to the political situation and took up its duty of training the rude peoples that had come within its fold.

The seventh and eighth centuries saw the completion of the revolution in the ecclesiastical situation. In the East, in the territories in which the national churches of the Monophysites were established, the Moslem rule protected them from the attempts of the orthodox emperors to enforce uniformity. The attempts made to recover their allegiance before they succumbed to Islam had only ended, in a serious dispute within the Orthodox Church, the Monothelete controversy, which ended in the Sixth General Council of 681. In Italy the Arian Lombards were gradually won to the Catholic faith, but the Roman see soon found itself embarrassed by the too near secular authority. Accordingly, when the controversy with the East over Iconoclasm broke out, the Roman Church became practically independent of the Eastern imperial authority, and in its conflict with the Lombards came into alliance with the rising Frankish power. With this, the transition to the Middle Ages may be said to have been completed. It was, however, only the last of a series of acts whereby the Church was severing itself from the ancient order and coming into closer alliance with the new order in the life of the West. Henceforth the Church, which found its centre in the Roman see, belongs to the West, and its relations to the East, although no formal schism had occurred, are of continued and increasing estrangement or alienation.

The *Cambridge Medieval History*, vol. II, will cover the entire period and give ample bibliographical references.

CHAPTER I. THE CHURCH IN THE EASTERN EMPIRE

The century extending from the accession of Justin I (518–528) to the end of the Persian wars of Heraclius (610–641), or from 518 to 628, is the most brilliant period of the Eastern Empire. The rise of Islam had not yet taken place, whereby the best provinces in Asia and Africa were cut off from the Empire. A large part of the West was recovered under Justinian, and under Heraclius the power of Persia, the ancient enemy of the Roman Empire, which had been a menace since the latter part of the third century, was completely overthrown in the most brilliant series of campaigns since the foundation of the Roman Empire. With the death of Justin II (565–578), the family of Justin came to an end after occupying the throne for sixty years. But under Tiberius (578–582) and Maurice (582–602) the policy of Justinian was continued in all essentials in the stereotyped form known as Byzantinism. The Church became practically a department of the State and of the political machinery. The only limitation upon the will of the Emperor was the determined resistance of the Monophysites and smaller factions. Maurice was succeeded by the rude Phocas (602–610), whom a military revolution placed upon the throne, and who instituted a reign of terror and blood. Upon his downfall, Heraclius (610–641) ascended the throne.

§ 93.   The Age of Justinian.
§ 94.   The Byzantine State Church under Justinian.
§ 95.   The Definitive Type of Religion in the East: Dionysius the Areopagite.

§ 93.   THE AGE OF JUSTINIAN

Justinian I, the greatest of all the rulers of the Eastern Empire, succeeded his uncle Justin I (518–527); but he had, from the beginning of the latter's reign, exercised an ever-increasing influence over the imperial policy, and to him can be attributed the direction of ecclesiastical affairs from the accession of Justin. No reign among the Eastern emperors was more filled with important events and successful undertakings. His first great work was the reduction of the vast mass of Roman law to what approached a system. This was accomplished in 534, resulting in the Digest, made up of the various decisions and opinions of the most celebrated Roman legal authorities, the Codex, comprising all the statute law then in actual force and applicable to the conditions of the Empire, and the Institutes, a revision of the excellent introductory manual of Gaius. No body of law reduced to writing has been more influential in the history of the world. The second great undertaking, or series of undertakings, was the reconquest of the West. In 533 Belisarius recovered North Africa to the Empire by the overthrow of the Vandal kingdom. In 554 the conquest of Italy by Belisarius and Narses was completed. Portions of Spain had also been recovered. No Eastern Emperor ruled over a larger territory than did Justinian at the time of his death. The third great line of work on the part of Justinian was his regulation of ecclesiastical and theological matters. In this he took an active personal part. The end of the schism with the West had been brought about under the reign of his uncle. Three controversies fill the reign of Justinian: the Theopaschite (519–533) over the introduction of the phrase into the Trisagion, stating that God was crucified for us, so that the Trisagion read as follows, "Holy God, Holy Mighty, Holy Immortal, who was crucified for us, have mercy upon us"; the Second Origenistic controversy (531–543) in which those elements of Origen's teaching which had never been accepted by the Church were condemned along with Origen himself; and the Three Chapters controversy, 544–553, in which, as an attempt to win back the Monophysites, which began even before the Conference with the Severians in 533, three of the leading Antiochians were condemned. In connection with the two last controversies, the Fifth General Council was held A. D. 553.

Additional source material: Evagrius, *Hist. Ec.*, Lib. IV–VI; John of Ephesus, *The Third Part of His Ecclesiastical History*, trans. by R. Payne Smith, Oxford, 1860; Percival, *Seven Ecumenical Councils* (PNF).

(*a*) Justinian, *Anathematisms against Origen.* Mansi, IX, 533. (MSG, 86 : 1013; MSL, 65 : 221.)

The Origenistic controversy arose in Palestine, where the learned monks were nicknamed Origenists by the more ignorant. The abbot St. Sabas was especially opposed to the group which had received this name. But several, among whom the more important were Domitian and Theodore Askidas, won the favor of Justinian and the latter received promotion, becoming bishop of Cæsarea in Cappadocia. Supported by them, struggles broke out in various places between the Sabaites and the Origenists. Ephraem, patriarch of Antioch, in a synodal letter thereupon condemned Origenism. The Origenists tried in vain to win the support of John, patriarch of Constantinople. But he turned to Justinian, who thereupon abandoned the Origenists and issued an edict condemning Origen and his writings, and appending a summary of the positions condemned in ten anathematisms. Text in Denziger, nn. 203 *f*. Synods were ordered for the condemnation of Origen, and among these was the synod under Menas, patriarch of Constantinople, in which were issued fifteen anathematisms based upon the ten of Justinian (Hefele, §§ 257, 258). With this action, the controversy may be said to be closed, were it not that in spite of the renewed condemnation at the Fifth General Council (see below) disputes and disturbances continued in Palestine until 563.

1. If any one says or thinks that human souls pre-existed, that is, that they had previously been spirits and holy powers, but that satiated with the vision of God, they turned to evil, and in this way the divine love in them became cold

[ἀποψυγείσας] and they were there named souls [ψυχάς] and were condemned to punishment in bodies, let him be anathema.

2. If any one says or thinks that the soul of the Lord pre-existed and was united with God the Word before the incarnation and conception of the Virgin, let him be anathema.

3. If any one says or thinks that the body of the Lord Jesus Christ was first formed in the womb of the holy Virgin, and that afterward there was united with it God the Word and the pre-existing soul, let him be anathema.

4. If any one says or thinks that the Word of God has become like to all heavenly orders, so that for the cherubim He was a cherub and for the seraphim a seraph, in short, like all the superior powers, let him be anathema.

5. If any one says or thinks that, at the resurrection, human bodies will arise spherical in form and not like our present form, let him be anathema.

6. If any one says or thinks that the heavens, the sun, moon, and stars, and the waters above the firmament have souls and are spiritual and rational beings, let him be anathema.

7. If any one says or thinks that Christ the Lord in a future age will be crucified for demons as He was for men, let him be anathema.

8. If any one says or thinks that the power of God is limited and that He created only as much as He was able to comprehend, let him be anathema.

9. If any one says or thinks that the punishment of demons and impious men is only temporary and will have an end, and that a restoration [apocatastasis] will take place of demons and impious men, let him be anathema.

10. Let Origen be anathema together with that Adamantius who set forth these opinions together with his nefarious and execrable doctrine, and whoever there is who thinks thus or defends these opinions, or in any way hereafter at any time shall presume to protect them.

(b) Vigilius, *Judicatum.* Mansi, IX, 181.

This important document was addressed to Menas of Constantinople and is dated April 11, 548. Unfortunately it exists only in detached fragments, which are given below, taken from the text as given by Hefele, § 259. The first is given in a letter of Justinian to the Fifth Council, an abridgment of which may be found in Hefele, § 267. Other fragments are from the *Constitutum* (see below), where they are quoted by Vigilius from his previous letter to Menas, which Hefele has identified with the *Judicatum.* In this opinion Krüger (art. "Vigilius" in PRE), and Bailey (art. "Vigilius" in DCB) and other scholars concur. The force of the first is that the writings condemned by the Three Chapters are heretical; of the others, that the credit of the Council of Chalcedon must be maintained. How the two positions were reconciled is not clear.

1. And because certain writings under the name of Theodore of Mopsuestia have been handed to us which contain many things contrary to the right faith, we, following the warnings of the Apostle Paul, who said: Prove all things, hold fast that which is good, therefore anathematize Theodore, who was bishop of Mopsuestia, with all his impious writings, and also those who defend him. We anathematize also the impious epistle which is said to have been written by Ibas to Maris the Persian, as contrary to the right faith, and also all who defend it and say that it is right. We anathematize also the writings of Theodoret which were written contrary to the right faith and against the capitula of Cyril.[1]

2. Since it is evident to us by sufficient reason, that whosoever attempts to do anything to the disparagement of the aforesaid council, will rather sin against himself.

3. If it had been shown conclusively by us to be contained in the acts [*i. e.*, of the Council of Chalcedon], no one would have dared to be the author of so great a presumption or would have regarded as doubtful or undecided anything which was brought before that most holy judgment; since it is to be believed that those then present could have investigated things diligently even apart from writing, and have defined them positively, which appears to us after so

[1] The Twelve Anathematisms of Cyril against Nestorius.

much time and on account of unknown causes still unsettled; since also it is a part of reverence for the synods that in those things which are less understood one recognizes their authority.

4. All things being accepted and remaining perpetually established which were defined in the venerable councils at Nicæa, and Constantinople, in the first at Ephesus, and at Chalcedon, and confirmed by the authority of our predecessors; and all who in the said holy councils were deposed are without doubt condemned, and those are no less absolved whose absolution was decreed by the same synods.

5. Subjecting also him to the sentence of anathema who accepts as of any force whatsoever may be found against the said synod of Chalcedon, written in this present letter, or in anything in the present case whatever done by us or by any one; and let the holy synod of Chalcedon, of which the authority is great and unshaken, perpetual and reverenced, have the same force as that which the synods of Nicæa, Constantinople, and the first at Ephesus have.

6. We anathematize also whoever does not faithfully follow and equally venerate the holy synods of Nicæa, of Constantinople, the first of Ephesus, and the synod of Chalcedon as most holy synods, agreeing in the one and immaculate faith of the Apostles, and confirmed by the pontiffs of the Apostolic See, and whoever wishes to correct as badly said, or wishes to supply as imperfect, those things which were done in the same councils which we have mentioned.

(c) Vigilius, *Oath to Justinian*, August 15, A. D. 550. Mansi, IX, 363. (MSL, 69 : 121.)

The *Judicatum* met with great opposition in the West. Vigilius, to still the clamor against it, withdrew it and proposed other measures in consultation with Justinian. In connection with this he bound himself with an oath to support Justinian in putting through the condemnation of the Three Chapters, and this oath Justinian produced later, when Vigilius had presented his *Constitutum* to him refusing to condemn the chapters. The Emperor thereupon suppressed the *Constitutum*.

The most blessed Pope Vigilius has sworn to the most pious lord Emperor in our presence, that is of me, Theodorus, bishop of Cæsarea, in Cappadocia [see DCB, *Theodorus of Askidas*], and of me, Cethegus, the patrician, by the sacred nails with which our Lord God Jesus Christ was crucified and by the four holy Gospels, as also by the sacred bridle,[1] so also by the four Gospels; that, being of one mind and will with your piety, we shall so will, attempt, and act, as far as we are able, so that the three chapters, that is, Theodore of Mopsuestia, the epistle attributed to Ibas, and the writings of Theodoret against the orthodox faith and his sayings against the twelve capitula of the holy Cyril, may be condemned and anathematized; and to do nothing, either by myself or by those whom we can trust, either of the clerical or lay order, in behalf of the chapters, against the will of your piety, or to speak or to give counsel secretly in behalf of those chapters. And if any one should say anything to me to the contrary, either concerning these chapters or concerning the faith, or against the State, I will make him known to your piety, without peril of death, and also what has been said to me, so that on account of my place you do not abandon my person; and you have promised, because I observe these things toward your piety, to protect my honor in all respects, and also to guard my person and reputation and to defend them with the help of God and to protect the privileges of my see. And you have also promised that this paper shall be shown to no one. I promise further that in the case of the three chapters, we shall treat in common as to what ought to be done, and whatsoever shall appear to us useful we will carry out with the help of God. This oath was given the fifteenth day of August, indiction XIII, the twenty-third year of the reign of our lord Justinian, the ninth year after the consulship of the illustrious Basil. I, Theodore, by the mercy of God bishop of Cæsarea, in Cappa-

---

[1] *Sanctum frenum.* Query: Does this refer to the tradition that Constantine made out of the nails of the cross a bit for his horse?

docia, have subscribed hereunto as a witness to this oath; I, Flavius Cethegus, patrician, have subscribed hereunto as a witness to this oath.

(d) Vigilius, *Constitutum*, May 14, 553. (MSL, 69 : 67.)

The synod known as the Fifth General Council met May 5, 553, and proceeded to condemn the Three Chapters, as directed by the Emperor. Vigilius refused to attend, but consented to pronounce his judgment on the matter apart from the council. This he did in his *Constitutum ad Imperatorem*, May 14, 553. In it he condemns the teaching of Theodore of Mopsuestia, but opposes the condemnation of Theodore himself, inasmuch as he had died in the communion of the Church. He also opposes the condemnation of Theodoret and Ibas, because both were acquitted at Chalcedon. This *Constitutum* is to be distinguished from the *Constitutum* of 554 (MSL, 69 : 143, 147), in which, after the council had acceded to the proposals of the Emperor and condemned the Three Chapters and had excommunicated Vigilius by removing his name from the diptychs, the latter confirmed the decisions of the council and joined in the condemnation of the Three Chapters. For a discussion of the whole situation, see Hefele, §§ 272–276. The devious course followed by Vigilius has been the subject of much acrimonious debate. The facts of the case are now generally recognized. The conclusion of Cardinal Hergenröther, KG. I, 612, is the best that can be said for Vigilius: "In the question as to the faith, Vigilius was never wavering; but he was so, indeed, in the question as to whether the action was proper or opportune, whether it was advisable or necessary to condemn subsequently men whom the Council of Chalcedon had spared, to put forth a judgment which would be regarded by the Monophysites as a triumph of their cause, which was most obnoxious for the same reason, and its supposed dishonoring of the Council of Chalcedon, and was likely to create new divisions instead of healing the old."

The portions of the *Constitutum* given below are the conclusions of Vigilius as to each of the Three Chapters. The whole is a lengthy document.

All these things have been diligertly examined, and although our Fathers speak in different phrases yet are guided by one sentiment, that the persons of priests, who have died in the peace of the Church, should be preserved untouched; likewise the constitutions of the Apostolic See, which we have quoted above, uniformly define that it is lawful for no one to judge anew anything concerning the persons of the dead, but each is left in that condition in which the last day finds him; and especially concerning the name of Theodore of Mopsuestia, what our Fathers determined is clearly shown above. Him, therefore, we dare not condemn by our sentence, and we do not permit him to be condemned by any one else; the above-written chapters of dogmas, which are damned by us, or any sayings of any one without name affixed, not agreeing with, or consonant with, the evangelical and apostolic doctrine and the doctrines of the four synods, of Nicæa, of Constantinople, of the first of Ephesus, and of Chalcedon, we, however, do not suffer to be admitted to our thought or even to our ears.

But concerning the writings which are brought forward under the name of that venerable man, Theodoret, late bishop, we wonder, first, why it should be necessary or with what desire anything should be done to the disparagement of the name of that priest, who more than a hundred years ago, in the judgment of the sacred and venerable Council of Chalcedon, subscribed without any hesitation and consented with profound devotion to the Epistle of the most blessed Pope Leo. . . . The truth of these things having been considered, we determine and decree that nothing be done or proposed by any one in judgment upon him to the injury and defamation of a man most approved in the synod of Chalcedon, that is to say, Theodoret of Cyrus. But guarding in all respects the reverence of his person, whatsoever writings are brought forward under his name or under that of another evidently in accord with the errors of the wicked Nestorius and Eutyches we anathematize and condemn.

Then follow these five anathematisms, the text of which may be found in Hahn, § 228:

1. If any one does not confess that the Word was made flesh, the inconvertibility of the divine nature having been preserved, and from the moment of conception in the womb of the Virgin united according to subsistence [hypostatically]

human nature to Himself, but as with a man already existing; so that, accordingly, the holy Virgin is not to be believed to be truly the bearer of God, but is called so only in word, let him be anathema.

2. If any one shall deny that a unity of natures according to subsistence [hypostatically] was made in Christ, but that God the Word dwelt in a man existing apart as one of the just, and does not confess the unity of natures according to subsistence, that God the Word with the assumed flesh remained and remains one subsistence or person, let him be anathema.

3. If any one so divides the evangelical, apostolic words in reference to the one Christ, that he introduces a division of the natures united in Him, let him be anathema.

4. If any one says that the one Jesus Christ, God the Word and the same true Son of Man, was ignorant of future things or of the day of the last judgment, and was able to know only so far as Deity revealed to Him, as if dwelling in another, let him be anathema.

5. If any one applies to Christ as if stripped of His divinity the saying of the Apostle in the Epistle to the Hebrews,[1] that He knew obedience by experience and with strong crying and tears offered prayers and supplications to God who was able to save Him from death, and who was perfected by the labors of virtue, so that from this he evidently introduces two Christs or two Sons, and does not believe the one and the same Christ to be confessed and adored Son of God and Son of Man, of two and in two natures inseparable and undivided, let him be anathema.

. . . We have also examined concerning the Epistle of the venerable man Ibas, once bishop of the city of Edessa, concerning which you also ask if in early times anything concerning it was undertaken by our Fathers, or discussed, or examined, or determined. Because it is known to all and especially to your piety, that we are ignorant of the Greek language, yet by

[1] Heb. 5 : 7, 8.

the aid of some of our company, who have knowledge of that tongue, we discover clearly and openly that in the same synod the affair of the venerable man Ibas was examined, from the action taken regarding Photius, bishop of Tyre, and Eustathius, bishop of Berytus, that this epistle, concerning which inquiry is made, was brought forward against him by his accusers; and when, after discussion of the affair was ended, it was asked of the venerable Fathers what ought to be done concerning the matter of the same Ibas, the following sentence was passed:

Paschasius and Lucentius, most reverend bishops, and Boniface, presbyter, holding the place of the Apostolic See (because the apostolic delegates are accustomed always to speak and vote first in synods), by Paschasius said: "Since the documents have been read, we perceive from the opinion of the most reverend bishops that the most reverend Ibas is approved as innocent; for now that his epistle has been read we recognize it as orthodox. And on this account we decree that the honor of the episcopate be restored to him, and the church, from which unjustly and in his absence he was driven out, be given back." [The patriarchs of Constantinople and Antioch agreed, and their opinions are also quoted by Vigilius from the Acts of the Council of Chalcedon.]

. . . Therefore we, following in all things the discipline and judgment of the holy Fathers, and the disposition of all things according to the account which we have given of the judgment of the Council of Chalcedon, since it is most evidently true, from the words of the Epistle of the venerable man Ibas, regarded with the right and pious mind, and from the action taken regarding Photius and Eustathius, and from the opinions of bishop Ibas, discussed in his presence by those present, that our Fathers present at Chalcedon most justly pronounced the faith of the same venerable man Ibas orthodox and his blaming the blessed Cyril, which they perceive to have been from error of human intelligence, purged by appropriate satisfaction, by the authority of our present sentence, we determine and decree in all things so also in the often-mentioned Epistle of the venerable Ibas, the judgment of the Fathers present at Chalcedon remain inviolate.

Conclusion of the *Constitutum*:

These things having been disposed of by us in every point with all caution and diligence, in order to preserve inviolate the reverence of the said synods and the venerable constitutions of the same; mindful that it has been written [*cf.* Prov. 22 : 26], we ought not to cross the bounds of our Fathers, we determine and decree that it is permitted to no one of any ecclesiastical rank or dignity to do anything contrary to these things which, by this present constitution, we assert and determine, concerning the oft-mentioned three chapters, or to write or to bring forward, or to compose, or to teach, or to make any further investigation after this present definition. But concerning the same three chapters, if anything contrary to these things, which we here determine and assert, is made in the name of any one, in ecclesiastical order or dignity, or shall be found by any one or anywheresoever, such a one by the authority of the Apostolic See, in which by the grace of God we are placed, we refute in every way.

(*e*) Council of Constantinople, A. D. 553, *Definition.* Mansi, IX, 367.

Condemnation of the Three Chapters.
This action is taken from the Definition of the council, a rather wordy document, but ending with a passage indicating the action of the council. From this concluding passage this condemnation is taken. See Hefele, § 274, also PNF, ser. II, vol. XIV, pp. 306–311.

We condemn and anathematize with all other heretics who have been condemned and anathematized by the before-mentioned four holy synods, and by the Catholic and Apostolic Church, Theodore, who was bishop of Mopsuestia, and his impious writings, and also those things which Theodoret impiously wrote against the right faith and against the twelve capitula of the holy Cyril, and against the first synod of Ephesus, and also those which he wrote in defence of Theodore and Nestorius. In addition to these, we also anathematize the impious epistle which Ibas is said to have written to Maris the Persian, which denies that God the Word was incarnate of the holy Theotokos and ever-virgin Mary, and accuses Cyril, of holy memory, who taught the truth, of being a heretic and of the same sentiments with Apollinaris, and blames the first synod of Ephesus for deposing Nestorius without examination and inquiry, and calls the twelve capitula of Cyril impious and contrary to the right faith, and defends Theodore and Nestorius, and their impious dogmas and writings. We, therefore, anathematize the three chapters before mentioned, that is the impious Theodore of Mopsuestia with his execrable writings, and those things which Theodoret impiously wrote, and the impious letter which is said to be by Ibas, together with their defenders and those who have written or do write in defence of them, or who dare to say that they are correct, and who have defended or do attempt to defend their impiety with the names of the holy Fathers or of the holy Council of Chalcedon.

(f) Council of Constantinople A. D. 553. *Anathematism* 11. Mansi, IX, 201. *Cf*. Denziger, n. 223.

Condemnation of Origen.
Appended to the Definition of the council are fourteen anathematisms, forming (1–10) an exposition of the doctrine of the two natures, and concluding with condemnation of Origen, together with other heretics, and of the Three Chapters (11–14). These anathematisms are based upon a confession of faith of the Emperor Justinian, a lengthy document, but containing thirteen anathematisms. This confession of faith was composed before the council, probably in 551. For an analysis of it, see Hefele, § 263. The text of the council's anathematisms may be found in Hefele, § 274, also in Hahn, § 148. Attempts have been made by older scholars to show that the name Origen was a later insertion. For arguments, see Hefele, *loc. cit*.

If any one does not anathematize Arius, Eunomius, Macedonius, Apollinaris, Nestorius, Eutyches, and Origen, with their impious writings, as also all other heretics already condemned and anathematized by the holy Catholic and Apostolic Church, and by the aforesaid four holy synods, and all those who have been or are of the same mind with the heretics mentioned, and who remain to the end in their impiety, let him be anathema.

§ 94. THE BYZANTINE STATE CHURCH UNDER JUSTINIAN

According to Justinian's scheme of Church government, the Emperor was the head of the Church in the sense that he had the right and duty of regulating by his laws the minutest detail of worship and discipline, and also of dictating the theological opinions to be held in the Church. This is shown, not merely in his conduct of the Fifth General Council, but also in his attempt, at the end of his life, to force Aphthartodocetism upon the Church. This position of the Emperor in relation to the Church is known as Cæsaropapism. (See Bury, *Later Roman Empire*, chap. XI.) The ecclesiastical legislation of Justinian should also be considered. At the same time Justinian strictly repressed the lingering heathenism and, in the interest of the schools at Constantinople, closed the schools at Athens, the last stronghold of paganism.

(a) Evagrius, *Hist. Ec.*, IV, 39. (MSG, 86 II : 2781.)

Aphthartodocetism of Justinian.

Among the many variations of Monophysitism flourishing under Justinian was Aphthartodocetism, according to which the body of Christ, before as well as after his resurrection, was "a glorified body," or incapable of suffering. See selection for description.

At that time Justinian, abandoning the right road of doctrine and following the path untrodden by the Apostles and Fathers, became entangled in thorns and briars; and he attempted to fill the Church also with these, but failed in his purpose, and thereby fulfilled the prediction of prophecy. . . . Justinian, after he had anathematized Origen, Didymus, and Evagrius, issued what the Latins call an edict, after the depo-

sition of Eustochius [A. D. 556], in which he termed the body
of the Lord incorruptible and incapable of the natural and
blameless passions; affirming that the Lord ate before His
passion in the same manner as after His resurrection, His holy
body having undergone no conversion or change from the
time of its actual formation in the womb, not even in respect
to the natural and voluntary passions, nor yet after the resurrection. To this he proceeded to compel bishops in all parts
to give their assent. However, they all professed to look to
Anastasius, the Bishop of Antioch, and thus avoided the first
attack.

(b) Justinian, *Novella VI* "Preface."

Church and State according to Justinian.

Among the greatest gifts of God bestowed by the kindness
of heaven are the priesthood and the imperial dignity. Of
these the former serves things divine; the latter rules human
affairs and cares for them. Both are derived from the one
and the same source, and order human life. And, therefore,
nothing is so much a care to the emperors as the dignity of
the priesthood; so that they may always pray to God for
them. For if one is in every respect blameless and filled with
confidence toward God, and the other rightly and properly
maintains in order the commonwealth intrusted to it, there
is a certain excellent harmony which furnishes whatsoever
is needful for the human race. We, therefore, have the greatest cares for the true doctrines of God and the dignity of the
priesthood which, if they preserve it, we trust that by it great
benefits will be bestowed by God, and we shall possess undis-
turbed those things which we have, and in addition acquire
those things which we have not yet acquired. But all things
are well and properly carried on, if only a proper beginning is
laid, and one that is acceptable to God. But this we believe
will be so if the observance of the sacred canons is cared for,
which also the Apostles, who are rightly to be praised, and the
venerated eye-witnesses and ministers of the word of God,

delivered, and which the holy Fathers have also preserved and explained.

(c) Justinian, *Novella CXXXVII*, 6.

The following section from the conclusion of a *novella* illustrates the manner in which Justinian legislated in matter of internal affairs for the Church and instituted a control over the priesthood which was other than that of the Church's own system of discipline.

We command that all bishops and presbyters shall offer the sacred oblation and the prayers in holy baptism not silently, but with a voice which may be heard by the faithful people, that thereby the minds of those listening may be moved to greater contrition and to the glory of God.   For so, indeed, the holy Apostle teaches (I Cor. 14 : 16; Rom. 10 : 10). . . . Therefore it is right that to our Lord Jesus Christ, to our God with the Father and the Holy Ghost, be offered prayer in the holy oblation and other prayers with the voice by the most holy bishops and the presbyters; for the holy priests should know that if they neglect any of those things they shall render an account at the terrible judgment of the great God and our Saviour Jesus Christ, and that we shall not quietly permit such things when we know of them and will not leave them unpunished.   We command, therefore, that the governors of the epachies, if they see anything neglected of those things which have been decreed by us, first urge the metropolitans and other bishops to celebrate the aforesaid synods, and do whatsoever things we have ordered by this present law concerning synods, and, if they see them delaying, let them report to us, that from us may come a proper correction of those who put off holding synods.   And the governors and the officials subject to them should know that if they do not observe these matters they will be liable to the extreme penalty [*i. e.*, death].   But we confirm by this present law all things which have been decreed by us in various constitutions concerning bishops, presbyters, and other clerics, and further concerning lodging-places for strangers, poor-houses, orphan asylums and others as many as are over the sacred buildings.

(d) Justinian, *Novella CXXIII*, 1.

Laws governing the ordination of bishops.

We decree that whenever it is necessary to ordain a bishop, the clergy and the leading citizens whose is the bishop who is to be ordained shall make, under peril of their souls, with the holy Gospels placed before them, certificates concerning three persons, testifying in the same certificates that they have not chosen them for any gifts or promises or for reasons of friendship, or any other cause, but because they know that they are of the true and Catholic faith and of honest life, and learned in science and that none of them has either wife or children, and know that they have neither concubine nor natural children, but that if any of them had a wife the same was one and first, neither a widow nor separated from her husband, nor prohibited by the laws and sacred canons; and know that they are not a curial or an official, or, in case they should be such, are not liable to any curial or official duty; and they know that they have in such case spent not less than fifteen years in a monastery. This also is to be contained in the certificate: that they know the person selected by them to be not less than thirty years of age; so that from the three persons for whom these certificates were made the best may be ordained by the choice and at the peril of him who ordains. But a curial or an official who, as has been said, has lived fifteen years in a monastery and is advanced to the episcopate is freed from his rank so that as freed from the curia he may retain a fourth part of his property, since the rest of his property, according to our law, is to be claimed by the curia and fisc. Also we give to those who make the certificate the privilege that if they deem a layman, with the exception of a curial or an official, worthy of the said election, they may choose such layman with the two other clergy or monks, but so, however, that the layman who has in this way been chosen to the episcopate shall not be ordained at once, but shall first be numbered among the clergy not less than three months, and so having learned the holy canons and the sacred ministry of the Church, he shall be ordained bishop; for he who ought to teach others ought not himself to be taught by others after his consecration. But if by chance there are not found in any place three persons eligible to such election, it is permitted those who make the certificates to make them for two or even for only one person, who shall each have the testimonials mentioned by us. But if those who ought to elect a bishop do not make this certificate within six months, then, at the peril of his soul, let him who ought to ordain ordain a bishop, provided, however, that all things which we have said be observed. But if any one is made bishop contrary to the aforesaid rules, we command that he be driven entirely from the episcopate; but as for him who dared to ordain him against these commands, let him be separated from the sacred ministry for a year and all his property, which at any time or in any way shall come into his possession, shall be seized on account of the crime he has committed against the rule of the Church of which he was a bishop.

Ch. 13. We do not permit clergy to be ordained unless they are educated, have the right faith, and an honorable life, and neither have, nor have had, a concubine or natural children, but who either live chastely or have a lawful wife and her one and only, neither a widow not separated from her husband, nor forbidden by laws and sacred canons.

Ch. 14. We do not permit presbyters to be made less than thirty years old, deacons and sub-deacons less than twenty-five, and lectors less than sixteen; nor a deaconess to be ordained[1] in the holy Church who is less than forty years old and who has been married a second time.

(e) Justinian, *Codex*, I, 11.

Law against paganism.
The following laws of Justinian, though of uncertain date, mark the

---

[1] Same word used as for ordination of clergy.

termination of the contest between Christianity and paganism. In the second of these laws there is a reference to the prohibition of pagan teachers. It is in line with the closing of the schools of the heathen teachers at Athens. The decree closing the schools has not been preserved.

Ch. 9.   We command that our magistrates in this royal city and in the provinces take care with the greatest zeal that, having been informed by themselves or the most religious bishops of this matter, they make inquiry according to law into all impurities of pagan[1] superstitions, that they be not committed, and if committed that they be punished; but if their repression exceed provincial power, these things are to be referred to us, that the responsibility for, and incitement of, these crimes may not rest upon them.

(1) It is permitted no one, either in testament or by gift, to leave or give anything to persons or places for the maintenance of pagan impiety, even if it is not expressly contained in the words of the will, testament, or donation, but can be truly perceived in some other way by the judges.   (2) But those things which are so left or given shall be taken from the persons and places to whom they have been given or left, and shall belong to the cities in which such persons dwell or in which such places are situated, so that they may be paid as a form of revenue.   (3) All penalties which have been introduced by previous emperors against the errors of pagans or in favor of the orthodox faith are to remain in force and effect forever and guarded by this present pious legislation.

Ch. 10.   Because some are found who are imbued with the error of the impious and detestable pagans, and do those things which move a merciful God to just wrath, and that we may not suffer ourselves to leave uncorrected matters which concern these things, but, knowing that they have abandoned the worship of the true and only God, and have in insane error offered sacrifices, and, filled with all impiety, have celebrated solemnities, we subject those who have committed these

---

[1] *Hellenic*, and so throughout.

things, after they have been held worthy of holy baptism, to the punishment appropriate to the crimes of which they have been convicted; but for the future we decree to all by this present law that they who have been made Christians and at any time have been deemed worthy of the holy and saving baptism, if it appear that they have remained still in the error of the pagans, shall suffer capital punishment.

(1) Those who have not yet been worthy of the venerable rite of baptism shall report themselves, if they dwell in this royal city or in the provinces, and go to the holy churches with their wives and children and all the household subject to them, and be taught the true faith of Christians, so that having been taught their former error henceforth to be rejected, they may receive saving baptism, or know, if they regard these things of small value, that they are to have no part in all those things which belong to our commonwealth, neither is it permitted them to become owners of anything movable or immovable, but, deprived of everything, they are to be left in poverty, and besides are subject to appropriate penalties.

(2) We forbid also that any branch of learning be taught by those who labor under the insanity of the impious pagans, so that they may not for this reason pretend that they instruct those who unfortunately resort to them, but in reality corrupt the minds of their pupils; and let them not receive any support from the public treasury, since they are not permitted by the Holy Scriptures or by pragmatic forms [public decrees] to claim anything of the sort for themselves.

(3) For if any one here or in the provinces shall have been convicted of not having hastened to the holy churches with his wife and children, as said, he shall suffer the aforesaid penalties, and the fisc shall claim his property, and they shall be sent into exile.

(4) If any one in our commonwealth, hiding himself, shall be discovered to have celebrated sacrifices or the worship of idols, let him suffer the same capital punishment as the Mani-

560 DISSOLUTION OF IMPERIAL STATE CHURCH

chæans and, what is the same, the Borborani [certain Ophitic Gnostics; *cf.* DCB], for we judge them to be similar to these.

(5) Also we decree that their children of tender years shall at once and without delay receive saving baptism; but they who have passed beyond their earliest age shall attend the holy churches and be instructed in the Holy Scriptures, and so give themselves to sincere penitence that, having rejected their early error, they may receive the venerable rite of baptism, for in this way let them steadfastly receive the true faith of the orthodox and not again fall back into their former error.

(6) But those who, for the sake of retaining their military rank or their dignity or their goods, shall in pretence accept saving baptism, but have left their wives and children and others who are in their households in the error of pagans, we command that they be deprived of their goods and have no part in our commonwealth, since it is manifest that they have not received holy baptism in good faith.

(7) These things, therefore, we decree against the abominable pagans and the Manichæans, of which Manichæans the Borborani are a part.

§ 95. The Definitive Type of Religion in the East: Dionysius the Areopagite

The works of Dionysius the Areopagite first appear in the controversies in the reign of Justinian, when they are quoted in the Conference with the Severians, 531 or 533. There are citations from the works of the Areopagite fifteen or twenty years earlier in the works of Severus, the Monophysite patriarch of Antioch. In this is given the latest date to which they may be assigned. They cannot be earlier than 476, because the author is acquainted with the works of Proclus (411–485) and uses them; also he refers to the practice of singing the Credo in divine service, which was first introduced by the Monophysites at Antioch in 476. No closer determination of the date is possible. The author is wholly unknown.

That he was Dionysius the Areopagite (Acts 17 : 34) is maintained by no scholar to-day. His standpoint is that of the
later Eastern religious feeling and practice, with its strong
desire for mysteries and sacramental system. But he brings
to it Neo-Platonic thought to such a degree as to color completely his presentation of Christian truth. The effect of
the book was only gradual, but eventually very great. In the
East it gave authority, which seemed to be that of the apostolic age, for its highly developed system of mysteries, which
had grown up in the Church. In the West it served as a
philosophical basis for scholastic mysticism. On account of
the connection between Dionysius and the later Greek philosophy and the mediæval philosophy, Dionysius the Areopagite occupies a place in the histories of philosophy quite out
of proportion to the intrinsic merit of the writer.

Additional source material: English translations of Dionysius the
Areopagite, Dean Colet, ed. by J. H. Lupton, London, 1869, and
J. Parker, Oxford, 1897 (not complete); a new translation into German appeared in the new edition of the *Kempten Bibliothek der Kirchenväter*, 1912.

(*a*) Dionysius Areopagita, *De Cælesti Hierarchia*, III, 2.
(MSG, 3 : 165.)
Dionysius thus defines "Hierarchy":

He who speaks of a hierarchy indicates thereby a holy
order . . . which in a holy manner works the mysteries of
illumination which is appropriate to each one. The order
of the hierarchy consists in this, that some are purified and
others purify; some are illuminated and others illuminate;
some are completed and others complete.

(*b*) *De Cælesti Hierarchia*, VI, 2. (MSG, 3 : 200.)
The heavenly hierarchy.

Theology has given to all heavenly existences new explan-
atory titles. Our divine initiator divides these into three
threefold ranks. The first is that, as he says, which is ever

about God, and which, as it is related (Ezek. 1), is permanently and before all others immediately united to Him; for the explanation of the Holy Scripture tells us that the most holy throne and the many-eyed and many-winged ranks, which in Hebrew are called cherubim and seraphim, stand before God in the closest proximity. This threefold order, or rank, our great leader names the one, like, and only truly first hierarchy, which is more godlike and stands more immediately near the first effects of the illuminations of divinity than all others. As the second hierarchy, he names that which is composed of authorities, dominions, and powers, and as the third and last of the heavenly hierarchies he names the order of angels, archangels, and principalities.

(c) *De Ecclesiastica Hierarchia*, I, 1.   (MSG, 3 : 372.)

The nature of the ecclesiastical hierarchy.

That our hierarchy . . . which is given by God, is God-inspired and divine, a divinely acting knowledge, activity, and completion, we must show from the supernal and most Holy Scriptures to those who through hierarchical secrets and traditions have been initiated into the holy consecration. . . . Jesus, the most divine and most transcendent spirit, the principle and the being and the most divine power of every hierarchy, holiness, and divine operation, brings to the blessed beings superior to us a more bright and at the same time more spiritual light and makes them as far as possible like to His own light. And through our love which tends upward toward Him, by the love of the beautiful which draws us up to Him, He brings together into one our many heterogeneities; that He might perfect them so as to become a uniform and divine life, condition, and activity, He gives us the power of the divine priesthood. In consequence of this honor we arrive at the holy activity of the priesthood, and so we ourselves come near to the beings over us, that we, so far as we are able, approximate to their abiding and unchangeable holy state and so look up to the blessed and divine brilliancy of

Jesus, gaze religiously on what is attainable by us to see, and are illuminated by the knowledge of what is seen; and thus we are initiated into the mystic science, and, initiating, we can become light-like and divinely working, complete and completing.

(d) *De Ecclesiastica Hierarchia*, V, 3. (MSG, 3 : 504.)

The most holy consecration of initiation has as the godlike power or activity the expiatory purification of the imperfect, as the second the illuminating consecration of the purified, and as the last, which also includes the other two, the perfecting of the consecrated in the knowledge of the consecrations that belong to them. . . .

5. The divine order of the hierarch[1] is the first under the God-beholding orders; it is the highest and also the last, for in it every other order of our hierarchy ends and is completed.[2] For we see that every hierarchy ends in Jesus, and so each one ends in the God-filled hierarchs.

6. The hierarchical order, which is filled full of the perfecting power, performs especially the consecrations of the hierarchy, imparts by revelation the knowledge of the sacred things, and teaches the conditions and powers appropriate to them. The order of priests which leads to light leads to the divine beholding of the sacred mysteries all those who have been initiated by the divine order of the hierarchs and with that order performs its proper sacred functions. In what it does it displays the divine working through the most holy symbols [*i. e.*, sacraments] and makes those who approach beholders and participants in the most holy mysteries, sending on to the hierarch those who desire the knowledge of those sacred rites which are seen. The order of the liturges [or deacons] is that which cleanses and separates the unlike

---

[1] By hierarch is to be understood in this connection the episcopal order, or the bishop.

[2] *Cf. Epistula*, VIII, 2. (MSG, 3 : 1092.) "Every order of the ecclesiastical hierarchy has relation to God and is more godlike than that which is further removed from God, and lighter and more illuminating in all that is nearer to the true light. Do not understand this nearness in a local sense: it has reference rather to the ability to receive God."

before they come to the sacred rites of the priests, purifies those who approach that it may render them pure from all that is opposing and unworthy of beholding and participating in the sacred mysteries.

(e) *De Ecclesiastica Hierarchia*, I, 3. (MSG, 3 : 373.)

The sacraments.

The mysteries or sacraments, according to Dionysius the Areopagite, are six in number: baptism, the eucharist, anointing or confirmation, the consecration of priests, the consecration of monks,[1] and the consecration of the dead. These he discusses in chs. 2–7 of the *Ecclesiastical Hierarchy*.

Salvation can in no other way come about than that the saved are deified. The deification is the highest possible resemblance to God and union with Him. The common aim of all the hierarchy is the love which hangs upon God and things divine, which fills with a divine spirit and works in godlike fashion; and before this is the complete and never retreating flight from that which is opposed to it, the knowledge of being as being, the vision and knowledge of the holy truth, the divinely inspired participation in the homogeneous perfection of the One himself, so far as man can come to that, the enjoyment of the holy contemplation, which spiritually nourishes and deifies every one who strives for it.

CHAPTER II. THE TRANSITION TO THE MIDDLE AGES. THE FOUNDATION OF THE GERMANIC NATIONAL CHURCHES

While the doctrinal system of the Church was being wrought out in the disputes and councils of Rome and the East, the foundations of the Germanic national churches were being laid in the West. In the British Isles the faith was extended from Britain to Ireland and thence to Scotland (§ 96). Among the inmates of the monasteries of these countries were many monks who were moved to undertake missionary journeys to various parts of Western Europe, and among them St.

[1] The highest order of all the consecrated orders is the holy order of monks.

Columbanus. But even more important for the future of Western Christendom was the conversion of the Franks from paganism to Catholic Christianity. At a time when the other Germanic rulers were still Arian, Clovis and the Franks became Catholics and, as a consequence, the champions of the Catholic faith. The Franks rapidly became the dominant power in the West, and soon other Germanic races either were conquered or followed the example of the Franks and became Catholics (§ 97). The State churches that thus arose were more under the control of the local royal authority than the Catholic Church had previously been, and the rulers were little disposed to favor outside control of the ecclesiastical affairs of their kingdoms (§ 98). Toward the end of the sixth century the greatest pontiff of the ancient Church, Gregory the Great, more than recovered the prestige and influence which had been lost under Vigilius. By his able administration he did much to unite the West, to heal the schism resulting from the Fifth Council, and to overcome the heresies which divided the Arians and the Catholics. At the same time he advanced the authority of the see of Rome in the East as well as in the West (§ 99). Of the many statesmanlike undertakings of Gregory none had more far-reaching consequences than the conversion of the Anglo-Saxons and the establishment in England of a church which would be in close and loyal dependence upon the Roman see, and in consequence of that close connection would be the heir of the best traditions of culture in the West (§ 100).

§ 96. The Celtic Church of the British Isles.
§ 97. The Conversion of the Franks: the Establishment of Catholicism in the Germanic Kingdoms.
§ 98. The State Church of the Germanic Kingdoms.
§ 99. Gregory the Great and the Roman Church in the Second Half of the Sixth Century and the Beginning of the Seventh Century.
§ 100. The Foundation of the Anglo-Saxon Church.

§ 96. The Celtic Church in the British Isles

Christianity was probably planted in the British Isles during the second century; as to its growth in the ante-Nicene period little is definitely known. Representatives of the British Church were at Arles in 314. The Church was in close connection with the Church on the Continent during the fourth century and in the fifth during the Pelagian controversy. The Christianity thus established was completely overthrown or driven into Wales by the invasion of the pagan Angles, Jutes, and Saxons *circa* 449–500. (For the conversion of the newcomers, *v. infra*, § 100.) Early in the fifth century the conversion of Ireland took place by missionaries from Britain. In this conversion St. Patrick traditionally plays an important part.

Additional source material: Bede, *Hist. Ec.*, Eng. trans. by Giles, London, 1894; by A. M. Sellar, London, 1907 (for Latin text, *v. infra, a*); Adamnani, *Vita S. Columbæ*, ed. J. T. Fowler, 1894 (with valuable introduction and translation); St. Patrick, *Genuine Writings*, ed. G. T. Stokes and C. H. H. Wright, Dublin, 1887; J. D. Newport White, *The Writings of St. Patrick*, 1904. For bibliography of sources, see Gross, *The Sources and Literature of English History*, 1900, pp. 221 *f*.

(*a*) Bede, *Hist. Ec. Gentis Anglorum*, I, 13. (MSL, 95 : 40.)

The Venerable Bede (672 or 673–735), monk at Jarrow, the most learned theologian of the Anglo-Saxon Church, was also the first historian of England. For the earliest period he used what written sources were available. His work becomes of independent value with the account of the coming of Augustine of Canterbury, 597 (I, 23). The history extends to A. D. 731. The best critical edition is that of C. Plummer, 1896, which has a valuable introduction, copious historical and critical notes, and careful discrimination of the sources. Wm. Bright's *Chapters on Early English Church History* is an elaborate commentary on Bede's work as far as 709, the death of Wilfrid. Translation of Bede's History by J. A. Giles, may be found in Bohn's *Antiquarian Library*, and better by A. M. Sellar, 1907.

In the following passage we have the only reference made by Bede to the conversion of Ireland, and his failure to mention Patrick has given rise to much controversy, see J. B. Bury, *The Life of St. Patrick and his Place in History,* 1905. This passage, referring to Palladius, is a quotation from the *Chronica* of Prosper of Aquitaine (403–463) ann. 431 (MSL, 51, critical edition in MGH, *Auct. antiquiss,* 9 : 1); from Gildas, *De excidio Britanniæ liber querulus* (MSL, 69 : 327, critical edition in MGH, *Auct. antiquiss,* 13. A translation by J. A. Giles in *Six Old English Chronicles,* in Bohn's *Antiquarian Library*), is the reference to the letter written to the Romans; from the *Chronica* of Marcellinus Comes (MSL, 51 : 913; critical edition in MGH, *Auct. antiquiss,* 11) is the reference to Blæda and Attila.

In the year of the Lord's incarnation, 423, Theodosius the younger received the empire after Honorius and, being the forty-fifth from Augustus, retained it twenty-six years. In the eighth year of his reign, Palladius was sent by Celestinus, the pontiff of the Roman Church, to the Scots[1] that believed in Christ to be their first bishop. In the twenty-third year of his reign (446), Aëtius, the illustrious, who was also patrician, discharged his third consulate with Symmachus as his colleague. To him the wretched remnants of the Britons sent a letter beginning: "To Aëtius, thrice consul, the groans of the Britons." And in the course of the letter they thus express their calamities: "The barbarians drive us to the sea; the sea drives us back to the barbarians; between them there have arisen two sorts of death; we are either slain or drowned." Yet neither could all this procure any assistance from him, as he was then engaged in a most dangerous war with Blæda and Attila, kings of the Huns. And though the year next before this, Blæda had been murdered by the treachery of his brother Attila, yet Attila himself remained so intolerable an enemy to the republic that he ravaged almost all Europe, invading and destroying cities and castles.

(*b*) Patrick, *Confessio,* chs. 1, 10.   (MSL, 53 : 801.)

The call of St. Patrick to be a missionary.
There is much dispute and uncertainty about the life and work of St. Patrick. Of the works of Patrick, two appear to be genuine, his *Confessio* and his *Epistola ad Coroticum.* The other works attributed to him are very probably spurious. The genuine works may be found

[1] The Irish were known as Scots. The name Scotland was given to that country on account of invaders from North Ireland.

in Haddan and Stubbs, *Councils and Ecclesiastical Documents relating to Great Britain and Ireland*, vol. II, pt. ii, 296 *ff*.

I, Patrick, a sinner, the most ignorant and least of all the faithful, and the most contemptible among many, had for my father Calpornius the deacon, son of the presbyter Potitus, the son of Odissus, who was of the village of Bannavis Tabernia; he had near by a little estate where I was taken captive. I was then nearly sixteen years old. But I was ignorant of the true God[1] and I was taken into captivity unto Ireland, with so many thousand men, according to our deserts, because we had forsaken God and not kept His commandments and had not been obedient to our priests who warned us of our salvation. And the Lord brought upon us the fury of His wrath and scattered us among many nations, even to the end of the earth, where now my meanness appears to be among strangers. And there the Lord opened the senses of my unbelief, that I might remember my sin, and that I might be converted with my whole heart to my Lord God, who looked upon my humbleness and had mercy upon my youth and ignorance, and guarded me before I knew Him, and before I knew and distinguished between good and evil, and protected me and comforted me as a father a son.

. . . And again after a few years[2] I was with my relatives in Britain, who received me as a son, and earnestly besought me that I should never leave them after having endured so many great tribulations. And there I saw in a vision by night a man coming to me as from Ireland, and his name was Victorinus, and he had innumerable epistles; and he gave me one of them and I read the beginning of the epistle as follows: "The voice of the Irish." And while I was reading the epistle, I think that it was at the very moment, I heard the voice of those who were near the wood of Fochlad,[3] which is near the

---

[1] *I. e.*, not necessarily a pagan, but he did not love God, or was not yet " converted."

[2] In the meanwhile he had escaped to France and lived there.

[3] Where Patrick had lived as a slave.

Western Sea. And thus they cried out with one voice: We beseech thee, holy youth, to come here and dwell among us. And I was greatly smitten in heart, and could read no further and so I awoke. Thanks be to God, because after many years the Lord granted them according to their cry.

(c) Bede, *Hist. Ec.*, III, 4. (MSL, 95 : 121.)

St. Ninian and St. Columba in Scotland.

In the year of our Lord 565, when Justin the younger, the successor of Justinian, took the government of the Roman Empire, there came into Britain a priest and abbot, distinguished in habit and monastic life, Columba by name, to preach the word of God to the provinces of the northern Picts, that is, to those who are separated from the southern parts by steep and rugged mountains. For the southern Picts, who had their homes within those mountains, had long before, as is reported, forsaken the error of idolatry, and ·embraced the true faith, by the preaching of the word to them by Ninian,[1] a most reverend bishop and holy man of the British nation, who had been regularly instructed at Rome in the faith and mysteries of the truth, whose episcopal see was named after St. Martin, the bishop, and was famous for its church, wherein he and many other saints rest in the body, and which the English nation still possesses. The place belongs to the province of Bernicia, and is commonly called Candida Casa,[2] because he there built a church of stone, which was not usual among the Britons.

Columba came to Britain in the ninth year of the reign of Bridius, the son of Meilochon, the very powerful king of the Picts, and he converted by work and example that nation to the faith of Christ; whereupon he also received the aforesaid island [Iona] for a monastery. It is not large, but contains about five families, according to English reckoning. His suc-

[1] This reference to Ninian is the most important there is; in fact, Bede is here the chief authority for the work of this missionary.
[2] Whitherne, Galloway.

cessors hold it to this day, and there also he was buried, when he was seventy-seven, about thirty-two years after he came into Britain to preach. Before he came into Britain he had built a noble monastery in Ireland, which from the great number of oaks is called in the Scottish tongue[1] Dearmach, that is, the Field of Oaks. From both of these monasteries many others had their origin through his disciples both in Britain and Ireland; but the island monastery where his body lies holds the rule.

That island always has for its ruler an abbot, who is a priest, to whose direction all the province and even bishops themselves are subject by an unusual form of organization, according to the example of their first teacher, who was not a bishop, but a priest and monk; of whose life and discourses some writings are said to have been preserved by his disciples. But whatever he was himself, this we regard as certain concerning him, that he left successors renowned for their great continency, their love of God, and their monastic rules. However, they followed uncertain cycles[2] in their observance of the great festival [Easter], for no one brought them the synodal decrees for the observance of Easter, because they were placed so far away from the rest of the world; they only practised such works of piety and chastity as they could learn from the prophetical, evangelical, and apostolical writings. This manner of keeping Easter continued among them for a long time, that is, for the space of one hundred and fifty years, or until the year of our Lord's incarnation 715.

§ 97. The Conversion of the Franks. The Establishment of Catholicism in the Germanic Kingdoms

Chlodowech (Clovis, 481–511) was originally a king of the Salian Franks, near Tournay. By his energy he became king of all the Franks, and, overthrowing Syagrius in 486, pushed his frontier to the Loire. In 496 he conquered a portion of the

---

[1] I. e., Irish tongue.   [2] Rules for computing Easter.

Alemanni. About this time he became a Catholic. He had for some time favored the Catholic religion, and with his conversion his rule was associated with that cause in the kingdoms subject to Arian rulers. In this way his support of Catholicism was in line with his policy of conquest. By constant warfare Chlodowech was able to push his frontier, in 507, to the Garonne. His death, in 511, at less than fifty years of age, cut short only for a time the extension of the Frankish kingdom. Under his sons, Burgundy, Thuringia, and Bavaria were conquered. The kingdom, which had been divided on the death of Chlodowech, was united under the youngest son, Chlotar I (sole ruler 558–561), again divided on his death, to be united under Chlotar II (sole ruler 613–628). In Spain the Suevi, in the northwest, became Catholic under Carrarich in 550. They were conquered in 585 by the Visigoths, who in turn became Catholic in 589.

(a) Gregory of Tours, *Historia Francorum*, II, 30, 31. (MSL, 71 : 225.)

Gregory of Tours (538–593) became bishop of Tours in 573. Placed in this way in the most important see of France, he was constantly thrown in contact with the Merovingian royal family and had abundant opportunity to become acquainted with the course of events at first hand. His most important work, the *History of the Franks*, is especially valuable from the fifth book on, as here he is on ground with which he was personally familiar. In Book II, from which the selection is taken, Gregory depends upon others, and must be used with caution.

The baptism of Chlodowech was probably the result of a long process of deliberation, beginning probably before his marriage with Chrotechildis, a Burgundian princess, who was a Catholic. While still a pagan he was favorably disposed toward the Catholic Church. About 496 he was baptized, probably on Christmas Day, at Rheims, by St. Remigius. The place and date have been much disputed of late. The earliest references to the conversion are by Nicetus of Trier (*ob. circa* 566), *Epistula ad Chlodosvindam reginam Longobardorum* (MSL, 65 : 375); and Avitus, *Epistula* 41, addressed to Chlodowech himself. (MSL, 59 : 257). A careful examination of all the evidence may be found in A. Hauck, *Kirchengeschichte Deutschlands*, fourth ed., I, 595 *ff.* Hauck concludes that "the date, December 25, 496, may be regarded as almost certainly the date of the baptism of Chlodowech. The connection as to time between the first war with the Alemanni and the baptism may have given occasion to seek for some actual connection between the two events." The selection is therefore given as the traditional version and is not to be relied upon as correct in detail. It represents what was probably the current belief within a few decades of the event.

Ch. 30. The queen (Chrotechildis) ceased not to warn Chlodowech that he should acknowledge the true God and forsake idols. But in no way could he be brought to believe these things. Finally war broke out with the Alemanni. Then by necessity was he compelled to acknowledge what before he had denied with his will. The two armies met and there was a fearful slaughter, and the army of Chlodowech was on the point of being annihilated. When the king perceived that, he raised his eyes to heaven, his heart was smitten and he was moved to tears, and he said: "Jesus Christ, whom Chrotechildis declares to be the Son of the living God, who says that Thou wilt help those in need and give victory to those who hope in Thee, humbly I flee to Thee for Thy mighty aid, that Thou wilt give me victory over these my enemies, and I will in this way experience Thy power, which the people called by Thy name claim that they have proved to be in Thee. Then will I believe on Thee and be baptized in Thy name. For I have called upon my gods but, as I have seen, they are far from my help. Therefore, I believe that they have no power who do not hasten to aid those obedient to them. I now call upon Thee and I desire to believe on Thee. Only save me from the hand of my adversaries." As he thus spoke, the Alemanni turned their backs and began to take flight. But when they saw that their king was dead, they submitted to Chlodowech and said: "Let not, we pray thee, a nation perish; now we are thine." Thereupon he put an end to the war, exhorted the people, and returned home in peace. He told the queen how by calling upon the name of Christ he had obtained victory. This happened in the fifteenth year of his reign (496).

Ch. 31. Thereupon the queen commanded that the holy Remigius, bishop of Rheims, be brought secretly to teach the king the word of salvation. The priest was brought to him secretly and began to lay before him that he should believe in the true God, the creator of heaven and earth, and forsake idols, who could neither help him nor others. But he replied: "Gladly do I listen to thee, most holy Father, but one thing remains, for the people who follow me suffer me not to forsake their gods. But I will go and speak to them according to thy words." When he met his men, and before he began to speak, all the people cried out together, for the divine power had anticipated him: "We reject the mortal gods, pious king, and we are ready to follow the immortal God whom Remigius preaches." These things were reported to the bishop, who rejoiced greatly and commanded the font to be prepared. . . . The king first asked to be baptized by the pontiff. He went, a new Constantine, into the font to be washed clean from the old leprosy, and to purify himself in fresh water from the stains which he had long had. But as he stepped into the baptismal water, the saint of God began in moving tone: "Bend softly thy head, Sicamber, reverence what thou hast burnt, and burn what thou hast reverenced." . . .

Therefore the king confessed Almighty God in Trinity, and was baptized in the name of the Father and of the Son and of the Holy Ghost, and was anointed with the holy chrism with the sign of the cross. Of his army more than three thousand were baptized. Also his sister Albofledis was baptized. . . . And another sister of the king, Lanthechildis by name, who had fallen into the heresy of the Arians, was converted, and when she had confessed that the Son and the Holy Ghost were of the same substance with the Father, she was given the chrism.

(b) Gregory of Tours, *Hist. Francorum*, II, 35–38. (MSL, 71 : 232.)

Clovis at the head of the anti-Arian party in Gaul.

Ch. 35. When Alarich, the king of the Goths, saw that King Chlodowech continually conquered the nations, he sent messengers to him saying: "If my brother wishes, it is also in my heart that we see each other, if God will." Chlodowech was not opposed to this and came to him. They met on an island in the Loire, in the neighborhood of Amboise, in the territory of Tours, and spake and ate and drank together, promised mutual friendship, and parted in peace.

Ch. 36. But already many Gauls wished with all their heart to have the Franks for their masters. It therefore happened that Quintianus, bishop of Rhodez, was driven out of his city on account of this. For they said to him: "You wish that the rule of the Franks possessed this land." And a few days after, when a dispute had arisen between him and the citizens, the rumor reached the Goths who dwelt in the city, for the citizens asserted that he wished to be subject to the rule of the Franks; and they took counsel and planned how they might kill him with the sword. When this was reported to the man of God, he rose by night, and with the most faithful of his servants left Rhodez and came to Arverne. . . .

Ch. 37. Thereupon King Chlodowech said to his men: "It is a great grief to me that these Arians possess a part of Gaul. Let us go forth with God's aid, conquer them, and bring this land into our power." And since this speech pleased all, he marched with his army toward Poitiers, for there dwelt Alarich at that time. . . . King Chlodowech met the king of the Goths, Alarich, in the Campus Vocladensis [Vouillé or Voulon-sur-Clain] ten miles from Poitiers; and while the latter fought from afar, the former withstood in hand to hand combat. But since the Goths, in their fashion, took to flight, King Chlodowech at length with God's aid won the victory. He had on his side a son of Sigbert the Lame, whose name was Chloderich. The same Sigbert, ever since he fought with the Alemanni near Zulpich [in 496], had been wounded in the knee and limped. The king killed King Alarich and put the Goths to flight. . . . From this battle Amalrich, Alarich's son, fled to Spain, and by his ability obtained his father's kingdom. Chlodowech, however, sent his son Theuderic to Albi, Rhodez, and Arverne, and departing he subjugated those cities, from the borders of the Goths to the borders of the Burgundians, to the rule of his father. But Alarich reigned twenty-two years. Chlodowech spent the winter in Bourdeaux, and carried away the entire treasure of Alarich from Toulouse, and he went to Angoulême. Such favor did the Lord show him that, when he looked on the walls, they fell of themselves. Thereupon when the Goths had been driven from the city he brought it under his rule. After the accomplishment of these victories he returned to Tours and dedicated many gifts to the holy Church of St. Martin.

Ch. 38. At that time he received from the Emperor Anastasius the title of consul, and in the Church of St. Martin he assumed the purple cloak and put on his head a diadem. He then mounted a horse and with his own hand scattered among the people who were present gold and silver in the greatest profusion, all the way from the door of the porch of the Church of St. Martin to the city gate. And from this day forward he was addressed as consul, or Augustus. From Tours Chlodowech went to Paris and made that the seat of his authority.[1]

(c) Third Council of Toledo, A. D. 589, *Acts*. Mansi, IX, 992.

This council is the most important event in the history of the Visigothic Church of Spain, marking the abandonment of Arianism by the ruling race of Spain and the formal acceptance of the doctrine of the Trinity or the Catholic faith and unity. The Suevi had accepted Catholicism more than thirty-five years before; see Synod of Braga, A. D. 563, in Hefele, § 285 (*cf.* also Hahn, § 176, who gives the text of the anathematisms in which, after a statement of the Catholic doctrine of the Trinity, the balance of the anathematisms are concerned with Priscillianism). Reccared, the Visigothic king (586–601), became a Catholic in 587, and held the council of 589 to effect the conversion of the nation to his new faith. For a letter of Gregory the Great on the conversion of Reccared, see PNF, ser. II, vol. XII, pt. 2, p. 87, and two from Gregory to Reccared himself (*ibid.*, vol. XIII, pp. 16, 35). The creed, as professed at Toledo, is the first instance of the authorized use of the term "and the Son" in a creed in connection with the doc-

[1] It had been at Soissons after 486, and before that at Tournay.

trine of the "procession of the Holy Spirit," the form in which the so-called Nicene creed came to be used in the West, and the source of much dispute between the East and the West in the ninth century and ever since.

I. From the Speech of Reccared at the Opening of the Council.

I judge that you are not ignorant, most reverend priests [*i. e.*, bishops] that I have called you into our presence for the restoration of ecclesiastical discipline; and because in time past the existence of heresy prevented throughout the entire Catholic Church the transaction of synodical business. God, who has been pleased by our action to remove the obstacle of the same heresy, warns us to set in order the ecclesiastical laws concerning church matters. Therefore let it be a matter of joy and gladness to you that the canonical order is being brought back to the lines of the times of our fathers, in the sight of God and to our glory.

II. From the Statement of Faith.

There is present here all the famous nation of the Goths, esteemed for their real bravery by nearly all nations, who, however, by the error of their teachers have been separated from the faith and unity of the Catholic Church; but now, agreeing as a whole with me in my assent to the faith, participate in the communion of that Church which receives in its maternal bosom a multitude of different nations and nourishes them with the breasts of charity. Concerning her the prophet foretelling said: "My house shall be called the house of prayer for all nations." For not only does the conversion of the Goths add to the amount of our reward, but also an infinite multitude of the people of the Suevi, whom under the protection of Heaven we have subjected to our kingdom, led away into heresy by the fault of an alien,[1] we have endeavored to recall to the source of truth. Therefore, most holy Fathers, I offer as by your hands to the eternal God,

[1] In 465, under the influence of the Visigoths, the Suevi, formerly Catholic, had embraced Arianism.

as a holy and pleasing offering, these most noble nations,
who have been attached by us to the Lord's possessions.
For it will be to me in the day of the retribution of the
just an unfading crown and joy if these peoples, who now by
our planning have returned to the unity of the Church, remain founded and established in the same. For as by the
divine determination it has been a matter of our care to bring
these peoples to the unity of the Church of Christ, so it is a
matter of your teaching to instruct them in the Catholic
dogmas, by which they may be instructed in the full knowledge of the truth, that they may know how to reject totally
the errors of pernicious heresy, to remain in charity in the
ways of the true faith, and to embrace with fervent desire the
communion of the Catholic Church. . . . As it is of benefit
to us to profess with the mouth what we believe in the heart
. . . therefore I anathematize Arius with all his doctrines . . .
so I hold in honor, to the praise and honor and glory of God,
the faith of the holy Council of Nicæa. . . . I embrace and
hold the faith of the one hundred and fifty Fathers assembled
at Constantinople. . . . I believe the faith of the first Council of Ephesus . . . likewise with all the Catholic Church I
reverently receive the faith of the Council of Chalcedon. . . .
To this my confession I have added the holy constitutions
[*i. e.*, confessions of faith] of the above-mentioned councils,
and I have subscribed with complete singleness of heart to
the divine testimony.

Here follows the faith of Nicæa, the so-called creed of Constantinople, with the words relating to the Holy Ghost, *ex Patre et Filio
procedentem* (proceeding from the Father and the Son); the actual form
filioque does not here occur.

III. From the *Anathemas*, Hahn, § 178.

3. Whosoever does not believe in the Holy Ghost and will
not believe that He proceeds from the Father and the Son, and
will not say that He is co-essential with the Father and the
Son, let him be anathema.

IV. From the *Canons*, Bruns, I, 212.

Canon 1. After the damnation of the heresy of Arius and the exposition of the Catholic faith, this holy council ordered that, because in the midst of many heretics and heathen throughout the churches of Spain, the canonical order has been necessarily neglected (for while liberty of transgressing abounded, and the desirable discipline was denied, and every one fostered excesses of heresy in the protection and continuation of evil times, a strict discipline was far off, but now the peace of the Church has been restored by the mercy of Christ), everything which by the authority of early canons may be forbidden is forbidden, discipline arising again, and everything is required which they order done. Let the constitutions of all the councils remain in their force, likewise all the synodical letters of the holy Roman prelates. Henceforth let no one aspire unworthily to ecclesiastical promotions and honors against the canons. Let nothing be done which the holy Fathers, filled with the Spirit of God, decreed should not be done. And let those who presume to violate the laws be restrained by the severity of the earlier canons.

Canon 2. Out of reverence for the most holy faith and to strengthen the weak minds of men, acting upon the advice of the most pious and glorious King Reccared[1] the synod has ordered that throughout the churches of Spain, Gaul, and Gallicia, the symbol of the faith be recited according to the form of the Oriental churches, the symbol of the Council of Constantinople, that is, of the one hundred and fifty bishops;

---

[1] "Let all the churches of Spain and Gallicia observe this rule, that at every time of offering of the sacrifice and before the communion of the body and blood of Christ, according to the custom of the Oriental parts, all should repeat together with a clear voice the most sacred symbol of the faith, that first the people may speak the faith which they hold, and they may bring hearts purified by faith to the reception of the body and blood of Christ. For so long as this constitution be perpetually observed in the Church of God, the entire belief of the faithful will be confirmed, and the false faith of the infidels be confuted, in order that one may be very easily inclined to believe what one hears very often repeated, neither shall any one excuse himself from all blame by pleading ignorance of the faith, when he knows from the mouth of all what the Catholic Church holds and believes." (From the Speech of Reccared, *cf.* Mansi, *loc. cit.*)

and before the Lord's prayer is said, let it be pronounced to the people in a clear voice, by which also the true faith may have a manifest testimony, and the hearts of the people may approach to the reception of the body and blood of Christ with hearts purified by faith.

§ 98.   The State Church in the Germanic Kingdoms

So long as the Germanic rulers remained Arian, the Catholic Church in their kingdoms was left for the most part alone or hindered in its synodical activity. But as the kingdoms became Catholic on the conversion of their kings, the rulers were necessarily brought into close official relations with the Church and its administration; and they exercised a strict control over the ecclesiastical councils and the episcopal elections. The Merovingians, on their conversion from paganism, at once became Catholics, and they consequently assumed this control immediately. With the extension of the Frankish kingdom, the authority of the king in ecclesiastical affairs was likewise extended. In Spain the Visigoths were Arians until 589. On the conversion of the nation at that date, the king at once assumed an extensive ecclesiastical authority (for Reccared's confirmation of the Third Synod of Toledo, 589, see Bruns, I, 393), and in the development of the system the councils of Toledo became at once the parliaments of the entire nation, now united through its common faith and the synods of the Church. This system was cut short by the Moslem invasion of 711, and the development of the Church and its relation to the State is to be studied in the Frankish kingdom in which from this time the ecclesiastical development of Western Europe is to be traced. The best evidence for the legal state of the Church under the Germanic rulers is chiefly in the acts of councils.

But there was also in the Catholic Church in the Germanic kingdoms a strong monastic spirit which was by no means willing to see the Church become an "establishment." This

fitted in poorly with the condition of the State Church. It
is illustrated by the career of St. Columbanus.

(a) Council of Orleans, A. D. 511, *Synodical Letter.* Bruns,
II, 160.

The king summons the council and approves its findings. Extract
from the synodical letter in which the canons are sent to Chlodowech.

To their Lord, the Son of the Catholic Church, Chlodowech,
the most glorious king, all the priests[1] whom you have commanded to come to the council.

Because your great care for the glorious faith so moves you
to reverence for the Catholic religion that from love of the
priesthood you have commanded the bishops to be gathered
together into one that they might treat of necessary things,
according to the proposals of your will and the titles [*i. e.,*
topics] which you have given, we reply by determining those
things which seem good to us; so that if those things which
we have decreed prove to be right in your judgment, the approval of so great a king and lord might by a greater authority
cause the determinations of so many bishops to be observed
more strictly.

(b) Council of Orleans, A. D. 549, *Canons.* Bruns, II, 211.

Canons regarding Episcopal elections. The first instance in canonical legislation in the West recognizing the necessity of royal consent to the election of a bishop. For the relation of the Pope to metropolitans, see in § 99 the Epistle of Gregory the Great to Vigilius of
Arles.

Canon 10. That it shall be lawful for no one to obtain
the episcopate by payment or bargaining, but with the permission of the king, according to the choice of the clergy and
the people, as it is written in the ancient canons, let him be
consecrated by the metropolitan or by him whom he sends in
his place, together with the bishops of the province. That if

[1] Here, as very often, the bishops attending a council are spoken of as
priests. The term "priest" had not become identified with "presbyter."
The bishop was a *sacerdos* or priest. The presbyter was also a *sacerdos.*

any one violates by purchase the rule of this holy constitution, we decree that he, who shall have been ordained for money, shall be deposed.

Canon 11. Likewise as the ancient canons decree, no one shall be made bishop of those who are unwilling to receive him, and neither by the force of powerful persons are the citizens and clergy to be induced to give a testimonial of election.[1] For this is to be regarded as a crime; that if this should be done, let him, who rather by violence than by legitimate decree has been ordained bishop, be deposed forever from the honor of the episcopate which he has obtained.

(c) Council of Paris, A. D. 557, *Canon.* Bruns, II, 221.

Canon 8. No bishop shall be ordained for people against their will, but only he whom the people and clergy in full election shall have freely chosen; neither by the command of the prince nor by any condition whatever against the will of the metropolitan and the bishops of the province shall he be forced in. That if any one with so great rashness presumes by royal appointment[2] to reach the height of this honor, let him not deserve to be received as a bishop by the bishops of the province in which the place is located, for they know that he was ordained improperly. If any of the fellow bishops of the province presume to receive him against this prohibition, let him be separated from all his brethren and be deprived of the charity of all.

(d) Gregory of Tours, *Hist. Francorum,* IV, 15. (MSL, 71 : 280.)

The difficulty of the Church in living under the Merovingian monarchs with their despotism and violence is illustrated by the following passage. The date of the event is 556.

---

[1] This testimonial, or certificate of election, was to be presented to the king that he might give his assent; *cf.* § 94.

[2] The kings appear to have attempted to appoint bishops without canonical election. This was never recognized by the Church as lawful on the part of the king and was always opposed. See next selection from Gregory of Tours.

582 DISSOLUTION OF IMPERIAL STATE CHURCH

When the clergy of Tours heard that King Chlothar [511–561; 558–561, as surviving son of Chlodowech, sole ruler of the Franks] had returned from the slaughter of the Saxons, they prepared the consensus[1] that they had chosen the priest Eufronius bishop and went to the king. When they had presented the matter, the king answered: "I had indeed commanded that the priest Cato should be ordained there, and why has our command been disregarded?" They answered him: "We have indeed asked him, but he would not come." And as they said this suddenly the priest Cato appeared and besought the king to command that Cautinus be removed and himself be appointed bishop of Arverne.[2] But when the king laughed at this, he besought him again, that he might be ordained for Tours, which he had before rejected. Then the king said to him: "I have already commanded that you should be consecrated bishop of Tours, but, as I hear, you have despised that church; therefore you shall be withheld from the government of it." Thereupon he departed ashamed. But when the king asked concerning the holy Eufronius, they said that he was a nephew of the holy Gregory, whom we have mentioned above.[3] The king answered: "That is a distinguished and very great family. Let the will of God and of the holy Martin[4] be done; let the election be confirmed." And after he had given a decree for the ordination, the holy Eufronius was ordained as the eighth bishop after St. Martin.[5]

(e) Gregory of Tours, *Hist. Franc.*, VIII, 22. (MSL, 71 : 464.)

Royal interference in episcopal elections was not infrequent under the Merovingians. Confused as the following account is, it is clear from it that the kings were accustomed to violate the canons and to exercise a free hand in episcopal appointments. See also the preceding selection. The date of the event is 585. For the Synod of Mâcon, A. D. 585, see Hefele, § 286.

[1] Testimonial of election.   [2] *I. e.*, Clermont-Ferrand.
[3] See Greg. Tour., III. 19. *Cf.* DCB, art. "Gregorius (29)." He was bishop of Langres.
[4] St. Martin of Tours, the patron saint of the church of Tours.
[5] Eufronius was the predecessor of Gregory of Tours, the author of this passage.

Laban, Bishop of Eauze,[1] died that year. Desiderius, a layman, succeeded him, although the king had promised with an oath that he would never again ordain a bishop from the laity. But to what will not the accursed hunger for gold drive human hearts? Bertchramnus[2] had returned from the synod,[3] and on the way was seized with a fever. The deacon Waldo was summoned, who in baptism had also been called Bertchramnus, and he committed to him the whole of his episcopal office, as he also committed to him the provisions regarding his testament, as well as those who merited well by him. As he departed the bishop breathed out his spirit. The deacon returned and with presents and the consensus[4] of the people, went to the king[5] but he obtained nothing. Then the king, having issued a mandate, commanded Gundegisilus, count of Saintes, surnamed Dodo, to be consecrated bishop; and so it was done. And because many of the clergy of Saintes before the synod had, in agreement with Bishop Bertchramnus, written various things against their Bishop Palladius to humiliate him, after his[6] death they were arrested by the bishop, severely tortured, and stripped of their property.

(f) Chlotar II, *Capitulary*, A. D. 614. MGH, Leges, II. *Capitularia Regum Francorum*, ed. Boretius, I, 20, MGH, Leges, 1883.

Not only did the councils admit the right of the king to approve the candidate for consecration as bishop, but the kings laid down the principle that their approval was necessary. They also legislated on the affairs of the Church, e. g., on the election of bishops. The text may also be found in Altmann und Bernheim, *Ausgewählte Urkunden*, Berlin, 1904, p. 1.

Ch. 1. It is our decree that the statutes of the canons be observed in all things, and those of them which have been

[1] At one time metropolis of Novempopulania; when it was destroyed in the ninth century, the dignity passed to Auch, where it remained.
[2] Bishop of Bourdeaux.　　　　　　　[3] At Mâcon.
[4] The formal certificate of election.　　[5] Guntrum.
[6] Bishop Bertchramnus's.

neglected in the past because of the circumstances of the times shall hereafter be observed perpetually; so that when a bishop dies one shall be chosen for his place by the clergy and people, who is to be ordained by the metropolitan and his provincials; if the person be worthy let him be ordained by the order of the prince; but if he be chosen from the palace[1] let him be ordained on account of the merit of his person and his learning.

Ch. 2. That no bishop while living shall choose a successor, but another shall be substituted for him when he become so indisposed that he cannot rule his church and clergy. Likewise, that while a bishop is living no one shall presume to take his place, and if one should seek it, it is on no account to be given him.

(g) Fredegarius Scholasticus, *Chronicon*, 75f. (MSL, 71 : 653.)

The Chronicon of Fredegarius is important, as it continues in its last book the *History of the Franks* by Gregory of Tours. The best edition is in the MGH, *Scriptores rerum Merovingicarum* II, ed. Krusch. An account of the work may be found in DCB, art. "Fredegarius Scholasticus." In the Frankish kingdom the higher clergy, especially the bishops, assembled with the great men of the realm in councils under the king to discuss affairs of State. These councils have been called *concilia mixta*. They are, however, to be distinguished from the strictly ecclesiastical assemblies in which the clergy alone acted. A change was introduced by Charles the Great. The following passage shows the king consulting with the bishops, along with the other nobles.

§ 75. In the eleventh year of his reign Dagobert came to the city of Metz, because the Wends at the command of Samo still manifested their savage fury and often made inroads from their territory to lay waste the Frankish kingdom, Thuringia, and other provinces. Dagobert, coming to Metz, with the counsel of the bishops and nobles, and the consent of all the great men of his kingdom, made his son, Sigibert, king of Austrasia, and assigned him Metz as his seat. To Chun-

---

[1] *I. e.*, if he be one of the court chaplains.

ibert, bishop of Cologne, and the Duke Adalgisel, he committed the conduct of his palace and kingdom.[1] Also he gave to his son sufficient treasure and fitted him out with all that was appropriate to his high dignity; and whatsoever he had given him he confirmed by charters specially made out. Since then the Frankish land was sufficiently defended by the zeal of the Austrasians against the Wends.

§ 76. When in the twelfth year of his reign a son named Chlodoveus was born by Queen Nantechilde to Dagobert, he made, with the counsel and advice of the Neustrians, an agreement with his Sigibert. All the great men and the bishops of Austrasia and the other people of Sigibert, holding up their hands, confirmed it with an oath, that after the death of Dagobert, Neustria and Burgundy, by an established ordinance, should fall to Chlodoveus; but Austrasia, because in population and extent it was equal to those lands, should belong in its entire extent to Sigibert.

(*h*) Jonas, *Vita Columbani*, chs. 9, 12, 17, 32, 33, 59, 60. (MSL, 87 : 1016.)

Columbanus (543–615) was the most active and successful of the Irish missionary monks laboring on the continent of Europe. In 585 Columbanus left Ireland to preach in the wilder parts of Gaul, and in 590 or 591 founded Luxeuil, which became the parent monastery of a considerable group of monastic houses. He came into conflict with the Frankish clergy on account of the Celtic mode of fixing the date of Easter [see Epistle of Columbanus among the Epistles óf Gregory the Great, to whom it is addressed, Bk. IX, Ep. 127, PNF, ser. II, vol. XIII, p. 38; two other epistles on the subject in MSL, vol. 80], his monastic rule [MSL, 80 : 209], and his condemnatory attitude toward the dissoluteness of life prevalent in Gaul among the clergy, as well as in the court. Banished from Burgundy in 610 partly for political reasons, he worked for a time in the vicinity of Lake Constance. In 612, leaving his disciple Gallus [see *Vita S. Galli*, by Walafrid Strabo, MSL, 114; English translation by C. W. Bispham, Philadelphia, 1908], he went to Italy and, having founded Bobbio, died in 615. Gallus (*ob. circa* 640) subsequently founded the great monastery of St. Gall in Switzerland, near Lake Constance. The Celtic monks on the continent abandoned their Celtic peculiarities in the ninth century and adopted the Benedictine rule.

[1] Sigibert appears to have been born 629.

Jonas, the author of the life of Columbanus, was a monk at Bobbio. His life of Columbanus was written about 640; see DCB, "Jonas (6)." In the following, the divisions and numbering of paragraphs follow Migne's edition. There is an excellent new edition in the MGH, *Script. rerum Merovin.*, ed. Krusch, 8vo, 1905.

Columbanus sets forth.

Ch. 9. Columbanus gathered such treasures of divine knowledge that even in his youth he could expound the Psalter in polished discourse and could make many other discourses, worthy of being sung and useful to teach. Thereupon he took pains to be received into the company of monks, and sought the monastery of Benechor [in Ulster] the head of which, the blessed Commogellus, was famous for his many virtues. He was an excellent father of his monks and highly regarded because of his zeal in religion and the maintenance of discipline according to the rule. And here he began to give himself entirely to prayer and fasting and to bear the yoke of Christ, easy to those who bear it, by denying himself and taking up his cross and following Christ, that he, who was to be the teacher of others, might himself learn by teaching, and by mortification to endure in his own body what he should abundantly show forth; and he who should teach what by others ought to be fulfilled, himself first fulfilled. When many years had passed for him in the cloister, he began to desire to wander forth, mindful of the command which the Lord gave Abraham: "Get thee out of thy country and from thy kindred and from thy father's house unto a land that I will show thee" [Gen. 12 : 1]. He confessed to Commogellus, the venerable Father, the warm desire of his heart, the desire enkindled by the fire of the Lord [Luke 12 : 49]; but he received no such answer as he wished. For it was a grief to Commogellus to bear the loss of a man so full of comfort. Finally Commogellus began to take courage and place it before his heart that he ought to seek more to advance the benefit of others than to pursue his own needs. It happened not without the will of the Almighty, who had trained His pupil for future wars, that from his victories he might obtain glorious triumphs and gain joyful victories over the phalanxes of slain enemies. The abbot called Columbanus unto him and said that though it was a grief to him yet he had come to a decision useful to others, that he would remain in peace with him, would strengthen him with consolation, and give him companions for his journey men who were known for their religion. . . .

So Columbanus in the twentieth[1] year of his life set forth, and with twelve companions under the leadership of Christ went down to the shore of the sea. Here they waited the grace of Almighty God that he would prosper their undertaking, if it took place with His consent; and they perceived that the will of the merciful Judge was with them. They embarked and began the dangerous journey through the straits, and crossed a smooth sea with a favorable wind, and after a quick passage reached the coasts of Brittany. . . .

Columbanus founds monasteries in Gaul.

Ch. 12. At that time there was a wide desert called Vosagus [the Vosges] in which there lay a castle long since in ruins. And ancient tradition called it Anagrates [Anegray]. When the holy man reached this place, in spite of its wild isolation, its rudeness, and the rocks, he settled there with his companions, content with meagre support, mindful of the saying that man lives not by bread alone, but, satisfied with the Word of Life, he would have abundance and never hunger again unto eternity.

Ch. 17. When the number of the monks had increased rapidly, he began to think of seeking in the same desert for a better place, where he might found a monastery. And he found a place, which had formerly been strongly fortified, at a distance from the first place about eight miles, and which was called in ancient times Luxovium.[2] Here there were

[1] Rather the thirtieth according to some MSS., which seems to be more in accord with what has gone before.
[2] Luxeuil.

warm baths erected with special art. A multitude of stone idols stood here in the near-by forest, which in the old heathen times had been honored with execrable practices and profane rites. Residing here, therefore, the excellent man began to found a cloister. On hearing of this the people came to him from all sides in order to dedicate themselves to the practice of religion, so that the great crowd of monks gathered together could hardly be contained in the company of one monastery. Here the children of nobles pressed to come, that, despising the scorned adornments of the world and the pomp of present wealth, they might receive eternal rewards. When Columbanus perceived this and that from all sides the people came together for the medicines of penance, and that the walls of one monastery could not without difficulty hold so great a body of converts to the religious life, and although they were of one mind and one heart, yet it was ill fitted to the intercourse of so great a multitude, he sought out another place, which was excellent on account of its abundance of water, and founded a second monastery, which he named Fontanæ,[1] and placed rulers over it, of whose piety none doubted. As he now settled companies of monks in this place, he dwelt alternately in each and, filled with the Holy Ghost, he established a rule which they should observe that the prudent reader or hearer of it might know by what sort of discipline a man might become holy.

The quarrel of Columbanus with the Court.

Ch. 32. It happened one day that the holy Columbanus came to Brunichildis, who was at that time in Brocariaca.[2] When she saw him coming to the court she led to the man of God the sons of Theuderich, whom he had begotten in adultery. He asked as he saw them what they wanted of him, and Brunichildis said: "They are the king's sons; strengthen them with thy blessing." But he answered: "Know then that these will never hold the royal sceptre, for they have sprung

---

[1] Fontenay or Fontaines.　　　　　[2] Near Autun.

from unchastity." In furious anger she commanded the boys to depart. The man of God thereupon left the royal court, and when he had crossed the threshold there arose a loud roar so that the whole house shook, and all shuddered for fear; yet the rage of the miserable woman could not be restrained. Thereupon she began to plot against the neighboring monasteries, and she caused a decree to be issued that the monks should not be allowed to move freely outside the land of the monastery, and that no one should give them any support or otherwise assist them with offerings.

Ch. 33. Against Columbanus Brunichildis excited the mind of the king and endeavored to disturb him; and she encouraged the minds of his princes, his courtiers, and great men to set the mind of the king against the man of God, and she began to urge the bishops that by vilifying the religion of Columbanus they might dishonor the rule he had given his monks to observe. . . .

Columbanus founds Bobbio.

§ 59. When the blessed Columbanus learned that Theudebert had been conquered by Theuderich, he left Gaul and Germany,[1] which were under Theuderich, and entered Italy where he was honorably received by Agilulf the Lombard king, who gave him permission to dwell where he wished in Italy. It happened by the will of God that, while he was in Milan, Columbanus wishing to attack and root out by the use of the Scripture the errors of the heretics, that is, the false doctrine of the Arians, lingered and composed an excellent work against them.[2]

§ 60. While things were thus going on, a man named Jocundus came before the king and reported to him that he knew of a church of the blessed Peter, prince of the Apostles, in a desert region of the Apennines, in which he learned that

[1] What is now Switzerland was then regarded as a part of Germany, Allemania.

[2] This has not been preserved. But Bobbio, subsequently founded, became a stronghold of the Catholic faith against Arianism.

there were many advantages, being uncommonly fruitful and supplied with water full of fish. It was called in old time Bobium[1] on account of the brook which flowed by it; another river in the neighborhood was called Trebia, on which Hannibal, spending a winter, suffered great losses of men, horses, and elephants. Thither Columbanus removed and restored with all possible diligence the already half-ruined church in all its former beauty. The roof and the top of the temple and the ruins of the walls he repaired and set to work to construct other things necessary for a monastery.

§ 99. Gregory the Great and the Roman Church in the Second Half of the Sixth Century.

Gregory the Great was born about 540. In 573 he was appointed prefect of the city of Rome, but resigned the following year to become a monk. Having been ordained deacon, he was sent in 579 to Constantinople as papal apocrisiarius, or resident ambassador at the court of the Emperor. In 586 he was back in Rome and abbot of St. Andrew's, and in 590 he was elected Pope. As Pope his career was even more brilliant. He reorganized the papal finances, carried through important disciplinary measures, and advanced the cause of monasticism. His work as the organizer of missions in England, his labors to heal the Istrian schism, his relations with the Lombards, his dealings with the Church in Gaul, his controversy with Constantinople in the matter of the title "Ecumenical Patriarch," and other large relations and tasks indicate the range of his interests and the extent of his activities. As a theologian Gregory interpreted Augustine for the Middle Ages and was the most important and influential theologian of the West after Augustine and before the greater scholastics. He did much to restore the prestige of his see, which had been lost in the earlier part of the sixth century. He died 604.

Additional source material: Selections from the writings of Gregory, including many of his letters, may be found in PNF, ser. II, vols.

[1] Bobbio, twenty-five miles southwest from Piacenza.

XII and XIII; see also *A Library of the Fathers of the Holy Catholic Church* (Oxford).

The selections under this section are arranged under four heads: (1) Relations with Gaul; (2) Relations with Constantinople; (3) Relations with the Schism in Northern Italy; (4) Relations with the Lombards; for English mission, *v. infra*, § 100.

1. *Relations with Gaul.*

(*a*) Gregory the Great, *Ep. ad Vigilium*, Reg. V, 53. (MSL, 77 : 782.)

The following letter was written in 595 in reply to a letter from Vigilius, bishop of Arles, asking for the pallium (DCA, art. "Pallium," also *Cath. Encyc.*) and the vicariate. For the relation of the Roman see to the bishop of Arles as primate of Gaul, see E. Loening, *Geschichte des deutschen Kirchenrechts.* The relation of the vicariate to the papacy and also to the royal power is indicated by the fact that the pallium is given in response to the request of the king. The condition of the church under Childebert is also shown; see § 98 for canons bearing on simony and irregularities in connection with ordination.

As to thy having asked therein [in a letter of Vigilius to Gregory] according to ancient custom for the use of the pallium and the vicariate of the Apostolic See, far be it from me to suspect that thou hast sought eminence of transitory power, or the adornment of external worship, in our vicariate and the pallium. But, since it is known to all whence the holy faith proceeded in the regiohs of Gaul, when your fraternity asks for a repetition of the early custom of the Apostolic See, what is it but that a good offspring reverts to the bosom of its mother? With willing mind therefore we grant what has been requested, lest we should seem either to withhold from you anything of the honor due to you, or to despise the petition of our most excellent son, King Childebert. . . .

I have learned from certain persons informing me that in the parts of Gaul and Germany no one attains to holy orders except for a consideration given. If this is so, I say it with tears, I declare it with groans, that, when the priestly order has fallen inwardly, neither will it be able to stand outwardly for long. . . .

Another very detestable thing has also been reported to us, that some persons being laymen, through the desire of temporal glory, are tonsured on the death of bishops, and all at once are made priests. . . .

On this account your fraternity must needs take care to admonish our most excellent son, King Childebert, that he remove entirely the stain of this sin from his kingdom, to the end that Almighty God may give him so much the greater recompense with himself as He sees him both love what He loves and shun what He hates.

And so we commit to your fraternity, according to ancient custom, under God, our vicariate in the churches which are under the dominion of our most excellent son Childebert, with the understanding that their proper dignity, according to primitive usage, be preserved to the several metropolitans. We have also sent a pallium which thy fraternity will use within the Church for the solemnization of mass only. Further, if any of the bishops should by any chance wish to travel to any considerable distance, let it not be lawful for him to remove to other places without the authority of thy holiness. If any question of faith, or it may be relating to other matters, should have arisen among the bishops, which cannot easily be settled, let it be ventilated and decided in an assembly of twelve bishops. But if it cannot be decided after the truth has been investigated, let it be referred to our judgment.

2. Relations with Constantinople.

(b) Gregory the Great, *Ep. ad Johannem Jejunatorem*, Reg. V, 44. (MSL, 77 : 738.) *Cf.* Mirbt, n. 180.

On the title "Ecumenical Patriarch."
The controversy over the title "Ecumenical Patriarch" was a result of Gregory's determination to carry through, as far as possible, the Petrine rights and duties as he conceived them. The title was prob-

ably intended to mark the superiority of Constantinople to the other
patriarchates in the East, according to the Eastern principle that the
political rank of a city determined its ecclesiastical rank.   It seemed
to Gregory to imply a position of superiority to the see of Peter.   As
it certainly might imply that, he consistently opposed it.   But it had
been a title in use for nearly a century.   (*Cf.* Gieseler, KG, Eng. trans.,
vol. I, p. 504.) Justinian in 533 so styled the patriarch of Constantinople (Cod. I, 1, 7).   For the difference in point of view between the
East and the West as to rank of great sees, see Leo's letters on
the 28th canon of Chalcedon, A. D. 451, *supra*, in § 86.

At the time when your fraternity was advanced in sacerdotal dignity, you recall what peace and concord of the
churches you found.   But, with what daring or with what
swelling of pride I know not, you have attempted to seize
upon a new name for yourself, whereby the hearts of all
your brethren would be offended.   I wonder exceedingly at
this, since I remember that in order not to attain to the
episcopal office thou wouldest have fled.   But now that thou
hast attained unto it, thou desirest so to exercise it as if
thou hadst run after it with ambitious desire.   And thou who
didst confess thyself unworthy to be called a bishop, hast at
length been brought to such a pitch that, despising thy brethren, thou desirest to be named the only bishop.   And in
regard to this matter, weighty letters were sent to thy
holiness by my predecessor Pelagius, of holy memory, and in
them he annulled the acts of the synod,[1] which had been assembled among you in the case of our former brother and
fellow priest, Gregory, because of that execrable title of pride,
and forbade the archdeacon whom he sent according to
custom to the feet of our Lord [2] to celebrate the solemnities
of the mass with thee.   But after his death, when I, an unworthy man, succeeded to the government of the Church, I
took care, formerly through thy representatives, and now
through our common son and deacon, Sabianus, to address thy
fraternity, not indeed in writing, but by word of mouth, desiring thee to refrain thyself from such presumption; and in

[1] Evagrius, *Hist. Ec.*, VI. 7.
[2] *I. e.*, to be the apocrisiarius at the court of the Emperor.

case thou wouldest not amend I forbade his celebrating the
solemnities of the mass with thee; that so I might appeal to
thy holiness through a certain sense of shame, and then, if
the execrable and profane assumption could not be corrected
through shame, I might resort to canonical and prescribed
measures. And because sores that are to be cut away should
first be stroked with a gentle hand, I beg of thee, I beseech
thee, and, as kindly as I can, I demand of thee that thy fraternity rebuke all who flatter thee and offer thee this name of
error, and not consent to be called by a foolish and proud
title. For truly I say it weeping, and out of deepest sorrow of
heart attribute it to my sins, that this my brother, who has
been placed in the episcopal order, that he might bring back
the souls of others to humility, has, up to the present time,
been incapable of being brought back to humility; that he
who teaches truth to others has not consented to teach himself, even when I implore him.

Consider, I pray thee, that by this rash presumption the
peace of the whole Church is disturbed, and that it is in contradiction to the grace poured out on all in common; in which
grace thou thyself wilt be able to grow so far as thou thyself
will determine to do so. And thou wilt become by so much
the greater as thou restrainest thyself from the usurpation of
proud and foolish titles; and thou wilt advance in proportion
as thou art not bent on arrogation by the humiliation of thy
brethren. . . . Certainly Peter, the first of the Apostles, was
a member of the holy and universal Church; Paul, Andrew,
John—what are they but the heads of particular communities?
And yet all are members under one Head. And to bind all
together in a short phrase, the saints before the Law, the
saints under the Law, the saints under grace, all these making
up the Lord's body were constituted as members of the
Church, and not one of them has ever wished himself to be
called "universal.". . .

Is it not the fact, as your fraternity knows, that the prelates of this Apostolic See, which by the providence of God I

serve, had the honor offered them by the venerable Council of Chalcedon of being called "universal"?[1] But yet not one of them has ever wished to be called by such a title, or seized upon this rash name, lest, if in virtue of the rank of the pontificate, he took to himself the glory of singularity, he might seem to have denied it to all his brethren.

(c) Gregory the Great, *Ep. ad Phocam*, Reg. XIII, 31. (MSL, 77 : 1281.)

Epistle to Phocas congratulating him on his accession.

Phocas (602–610) was a low-born, ignorant centurion whom chance had placed at the head of a successful rebellion originating in the army of the Danube. The rebellion was successful, and the Emperor Maurice was murdered, together with his sons. Maurice had been unsuccessful in war, unpopular with the army, and his financial measures had been oppressive. Phocas was utterly incompetent as a ruler, licentious and sanguinary as a man. His reign was a period of horror and blood.

Gregory to Phocas. Glory to God in the highest, who, according as it is written, changes times, and transfers kingdoms, because He has made apparent to all what He has vouchsafed to speak by His prophet, that the most High ruleth in the kingdom of men, and giveth it to whomsoever He will [Dan. 4 : 17]. For in the incomprehensible dispensation of Almighty God there is an alternating control of human life, and sometimes, when the sins of many are to be smitten, one is raised up through whose hardness the necks of subjects may be bowed down under the yoke of tribulation, as in our affliction we have long had proof. But sometimes, when the merciful God has decreed to refresh with His consolation the mourning hearts of many, He advances one to the summit of government, and through the bowels of His mercy infuses in the minds of all the grace of exultation in Him. In which abundance of exultation we believe that we, who rejoice that the benignity of your piety has arrived at imperial supremacy, shall speedily be confirmed. "Let the heavens rejoice and let the earth be glad" [Psalm 96 : 11], and let the whole people

[1] See Gieseler, KG, Eng. trans. I, p. 396, n. 72.

of the republic, hitherto afflicted exceedingly, grow cheerful for your benignant deeds. Let the proud minds of enemies be subdued to the yoke of your domination. Let the sad and depressed spirit of subjects be relieved by your mercy. Let the power of heavenly grace make you terrible to your enemies; let piety make you kind to your subjects. Let the whole republic have rest in your most happy times, since the pillage of peace under the color of legal processes has been exposed. Let plottings about testaments cease, and benevolences extorted by violence end. Let secure possession of their own goods return to all, that they may rejoice in possessing without fear what they have acquired without fraud. Let every single person's liberty be now at length restored to each one under the yoke of the holy Empire. For there is this difference between the kings of the nations and the emperors of the republic: the kings of the nations are lords of slaves, but the emperors lords of free men. But we shall better speak of these things by praying than by putting you in mind of them. May Almighty God keep the heart of your piety in the hand of His grace in every thought and deed. Whatsoever things should be done justly, whatever things with clemency, may the Holy Ghost, who dwells in your breast direct, that your clemency may both be exalted in a temporal kingdom and after the course of many years attain to heavenly kingdoms. Given in the month June, indiction six.

3. *Gregory and the Schism in North Italy.*

Among the results of the Fifth General Council of Constantinople, 553, was a wide-spread schism in the northern part of Italy and adjacent lands. The bishops of the western part of Lombardy, under the lead of the bishop of Milan, together with the bishops of Venetia, Istria, and a portion of Illyricum, Rhætia Secunda, and Noricum, under the bishop of Aquileia, renounced communion with the see of Rome, and became autocephalic. Even bishops in Tuscany abandoned communion with the see of Rome because the council and Vigilius had condemned Theodore, Theodoret, and Ibas (*v. supra*, § 93). Justin II attempted to heal the schism, and his verbose edict may be found in Evagrius, *Hist. Ec.*, V, 4. A serious problem was presented to the Roman see. In dealing with them, however, it was possible to treat each group separately. On account of the Lombard invasion the bishop of Aquileia removed his see to Grado. Gregory the Great had some success in drawing the schismatics into more friendly relations. But not till 612 was the see of Aquileia-Grado in communion with Rome. A rival bishop was elected, who removed his see to old Aquileia. See extract from Paulus Diaconus (*f*). And the opposition was maintained until about 700. The Milanese portion of the schism had long since ended. Of Gregory's epistles several bearing on the schism are available in PNF, ser. II, vols. XII and XIII: Reg. I, 16; II, 46, 51; IV, 2, 38, 39; V, 51; IX, 9, 10; XIII, 33.

(*d*) Gregory the Great, *Ep. ad Constantium*, Reg. IV, 2. (MSL, 77 : 669.)

Gregory to Constantius, Bishop of Milan. My beloved son, the deacon Boniface, has given me information from a private letter of thy fraternity: namely, that three bishops, having sought out rather than having found an occasion, have separated themselves from the pious communion of thy fraternity, saying that thou hast assented to the condemnation of the three chapters and hast given a solemn pledge. And, indeed, whether there has been any mention made of the three chapters in any word or writing whatever, thy fraternity remembers well; although thy fraternity's predecessor, Laurentius (*circa* 573), did send a most strict security to the Apostolic See, and to it a legal number of the most noble men subscribed; among whom, I also, at that time holding the prætorship of the city, likewise subscribed; because, when such a schism had taken place about nothing, it was right that the Apostolic See should be careful to guard in all respects the unity of the universal Church in the minds of priests. But as to its being said that our daughter, Queen Theodelinda,[1] after hearing this news has withdrawn herself from thy communion, it is perfectly evident that though she has been seduced to some little extent by the words of wicked men, yet

---

[1] Theodelinda held to the schismatic party in Northern Italy. Gregory is careful to touch this point very delicately, and not to allow it to become such a point of contention as might disturb favorable political relations.

when Hippolytus the notary and John the abbot arrive, she will seek in all ways the communion of thy fraternity.

(e) Gregory the Great, *Ep. ad Constantium*, Reg. IV, 39. (MSL, 77 : 713.)

In reply to a letter from Constantius of Milan informing Gregory that the demand had been made upon him by the clergy of Brescia that he should take an oath that he, Constantius, had not condemned the Three Chapters, *i. e.*, had not accepted the Fifth General Council, Gregory advises him to take no such oath.

But lest those who have thus written to you should be offended, send them a letter declaring under an imposition of an anathema that you neither take away anything from the faith of the synod of Chalcedon nor receive those who do, and that you condemn whatsoever it condemned and absolve whatsoever it absolved. And thus I believe that they may soon be satisfied. . . . As to what you have written to the effect that you are unwilling to transmit my letter to Queen Theodelinda on the ground that the fifth synod is named in it, for you believed that she might be offended, you did right not to transmit it. We are therefore doing now as you recommended, namely, only expressing approval of the four synods. Yet as to the synod which was afterward called at Constantinople, which is called by many the fifth, I would have you know that it neither ordained nor held anything in opposition to the four most holy synods, seeing that nothing was done in it with respect to the faith, but only with respect to three persons, about whom nothing is contained in the acts of the Council of Chalcedon;[1] but after the canons had been promulgated, discussion arose, and final action was ventilated concerning persons.

[1] Gregory is not correct here. In the eighth, ninth, and tenth sessions of the Council of Chalcedon, the cases of Theodoret and Ibas were examined, they were heard in their own defence and were acquitted or excused without censure. See Hefele, §§ 195, 196. The case of Theodore of Mopsuestia, however, did not come before the Council of Chalcedon, because he was dead, *v. supra*, § 93, the *Constitutum* of Vigilius.

(f) Paulus Diaconus, *Historia Langobardorum*, IV, 32, 33, 36. (MSL, 95 : 657.)

The continuation of the schism in Istria and the rise of the two patriarchates of Aquileia. The Emperor Phocas and the title "Head of All the Churches."

32. In the following month of November [A. D. 605] King Agilulf concluded peace with the Patrician Smaragdus for a year, and received from the Romans twelve thousand solidi. Also the Tuscan cities Balneus Regis [Bagnarea] and Urbs Vetus [Orvieto] were conquered by the Lombards. Then appeared in the heavens in the months of April and May a star which is called a comet. Thereupon King Agilulf again made a peace with the Romans for three years.

33. In the same days after the death of the patriarch Severus, the abbot John was made patriarch of old Aquileia in his place with the approval of the king and Duke Gisulf. Also in Grados [Grado] the Roman[1] Candidianus was appointed bishop. In the months of November and December a comet was again visible. After the death of Candidianus, Epiphanius, who had formerly been the papal chief notary, was elected patriarch by the bishops who stood under the Romans; and since this time there were two patriarchs.

36. Phocas, as also has been related above, after the murder of Maurice and his sons, obtained the Roman Empire and ruled for eight years. At the request of Pope Boniface[2] he decreed that the seat of the Roman and Apostolic Church should be the head of all churches [*caput omnium ecclesiarum*], because the Church of Constantinople in a proclamation had named itself first of all. At the request of another Pope Boniface,[3] he commanded that the idolatrous rubbish should be removed from the old temple which bore the name of the Pantheon, and from it a church should be made to the holy Virgin Mary and all martyrs, so that where formerly the serv-

---

[1] *I. e.*, in communion with the Roman see.   [2] Boniface III, 606–607.
[3] Boniface IV, 607–615.

ice not of all gods but of all idols was celebrated, now only the memory of all saints should be found.

4. *Gregory the Great and the Lombards.*

The Lombards entered Italy 568, and gradually spread over nearly all the peninsula. The territories retained by the Emperor from the conquests of Justinian were only the Exachate of Ravenna, the Ducatus Romanus, and the Ducatus Neapolitanus, the extreme southern parts of the peninsula and Liguria. The Lombards were the last Germanic tribe to settle within the Empire, and like so many others they were Arians. Theodelinda, the queen of the Lombards, was a Bavarian princess and a Catholic. Her second husband, Agilulf, seems to have been favorably disposed to Catholicism, far more so than Authari, her first husband.

(g) Paulus Diaconus, *Historia Langobardorum*, IV, 5–9. (MSL, 95 : 540.)

Paulus Warnefridi, known as Paulus Diaconus (circa 720–circa 800), was himself a Lombard, and in writing his *History of the Lombards* shows himself the patriot as well as the loyal son of the Roman Church. To do this was at times difficult. The work is one of the most attractive histories written in the Middle Ages. For nearly all of his history, Paulus is dependent upon older sources, but he restates the older accounts in clear and careful fashion. The connection between the various extracts is not always felicitous, yet he has succeeded in producing one of the great books of history. For an analysis of the sources, see F. H. B. Daniell, art. "Paulus (70) Diaconus" in DCB. The best edition is that by Bethmann and Waitz in the MGH, *Scriptores rerum Langobardorum et Italicarum sæc.* VI–IX, also in the 8vo edition. There is an English translation of the entire work in the *Translations and Reprints of the Historical Department of the University of Pennsylvania.*

5. At that time the learned and pious Pope Gregory, after he had already written much for the benefit of the holy Church, wrote also four books concerning the lives of the saints; these books he called *Dialogus*, that is, conversation, because in them he has introduced himself speaking with his deacon Peter. The Pope sent these books to Queen Theodelinda, whom he knew to be true in the faith in Christ and abounding in good works.

6. Through this queen the Church of God obtained many and great advantages. For the Lombards, when they were still held by heathen unbelief, had taken possession of the entire property of the Church. But, induced by successful requests of the queen, the king, holding fast to the Catholic faith,[1] gave the Church of Christ many possessions and assigned to the bishops, who had theretofore been oppressed and despised, their ancient place of honor once more.

7. In these days Tassilo was made king of Bavaria by the Frankish king Childebert. With an army he immediately marched into the land of the Slavs, and with great booty returned to his own land.

9. At the same time the patrician and exarch of Ravenna, Romanus,[2] went to Rome. On his return to Ravenna he took possession of the cities which had been taken by the Lombards. The names of them are: Sutrium [Sutri], Polimarcium [near Bomarzio and west of Orte], Horta [Orte], Tuder [Todi], Ameria [Amelia], Perusia [Perugia], Luceoli [near Gubbio], and several others. When King Agilulf received word of this, he at once marched forth from Ticinus with a strong army and pitched before the city of Perusia. Here he besieged several days the Lombard duke Marisio, who had gone over to the side of the Romans, took him prisoner, and without delay had him executed. On the approach of the king, the holy Pope Gregory was so filled with fear that, as he himself reports in his homilies, he broke off the explanation of the temple, to be read about in Ezekiel; King Agilulf returned to Ticinus after he had settled the matter, and not long after, chiefly on account of the entreaties of his wife, Queen Theodelinda, who had often been advised in letters by the holy Father Gregory to do so, he concluded with Gregory and the Romans a last-

[1] He was not a professed Catholic. It probably means either that he held fast to his political alliance with Rome, or that he was determined to favor the Catholic faith professed by his spouse.
[2] There are several letters written by Gregory to Romanus available in translation, see above.

ing peace. To thank her for this, the venerable priest sent the following letter to the queen:

Gregory to Theodelinda, queen of the Lombards. How your excellency has labored earnestly and kindly, as is your wont, for the conclusion of peace, we have learned from the report of our son, the abbot Probus. Nor, indeed, was it otherwise to be expected of your Christianity than that you would in all ways show assiduity and goodness in the cause of peace. Wherefore, we give thanks to Almighty God, who so rules your heart with His lovingkindness that, as He has given you a right faith, so He also grants you to work always what is pleasing in His sight. For you may be assured, most excellent daughter, that for the saving of much bloodshed on both sides you have acquired no small reward. On this account, returning thanks for your good-will, we implore the mercy of God to repay you with good in body and soul here and in the world to come. Moreover, greeting you with fatherly affection, we exhort you so to deal with your most excellent consort that he may not reject the alliance of the Christian republic. For, as I believe you yourself know, it is in many ways profitable that he should be inclined to betake himself to its friendship. Do you then, after your manner, always strive for what tends to good-will and conciliation between the parties, and labor wherever an occasion of reaping a reward presents itself, that you may commend your good deeds the more before the eyes of Almighty God.

§ 100. The Foundation of the Anglo-Saxon Church

The Anglo-Saxon Church owes its foundation to the missionary zeal and wise direction of Gregory the Great. Augustine, whom Gregory sent, arrived in the kingdom of Kent 597, and established himself at Canterbury. In 625, Paulinus began his work at York, and Christianity was accepted by the Northumbrian king and many nobles. On the death of King Eadwine, Paulinus was obliged to leave the kingdom. Missionaries were brought into Northumbria in 635 from the Celtic Church, the centre of which was at Iona, where the new king Oswald had taken refuge on the death of Eadwine. Aidan now became the leader of the Northern Church. As the Christianization of the land advanced and Roman customs were introduced into the northern kingdom, practical inconveniences as to the different methods of reckoning the date of Easter, in which the North Irish and the Celts of Scotland differed from the rest of the Christian Church, came to a settlement of the difficulty at Streaneshalch, or Whitby, 664. Colman, Bishop of Lindisfarne, the leader of the Celtic party, withdrew, and Wilfrid, afterward bishop of York, took the lead under the influence of the Roman tradition. The Church of the Anglo-Saxon kingdoms, now in agreement as to custom, was organized by Theodore of Canterbury (668–690), and developed a remarkable intellectual life, becoming, in fact, for the first part at least of the eighth century, the centre of Western theological and literary culture.

Additional source material: Bede, *Ecclesiastical History of the English People*, for editions, *v. supra*, § 96. This is the best account extant of the conversion of a nation to Christianity. H. Gee and W. J. Hardy, *Documents Illustrative of English Church History*, London, 1896; A. W. Haddan and W. Stubbs, *Councils and Ecclesiastical Documents*, 1869 *ff*.

(*a*) Bede, *Hist. Ec.*, I, 29. (MSL, 95 : 69.)

The scheme of Gregory the Great for the organization of the English Church A. D. 601.

Gregory, in planning his mission, seems not to have been aware of the profound changes in the kingdom resulting from the Anglo-Saxon invasion. He selected York as the seat of an archbishop, because it was the ancient capital of the Roman province in the North, and London, because it was the great city of the South. The rivalries of the two archbishops caused difficulties for centuries, and was a hinderance to the efficiency of the ecclesiastical system. By this letter, the British bishops were to be under the authority of Augustine, a position which was distasteful to the British, who were extremely hostile to the Anglo-Saxons, and incomprehensible to them, as they saw no reason or justification in any such arrangement without their consent. They withdrew from all intercourse with the new Anglo-Saxon Church and retired into Wales.

To the most reverend and holy brother and fellow bishop, Augustine, Gregory, servant of the servants of God.

Although it is certain that the unspeakable rewards of the eternal kingdom are laid up for those who labor for Almighty God, yet it is necessary for us to render to them the benefits of honors, that from this recompense they may be able to labor more abundantly in the zeal for spiritual work. And because the new Church of the English has been brought by thee to the grace of Almighty God, by the bounty of the same Lord and by your toil, we grant you the use of the pallium, in the same to perform only the solemnities of the mass, in order that in the various places you ordain twelve bishops who shall be under your authority, so that the bishop of the city of London ought always thereafter to be consecrated by his own synod and receive the pallium of honor from the holy Apostolic See, which by God's authority I serve.[1] Moreover, we will that you send to York a bishop whom you shall see fit to ordain, yet so that if the same city shall have received the word of God along with the neighboring places, he shall ordain twelve other bishops, and enjoy the honor of metropolitan, because if our life last, we intend, with the Lord's favor, to give him the pallium also. And we will that he be subject to your authority, my brother. But after your decease he shall preside over the bishops he has ordained, so that he shall not be subject in anywise to the bishop of London. Moreover, let there be a distinction of honor between the bishops of the city of London and of York, in such a way that he shall take the precedence who has been ordained first. But let them arrange in concord by common counsel and harmonious action the things which need to be done for the zeal for Christ; let them determine rightly and let them accomplish what they have decided upon without any mutual misunderstandings.

But you, my brother, shall have subject to you not only the

---

[1] Augustine had been consecrated in Gaul. His successors in the see of London were to be consecrated by the suffragans of that archiepiscopal see.

bishops whom you have ordained and those ordained by the bishop of York, but also, by the authority of our Lord Jesus Christ, the priests [*i. e.*, the bishops] of Britain; so that from the lips of your holiness they may receive the form both of correct faith and of holy life, and fulfilling the duties of their office in faith and morals may, when the Lord wills, attain to the kingdom of heaven. May God keep you safe, most reverend brother. Dated the 22d June in the nineteenth year of the reign of Mauritius Tiberius, the most pious Augustus, in the eighteenth year of the consulship of the same Lord, indiction four.

(*b*) Bede, *Hist. Ec.*, III, 25 *f.* (MSL, 95 : 158.)

The Easter dispute and the synod of Whitby. The triumph of the Roman tradition.

The sharpest dispute between the Celtic and the Roman churches was on the date of Easter as presenting the most inconveniences. The principal points were as follows: Both parties agreed that it must be on Sunday, in the third week of the first lunar month, and the paschal full moon must not fall before the vernal equinox. But the Celts placed the vernal equinox on March 25, and the Romans on March 21. The Celts, furthermore, reckoned as the third week the 14th to the 20th days of the moon inclusive; the Romans the 15th to the 21st inclusive. The Irish Church in the southern part of Ireland had already adopted the Roman reckoning at the synod of Leighlin, 630–633 [Hefele, § 289]. The occasion of the difference of custom was, in reality, that the Romans had adopted in the previous century a more correct method of reckoning and one that had fewer practical inconveniences. For a statement by a Celt, see Epistle of Columbanus to Gregory the Great, in the latter's *Epistolæ*, Reg. IX, Ep. 127 (PNF, ser. II, vol. XIII, p. 38). In the following selection space has been saved by omissions which are, however, indicated.

At this time [*circa* 652] a great and frequent controversy happened about the observance of Easter; those that came from Kent or France asserting that the Scots kept Easter Sunday contrary to the custom of the universal Church. Among them was a most zealous defender of the true Easter, whose name was Ronan, a Scot by nation, but instructed in ecclesiastical truth, either in France or Italy, who disputed with Finan,[1] and convinced many, or at least induced them, to make a stricter inquiry after the truth; yet he could not prevail upon Finan . . . James, formerly the deacon of the venerable archbishop Paulinus . . . kept the true and Catholic Easter, with all those that he could persuade to adopt the right way. Queen Eanfleda [wife of Oswy, king of Northumbria] and her attendants also observed the same as she had seen practised in Kent, having with her a Kentish priest that followed the Catholic mode, whose name was Romanus. Thus it is said to have happened in those times that Easter was kept twice in one year;[2] and that when the king, having ended the time of fasting, kept his Easter, the queen and her attendants were still fasting and celebrating Palm Sunday. . . .

After the death of Finan [662] . . . when Colman, who was also sent out of Scotland, came to be bishop, a great controversy arose about the observance of Easter, and the rules of ecclesiastical life. . . . This reached the ears of King Oswy and his son Alfrid; for Oswy, having been instructed and baptized by the Scots, and being very perfectly skilled in their language, thought nothing better than what they taught. But Alfrid, having been instructed in Christianity by Wilfrid, a most learned man, who had first gone to Rome to learn the ecclesiastical doctrine, and spent much time at Lyons with Dalfinus, archbishop of France, from whom he had received the ecclesiastical tonsure, rightly thought this man's doctrine ought to be preferred to all the traditions of the Scots. . . .

The controversy having been started concerning Easter, the tonsure, and other ecclesiastical matters, it was agreed that a synod should be held in the monastery of Streaneshalch, which signifies the bay of the lighthouse, where the Abbess Hilda, a woman devoted to God, presided; and that there the controversy should be decided. The kings, both father and son, came hither. Bishop Colman, with his Scottish clerks,

---

[1] Bishop of Lindisfarne, 652–662.
[2] In 645, 647, 648, 651. It would occur again in 665.

and Agilbert,[1] and the priests Agatho and Wilfrid, James and Romanus were on their side. But the Abbess Hilda and her associates were for the Scots, as was also the venerable bishop Cedd, long before ordained by the Scots. . . . Then Colman said: " The Easter which I keep, I received from my elders who sent me hither as bishop; all our fathers, men beloved of God, are known to have kept it in the same manner; and that the same may not seem to any to be contemptible or worthy of being rejected, it is the same which St. John the Evangelist, the disciple especially beloved of our Lord, with all the churches over which he presided, is recorded as having observed. . . ."

Wilfrid, having been ordered by the king to speak, said: " The Easter which we observe we saw celebrated by all at Rome, where the blessed Apostles, Peter and Paul, lived, taught, suffered, and were buried; we saw the same done in Italy and France, when we travelled through those countries for pilgrimage and prayer. We found the same practised in Africa, Asia, Egypt, Greece, and in all the world, wherever the Church of Christ is spread abroad, through several nations and tongues, at one and the same time . . . except only these and their accomplices in obstinacy, I mean the Picts and the Britons, who foolishly, in these two remote islands of the world, and only in part of them, oppose all the rest of the universe. . . . John, pursuant to the custom of the law, began the celebration of the feast of Easter on the fourteenth day of the month, in the evening, not regarding whether the same happened on a Saturday or any other day. . . . Thus it appears that you, Colman, neither follow the example of John, as you imagine, nor that of Peter, whose traditions you knowingly contradict. . . . For John, keeping the paschal time according to the decree of the Mosaic law, had no regard to the first day after the Sabbath [i. e., that it should fall on Sunday], and you who celebrate Easter only on the first day after the Sabbath do not practise this. Peter kept Easter

---

[1] Bishop of the West Saxons, temporarily in Northumbria.

Sunday between the fifteenth and the twenty-first day of the moon, and you do not do this, but keep Easter Sunday from the fourteenth to the twentieth day of the moon, so that you often begin Easter on the thirteenth moon in the evening . . . besides this in your celebration of Easter, you utterly exclude the twenty-first day of the moon, which the law ordered to be especially observed."

To this Colman rejoined: " Did Anatolius, a holy man, and much commended in ecclesiastical history, act contrary to the Law and the Gospel when he wrote that Easter was to be celebrated from the fourteenth to the twentieth? Is it to be believed that our most reverend Father Columba and his successors, men beloved of God, who kept Easter after the same manner, thought or acted contrary to the divine writings? Whereas there were many among them whose sanctity was attested by heavenly signs and the workings of miracles, whose life, customs, discipline I never cease to follow, not questioning that they are saints in heaven."

Wilfrid said: " It is evident that Anatolius was a most holy and learned and commendable man; but what have you to do with him, since you do not observe his decrees? For he, following the rule of truth in his Easter, appointed a cycle of nineteen years, which you are either ignorant of, or if you know yet despise, though it is kept by the whole Church of Christ. . . . Concerning your Father Columba and his followers. . . . I do not deny that they were God's servants, and beloved by Him, who, with rustic simplicity but pious intentions, have themselves loved Him. . . . But as for you and your companions, you certainly sin, if, having heard the decrees of the Apostolic See, or rather of the universal Church, and the same confirmed by Holy Scripture, you refuse to follow them. For though your Fathers were holy, do you think that their small number in a corner of the remotest island is to be preferred before the universal Church of Christ throughout the world? And if that Columba of yours (and, I may say, ours also, if he was Christ's servant) was a holy man and powerful in miracles, yet could he be preferred before the most blessed prince of the Apostles, to whom our Lord said: 'Thou art Peter, and upon this rock I will build my Church, and the gates of hell shall not prevail against it, and to thee I will give the keys of the kingdom of heaven'?"

When Wilfrid had thus spoken, the king said: "Is it true, Colman, that these words were spoken to Peter by our Lord?" He answered: "It is true, O king." Then he said: "Can you show any such power given to your Columba?" Colman answered: "None." Then the king added: "Do you both agree that these words were principally directed to Peter, and that the keys of heaven were given to him by our Lord?" They both answered: "We do." Then the king concluded: "And I also say unto you that he is the doorkeeper whom I will not contradict, but will, as far as I know and am able in all things, obey his decrees, lest, when I come to the gates of the kingdom of heaven, there should be one to open them, he being my adversary who is proved to have the keys." The king having said this, all present, both small and great, gave their assent, and renounced the more imperfect institution, and resolved to conform to that which they found to be better . . . [ch. 26]. Colman, perceiving that his doctrine was rejected and his sect despised, took with him such as would not comply with the Catholic Easter and the tonsure (for there was much controversy about that also) and went back to Scotland to consult with his people what was to be done in this case. Cedd, forsaking the practices of the Scots, returned to his bishopric, having submitted to the Catholic observance of Easter. This disputation happened in the year of our Lord's incarnation, 664.

(c) Bede, *Hist. Ec.*, IV, 5. (MSL, 95 : 180.)

The Council of Hertford A. D. 673. The organization of the Anglo-Saxon Church by Theodore.

As the important synod of Whitby marks the beginning of conformity of the Anglo-Saxon Church under the leadership of the kingdom of Northumbria to the customs of the Roman Church, so the synod of Hertford brings the internal organization of the Church into conformity with the diocesan system of the Continent and of the East, where the principles of the general councils were at this time most completely enforced. Theodore of Canterbury was a learned Greek who was sent to England to be archbishop of Canterbury by Pope Vitalian in 668. The Council of Hertford was the first council of all the Church among the Anglo-Saxons. For the council, see also Haddan and Stubbs, *Councils and Ecclesiastical Documents*, III, 118–122. The text given is that of Plummer.

In the name of our Lord God and Saviour Jesus Christ, in the perpetual reign of the same Lord Jesus Christ and His government of His Church. It seemed good that we should come together according to the prescription of the venerable canons, to treat of the necessary affairs of the Church. We are met together on this 24th day of September, the first indiction in the place called Hertford. I, Theodore, although unworthy, appointed by the Apostolic See bishop of the church of Canterbury, and our fellow priest the most reverend Bisi, bishop of the East Angles, together with our brother and fellow bishop Wilfrid, bishop of the nation of the Northumbrians, present by his proper legates, as also our brethren and fellow bishops, Putta, bishop of the Castle of the Kentishmen called Rochester, Leutherius, bishop of the West Saxons, and Winfrid, bishop of the province of the Mercians, were present. When we were assembled and had taken our places, each according to his rank, I said: I beseech you, beloved brethren, for the fear and love of our Redeemer, that we all labor in common for our faith, that whatsoever has been decreed and determined by the holy and approved Fathers may be perfectly followed by us all. I enlarged upon these and many other things tending unto charity and the preservation of the unity of the Church. And when I had finished my speech I asked them singly and in order whether they consented to observe all things which had been canonically decreed by the Fathers? To which all our fellow priests answered: We are all well agreed readily and most cheerfully to keep whatever the canons of the holy Fathers have prescribed. Whereupon I immediately produced the book of canons,[1] and pointed out ten chapters from the same book, which I had marked, because I knew that they were especially necessary for us, and proposed that they should be diligently observed by all, namely:

Ch. 1. That we shall jointly observe Easter day on the Lord's day after the fourteenth day of the moon in the first month.

Ch. 2. That no bishop invade the diocese of another, but be content with the government of the people committed to him.

Ch. 3. That no bishop be allowed to trouble in any way any monasteries consecrated to God, nor to take away by violence anything that belongs to them.

Ch. 4. That the monks themselves go not from place to place; that is, from one monastery to another, without letters dismissory of their own abbot;[2] but that they shall continue in that obedience which they promised at the time of their conversion.

Ch. 5. That no clerk, leaving his own bishop, go up and down at his own pleasure, nor be received wherever he comes, without commendatory letters from his bishop; but if he be once received and refuse to return when he is desired so to do, both the receiver and the received shall be laid under an excommunication.

Ch. 6. That stranger bishops and clerks be content with the hospitality that is freely offered them; and none of them be allowed to exercise any sacerdotal function without permission of the bishop in whose diocese he is known to be.

Ch. 7. That a synod be assembled twice in the year. But, because many occasions may hinder this, it was jointly agreed by all that once in the year it be assembled on the first of August in the place called Clovesho.

---

[1] Coming from Rome under the circumstances in which he was sent, this book of the canons can be no other than the collection of Dionysius Exiguus.

[2] See below, § 105.

Ch. 8. That no bishop ambitiously put himself before another, but that every one observe the time and order of his consecration.

Ch. 9. The ninth chapter was discussed together: That the number of bishops be increased as the number of the faithful grew;[1] but we did nothing as to this point at present.

Ch. 10. As to marriages: That none shall be allowed to any but what is a lawful marriage. Let none commit incest. Let none relinquish his own wife but for fornication, as the holy Gospel teaches. But if any have dismissed a wife united to him in lawful marriage, let him not be joined to another if he wish really to be a Christian, but remain as he is or be reconciled to his own wife.

After we had jointly treated on and discussed these chapters, that no scandalous contention should arise henceforth by any of us, and that there be no changes in the publication of them, it seemed proper that every one should confirm by the subscription of his own hand whatever had been determined. I dictated this our definitive sentence to be written by Titillus, the notary. Done in the month and indiction above noted. Whosoever, therefore, shall attempt in any way to oppose or infringe this sentence, confirmed by our present consent, and the subscription of our hands as agreeable to the decrees of the canons, let him know that he is deprived of every sacerdotal function and our society. May the divine grace preserve us safe living in the unity of the Church.

(d) Bede, *Hist. Ec.*, IV, 17. (MSL, 95 : 198.)

Council of Hatfield, A. D. 680.
At the Council of Hatfield the Anglo-Saxon Church formally recognized the binding authority of the five general councils already held, and rejected Monotheletism in accord with the Roman synod A. D. 649. It seems to have been, as stated in the introduction to the Acts of the council, a preventive measure. In Plummer's edition of Bede this chapter is numbered 15.

[1] *Cf.* Bede, *Epistula ad Egbertum Episcopum;* Plummer, *op. cit.*, I, 412 *f.*

At this time Theodore, hearing that the faith of the Church of Constantinople had been much disturbed by the heresy of Eutyches,[1] and being desirous that the churches of the English over which he ruled should be free from such a stain, having collected an assembly of venerable priests and very many doctors, diligently inquired what belief they each held, and found unanimous agreement of all in the Catholic faith; and this he took care to commit to a synodical letter for the instruction and remembrance of posterity. This is the beginning of the letter:

In the name of our Lord and Saviour Jesus Christ, in the reign of our most pious lords, Egfrid, king of the Humbrians, in the tenth year of his reign, on the fifteenth day before the Kalends of October [September 17] in the eighth indiction, and Ethelred, king of the Mercians, in the sixth year of his reign; and Adwulf, king of the Kentishmen, in the seventh year of his reign; Theodore being president, by the grace of God, archbishop of the island of Britain and of the city of Canterbury, and other venerable men sitting with him, bishops of the island of Britain, with the holy Gospels laid before them, and in the place which is called by the Saxon name of Hatfield, we, handling the subject in concert, have made an exposition of the right and orthodox faith, as our incarnate Lord Jesus Christ delivered it to His disciples, who saw Him present and heard His discourses, and as the creed of the holy Fathers has delivered it, and all the holy and universal synods and all the chorus of approved doctors of the Catholic Church teach. We therefore piously and orthodoxly following them and, making our profession according to their divinely inspired teaching, believe in unison with it, and confess according to the holy Fathers that the Father and the Son and the Holy Ghost are properly and truly a consubstantial Trinity in unity, and unity in Trinity; that is, in one God in three consubstantial subsistencies or persons of equal glory and honor.

---

[1] The Monothelete doctrine, which appeared to be a form of Eutychianism because of its close connection with Monophysitism, v. infra, § 108.

And after many things of this kind that pertained to the confession of the right faith, the holy synod also adds these things to its letter:

We have received as holy and universal five synods of the blessed Fathers acceptable to God; that is, of the three hundred and eighteen assembled at Nicæa against the most impious Arius and his tenets; and of the one hundred and fifty at Constantinople against the madness of Macedonius and Eudoxius and their tenets; and of the two hundred in the first Council of Ephesus against the most wicked Nestorius and his tenets; and of the six hundred and thirty at Chalcedon against Eutyches and Nestorius and their tenets; and again of those assembled in a fifth council at Constantinople [A. D. 553], in the time of the younger Justinian, against Theodore and the epistles of Theodoret and Ibas and their tenets against Cyril.

And a little after: Also we have received the synod[1] that was held in the city of Rome in the time of the blessed Pope Martin in the eighth indiction, in the ninth year of the reign of the most pious Constantine.[2] And we glorify our Lord Jesus Christ as they glorified Him, neither adding nor subtracting anything; and we anathematize with heart and mouth those whom they anathematized; and those whom they received we receive, glorifying God the Father without beginning, and his only begotten Son, begotten of the Father before the world began, and the Holy Ghost proceeding ineffably from the Father and the Son, as those holy Apostles, prophets, and doctors have declared whom we have mentioned above. And we all who with Theodore have made an exposition of the Catholic faith have subscribed hereto.

[1] A. D. 649, Against the Monotheletes, see Hefele, § 307; *v. infra*, § 108; see Hahn, § 181, for the Anathematism of the Council; Haddan and Stubbs, *op. cit.*, III, 145–151.

[2] Constans II, also known as Constantine IV; see DCB.

CHAPTER III.   THE FOUNDATION OF THE ECCLESIAS-
TICAL INSTITUTIONS OF THE MIDDLE AGES

In the period between the conversion of the Franks and the
rise of the dynasty of Charles Martell, or the period comprising the sixth and seventh centuries, the foundation was laid
for those ecclesiastical institutions which are peculiar to the
Middle Ages, and found in the mediæval Church their full
embodiment. In the Church the Latin element was still more
or less dominant, and society was only slowly transformed
by the Germanic elements. In the adjustment of Roman institutions to the new political conditions in which Germanic
factors were dominant, the Germanic and the Roman elements are accordingly found in constantly varying proportions. In the case of the diocesan and parochial organization, only very slowly could the Church in the West attain
that complete organization which had long since been established in the East, and here Roman ideas were profoundly
modified by Germanic legal principles (§ 101). But at the
same time the Church's body of teaching and methods of
moral training were made clearly intelligible and more applicable to the new conditions of Christian life. The teaching of
Augustine was received only in part at the Council of Orange,
A. D. 529 (v. supra, § 85), and it was profoundly modified by
the moralistic type of theology traceable to Tertullian and
even further back (v. supra, § 39). It was, furthermore, completed by a clearer and more precise statement of the doctrines of purgatory and the sacrifice of the mass, and to the
death of Christ was applied unequivocally the doctrine of
merit which had been developed in the West in connection
with the early penitential discipline, and which was seen to
throw a new light upon the sacrifice of Christ upon the cross.
These conceptions served as a foundation for new discussions,
and confirmed tendencies already present in the Church
(§ 102). Connected with this theology was the penitential
discipline, which, growing out of the ancient discipline as

modified by the earlier form of monastic life, especially in Ireland, came under the influence of the Germanic legal conceptions (§ 103). In the same period monasticism was organized upon a new rule by Benedict of Nursia (§ 104), and the need of provision for the education of the young and for the training of the clergy was felt and, to some extent, provided for by monastery schools and other methods of education (§ 105).

§ 101. The Foundation of the Mediæval Diocesan and Parochial Constitution.

§ 102. Western Piety and Thought in the Period of the Conversion of the Barbarians.

§ 103. Foundation of the Mediæval Penitential System.

§ 104. The New Monasticism and the Rule of Benedict of Nursia.

§ 105. Foundation of Mediæval Culture and Schools.

§ 101. FOUNDATION OF THE MEDIÆVAL DIOCESAN AND PAROCHIAL CONSTITUTION

An outline of some of the legislation is here given, whereby the parish as organized in the West was built up, and the diocese was made to consist of a number of parishes under the bishop, who, however, did not exercise an absolute control over the incomes and position of the priests under him.

The selections are given in chronological order.

(a) Council of Agde, A. D. 506, *Canons.* Bruns, II, 145.

This is one of the most important councils of the period. Its various canons have all been embodied in the Canon Law; for the references to the Decretum of Gratian, in which they appear, see Hefele, § 222. It is to be noted that it was held under Alarich, the Arian king of the Visigoths. The preface is, therefore, given as being significant.

Since this holy synod has been assembled in the name of the Lord and with the permission of our most glorious, magnificent, and most pious king in the city of Agde, there, with knees bent and on the ground, we have prayed for his kingdom, his long life, for the people, that the lord who has given us permission to assemble, may happily extend his kingdom, that he may govern justly and protect valiantly; we have assembled in the basilica of St. Andrew to treat of the discipline and the ordination of pontiffs and other things of utility to the Church.

Canon 21. If any one wishes to have an oratory in the fields outside of the parishes, in which the gathering of the people is lawful and appointed, we permit him to have a mass there with the proper license on the other festivals, on account of the weariness of the family [*i. e.*, in going to the distant parish church], but on Easter, Christmas, Epiphany, Ascension Day, Pentecost and the Nativity of St. John the Baptist, or if there are any other very high festival days observed, let them hold no masses except in the cities and parishes. But if the clergy, without the command or permission of the bishop, hold and perform the masses on the festivals above mentioned in the oratories, let them be driven from the communion.

Canon 30. Because it is appropriate that the service of the Church be observed in the same way by all, it is to be desired that it be done so everywhere. After the antiphones the collects shall be said in order by the bishops and presbyters, and the hymns of Matins and Vespers be sung daily; and at the conclusion of the mass of Matins and Vespers,[1] after the hymns a chapter of the Psalms shall be read, and the people who are gathered shall, after the prayer, be dismissed with a benediction of the bishop until Vespers.

Canon 38. Without letters commendatory of their bishops, it is not permitted to the clergy to travel. The same rule is to be observed in the case of monks. If reproof of words does not correct them, we decree that they shall be beaten with rods. It is also to be observed in the case of monks that it

---

[1] *Matitutinarum vel vespertinarum missarum.* The term "mass" is here applied, not to the eucharist, but to Matins and Vespers. See Hefele, § 222, on this canon.

is not permitted them to leave the community for solitary cells, unless the more severe rule is remitted by their abbot to them who have been approved in the hermit life, or on account of the necessity of infirmity; but only then let it be done so that they remain within the walls of the same monastery, and they are permitted to have separate cells under the authority of the abbots. It is not permitted abbots to have different cells or many monasteries, or except on account of the inroads of enemies to erect dwellings within walls.

(b) I Council of Orleans, A. D. 511, *Canons*. Bruns, II, 160.

Canon 15. Concerning those things which in the form of lands, vineyards, slaves, and other property the faithful have given to the parishes, the statutes of the ancient canons are to be observed, so that all things shall be in the control of the bishop; but of those things which are given at the altar, a third is to be faithfully given to the bishop.

Canon 17. All churches which in various places have been built and are daily being built shall, according to the law of the primitive canons, be in the control of the bishop in whose territory they are located.

(c) IV Council of Orleans, A. D. 541, *Canons*. Bruns, II, 208.

Canon 7. In oratories on landed estates, the lords of the property shall not install wandering clergy against the will of the bishop to whom the rights of that territory belong, unless, perchance, they have been approved, and the bishop has in his discretion appointed them to serve in that place.

Canon 26. If any parishes are established in the houses of the mighty, and the clergy who serve there have been admonished by the archdeacon of the city, according to the duty of his office, and they neglect to do what they ought to do for the Church, because under the protection of the lord of the house, let them be corrected according to the ecclesiastical discipline; and if by the agents of these lords, or by these

lords themselves of the place, they are prevented from doing
any part of their duty toward the Church, those who do this
iniquity are to be deprived of the sacred rites until, having
made amends, they are received back into the peace of the
Church.[1]

Canon 33. If any one has, or asks to have, on his land a
diocese [*i. e.*, parish], let him first assign to it sufficient lands
and clergy who may there perform their duties, that suitable
reverence be done to the sacred places.

(*d*) V Council of Orleans, A. D. 549, *Canons*. Bruns, II,
208.

At this council no less than seven archbishops, forty-three bishops
and representatives of twenty-one other bishops were present. It was,
therefore, a general council of the Frankish Church, although politically the Frankish territory was divided into three kingdoms held
respectively by Childebert, Chlothar, and Theudebald. Orleans itself was in the dominion of Childebert. *Cf.* preface to the canons of
II Orleans, A. D. 533, which states that that council was attended by
five archbishops and the deputy of a sixth, as well as by bishops from
all parts of Gaul, and was called at the command of the "Glorious
kings," *i. e.*, Childebert, Chlothar, and Theudebert.

Canon 13. It is permitted to no one to retain, alienate, or
take away goods or property which has been lawfully given
to a church, monastery, or orphan asylums for any charity;
that if any one does do so he shall, according to the ancient
canons [*cf.* Hefele, §§ 220, 222], be regarded as a slayer of the
poor, and shall be shut out from the thresholds of the Church
so long as those things are not restored which have been taken
away or retained.

(*e*) Council of Braga, A. D. 572, *Canons*. Bruns, II, 37.

Canon 5. As often as bishops are requested by any of the
faithful to consecrate churches, they shall not, as having a
claim, ask any payment of the founders; but if he wishes to
give him something from a vow he has made, let it not be de-

[1] *Cf.* canon 4, Council of Clermont, A. D. 535 (Bruns, II, 188): "The clergy
are not in any way to be set against their bishops by the secular potentates."

spised; but if poverty or necessity prevent him, let nothing be demanded of him. This only let each bishop remember, that he shall not dedicate a church or basilica before he shall have received the endowment of the basilica and its service confirmed by an instrument of donation; for it is a not light rashness for a church to be consecrated, as if it were a private dwelling, without lights and without the support of those who are to serve there.

Canon 6. In case of any one who builds a basilica, not from any faithful devotion, but from the desire of gain, that whatsoever is there gathered of the offerings of the people he may share half and half with the clergy, on the ground that he has built the basilica on his own land, which in various places is said to be done quite constantly, this therefore ought hereafter to be observed, that no bishop consent to such an abominable purpose, that he should dare to consecrate a basilica which is founded not as the heritage of the saints but rather under the condition of tribute.

(*f*) II Council of Toledo, A. D. 589, *Canons*. Bruns, I, 217.

Canon 19. Many who have built churches demand that these churches, contrary to the canons, shall be consecrated in such a way that they shall not allow the endowment, which they have given the church, to belong to the control of the bishop; when this has been done in the past, let this be void, and in the future forbidden; but let all things pertain to the power and control of the bishop according to the ancient law.

§ 102. WESTERN PIETY AND THOUGHT IN THE PERIOD OF THE CONVERSION OF THE BARBARIANS

In the century following Augustine, the dogmatic interest of the Church was chiefly absorbed in the Christological controversies in the East. There were, however, some discussions in the West arising from the manifest difficulty of reconciling the doctrine of predestination, as drawn from Augustine, with the efficacy of baptism. For the adjustment of the teaching of Augustine to the sacramental system of the Church and to baptism more particularly, see the Council of Orange, A. D. 529, of which the principal conclusions are given above (§ 85). In the sixth century and in the early part of the seventh, doctrines were clearly enunciated which had been abundantly foreshadowed by earlier writers, but had not been fitted into an intelligible and practical system. These were especially the doctrine of purgatory and the sacrifice of the mass. The doctrine of purgatory completed the penitential system of the early Church by making it possible to expiate sin by suffering in a future existence, in the case of those who had died without completely doing penance here. By the sacrifice of the mass the advantages of Christ's death were constantly applied, not merely to the sin of the world in general, but to specified objects; the believer was brought into closest contact with the great act of redemption, and a centre was placed around which the life of the individual and the authority of the hierarchy could be brought into relation.

Additional source material: The works of Gregory the Great, PNF.

(a) Cæsarius of Arles, *Sermon* 104. (MSL, 39 : 1947, 1949.)

Cæsarius presided at the Council of Orange A. D. 529. He died in 543. Not a few of his sermons have been mixed up with those of Augustine, and this sermon is to be found in Appendix to the works of Augustine in the standard editions of that Father. It should be noted that this conception of purgatory is not wholly unlike that of St. Augustine; see his *Enchiridion*, chs. 69, 109 (*v. supra*, § 84); also *De Civ. Dei*, 20: 25; 21 : 13.

Ch. 4. By continual prayers and frequent fasts and more generous alms, and especially by forgiveness of those who sin against us, we diligently redeem our sins, lest by chance when collected together against us at once they make a great mass and overwhelm us. Whatsoever of these sins shall not have been redeemed by us is to be purged by that fire concerning which the Apostle said: " Because it will be revealed by fire, and if any man's work is burned he will suffer loss" (I Cor. 3 : 15). If in tribulation we do not give thanks to God, if by good works we do not redeem our sins, we will remain so long in that fire of purification[1] until the little, trifling sins, as hay, wood, and stubble are consumed.

Ch. 8. All saints who serve God truly strive to give themselves to reading and prayer, and to perseverance in good works, and building no mortal sins and no little sins, that is, wood, hay, and stubble, upon the foundation of Christ; but good works, that is, gold, silver, and precious stones, will without injury go through that fire of which the Apostle spoke: "Because it will be revealed by fire." But those who, although they do not commit capital sins, yet are prone to commit very little sins and are negligent in redeeming them, will attain to eternal life because they believed in Christ, but first either in this life they are purified by bitter tribulation, or certainly in that fire of which the Apostle speaks they are to be tormented, that they may come to eternal life without spot or wrinkle. But those who have committed homicide, sacrilege, adultery, and other similar sins, if there does not come to their aid suitable penitence, will not deserve to go through that fire of purification to life, but they will be thrown into death by eternal fire.

(b) Gregory the Great, *Dialogorum libri IV, de Vita et Miraculis Patrum Italicorum*, IV, 56. (MPL, 77 : 425.)

The sacrifice of the mass.
See also the selection below on the doctrine of purgatory.

It should be considered that it is safer to do to men, while one is living, the good which one hopes will be done by others after one's death. It is more blessed to depart free than to seek liberty after chains. We ought, with our whole mind, despise the present world, especially since we see it already

---

[1] The employment of the technical term *purgatorium* to designate the place and fires of purification is very much later, and not defined until the thirteenth century as the official and technical word, although used long before that time in theological discussion.

passing away. We ought to immolate to God the daily sacrifice of our tears, the daily offerings of His flesh and blood.
For this offering peculiarly preserves the soul from eternal
death, and it renews to us in a mystery the death of the Only
begotten, who, although being risen from the dead, dieth no
more, and death hath no more dominion over Him (Rom. 6 : 9);
yet, while in Himself He liveth immortal and incorruptible,
for us He is immolated again in this mystery of the sacred
oblation. For it is His body that is there given, His flesh
that is divided for the salvation of the people, His blood that
is poured, no longer into the hands of unbelievers, but into the
mouths of the faithful. For this let us ever estimate what
this sacrifice is for us, which for our absolution ever imitates
the passion of the only begotten Son. For what one of the
faithful can have any doubt that at the very hour of the offering [*immolatio*], at the word of the priest, the heavens are
opened, the choirs of angels are present at the mystery of
Jesus Christ, the lowest things are united to the highest,
earthly things with heavenly, and from the invisible and the
visible there is made one ?

(c) Gregory the Great, *Dialog.*, IV, 39. (MSL, 77: 393.)

The doctrine of purgatory.
Gregory hardly adds anything to Augustine more than a clearer
definition after the lines laid down by Cæsarius of Arles.

From these sayings [John 12:35; II Cor. 6:2; Eccles. 9:10]
it is evident that as one left the earth so one will appear
before the judgment. Yet still it is to be believed that for
certain slight sins there is to be before that judgment a fire
of purification, because the Truth says that, if one utters blasphemy against the Holy Ghost, his sin will be forgiven him
neither in this world nor in the future [Matt. 12 : 31]. From
this saying one is given to understand that some sins can be
forgiven in this life, others in a future life.

(d) Gregory the Great, *In Evangelia*, II, 37, 8. (MSL,
76 : 1279.)

The application of the sacrifice of the mass to persons in purgatory.

Not long before our time the case is told of a certain man who, having been taken captive, was carried far away [*cf. Dialog.*, IV, 57], and because he was held a long time in chains his wife, since she had not received him back from that captivity, believed him to be dead and every week she had the sacrifice offered for him as already dead. And as often as the sacrifice was offered by his spouse for the absolution of his soul, the chains were loosed in his captivity. For having returned a long time after, greatly astonished he told his wife that on certain days each week his chains were loosed. His wife considered the days and hours, and then knew that he was loosed when, as she remembered, the sacrifice was offered for him. From that perceive, my dearest brothers, to what extent the holy sacrifice offered by us is able to loose the bonds of the heart, if the sacrifice offered by one for another can loose the chains of the body.

§ 103. THE FOUNDATION OF THE MEDIÆVAL PENITENTIAL SYSTEM

The penitential system, as it was organized in the Western Church in the sixth, seventh, and eighth centuries, was but the carrying out of principles which had appeared elsewhere in Christendom and were involved in the primitive method of dealing with moral delinquents by the authorities of the Church. [See the epistles of Basil the Great to Amphilochius (Ep. 189, 199, 217) in PNF, ser. II, vol. VIII.] Similar problems had to be handled everywhere whenever the Church came to deal with moral conduct, and much the same solution was found everywhere. There is, however, no known connection between the earliest penitentials of the Western Church, those of Ireland, and the similar books of the East. There is no need of supposing that there was a connection. But in the case of the works attributed to Theodore of Tarsus, archbishop of Canterbury, himself a Greek and probably a native of Tarsus, there is a provable connection which is evident to any one reading his work, as he refers to Basil and others. The characteristics of the Western penitentials are their minute division of sins, their exact determination of penances for each sin, and the great extent to which they were used in the practical work of the Church. They serve as the first crude beginnings of a moral theology of a practical character, such as would be needed by the poorly trained parish clergy of the times in dealing with their flocks. On account of the nature of these works, it is hardly necessary or expedient to give more than a few brief extracts in addition to references to sources. Much of the matter is extremely offensive to modern taste.

(a) King Æthelberht, *Laws*. Thorpe, *Ancient Laws and Institutes* (Rolls Series), 1 *ff.*

The Early Germanic Codes are full of regulations whereby for an injury the aggrieved party, or his family in case of his death, could be prevented from retaliating in kind upon the aggressor and his family. This was effected by a money payment as compensation for damages sustained, and the amount for each sort of injury was carefully regulated by law, *i. e.*, by ancient custom, which was reduced to writing in the sixth century in some cases. The *Laws of Æthelberht* are written in Anglo-Saxon and are probably the earliest in a Teutonic language. For a translation of characteristic portions of the *Salic Law*, which should be compared with the *Laws of Æthelberht* to show the universality of the same system, see Henderson, *Select Historical Documents of the Middle Ages*, p. 176, London, 1892; also Hodgkin, *Italy and Her Invaders*, VI, 183, for the Lombard law of Rothari, a little later, but of the same spirit.

21. If any man slay another, let him make bot with a half leod-geld of 100 shillings.

22. If any man slay another at an open grave, let him pay 20 shillings and pay the whole leod within 40 days.

23. If a stranger retire from the land, let his kindred pay a half leod.

24. If any one bind a freeman, let him make bot with 20 shillings.

25. If any one slay a ceorl's hlaf-aeta,[1] let him make bot with 5 shillings.

38. If a shoulder be lamed,[2] let bot be made with 12 shillings.

39. If the ear be struck off, let bot be made with 12 shillings.

40. If the other ear hear not, let bot be made with 25 shillings.

41. If an eye be struck out, let bot be made with 50 shillings.

51. For each of the four front teeth, 6 shillings; for the tooth that stands next to them, 4 shillings; for that which stands next to that, 3 shillings, and then afterward 1 shilling.

(b) Vinnian, *Penitential*. Wasserschleben, *Die Bussordnungen der abendländischen Kirche*, 108 ff.

This is one of the earliest of the penitentials and belongs to the Irish Church.

1. If one has committed in his heart a sin of thought and immediately repents of it, let him smite his breast and pray God for forgiveness and perform satisfaction because he has sinned.

2. If he has often thought of the sins and thinks of committing them, and is then victor over the thought or is overcome by it, let him pray God and fast day and night until the wicked thought disappears and he is sound again.

3. If he has thought on a sin and determines to commit it, but is prevented in the execution, so is the sin the same, but not the penance.[3]

6. If a cleric has planned in his heart to smite or kill his neighbor, he shall do penance half a year on bread and water according to the prescribed amount, and for a whole year

[1] Member of household, a servant.   [2] In case of assault and battery.
[3] The preceding rules are clearly matter of moral direction, and indicate the transition from general advice to a scale of sins and punishments, such as follows.

abstain from wine and the eating of meat, and then may he be permitted again to approach the altar.

7. If it is a layman, he shall do penance for a whole week; for he is a man of this world and his guilt is lighter in this world and his punishment in the future is less.

8. If a cleric has smitten his brother [*i. e.*, a clergyman] or his neighbor and drawn blood . . . he shall do penance a whole year on bread and water; he may not fill any clerical office, but must with tears pray to God for himself.

9. Is he a layman, he shall do penance for 40 days, and according to the judgment of the priest or some other righteous man pay a determined sum of money.

(*c*) Theodore of Tarsus, *Penitential*, I. Haddan and Stubbs, III, 73 *ff*.

For Theodore of Tarsus, archbishop of Canterbury, see W. Stubbs, art. "Theodorus of Tarsus" in DCB. That he wrote a penitential is not certain. But that he was regarded as the author of a penitential is clear enough. In fact, his name is attached to penitentials in much the same way as David's name is attached to the whole book of Psalms. For a discussion of the various works attributed to Theodore, see Haddan and Stubbs, *Councils and Ecclesiastical Documents*, *loc. cit.* This is a characteristic penitential and may be regarded as following closely the decisions and opinions of Theodore. Much of it is unprintable in English.

Cap. I. *On drunkenness.* 1. If any bishop or other person ordained is customarily given to the vice of drunkenness, let him cease from it or be deposed.

2. If a monk vomit from drunkenness, let him do 30 days, penance.

3. If a presbyter or deacon do the same, let him do 40 days' penance.

4. If any one by infirmity or because he has abstained for a long time, and it is not his habit to drink or eat much, or for joy at Christmas or at Easter, or for the commemoration of any of the saints, does this, and he has not taken more than is decreed by the elders, he has done no wrong. If the bishop

should have commanded, he does no harm to him unless he himself does likewise.

5. If a believing layman vomits from drunkenness, let him do 15 days' penance.

6. He who becomes drunk against the commandment of the Lord, if he has a vow of holiness let him do penance 7 days on bread and water, and 70 days without fat; the laity without beer.

7. Whoever out of malice makes another drunk, let him do penance 40 days.

8. Whoever vomits from satiety let him do penance 3 days.

9. If with the sacrifice of the communion, let him do penance 7 days; but if out of infirmity, he is without guilt.

Cap. II. *On fornication.*

Cap. III. *On theft.*

Cap. IV. *On the killing of men.* [This should be compared with the secular laws.]

1. If any one out of vengeance for a relative kill a man, let him do penance as for homicide 7 or 10 years. If, however, he is willing to return to relatives the money of valuation [Weregeld, according to the secular rating], the penance will be lighter, that is by one-half the length.

2. He who kills a man for vengeance for his brother, let him do penance 3 years; in another place he is said to do penance 10 years.

3. But homicides 10 or 7 years.

4. If a layman kills another man with thoughts of hatred, if he does not wish to relinquish his arms, let him do penance 7 years, without flesh and wine 3 years.

5. If any one kills a monk or a clergyman, let him relinquish his arms and serve God[1] or do 7 years' penance. He is in the judgment of the bishop. But he who kills a bishop or a presbyter, the judgment concerning him is in the king.

6. He who by the command of his lord kills a man, let

---

[1] *I. e.*, in a monastery.

him keep away from the church 40 days; and he who kills a man in a public war, let him do penance 40 days.

7. If out of wrath, 3 years; if by chance, 1 year; if by drink or any contrivance, 4 years or more; if by strife, let him do penance 10 years.[1]

Cap. V. *Concerning those who are deceived by a heresy.*

Cap. VI. *Concerning perjury.*

Cap. VII. *Concerning many and various wrong acts and those necessary things which are not harmful.*

Cap. VIII. *Concerning various failings of the servants of God.*

Cap. IX. *Concerning those who are degraded or cannot be ordained.*

Cap. X. *Concerning those who are baptized twice, how they shall do penance.*

Cap. XI. *Concerning those who violate the Lord's Day and the appointed fasts of the Church.*

Cap. XII. *Concerning the communion of the eucharist or the sacrifice.*

Cap. XIII. *Concerning reconciliation.*

Cap. XIV. *Especially concerning the penance of those who marry.*

Cap. XV. *Concerning the worship of idols.*

(d) Bede, *Penitential*, ch. XI. Haddan and Stubbs, *Councils and Ecclesiastical Documents*, III, 32.

The Penitential of Bede is to be distinguished from the *Liber de Remediis Peccatorum* attributed to him, *cf.* Haddan and Stubbs, *op. cit.*, who print the genuine penitential. It belongs to the period before 725. In not a few points it closely resembles that of Theodore. The concluding passage here given is to be found in many penitentials with but little variation. It is probably as early as the work itself, although apparently not by Bede. It is a method of commuting penances. In place of fasting inordinate or impossible lengths of time, other penances could be substituted. In later ages still other forms of commutation were introduced. Even money payments were used as commutation of penance.

[1] Another reading, 4.

XI. *On Counsel to be Given.*

We read in the penitential of doing penance on bread and water, for the great sins one year or two or three years, and for little sins a month or a week. Likewise in the case of some the conditions are harsh and difficult. Therefore to him who cannot do these things we give the counsel that psalms, prayers, and almsgiving ought to be performed some days in penance for these; that is, that psalms are for one day when he ought to do penance on bread and water. Therefore he should sing fifty psalms on his knees, and if not on his knees seventy psalms inside the church or in one place. For a week on bread and water, let him sing on his knees three hundred psalms in order and in the church or in one place. And for one month on bread and water, one thousand five hundred psalms kneeling, or if not kneeling one thousand eight hundred and twenty, and afterward let him fast every day until the sixth hour and abstain from flesh and wine; but whatsoever other food God has given him let him eat, after he has sung the psalms. And he who does not know psalms ought to do penance and to fast, and every day let him give to the poor the value of a denarius, and fast one day until the ninth hour, and the next until vespers, and after that whatsoever he has let him eat.

§ 104. THE NEW MONASTICISM AND THE RULE OF BENE-
DICT OF NURSIA

In the first centuries of monasticism in the West, the greatest variety was to be found among the constitutions of the various monastic houses and the rules drawn up by great leaders in the ascetic movement. This variety extended even to the nature of the vows assumed and their obligation. Benedict of Nursia (circa 480 to circa 544), gave the rule according to which for some centuries nearly all the monasteries of the West were ultimately organized. The first great example of this rule in operation was Benedict's own monastery at Monte Cassino. For a time the rule of Benedict came into conflict with that of Columbanus in Gaul.[1] But the powerful recommendation of Gregory the Great, who had introduced it in Rome, and the intrinsic superiority of the rule itself made the Benedictine system triumphant. It should be noted that the Benedictine cloisters were for centuries independent establishments and only formed into organized groups of monasteries in the great monastic reforms of the tenth and following centuries. It is a question how far the Benedictine rule was introduced into England in the early centuries of the Anglo-Saxon Church, although it is often taken for granted that it was introduced by Augustine. Critical edition of the Benedictine rule by Wölfflin, Leipsic, 1895; in Migne's edition there is an elaborate commentary with many illustrative extracts and formulæ, as well as traditional glosses.

Additional source material: An abbreviated translation of the Benedictine rule may be found in Henderson, *Select Historical Documents*, 1892, and in full in Thatcher and McNeal, *A Source Book for Mediæval History*, 1905.

(*A*) Benedict of Nursia, *Regula*. (MSL, 66 : 246.)

1. *Concerning the kinds of monks and their modes of living.* It is manifest that there are four kinds of monks. The first is that of the cenobites, that is the monastic, serving under a rule and an abbot. The second kind is that of the anchorites, that is the hermits, those who have learned to fight against the devil, not by the new fervor of conversion, but by a long probation in a monastery, having been taught already by association with many; and having been well prepared in the army of the brethren for the solitary fight of the hermit, and secure now without the encouragement of another, they are able, God helping them, to fight with their own hand or arm against the vices of the flesh or of their thoughts. But a third and very bad kind of monks are the sarabites, not tried as gold in the furnace by a rule, experience being their teacher, but softened after the manner of lead;

[1] For the rule of Columbanus, see MSL, 80: 209 *ff.*

keeping faith with the world by their works, they are known by their tonsure to lie to God. Being shut up by twos and threes alone and without a shepherd, in their own and not in the Lord's sheepfold, they have their own desires for a law. For whatever they think good and choose, that they deem holy; and what they do not wish, that they consider unlawful. But the fourth kind of monk is the kind called the *gyrovagi*, who during their whole life are guests for three or four days at a time in the cells of different monasteries throughout the various provinces; they are always wandering and never stationary, serving their own pleasures and the allurements of the palate, and in every way worse than the sarabites. Concerning the most wretched way of all, it is better to keep silence than to speak. These things, therefore, being omitted, let us proceed with the aid of God to treat of the best kind, the cenobites.

2. *What the abbot should be like.* An abbot who is worthy to preside over a monastery ought always to remember what he is called and to carry out in his deeds the name of a superior. For in the monastery he is believed to be Christ's representative, since he is called by His name, the Apostle saying: " We have received the spirit of adoption of sons, whereby we cry Abba, Father" [Rom. 8 : 15]. And so the abbot ought not (and oh that he may not!) teach or decree or order anything apart from the precepts of the Lord; but his order or teaching should be sprinkled with the leaven of divine justice in the minds of his disciples. . . . No distinctions of persons shall be made by him in the monastery. One shall not be loved by him more than another, unless the one whom he finds excelling in good work and obedience. A freeborn man shall not be preferred to one coming from servitude, unless there be some reasonable cause. But when it is just and it seems good to the abbot he shall show preference no matter what the rank shall be. But otherwise they shall keep their own places; for, whether we be bound or free, we are all one in Christ, and under God we perform an equal

service of subjection; for God is no respecter of persons
[Acts 10 : 34]. . . .

3. *Concerning calling the brethren to take counsel.* As often as
anything unusual is to be done in the monastery, let the abbot
call together the whole congregation and himself explain the
question before them. And having heard the advice of the
brethren, he shall consider it by himself, and let him do what
he judges most advantageous. And for this reason, moreover, we have said that all ought to be called to take counsel;
because it is often to a younger person that the Lord reveals
what is best. The brethren, moreover, ought, with all humble
subjection, to give their advice so that they do not too boldly
presume to defend what seems good to them, but it should
rather depend upon the judgment of the abbot; so that, whatever he decides upon as the more salutary, they should all
agree to it. . . .

4. *Concerning the instruments of good works.*

5. *Concerning obedience.* The first grade of humility is
prompt obedience. This becomes those who, on account of
the holy service which they professed, or on account of the
fear of hell or the glory of eternal life, consider nothing dearer
to them than Christ; so that as soon as anything is commanded
by their superior, they may not know how to suffer delay in
doing it, even as if it were a divine command. . . .

6. *Concerning silence.* 7. *Concerning humility.* 8. *Concerning the Divine Offices at night.* 9. *How many Psalms are
to be said at night.* 10. *How in summer the Nocturnal Praises
shall be carried on.* 11. *How Vigils shall be conducted on Sunday.* 12. *Concerning the order of Matins on Sunday.* 13.
Concerning the order of Matins on week days. 14. *Concerning
the order of Vigils on Saints' days.* 15. *Concerning the occasions when the Alleluias shall be said.* 16. *Concerning the order
of Divine Worship during the day.* 17. *On the number of
Psalms to be said at these times.* 18. *Concerning the order in
which the Psalms are to be said.* 19. *Concerning the art of singing.* 20. *Concerning the reverence in prayer.* 21. *Concern-*

ing the Deans of monasteries. 22. *How monks shall sleep.* 21. *Concerning excommunication for faults.* 24. *What ought to be the measure of excommunication.* 25. *Concerning graver faults.* 26. *Concerning those who without being ordered by the Abbot, associate with the excommunicated.* 27. *What care the Abbot should exercise with regard to the excommunicated.* 28. *Concerning those who, being often rebuked, do not amend.* 29. *Whether brothers who leave the monastery ought to be received back.* 30. *Concerning boys under age, how they should be corrected.* 31. *Concerning the Cellarer of the monastery, what sort of person he should be.* 32. *Concerning the utensils or property of the monastery.*

33. *Whether monks should have anything of their own.* More than anything else is this special vice to be cut off root and branch from the monastery, that one should presume to give or receive anything without order from the abbot, or should have anything of his own; he should have absolutely nothing, neither a book nor tablets nor a pen, nothing at all—for indeed it is not allowed to have their own bodies or wills in their own power. But all things necessary they must receive from the father of the monastery; nor is it allowable to have anything which the abbot has not given or permitted. . . .

34. *Whether all ought to receive necessaries equally.* 35. *Concerning the weekly officers of the kitchen.* 36. *Concerning infirm brothers.* 37. (Mitigation of the rule for the very old and the very young.) 38. *Concerning the weekly reader.*

39. *Concerning the amount of food.* We believe, moreover, that for the daily refection of the sixth and for that of the ninth hour as well two cooked dishes, on account of the infirmities of the different ones, are enough in all months for all tables; so that whoever, perchance, cannot eat of one may partake of the other. Therefore let two cooked dishes suffice for all the brethren; and if it is possible to obtain apples or fresh vegetables, a third may be added. One full pound of bread shall suffice for a day, whether there be one refection or breakfast and supper. But if they are to have supper, the

third part of that same pound shall be reserved by the cellarer to be given back to those when they are about to sup. But if perchance some greater labor shall have been performed, it shall be in the will and power of the abbot, if it is expedient, to increase anything. . . . But to younger boys the same quantity shall not be served, but less than to the older ones, as moderation is to be observed in all things. But every one shall abstain altogether from eating the flesh of four-footed beasts except alone in the case of the weak and the sick.

40. *Concerning the amount of drink.* Each one has his own gift from God, one in this way and another in that. Therefore it is with some hesitation that the amount of daily sustenance for others is fixed by us. Nevertheless, considering the weakness of the infirm, we believe that a half pint of wine a day is enough for each one. Those, moreover, to whom God has given the ability of enduring abstinence should know that they will have their own reward. But the prior shall judge if either the needs of the place, or labor, or heat of the summer require more; considering, in all things, lest satiety or drunkenness creep in. Indeed, we read that wine is not suitable for monks at all. But, because in our times it is not possible to persuade monks of this, let us agree at least as to the fact that we should not drink until we are sated, but sparingly. For wine can make even the wise to go astray. Where, moreover, the limitations of the place are such that the amount written above cannot be found, but much less or nothing at all, those who live there shall bless God and shall not murmur. And we admonish them as to this, above all, that they be without murmuring.

41. *At what hours the brethren ought to take their refection.* 42. *That after Compline no one shall speak.* 43. *Concerning those who come late to Divine Service or to table.* 44. *Concerning those who are excommunicated and how they shall render satisfaction.* 45. *Concerning those who make mistakes in the oratory.* 46. *Concerning those who err in other matters.* 47. *Concerning the announcement of the hour of Divine Service.*

48. *Concerning the daily manual labor.* Idleness is the enemy of the soul. Therefore at fixed times the brethren ought to be occupied in manual labor; and again at fixed times in sacred reading. Therefore we believe that according to this disposition both seasons ought to be so arranged that, from Easter until the first of October, going out early from the first until about the fourth hour, they shall labor at what might be necessary. Moreover, from the fourth until about the sixth hour, they shall give themselves to reading. After the sixth hour, moreover, rising from table, they shall rest in their beds with all silence; or perchance he that wishes to read may so read to himself that he shall not disturb another. And nones shall be said rather early, about the middle of the eighth hour; and again they shall work at what is necessary until vespers. But if the exigency or the poverty of the place demands that they shall be occupied by themselves in picking fruits, they shall not be cast down; for then they are truly monks if they live by the labor of their hands, as did also our Fathers and the Apostles.

From the first of October until the beginning of Lent, they shall give themselves unto reading until the second full hour. At the second hour tierce shall be said, and all shall labor at the task which is enjoined upon them until the ninth. When the first signal of the ninth hour shall have been given they shall each leave off his work and be ready when the second signal strikes. Moreover, after the refection they shall give themselves to their reading or to the Psalms.

And in the days of Lent, from dawn until the third full hour, they shall give themselves to their reading; and until the tenth hour they shall do the labor that is enjoined upon them. In the days of Lent they shall all receive separate books from the library, which they shall read through completely in order; these books shall be given out on the first day of Lent. Above all, there shall certainly be appointed one or two elders to go around the monastery at the hours in which the brethren are engaged in reading and see to it that no troublesome brother is to be found who is given to idleness and chatting and is not intent upon his reading and is not only of no use to himself but disturbing the others. If such an one (and may there not be such!) be found, he shall be admonished once and a second time. If he does not amend, he shall be subject under the rule to such punishment that others may fear. Nor shall the brethren assemble at unsuitable hours.

On Sundays all shall give themselves to reading except those who are deputed to various duties. But if any one be so negligent and lazy that he will not or cannot meditate or read, some task shall be imposed upon him which he can perform, so that he be not idle. On feeble and delicate brothers such a labor or art is to be imposed that they shall neither be idle nor so oppressed by the burden of labor as to be driven to take to flight. Their weakness is to be taken into consideration by the abbot.

49. *The observance of Lent.* 50. *Concerning brothers who labor far from the oratory or are on a journey.* 51. *Concerning brothers who do not journey very far.* 52. *Concerning the oratory of the monastery.* 53. *Concerning the reception of guests.* 54. *As to whether a monk should be allowed to receive letters or anything.* 55. *Concerning the Vestiarius and Calciarius.* 56. *Concerning the table of the Abbot.* 57. *Concerning the artificers of the monastery.*

58. *Concerning the manner of receiving brethren.* When any one newly comes for conversion of life, an easy entrance shall not be granted him, but as the Apostle says: "Try the spirits whether they be of God" [I John 4 : 1]. Therefore if one who comes perseveres in knocking, and is seen after four or five days to endure patiently the insults heaped upon him and the difficulty of ingress and to persist in his request, let entrance be granted him, and let him be for a few days in the guest cell. After this let him be in the cell of the novices, where he shall meditate and eat and sleep. And an elder shall be appointed for him such as shall be capable of winning

souls, who shall altogether intently watch him, and be zealous to see if he in truth seek God, if he be zealous for the work of God, for obedience, for suffering shame. And above all the harshness and roughness of the means through which one approaches God shall be told him in advance. If he promise perseverance in his steadfastness after the lapse of two months, this Rule shall be read over to him in order, and it shall be said to him: Behold the law under which thou didst wish to serve; if thou canst observe it, enter; but if thou canst not, depart freely. If he shall have stood firm thus far, then he shall be led into the aforesaid cell of the novices, and again he shall be proven with all patience.

And after the lapse of six months, the Rule shall be reread to him, that he may know upon what he is entering. And if he persist thus far, after four months the same Rule shall still again be read to him. If, after deliberating with himself, he shall promise that he will observe all things and to obey all the commands laid upon him, then he shall be received into the congregation, knowing that it is decreed that by the law of the Rule he shall from that day not be allowed to depart from the monastery, nor to shake free from his neck the yoke of the Rule, which after such painful deliberation he was at liberty to refuse or receive.

He who is to be received shall make in the oratory, in the presence of all, a promise before God and His saints concerning his stability [*stabilitas loci*] and the change in the manner of his life [*conversio morum*] and obedience [*obedientia*],[1] so that if at any time he act contrary he shall know that he shall be condemned by Him whom he mocks. And concerning this, his promise, he shall make a petition addressed by name to the saints whose relics are there, and to the abbot who is present. And this petition he shall write out with his own hand; or, if he be really unlearned in letters, let another at his request write it, and to that the novice shall make his sign. With his own hand he shall place it upon the altar. And when

---

[1] This with the two preceding are the three vows of the Benedictine monk.

he has placed it there, the novice shall immediately begin this verse: "Receive me O Lord according to Thy promise and I shall live; and cast me not down from my hope" [Psalm 119 : 116, Vulgate version]. And this verse the whole congregation shall repeat three times adding: Glory be to the Father, etc. Then that brother novice shall prostrate himself at the feet of each one that they may pray for him. And already from that day he shall be considered as in the congregation.

If he have any property, he shall first either present it to the poor or, making a solemn donation, shall confer it on the monastery, receiving nothing at all for himself; and he shall know for a fact that from that day he shall have no power even over his own body. Immediately thereafter, in the monastery, he shall take off his own garments in which he was clad, and shall put on the garments of the monastery. Those garments, furthermore, which he has taken off shall be placed in the vestiary to be preserved; so that if, at any time, on the devil's persuasion, he shall wish to go forth from the monastery (and may it never happen) then, taking off the garments of the monastery let him be cast out. But the petition he made and which the abbot took from upon the altar, he shall not receive again, but it shall be preserved in the monastery.

59. *Concerning the sons of nobles and poor men who are presented.* If by chance any one of the nobles offers his son to God in the monastery, and the boy himself is a minor in age, his parents shall make the petition of which we have spoken above. And with an oblation, they shall wrap the petition and the hand of the boy in the linen cloth of the altar; and thus shall they offer him. Concerning their property, either they shall promise in the present petition, under an oath, that they will never, either indirectly or otherwise, give him anything at any time, or furnish him with means of possessing it. Or, if they be unwilling to do this, and wish to offer something as alms to the monastery for their salvation, they shall make a donation of those things which they wish to give to the mon-

astery, retaining for themselves the usufruct if they so wish. And let all things be so observed that no suspicion may remain with the boy; by which, as we have learned from experience, being deceived, he might perish (and may it not happen). The poorer ones shall do likewise. Those who have nothing at all shall simply make their petitions; and with an oblation they shall offer their sons before witnesses.

60. *Concerning priests who may wish to dwell in the monastery.* 61. *Concerning pilgrim monks, how they are to be received.* 62. *Ordination of monks as priests.* 63. *Concerning rank in the congregation.* 64. *Concerning the ordination of an Abbot.* 65. *Concerning the Prior of the monastery.* 66. *Concerning the Doorkeepers of the monastery.* 67. *Concerning brothers sent on a journey.* 68. *If impossibilities are imposed on a brother.* 69. *That in the monastery one shall not presume to defend another.* 70. *That no one shall presume to strike another.* 71. *That they shall be obedient to one another.* 72. *Concerning the good zeal which monks ought to have.*

73. *Concerning the fact that not every just observance is decreed in this Rule.* We have written down this Rule, that we may show those observing it in the monasteries how to have some honesty of character or beginning of conversion. But for those who hasten to the perfection of living, there are the teachings of the holy Fathers; the observance of which leads a man to the heights of perfection. For what page or what discourse of divine authority in the Old or New Testament is not a more perfect rule of human life? Or what book of the holy and Catholic Fathers does not trumpet forth how by the right road we shall come to our Creator?

Also the reading aloud of the Fathers, and their decrees and lives; also the Rule of our holy Father Basil—what else are they except instruments of virtue for good living and obedient monks? But to us who are idle and evil livers and negligent there is the blush of confusion. Thou, therefore, whoever hastens to the heavenly fatherland, perform with Christ's aid this Rule written out as the least beginnings; and then at length, under God's protection, thou wilt come to the greater things that we have mentioned—to the summits of teaching and virtue.

(B) Formulæ.

The following *formulæ* are given to illustrate the Rule in its working. The first group bear upon the vow of *stabilitas loci*. The case not infrequently arose that a brother wished to go to a monastery in which the observance of the Rule was stricter. In case a new foundation was begun anywhere, the first monks were almost always from another monastery. If therefore the monk is to remove, he must obtain permission of his abbot, and this was not regarded as a violation of the vow of *stabilitas loci* and obedience to his abbot. These *formulæ* were not uniform throughout the Church, but the following are given as samples of early practice.

1. *Letters dimissory.* (MSL, 66 : 859.)

(a) To all bishops and all orders of the holy Church, and to all faithful people.

Be it known unto you that I have given license to this our brother, John or Paul by name, that where he finds it agreeable to dwell in order to lead the monastic life, he shall have license to dwell for the benefit of himself and the monastery.

(b) Since such a brother desires to dwell in another monastery, where, as it seems to him, he can save his soul and serve God, know then that by these letters dimissory, we have given him license to go to another monastery.

(c) From the *Consuetudines* of the Monastery of St. Paul at Rome.

I, a humble abbot. You should know, beloved, that this brother, John or Paul by name, has asked us to give him permission to dwell with you. And, because we know that you observe the Rule of the order, we assent to his dwelling with you. I now commend him to you, that you may treat him as I would, and for him you are to render an account to God as I would have had to render.

(*d*) Another from the same.

To the venerable father the abbot of (. . .) monastery, the abbot of (. . .) monastery greeting with a holy kiss. Since our monastery has been burdened with various embarrassments and poverty, we beseech your brotherliness that you will receive our brother to dwell in your monastery, and we commend him by these letters of commendation and dismission to your jurisdiction and obedience.

Alternate conclusion:

We send him from our obedience to serve the Lord under your obedience.

2. *Offering of a child to a monastery.* (MSL, 66 : 842.)

The following forms should be compared with chapter 59 of the Rule. Children so offered were known as *oblati, i. e.,* offered. These forms are from a manuscript of the ninth century.

(*a*) To offer children to God is sanctioned in the Old and New Testaments as Abraham[1] . . . are related to have done. Moved by the example of these and many others, I (. . .) do now, for the salvation of my soul and for the salvation of the souls of my parents, offer in the presence of the abbot (. . .) this my son (. . .) to Almighty God and to St. Mary His mother, according to the Rule of the blessed Benedict in the Monastery of Mons Major, so that from this day forth it shall not be lawful for him to withdraw his neck from the yoke of this service; and I promise never, by myself or by any agent, to give him in any way opportunity of leaving, and that this writing may be confirmed I sign it with my own hand.

(*b*) Brief form.

[1] Lacuna in text.

I give this boy in devotion to our Lord Jesus Christ, before God and His saints, that he may remain all the days of his life and become a monk until his death.

3. *Ceremony of receiving a monk into a Benedictine monastery.* (MSL, 66 : 829.)

(a) From Peter Boherius, *Commentary on the Regula S. Benedicti*, ch. 58 of the Rule, *v. supra*.

When the novice makes his solemn profession, the abbot vests to say mass, and after the offertory the abbot interrogates him saying:

Brother (such a one): Is it your will to renounce the world and all its pomps ?

He answers: It is.

Abbot: Will you promise obedience according to the Rule of St. Benedict?   Answer: I will.

Abbot: May God give you his aid.

Then the novice, or some one at his request, reads the aforesaid profession, and when it has been read he places it upon his head, and then upon the altar.   After this, when he has prostrated himself on his knees in four directions in the form of a cross, he says the verse: Receive me, O Lord, etc.   And then the *Gloria Patri*, the *Kyrie Eleison*, the *Pater Noster* and the Litany are said, the novice remaining prostrate on the ground before the altar, until the end of the mass.   And the brothers ought to be in the choir kneeling while the Litany is said.   When the Litany has been said, then shall follow very devoutly the special prayers as commanded by the Fathers, and immediately after the communion and before the prayer is said, the garments of the novice, which have been folded and placed before the altar, shall be blessed with their proper prayers; and they shall be anointed and sprinkled with holy water by the abbot.   After "*Ite, missa est*"[1] the novice rises from the ground, and having put off his old garments which were not blessed he puts on those which have been blessed, while the abbot recites: *Exuat te Dominus*, etc.

[1] The conclusion of the mass.

And when the kiss has been given by the abbot, all the brothers in turn give him the kiss of peace, and he shall keep silence for three days continuously after this, going about with his head covered and receiving the communion every day.

(b) From Theodore of Canterbury, *ibid.*, 827.

In the ordination of monks the abbot ought to say mass, and say three prayers over the head of the novice; and for seven days he veils his head with his cowl, and on the seventh day the abbot takes the veil off.

(c) The Vow. From another form, *ibid.*

I promise concerning my stability and conversion of life and obedience according to the Rule of St. Benedict before God and His saints.

§ 105. FOUNDATION OF MEDIÆVAL CULTURE AND SCHOOLS

Schools never wholly disappeared from Western society, either during the barbarian invasion or in the even more troublous times that followed. Secular schools continued throughout the fifth century. During the sixth century they gave way for the most part to schools fostered by the Church, or were thoroughly transformed by ecclesiastical influences. In the fifth and sixth centuries, the great compends were made that served as text-books for centuries. Boethius, Cassiodorus, Isidore of Seville, and Bede represent great steps in the preparation for the mediæval schools. But, apart from the survival of old schools, there was a real demand for the establishment of new schools. The new monasticism needed them. It required some reading and study every day by the monks. As children were constantly being received, ordinarily at the age of seven, these *oblati* needed instruction. The monastic schools, which thus arose, early made provision for the instruction of those not destined for the monastic life in the external schools of the monasteries. Then again, the need of clergy with some literary training, however simple, was felt, especially as the secular schools declined or were found not convenient, and conciliar action was taken in various countries to provide for such education. In the conversion of the English, schools seem very early to have been established, and the encouragement given these schools by the learned Theodore of Tarsus, archbishop of Canterbury, bore splendid fruit, not merely in the great school of Canterbury but still more in the monastic schools of the North, at Jarrow and Wearmouth and at York. It was from the schools in the North that the culture of the Frankish kingdom under Charles the Great largely came. There was always a marked difference of opinion as to the value of secular literature in education, as is shown by the attitude already taken by Gregory the Great in his letter to Desiderius of Vienne, a letter which did much to discourage the literary study of the classics.

(a) Augustine, *De Doctrina Christiana*, II, 40 (§ 60). (MSL, 34 : 63).

The Christian's use of heathen writers.

The whole book should be examined carefully to see the working out of the same idea in detail. St. Augustine was a man of literary culture, although he was imperfectly acquainted with Greek. He speaks from his own experience of the help he had derived from this culture. The work *On Christian Doctrine* is, in fact, not at all a treatise on theology but on pedagogy, and was of immense influence in the Middle Ages.

If those who are called philosophers and especially the Platonists have said anything true and in harmony with the faith, we ought not only not to shrink from it, but rather to appropriate it for our own use, taking it from them as from unlawful possessors. For as the Egyptians had not only the idols and heavy burdens, which the people of Israel hated and fled from, but also vessels and ornaments of gold and silver and clothing which the same people on going out of Egypt secretly appropriated to themselves as for a better use, not on their own authority but on the command of God, for the Egyptians in their ignorance lent those things which they themselves were not using well [Ex. 3 : 22; 12 : 35]; in the same way all branches of heathen learning have not only false and superstitious fancies and heavy burdens of unnecessary toil which each of us, in going out under the leadership of Christ from the fellowship of the heathen, ought to hate and avoid; but they contain also liberal instruction which it is well to adapt to the use of truth and some most useful precepts of morality; and some truths in regard even to the worship of the one God are found among them. Now these are, so to speak, their gold and silver, which they themselves did not create, but dug, as it were, out of certain mines of God's providence, which are everywhere scattered abroad, and are perversely and unlawfully misused to the worship of devils. These, therefore, the Christian, when he separates himself in spirit from the miserable fellowship of these men, ought to take away from them for their proper use in preaching the Gospel. Their clothing also, that is, human institutions, adapted to that intercourse with men which is indispensable for this life, it is right to take and to have so as to be turned to Christian use.

(b) John Cassian, *Institutiones*, V, 33, 34. (MSL, 49 : 249.)

Cassian, born 360, was one of the leaders of the monastic movement. He founded monasteries near Marseilles, and did much to spread the monastic movement in Gaul and Spain. His *Institutiones* and *Collationes* were of influence, even after his monasteries had been entirely supplanted by the Benedictines. The opinion here given is probably that prevalent in the monasteries in Egypt. It is utterly different from the spirit of Basil, and the great theologians of Asia Minor who, in the matter of secular studies, hold the same opinion as the older Alexandrian school of Clement and Origen.

Ch. 33. We also saw the abbot Theodore, a man endowed with the utmost holiness and with perfect knowledge not only of things of the practical life but also of the meaning of the Scriptures, which he had acquired, not so much by study and reading, or secular scholarship, as by purity of heart alone;

since he was able only with difficulty to understand or speak even but a few words in the Greek language. This man, when he was seeking an explanation of some most difficult question, continued indefatigably seven days and nights in prayer until, by a revelation of the Lord, he knew the answer to the question propounded.

Ch. 34. This man, therefore, when some of the brethren were wondering at the splendid light of his knowledge, and were asking him some meanings of Scripture, said: "A monk desiring to attain to a knowledge of the Scriptures ought in no wise to spend his labor on the books of the commentators, but rather to keep all the efforts of his mind and the intentions of his heart set on purification from carnal vices. When these are driven out, at once the eyes of the heart, when the veil of passions has been removed, will begin, as it were, naturally to gaze on the mysteries of Scripture, since these were not declared unto us by the grace of the Holy Ghost to remain unknown and obscure; but they are rendered obscure by our vices, as the veil of our sins cover the eyes of the heart, and for these, when restored to their natural health, the mere reading of Holy Scripture is amply sufficient for the perception of the true knowledge; nor do they need the instruction of commentators, just as these eyes of flesh need no man's assistance to see provided they are free from the dimness or darkness of blindness."

(c) Gregory the Great, *Ep. ad Desiderium*, Reg. XI, ep. 54. (MSL, 77 : 1171.)

Desiderius was bishop of Vienne. This letter was sent with several others written in connection with the sending of Mellitus to England; see Bede, *Hist. Ec.*, I, 27, 29.

Many good things have been reported to us regarding your pursuits, and such joy arose in our hearts that we could not bear to refuse what your fraternity had requested to have granted you. But afterward it came to our ears, what we cannot mention without shame, that thy fraternity is in the habit

of expounding grammar to certain persons.   This thing pained
us so and we so strongly disapproved of it that we changed
what had been said before into groaning and sadness, since
the praises of Christ cannot find room in the one mouth with
the praises of Jupiter.   And consider thyself what a grave
and heinous offence it is for bishops to sing what is not becoming even for a religious layman.   And, though our most
beloved son Candidus, the presbyter, who was strictly examined
on this matter when he came to us, denied it and endeavored to excuse you, yet still the thought has not left our
mind that, in proportion as it is execrable for such a thing
to be related of a priest, it ought to be ascertained by strict
and veracious evidence whether or not it be so.   If, therefore, hereafter what has been reported to us should prove to be
evidently false, and it should be clear that you do not apply
yourself to trifles and secular literature, we shall give thanks
to God, who has not permitted your heart to be stained with
the blasphemous phrases of what is abominable; and we will
treat without misgiving or hesitation concerning granting
what you have requested.

We commend to you in all respects the monks whom, together with our most beloved son Laurentius, the presbyter,
and Mellitus, the abbot, we have sent to our most reverend
brother and fellow-bishop Augustine, that by the help of your
fraternity no delay may hinder their journey.

(d) Council of Vaison, A. D. 529, *Canon* 1. Bruns, II, 183.

Vaison is a small see in the province of Arles.   The synod was attended by about a dozen bishops.   It is, therefore, not authoritative
for a large district, but when taken in connection with the following
selection indicates a wide-spread custom.

That presbyters in their parishes shall bring up and instruct young readers in their houses.   It was decided that all
presbyters who are placed in parishes should, according to a
custom which we learn is very beneficially observed throughout Italy, receive young readers, as many as they have who

are unmarried, into their house where they dwell, and as good fathers shall endeavor to bring them up spiritually to render the Psalms, and to instruct them in the divine readings, and to educate them in the law of the Lord, that so they may provide for themselves worthy successors, and receive from the Lord eternal rewards. But when they come to full age, if any of them, on account of the weakness of the flesh, wish to marry, they shall not be denied the right of doing so.

(e) II Council of Toledo, A. D. 531, *Canon* 1. Bruns, I, 207.

Concerning those whom their parents voluntarily give in the first years of their childhood to the office of the clergy, we have decreed this to be observed; namely, that as soon as they have been tonsured or have been given to the care of appointed persons, they ought to be educated by some one set over them, in the church building, and in the presence of the bishop. When they have completed their eighteenth year, they shall be asked by the bishop, in the presence of all the clergy and people, their will as to seeking marriage. And if by God's inspiration they have the grace of chastity, and shall have promised to observe the profession of their chastity without any necessity of marriage, let these who are more desirous of the hardest life put on the most gentle yoke of the Lord, and first let them receive from their twentieth year the ministry of the subdiaconate, probation having been made of their profession, that, if blamelessly ànd without offence they attain the twenty-fifth year of their age, they may be promoted to the office of the diaconate, if they have been proved by their bishop to be able to fulfil it. . . .

(f) Bede, *Hist. Ec.*, III, 18. (MSL, 95 : 144.)

Sigebert became king of the East Angles about 631 and died 637. The facts known of him are briefly recorded in DCB.

At this time the kingdom of the East Angles, after the death of Earpwald, the successor of Redwald, was subject to his brother Sigebert, a good and religious man, who long before had been baptized in France, whilst he lived in banishment, flying from the enmity of Redwald; when he returned home and had ascended the throne he was desirous of imitating the good institutions which he had seen in France, and he set up a school for the young to be instructed in letters, and was assisted therein by Bishop Felix, who had come to him from Kent and who furnished him with masters and teachers after the manner of that country.

(g) Bede, *Hist. Ec.*, IV, 2. (MSL, 95 : 173.)

Theodore arrived at his church the second year after his consecration, on Sunday, May 27, and held the same twenty-one years, three months and twenty-six days. Soon after he visited all the islands, wherever the tribes of the Angles dwelt, for he was willingly entertained and heard by all persons. Everywhere he was attended and assisted by Hadrian, and he taught the right rule of life and the canonical custom of celebrating Easter.[1] This was the first archbishop whom all the English Church obeyed. And forasmuch as both of them were, as has been said, well read in sacred and secular literature, they gathered a crowd of scholars and there daily flowed from them rivers of knowledge to water the hearts of their hearers; and together with the books of the holy Scriptures they also taught them the arts of ecclesiastical poetry, astronomy, and arithmetic. A testimony of which is that there are still living at this day [*circa* A. D. 727] some of their scholars who are as well versed in the Greek and Latin tongues as in their own, in which they were born. Never were there happier times since the English came to Britain; for their kings were brave men and good Christians and were a terror to all barbarous nations, and the minds of all men were bent upon the joys of the heavenly kingdom of which they had just heard. And all who desired instruction in sacred reading had masters at hand to teach them. From that time also they began in all the churches of the English

[1] *V. supra*, § 100.

to learn sacred music which till then had been only known in Kent. And excepting James, mentioned above, the first singing-master[1] in the churches of the Northumbrians was Eddi, surnamed Stephen, invited from Kent by the most reverend Wilfrid, who was the first of the bishops of the English nation that taught the churches of the English the Catholic mode of life.

(h) Council of Clovesho, A. D. 747, *Canon* 7. Haddan and Stubbs, III, 360.

They decreed in the seventh article of agreement that bishops, abbots, and abbesses should by all means take care and diligently provide that their families should incessantly apply their minds to reading, and that knowledge be spread by the voices of many to the gaining of souls and to the praise of the eternal King. For it is sad to say how few[2] in these times do heartily love and labor for sacred knowledge and are willing to take pains in learning, but they are from their youth up rather employed in divers vanities and the affectation of vainglory; and they rather pursue the amusements of this present unstable life than the assiduous study of holy Scriptures. Therefore let boys be kept and trained up in such schools, to the love of sacred knowledge, and that, being by this means well learned, they may become in all respects useful to the Church of God.

[1] Further on, Bede mentions Putta, bishop of Rochester, who was "extraordinarily skilful in the Roman style of church music, which he had learned from the pupils of the holy pope Gregory."

[2] Monasticism had already begun to decline as the monasteries increased in wealth and numbers. The decline continued into the next century, when the Church was at its worst condition about the beginning of the reign of Alfred. The revival of monasticism was not until the tenth century as a result of the Cluny Reform.

CHAPTER IV. THE REVOLUTION IN THE ECCLESIAS-
TICAL AND POLITICAL SITUATION DUE TO THE
RISE OF ISLAM AND THE DOCTRINAL DISPUTES IN
THE EASTERN CHURCH

In the course of the seventh and eighth centuries, the ecclesiastical and political situation altered completely. This
change was due, in the first place, to the rise of the religion
and empire of the Moslems, whereby a very large part of the
Eastern Empire was conquered by the followers of the Prophet,
who had rapidly extended their conquests over Syria and the
best African provinces. Reduced in extent and exposed to
ever fresh attacks from a powerful enemy, the Eastern Empire
had to face new political problems. In the second place, as
the provinces overrun contained the greater number of those
dissatisfied with the doctrinal results of the great councils,
the apparently interminable contests over the question as
to the two natures of Christ came to an unexpected end.
This did not take place until a new cause for dispute had arisen
among the adherents of Chalcedon, due to an attempt to win
back the Monophysites by accounting for the unity of the person of Christ by positing one will in Jesus. Monotheletism at
once became among the adherents of Chalcedon a burning question. It was finally condemned at the Sixth General Council,
Constantinople, A. D. 683, at which Pope Agatho played a part
very similar to that played by Pope Leo at Chalcedon, but at
the cost of seeing his predecessor, Honorius, condemned as a
Monothelete. It was the last triumph of the West in the dogmatic controversies of the East. The Eastern ecclesiastics,
irritated at the diplomatic triumph of Rome, expressed their
resentment at the Concilium Quinisextum, in 692, where, in
passing canons to complete the work of the Fifth and Sixth
Councils, an opportunity was embraced of expressly condemning several Roman practices. In the confusion resulting in
the next century from the attempt of Leo the Isaurian to put

an end to the use of images in the churches, the Roman see was able to rid itself of the nominal control which the Emperor still had over the papacy by means of the exarchate of Ravenna. When the Lombards pressed too heavily upon the papacy it was easy for the Bishop of Rome to make an alliance with the Franks, who on their side saw that it was profitable to employ the papacy in the advancement of their own schemes. In this way arose that alliance between the pontiff and the new Frankish monarchy upon which the ecclesiastical development of the Middle Ages rests. But Iconoclasm suffered defeat at the Seventh General Council, 787, in which the doctrinal system of the East was completed. As this was the last undisputed general council, it may be taken as marking the termination of the history of the ancient Church. In following the further course of the Western Church there is no longer need of a detailed tracing of the history of the Eastern Church, which ceased to be a determining factor in the religious life of the West. The two parts of Christendom come in contact from time to time, but without formal schism they have ceased to be organically united.

§ 106. The Rise and Extension of Islam.
§ 107. The Monothelete Controversy and the Sixth General Council, Constantinople, A. D. 681.
§ 108. Rome in Relation to the Eastern Empire and the Lombard State.
§ 109. Rome, the Eastern Empire, and the Lombard State in the First Iconoclastic Controversy. The Seventh General Council, Nicæa, A. D. 787.

§ 106. The Rise and Extension of Islam

Mohammed (571–632) began his work as a prophet at Mecca about 613, having been "called" about three years earlier. He was driven from Mecca in 622 and fled to Yathrib, afterward known as Medina. Here he was able to unite warring factions and, placing himself at their head, to build up despotic authority over the surrounding country. He steadily increased the territory under his sway, and by conquests and diplomacy was able to gain Mecca in 629. Before his death in 632 he had conquered all Arabia. His authority continued in his family after his death, and the course of conquest went on. Damascus was conquered in 635; in 636 the Emperor Heraclius was driven to abandon Syria, which now fell into the hands of the Moslems. In 637 the Persians were forced back. In 640 Egypt was taken, and by 650 all between Carthage and the eastern border of Persia had been acquired for Islam. In 693, after a period of civil war, the work of conquest was resumed. In 709 all the African coast as far as the Straits of Gibraltar was gained, and in 711 the Moslems entered Spain. They at once made themselves masters of the peninsula with the exception of a small strip in the north in the mountains of Asturias, the kingdom of Gallicia. Crossing the Pyrenees, they attempted to possess Gaul, but were forced to retreat from central Gaul by Charles Martel at the battle at Tours and Poitiers in 732. They maintained themselves north of the Pyrenees until 759 when they were driven out of Narbonne and across the mountains.

Additional source material: *The Koran*, standard translation by E. H. Palmer, in the *Sacred Books of the East;* Stanley Lane-Poole, *Speeches and Table Talk of the Prophet Mohammed.*

(a) Mohammed, *Koran* (translation of E. H. Palmer).

Surah CXII.

The Unity of God.
The following surah or chapter of the Koran, entitled "The Chapter of Unity," Mohammed regarded as of value equal to two-thirds of the whole book. It is one of the shortest and most famous.

In the name of the merciful and compassionate God, say:
"He is God alone!
God the Eternal.
He begets not and is not begotten!
Nor is there like unto Him any one."

Surah V, 73, 76, 109 *ff.*

The teaching as to the nature and mission of Jesus.

[73.] Verily, those who believe and those who are Jews, and the Sabæans, and the Christians, whosoever believes in God and the last day and does what is right, there is no fear for them, nor shall they grieve.

[76.] They misbelieve who say, "Verily, God is the Messiah, the son of Mary"; but the Messiah said, "O Children of Israel, worship God, my Lord and your Lord." Verily he who associates aught with God, God hath forbidden him paradise, and his resort is the fire, and the unjust shall have none to help them.

They misbelieve who say, "Verily, God is the third of three"; for there is no God but one, and if they do not desist from what they say, there shall touch those who misbelieve amongst them grievous woe.

Will they not turn toward God and ask pardon of Him? for God is forgiving and merciful.

The Messiah, the son of Mary, is only a prophet; prophets before him have passed away: and His mother was a confessor.

[109.] When God said, "O Jesus, son of Mary! remember my favors towards thee and towards thy mother, when I aided thee with the Holy Ghost, till thou didst speak to men in the cradle and when grown up.

"And when I taught thee the Book and wisdom and the law and the gospel; when thou didst create of clay, as it were, the likeness of a bird, by my power, and didst blow thereon, it became a bird;[1] and thou didst heal the blind from birth, and the leprous by my permission; and when thou didst bring forth the dead by my permission; and when I did ward off the children of Israel from thee, and when thou didst come to them with manifest signs, and those who misbelieved among them said: 'This is naught but obvious magic.'

"And when I inspired the Apostles that they should believe

[1] See *Arabic Gospel of the Infancy*, c. 46; ANF, viii, 415.

in Him and in my Apostle, they said, 'We believe; do thou bear witness that we are resigned.'"

[116.] And when God said, "O Jesus, son of Mary! is it thou who dost say to men, take me and my mother for two gods, beside God?" He said: "I celebrate thy praise! what ails me that I should say what I have no right to? If I had said it, Thou wouldest have known it; Thou knowest what is in my soul, but I know not what is in Thy soul; verily Thou art one who knoweth the unseen. I never told them save what Thou didst bid me, 'Worship God, my Lord and your Lord,' and I was a witness against them so long as I was among them, but when Thou didst take me away to Thyself Thou wert the watcher over them, for Thou art witness over all." . . .

Surah IV, 152.

Relation of Islam to Judaism and Christianity.

[152.] The people of the Book will ask thee to bring down for them a book from heaven; but they asked Moses a greater thing than that, for they said, "Show us God openly"; but the thunderbolt caught them in their injustice. Then they took a calf, after what had come to them of manifest signs; but we pardoned that, and gave Moses obvious authority. And we held over them the mountain at their compact, and said to them, "Enter ye the door adoring," and we said to them, "Transgress not on the Sabbath day," and we took from them a rigid compact.

But for that they broke their compact, and for their misbelief in God's signs, and for their killing the prophets undeservedly, and for their saying, "Our hearts are uncircumcised" —nay, God hath stamped on them their misbelief, so that they cannot believe, except a few—and for their misbelief, and for their saying about Mary a mighty calumny, and for their saying, "Verily we have killed the Messiah, Jesus the son of Mary, the apostle of God," but they did not kill Him, and they did not crucify Him, but a similitude was made for them. And verily, those who differ about Him are in doubt concerning Him; they have no knowledge concerning Him, but only follow an opinion. They did not kill Him, for sure! nay God raised Him up unto Himself; for God is mighty and wise! . . .

[164.] O ye people of the Book! do not exceed in your religion, nor say against God save the truth. The Messiah, Jesus, the son of Mary, is but the apostle of God and His Word, which He cast into Mary and a spirit from Him; believe then in God and His apostles, and say not "Three." Have done! it were better for you. God is only one God, celebrated be His praise that He should beget a Son!

Surah LVI.

The delights of heaven and the pains of hell.
This description of the future life has been taken as characteristic of the religion of Mohammed, but not quite fairly. It is simply the Bedouin's idea of complete happiness, and is by no means characteristic of the religion as the whole.

In the name of the merciful and compassionate God.

When the inevitable [day of judgment] happens; none shall call its happening a lie!—abasing—exalting!

When the earth shall quake, quaking! and the mountains shall crumble, crumbling, and become like motes dispersed!

And ye shall be three sorts;

And the fellows of the right hand—what right lucky fellows!

And the fellows of the left hand—what unlucky fellows!

And the foremost foremost!

These are they who are brought nigh,

In gardens of pleasure!

A crowd of those of yore, and a few of those of the latter day!

And gold-weft couches, reclining on them face to face.

Around them shall go eternal youths, with goblets and ewers and a cup of flowing wine; no headache shall feed therefrom, nor shall their wits be dimmed!

And fruits such as they deem the best;

And flesh of fowl as they desire;

And bright and large-eyed maids like hidden pearls;
A reward for that which they have done!
They shall hear no folly there and no sin;
Only the speech, "Peace, Peace!"
And the fellows of the right—what right lucky fellows!
Amid thornless lote trees.
And tal'h[1] trees with piles of fruit;
And outspread shade,
And water poured out;
And fruit in abundance, neither failing nor forbidden;
And beds upraised!
Verily we have produced them[2] a production,
And made them virgins, darlings of equal age (with their
spouses) for the fellows of the right!
A crowd of those of yore, and a crowd of those of the latter
day!
And the fellows of the left—what unlucky fellows!
In hot blasts and boiling water;
And a shade of pitchy smoke,
Neither cool nor generous!
Verily they were affluent ere this, and did persist in mighty
crime; and used to say, "What, when we die, have become
dust and bones, shall we indeed be raised? or our fathers of
yore?"
Say, "Verily, those of yore and those of the latter days
shall surely be gathered together unto the tryst of the well-
known day."
"Then ye, O ye who err! who say it is a lie! shall eat of the
Zaqqum[3] tree and fill your bellies with it! a drink of boiling
water! and drink as drinks the thirsty camel!"

(b) Paulus Diaconus, *Historia Langobardorum*, VI, 46 ff.
(MSL, 95 : 654.)

The Advance of the Saracens.

---

[1] Probably banana is meant.
[3] An intensely bitter tree.

[2] *I. e.*, the celestial damsels.

Ch. 46. At that time [A. D. 711] the people of the Saracens, crossing over from Africa at a place which is called Ceuta, invaded all Spain. Then after ten years, coming with their wives and children, they invaded as if to settle in Aquitania, a province of Gaul. Charles[1] had at that time a dispute with Eudo, prince of Aquitania. But they came to an agreement and fought with perfect harmony against the Saracens. For the Franks fell upon them[2] and slew three hundred and seventy-five thousand of them; but on the side of the Franks only fifteen hundred fell. Eudo with his men broke into their camp and slew many and laid waste all.

Ch. 47. At the same time [A. D. 717], the same people of the Saracens with an immense army came and encompassed Constantinople and for three years besieged it until, when the people had called upon God with great earnestness, many of the enemy perished from hunger and cold and by war and pestilence and so wearied out they abandoned the siege. When they had left they carried on war against the people of the Bulgarians who were beyond the Danube, but, vanquished by them also, they fled back to their ships. But when they had put out to the deep sea, a sudden storm fell upon them and many were drowned and their vessels were destroyed. But in Constantinople three hundred thousand men died of the pestilence.

Ch. 48. Now when Liutprand heard that the Saracens, when Sardinia had been laid waste, had also polluted those places where the bones of the holy bishop Augustine, on account of the devastation of the barbarians, had formerly been transported and solemnly buried, he sent thither and when he had given a large sum obtained them and transported them to the city of Pavia, where he buried them with the honor due so great a father.[3] In these days the city of Narnia was conquered by the Lombards.

---

[1] Charles Martel.   [2] A. D. 732, Battle of Tours and Poitiers.
[3] The shrine of later construction may still be seen in the Cathedral of Pavia. It is not improbable that the genuine relics of St. Augustine are here.

§ 107. The Monothelete Controversy and the Sixth
General Council, Constantinpole A. D. 681

The Monothelete controversy was the natural outcome of
the earlier Christological controversies. With the assertion
of the two complete and persisting natures of Christ, the question must sooner or later arise as to whether there was one will
or two in Christ. If there were two wills, it seemed to lead
back to Nestorianism; if there was but one, either the humanity was incomplete or the position led to virtual monophysitism. But political causes played even a greater part than
the theological dialectic. The Emperor Heraclius, in attempting to win back the Monophysite churches, on account of the
war with Persia and later on account of the advancing Moslems, proposed that a union should be effected on the basis of
a formula which asserted that there was but one will in the
God-man. This had been suggested to him in 622 by
Sergius, patriarch of Constantinople [Hefele, §§ 291, 295].
In 633 Cyrus of Phasis, since 630 patriarch of Alexandria,
brought about a union between the Orthodox Church and the
Egyptian Monophysites on the basis of a Monothelete formula, i. e., a statement that there was but one will or energy
in Christ. At once a violent controversy broke out. The
formula was supported by Honorius of Rome, but attacked
by Sophronius, patriarch of Jerusalem, and after the fall of
Jerusalem in 638, by the monk Maximus Confessor. In 638
Heraclius tried to end the controversy by an *Ecthesis* [*Hefele*,
§ 299], and Constans II (641–668) attempted the same in 648,
by his *Typos*. But at the Lateran Council of 649, under Martin
I, Monotheletism as well as the *Ecthesis* and *Typos* were condemned. For this Martin was ultimately banished, dying in
misery, 654, in the Chersonesus, and Maximus, after a long,
cruel imprisonment, and horrible torture and mutilation, died
in exile, 662. But Constantius Pogonatus (668–685), the successor of Constans II, determined to settle the matter by a

general council. Pope Agatho (678–682) thereupon held a great council at Rome, 679, at which it was decided to insist at the coming general council upon the strictest maintenance of the decisions of the Roman Council of 649. On this basis Agatho dictated the formula which was accepted by the Council of Constantinople, A. D. 681, which sent its proceedings and conclusions to the Pope to be approved. Along with them was an express condemnation of Honorius. Leo II (682–683), Agatho's successor, approved the council with special mention of Honorius as condemned for his heresy.

(a) Cyrus of Alexandria, *Formula of Union*, A. D. 633, Hahn, § 232.

The author of this formula, known also as Cyrus of Phasis, under which name he was condemned at Constantinople, A. D. 680, attempted to win over the Monophysites in Alexandria and met with great success on account of his formula of union. The first five anathemas, the form in which the formula is composed, are clearly based upon the first four councils. The sixth is slightly different; and the seventh, the most important, is clearly tending toward Monotheletism. The document is to be found in the proceedings of the Sixth General Council in Mansi, and also in Hardouin. For a synopsis, see Hefele, § 293, who is most valuable for the whole controversy.

6. If any one does not confess the one Christ, the one Son, to be of two natures, that is, divinity and humanity, one nature become flesh[1] of God the Word, according to the holy Cyril, unmixed, unchanged, unchangeable, that is to say, one synthetic hypostasis, who is the same, our Lord Jesus Christ, being one of the holy homoousian Triad, let such an one be anathema.

7. If any one, saying that our one Lord Jesus Christ is to be regarded in two natures, does not confess that He is one of the Holy Triad, God the Word, eternally begotten of the Father, in the last times of the world made flesh and born of our all-holy and spotless lady, the Theotokos and ever-virgin

---

[1] Note that this is not "the one nature of the Word of God become flesh," the formula most commonly employed by Cyril, and to be distinguished from this, though Cyril sometimes appears to use the two contrary to his own distinction.

Mary; but is this and another and not one and the same, according to the most wise Cyril, perfect in deity and the same perfect in humanity, and accordingly only to be thought of as in two natures; the same suffering and not suffering, according to one or the other nature, as the same holy Cyril said, suffering as a man in the flesh, inasmuch as he was a man, remaining as God without suffering in the sufferings of His own flesh; and the one and the same Christ energizing the divine and the human things with the one theandric energy,[1] according to the holy Dionysius; distinguishing only in thought those things from which the union has taken place, and viewing these in the mind as remaining unchanged, unalterable, and unmixed after their union according to nature and hypostasis; and recognizing in these without division or separation the one and the same Christ and Son, inasmuch as he regards in his mind two as brought together to each other without commingling, making the theory of them as a matter of fact, but not by a lying imagination and vain combinations of the mind; but in nowise separating them, since now the division into two has been destroyed on account of the indescribable and incomprehensible union; saying with the holy Athanasius: for there is now flesh and again the flesh of God the Word, now flesh animated and intelligent, and again the flesh of the animated and intelligent God the Word; but should under such expressions understand a distinction into parts, let such an one be anathema.

(b) Constans II, *Typos*, A. D. 648, Mansi, X, 1029. *Cf.* Kirch, nn. 972 *f*.

The attempt to end the controversy by returning to the condition of things before the controversy broke out, an entirely futile undertaking. The question having been raised had to be discussed and settled by rational processes. See Hefele, § 306.

Since it is our custom to do everything and to consider everything which can serve the welfare of the Christian State,

---

[1] The phrase of Dionysius was not "one theandric energy" but "a new theandric energy."

and especially what concerns our true faith, by which we believe all our happiness is brought about, we perceive that our orthodox people are greatly disturbed, because some in respect to the Economy[1] of our great God and Saviour Jesus Christ assert that there is only one will, and that one and the same affects both the divine and human deeds; but others teach two wills and two operations in the same dispensation of the incarnate Word. The former defend their views by asserting that our Lord Jesus Christ was only one person in two natures, and therefore without confusion or separation, working and willing as well the divine as the human deeds. The others say that because in one and the same person two natures are joined without any separation, so their differences from each other remain, and according to the character of each nature one and the same Christ works as well the divine as the human; and from this our Christian State has been brought to much dissension and confusion, so that differing from one another they do not agree, and from this the State must in many ways needs suffer.

We believe that, under God's guidance, we must extinguish the flames enkindled by discord, and we ought not to permit them further to destroy human souls. We decree, therefore, that our subjects who hold our immaculate and orthodox Christian faith, and who are of the Catholic and Apostolic Church, shall from the present moment on have no longer any permission to raise any sort of dispute and quarrel or strife with one another over the one will and energy, or over two wills and two energies. We order that this is not in any way to take anything from the pious teaching, which the holy and approved Fathers have taught concerning the incarnation of God the Word, but with the purpose that all further strife in regard to the aforesaid questions cease, and in this matter we follow and hold as sufficient only the Holy Scriptures and the tradition of the five holy general councils and the simple statements and unquestioned usage and expressions of

[1] I. e., the incarnation, term so used constantly in Greek theology.

the approved Fathers (of which the dogmas, rules, and laws of God's holy Catholic and Apostolic Church consists), without adding to or taking from them anything, or without explaining them against their proper meaning, but everywhere shall be preserved the former customs, as before the disputes broke out, as if no such dispute had existed. As to those who have hitherto taught one will and one energy or two wills and two energies, there shall be no accusation on this account; excepting only those who have been cast forth as heretics, together with their impious doctrines and writings, by the five holy universal councils and other approved orthodox Fathers. But to complete the unity and fellowship of the churches of God, and that there remain no further opportunity or occasion to those who are eager for endless dispute, we order that the document,[1] which for a long time has been posted up in the narthex of the most holy principal church of this our God-preserved royal city, and which touches upon the points in dispute, shall be taken down. Whoever dares to transgress this command is subject before all to the fearful judgment of Almighty God, and then also will be liable to the punishment for such as despise the imperial commands. If he be a bishop or clergyman, he will altogether be deposed from his priesthood or clerical order; if a monk, excommunicated and driven out of his residence; if a civil or military officer, he shall lose his rank and office; if a private citizen, he shall, if noble, be punished pecuniarily, if of lower rank, be subjected to corporal punishment and perpetual exile.

(c) Council of Rome, A. D. 649, *Canons*, Mansi, X, 1150. *Cf.* Denziger, nn. 254 *ff.*

Condemnation of Monotheletism, the *Ecthesis*, and the *Typos*, by Martin I.

Text of canons or anathematisms and abstract of proceedings in Hefele, § 307.

Canon 18. If any one does not, according to the holy Fathers, and in company with us, reject and anathematize

---
[1] The *Ecthesis*.

with mind and mouth all those whom as most wicked heretics
the holy Catholic and Apostolic Church of God, that is, the
five universal synods and likewise all approved Fathers of the
Church, rejects and anathematizes, with all their impious
writings even to each point, that is, Sabellius, etc. . . . and
justly with these, as like them and in equal error . . . Cyrus
of Alexandria, Sergius of Constantinople, and his successors
Pyrrhus and Paul, persisting in their pride, and all their
impious writings, and those who to the end agreed with them
in their thought, or do so agree, that there is one will and one
operation of the deity and manhood of Christ; and in addition to these the most impious *Ecthesis*, which, by the persuasion of the same Sergius, was put forth by the former Emperor Heraclius against the orthodox faith, defining, by way
of adjustment, one will in Christ our God, and one operation
to be venerated; also all those things which were impiously
written or done by them; and those who received it, or any
of those things which were written or done for it; and along
with these, furthermore, the wicked *Typos*, which, on the persuasion of the aforesaid Paul, was recently issued by our most
serene prince Constans against the Catholic Church, inasmuch
as it equally denies and excludes from discussion the two
natural wills and operations, a divine and a human, which
are piously taught by the holy Fathers to be in Christ,
our God, and also our Saviour, and also the one will and
operation, which by the heretics is impiously venerated in
Him, and therefore declaring that with the holy Fathers
also the wicked heretics are unjustly freed from all rebuke
and condemnation, to the destruction of the definitions of
the Catholic Church and its rule of faith . . . let him be
condemned.

(*d*) Sixth General Council, Constantinople, A. D. 681,
Definition of Faith. Mansi, XI, 636 *ff.*

The concluding, more strictly dogmatic portion of this symbol is to
be found in Greek in Hahn, § 150, and in Latin and Greek in Denziger,
nn. 289 *ff.* See also PNF, ser. II, vol. XIV.

The holy, great, and ecumenical synod assembled by the grace of God and the religious decree of the most religious, faithful, and mighty Emperor Constantine, in this God-preserved and royal city of Constantinople, New Rome, in the hall of the imperial palace called Trullus, has decreed as follows:

The only begotten Son and Word of God the Father, who was made man, like unto us in all things, without sin, Christ our true God, has declared expressly in the words of the Gospel: "I am the light of the world; he that followeth Me shall not walk in darkness, but shall have the light of life" [John 8 : 12]; and again: "My peace I leave with you, My peace I give unto you" [John 14 : 27]. Our most gracious Emperor, the champion of orthodoxy and opponent of evil doctrine, being reverentially led by this divinely uttered doctrine of peace, and having assembled this our holy and ecumenical synod, has united the judgment of the whole Church. Wherefore this our holy and ecumenical synod, having driven away the impious error which has prevailed for a certain time until now, and following closely the straight path of the holy and approved Fathers, has piously given its assent to the five holy and ecumenical synods—that is to say, to that of the three hundred and eighteen holy Fathers assembled at Nicæa against the insane Arius; and the next at Constantinople of the one hundred and fifty God-inspired men against Macedonius, the adversary of the Spirit, and the impious Apollinaris; and also the first at Ephesus of two hundred venerable men assembled against Nestorius, the Judaizer; and that in Chalcedon of six hundred and thirty God-inspired Fathers against Eutyches and Dioscurus, hated of God; and in addition to these the last, that is the fifth, holy synod assembled in this place against Theodore of Mopsuestia, Origen, Didymus, and Evagrius, and the writings of Theodoret against the twelve chapters of the celebrated Cyril, and the epistle which was said to have been written by Ibas to Maris the Persian—without alteration this synod renews in all points the ancient decrees of religion, chasing away the impious doctrines of irreligion. And this our holy and ecumenical synod, inspired of God, has set its seal to the creed of the three hundred and eighteen Fathers, and again religiously confirmed by the one hundred and fifty, which also the other holy synods gladly received and ratified for the removal of every soul-destroying heresy.

Then follow:
The Nicene Creed of the three hundred and eighteen holy Fathers. *We believe*, etc.
The Creed of the one hundred and fifty holy Fathers assembled at Constantinople. *We believe*, etc., but without the *filioque*.

The holy and ecumenical synod further says that this pious and orthodox creed of the divine grace would be sufficient for the full knowledge and confirmation of the orthodox faith. But as the author of evil, who in the beginning availed himself of the aid of the serpent, and by it brought the poison of death upon the human race, has not desisted, but in like manner now, having found suitable instruments for the accomplishment of his will—that is to say, Theodorus, who was bishop of Pharan; Sergius, Pyrrhus, Paul and Peter, who were prelates of this royal city; and also Honorius, who was pope of Old Rome; Cyrus, bishop of Alexandria, Marcarius, lately bishop of Antioch, and Stephen, his disciple—has not ceased with their aid to raise up for the whole Church the stumbling-blocks of one will and operation in the two natures of Christ, our true God, one of the holy Trinity; thus disseminating in novel terms among orthodox people a heresy similar to the mad and wicked doctrine of the impious Apollinaris, Severus, and Themistius, and endeavoring craftily to destroy the perfection of the incarnation of the same our Lord Jesus Christ, our God, by blasphemously representing His flesh as endowed with a rational soul devoid of will and operation. Christ, therefore, our God, has raised up our faithful Emperor, a new David, having found him a man after His own heart, who, as it is written, has not suffered his eyes to sleep nor his eyelids to slumber [*cf.* Psalm 132 : 4] until he had found a perfect declaration of orthodoxy by this our God-assembled and holy synod; for according to the sentence spoken of God: "Where two or three are gathered together in My name, there am I in the midst of them " [Matt. 18 : 20], the present[1] holy and ecumenical synod, faithfully receiving and saluting with uplifted hands also the suggestion which by the most holy and blessed Pope Agatho, Pope of Old Rome, was sent to our most pious and faithful Emperor Constantine, which rejected by name those who taught or preached one will and operation in the dispensation of the incarnation of Christ[2] our very God, has likewise adopted that other synodal suggestion which was sent by the council held under the same most holy Pope, composed of one hundred and twenty-five bishops beloved of God,[3] to his God-instructed tranquillity [i. e., the Emperor], as consonant to the holy Council of Chalcedon and the *Tome* of the most holy and blessed Leo, Pope of the same Old Rome, which was directed to the holy Flavian, which also the council called the pillar of a right faith; and also agrees with the synodical letters written by the blessed Cyril against the impious Nestorius and addressed to the Oriental bishops.

Following[4] the five holy and ecumenical synods and the most holy and approved Fathers, with one voice defining that our Lord Jesus Christ must be confessed to be our very God, one of the holy and consubstantial and life-giving Trinity, perfect in deity and the same perfect in humanity, truly God and truly man, of a reasonable soul and body; consubstantial with His Father as to His godhead, and consubstantial with us as to His manhood; in all things like unto us, without sin [Heb. 4 : 15]; begotten of His Father before the ages according to His godhead, but in these last days for us men and for our salvation begotten of the Holy Ghost and of the Virgin Mary, strictly and in truth Theotokos, according to the flesh; one and the same Christ, Son, Lord, Only begotten, in two

---

[1] From here text in Denziger.   [2] Latin reads: *our Lord Jesus Christ.*
[3] For this council, see Hefele, § 314.
[4] From here the text may be found also in Hahn, § 150.

natures unconfusedly, unchangeably, inseparably, indivisibly
to be recognized; the peculiarities of neither nature lost
by the union, but rather the properties of each nature preserved, concurring in one person,[1] and in one subsistence,[2]
not parted or divided into two persons, but one and the same
only begotten Son, the Word of God,[3] the Lord Jesus Christ,
according as the prophets of old have taught, and as Jesus
Christ Himself hath taught, and the creed of the holy Fathers
hath delivered to us;[4] we likewise declare that in Him are
two natural wills or willings and two natural operations indivisibly, unchangeably, inseparably, unconfusedly, according
to the teaching of the holy Fathers. And these two natural
wills are not contrary one to the other (which God forbid), as
the impious heretics say, but His human will follows, not as
resisting or reluctant, but rather therefore as subject to His
divine and omnipotent will. For it was right that the will
of the flesh should be moved, but be subject to the divine will,
according to the most wise Athanasius. For as His flesh is
called and is the flesh of God the Word, so also the natural
will of His flesh is called and is the proper will of God the Word,
as He Himself says: "I came down from heaven, not to do
Mine own will, but the will of the Father which sent Me,"[John
6 : 38], wherein he calls His own will the will of the flesh,
inasmuch as His flesh was also His own. For as His most
holy and immaculately animated flesh was not destroyed because it was deified [θεωθεῖσα], but continued in its own state
and nature, so also His human will, although deified, was not
taken away, but rather was preserved according to the saying of Gregory the Theologian:[5] "His will, namely that of the
Saviour, is not contrary to God, but altogether deified."

We glorify two natural operations, indivisibly, unchangeably, inseparably, unconfusedly, in the same our Lord Jesus
Christ, our true God, that is to say, a divine operation and a

---

[1] *Prosopon*, and so throughout.   [2] *Hypostasis*, and so throughout.
[3] Latin: *God the Word*.
[4] The preceding is but a recapitulation of Chalcedon; see above, § 90.
[5] *I. e.*, Gregory Nazianzus.

human operation, according to the divine preacher Leo, who most distinctly says as follows: "For each form does in communion with the other what pertains to it, namely the Word doing what pertains to the Word, and the flesh what pertains to the flesh."[1] For we will not admit one natural operation of God and of the creature, that we may not exalt into the divine essence what is created, nor will we bring down the glory of the divine nature to the place suited for those things which have been made. We recognize the miracles and the sufferings as of one and the same person, but of one or of the other nature of which He is, and in which He has His existence, as the admirable Cyril said. Preserving in all respects, therefore, the unconfusedness and indivisibility, we express all in brief phrase: Believing that our Lord Jesus Christ, one of the Trinity also after the incarnation, is our true God, we say that His two natures shone forth in His one subsistence [hypostasis], in which were both the miracles and the suffering throughout the whole incarnate life,[2] not in appearance merely but in reality, the difference as to nature being recognized in one and the same subsistence; for, although joined together, each nature wills and operates the things proper to it.[3] For this reason we glorify two natural[4] wills and operations concurring most fitly in Him for the salvation of the human race.

Since these things have been formulated by us with all diligence and care, we decree that to no one shall it be permitted to bring forward or write or to compose or to think or to teach otherwise. Whosoever shall presume to compose a different faith or to propose, or to teach, or to hand to those wishing to be converted to the knowledge of the truth from the heathen or the Jews or from any heresy any different symbol, or to introduce a new mode of expression to subvert

---

[1] Leo, *Ep. ad Flavianum*, ch. 4: Agit enim utraque forma cum alterius communione quod proprium est, Verbo scilicet operante quod Verbi est, et carne exsequente quod carnis est; unum horum coruscat miraculis, aliud succumbit iniuriis; *v. supra*, § 90, *b*.

[2] Greek: *economic life*.   [3] Latin adds: *indivisibly and unconfusedly*.

[4] Here, as elsewhere, "natural will" means such a will as belongs to a nature, divine or human.

these things which have now been determined by us, all these, if they be bishops or clergy, shall be deposed, the bishops from the episcopate, the clergy from the clerical office; but if they be monks or laymen, they shall be anathematized.

(e) Council of Constantinople, A. D. 681, *Sessio* XIII. Mansi, XI, 1050. *Cf.* Mirbt, n. 188.

The condemnation of the Monotheletes, including Honorius of Rome. The condemnation of Honorius has become a *cause célèbre*, especially in connection with the doctrine of papal infallibility. It should be observed, however, that the doctrine of papal infallibility, as defined at the Vatican Council, A. D. 1870 (*cf.* Mirbt, n. 509), requires that only when the Pope speaks *ex cathedra* is he infallible, and it has not been shown that any opinion whatever held by Honorius was an *ex cathedra* definition of faith and morals according to the Vatican Council. The matter is therefore a mere question of fact and may be treated apart from the Vatican dogma. It should be borne in mind, further, that the Sixth General Council was approved by Pope Leo II, A. D. 682 (*cf.* Mirbt, n. 189), who included Honorius by name among those whose condemnation was approved. That he did so approve it is also stated in the *Liber Pontificalis* (*cf.* Mirbt, n. 190), and according to the *Liber Diurnus*, the official book of formulæ used in the papal business, the Pope took an oath recognizing among others the Sixth General Council, and condemning Honorius among other heretics (*cf.* Mirbt, n. 191). That Honorius was actually a heretic is still another matter; for it seems not at all unlikely that he misunderstood the point at issue and his language is quite unscientific. The text of the letters of Honorius may be found in Kirch, nn. 949–965, and in Hefele in a translation, §§ 296, 298. On the condemnation of Honorius, see Hefele, § 324.

The holy council said: After we had reconsidered, according to our promise made to your highness,[1] the doctrinal letter written by Sergius, at one time patriarch of this royal God-preserved city, to Cyrus, who was then bishop of Phasis, and to Honorius, sometime Pope of Old Rome, as well as the letter of the latter to the same Sergius, and finding that the documents are quite foreign to the apostolic dogmas, to the definitions of the holy councils, and to all the approved Fathers, and that they follow the false teachings of the heretics, we entirely reject them, and execrate them as hurtful to the soul.

[1] The Emperor to whom the report is made.

But the names of those men whom we execrate must also be thrust forth from the holy Church of God, namely, that of Sergius, sometime bishop of this God-preserved royal city, who was the first to write on this impious doctrine; also that of Cyrus of Alexandria, of Pyrrhus, Paul, and Peter, who died bishops of this God-preserved city, and were like-minded with them; and that of Theodore, sometime bishop of Pharan, all of whom the most holy and thrice-blessed Agatho, Pope of Old Rome, in his suggestion to our most pious and God-preserved lord and mighty Emperor, rejected because they were minded contrary to our orthodox faith, all of whom we declare are subject to anathema. And with these we decree that there shall be expelled from the holy Church of God and anathematized Honorius, who was Pope of Old Rome, because of what we found written by him to Sergius, that in all respects he followed his view and confirmed his impious doctrine.

We have also examined the synodal letter[1] of Sophronius, of holy memory, sometime patriarch of the holy city of our God, Jerusalem, and have found it in accordance with the true faith and with apostolic teachings, and with the teachings of the holy and approved Fathers. Therefore, we have received it as orthodox and salutary to the holy and Catholic and Apostolic Church, and have decreed that it is right that his name be inserted in the diptychs of the holy churches.

§ 108. ROME, CONSTANTINOPLE, AND THE LOMBARD STATE CHURCH IN THE SEVENTH CENTURY

The Sixth General Council was the last great diplomatic triumph of Rome in the East in matters of faith, though two centuries after, in the matter of Photius, Rome played a brilliant part in the internal affairs of the Eastern Church. Immediately after the council of 681, it was felt that the West, of which the Greeks had grown very jealous, had triumphed

[1] The most important parts of this are to be found in Hahn, § 233.

over the East, especially as several of the leading patriarchs
had been condemned. Monotheletism, furthermore, was too
strongly intrenched in the East to be removed by a single
conciliar action. It was felt necessary to take action to confirm the results of Constantinople in 681. The fifth and
sixth general councils had been occupied entirely with doctrinal matters and had not issued any disciplinary canons.
A new council might be gathered to complete the work of the
Sixth General Council, not only to reaffirm it, but in connection with some much-needed legislation to retort upon the
West by condemning some Roman practices. In this way
the Second Trullan Council, or Concilium Quinisextum, came
about in 692. The Roman see, in the meanwhile, although it
had triumphed at Constantinople in 681, did not enjoy an
independent political position in Italy. It was still under the
Roman Emperor at Constantinople, as had been most pain-
fully perceived in the treatment of Martin I by Constans.
Although the Pope had his apocrisarius, or nuncio, at Constantinople, he came into immediate contact with the exarch
of Ravenna, the Emperor's representative in Italy. In Italy,
furthermore, the Arian heresy long persisted among the Lombards, although greater toleration was shown the Catholic
Church.

Additional source material: The canons of the Quinisext Council
may be found complete in Percival, *Seven Ecumenical Councils*, PNF,
ser. II, vol. XIV.

(a) Concilium Quinisextum, A. D. 692, *Canons*. Bruns,
I, 34 *ff*.

This council was commonly regarded as the continuation of the
Sixth General Council, and has been received in the East, not as a
separate council, but as a part of the sixth. The West has never accepted this opinion and has only to a limited extent admitted the authority of its canons, though some have been current in the West because, like much conciliar action, they were re-enactments of older
canons. Occasionally some of the canons have been cited by popes
as belonging to the Sixth Council. The canons given here are, for the
most part, those which were in some point in opposition to the Roman
practice.

Canon 1. *Renewal of the Condemnations of the Sixth Council.*
. . . We, by divine grace at the beginning of our decrees,
define that the faith set forth by the God-chosen Apostles,
who themselves had both seen the Word and were ministers
of the Word, shall be preserved without any innovation, unchanged and inviolate. Moreover the faith of the three hundred and eighteen holy and blessed Fathers, etc.

[Here follows a detailed statement of the first five general councils.]

Also we agree to guard untouched the faith of the Sixth
Holy Synod, which first assembled in this royal city in the time
of Constantine, our Emperor, of blessed memory, which faith
received still greater confirmation from the fact that the pious
Emperor ratified with his own signet what was written, for
the security of every future age. And again we confess that
we should guard the faith unaltered and openly acknowledged;
that in the Economy of the incarnation of our one Lord Jesus
Christ, the true God, there are two natural wills or volitions
and two natural operations; and have condemned by a just
sentence those who adulterated the true doctrine and taught
the people that in the one Lord, our God, Jesus Christ, there is
but one will and operation, that is to say, Theodore of Pharan,
Cyrus of Alexandria, Honorius of Rome, Sergius, Pyrrhus,
Paul, and Peter, who were bishops of this God-preserved city,
Macarius, who was bishop of Antioch, Stephen who was his
disciple, and the insane Polychronius, depriving them henceforth of the communion of the body of Christ our God. . . .

Canon 2. *On the Sources of Canon Law.*

This canon opposed Rome in two respects: it accepted eighty-five
Apostolic Canons, whereas Rome received but fifty; it drew up a list
of councils and of Fathers whose writings should have authority as
canons, and omitted the important Western councils, except Carthage,
and all the papal decrees. With this canon should be compared the
decretal of Gelasius, *De Libris Recipiendis, v. supra*, § 92.

It has also seemed good to this holy synod that the eighty-
five canons received and ratified by the holy and blessed

Fathers before us, and also handed down to us in the name of the holy and glorious Apostles, should from this time forth remain firm and unshaken for the cure of souls and the healing of disorders. And since in these canons we are bidden to receive the *Constitutions of the Holy Apostles* by Clement, in which, in old time, certain spurious matter entirely contrary to piety was introduced by heterodox persons for the polluting of the Church, which obscures to us the elegance and beauty of the divine decrees; we, therefore, for the edification and security of the most Christian flock, reject properly such constitutions; by no means admitting the offspring of heretical error, and cleaving to the pure and perfect doctrine of the Apostles. But we set our seal likewise upon all the other holy canons set forth by our holy and blessed Fathers, that is, by the three hundred and eighteen God-fearing Fathers assembled at Nicæa, and those at Ancyra; further, those at Neo-Cæsarea and at Gangra, and besides these those at Antioch in Syria [A. D. 341], those too at Laodicea in Phrygia, and likewise those of the one hundred and fifty assembled in this God-preserved imperial city and of the two hundred, who assembled for the first time in the metropolis of the Ephesians, and of the six hundred and thirty holy and blessed Fathers at Chalcedon; in like manner those of Sardica and those of Carthage; those also who assembled in this God-preserved imperial city under Nectarius [A. D. 394], and under Theophilus, archbishop of Alexandria; likewise too the canons[1] of Dionysius, formerly archbishop of the great city of Alexandria, and of Peter, archbishop of Alexandria, and martyr; of Gregory the Wonder-worker, archbishop of Neo-Cæsarea; of Athanasius, archbishop of Alexandria; of Basil, archbishop of Cæsarea in Cappadocia; of Gregory, bishop of Nyssa; of Gregory the Theologian;[2] of Amphilochius of Iconium; of Timothy, archbishop of Alexandria; of the first Theophilus, archbishop of the same metropolis of Alexandria; of Gennadius, patriarch of the God-preserved imperial city;

---

[1] Decretal letters.   [2] *I. e.*, Gregory Nazianzus.

676 DISSOLUTION OF IMPERIAL STATE CHURCH

moreover the canons set forth by Cyprian, archbishop of the country of the Africans, and martyr, and by the synod under him,[1] which have been kept in the country of the aforesaid bishops and only according to the custom delivered down to them. And that no one be allowed to transgress the aforesaid canons, or to receive other canons besides them, supposititiously set forth by some who have attempted to make a traffic of the truth. But should any one be convicted of innovating upon them, or attempting to overturn any of the aforementioned canons, he shall be condemned to receive the penalty which the canon imposes and so to be cured of his transgressions.

Canon 13. *On the Marriage of the Clergy.*

The following canon permits subdeacons and priests if married before ordination to continue to live in marriage relations with their wives. But they are not allowed to marry a second time or to marry a widow. Neither are bishops to remain married; but if they are married when elected, their wives must enter a monastery at a distance. With this canon should be compared the earlier legislation of Nicæa, *v. supra*, § 78, and also the law of Justinian, *v. supra*, § 94.

Since we know that it is handed down in the canonical discipline in the Roman Church that those who are about to be deemed worthy of ordination to the diaconate or presbyterate should promise no longer to live maritally with their wives, we, pursuing the ancient rule of apostolic discipline and order, will that henceforth the lawful marriage of men in holy orders remain firm, by no means dissolving their union with their wives, nor depriving them of intercourse with each other at a convenient season. . . . Therefore, if any one shall have dared, contrary to the Apostolic Canons, to deprive any one in holy orders, that is, any presbyter, deacon, or subdeacon, of cohabitation and intercourse with his lawful wife, let him be deposed; likewise also if any presbyter or deacon, on pretence of piety, puts away his wife, let him be excluded from communion; but if he persists let him be deposed.

[1] Probably that of 256.

Canon 36. *On the Rank of the Patriarchal Sees.*

Rome always rejected the claim of Constantinople to rank as second. *Cf.* Leo's opinion, *v. supra*, § 87.

Renewing the enactments of the one hundred and fifty Fathers assembled in the God-preserved and imperial city, and the six hundred and thirty assembled at Chalcedon, we decree that the see of Constantinople shall enjoy equal privilege with the see of Old Rome, and in ecclesiastical matters shall be as highly regarded as that is, and second after it. And after this [Constantinople] shall be ranked the see of the great city of Alexandria, and after that the see of Antioch, and after that the see of Jerusalem.

Canon 37. *On Bishops of Sees among Infidels.*

This canon is cited here, though not entering into the controversy between the East and the West, because it is significant of the changed position of the Eastern Church at this time, due to the Moslem and other conquests. The Monophysite bishops in Egypt and Syria were not molested by the Moslems. This canon marks the beginning of the practice of ordaining bishops *in partibus infidelium.*

Since at different times there have been invasions of the barbarians, and consequently very many cities have come into the possession of the infidels, so that as a consequence the prelate of a city may not be able, after he has been ordained, to take possession of his see and to be settled in it in sacerdotal order, and so to perform and manage, according to custom, the ordinations and all other things which appertain to the bishop; we, preserving the honor and veneration of the priesthood, and in nowise wishing to make use of the heathen injury to the ruin of ecclesiastical rights, have decreed that they who have been thus ordained, and for the aforesaid causes have not settled in their sees, may be kept from any prejudice from this thing, so that they may canonically perform the ordination of the different clerics and use the authority of their offices according to proper limits, and that whatever administration proceeds from them may be valid and

legitimate. For the exercise of his office shall not be circumscribed by reason of necessity, when the exact observance
of the law is circumscribed.

Canon 55.   *On Fasts in Lent.*

As stated in the canon, this enactment is aimed at the Roman
usage, and refers to the 64th Apostolic Canon, which Rome rejected.
For the Apostolic Canons, see ANF, VII, 504.

Since we have learned that in the city of the Romans, in
the holy fast of Lent, they fast on the Sabbaths[1] contrary to
the traditional ecclesiastical observance, it seemed good to
the holy synod that also in the Church of the Romans the
canons shall be in force without wavering which says: If any
cleric shall be found to fast on Sunday or on the Sabbath
except on one occasion only,[2] he shall be deposed; and if a
layman he shall be excommunicated.

Canon 67.   *On Eating Blood.*

This canon is less distinctly aimed at Rome. In the West the prohibition against eating blood seems to have been little observed, as it
had been given another interpretation. At the time of the Second
Trullan Council the practice was very common. Augustine, it might
be said, did not consider the apostolic command as binding except in
the special circumstance in which it was issued. *Cf.* Augustine,
Contra Faustum, 32 : 13.

The divine Scriptures command us to abstain from blood,
from things strangled, and from fornication. Those, therefore, who, on account of a dainty stomach, prepare by any
art for food the blood of animals and so eat it, we punish suit-
ably. If any one henceforth venture to eat in any way the
blood of an animal, if he be a clergyman let him be deposed;
if a layman, let him be excommunicated.

Canon 82.   *On Pictures of the Lamb of God.*

The custom which is here condemned was prevalent in the West.

[1] *I. e.*, Saturdays.
[2] See canon 69 of the Apostolic Canons, which prescribed fasting on the Saturday before Easter, or the Preparation.

In some pictures of the holy icons, a lamb is painted to which the Forerunner[1] points his finger, and this is received to serve as a type of grace, indicating beforehand through the Law our true lamb, Christ our God. Embracing therefore the ancient types and shadows as symbols and patterns of the truth, which have been given to the Church, we prefer "grace and truth," receiving it as the fulfilment of the Law. In order, therefore, that what is perfect may be delineated to the eyes of all, at least in colored expression, we decree that the figure of the lamb who taketh away the sin of the world, Christ our God, be henceforth exhibited according to human form in the icons, instead of the ancient lamb, so that all may understand, by means of it, the depth of the humiliation of the Word of God, and that we may recall to our memory His life in the flesh, His passion and salutary death, and the redemption resulting therefrom for the whole world.

(*b*) *Liber Diurnus Romanorum Pontificum*, n. 58.

Notification to the Emperor of an Election of a Pontiff.
The *Liber Diurnus* was the book of official formulæ used on occasions such as elections of pontiffs and the conferring of the pallium. It was composed between 685 and 751, and was employed in the papal chancellery down to the eleventh century, when it became antiquated on account of the changes in the position of the popes. The modern editions of the book are by Rozière, Paris, 1869, and by Sickel, Vienna, 1889. The text may be found in Mirbt, n. 195, where may also be found numerous other useful extracts.

Although it has not been without the merciful divine ordering that, after the death of the supreme pontiff, the votes of all should agree in the election of one, and that there be perfect harmony so that no one at all is to be found who would oppose it, it is yet necessary that we ought obediently to pour forth the prayers of our petitions to our most serene and most pious lord, who is known to rejoice in the concord of his subjects, and graciously to grant what has been asked by them in unanimity. And so when our Pope (*name*) of most blessed

---

[1] John the Baptist.

memory died, the assent of all was given, by the will of God, to the election of (*name*), the venerable archdeacon of the Apostolic See, because from the beginning of his life he had so served the same church, and in all things shown himself so able that he ought deservedly to be placed, with the divine approval, over the ecclesiastical government, especially since by his constant association with the aforesaid most blessed pontiff (*name*), he has been able to attain to the same distinctions of so great merit, by which the same prelate of holy memory is known to have been adorned, who by his words always stirred up his mind, being desirous of heavenly joys, so that whatsoever good we have lost in his predecessor we are confident that we have certainly found in him. Therefore, in tears, all we your servants pray that the piety of the lords may deign to hear the supplication of their servants, and the desires of their petitioners may be granted by the command of their piety, for the benefit of the Empire, that command may be given for his ordination; so that when we have been placed by your sacred and exalted clemency under him as our pastor, we may always pray for the life and empire of our most serene lords to the Lord Almighty and to the blessed Peter, prince of the Apostles, to whose church it has been granted that a worthy ruler be ordained.

Subscription of the priests.

I (*name*), by the mercy of God, presbyter of the holy Roman Church, consenting to this action made by us in regard to (*name*), the venerable archdeacon of the holy Apostolic See and our elected Pope, have subscribed.

Subscription of the laity.

I (*name*), servant of your piety, consenting to this action drawn up by us in regard to (*name*), the venerable archdeacon of the holy Apostolic See and our elected Pope, have subscribed.

(*c*) *Liber Diurnus Romanorum Pontificum*, ch. 60.

Notification of the Election of a Pontiff to the Exarch of Ravenna. The text may be found in part in Mirbt, *loc. cit.*

To the most excellent and exalted lord, graciously to be
preserved to us for a long life in his princely office (*name*),
exarch of Italy, the priests, deacons, and all the clergy of Rome,
the magistrates, the army, and the people of this city of Rome
as suppliants send greeting.

Providence is able to give aid in human affairs and to
change the weeping and groaning of the sorrowing into rejoicing. . . .

Inasmuch as (*name*), of pontifical memory, has been called
from present cares to eternal rest, as is the lot of mortals, a
great load of sorrow oppressed us, for as guardians we were
deprived of our own guardian. But the accustomed kindness
of our God did not permit us to remain long in this affliction
because we hoped in Him. For after we had humbly spent
three days in prayer that the heavenly kindness might, for
the merits of all, make known whom as worthy it commanded
to be elected to succeed to the apostolic office, with the aid
of His grace which inspired the minds of all; and after we had
assembled as is customary, that is, the clergy and the people
of Rome with the presence of the nobility and the army, from
the least to the greatest, so to speak; and the election, with
the help of God and the aid of the holy Apostles, fell upon the
person of (*name*), the most holy archdeacon of this holy Apostolic See of the Roman Church. The good and chaste life
of this man, beloved of God, was in the opinion of all so deserving that none opposed his election, no one was absent,
and none dissented from it. For why should not men agree
unanimously upon him whom the incomparable and unfail-
ing providence of our God had foreordained to this office?
For without doubt this had been determined upon in the
presence of God. So solemnly performing his decrees and
confirming with our signatures the desires of hearts concerning his election, we have sent you our fellow-servants as the
bearers of this letter (*names*), most holy bishop (*name*), venerable presbyter (*name*), regionary notary (*name*), regionary
subdeacons (*names*), honorable citizens, and from the most

flourishing and successful Roman army (*name*), most eminent consul, and (*names*) chief men, tribunes of the army, begging and praying together that your excellency, whom may God preserve, may with your accustomed goodness agree with our pious choice; because he, who has been unanimously elected by our humility, is such that so far as human discernment is able to see, no spot of reproach appears in him. And therefore we beg and beseech you, by God's inspiration, to grant our petition quickly, because there are many questions and other matters arising daily which require for remedy the care of pontifical favor. And the affairs of the province and the need of causes connected therewith also seek and await the control of due authority. Besides we need some one to keep the neighboring enemy in check, which can only be done by the power of God, and of the Prince of the Apostles through his vicar, the bishop of Rome; since it is well known that at various times the bishop of Rome has driven off enemies by his warnings, and at other times he has turned aside and restrained them by his prayers; so that by his words alone, on account of their reverence for the Prince of the Apostles, they have offered voluntary obedience, and thus they, whom the force of arms had not overcome, have yielded to the warnings and prayers of the Pope.

Since these things are so, we again and again beseech you, our exalted lord, preserved by God, that, with the aid and inspiration of God in your heart, you may quickly give orders to adorn the Apostolic See by the completed ordination of the same, our father. And we, your humble servants, on seeing our desires fulfilled, may then give unceasing thanks to God and to you, and with our spiritual pastor, our bishop, enthroned in the Apostolic Seat, we may pour out prayers for the life and health and complete victories of our most exalted and Christian lords (*names*), the great and victorious emperors, that the merciful God may give manifold victories to their royal courage, and cause them to triumph over all peoples, and that God may give them joy of heart, because the ancient rule of Rome has been restored. For we know that he whom we have elected Pope can, with his prayers, influence the divine omnipotence; and he has prepared a joyful increase for the Roman Empire, and he will aid you in this, in the government of this province of Italy, which is subject to you, and will aid and protect all of us, your servants, through many years.

Subscription of the priests.

I, (*name*), the humble archpriest of the holy Roman Church, have with full consent subscribed to this document which we have made concerning (*name*), most holy archdeacon, our bishop elect.

And the subscription of the laity.

I, (*name*), in the name of God, consul, have with full consent subscribed to this document which we have made concerning (*name*), most holy archdeacon, our bishop-elect.

(*d*) Paulus Diaconus, *Hist. Langobardorum*, IV, 44. (MSL, 95 : 581.)

Agilulf may have been a convert to the Catholic faith, *v. supra*, § 99. His successors were not. In fact, not until 653, when Aribert, the nephew of Theodelinda, ascended the throne, were the Lombards permanently under Catholic rulers.

44. After Ariwald (626–636) had reigned twelve years over the Lombards he departed this life, and Rothari of the family of Arodus took the kingdom of the Lombards. He was a strong, brave man, and walked in the paths of justice; in Christian faith, however, he did not hold to the right way, but was polluted by the unbelief of the Arian heresy. The Arians say, to their confusion, that the Son is inferior to the Father and, in the same way, the Holy Ghost is inferior to the Father and the Son; we, Catholic Christians, on the contrary, confess that the Father and the Son and the Holy Ghost are one true God in three persons, equal in power and glory. In the times of Rothari there were in nearly all the cities of his kingdom two bishops, a Catholic and an Arian.

To this very day there is shown in the city of Ticinus [Pavia] the place where the Arian bishop resided, at the church of St. Eusebius, and held the baptistery while the Catholic bishop was at the head of another church. The Arian bishop, however, who was in this city, whose name was Anastasius, accepted the Catholic faith and afterward ruled the Church of Christ. This king Rothari caused the laws of the Lombards to be reduced to writing and named the book *The Edict;* the laws of the Lombards up to that time had been retained merely in. memory and by their use in the courts. This took place, as the king in the preface to his law-book says, in the seventy-seventh year[1] after the Lombards came into Italy.

§ 109. Rome, Constantinople, and the Lombards in the Period of the First Iconoclastic Controversy; the Seventh General Council, Nicæa, A. D. 787

By the eighth century the veneration of pictures or icons had become wide-spread throughout the Eastern Church. Apart from their due place in the cultus, grave abuses and superstitions had arisen in many parts of the Church in connection with the icons. To Leo III the Isaurian (717-741), and to the army, the veneration of the icons, as practised by the populace, and especially by the monks, seemed but little removed from the grossest idolatry. Accordingly, in an edict issued in 726, Leo attempted to put an end to the abuses by preventing all veneration of the icons. Meeting with opposition, his measures passed from moderate to severe. In Italy, although the use of icons was not developed to the same extent as in the East, sympathy was entirely against the Iconoclasts. Gregory II (715–731) and Gregory III (731–741) bitterly reproached and denounced the action of the Emperor. Nearly all the exarchate willingly passed under the power of the Lombards. Other parts of northern Italy also broke with the Emperor. Leo retaliated by annex-

---

[1] *The Edict* says seventy-sixth year.

ing Illyricum to the see of Constantinople and confiscating the papal revenues in southern Italy. From that time the connection between the Pope and the Emperor was very slight. The Emperor Constantine V Copronymus (741–775) was more severe than his father, and in many respects even fiercely brutal in his treatment of the monks. A synod was assembled at Constantinople, 754, attended by three hundred and thirty-eight bishops, who, as was customary in Eastern synods, supported the Emperor. His son, Leo IV Chazarus (775–780), was less energetic and disposed to tolerate the use of icons in private. But his widow, Irene, the guardian of her infant son, Constantine VI, was determined to restore the images or icons. A synod held at Constantinople in 786 was broken up by the soldiery of the capital. In 787 at Nicæa a council was called at a safe distance and Iconoclasm was condemned.

Additional source material: *St. John Damascene on Holy Images,* Eng. trans. by Mary H. Allies, 1898; St. John of Damascus, *Exposition of the Orthodox Faith,* PNF, ser. II, vol. IX; Percival, *Seven Ecumenical Councils* (PNF).

(*a*) *Liber Pontificalis, Vita Gregorii* II. Ed. Duchesne, I, 403.

Disorders in Italy consequent upon Iconoclasm.
The following passage from the *Liber Pontificalis* gives a vivid and, on the whole, accurate picture of the confusion in Italy during the last years of the authority of the Eastern Roman Empire in the peninsula. It is hardly likely that the Emperor ordered the death of the pontiff as recorded, and more probable that his over-officious representatives regarded it as a means of ingratiating themselves with their master. The passage is strictly contemporaneous, as the *Liber Pontificalis,* at least in this part, is composed of brief biographies of Popes written immediately after their decease and in some instances during their lives. For a fuller statement of the whole period, see Hefele, §§ 332 *ff.,* who gives an abstract of the following and also of two letters alleged to have been written by Gregory II to the Emperor, which Hefele accepts as genuine. For a criticism of these letters, see Hodgkin, *op. cit.,* VI, 501–505. Hodgkin gives an excellent account of King Liutprand in ch. XII of the same volume, pp. 437–508, and throws much light on the following passage.
For the events immediately preceding this, see Paulus Diaconus, *Hist. Langobardorum,* VI, 46–48, given above in § 106. Paulus refers

to the capture of Narnia in the last sentence of ch. 48, and his next chapter is apparently a condensation of the following sections of the official papal biography.

At that time [*circa* A. D. 725] Narnia[1] was taken by the Lombards. And Liutprand, the king of the Lombards, advanced upon Ravenna with his entire army, and besieged it for some days. Taking the fortress of Classis, he bore off many captives and immense booty. After some time the duke Basilius, the chartularius Jordanes, and the subdeacon John, surnamed Lurion, conspired to kill the Pope; and Marinus, the imperial spatarius, who at that time held the government of the duchy of Rome, having been sent by the command of the Emperor to the royal city, joined their conspiracy. But they could not find an opportunity. The plot was broken up by the judgment of God, and he therefore left Rome. Later Paulus, the patrician, was sent as exarch to Italy, who planned how at length he might accomplish the crime; but their plans were disclosed to the Romans. These were so enraged that they killed Jordanes and John Lurion. Basilius, however, became a monk and ended his life hidden in a certain place. But the exarch Paulus, on the command of the Emperor, tried to kill the pontiff because he hindered the levying of a tax upon the province, intending to strip the churches of their property, as was done in other places, and to appoint another [Pope] in his place. After this another spatarius was sent with commands to remove the pontiff from his seat. Then again the patrician Paulus sent, for the accomplishment of this crime, such soldiers as he could withdraw from Ravenna, with his guard and some from the camps. But the Romans were aroused, and from all sides the Lombards gathered for the defence of the pontiff at the bridge of Solario, in the district of Spoleto, and the dukes of the Lombards, surrounding the Roman territories, prevented this crime.

In a decree afterward sent, the Emperor ordered that there

[1] In the duchy of Spoleto.

no longer should be in any church an image[1] of any saint, or martyr, or angel (for he said that all these were accursed); and if the pontiff assented he should enjoy his favor, but if he prevented the accomplishment of this also he should fall from his position. The pious man, despising therefore the profane command of the prince, armed himself against the Emperor as against an enemy, rejecting this heresy and writing everywhere to warn Christians of the impiety which had arisen.

Aroused by this, the inhabitants of the Pentapolis[2] and the armies of Venetia resisted the command of the Emperor, saying that they would never assent to the murder of the pontiff, but on the contrary would strive manfully for his defence. They anathematized the exarch Paulus, him who had sent him, and those who sided with him, refusing to obey them; and throughout Italy all chose leaders[3] for themselves, so eager were all concerning the pontiff and his safety. When the iniquities of the Emperor were known, all Italy started to choose for itself an emperor and conduct him to Constantinople, but the pontiff prevented this plan, hoping for the conversion of the prince.

Meanwhile, in those days, the duke Exhiliratus,[4] deceived by the instigation of the devil, with his son Adrian, occupied parts of Campania, persuading the people to obey the Emperor and kill the pontiff. Then all the Romans pursued after him, took him, and killed both him and his son. After this they chased away the duke Peter [governor of Rome under the Emperor], saying that he had written against the pontiff to the Emperor. When, therefore, a dissension arose in and about Ravenna, some consenting to the wickedness of the Emperor and some holding to the pontiff and those faithful to him, a great fight took place between them and they killed the patrician Paulus [exarch at that time]. And the cities of Castra Æmilia, Ferrorianus, Montebelli, Verabulum, with

[1] *I. e.*, a picture, and not a statue, for these had been forbidden long since.
[2] Rimini, Pesaro, Fano, Sinigaglia, and Ancona.
[3] *Duces* can hardly mean dukes here.
[4] Governor of Naples under the Emperor.

its towns, Buxo, Persiceta, the Pentapolis, and Auximanum, surrendered to the Lombards.[1] After this the Emperor sent to Naples Eutychius Fratricius, the eunuch, who had formerly been exarch, to accomplish what the exarch Paulus, the spatarii, and the other evil counsellors had been unable to do. But by God's ordering his miserable craft was not so hidden but that his most wicked plot was disclosed to all, that he would attempt to violate the churches of Christ, to destroy all, and to take away the property of all. When he had sent one of his own men to Rome with written instructions, among other things, that the pontiff should be killed, together with the chief men of Rome, this most bloody outrage was discovered, and the Romans would at once have killed the messenger of the patrician if the opposition of the Pope had not prevented them. But they anathematized the same exarch Eutychius, binding themselves, great and small, by an oath, never to permit the pontiff, the zealous guardian of the Christian faith and the defender of the churches, to be killed or removed, but to be ready all to die for his safety. Thereupon the patrician [Eutychius], promising many gifts to the dukes and to the king of the Lombards, attempted to persuade them by his messengers to abandon the support of the pontiff. But they despised the man's detestable wiles contained in his letters; and the Romans and the Lombards bound themselves as brothers in the bond of faith, all desiring to suffer a glorious death for the pontiff, and never to permit him to receive any harm, contending for the true faith and the salvation of Christians. While they were doing this that father chose, as a stronger protection, to distribute with his own hand such alms to the poor as he found; giving himself to prayers and fastings, he besought the Lord daily with litanies, and he remained always more supported by this hope than by men; however, he thanked the people for their offer, and with gentle

---

[1] These names are not all to be identified. Auximanum, however, is Osimo, south of Ancona; Ferronianus is Fregnano, near Modena; Montebelli or Monte Veglio is west of Bologna; Persiceta is also near Bologna, which Paulus Diaconus says was taken by the Lombards, *op. cit.*, VI, 49.

words he besought all to serve God with good deeds and to remain steadfast in the faith; and he admonished them not to renounce their love and fidelity to the Roman Emperor.

At that time in the eleventh indiction,[1] the castle of Sutri was taken by the Lombards by craft, and was held by them for a period of forty days,[2] but urged by the constant letters of the pontiff and warnings sent to the king, when very many gifts had been made, as a gift at least for all the towns, the king of the Lombards restored them and gave them as a donation to the most blessed Apostles Peter and Paul. At the same time, in the twelfth indiction [A. D. 729], in the month of January, for ten days and more, a star, called Gold-bearing,[3] with rays, appeared in the west. Its rays were toward the north and reached to the midst of the heavens. At that time, also, the patrician Eutychius and King Liutprand made a most wicked agreement, that when an army had been gathered the king should subject Spoleto and Beneventum,[4] and the exarch of Rome, and they should carry out what was already commanded concerning the pontiff. When the king came to Spoleto, oaths and hostages were received from both [i. e., the dukes of Spoleto and Beneventum], and he came with all his troops to the Campus Neronis.[5] The pontiff went forth and presented himself before him and endeavored to the extent of his ability to soften the mind of the king by pious warnings, so that the king threw himself at his feet and promised to harm no one; and he was so moved to compunction by the pious warnings that he abandoned his undertaking and laid on the grave of the Apostle his mantle, his military cloak, his sword belt, his short two-edged sword, and his golden sword, as well as a golden crown and a silver cross. After prayer he besought the pontiff to consent to make peace with

---

[1] From Sept. 1, A. D. 727, to Sept. 1, A. D. 728.

[2] One hundred and forty, according to another reading.

[3] Aurifer, or, according to another reading, Lucifer.

[4] Both duchies were nominally under the king of the Lombards, but it is very probable that they were attempting to free themselves from his rule.

[5] The Campus Neronis was outside the walls of Rome, as they then extended, and adjoined the Vatican.

the exarch, which also was done. So he departed, for the king forsook the bad designs with which he had entered into the plot with the exarch. While the exarch remained in Rome, there came into Tuscany to Castrum Maturianense,[1] a certain deceiver, Tiberius by name, called also Petasius,[2] who attempted to usurp the rule of the Roman Empire and deceived some of the less important, so that Maturianum, Luna, and Blera [Bieda] took oath to him. The exarch, hearing of this, was troubled, but the most holy Pope supported him, and, sending with him his chief men and an army, he advanced and came to Castrum Maturianense. Petasius was killed, his head was cut off and sent to Constantinople, to the prince; nevertheless the Emperor showed no great favor to the Romans.

After these things the malice of the Emperor became evident, on account of which he had persecuted the pontiff. For he compelled all the inhabitants of Constantinople, by force and persuasion, to displace the images of the Saviour as well as of His holy mother, and of all saints, wherever they were, and (what is horrible to tell) to burn them in the fire in the middle of the city, and to whitewash all the painted churches. Because very many of the people of the city withstood the commission of such an enormity, they were subjected to punishment; some were beheaded, others lost a part of their body. For this reason also, because Germanus, the prelate of the church of Constantinople, was unwilling to consent to this, the Emperor deprived him of his pontifical position, and appointed in his place the presbyter Anastasius, an accomplice. Anastasius sent to the Pope a synodical letter, but when that holy man saw that he held the same error, he did not regard him as brother and fellow-priest, but wrote him warning letters, commanding him to be put out of his sacerdotal office unless he returned to the Catholic faith. He also charged the Emperor, urging wholesome advice, that he should desist from such execrable wickedness, and he warned him by letter.[3]

---

[1] Barberino, fifteen miles east of Civita Vecchia.
[2] This was his real name.   [3] See introduction to this extract.

(b) John of Damascus, *De Fide Orthodoxa*, IV, 16. (MSG, 94 : 1168.)

John of Damascus (*ob. ante* 754) was the last of the Church Fathers of the East. He became the classical representative of the theology of the Eastern Church, and his system forms the conclusion and summing up of the results of all the great controversies that had distracted that part of the Church. His greatest work, *De Fide Orthodoxa*, may be found translated in PNF. In the following chapter John sums up briefly the arguments which he uses in his three orations *In Defence of Images* (to be found in MSG, 94 : 1227 *ff*.; for translation see head of section). By images one should understand pictures rather than statues. The latter were never common and fell entirely out of use and were forbidden. They seemed too closely akin to idols. In the translation, the phrase "to show reverence" is the equivalent of the Greek προσκυνέω.

Since some find fault with us for showing reverence and honoring the image of our Saviour and that of our Lady, and also of the rest of the saints and servants of Christ, let them hear that from the beginning God made man after His own image. On what other grounds, then, do we show reverence to each other than that we are made after God's image? For as Basil, that most learned expounder of divine things, says: "The honor given to the image passes over to the prototype."[1] Now a prototype is that which is imaged, from which the form is derived. Why was it that the Mosaic people showed reverence round about the tabernacle which bore an image and type of heavenly things, or rather the whole creation? God, indeed, said to Moses: "Look that thou make all things after the pattern which was shewed thee in the mount" [Ex. 33 : 10]. The Cherubim, also, which overshadowed the mercy-seat, are they not the work of men's hands? What is the renowned temple at Jerusalem? Is it not made by hands and fashioned by the skill of men? The divine Scriptures, however, blame those who show reverence to graven images, but also those who sacrifice to demons. The Greeks sacrificed and the Jews also sacrificed; but the Greeks to demons; the Jews, however, to God. And the sacrifice of the Greeks was rejected and con-

[1] See next selection.

demned, but the sacrifice of the just was acceptable to God. For Noah sacrificed, and God smelled a sweet savor of a good purpose, receiving, also, the fragrance of a good-will toward Him. And so the graven images of the Greeks, since they were the images of demon deities, were rejected and forbidden.

But besides this, who can make an imitation of the invisible, incorporeal, uncircumscribed, and formless God? Therefore to give form to the Deity is the height of folly and impiety. And therefore in the Old Testament the use of images was repressed. But after God, in the bowels of His mercy, became for our salvation in truth man, not as He was seen by Abraham in the semblance of a man, or by the prophets, but He became in truth man, according to substance, and after He lived upon earth and dwelt among men, worked miracles, suffered, and was crucified, He rose again, and was received up into heaven; since all these things actually took place and were seen by men, they were written for the remembrance and instruction of us who were not present at that time, in order that, though we saw not, we may still, hearing and believing, obtain the blessing of the Lord. But since all have not a knowledge of letters nor time for reading, it appeared good to the Fathers that those events, as acts of heroism, should be depicted on images[1] to be a brief memorial of them. Often, doubtless, when we have not the Lord's passion in mind and see the image of Christ's crucifixion, we remember the passion and we fall down and show reverence not to the material but to that which is imaged; just as we do not show reverence to the material of the Gospel, nor to the material of the cross, but that which these typify.[2] For wherein does the cross that typifies the Lord differ from a cross that does not do so? It is the same also as to the case of the Mother of God.[3] For the honor which is given her is referred to Him who was incarnate of her. And similarly also the brave acts of holy men stir us to bravery

[1] *I. e.*, in pictures.
[2] John had a strong argument here as the Iconoclasts reverenced the true cross.
[3] Θεομήτωρ, not Θεοτόκος.

and to emulation and imitation of their valor and to the glory of God. For, as we said, the honor that is given to the best of fellow servants is a proof of good-will toward our common lady, and the honor rendered the image passes over to the prototype. But this is an unwritten tradition, just as is also to show reverence toward the East and to the cross, and very many similar things.[1]

A certain tale is told also that when Augarus [*i. e.*, Abgarus] was king over the city of the Edessenes, he sent a portrait-painter to paint a likeness of the Lord; and when the painter could not paint because of the brightness that shone from His countenance, the Lord himself put a garment over His divine and life-giving face and impressed on it an image of Himself, and sent this to Augarus to satisfy in this way his desire.

Moreover, that the Apostles handed down much that was unwritten, Paul the Apostle of the Gentiles writes: Therefore, brethren, stand fast and hold the traditions which ye have been taught of us, whether by word or by epistles [II Thess. 2 : 14]. And to the Corinthians he writes: Now I praise you, brethren, that ye remembered me in all things and keep the traditions as I have delivered them to you [I Cor. 2 : 2].

(*c*) Basil the Great, *De Spiritu Sancto*, ch. 18. (MSG, 32 : 149.)

Basil is speaking of the three persons of the Trinity, and says that although we speak of the Father, Son and Holy Spirit, we must not count up "by way of addition gradually increasing from unity to multitude," but that number must be understood otherwise in speaking of the three divine persons.

How then, if one and one, are there not two Gods? Because we speak of a king and of the king's image, and not of two kings. The power is not parted nor the glory divided. The power ruling over us is one, and the authority one, and so also the doxology ascribed by us is one and not plural; because the honor paid to the image passes over to the prototype.

---

[1] *Cf.* Basil, *De Spiritu*, ch. 27; *v. supra*, § 87, for Basil on the force of tradition.

Now what in the one case the image is by reason of imitation, that in the other case the Son is by nature; and as in works of art the likeness is dependent upon the form, so in the case of the divine and uncompounded nature the union consists in the communion of the godhead.

(d) The Seventh General Council, Nicæa, A. D. 787, *Definition of Faith*. Mansi, XIII, 398 *ff*.

In addition to Hefele, and PNF, ser. II, vol. XIV, see Mendham, *The Seventh General Council, the Second of Nicæa, in which the Worship of Images was Established; with copious notes from the "Caroline Books," compiled by order of Charlemagne for its Confutation*, London, n. d.

The holy, great and ecumenical synod which, by the grace of God and the command of the pious and Christ-loving Emperors, Constantine, and Irene his mother, was gathered together for the second time at Nicæa, the illustrious metropolis of the eparchy of Bithynia, in the holy Church of God which is named Sophia, having followed the tradition of the Catholic Church, hath defined as follows:

Christ our Lord, who hath bestowed upon us the light of the knowledge of Himself, and hath redeemed us from the darkness of idolatrous madness, having espoused to Himself His holy Catholic Church without spot or defect, promised that He would so preserve her; and assured His holy disciples, saying, "I am with you always, even unto the end of the world" [Matt. 28 : 20], which promise He made, not only to them, but to us also who through them should believe in His name. But some, not considering this gift, and having become fickle through the temptation of the wily enemy, have fallen from the right faith; for, withdrawing from the tradition of the Catholic Church, they have erred from the knowledge of the truth, and as the proverb saith: "The husbandmen have gone astray in their own husbandry, and have gathered in their hands sterility," because certain priests in deed, but not priests in reality, had dared to slander the God-approved ornaments of the sacred monuments. Of whom God

ICONOCLASTIC PERIOD 695

cries aloud through the prophet: "Many pastors have corrupted my vineyard, they have polluted my portion" [Jer. 12 : 10; *cf.* LXX]. And, forsooth, following profane men, trusting to their own senses, they have calumniated His holy Church espoused to Christ our God, and have not distinguished between holy and profane, styling the images of the Lord and of His saints by the same name as the statute of diabolical idols. Seeing which things, our Lord God (not willing to behold His people corrupted by such manner of plague) hath of His good pleasure called us together, the chief of His priests, from every quarter, moved with a divine zeal and brought hither by the will of our Emperors, Constantine and Irene, to the end that the divine tradition of the Catholic Church may receive stability by our common decree. Therefore, with all diligence, making a thorough examination and investigation, and following the trend of the truth, diminishing naught, adding naught, we preserve unchanged all things which pertain to the Catholic Church, and following the six ecumenical synods, especially that which met in this illustrious metropolis of Nicæa, as also that which was afterward gathered together in the God-preserved royal city.

We believe in one God . . . life of the world to come. Amen.[1]

We detest and anathematize Arius and all who agree with him and share his absurd opinion; also Macedonius and those who, following him, are well styled foes of the Spirit.[2] We confess that our lady, St. Mary, is properly and truly the Theotokos, because she bore, after the flesh, one of the Holy Trinity, to wit, Christ our God, as the Council of Ephesus has already defined, when it cast out of the Church the impious Nestorius with his allies, because he introduced a personal [προσωπικὴν] duality [in Christ]. With the Fathers of this synod we confess the two natures of Him who was incarnate for us of the immaculate Theotokos and ever-Virgin Mary,

---

[1] The creed of Nicæa is not here recited, only the so-called creed of Constantinople, but without the *filioque* in the Greek.

[2] Pneumatomachians.

recognizing Him as perfect God and perfect man, as also the Council of Chalcedon hath promulgated, expelling from the divine Atrium as blasphemers, Eutyches and Dioscurus; and placing with them Severus, Peter, and a number of others blaspheming in divers fashions. Moreover, with these we anathematize the fables of Origen, Evagrius, and Didymus, in accordance with the decision of the Fifth Council held at Constantinople. We affirm that in Christ there are two wills and operations according to the reality of each nature, as also the Sixth Council held at Constantinople taught, casting out Sergius, Honorius, Cyrus, Pyrrhus, Macarius, and those who are unwilling to be reverent and who agree with these.

To make our confession short, we keep unchanged all the ecclesiastical traditions handed down to us, written or unwritten, and of these one is the making of pictorial representations, agreeable to the history of the preaching of the Gospel, a tradition useful in many respects, but especially in this, that so the incarnation of the Word of God is shown forth as real and not merely fantastic, for these have mutual indications, and without doubt have also mutual significations.

We, therefore, following the royal pathway and the divinely inspired authority of our holy Fathers and the traditions of the Catholic Church for, as we all know, the Holy Spirit dwells in her, define with all certitude and accuracy, that just as the figure of the precious and life-giving cross, so also the venerable and holy images, as well in painting and mosaic, as of other fit materials, should be set forth in the holy churches of God, and on the sacred vessels and on the vestments and on hangings and in tablets both in houses and by the wayside, to wit, the figure of our Lord God and Saviour Jesus Christ, of our spotless lady, the Theotokos, of the venerable angels, of all saints, and of all pious people. For by so much the more frequently as they are seen in artistic representation, by so much the more readily are men lifted up to the memory of their prototypes, and to a longing after them; and to these should be given due salutation and honorable reverence [ἀσπασμὸν καὶ τιμητικὴν προσκύνησιν], not indeed that true worship [τὴν ἀληθινὴν λατρείαν] which pertains alone to the divine nature; but to these, as to the figure of the precious and life-giving cross, and to the book of the Gospels and to other holy objects, incense and lights may be offered according to ancient pious custom. For the honor which is paid to the image passes on to that which the image represents, and he who shows reverence [προσκυνεῖ] to the image shows reverence to the subject represented in it. For thus the teaching of our holy Fathers, which is called the tradition of the Catholic Church, which from one end of the earth to the other hath received the Gospel, is strengthened. Thus we follow Paul, who spake in Christ, and the whole divine Apostolic company and the holy Fathers, holding fast the traditions which we have received. So we sing prophetically the triumphal hymns of the Church: Rejoice greatly, O daughter of Sion; Shout, O daughter of Jerusalem. Rejoice and be glad with all thy heart. The Lord hath taken away from thee the oppression of thy adversaries; thou art redeemed from the hand of thy enemies: The Lord is a king in the midst of thee; thou shalt not see evil any more, and peace be unto thee forever.

Those, therefore, who dare to think or teach otherwise, or as wicked heretics dare to spurn the traditions of the Church and to invent some novelty, or else to reject some of those things which the Church hath received, to wit, the book of the Gospels, or the image of the cross, or the pictorial icons, or the holy relics of a martyr, or evilly and sharply to devise anything subversive of the lawful traditions of the Catholic Church, or to turn to common uses the sacred vessels and the venerable monasteries, if they be bishops or clerics we command that they be deposed; if religious[1] or laics, that they be cut off from communion.

[1] I. e., monks.

INDEX

The Analytical Table of Contents at the opening of this volume should be used to supplement this Index.

Acacius of Constantinople, 526, 536.
Adoptionists, 172.
Advent, second. See "Chiliasm."
Ælia Capitolina, 361.
Æons. See "Gnosticism," "Basilides," "Valentinus."
Africa, North, Church of, 157, 281. See also "Tertullian," "Cyprian," "Donatism," "Augustine."
Agape, 41.
Agatho of Rome, 652.
Agde, council of (A. D. 506), canons, 616.
Alexander of Alexandria, 300 *f.*, 302.
Alexander of Jerusalem, 207.
Alexandria, catechetical school of, 189-202.
Alexandria, councils of (A. D. 320), 304; (A. D. 362), 349-352; (A. D. 430), anathematisms, 505 *ff.*
Allegorism, or Allegorical Exegesis, 15 *f.*, 120; Origen on, 199 *f.*; Nepos on, 219 *f.*; Methodius on, 230; Augustine on, 442 *f.*
Alms, as expiation of sin, 48, 169-171.
Ambrose of Milan, reply to Symmachus, 342-346; epistle to Theodosius, 390 *f.*; invocation of saints, 397; patron of monasticism, 409; on Fall of Man, 438.
Anastasius, emp., 527, 530, 575.
Anastasius of Rome, condemnation of Origen, 487 *f.*
Ancyra, council of (A. D. 358), 348, 412, 675.
Angels, invocation of, 400.
Anicetus of Rome, 164.
Anointing, 484.
Anthony, hermit, 248-251, 409.
Antioch, council of (A. D. 269), 225 *ff.*;

(A. D. 341), creed, 313 *f.*; canons, 362-364, 675.
Antioch, school of, 504, 511.
Apelles, 105.
Aphthartodocetism, 553.
Apollinaris the Elder, 334.
Apollinaris of Laodicæa, 354, 494 *f.*, 498.
Apollinarius of Hierapolis, 111.
Apollonius, Antimontanist, 108.
Apologist, 69 *ff.*; theology of, 130 *ff.*
Apostles, 8 *ff.*, 40.
Apostles' Creed, 123-126.
Apostolic Age, 5-12.
Apostolic churches, 111 *ff.*
Apostolic Fathers, 13.
Apostolic succession, 112-115, 122.
Appeals to Emperor, 359, 370; to Rome, Sardica on, 364-366; rescript of Gratian and Valentinian on, 366 *f.*
Archelaus, 82.
Arian controversy, 297-320, 348-356.
Arianism among the Germans: among the Goths, 426 *f.*; among the Lombards, 683 *f.*
Aristides, Apology of, 69-72.
Aristotelian philosophy, 174.
Arius, 269, 293, 299 *f.*; epistle to Eusebius of Nicomedia, 302; *Thalia*, 303; confession, 307, 308.
Arles, council of, 289-292.
Artemon, 173.
Asceticism, 46 *ff.*, 105, 248.
Asia Minor, theology of, 30-32, 135-139, 229 *ff.*
Askidas, Theodore of, 546.
Athanasius, on Sabellianism, 180; on Dionysius of Alexandria, 223-225; exile, 308, 310.
Athenagoras, 133.

Audientia Episcopalis, 380, 382 f.
Augustine of Canterbury, 602–605.
Augustine of Hippo, life and conversion, 433–436; his type of piety, 437; on Fall of Man and original sin, 438; predestination, 440; allegory, 442; merit, 444; on baptism, 448; sacraments, 449; repression of heresy, 450–453.
Aurelian, emp., 227.

Baptism, 39, 116, 167, 179 f., 184, 186, 213, 231–234, 292, 447 f., 450, 452, 464.
Baptism, rite of, 33, 38, 232, 484 f.
Baptism of heretics, 243, 245–248, 292.
Barbarian invasions, 420–423.
Bardesanes, 54.
Barnabas, epistle of, 14.
Bartholomew, Apostle, 55.
Basil of Cæsarea, on Sabellianism, 181; his charities, 395; monastic rule, 405; on tradition, 484; on reverence shown images, 693.
Basilides the Gnostic, 82 ff., 89, 91, 120.
Basiliscus, emp., *Encyclion* of, 523–526.
Bede, the Venerable, 566, 569, 603 ff.; his Penitential, 629 f.
Benedict of Nursia, *Rule* of, 631–641.
Bishops, apostolic appointment of, 37; authority of, 31, 41, 42, 237–239, 265–270, 361–364; election of, 556, 580 f.; State service of, 383 f.; succession of, 111, 115, 122, 128.
Boniface II of Rome, 473.
Braga, council of (A. D. 572), 619.
Britain, Church in, 53, 566–570, 602–614.

Cælestinus, the Pelagian, 455 f., 460.
Cæsarius of Arles, 621 f.
Cæsaropapism, 552 ff.
Caius of Rome, 8.
Callistus of Rome, 69, 175–177, 186.
Canon. See "Council."
Canon law, Quinisext Council on, 674–676.
Canon of New Testament, 117 ff., 120, 122 f., 532.

Caracalla, emp., 142 f., 149.
Carthage, councils of (A. D. 256), 238; (A. D. 390), 417; (A. D. 418), 463–466.
Cassian, on grace, 467–469; on secular studies, 646 f.
Cassiodorus, 530.
Cassius, Dio, 11.
Cataphrygians. See "Montanists."
Cathari. See "Novatians."
Celestinus of Rome, 374.
Celibacy, laws permitting, 285; of clergy, 411–418, 676.
Celsus, 55–59, 158.
Celtic Church in British Isles, 566–570.
Cerdo, 102 f.
Cerinthus, 81, 114.
Chalcedon, council of (A. D. 451), 511–522.
Character, doctrine of, 452.
Charity, 24, 35, 41, 48, 71 f., 145, 157, 333, 394 ff.
Chastity, 47, 344.
Chiliasm, 25–27, 219–221.
Chorepiscopoi, 364.
Christology. See "Apollinaris," "Logos," "Monarchians," "Monophysites," "Monotheletes," "Sabellius."
Christotokos, Mary as the, 501.
Chrysostom, John, 372, 491 f.
Church, authority of, Augustine on, 454.
Church, organization of, Post-Apostolic age, 36–42.
Church and State, mutual relations, 530, 554.
Circumcelliones, 323.
Classical Literature, Christian use of, 334 ff., 645–648.
Clemens, Flavius, 11 f.
Clement of Alexandria, on Gnosticism, 84, 89, 92, 189; on Greek philosophy, 190; Christian Gnosticism, 191 ff.
Clement of Rome, 7, 24, 36, 47, 129.
Clergy, distinguished from laity, 167, 181 f.; exemption from civil burdens, 283 f.; subjection to bishops, 361. See "Ordination."
Clovesho, council of (A. D. 747), 611, 651.

Clovis, king, 570–575.
Code, of Justinian, 541; of Theodosius II, 424.
Cœnobites, 405.
Columba, 569.
Columbanus, 585–590.
Commodus, emp., 69.
Confession, auricular, 384 f.; public, see "Penitential Discipline."
Constans II, *Typos* of, 662–664.
Constantine I, Edict of Milan, 263; fiscal policy, 277–281; ecclesiastical patronage, 281–285; repression of heathenism, 285–287; ecclesiastical policy, 289–296.
Constantinople, councils of (A. D. 381), 353, 369, 480; (A. D. 382), 359, 498; (A. D. 448), 512 f.; (A. D. 553), 551 f.; (A. D. 681), 665–671; (A. D. 691), 673–679.
Constantinople, see of, 354, 477–480, 521 f.
Constantius, emp., 326–329, 331.
Corinth, church of, 7–9.
Cornelius of Rome, 157, 217.
Councils, ecclesiastical, 110 f., 157, 177, 289; general, in North Africa, 463; provincial, 359 f.; relation of, to secular rulers, 369 f., 580.
Creed, forms approximating to the Apostles', 32, 123–126.
Creeds and confessions of faith, of Gregory Thaumaturgus, 222; of Eusebius of Cæsarea, 305; of Nicæa (A. D. 325), 305; of Arius, 307; II Antioch (A. D. 341), 313; IV Antioch (A. D. 341), 314; Nice (A. D. 359), 318; Cyril of Jerusalem, 354; Epiphanius of Salamis, 355; Ulfilas, 426; Antioch (A. D. 433), 510.
Cyprian, on almsgiving, 169–171; on the lapsed, 208–210, 214–217; on the eucharist, 234–237; on the episcopate, 237–242; on the unity of the Church, 240–245; on baptism by heretics, 245–248.
Cyril of Alexandria, 373, 494, 504; anathematisms against Nestorius, 505–507, 510, 520, note.
Cyril of Jerusalem, 348, 354.
Cyrus of Alexandria, 520, 660; formula of union, 661 f.

Dacia, Church in, 53.
Damasus of Rome, 270, 366, 380 f.
Deacon, 35, 37, 41.
Deaconess, 21.
Dead, prayers for, 169, 444 f., 624.
Decius, emp., persecution under, 206–212.
Decretals, Siricius on the force of, 417.
Decretum Gelasii, 532–536.
Demiurge, 90, 96.
Deposition, 239, 363.
Didache, 37, 46.
Dio Cassius, on Domitian persecution, 11.
Diocese, 354, 362, 611, 616–620.
Diocletian, reorganization of the Empire, 257 f.
Diocletian persecution, 258–262.
Diognetus, Epistle to, 28.
Dionysius of Alexandria, 219 f., 223 ff.
Dionysius the Areopagite, 560–564.
Dionysius of Corinth, 9, 24.
Dionysius Exiguus, 530, 611, note.
Dionysius of Rome, 223 ff., 226.
Dioscurus of Alexandria, 511 f.
Discipline, penitential, 42–49, 166 f., 169 f., 183–188, 213, 215 ff., 362, 384 f., 624–630.
Divorce, 169, 391, 393, 612.
Docetism, 32, 92.
Domitian, emp., 7, 11.
Donatus and Donatism, 245, 287 f., 289 ff., 322–325, 445–454.
Dynamistic Monarchianism, 172–175, 221, 225–229, 298.

Easter, worship on, 164.
Easter, controversy as to date, 161–165, 291, 295, 375, 570, 605 ff.
Ecumenical Patriarch, Gregory the Great on the title, 592–595.
Edessa, Christianity in, 54.
Elvira, council of (A. D. 309), 386, 415.
Emanations, Gnostic theory of, 85 f., 94 f.
Encratites, 105.
Encyclion. See "Basiliscus."
Ephesus, church of, 9 ff., 116.
Ephesus, council of (A. D. 431), 507–509; (A. D. 449), 512.
Epiphanius of Salamis, 228, 355.

Episcopal courts of arbitration. See "*Audientia Episcopalis.*"
Episcopate, 237–239.
Epistula pacis, 215.
Eucharist, 18, 21, 30 f., 34, 38, 41, 42, 116, 138 f., 231–237, 449, 622–624.
Eusebius of Cæsarea, 8, 305, 309.
Eusebius of Nicomedia, 299, 302, 308, 310.
Eusebius of Rome, 270.
Eustathius, 309, 348.
Eutyches and Eutychian controversy, 511–522.
Evagrius Scholasticus, 274.
Exomologesis, 185.
Extension of Christianity, 18, 52–55, 156–159, 425–429, 566–570, 570–573, 602–605.

Fasting, 33, 38, 48 f., 71, 99, 166, 171, 232, 678.
Felicissimus, 212, 215–217.
Felicitas. See "Perpetua."
Felix of Aptunga, 291.
Fihrist of An Nadim, on Mani, 252–256.
Filioque, addition of, to the Creed, 577.
Firmilian, epistle of, on Stephen of Rome, 242–245.
Flavian of Constantinople, 512 ff.
Flora, Epistle of Ptolomæus to, 95–102.
Formula Macrostichos, 180.
Franks, conversion of, 570 ff.

Galen, 174.
Galerius, emp., 260, 262.
Gangra, council of, canons, 386, 413.
Gelasius of Rome, 531, 532–536.
Germans, Christianity among, 53.
Germanic State Church, 579–589.
Gladiatorial combats, abolishment of, 389.
Gnosticism, 50, 75–106, 126 f. See also "Simon," "Menander," "Cerdo," "Basilides," "Valentinus," "Ptolomæus."
Gospels, 35, 118, 120, 123.
Grace, controversy on. See "Augustine," "Pelagian Controversy," "Semi-Pelagian Controversy."
Gratian, emp., 366.

Gregory of Nazianzus, 353, 496 f.
Gregory of Nyssa, 502 f.
Gregory of Tours, 571 ff., 581 ff.
Gregory Thaumaturgus, 221 f.
Gregory the Great, 388, 590–602.

Hadrian, emp., 153.
Hatfield, council of (A. D. 680), 612.
Heathen slanders against Christianity, 61–64.
Heathenism, repression of, 285–287, 320–322, 346 f., 370–374, 557.
Heathenism, revival of, 330–336, 339.
Heathenism in the Church, 396 f., 400 f.
Heliogabalus, emp., religious policy of, 152.
Henoticon of Zeno, 526–529.
Heraclius, emp., 540, 660.
Heraclius, schism of, 270.
Heresy, laws against, 368, 372, 450–453.
Heretics, baptism of. See "Baptism."
Hermas, 43, 47, 48, 184.
Hertford, council of (A. D. 672), 609 ff.
Hierapolis, council of, 110.
Hierarchy, 128 f., 237 f., 360 ff., 562 f.
Hieronymus. See "Jerome."
Hilary of Poitiers, 316, 319.
Hippolytus, 68, 105, 108, 175–178.
Homoiousian party, rise of, 315–320.
Homoiousios, 316, 319, 348.
Homoousios, 306, 309, 316, 319, 348.
Honorius, emp., 420
Honorius of Rome, 671 f.
Hormisdas of Rome, 536.
Hosius, 299.
Hospitality, 40.
Hylics, 92 f.
Hymns, Christian, 21, 173.
Hypatia, 373.
Hypostasis, 193, 300, 306, 309, 315, 319, 349 ff.

Ibas. See "Three Chapters, controversy on."
Iconoclasm, 684 ff.
Ignatius of Antioch, 22, 30, 41 f.
Images, controversy on, 684 ff.
Incorruptibility, 136 ff.
India, Christianity in, 55.

Irenæus, on John, 26; on Gnosticism, 78–81, 85 f., 92 f.; on apostolic tradition and churches, 112–114; on the gospels, 120; on Apostles' Creed, 123 ff.; on redemption, 136–138; on eucharist, 139 f.; on Easter controversy, 163 f.
Irene, empress, 685.
Istrian schism, 596–600.

Jerome, on fall of Rome, 421–423; on text of New Testament, 485; on Origen, 486 f.
Jews, relation of, to the Christians, 14–18.
John, Apostle, death of, 9, 10; chiliastic teaching, 26 f.; in Ephesus, 114, 116, 118; founds order of bishops, 122.
John of Damascus on images, 691–693.
Jovian, emp., 337, 339.
Julia Mammæa, 153 f.
Julian, emp., early life, 325–329; habits, 329 f.; opens temples, 330; his ecclesiastical and religious policy, 330–334; forbids Christians to teach classics, 334–336.
Julius of Rome, 310; epistle of, 311; appeals allowed to, 364.
Justin Martyr, on Jews, 16; extension of Christianity, 18; chiliastic views, 27; on Christian worship, 32–35; defence of Christianity, 72–75, 135.
Justin I, emp., 540.
Justinian I, emp., 541; anathematisms against Origen, 542 f.; Aphthartodocetism, 553 f.; ecclesiastical legislation, 383, 554–560.

Lactantius, 206.
Lamb as image of Christ, 678 f.
Laodicæa, council of (c. A. D. 343), 399 f.
Lapsi, 208–212, 214–217.
Law, Mosaic, Gnostic conception of, 95 ff., 104.
Laws against Christianity, 19–22, 56, 145, 211.
Laws in favor of the Church, 281–285.
Legacy-hunting by clergy forbidden, 381 f.

Legislation, influence of the Church on, 284 f., 385 f.
Leo of Rome, on the Priscillianists, 378; on auricular confession, 384; on clerical celibacy, 417 f., represents Roman people, 476; on Petrine prerogatives, 476 f.; condemns 28th canon of Chalcedon, 478 f.; on apostolic sees, 480; his course in Eutychian controversy, 511 f.; his Tome, 514.
Libellatici, 158, 209 f., 214 f.
Libelli pacis, 187, 215, 292.
Libri pœnitentiales, 626–630.
Licinius, emp., 263–265.
Little Labyrinth, 173–175.
Liutprand, king, 659, 686–690.
Logos, 72 f., 130–132, 171, 176, 193 f., 227 ff., 298 f., 304, 313.
Lombard Church, 597 ff., 683 f.
Lombards, 589, 600–602.
Lord's Day, 41, 232, 284.
Lord's Prayer with Doxology, 38.
Lord's Supper. See "Eucharist."
Lucian of Samosata, 55, 59–61.
Lucian the martyr, 303; creed of, 313.
Luke, Gospel of, mutilated by Marcion, 103.
Luxeuil, foundation of, 587 f.

Macedonian heresy, 353 f., 524, 552, 666.
Magic among the Gnostics, 80, 87.
Malchion, 225 ff.
Mani and Manichæanism, 127, 252–256, 372; laws against, 375, 559 f.; persecution of, 376; Augustine on, 454 f.
Marcellus of Ancyra, 310 ff.
Marcia, concubine of Commodus, 69.
Marcian, emp., 510.
Marcion, Gnostic, 103–106, 114, 119, 122.
Marcionites, 127.
Marius Mercator, on Pelagianism, 460.
Mark, Gospel of, 123.
Marriage, Christian, 106, 108, 168 f.; compared with virginity, 168, 393; indissolubility of, 43, 169, 392 f., 612; second, 47, 169, 182.
Martin of Rome, 660.
Martin of Tours, 410, 427 ff.

Martyrdom, 65 *f.*, 66–68.
Martyrs, anniversaries of, 401; merits of, 167, 187, 212 *f.*; intercession of, 399.
Mary, the Virgin, 30, 70, 81; is Theotokos, 505, 511, 518, 520.
Massilians, 467.
Maximilla, Montanist prophetess, 107 *f.*, 110.
Maximinus Thrax, emp., persecution under, 154 *f.*
Maximus the Confessor, 660.
Melchizedek, 173.
Meletius and the Meletian schism, 266–270, 293 *f.*
Meletius, Bishop of Antioch, 349.
Memnon of Ephesus, 504.
Menander, 81.
Merovingian Church, 581 *ff.*
Methodius of Olympus, his theory of recapitulation, 229 *f.*; on the resurrection of the body, 230.
Metropolitans, 361, 363 *f.*
Milan, church of, 596 *ff.*
Milan, edict of, 263–265.
Minucius Felix, 61–64.
Miracles, Christian, 56, 153.
Mithras, 34, 150 *f.*
Monarchian controversies, 171–181, 221–229.
Monasteries, subject to bishops, 407. See also "Monasticism."
Monastic rules. See "Basil," "Benedict of Nursia," "Pachomius," "Columbanus."
Monasticism, 248–251, 401–411, 586 *ff.*, 617 *f.*, 630–644.
Monophysite churches, 538 *f.*
Monophysite controversies, 511–514, 516 *f.*, 522–529.
Monothelete controversy, 516, 539, 652 *f.*, 660–672.
Montanism in the West, 145, 179, 181 *f.*
Montanus and Montanism, 106 *ff.*, 109 *ff.*, 120, 127, 372.
Moralism and moralistic Christianity, 45 *ff.*, 134, 165 *ff.*
Morality, Christian, 28, 70 *ff.*, 188.
Morality, double, 46, 48.
Moslems, 653–659.
Muratorian Fragment, 117–120.

Natalius, confessor, 174.
Neo-Platonism, 202–204, 430 *ff.*
Nepos, schism of, 219–221.
Nero, emp., persecution by, 5–7, 9.
Nestorian controversy, 504–511.
Nestorius, fragments on the doctrine of, 501 *f.*
New-Nicene Party, 348 *f.*
Nicæa, council of (A. D. 325), 292–295; creed of, confirmed at Constantinople, A. D. 381, 353; canons of, 360–362, 412; doctrine of, enforced by law, 368; Goths present at, 425; (A. D. 787), definition of, 694–697.
Nice, Creed of, 318.
Ninian, 569.
Noetus, 109, 175, 178.
Novatian and Novatians, 217, 245, 247, 295 *f.*, 374.

Oak, synod of the, 492.
Oblati, 639, 642.
Oblation, 168.
Offerings, 41.
Optatus, on sacraments and the Catholic Church, 446 *f.*
Orange, council of (A. D. 529), canons of, against Pelagianism, 472–476.
Ordination, of clergy, 41; of bishops, 239.
Origen, 144, 153; on eternal generation of the Son, 193; eternal creation, 194; pre-existence of souls, 195; redemption, 196 *f.*; universal salvation, 198 *f.*; allegorism, 199; persecution, 206; martyrdom, 212 *f.*; errors of, 486, 489; condemnation of by Anastasius, 487 *f.*
Origenistic controversies, first, 483, 486–493; second, 541 *ff.*
Original Sin, Augustine on, 438–440; Pelagius on, 458, 460, 464 *f.*; council of Orange, 473–475.
Orleans, council of (A. D. 511), 580, 618; (A. D. 541), 618; (A. D. 549), 580, 619.
Orthodoxy, enforcement of, 367, 370.
Ostrogoths, Church under, 529, *f.*
Ousia distinguished from *hypostasis*, 348 *f.*

Pachomius, *Rule* of, 402–405.
Palladius, bishop in Ireland, 567.
Pallium, 591, 604.
Pantænus, 55, 189.
Papias, chiliastic ideas of, 25 *f.*
Paris, council of (A. D. 557), 581.
Parish, 616–620.
Patriarchates, 354, 359, 361.
Patrick, Irish missionary, 567–569.
Patripassianism, 125, 175 *ff.*
Paul, Apostle, death of, 8, 9, 23, 112 *f.*, 116; epistles of, 68, 103 *f.*, 119, 122.
Paul of Samosata, 221, 225–229.
Paulinus of Antioch, 349.
Paulus Diaconus, 600 *ff.*
Pelagian controversy, 455–466.
Pelagius, 455; Augustine on, 456 *f.*; statement of position, 457 *f.*; epistle to Demetrias, 458–460; his confession of faith, 461; condemnation at Carthage, 463–465; condemnation at Ephesus, 508.
Penances, 626–630.
Penitential discipline. See "Discipline, penitential."
Pentecost, feast of, 165 *f.*
Peregrinus Proteus, 59–61.
Perpetua and Felicitas, Passion of, 145–149.
Persecution. See under name of Emperor.
Persia, Christians in, 54.
Peter, Apostle, death of, 8; at Rome, 9, 23, 112 *f.*, 116, 123.
Peter of Alexandria, 270.
Peter Fullo, 535 *f.*
Peter Mongus, 535 *f.*
Petrine authority, 180, 186, 243 *f.*, 447, 477–481, 532.
Philip, Apostle, death of, 11.
Philip the Arabian, emp., religious policy of, 156.
Philippopolis, council of (A. D. 343), 364.
Philo Judæus, 135.
Philosophy, 72 *f.*, 78, 174, 190, 192.
Phocas, emp., 595.
Phrygian heresy, 375. See "Montanism."
Pictures. See "Icons."
Plato, 73 *f.*

Pleroma, Gnostic doctrine of, 90.
Pliny the Younger, epistle to Trajan, 19.
Pneumatics, 93.
Polycarp, 113, 129, 163 *f.*
Polycrates, 10, 162.
Poor. See "Charity."
Pope. See "Rome, Bishop of," also name of individual popes.
Pope, title of, 215, 408, note.
Porphyry, epistle to Marcella, 202–204.
Praxeas, 125 *f.*, 178 *f.*
Prayer, 33 *f.*, 38, 72, 165, 184.
Prayer, times of, 38, 166.
Prayers to saints, 397–399.
Predestination, 136, 440–442.
Presbyter, 31, 37, 41, 82.
Priscilla, Montanist, 107, 110.
Priscillianists, 375, 378 *ff.*
Prophecy, argument from Hebrew, 74, 134.
Prophets, Christian, 40 *f.*
Prosecution of Christians, 20, 66–68.
Pseudo-Dionysius. See "Dionysius the Areopagite."
Psychics, 92 *f.*
Ptolomæus, martyr, 65 *f.*
Ptolomæus, 93; epistle to Flora, 95–102.
Pulcheria, empress, 512.

Quartodecimans, 108.
Quinisext Council (A. D. 692), 413–415, 673–679.

Ravenna, exarchate of, 653, 680, 684, • 686 *ff.*
Real Presence, 31, 34, 231, 235.
Reccared, Visigothic king, 575–579.
Redemption, Asia Minor conception of, 136; Origen's conception, 196 *f.*
Regula fidei, 125.
Relics, 398.
Remission of sin after baptism, 44, 184.
Resurrection of Christ, 59.
Resurrection of the body, 116, 230.
Rhodon, 104 *f.*
Robber synod of Ephesus (A. D. 449), 512.
Roman government, attitude of, to-

ward Christians, 20–22, 64–69, 142–145, 151–154, 205–208, 258 *f.*
Rome, appeals to, 364–366.
Rome, bishops of, list of, 113; election of, 679–683.
Rome, councils of, under Cornelius, 217; under Julius, 310; under Martin, 614, 664 *f.*
Rome, see of, and the Unity of the Church, 240–245.
Rome, see of, authority of, *potior principalitas*, 113; statement of Siricius on, 416; *causa finita est*, 462 *f.*; statement of Leo the Great, 480 *f.*; of Gelasius, 532.
Rome, see of, separation from the Churches of Asia Minor, 161–165.
Rufinus, 489.

Sabellius and Sabellianism, 180 *f.*, 223 *ff.*, 300, 309, 352, 354.
Sacraments, nature of, 447, 449 *f.*, 564. See also "Baptism" and "Eucharist."
Sacrifice of the mass, 622.
Saints, prayers to, 397, 399.
Sardica, council of (A. D. 343), canons, 364.
Saturninus, Gnostic, 106.
Schism. See under "Novatian," "Felicissimus," "Meletius," "Heraclius," "Donatism," "Istrian."
Schools, mediæval, 644, 650 *f.*
Scilitan Martyrs, 66–68.
Semi-Arians, 316.
Semi-Pelagians, 466–476.
Severus, Alexander, emp., religious policy of, 152 *ff.*
Severus, Septimius, emp., 141–149.
Simon Magus, 78 *f.*, 103.
Siricius of Rome, decretal of, 415–417.
Sirmium, council and creed of (A. D. 357), 316.
Sixtus of Rome, 211.
Slaves, manumission of, 385, 387; canons on treatment of, 386–388.
Socrates, Greek philosopher, 72 *f.*, 131 *f.*
Socrates, ecclesiastical historian, 274.
Soter of Rome, 24.
Sozomen, ecclesiastical historian, 274.
Spain, Church in, 53, 158, 575 *ff.*

Spirit, Holy, 133, 187, 349, 351, 353, 577 *ff.* See also "Trinity."
State Church, 356, 358–384, 553–557, 579–585.
Stephen of Rome, 242–245.
Subintroductæ, 226, 412.
Suevi, 571, 575 *f.*
Sulpicius Severus, 410 *f.*, 427 *ff.*
Sunday, 35, 284.
Sylvester of Rome, 291.
Symbol. See "Creed."
Symmachus of Rome, 530.
Symmachus, prefect of Rome, 339–342.
Synods. See "Council" and under place-name.
Syria, Christianity in, 54.
Syzygies, Gnostic doctrine of, 90, 94.

Tabenna, first cloister, 402.
Tacitus on Christians, 6.
Tatian, 106 *f.*
Telemachus, monk, 389.
Temples, destruction of, 372 *f.*
Tertullian, on extension of Christianity, 52–54; on Gnostics, 77 *f.*; on Marcion, 104; on apostolic churches, 114–116, 122, 129; on the creed, 125 *f.*; in defence of Christians, 142 *f.*, 145; on prayer, 165; on fasting, 166; on baptism, 167, 232 *f.*; on merit, 167 *f.*; on marriage, 168 *f.*; against Praxeas, 178 *f.*; on discipline, 184–188.
Theodelinda, Lombard queen, 597 *f.*
Theodore of Canterbury, organization of English Church, 609–614; penitential, 627–629; founds schools, 650.
Theodore of Mopsuestia, his creed, 498–500; fragments on Christology, 500 *f.* See also "Three Chapters."
Theodoret of Cyrus, 127; creed, 510. See also "Three Chapters."
Theodosius I, ecclesiastical policy, 352 *f.*; requires orthodoxy, 367; represses heathenism, 368; massacre at Thessalonica, 390 *f.*; dynasty of, 420 *f.*
Theodosius II, issues Theodosian code, 424 *f.*; engages in Nestorian controversy, 504, 510; in Eutychian controversy, 511 *f.*

Theodotus of Byzantium, 172.
Theodotus the leather-worker, 110, 173 f.
Theopaschites, 523, 541 f.
Theophilus of Alexandria, attacks Chrysostom, 491–493.
Theophilus of Antioch, on Logos doctrine, 132; on Trinity, 134.
Theotokos, Mary as the, 505, 511, 518, 520.
Three Chapters, controversy on, 544–552; condemnation of, 551 f.; schisms resulting from condemnation, 596 ff.
Toledo, council of (A. D. 531), on schools, 649; (A. D. 589), conversion of Visigoths, 575–579.
Toleration of Christians by Edict of Milan, 263 ff.
Tradition, 109, 111 ff.; Basil on, 484.
Traditores, 291 f.
Trajan, emp., epistle to Pliny, 22.
Trinity, 132 ff., 171–181, 222–225, 368.
Trisagion, 541 f.
True Word of Celsus, 56–59.
Typos of Constans II, 662–664.

Ulfilas, 425–427; his creed, 426.
Unity of the Church, 240–245.
Universal salvation, 198.

Valens, emp., 337, 339.
Valentinian I, emp., 337 ff.
Valentinus, Gnostic, 78, 88–95, 106, 120.
Valerian, emp., persecution under, 205, 210 f.
Vicariate of Arles, 591 f.
Victor of Rome, 162 ff., 174.
Victorinus, philosopher, 431–433.
Vigilantius, 397 ff.
Vigilius of Rome, his Judicatum, 544; oath to Justinian, 545; Constitutum, 547–551.
Vincent of Lerins, rule of Catholic faith, 471; on grace, 472.
Virgin-birth of Jesus, 30, 31.
Virginity compared with marriage, 168, 393 f.
Visigothic Church, 575–579.

Whitby, council of, 605 ff.
Will, freedom of, Theophilus on, 134; Pelagius on, 457 ff.; John Cassian on, 469.
Worship, Christian, 21, 32–35, 38 f. 156, 165, 231–237, 578.

Xystus of Rome. See "Sixtus."

Zeno, emp., Henoticon, 526–529.
Zephyrinus of Rome, 176 f.
Zosimus of Rome, on Pelagius, 46: